WORLD HISTORY

FIFTH EDITION

bju press®

Greenville, South Carolina

Note: The fact that materials produced by other publishers may be referred to in this volume does not constitute an endorsement of the content or theological position of materials produced by such publishers. Any references and ancillary materials are listed as an aid to the student or the teacher and in an attempt to maintain the accepted academic standards of the publishing industry.

WORLD HISTORY Student Edition
Fifth Edition

Dennis Bollinger, PhD

Editor
Manda Kalagayan, MEd

Biblical Worldview
Brian Collins, PhD
Bryan Smith, PhD

Cover
Drew Fields

Book Design
Dan Van Leeuwen

Page Layout
Jessica Johnson
Carrie Walker

Project Coordinator
Dan Berger

Permissions
Sharon Belknap
Sarah Gundlach
Ashleigh Schieber

Illustration
Preston Gravely Jr.
David Schuppert

Consultants
Carl Abrams, PhD
Mark Sidwell, PhD

Academic Oversight
Jeff Heath, EdD

Photograph credits appear on pages 590–93.

© 2019 BJU Press
Greenville, South Carolina 29609

Fourth Edition © 2013 BJU Press
First Edition © 1984 BJU Press

Printed in the United States of America

ISBN: 978-1-62856-344-3

15 14 13 12 11 10 9 8 7 6 5 4

CONTENTS

FEATURES OF THE BOOK

UNIT

3

CULTURES OF THE WORLD
500–1100

6 The Byzantine and Islamic Empires

7 The Civilizations of Asia

8 The Civilizations of the Americas

9 The Making of Medieval Europe

Medieval Europeans thought of Asia as a mysterious place. This unit progresses eastward from Rome into the mysterious, alluring Asia as well as west to the American continents. Beginning with the Byzantine Empire (a blending of Eastern and Western culture), we will move to the Middle East (the realm of Islam), to the faraway lands of India and China, to a brief examination of early American civilizations, and then back to medieval Europe.

Great Wall of China

ca. 250–900
Classic period in Mayan history

618–907
Tang Dynasty

622
Muhammad flees to Medina

661–750
Umayyad Caliphate

732
Battle of Tours

500

600

700

476–1453
Byzantine Empire

Development of the Eastern Woodlands Indian culture

ca. 700
ca. 700–1200
Ghana Empire

750–
Abb

ca. 950–1539
postclassic period in Mayan history

1066

CHAPTER

4

The Roman Civilization

I. Beginning of Roman Civilization

II. The Roman Empire Emerges

III. Rise of the Christian Church

IV. Collapse of the Roman Empire

V. Roman Culture and Achievement

Roman aqueduct at Pont du Gard, France

Big Ideas

1. What were the strengths and weaknesses of the Roman Republic?
2. What was the significance of the *Pax Romana*?
3. How was Christ's coming the turning point of history?
4. Why did the Roman Empire decline and collapse?
5. What impact has Roman culture had on modern society?

Unit openers offer a glimpse of major events with a photo and timeline. In addition, the unit outline lists the chapters that will be covered.

The **chapter outline** lists the major topics that will be covered.

Each chapter includes **Big Ideas** to provide the student with important topics covered in the chapter.

Guiding Questions

1. What led to the rise and fall of the Mongol Empire and the Yuan and Ming dynasties?
2. What were the cultural accomplishments of the Mongols and the Chinese during this period?
3. What role did justice, power, and citizenship play in these empires?

III. Asia

The Mongols

You first read about the inhabitants of Mongolia in chapter 7. During this period a Mongol teenager harnessed their vast numbers and great potential and turned them into an unstoppable military force. From an obscure land and humble beginnings, this youth conquered or influenced a large percentage of the world's population and built a vast empire spanning thousands of miles.

Building the Mongol Empire

The Mongol people arose north of China, in the land known today as Mongolia. Their round felt tents dotted the eastern portion of the Asiatic grasslands. They raised sheep, goats, and horses. They had no central government and were divided into small tribes. In approximately 1162, **Temujin** (TEM yoo jin) was born to the family of a tribal chief. Overcoming many hardships in his youth, Temujin succeeded his father as leader of his tribe at the age of thirteen. He gradually united all the Mongol tribes under his authority and established an empire in Mongolia. He became "lord of all the people dwelling in felt tents." In 1206 the Mongols gave him the title "**Genghis Khan**" (GENG-gis KAHN), meaning "universal ruler."

Genghis Khan was one of the greatest conquerors in history. He believed that he had a divine commission to conquer the world. Having organized the Mongols into a well-disciplined fighting force, he conquered northern China. He then turned his army westward. The Mongols overran central Asia, advanced to the banks of the Indus River, pushed into Persia, and crossed into southern Russia. Returning from his western conquests, Genghis Khan renewed his campaign against China. His death in 1227, however, prevented him from seeing the whole of China fall under Mongol control.

Much of Genghis Khan's success lay in the organization and mobility of his army. He skillfully deployed his forces in battle. His army, which he divided into groups of tens, hundreds, and thousands, could strike with great speed. In addition, the Mongols were e... int...

Genghis Khan

Artist's conception of a mound village

Monks Mound

Iroquois longhouse

some of the mounds, which indicate they were, at least in part, used as burial mounds.

Artifacts from the Hopewell culture reveal a wealth of fine craftsmanship and artwork. Many of the discovered items appear to be linked to religious activities. Items made from mica and copper and carved from bone have been found in the burial chambers, in addition to many types of statues and smoking pipes.

Mississippian (ca. 800–1600)

The Indian culture broadly named **Mississippian** covered the central Mississippi River Valley and extended to the Ohio River Valley and south to parts of Kentucky, Tennessee, Alabama, and Mississippi. Indian sites contained large platform mounds probably used for Indian ceremonies and homes. Often these mounds were surrounded by ditches and fencing for security. The Cahokia settlement is believed to be the largest Mississippian site, with eighty mounds and indications that the Indian population had developed a city that covered about six square miles. Some have estimated that Cahokia sustained a population of up to forty thousand.

Eastern Woodlands

Another diverse American Indian civilization developed in the Southeast and along the Atlantic coast into the Northeast. These tribes were called the **Eastern Woodlands Indians**. The civilization may have developed around AD 700 and spread throughout the Southeast, especially after 1200. They tended to settle along the rich bottomlands of the Mississippi, Ohio, and Tennessee Rivers and developed tight-knit agricultural communities. The women grew crops while the men hunted and served as warriors when necessary. These Indians had a matriarchal society, meaning that the women held an unusual degree of power in the social structure and political decision-making. They were politically engaged and developed a high level of civilization among the Indian tribes.

Section Review

1. What is the name of the possible land bridge that many believe was the migration route to America?
2. Whom did the Indians look to as religious leaders?
3–4. List the names of two Native American groups.
5. What type of burial did many Indians along the Ohio River Valley use?
★ Why do you think many tribes passed down creation and flood stories?
★ How did geography influence the North American Indians?

Guiding Questions focus the students and prepare them for reading each section in the chapter.

Terms in bold type draw attention to important facts, ideas, people, or definitions.

Amazing **color artwork** helps the students see the sites, people, and events discussed in the text.

Vivid **color photographs** take students on a visual tour of the cultures they are learning about.

General feature boxes provide a more detailed look at a person, event, or concept mentioned in the chapter.

Margin info boxes offer fascinating bits of extra information.

---

268 • Chapter 12

Sikhism

Sikhism (from the Punjabi term meaning "disciple" or "learner") was founded around 1500 by a Hindu man named Nanak (1469–1539) in the Punjab region of India. Sikhs retained ideas of reincarnation and karma but rejected the caste system. Nanak and ten other successive leaders were known as *gurus* (teachers or experts). The tenth successor of Nanak declared himself the final *guru* and placed his authority in the Sikh scriptures, *Granth Sahib*, composed of hymns. These scriptures also contain the traditions and teachings of several Hindu Bhakti saints.

Sikhs meditate on the words of the Sikh scriptures through music or by silently repeating their god's name. They believe that this enables the disciple to sense their god's presence and maintain control over the "Five Thieves"—lust, rage, greed, attachment, and conceit. Positive Sikh attributes include being truthful, faithful, self-controlled, and pure.

This religion formed in a region of India controlled by the Mughal Empire and experienced treatment varying from patronization (during Akbar's reign) to violent persecution (during Aurangzeb's reign). Mughal rulers executed two of the ten gurus who succeeded Nanak, and many Sikhs became skilled warriors to preserve their way of life. One of the desired qualities of a Sikh was to become a "sant-Sipahi," a saint-soldier. Members of the *khalsa* (army of the pure) distinguished their appearance by refraining from cutting their beards or their hair, wearing a steel bracelet on the right wrist, and carrying a sword.

Sikh guard near the Golden Temple

period of achievement in art and architecture. The most successful Mughal ruler was Babur's grandson **Akbar** (r. 1556–1605). He became ruler around the age of thirteen and ruled the Mughal Empire under the watchful eye of a regent. Akbar proved to be a brilliant military strategist and expanded the empire to include all of northern and central India north of the Krishna River.

Initially Akbar was a dedicated Muslim and approved the slaughter of nearly half a million Hindus and the enslavement of many women and children in the name of Islam. Gradually he interacted with other religions and concluded that Islam did not possess exclusive truth. This abandonment of Islam alienated many Muslim rulers and threatened Akbar's rule. Akbar protected himself by removing Muslim clerics from places of influence, by ending the collection of the tax on non-Muslims (*jizya*), and by promoting many Hindus to key positions in his government. He restricted access to the empire's wealth to those who could pose no political threat and gave political power to those who had no access to soldiers or the empire's wealth. Akbar also encouraged emperor worship and initiated the adding of halos to the paintings of the royal family.

Akbar's grandson, Shah Jahan (r. 1627–1658), is best remembered for commissioning the construction of a mausoleum for his

---

988. He ordered the destruction of pagan idols and temples and established Orthodox Christianity as the official state religion. By adopting Eastern Orthodoxy rather than Roman Catholicism, Russia cut itself off from the mainstream of Western thought and instead came under the influences of the Eastern church and Byzantine culture.

The influence of the Orthodox church upon Russia was great. The Russian language profited from the Slavic alphabet, which the Byzantine missionaries Cyril and Methodius had adapted from the Greek alphabet. The Slavic alphabet enabled the Russians to translate late Greek works into their Slavic language. It also prompted the growth of native Russian literature. Russian artists made beautiful icons like those adorning Byzantine churches. The Russians even patterned their cathedrals after Byzantine models. One feature of their cathedrals, however, is uniquely Russian—the onion-shaped dome.

Russian Orthodox Church

Height of Kievan Russia

Kiev reached the zenith of its power and prestige during the reign of Yaroslav (yuh ruh SLAHV) "the Wise" (r. 1036–1054). Yaroslav greatly strengthened the city's position of leadership; Kiev became known as the "Mother of Russian cities." His reign saw the greatest territorial expansion of the early Russian state. He gained international recognition by negotiating marriage alliances between his princely house and the royal families of France, Sweden, Norway, Poland, Hungary, and the Byzantine Empire. He also sponsored the earliest known Russian code of laws, which combined Slavic tribal law and Byzantine law.

Yaroslav desired to make Kiev a rival of Constantinople. In size, wealth, and culture, Kiev became one of the leading cities of its day. It was a prosperous center of commerce—a meeting place of the world's merchants. Yaroslav's patronage of art, education, and the church attracted Byzantine painters, architects, teachers, and priests. With the aid of Byzantines, the Russians constructed their own cathedral of Hagia Sophia. Kiev also boasted schools, libraries, monasteries, cathedrals, and fortifications that Yaroslav built.

After the death of Yaroslav, Kiev lost its prominence among the Russian cities when his heirs fought to determine who would succeed him on the throne. Cities that had formerly looked to the Kievan rulers as the Grand Princes of Russia began to assert their independence. New trade routes and commercial centers drew away much of Kiev's wealth and population. Kiev's declining influence suffered a deathblow in the thirteenth century, when the Tartars—fierce Mongolian warriors from central Asia—swept into Russia (see ch. 12). They destroyed Kiev in 1240 and ruled Russia until the late 1400s. After the decline of Mongol power, a new center of Russian society—Moscow—arose in the north.

The Byzantine & Islamic Empires • 129

Vladimir and the Orthodox Church

According to legend, the Russian ruler Vladimir decided that he would establish a monotheistic religion among his people to replace their polytheistic, pagan beliefs. Before he decided what that new religion would be, he investigated what the world had to offer. He summoned representatives of Islam, Judaism, Roman Catholicism, and Eastern Orthodoxy and had each of them explain why their particular religion was best. After listening to the claims of each, Vladimir sent out envoys to observe these religions on a firsthand basis. When they returned, he made his decision.

First of all, Vladimir rejected Islam because the Qur'an forbade the drinking of alcoholic beverages. Second, he rejected Judaism because the Jewish people had been defeated and scattered across the world. Since their God did not seem strong enough to protect them, He could not be counted on to protect the Russian people, thought Vladimir. Third, the king rejected Roman Catholicism because the Catholic churches were dark and damp and the services were dull. Vladimir chose Eastern Orthodoxy.

The reason for his choice was simple. When his envoys returned from Constantinople, they enthusiastically described a service they had attended at the Hagia Sophia. They told him how the whole church seemed to shine as the mosaics reflected the light of the burning candles. They told him of the beautiful music, the clouds of incense, and the gorgeous robes of the patriarch who led the service. Impressed by what he heard, Vladimir adopted Eastern Orthodoxy. The Russian Orthodox Church was established.

Maps help the students visualize geographic locations.

POLAND
UKRAINE
GERMANY
CZECH. REP.
Prague
SLOVAKIA
MOLDOVA
Vienna
Bratislava
Kishinev
Danube R.
AUSTRIA
HUNGARY
Budapest
ROMANIA
Black Sea
Bern
SWITZ.
SLOVENIA
Zagreb
CROATIA
Bucharest
Ljubljana
BOSNIA
AND HERZ.
Belgrade
Ankara
ITALY
Sarajevo
YUGOSLAVIA
Sofia
BULGARIA
Rome
Skopje
MACEDONIA
Tirane
ALBANIA
TURKEY
GREECE
Dnieper R.

Immediate Post-Communist Eastern Europe

and Muslim). Without the unifying force of the Communist regime, the different regions of that nation began to pursue independence. Slovenia, Croatia, Macedonia, and Bosnia and Herzegovina claimed independence in 1991. Only Serbia and Montenegro temporarily combined under the name "Federal Republic of Yugoslavia." Violence marred the breakup of Yugoslavia. The Serbs particularly resented the reduction of their power and feared for the fate of Serbs, who were now minorities in the other former Yugoslav republics.

The result was bloody civil war. Thousands of civilians died, particularly in Bosnia, where the Serbs sent arms and troops to "protect" Serb minorities—and carve out more territory for the Serb-dominated government of Yugoslavia. To help knit the acquired regions to Yugoslavia, the Serbs began the forced removal or even killing of non-Serbs in the conquered regions. Anarchy reigned even as the UN sought a peaceful solution. Described as the powder keg of Europe before World War I, the Balkans had again become a center of terror and violence by the end of the twentieth century. Years of Communist rule had done little to bring a sense of unity to that troubled region.

Section Review

1–2. Which of the former Soviet republics became the most important player in world politics? Who was its first president?

Over what European country did dictator Nicolae Ceausescu rule? How did his rule end?

5. After the collapse of communism in Eastern Europe, what former Communist nation broke into several smaller republics and engaged in ethnic civil war?

★ Analyze the difficulties of transitioning away from communism after the collapse of the USSR.

★ Why have the Balkans been described as the powder keg of Europe, what forces have restrained this region in the past, and how did the collapse of the USSR lead to renewed hostilities?

The **Chapter Review** asks students to think in terms of higher learning, including understanding, analyzing, evaluating, and creating.

CHAPTER REVIEW 17

Making Connections

1–2. Give two reasons the Vienna peace settlement failed to accomplish its goals.

3–6. List three goals of liberalism and explain why the middle class supported these goals.

7. Why did Giuseppe Mazzini start a patriotic society called Young Italy?

8. Explain how Beethoven bridged the gap between classical and romantic music.

Developing History Skills

1. What were the long-term results of the revolts of Latin American colonies from Spain?

2. What significant events in this chapter led to the unification of Germany?

Thinking Critically

1. Should national interests come before international cooperation? Explain your answer.

2. Evaluate the romantic attitude toward freedom in light of God's instruction to Adam in Genesis 2:16–17.

Living in God's World

1. During the late nineteenth century, an anti-revolutionary party was started by Christians in the Netherlands as an alternative to both the Conservative and Liberal Parties. Imagine that you are a newspaper editor for the *De Standaard*, the party newspaper. Write a brief article explaining why the Anti-Revolutionary Party would disagree with both liberals and conservatives. Explain why the name Anti-Revolutionary was chosen for the party.

2. Outline some of the key unbiblical tenets of romanticism and formulate biblical alternatives.

People, Places, and Things to Know

Congress of Vienna
Lord Castlereagh
Alexander I
Prince Klemens von Metternich
Charles Maurice de Talleyrand
Quadruple Alliance
Monroe Doctrine
peninsulares
criollos
mestizos
Simón Bolívar
José de San Martín
Dom Pedro
caudillos
liberalism
nationalism
Louis XVIII
Charles X
July Revolution
Louis Philippe
Treaty of London
Louis Napoleon
Franz Josef I
Nicholas I
Russification
realpolitik
Risorgimento
Giuseppe Mazzini
Camillo di Cavour
Giuseppi Garibaldi
Victor Emmanuel II
Zollverein
Otto von Bismarck
Austro-Prussian War
Franco-Prussian War
Dual Monarchy
Alexander II
romanticism
Ludwig van Beethoven
Jacques Louis David

Section Review questions provide reinforcement to help the students remember what they have learned so far. In addition, critical-thinking questions challenge the students to combine details and demonstrate higher thinking skills.

HOW TO USE THIS BOOK

Units and Chapters

WORLD HISTORY is divided into eight units. The main theme of each unit is presented in a brief summary and timeline and illustrated by a two-page color picture. Each unit in turn contains from two to four chapters. These begin with a brief introduction and an outline of the period to be studied. The chapters are divided into main sections and subsections. For instance, one of the main sections in chapter 2 is Mesopotamia. The first subsection under this is Sumerian Civilization. Often subsections are further divided to help you quickly identify the major topics of discussion.

Section Reviews

At the end of each major section of a chapter is a section review. The numbered questions are primarily recall questions designed to test your understanding of the material you have just read. Final questions are critical-thinking questions that require you to analyze, evaluate, or apply information from the section in order to answer the question. There are normally three to four section reviews in each chapter. In addition, if a section is unusually long, a section quiz will be inserted in the middle as well as at the end.

Chapter Reviews

Each chapter ends with a review section that should help you study the chapter and demonstrate your ability to analyze and apply the chapter content. The Chapter Review is divided into five parts: Making Connections; Developing History Skills; Thinking Critically; Living in God's World; and People, Places, and Terms to Know.

1. Questions from Making Connections help you recall what you have read in the chapter and demonstrate understanding by combining details to answer the questions.

2. Questions from Developing History Skills help you develop skills in applying and analyzing information in the chapter.

3. Questions from Thinking Critically help you develop skill in evaluating information in the chapter.

4. Questions from Living in God's World help you develop creative skill through a practical application of information in the chapter.

5. People, Places, and Terms to Know are listed in the order in which they appear in the text. You should be able to define, identify, or state the importance of the terms depending on their context in the chapter. All the terms in this list are in boldface type in the text.

Illustrations, Charts, Timelines, and Maps

Each illustration and chart in the book has been included to aid you in your understanding of world history. Take time to look at these and read the captions associated with them. The timelines will help you place events in a broader historical context. The maps will help you visualize the size and location of various countries or regions.

Highlights

Each chapter has a number of interesting articles contained in feature boxes. Not only will these help to broaden your knowledge of history, but many will also make your reading of *WORLD HISTORY* more exciting. If you are curious, for instance, about how we got our calendar or how during World War II the United States knew ahead of time that the Japanese were going to attack Midway, you will be able to read all about it in these boxes.

Dates

In your reading of this *WORLD HISTORY* textbook, you will encounter many dates. We do not intend for you to memorize all of them. The dates are provided so that you will be able to fit people and events into a time frame.

How to use BC and AD

Today it is customary to label events that happened before the birth of Christ *BC* (meaning "before Christ") and events that happened after His birth AD ("*Anno Domini*," Latin for "in the year of our Lord"). BC is written after a date (e.g., 509 BC), and AD typically appears before the date (e.g., AD 70). However, we do not write AD next to a date unless it might be confused with a BC date. Therefore, when you see a date in the book without BC after it or AD before it, you may assume it is AD. Some contemporary writers use "Before the Common Era" (BCE) and "Common

Era" (CE) for their dating schemes to stand for BC and AD, respectively.

How to count in BC

The dates of events before the birth of Christ are much like the countdown of a rocket launch (10, 9, 8, . . . 3, 2, 1). Ancient civilizations, of course, did not count backward like this. But because of the historical significance of the birth of Christ, we now date ancient events from the number of years before His birth.

How to recognize an approximate date

Because of incomplete historical records, it is sometimes impossible to establish an exact date for a historical event. When this is the case, we express an approximate date by placing the abbreviated form of *circa* (Latin for "around") before the date (e.g., ca. 1446).

How to understand dates printed after a person's name

The dates in parentheses after a person's name usually indicate his lifespan. Dates for monarchs or popes, however, are often the dates they held office. The abbreviation *r.* before a date stands for "ruled" (e.g., r. 1307–78). If a question mark appears after a date, it means we are uncertain about the time of a person's birth or death—for example, John Wycliffe (1320?–1384).

How to determine the century in which an event took place

The first century includes the years 1 to 100; the second, 101 to 200; the third, 201 to 300; and so on. The twenty-first century will therefore be from 2001 to 2100. The same procedure is used for establishing centuries BC. Try to determine the centuries for the following dates: 586 BC, ca. 1446, 1900.

PRONUNCIATION GUIDE

Vowels			
symbol	example	symbol	example
a	cat = KAT	aw	all = AWL
a_e	cape = KAPE	o	potion = PO shun
ay	paint = PAYNT	oa	don't = DOANT
e	jet = JET	o_e	groan = GRONE
eh	spend = SPEHND	oh	own = OHN
ee	fiend = FEEND	u	some = SUM
i	swim = SWIM	uh	abet = uh BET
ih	pity = PIH tee	oo	crew = CROO
eye	icy = EYE see	oo	push = POOSH
i_e	might = MITE	ou	loud = LOUD
ah	cot = KAHT	oy	toil = TOYL
ar	car = KAR		

Consonants			
symbol	example	symbol	example
k	cat = KAT	th	thin = THIN
g	get = GET	th	then = THEN
j	gentle = JEN tul	zh	fusion = FYOO zhun

The pronunciation key used in this text is designed to give the reader a self-evident, acceptable pronunciation for a word as he reads it from the page. For more accurate pronunciations, the reader should consult a good dictionary.

Stress: Syllables with primary stress appear in LARGE CAPITAL letters. Syllables with secondary stress and one-syllable words appear in SMALL CAPITAL letters. Unstressed syllables appear in lowercase letters. Where two or more words appear together, hyphens separate the syllables within each word. For example, the pronunciation of Omar Khayyám appears as (O-mar keye-YAHM).

THE ANCIENT WORLD
Creation–500 BC

1 Foundations of World History

2 Early Civilizations

Columns of Luxor temple in Luxor, Egypt

ca. 2270 BC
Sargon and the first known empire

ca. 2000 BC
Hittites settle
in Asia Minor

Phoenician civilization
appears

Creation

Flood

ca. 3000 BC
Rise of early civilizations

ca. 2300 BC
Indian civilizations flourish

3000 BC

2500 BC

2000 BC

ca. 2700–2200 BC
Old Kingdom (Egypt)

2166 BC
Abraham born

ca. 2040–1650 BC
Middle Kingdom
(Egypt)

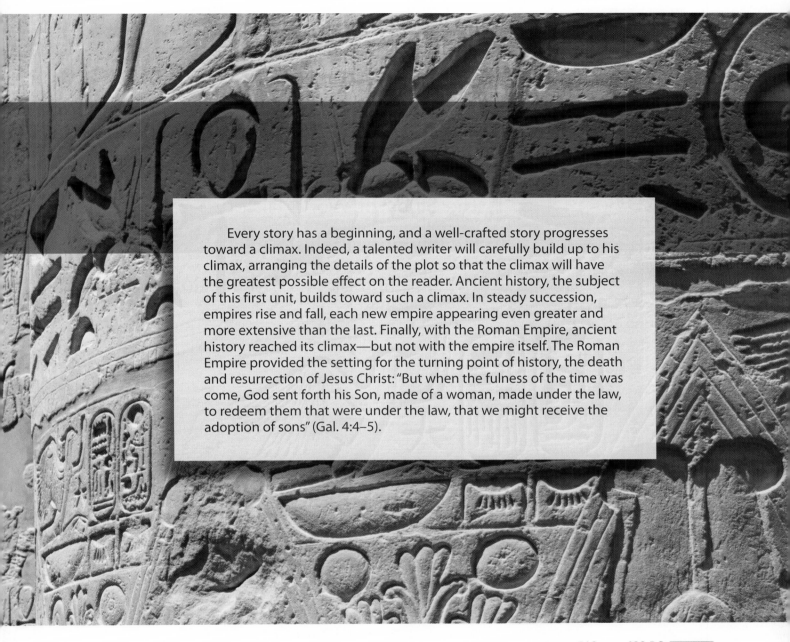

Every story has a beginning, and a well-crafted story progresses toward a climax. Indeed, a talented writer will carefully build up to his climax, arranging the details of the plot so that the climax will have the greatest possible effect on the reader. Ancient history, the subject of this first unit, builds toward such a climax. In steady succession, empires rise and fall, each new empire appearing even greater and more extensive than the last. Finally, with the Roman Empire, ancient history reached its climax—but not with the empire itself. The Roman Empire provided the setting for the turning point of history, the death and resurrection of Jesus Christ: "But when the fulness of the time was come, God sent forth his Son, made of a woman, made under the law, to redeem them that were under the law, that we might receive the adoption of sons" (Gal. 4:4–5).

ca. 563–ca. 483 BC
Siddhartha Gautama (Buddha)

1446 BC
Hebrew Exodus from Egypt

722 BC
Assyria destroys Samaria
and threatens Judah

539 BC
Cyrus the Great
frees Hebrews

ca. 1810–1750 BC
Hammurabi

1500–1000 BC
Shang Dynasty (China)

750–500 BC
Development of Greek city-states

1500 BC　　　　　　　　　　**1000 BC**　　　　　　　　　　**500 BC**

ca. 1570–1075 BC
New Kingdom (Egypt)

1000–ca. 500 BC
Zhou Dynasty (China)

753 BC
Rome founded

551–479 BC
Confucius

605–586 BC
Hebrew captivity in Babylon begins

Foundations of World History

I. The Study of World History

II. Evolutionary Prehistory?

III. The Beginnings of World History

"The heavens declare the glory of God"; a view of earth from space

Big Ideas

1. How should a biblical worldview affect the way a believer interprets history?

2. How does a secular view of origins differ from the biblical account?

3. How do Creation, Fall, and Redemption affect the development of civilization?

A building cannot be stronger than its foundation. This statement is certainly true in architecture, and it is also true in the study of history. Every telling of history—whether by a grandfather at a fireside or by a college professor in front of a classroom—is based on a number of "foundation stones." This chapter will talk about the foundational concepts that form the basis for this study of world history. One foundation is the method that a historian uses to understand the past. A faulty approach to doing historical research will lead to faulty conclusions. Another foundation is the world's earliest events. These events are foundational because they form the bedrock on which all the rest of world history is built.

I. The Study of World History

The Historian and His Task

History is the inquiry into what has happened in the past and why it has happened. But how do historians know what happened in the past? Historians act a lot like detectives. They search for clues that they hope will unlock the secrets of the past. These clues, or resources, provide the raw material of historical study. By collecting, analyzing, and interpreting this material, the historian can produce an account of the past that others may use.

The Historian's Resources

The resources that historians use are of two basic kinds. First, historians examine **primary sources**, which are records produced during the time period being studied and often produced by the people involved in the events. Second, historians study **secondary sources**, which are records that explain or interpret primary sources. Obviously, historians prefer to base their work on primary sources, but for some periods they are unable to do so. Primary sources may be derived from three basic historical resources: artifacts, oral tradition, and written records.

Sources	
Primary	Secondary
Manuscripts of Bach's choral pieces	Article analyzing the music of Bach
Emancipation Proclamation	Biography of Abraham Lincoln
Poems by American Puritans	Books about the Puritans
Memoirs of Napoleon	Essay on Napoleon's military tactics

Artifacts

The historian studies **artifacts** to learn about the background and culture of a people. Artifacts are objects made by man. They may be small relics, towering monuments, or priceless works of art. Most artifacts are simple, everyday items. Pottery, tools, weapons, furniture, clothing, coins, and jewelry unearthed by archaeologists (those who search for and study the artifacts of the past) give us valuable information about everyday life in past centuries.

The historian also derives information from architecture. He considers, for example, the pyramids in Egypt, the Acropolis in Athens, the Colosseum in Rome, the Great Wall in China, the Mayan temples in Central America, the soaring cathedrals in Europe, the

Guiding Questions

1. Why should we study world history?
2. What processes do historians use to analyze various sources?
3. How do making moral judgments and discerning divine providence shape the Christian historian's conclusions?

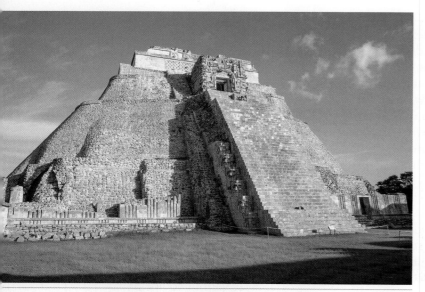

As a historical artifact, this Mayan pyramid contains important clues for understanding the culture that produced it.

A portion of Thucydides'
History of the Peloponnesian War

Taj Mahal in India, or the towering skyscrapers of New York City. These impressive structures reflect the creative skill that God has given to men as well as the character of the people who built them.

Even works of art aid the historian in understanding the past. Statues, drawings, paintings, and tapestries—"pictures of the past"—depict the customs, beliefs, hobbies, fashions, and ways of life of past generations.

Tradition

Think of your own family's history. You may be able to trace your heritage back many generations. How did you learn about your family's past? Most likely this information was passed down by parents or grandparents who talked of the "good old days." Such oral communication was the earliest method of transmitting historical information. It is called **tradition**, which is simply the handing down of information by word of mouth from generation to generation. Over the centuries tradition has taken many forms. Legends, ballads, folk songs, and tales are but a few of these forms. But tradition is more than the reciting of songs and stories about the past. It includes the imparting of religious beliefs, family heritage, and social customs.

Written Records

Because word-of-mouth information can easily be forgotten or distorted, people have written down their accounts of the past to preserve a more accurate record for future generations. These **written records** are often abundant and diverse. They include private letters, inventory lists, inscriptions, diaries, and journals. Historians also use information preserved in family and church records, in lists of kings and dynasties, and in political and legal documents. They gain insight into the thoughts, attitudes, and feelings of past generations by examining their works of literature. They also make use of historical works—detailed accounts of people, places, and events written during the period being investigated. These are valuable tools in understanding the past.

Of the three kinds of primary sources, written records are by far the most important to the historian. Artifacts usually give only a sketchy testimony to the past that can be interpreted in very different ways. Tradition tends to offer detailed accounts, but since these accounts are subject to the embellishing of hundreds (sometimes thousands) of retellings, the testimony they yield is often not reliable. However, written records produced by those who lived during the period often give a clearer testimony than artifacts, and since they do not have to be retold generation after generation, they are usually more reliable than tradition. The great importance of written records is demonstrated by the fact that most historians consider it impossible to write a reliable history of a period unless written records are available.

The Historian's Use of His Resources

Producing a historical account, however, involves more than just collecting primary and secondary sources. The historian must also make proper use of what he has amassed. He does this, first of all, by **evaluation of historical sources**. He examines a given record for its internal consistency and believability. Then he compares that record to others like it, examining their points of agreement and disagreement. Having exposed the strengths and weaknesses of what is available to him, the historian is ready for the next step—**historical synthesis**. In this step he gathers the useful information he has found in his investigations and weaves that information together into a narrative of the past. The narrative he produces constitutes the vast majority of his history. But the historian's task is not yet complete. He must also engage in **historical interpretation**. He needs to interpret the events he records by integrating into that account what he believes is the meaning and significance of the events. He must not simply state what happened; he must also explain why it happened and how that explanation remains significant for humans today. Once the historian has completed the steps of evaluation, synthesis, and interpretation, his work is ready to be studied, critiqued, and perhaps received by those who desire to know more about the subject of his work.

The Historian's Philosophy

In working through the previously mentioned steps, the historian quickly realizes that he is limited. He cannot know everything about the past. Furthermore, he cannot (and should not) record every bit of knowledge that is available about a given subject. He must select the events and facts that he will record. After selecting his information, he must then decide which areas will receive more emphasis. Some facts and events require several pages of description while others need only a paragraph. Decisions about selection and emphasis are driven by a historian's philosophy of life—how he answers life's most important questions. Where did the universe come from? Why is it here? Where is this world headed? These are questions that humans can answer only by faith. A historian's faith—whether the faith of a Hindu, Muslim, atheist, or Christian—will profoundly shape his telling of history.

Studying History with a Christian Worldview

The Bible gives Christians a **worldview**, a perspective from which they may examine and interpret the universe and everything in it. The Christian worldview presented in the Bible is composed of three central truths: (1) God made the world and everything in it; (2) this world has fallen into a sad and broken condition because of human sin; and (3) God is working to redeem this world to Himself. The paragraphs that follow show you how this Christian worldview shapes our telling of history and how it enables us to face with confidence the limits of historical research.

Divine Control of History

The Bible teaches that God controls all of human history. This biblical teaching is often referred to as the doctrine of **divine providence**. There is no event that is out of God's control or that does not help to accomplish His purpose for this world.

One of the best demonstrations of this truth in Scripture is found in the book of Daniel. At that time in history, God's people found themselves a conquered nation living in exile in the great Neo-Babylonian Empire. But Israel's captivity did not mean God had lost control. When the ruler of the Neo-Babylonian Empire,

Modeling

When a person summarizes complex information, he often forms a model. Given the limitations of historians, their models are based on incomplete information and imperfect understanding. Recognition of these human constraints should temper the assessment of models that are designed to explain history.

Nebuchadnezzar's Babylon was the glory of the ancient world.

Nebuchadnezzar, spoke with pride of his achievements, God struck his mind with a strange malady that caused him to think he was an animal. After seven years, God healed him. Then Nebuchadnezzar confessed of the God of the Bible, "He doeth according to his will in the army of heaven, and among the inhabitants of the earth: and none can stay his hand, or say unto him, What doest thou?" (Dan. 4:35). All who are able to think and reason clearly about history should arrive at the same conclusion. The Christian God is the One who "worketh all things after the counsel of his own will" (Eph. 1:11).

The reality of divine providence affects our study of history in two important ways. First, it reminds us that we should be historical optimists. As we learn about the problems of the past (and there are more than anyone can count), we will be tempted to become very pessimistic about human history. But the fact that God is in control teaches us that we have no good reason to despair about the condition or direction of our world. Divine providence does not deny that the world is evil; it does, however, deny that the world is out of control.

Second, divine providence encourages us to develop the habit of studying history with God's will in mind. The Christian should regularly ask himself, "What was God doing in this part of history?" Certainly we face limitations in seeking to answer this question. Aside from the history recorded in the Bible, we do not have revelation about God's purposes. The historian may not even have all of the information about what happened. Even so, the historian may compare events to Scripture and conclude that certain events benefited the spread of the gospel or strengthened the church, whereas other events brought about times of chastening for God's people.

When attempting to discern God's role in history, two cautions are in order. First, when dealing with aspects of history where God has not revealed His providential purposes, the historian may only humbly suggest what God's intentions might have been. Events are often complex, and historians don't have access to all relevant information. Second, historians should avoid the temptation to declare that all calamities are God's judgments and all victories prove that God is on the side of the victors. To determine God's purposes in history, the historian needs to look not at who appears to succeed or fail, but at God's own statements of His purposes in Scripture and how they are advanced in history.

Man's Fall into Sin

We cannot understand history unless we understand what the Christian worldview teaches regarding the source of the world's problems. Ultimately, it is not scarcity, disease, social inequality, or lack of education that is to blame for pain in the world. The problem lies within each of us. Our world is a troubled place because of our fall into sin. Because our first parents disobeyed and were cursed, all of us are sinful. An understanding of human sinfulness will prevent the Christian from having an overly optimistic view about past generations. He will resist the temptation to accept an unrealistic picture of the past. The Christian can also evaluate the morality of historical actions, not merely by the standards of the time or by his personal preferences but by the moral standards of Scripture.

Because of the existence of evil in our world, all historians make moral judgments as they interpret history. Christian historians base their moral judgments on what the Bible teaches about good and evil. The movements, institutions, and leading individuals of the past should be judged on their response to two divine commands: (1) people are to love God with their entire being, and (2) people are to love their fellow humans as much as they love themselves (Mk. 12:30–31).

In judging the past by the command to love, student historians should learn three lessons. First, moral behavior without love for the one true God is not true morality, and in time it will deteriorate into immoral behavior. Second, moral judgments in history must be made cautiously. A person's loves are a matter of the heart, and determining the condition of a person's heart is not possible (Jer. 17:9). Third, as we judge history by love, we will realize that no human is completely good—none but One, that is. Because Jesus Christ is the only entirely good human being, He alone is the hero of human history, and He alone can succeed as mankind's Savior.

Redemption in Christ as the Goal of History

We have already mentioned that God is in control of history, and have suggested that Christians studying history should attempt to discern what God has been doing in the past. We cannot, of course, discern God's working unless we know the final goal that He is guiding this world toward. We cannot suggest *what* God may have done in the past unless we first know *why* He has chosen to be in control in the first place. Repeatedly, Scripture teaches that God is in control of history to redeem this world to Himself through the work of His Son. Or to state it more fully, God allows all that happens in order to establish Christ's kingdom on earth so that through that kingdom He may declare His own glory (Rom. 11:36; 1 Cor. 15:28; Eph. 1:10). The goal of human history is Redemption in Christ.

A historian may not be able to determine God's purpose in specific historical events. However, the Christian historian should begin by considering the historical details of the event in addition to the fact that God is in control. Believers, including historians, can rest in the knowledge that God's ultimate goal is to glorify Himself through redeeming a people. History will conclude with the Father establishing a kingdom of redeemed sinners to be ruled by His Son.

A Final Word About Studying History

As we think about our Christian worldview and how it affects our investigation of the past, we conclude that **history** is the study of the record of the past acts of God and man on earth from its creation to the present, based on the best surviving evidence. The primary purpose for presenting to you a Christian view of history is not to enable you to do well on standardized tests or to make you appear educated before unbelievers (though we believe that if this book is used properly both will result). Our primary goal is to accomplish what the biblical historians sought to accomplish. When

Where Is This World Headed?

A hymn composed by Isaac Watts eloquently reminds the believer where this world is headed. This hymn is based on Psalm 72.

Jesus shall reign where'er the sun
Doth his successive journeys run;
His kingdom stretch from shore to shore,
Till moons shall wax and wane no more.

People and realms of every tongue
Dwell on His love with sweetest song;
And infant voices shall proclaim
Their early blessings on His name.

Where He displays His healing power,
Death and the curse are known no more;
In Him the tribes of Adam boast
More blessings than their father lost.

the psalmist Asaph introduced his survey of Israelite history, he told his readers, "I will utter dark sayings of old: which we have heard and known, and our fathers have told us. We will not hide them from their children, shewing to the generation to come the praises of the Lord . . . that they might set their hope in God, and not forget the works of God, but keep his commandments" (Ps. 78:2–4, 7).

If you are trusting in Christ for salvation from sin, then you are part of the next generation of the people of God. We sincerely hope that this year of studying world history will motivate you to set your hope in God. He has never failed His people, and He will not begin to do so in your generation. May the chapters that follow give you hundreds of reasons to live in obedience to His commands, and may they open your eyes to the ways in which God can use you to extend the kingdom of His Son. Some of you may exercise great influence on the future course of history. Many of you will have a small sphere of power. But all of you will have an impact, and that influence will have meaning and will be significant. May the history books of the next century be filled with hope because you used your life for the glory of God.

Section Review

1. How do primary and secondary sources differ?
2–4. What are the three steps a historian must go through in order to produce a historical account?
5. What drives a historian's decisions about selection and emphasis?
6. What question should Christians regularly ask themselves as they study various periods in history?
★ How would you define *history*?
★ How should Isaac Watts's Christian viewpoint shape your attitude toward history?

Guiding Questions

1. How would you summarize evolutionary prehistory?
2. How would you evaluate evolutionary prehistory from a biblical worldview?

II. Evolutionary Prehistory?

Most world history textbooks offer an evolutionary account of the beginnings of the human race. These accounts are called "prehistory" because they describe events that took place before humans developed writing. For these periods there are only artifacts: tools, clothing, weapons, and skeletons. These scant pieces of evidence are supposed to tell a story millions of years in length.

According to this view of the past, hominids (early humanlike creatures) first lived in East Africa as far back as three million years ago. From this time to about 10,000 BC is called the Early Stone Age (or the **Paleolithic Age**) because humans during this period used very simple stone tools. From the early hominids evolved the species *Homo erectus* ("upright human"). These hominids had more advanced tools than their predecessors, and they were the first to leave Africa for Asia and Europe. About 250,000 years ago, another human species arose, *Homo sapiens* ("wise human"). All humans today are members of this species.

Toward the end of the Early Stone Age, two kinds of *Homo sapiens* are said to have become prominent. In the caves of Europe and Southwest Asia, Neanderthals lived from about 130,000 BC to 35,000 BC. Their significant contribution to human history was

"Lucy," named after a famous Beatles song, was discovered in Ethiopia in 1974. Considered an early hominid skeleton (two or three million years old), it is one of the most complete ever found.

Though primitive to the untrained eye, the cave paintings attributed to Cro-Magnons show remarkable artistic sensitivity and skill.

the great care that they took in burying their dead. Anthropologists believe that this practice is the first indication of belief in life after death—and thus some take it as the first evidence of religion in human history. About 35,000 years ago, the Cro-Magnons arose in Europe. These humans made advancements in tools and weapons. But perhaps their most interesting advancements were in art. Paintings attributed to Cro-Magnons have been found in the caves of Spain and southern France.

The period from 10,000 BC to about 4,000 BC is called the New Stone Age (or the **Neolithic Age**). The most significant development during this period was the agricultural revolution. Prior to this time, humans were hunter-gatherers. They wandered from place to place hunting animals for food. But somehow, during the New Stone Age, humans learned that if certain seeds were planted, they could grow into edible plants. As agriculture and the domestication of animals developed, humans began settling into permanent communities. These communities became the forerunners of the cities of antiquity. With the founding of the first cities between 4,000 and 3,000 BC, human civilization began.

It is difficult to imagine an account more at odds with biblical history. The Bible presents the human race as intelligent and able to engage in agricultural pursuits from its earliest times. Art and religion did not take millennia to develop. Toward the end of mankind's first day, the first man spontaneously authored a poem (Gen. 2:23), and both man and woman spoke daily with God while in the Garden of Eden (Gen. 3:8). Genesis 4 describes the early development of civilization with the construction of cities, animal husbandry, development of metallurgy (bronze and iron), and the invention of musical instruments. These aspects of civilization did not take centuries to develop as in secular models of history, though after the Flood it seems to have taken time for some of these technologies to be re-established.

But the greatest problem with evolutionary accounts is that they attempt to show that humans came into being apart from God. In so doing, they remove from the history of humanity the Person who gives our race meaning and significance. God has made us in His image; therefore, we have dignity, and therefore we can experience peace and happiness only as we serve and love Him. Without Him we are nothing, and without Him in our history, our history has no meaning.

Section Review

1. What separates "prehistory" from "history"?
2. What is said to be the time period for the Paleolithic Age?
3. What is the period from 10,000 to 4,000 BC called?
4. How does the Bible present the beginning of the human race?
✶ Evaluate the concept of "prehistory" from a biblical worldview.

Guiding Questions

1. How did the Creation Mandate affect the development of civilizations?
2. What are the features and themes of civilizations?
3. How does the Fall affect the development of civilizations?

Octopus

III. The Beginnings of World History

As previously mentioned, the first pages in most world history textbooks are some of the most difficult to read because they deal with events in the very distant past for which historians have only theories. Paragraph after paragraph presents impersonal accounts of human-like groups struggling to move their race toward civilization.

The Bible's opening chapters present a very different account of long ago. Genesis 1–11 is anything but impersonal. It tells the story of individuals known to us by name: Adam, Eve, Cain, Abel, and Noah, to name a few. More importantly, however, these chapters introduce us to history's most important person. This person too we know by name—**Yahweh**, the only true God. And unlike the cautious presentation of most history books, the Bible's record is bold, going far beyond the "shadowy past" to a time when there were no cities, no farms, no humans, and no earth.

Creation

The Bible begins where it must: "In the beginning God." Before the universe was made, there was God and God alone. If the universe came about by chance—as many have claimed—its inhabitants are not responsible to anyone. But if the world has been made by an almighty God—as the Bible claims—then this Supreme Being holds the title deed to every galaxy, every planet, and every human. All are responsible to honor and obey the One who has graciously chosen to let them exist.

God completed His world simply by speaking. In six days the earth went from nothing to a dark, watery sphere to a beautiful, inhabited world that God Himself could describe as "very good" (Gen. 1:31). And God accomplished all this work with only a series of commands. Yahweh's voice of command is more than law. It determines what is and what will be. Although rebels within His creation may seem to triumph, He will in His own time prove to all that He alone is victorious, "for he spake, and it was done; he commanded, and it stood fast" (Ps. 33:9).

The Climax of Creation—The Human Race

The climax of God's creative work came after He made the land animals on the sixth day. To that point, all that God had made came into existence with some form of the impersonal command, "Let there be." Just before His final creation, however, God expressed special interest in what He was about to do: "Let us make man" (Gen. 1:26).

Mankind's Distinction

The reason for this special interest was that man was to be God's great masterpiece. Unlike the mammoth whales of the ocean, the majestic peaks of the mountains, and the brilliant stars scattered across the expanse of space, man would be made in God's own image: "So God created man in his own image, in the image of God created he him; male and female created he them" (Gen. 1:27). The **image of God** in man is one of the qualities that set humans apart from the rest of creation and that reflect part of God's own personality. Like God, humans would possess the characteristics of reason, moral consciousness, spiritual desire, sociability, and emotion. By mirroring part of His own being in man's, God set in this creature's soul both the desire and the ability to know Him intimately. The other creatures praise God for being the mighty Creator. Man, however, is privileged to praise Him for being both Creator and Friend.

Mankind's Purpose

The image of God in man also equipped the human race to fulfill its calling on earth. God did not make humans simply with the ability to fellowship with Him; He also made them with a job to do. After making the first man and woman, God told them, "Be fruitful, and multiply, and replenish the earth, and subdue it: and have dominion over the fish of the sea, and over the fowl of the air, and over every living thing that moveth upon the earth" (Gen. 1:28). This first command from God, often called the **Creation Mandate**, reveals mankind's reason for being.

The Meaning of the Creation Mandate—The central command of Genesis 1:28 is the command to "subdue" the earth by exercising "dominion" over it. Whether the item to be subdued is a tomato or Niagara Falls, humans are called by God to imagine and implement prudent ways to tame the earth and make it useful.

To exercise good and wise dominion requires all sorts of knowledge and skill—knowledge of science, math, technology, language, and history, to name a few. These areas of human endeavor are not found explicitly in Genesis 1–2, but they are implied in the Creation Mandate. Properly understood, the Creation Mandate is not a command about fish and birds only. It is a command about pursuing the advancement of culture—the physical and mental environment developed through human thought and labor.

Historians who reject the Bible's history usually assert that humans had to evolve over thousands of years before they were capable of changing their environment. The Bible, however, teaches that human management of the environment—one of the leading themes of world history—goes back to the human race's first days. At that time God placed in man's heart the desire and the ability to pursue every aspect of culture. This pursuit was never meant to serve man's selfishness or pride. It was to be God's way of declaring His glory through us. All of creation exists to declare God's glory (Rom. 11:36). But humans are special. The stars glorify God by declaring the greatness of His power and creativity. Humans glorify God by being like Him and imitating His deeds. He is the infinite Lord of the universe; we are the finite lords of His earth.

The Creation Mandate and Civilization—Central to the study of world history is the study of civilization. The word **civilization** comes from a Latin word (*civitas*) meaning "city," and it refers to human culture

Ultimately, even the skyline of a city is not of human origin. The specialization and organization that make a city a city have their roots in the Creation Mandate of Genesis 1:28.

lived in cities or under their influence. Historically, a city is more than a place where many people live. It is a complex cultural institution in which humans share core values and a desire to improve the quality of their existence through specialization and organization.

Modern automotive plant

Specialization refers to the division of labor that is part of the culture of every city. Individuals can specialize in a given endeavor necessary for human existence. The benefit of specialization is that individuals no longer need to do everything for themselves. Some specialize in food production, some in education, some in housing, some in the making of tools, and so forth; and each one benefits from the achievements of the others. To keep the network of specialization from unraveling, organization is necessary. This **organization** refers to a system of rules, regulations, and accountability that governs all who take part in the functions of the city. The results of specialization and organization are great advancements in science, technology, government, language, art, philosophy, and the accumulation of wealth.

It is important for Christians to realize that the city is ultimately not a human invention. Civilization—the object of study in this course—has its roots in the Creation Mandate. The specialization and organization that make a city possible are suggested in the opening commands of Genesis 1:28: "Be fruitful, and multiply, and replenish the earth, and subdue it." God recognized that the earth was a huge, complex place. If humans were to exercise the kind of dominion that would glorify Him, there would need to be a network of humans working together to maximize the usefulness of God's world. While it is true that the first city was still many years away (the first mention of a city is in Genesis 4:17), God intended from the beginning that civilization—and the enrichment that it brings—be part of human experience. It is not by accident that the Bible closes with saints in a city—the new Jerusalem.

The Features of Civilization

Features of a civilization include organized cities, government, social classes, job specialization, arts, sciences, written language, and religion. **Cities** are central locations for a particular group of people where government, religion, and culture are found. **Social classes** are composed of people with specific functions. An example is job **specialization** where people focus on a specific job or skill. Then the items produced are traded with others to supply goods and services to meet people's needs. When people work together in a civilization they communicate through art, music, and **written language** in addition to their spoken language. Many also use sciences to develop technology and learn about their world. **Religion** can be defined as a system of basic values, beliefs, and behaviors that are directed in worship toward God and lived out in community with others. False religion worships that which is not God or worships God in a way that contradicts His revealed will. False religion results in corrupted values, beliefs, and behaviors.

The Themes of Civilization

This textbook will highlight four themes of civilization: justice, power, citizenship, and environment. **Justice** is a social condition in which people do right and respect the rights of others. In a Christian worldview this is based on the image of God in man and our obligation to love others as much as we love ourselves. **Power** can be defined as the ability to bring things under one's control. Power is essential to any civilization because its leaders must maintain order in the community and exercise some control over nature. **Citizenship** is the status a person has within a community that gives this person certain rights, privileges, and duties. Citizenship gives people a voice in how their community functions, but it also imposes duties that require sacrifice. **Environment** is the physical geography in which civilizations are located. God made man to live on the earth and rule over the earth.

The Fall

Adam and his wife, whom he later named **Eve** (Gen. 3:20), were part of a wonderful paradise. The best aspect for Adam and Eve was not the beauty of the garden or the pleasures of a perfect marriage. Their greatest joy must have come from the relationship they had with their Creator. Genesis 3:8 indicates that Yahweh came regularly to visit with Adam and Eve, perhaps much like a parent spending time with a child. There was no fear and no danger. God and His highest creation enjoyed unbroken, holy communion.

The First Sin

All of this changed in a moment. When God called the human race to govern the earth, He called it also to govern itself. God had prohibited Adam and Eve from eating from the tree of the knowledge of good and evil (Gen. 2:16-17). This divine demand for self-control was taken by Satan as an opportunity to tempt the first woman to sin.

After listening to Satan's lies, Eve found herself doubting the only person who is completely trustworthy and trusting the person who can never be trusted. She was then ready to commit the act that would change the world: "She took of the fruit thereof, and did eat, and gave also unto her husband with her; and he did eat" (Gen. 3:6).

The Consequences of Sin

Immediately Adam and Eve became painfully aware that they had made the wrong decision. The consequences of their sinful choice affected both their inner being and their physical existence. As the apostle Paul explained centuries later, the consequences of that choice have been passed on to all humans: "Wherefore, as by one man sin entered into the world, and death by sin; and so death passed upon all men, for that all have sinned" (Rom. 5:12).

Twisted Affections

Since God had made the man and the woman good, they originally obeyed God's most basic moral commands naturally. They naturally loved God with their entire being and loved each other as much as themselves (cf. Mk. 12:30–31). But when they chose to disobey, these affections became twisted. As a result, humans love themselves supremely, and they cannot love God or their fellow humans as they should. This central moral defect has characterized all of human culture ever since. The histories of science, technology,

Like these plum mangoes, the fruit of the tree of the knowledge of good and evil looked beautiful and delicious.

art, politics, religion, and philosophy all bear the tragic marks of mankind's inability to love as he was meant to love.

Thwarted Dominion

God had made Adam and Eve to have dominion over the earth. Just as they had rebelled against God, so God made the earth rebel against them: "Cursed is the ground for thy sake. . . . Thorns also and thistles shall it bring forth to thee" (Gen. 3:17–18). In this struggle Adam—along with all his offspring—was destined for defeat. Though called to subdue the earth, he would in the end be subdued by it: "In the sweat of thy face shalt thou eat bread, till thou return unto the ground; for out of it wast thou taken: for dust thou art, and unto dust shalt thou return" (v. 19).

The couple's most tragic punishment came last. Because they were now sinners, Adam and Eve were no longer fit to enjoy the bliss of the garden and the unhindered fellowship with God that it provided. Yahweh expelled them from paradise and stationed angels with flaming swords at its entrance. To gain the knowledge of good and evil, our first parents chose to disobey God. They got what they wanted; they lost what they had.

Redemption

In the middle of this devastating tragedy, God gave humans a glimmer of hope. While pronouncing His curse on Satan and the serpent he used, God offered a glimpse of the gracious salvation He had planned for mankind: "I will put enmity between thee [Satan] and the woman, and between thy seed and her seed; it shall bruise thy head, and thou shalt bruise his heel" (Gen. 3:15). The human race had chosen its own destruction by sinning. But God revealed only moments after confronting this sin that those made in His image would have the hope of future triumph.

The Two "Seeds"

God promised both the serpent and the woman a "seed," or a group of descendants. Most likely, the **seed of the serpent** is a phrase referring to humans yet to be born who would prove to have the same deceptive, God-defying nature that Satan evidenced that day in the garden. The **seed of the woman**, on the other hand, refers primarily to Christ but also includes future humans who are united to Him in faith.

The Central Conflict of History

Genesis 3:15 is the Bible's thesis statement for human history. Man had been called to exercise dominion over God's creation. But because of sin there would now be two dominions: the seed of the woman and the seed of the serpent. God predicted that these two seeds were destined for conflict ("enmity"). Through the long centuries ahead, Satan's offspring would wound the followers of Yahweh many times. Often Satan's bruising of God's people would seem more like fatal blows to the head than injuries to the foot. And at such times Satan and his followers would seem to go on with no injuries at all. During these periods—and there would be many—the seed of the woman would be able to discern God's working in the world only through eyes of faith. Yahweh had promised victory for His followers, but that victory would be many battles away.

Moral Decay and Judgment

The effects of sin on humanity soon manifested themselves. Within the first generation after Adam and Eve, one son, Cain, murdered his brother Abel.

Cain fathered a line of descendants whose activities are in many ways typical of human history. The Cainites, it seems, were the first to live in civilization. The first city mentioned in Scripture was built by Cain. The specialization that is always part of city life was carried on by Cain's descendants. One of them, Jabal, worked in agriculture as a herdsman. Another, Jubal, labored in the arts, making musical instruments. Another, Tubal-cain, worked in industry, producing all sorts of objects made of brass and iron. Whether they realized it or not, they were demonstrating the implications of the Creation Mandate. They had been fruitful and therefore had multiplied over the face of the earth. Through specialization and organization, they had developed the earliest human civilization.

Nevertheless, their civilization was not pleasing to God. Their sin was not building and maintaining a city. Their sin was attempting to fulfill the Creation Mandate independent of God. Perhaps the best summary statement in Genesis for the problem with Cainite culture is the verse that introduces us to that culture: "And Cain went out from the presence of the Lord, and dwelt in the land of Nod" (Gen. 4:16). Living apart from the will and love of Yahweh was one of the core values that held Cainite civilization together.

Ruins of the Roman Forum in Rome

Seth and His Seed

The story of Cain and his descendants is only part of the history of mankind after the Fall. God gave Adam and Eve another son. Eve named him **Seth** ("appointed"). She explained, "God . . . hath appointed me another seed instead of Abel" (Gen. 4:25). Seth proved to be a spiritual as well as a physical replacement for Abel. Just as Abel worshiped God in an acceptable manner, so Seth fathered a line of people who were known to "call upon the name of the Lord" (v. 26). Through Seth, the seed of the woman increased and prospered.

The Sethites, however, did not remain true to God. Because of the reality of death, a godly people cannot remain godly unless it passes on to each new generation its love and devotion to God. At some point in their history, the Sethites allowed their children to intermarry with the Cainites. The Bible explains that Seth's descendants ("the sons of God") were attracted to the Cainite women ("the daughters of men") because "they were fair" (Gen. 6:2). As the previous generations of godly Sethites died and were replaced by the children of religiously mixed marriages, the line of Seth was transformed. Soon the behavior of Seth's descendants was no different from that of Cain's people. The entire human race became morally corrupt. Eventually, as the Bible declares, "every imagination of the thoughts of [man's] heart was only evil continually" (v. 5).

The Great Flood

Since the earth was no longer serving its purpose, God determined to remake His world. God was now preparing to cover the whole earth with a great flood. One man remained a committed worshiper of his Creator. **Noah** rejected the corrupting influences of the world and, like Enoch, "walked with God" (Gen. 6:9). To Noah God revealed His plan for the survival of the human race. He instructed Noah to build a massive ark. God told Noah that when he completed this project, he was to take his family and representatives of the animal kingdom into the ark, where they would be safe. Noah and his family obeyed. God held back His judgment for 120 years (Gen. 6:3). The human race had more than a century to repent and accept the promise of life offered through the ark. But in the end only Noah, his wife, his three sons, and their wives entered the ark. At the predetermined moment, the "foundations of the great deep" (Gen. 7:11) were broken up, and torrents of rain fell to the earth. It rained for forty days, and by the time it stopped, the entire earth was covered in water. The almighty Creator had caused the earth to return to its original state. Once again it was "without form, and void" (Gen. 1:2).

Following the Flood, God made a covenant with Noah and his descendants (Gen. 9). Yahweh promised to preserve the regular seasons, and to never destroy the earth with another flood. God affirmed that man was still bearing His image and repeated the principles of the Creation Mandate. This covenant established the earth as a place for God to implement His plan of redemption rather than a place that would be continually overturned by divine judgment.

A Second Beginning

As the flood waters receded, the ark came to rest on the Ararat mountain range. As Noah left the ark, he entered a world newly reborn. The contaminating vestiges of the old world had been purged away. But sin still resided in the human heart.

One of Noah's earliest actions after the Flood was less than noble. He became intoxicated from the fruit of his own vineyard and fell asleep naked in his tent. Noah's son **Ham** saw his father in his shameful stupor and talked about him to his brothers, **Shem** and **Japheth**. Having proper respect and love for their father, these two sons entered Noah's tent with their backs turned and covered him with a garment.

Noah's Prophecy

When Noah realized what had happened, he punished Ham by placing a curse on **Canaan**, one of Ham's sons: "Cursed be Canaan; a servant of servants shall he be unto his brethren" (Gen. 9:25). But

Artist's rendering of what the ark may have looked like. The foil in the front would have kept the ark facing the wind and the waves.

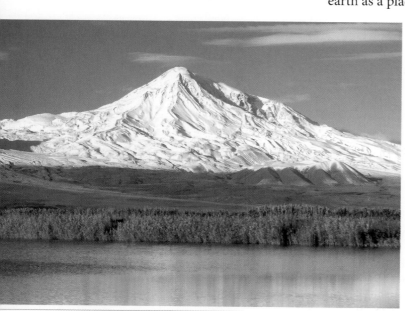

Mt. Ararat is located in modern-day Turkey, near its eastern border.

recognizing the noble deed of the other two sons, Noah blessed Shem and Japheth. He first spoke of Shem's future: "Blessed be the Lord God of Shem; and Canaan shall be his servant" (v. 26). Thus Noah indicated that Shem's future blessing would consist in his descendants' special relationship to Yahweh and that God would use the curse on Canaan to benefit Shem. Concerning Japheth, Noah prophesied, "God shall enlarge Japheth, and he shall dwell in the tents of Shem" (v. 27). Japheth would be blessed with wealth and power, and he would find additional blessing by sharing in Shem's blessing.

Here God suggested that Shem would somehow play a special role in the triumph of the seed of the woman. This triumph is foreshadowed in the curse on Canaan. The Canaanites, who eventually settled in a land they named for their ancestor, would end up serving the descendants of Shem. It should not surprise us, therefore, to find that much of biblical history traces God's working among the Hebrews, descendants of Shem, in a land that God took from the Canaanites.

Babel and Its Consequences

As years passed into decades, mankind once again multiplied and began to fill the earth. Civilization reemerged as city building began again. But mankind did not want to establish many different civilizations. The race desired to live together and form a single, unified society.

At this time all of mankind spoke the same language. It was not difficult, therefore, for people to organize themselves. They gathered in the land of Shinar (probably located in southeastern Mesopotamia) and began to build the city that would later be called **Babel**. Central to this city was to be a magnificent tower, which would serve as this civilization's religious center. The reasons they gave for this undertaking are revealing: "Let us build us a city and a tower, whose top may reach unto heaven; and let us make us a name, lest we be scattered abroad upon the face of the whole earth" (Gen. 11:4).

The tower of Babel may have looked something like this artist's rendering of the Ziggurat of Ur.

God did not feel threatened by what was happening at Babel. But rather than unleashing His righteous anger, He chose to restrain humans' ability to do evil. He confused the minds of those at Babel so that they could no longer communicate with one another. In that hour, long ago, the complex and confusing differences among human languages were born.

The Rise of Nations

The human race eventually reorganized itself into people groups, each having a common language. It was probably during this period that the first nations arose. A **nation** is a very large group of people (usually including many cities) who have in common the same land area and the same language. Genesis 10 is often referred to as the Bible's **Table of Nations** because it lists the descendants of Shem, Ham, and Japheth according to the nations that arose from their families. There we learn that Japheth's descendants

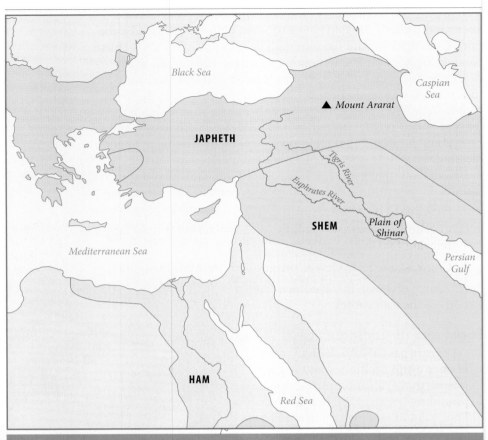

The Post-Flood World

founded nations in eastern Europe. Ham's descendants founded nations in eastern Asia and Africa. And Shem's descendants founded nations to the east and north of Ham's descendants.

Much of the remainder of human history would be the story of one nation after another attempting to reestablish the ideal that the men of Babel sought. But as one nation would begin to succeed in establishing a man-centered one-world civilization, another would rise up and overthrow it. God manifests His mercy to humans beyond merely meeting humans' daily needs. His mercy is also evident in the decline and fall of great civilizations. By bringing them to an end before they gain permanent, worldwide authority, He restrains man from much of his destructive sinfulness.

Section Review

1. Who is history's most important person?

2–3. Where does the Creation Mandate appear in Scripture, and what does this command include?

4–7. List and describe four themes of civilization.

8. Where in the Bible do you find the thesis statement for human history?

✶ How did the Fall affect the development of civilizations, beginning with Cain?

Making Connections

1–3. Classify the historian's three types of primary sources.

4–7. Briefly outline the history of man from the birth of Seth to the Flood.

8–15. Identify the features of civilization.

Developing History Skills

1. Using Genesis 9, respond to the following statement: "The Creation Mandate was nullified by the Flood and is no longer relevant for Christians today."

2. Contrast a secular view of origins with the biblical account.

Thinking Critically

1. Referring to Genesis 11, answer this question: "From the definition of a city as a cultural institution where people share core values and develop specialization and organization, which of these features was flawed in the city of Babel?" Explain your answer.

2. Using John 8:39–45 and 1 John 3:9–12, write a brief essay surveying the differences between the seed of the woman and the seed of the serpent.

Living in God's World

1. Write a brief essay about why you as a Christian should study history.

2. Create a flow chart of history from the Fall to the rise of nations that visualizes how Genesis 3:15 is the thesis statement for human history.

People, Places, and Things to Know

primary sources
secondary sources
artifacts
tradition
written records
evaluation of historical sources
historical synthesis
historical interpretation
worldview
divine providence
history
Paleolithic Age
Neolithic Age
Yahweh
image of God
Creation Mandate
civilization
organization
cities
social classes
specialization
written language
religion
justice
power
citizenship
environment
Adam
Eve
seed of the serpent
seed of the woman
Seth
Noah
Ham
Shem
Japheth
Canaan
Babel
nation
Table of Nations

Early Civilizations

The Plain of Gennesaret and the Sea of Galilee

Big Ideas

1. What were the major cultural achievements of the Fertile Crescent civilizations?

2. How did Egypt's geography shape its history and culture?

3. What role did the Assyrian, Chaldean, and Persian empires play in God's plan for history?

4. What role did religion play in the development of early Indian and Chinese civilizations?

Israel is unique among the nations. All other nations followed after false gods, but God chose Israel to bring His blessings to these other nations. This blessing came primarily through the revelation that God gave to Israelite prophets (much of which is now preserved in the Old Testament). During this period of history, Israel was also to bless the nations by obeying God's law. When the other nations saw the wisdom of God's law, they would be drawn to worship Israel's God. Sadly, aside from a few brief, shining moments in the reigns of David and Solomon, Israel failed at this mission. The nations which Israel was to bless became instruments of God to judge His wayward people.

I. The Fertile Crescent

After God scattered the nations at the Tower of Babel, many of the descendants of Ham and Shem remained and settled in the fertile region of the Tigris and Euphrates Rivers (Gen. 10:6–32). Later the Greeks described this region with the word *Mesopotamia* (MES uh puh TAY mee uh), meaning the "land between the rivers." By about 3000 BC the people in the southern part of this area had established the Sumerian culture.

Sumerian Civilization

Sumer consisted of about a dozen independent city-states that had no political unity but possessed a similar culture. The cities fought among themselves, each trying to gain dominance over the others. The Sumerians believed that their cities belonged to the gods. For this reason the temple was not only a place of worship but also the center of education, government, and trade. Each city had its own ruler, usually a priest, who acted as the representative of the gods.

The Sumerians were historically near the event of the Flood and should have retained a cultural remembrance of true religion as passed down by Noah and his descendants. However, by the time of the tower of Babel incident, true worship had been replaced by false worship. **Polytheism** (belief in many gods) was a natural result of the scattering of the people into separate ethnic groups, with each developing its own religion. In Sumer, as with almost every other civilization until the coming of Christ, the religion of the people was polytheistic, with the power and actions of the true God being divided among invented deities. These gods were a pale reflection of the true God. They were in many ways like all-powerful humans who fought and fathered children and did many other things that humans do. Genesis 1 says that God made man in His image, but the Sumerians made gods in the image of man.

Cuneiform

Much of what we know about Sumer has come from the discovery of thousands of clay tablets bearing **cuneiform** (KYOO nee uh form), the earliest known form of writing. Using a wedge-shaped stylus (a split reed), the Sumerians made impressions on tablets of wet clay, which they later baked until hard. They could express ideas by the manner in which they

Guiding Questions

1. What were the major cultural achievements of the civilizations of the Fertile Crescent?
2. What role did justice, power, citizenship, and the environment play in the civilizations of the Fertile Crescent?
3. What was the significance of the Hebrew civilization for the development of world history?

Early cuneiform tablet

arranged these wedge-shaped impressions. Young men learned this complex writing in a formal educational system. Teachers were called "school-fathers," and the students were called "school-sons." Sumerian boys who learned cuneiform also studied the Sumerians' numerical system—a system based not on ten like ours today, but on the number sixty.

Reconstructed ziggurat at Ur

Epic of Gilgamesh

A noted example of Sumerian literature is the *Epic of Gilgamesh*. This epic poem describes the adventures of the legendary hero Gilgamesh (GIL guh mesh) and his search for eternal life. In his travels Gilgamesh meets Utnapishtim (oot nah PEESH teem), the only man to have attained immortality.

One of the most interesting sections of the poem is Utnapishtim's account of how Ea, one of the gods, delivered him from a universal flood. Ea warned him that Enlil, one of the other gods, was angry and was planning to cover the earth with water. He told Utnapishtim to tear down his house and build a boat. Utnapishtim was also to take "the seed of all living things" aboard his boat.

Having built a boat, Utnapishtim gathered aboard his family, the craftsmen who helped him, and the animals of the field. The rains and flood raged for six days and nights and subsided on the seventh day.

Farming and Architecture

The major occupation of the Sumerians was farming. They built an elaborate network of canals and dikes to provide irrigation for their crops. Although agriculture was the basis of their economy, the people lived in fortified cities. They built their homes and public buildings with baked clay bricks. Temple towers called **ziggurats** (ZIG uh rats) were outstanding examples of Sumerian architecture. These impressive pyramid-like structures had terraces at different levels along their exterior. The bricks used in these buildings were often glazed in different colors.

Sargon

Near the end of Sumerian dominance, a new people migrated to the northern Sumerian cities. They adopted much of the Sumerian culture but also asserted their own influence on the cities in which they settled. Around 2270 BC the ruler **Sargon** came to power in the city-state of Kish. Sargon conquered other city-states and established an **empire**—the rule of one people over another. Making the city of Akkad his capital, he created a united kingdom—the Akkadian (uh KAY dee un) Empire—which stretched from the Persian Gulf to northern Mesopotamia. Under Sargon, the king's authority surpassed that of the priests. The people were encouraged to view the king as a god.

About a century after Sargon's death, the city of Ur rose to prominence. This powerful city-state may have been the same Ur that is mentioned in Genesis 11:31 as the birthplace of Abraham, the father of the Hebrew people. But whether "Ur of the Chaldees" (as the Bible calls it) was the well-known city of southern Mesopotamia is ultimately of little importance. What is important to know and remember is that Abraham's world was dominated by polytheism and idolatry. When God revealed Himself to Abraham around 2100 BC

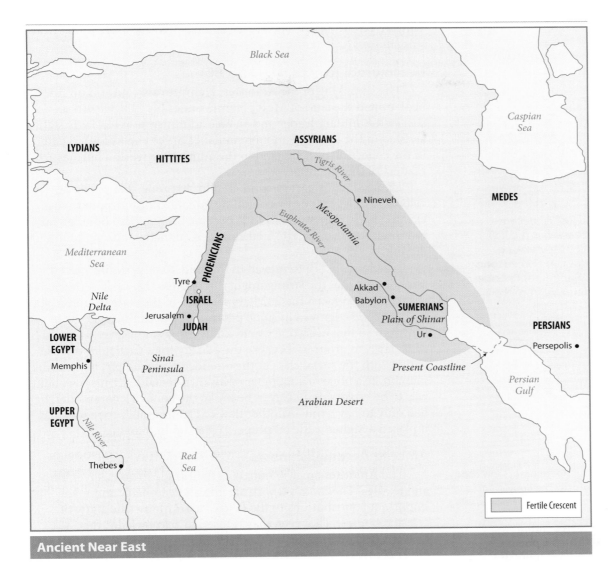

Ancient Near East

and called him to move out of Ur, He was not simply telling Abraham to leave his home. God was also telling him to leave his way of life—probably the only way of life Abraham had known.

Sumerian Contributions

By 2000 BC the Sumerian civilization had disappeared, but aspects of its culture continued in later civilizations. For example, the Amorites, Hittites, Assyrians, and Persians used a version of cuneiform. Roman architects adopted Sumerian building techniques such as the arch. Even today we use Sumerian inventions: the wheel, the division of a circle into 360 degrees, and the division of hours and minutes into sixty units. These influences testify of Sumerian knowledge and technological skill.

Amorite Civilization

Weakened by a series of wars with its neighbors, the Sumerian civilization, centered at Ur, fell to Amorite invaders. The Amorites established what is now referred to as the "Old Babylonian" Empire. Its capital was the city of Babylon (BAB uh lun), one of the greatest cities of the ancient world. The history of this city began shortly after the Flood, when Nimrod established a kingdom that included

Babylon (Gen. 10:10). The Tower of Babel may have been built near this city.

Hammurabi (ca. 1810–1750 BC)

The sixth king of the Amorites, **Hammurabi** (HAH moo RAH bee), united the land of Mesopotamia under his rule. He was a successful military leader and an able administrator. His large staff assisted in the building and maintenance of the canals for irrigation, in the collection of taxes, and in the administrative and business matters of the kingdom.

Hammurabi is best remembered for his code of laws. He developed this legal code by compiling, organizing, and simplifying existing laws. Hammurabi's code became the standard of judgment in moral, social, domestic, and commercial matters throughout the empire.

"To cause justice to prevail in the land, to destroy the wicked and the evil, that the strong might not oppress the weak"—this inscription introduced the 282 laws set forth in the code. Hammurabi had the code engraved in stone pillars and placed throughout the kingdom so that everyone would know the law. However, Hammurabi's law was arbitrary because the penalty for a particular offense varied with the social class of the offender. For example, if a wealthy man broke a bone of a member of his own social class, his own bone was to be broken. If, however, he broke the bone of a commoner, he had only to pay a fine. Another flaw of Hammurabi's code was that it placed a higher value on property than on human life.

Amorite Accomplishments

The Amorites are also noted for their trade in gold, silver, tin, and textiles. They worked with algebra and geometry and made important contributions to the field of **astronomy** (the study of celestial bodies). However, they refused to acknowledge that "the heavens declare the glory of God" (Ps. 19:1). Instead of trusting God's control over the events of life, the Amorites resorted to a false method of interpreting human events and destiny by the position of the planets and stars—a practice that is called **astrology**.

Lacking able leadership after the death of Hammurabi, the Amorite civilization declined in both power and influence. Invaders came into the land and seized control of the territory of this once powerful kingdom.

Justice

Law codes contribute to justice because they make public and clear what the laws are and the consequences for violating them. However, law codes can also encode injustices. For instance, Hammurabi's Code treated the wealthy differently from the poor.

Stele containing Hammurabi's law code; the carving portrays the Babylonian god Shamash presenting the law to Hammurabi.

Section Review

1. What did the Greeks call the fertile region between the Tigris and Euphrates Rivers?

2. What is the name of the Sumerian, wedge-shaped form of writing?

3–4. Who established the first known empire? What became his capital city?

5. The Amorite civilization was centered in what capital city?

★ An empire is often held together by force of arms. One people has the military might to maintain rule over other people. How might this use of power lead to injustice? Could it ever lead to more justice?

★ What role did rivers play in ancient civilizations?

The Hittites

Before the twentieth century, little was known about the Hittites. Many people did not even believe they had ever existed because the Old Testament was the only source of information concerning them. The Hittites were the descendants of Heth, the son of Canaan and the grandson of Ham (Gen. 10:15). Biblical references to the Hittites include Abraham's purchase of a burial site from Ephron the Hittite (Gen. 23:1–20; 25:7–10) and King David's murder of Uriah the Hittite to cover up his sin with Bathsheba (2 Sam. 11:3–27).

Archaeological discoveries around the turn of the twentieth century confirmed the existence of the Hittite Empire. The Hittites may have begun to settle in Asia Minor (modern-day Turkey) about 2000 BC. The Hittite king was the commander of the army. His power rested upon the support of the chief warriors. Controlling rich supplies of iron ore, the Hittites excelled in the production of iron. With their military skill and their work in iron, they became feared by other people.

Using iron weapons and horse-drawn chariots, the Hittites extended their empire throughout Asia Minor and into the **Fertile Crescent** (which takes its name from the crescent-shaped fertile region encompassing Mesopotamia and the land of Canaan). They raided the Amorite capital of Babylon and later took control of modern-day Syria. This expansion brought them into conflict with the Egyptian empire, which was also expanding into that area. Frequent fighting between the Hittites and the Egyptians weakened both and led to their mutual decline. This event gave the Phoenicians, the Arameans, and the Hebrews an opportunity to establish independent kingdoms. Once a major power in Asia Minor and the northern Fertile Crescent, the Hittites were absorbed by more advanced cultures and gradually passed into obscurity.

Hittite metalwork

The Phoenicians

In Ezekiel 27:3–4 and verse 33, the prophet Ezekiel described the city of Tyre as proud and enamored with acquiring wealth. For more than a thousand years, Tyre was one of the leading city-states of Phoenicia. Containing many independent city-states, Phoenicia was located along the eastern coast of the Mediterranean Sea (where Lebanon is today). The Phoenicians were a Canaanite people. One of the earliest Phoenician cities was probably Sidon, founded by Canaan's firstborn son, Sidon (Gen. 10:15).

Merchants of the Mediterranean

The Phoenicians appeared around 2000 BC and later became the greatest merchants of their day. With their large merchant fleet, they traded with areas all around the Mediterranean Sea—Egypt, Greece, Sicily, Spain, and North Africa. Spices, fine linen, wheat, cattle, horses, ivory, gold, precious stones, and tin (used to harden copper) were just some of the items handled by these traders.

The Phoenicians also gained great wealth through two valuable natural resources. The first was a type of mollusk (a sea animal similar to a snail) found off the Phoenician coast. The Phoenicians obtained a purple dye from this sea animal. Purple-dyed cloth became one of their chief

> ### Environment
> Part of human dominion over the earth (Gen. 1:28) is making use of physical features to advance civilization. The Phoenicians used their location on the Mediterranean Sea to build a trading empire, and the city of Tyre transformed an island into a fortress.

Mollusk

Land of Canaan

exports. (The word *Phoenicia* comes from the Greeks, who called the Phoenicians the "purple people" or the "traders of purple.") The second natural resource was the cedar and fir trees found in the Lebanon mountains. Phoenicia supplied the cedars that King Solomon used to build the temple in Jerusalem. In fact, Solomon used many precious materials from the commercial city of Tyre in building the temple (1 Kings 5).

The Phoenician Alphabet

The Phoenicians are believed to be the originators of the alphabet. By the eleventh century BC, the cuneiform writing of the Sumerians and the hieroglyphics of the Egyptians had been in use for centuries. The Phoenicians developed uniform symbols to stand for distinct sounds. By arranging the letters, they could form an almost infinite number of words. Writing then became simple enough for most people to understand. The Greeks and the Romans later adapted this alphabet for their own use and passed it on to future generations.

The City of Tyre

The Phoenicians lost their independence during the ninth and eighth centuries BC as the Assyrians invaded the territory along the coast and exacted tribute from the wealthy city-states. However, Tyre, a leading Phoenician city-state, continued to thrive, its trade unhampered by the Assyrians. Long before the Assyrian invasion, Tyre had expanded to an island about a half mile off the coast. From this island fortress it was safe from land attack. Massive walls around the island city and a strong navy protected Tyre from sea attack as well.

The wealth and prosperity of Tyre was short-lived. The people of Tyre and the other Phoenician cities rejected the knowledge of the true God by worshiping **Baal,** one of the Canaanites' gods. The Phoenicians were also largely responsible for the growth of paganism in Israel. It was Jezebel, the daughter of the king of Sidon, who married Ahab, an Israelite king, and introduced Baal-worship in Israel. Because of Tyre's great commerce, pride entered the people's hearts. The prophet Ezekiel addressed them, "Thine heart is lifted up because of thy riches" (Ezek. 28:5). Tyre also laughed at the calamity of the people of God when Nebuchadnezzar destroyed Jerusalem. For these reasons the prophet Ezekiel declared that God would cause many nations to destroy this city (Ezekiel 26:3–5).

Ezekiel foretold that Nebuchadnezzar, king of Babylon, would come and besiege the city (Ezek. 26:7–11). Nebuchadnezzar did come, and he besieged Tyre for thirteen years. He destroyed the mainland portion of the city but failed to destroy the island portion. Alexander the Great, more than two hundred years later, continued the fulfillment of this prophecy against Tyre. By pushing the ruins of mainland Tyre into the sea, Alexander's men built a causeway out to the island city. His forces conquered the city, killing thousands and taking many thousands captive. The plunder of Tyre continued in the centuries to follow.

The Hebrews
The Call of Abraham

"Get thee out of thy country, and from thy kindred, and from thy father's house, unto a land that I will shew thee: and I will make

Ruins of Tyre

of thee a great nation, and I will bless thee, and make thy name great; and thou shalt be a blessing: and I will bless them that bless thee, and curse him that curseth thee: and in thee shall all families of the earth be blessed" (Gen. 12:1–3). With these words God called Abraham out of Mesopotamian paganism and preserved through Abraham and his offspring the worship of the true God. Unlike the surrounding polytheistic religions, the religion of Abraham and his offspring was monotheistic. God also made a covenant with Abraham (called the **Abrahamic Covenant**) that expresses very briefly God's plan for redeeming His fallen world to Himself. The covenant is composed of three basic promises. First, God promised Abraham a great seed, or group of descendants. This seed would grow to become a mighty nation from which God would raise up the Messiah (Hebrew for "the anointed one"). The Messiah would bless God's people by saving them from their sins and ruling over them in goodness and justice. Second, God promised to give Abraham's seed a land in which to live, the land of Canaan. Third, God promised that the blessings given to Abraham would benefit all the nations of the world because the Messiah would bring salvation to people from every nation who turned from their false religions to the true God.

For the Christian, this final promise is the summary statement for human history. It is a declaration that finds its earliest expression in God's promise to the serpent in Eden: "I will put enmity between thee and the woman, and between thy seed and her seed; it shall bruise thy head, and thou shalt bruise his heel" (Gen. 3:15). And it finds its consummation in history's greatest "Hallelujah": "The kingdoms of this world are become the kingdoms of our Lord, and of his Christ; and he shall reign for ever and ever" (Rev. 11:15). The story of the human race is the story of how God is working to make the disobedient kingdoms of this world the kingdom of His Messiah, His own Son.

Abraham was born in 2166 BC. When God called him (ca. 2091 BC), Abraham was himself an idolater (cf. Josh. 24:2–3). God chose Abraham not because he was a better person than the other inhabitants of Ur but because He is gracious. He told Abraham that he would be the father of a great nation, even though, at the time, his wife could not have children and the land God brought him to was occupied by other people groups. Nevertheless, Abraham believed God and obeyed. In time God fulfilled His promise by providing the aged Abraham with a son, Isaac, through whom the chosen line was to come. This line of blessing continued through Isaac's son Jacob. The descendants of these patriarchs are called the children of Israel, taking their name from Jacob, whose name God changed to Israel.

Bondage in Egypt

Jacob and his family went down into Egypt to escape a famine in Canaan. God had already provided for His people in Egypt by giving Joseph (one of Jacob's sons) a place of leadership. It was in Egypt that God revealed through Jacob that the future nation of Israel would be composed of twelve tribes, each descending from one of Jacob's twelve sons (Gen. 49). The most important of these tribes would be Judah. From this patriarch Israel's kings would come, the greatest being the Messiah Himself (v. 10). In Egypt Jacob's descendants grew from a family into a nation—the Israelites. Once a place of refuge for the Israelites, Egypt became a place of hardship. An Egyptian leader who did not remember (or acknowledge) what

No Egyptian Record?

No Egyptian record has been found of the Israelites in Egypt or the events of the Exodus. This leads some to doubt the accuracy of God's Word in the Book of Exodus. However, the Egyptians rarely recorded losses in battle or invasions by other countries. Rather, they emphasized victories and conquests. Therefore, it would have been out of character for them to record the fact that a large number of people they had enslaved had been led to freedom by an omnipotent God.

We should also note that the archaeological research for the era and location of the Israelite occupation is still underdeveloped. Future research could reveal evidence affirming the biblical account.

Mount Sinai

Joseph had done for Egypt enslaved the Hebrew people. God remembered his people, however, and raised up **Moses** to lead them out of bondage. The children of Israel left Egypt in 1446 BC and crossed the Red Sea, bound for the land of Canaan.

The Covenant at Sinai

One of the most important events in Hebrew history occurred at Mount Sinai (Exod. 19–20). There God established Israel as a theocracy—a people governed directly by God. God established His covenant with the children of Israel, promising to be ever present with them. God communicated His will through leaders He ordained, such as Moses and Joshua. The centerpiece of the covenant at Sinai was the law of God, which provided instruction, guidelines, and judgments in moral, civil, and ceremonial matters. It established for all time a perfect moral standard for distinguishing right from wrong.

The Conquest of Canaan

Though blessed with the very presence of God, the children of Israel often chose to sin. This was illustrated when Moses sent twelve spies into Canaan to search the land (Num. 13:1–16). As the reports came back that the land was filled with giants and walled cities, the people forgot God's promises and rebelled against the Lord out of fear. Because of this rebellion, the children of Israel had to wander in the wilderness. That generation died along the way, never inhabiting the Promised Land (Num. 14:20–35). After forty years the next generation of Israelites crossed the Jordan River into the land "flowing with milk and honey." Under a new leader, Joshua, they destroyed the cities of Jericho and Ai and defeated the many different peoples of the land. Then they divided the land among the twelve tribes of Israel (Josh. 14–22).

The Judges

After the death of Joshua, "every man did that which was right in his own eyes" (Judges 17:6, 21:25). God had intended that the Hebrew people demonstrate to the ancient world that there is but one living God. In an age dominated by polytheism, He wanted them to be sincerely committed to **monotheism** (belief in only one God). But the children of Israel turned from the true God to worship the false gods of the Canaanites. Because of their disobedience, God raised up enemies to oppress Israel. This oppression caused the children of Israel to turn back to God and cry out for mercy. God heard their cries and raised up leaders, called judges, through whom He ruled His people and delivered them from their oppressors (Judges 2:16–18).

During the judgeship of Samuel, the Israelites again rejected God's rule, desiring a human king to rule over them instead (1 Sam. 8:4–8). Saul became the first king of Israel. He united all the tribes of Israel under his leadership and led Israel in victories over the Philistines and the Amalekites. Nevertheless, he failed to obey the commands of God, and God rejected him as king (1 Sam. 15).

David and Solomon

God chose **David**, a man "after God's own heart," as the next king. From his family the promised Messiah would come. King David conquered Israel's enemies, enlarged Israel's borders, and established peace throughout the land. Jerusalem, the "city of David," became the center of worship and government for the Hebrew kingdom (2 Sam. 5:6–10).

The kingdom of Israel reached its peak during the reign of David's son Solomon. Visiting dignitaries, such as the Queen of Sheba, marveled at the wealth and wisdom of this Hebrew king (1 Kings 10:1–13). Supplied with materials from Phoenicia, Solomon built the magnificent temple of God that his father David had planned. Before the end of Solomon's reign, however, he began to permit the worship of false gods in Israel. God, therefore, revealed to Solomon that He would judge Israel by dividing the nation in two.

Ruins of Solomon's fortress at Megiddo

Division and Judgment

God used Solomon's oppressive taxation policy to bring this division about. Following the death of Solomon, the Hebrew people came to Rehoboam, the new king, and begged him to lower their taxes. Rehoboam decided to increase the taxes instead (1 Kings 12:1–15). Outraged at this decision, the ten northern tribes of Israel rebelled and made Jeroboam their king. The southern tribes of Benjamin and Judah became the kingdom of Judah, remaining loyal to Rehoboam and the house of David (1 Kings 12:19–24).

The Hebrew nation, now divided, lost the greatness and peace achieved under the reigns of David and Solomon. Wickedness increased among both the people of Israel and the people of Judah. Peace was replaced by strife and warfare. Isaiah and Jeremiah, as well as other prophets, warned God's people of coming judgment, but their warnings went unheeded.

Judgment came upon the disobedient people of God. In 722 BC the Assyrians destroyed Samaria (the capital of the Northern Kingdom of Israel) and carried its people away captive. The Chaldeans (kal DEE unz) under Nebuchadnezzar (r. 605–562 BC) destroyed Jerusalem in 586 BC and carried many of the Jews back to Babylon. This period of exile, known as the **Babylonian Captivity**, lasted seventy years.

Nevertheless, God did not forsake His people, and He did not forget the Abrahamic Covenant. God raised up the Persians to free His people and restore them once again to their land. By renewing His promise of a seed for Abraham and of a land for that seed, God was keeping alive His promise to bless all the nations of the earth through the coming of the Messiah.

Section Review

1–2. What two weapons did the Hittites use as they expanded their empire into Asia Minor?

3–6. Name the three promises that make up the Abrahamic Covenant. What is special about the third promise?

7. Define *theocracy*.

✶ God promised to bless David (2 Samuel 7) and Solomon (1 Kings 3). Which promise was unconditional?

✶ Assess the importance of the Hebrew civilization for the development of world history.

Guiding Questions

1. How did Egypt's geography shape the development of its civilization?
2. What are the three periods of Egypt's history?
3. What are key aspects of Egypt's culture?
4. How did the Egyptians view the afterlife?

The Nile

II. Egypt

Egypt is a desert land. Had it not been for the dry climate, the remains of Egypt—the monuments, the documents, and even the bodies of its rulers—would have crumbled or decayed long ago. Because so much has been preserved from this ancient civilization, we can learn a great deal about its fascinating history and culture.

The Land of Egypt

Ancient Egypt was not the square-shaped territory that we call Egypt today. It was the narrow strip of land along the banks of the Nile River. It was about 750 miles long but in many places less than twelve miles wide. Because the Nile flows northward from the southern plateau, the southern region is called "Upper Egypt" and the northern region "Lower Egypt." These were really two entirely different lands. Upper Egypt lay close against the Nile, completely cut off from the outside world by desert to the east and west and by rapids (called "cataracts") to the south. Lower Egypt, on the other hand, spread out across the Nile Delta in easy contact with other nations by way of the Mediterranean Sea and the Sinai Peninsula.

One Greek historian called Egypt the "gift of the river." He was right. If there were no Nile, there would have been no Egypt. Because there was almost no rain there, only the Nile held back the menacing desert wasteland. The river rose and fell every year. As the snow at the river's source in the mountains melted every spring, the river flooded its banks from June through August. This flooding deposited tons of rich silt on Egypt, annually providing fertile soil for the crops.

The Nile was also important as a highway. Boats at the northern end of the river (called the "delta" after the triangular Greek letter delta, Δ) could hoist sails and let the winds from the north push them upriver. To return they needed simply to drop their sails and let the current carry them back. Since nearly all ancient Egyptians lived on the banks of the river, it was easy for those living at one end of the kingdom to communicate with those at the other end. Thus the Nile greatly contributed to a unified Egypt.

The History of Egypt

The people of Egypt were descended from Mizraim, the son of Noah's son Ham. In fact, the Hebrews called Egypt "Mizraim." Around 3000 BC a man named **Menes** (MEE neez) is believed to have united the two lands of Upper and Lower Egypt, ruling them from a capital that he called "White Walls" (later named Memphis). Historians refer to this time as the Early Dynastic Period.

Old Kingdom

Many historians divide ancient Egyptian history into three major phases: the Old, Middle, and New Kingdoms. These phases are separated by times of unrest generally known as intermediate periods. The Old Kingdom (ca. 2700–2200 BC) has been called "The Age of the Pharaohs." There were **pharaohs**, or rulers, throughout all of ancient Egyptian history, of course, but in the Old Kingdom they were especially powerful. The people considered them to be gods in human form. As "gods" they owned all of Egypt and used it for their own purposes. It was during this time that the great pyramids were built—huge tombs attesting to the splendor and might

The Great Pyramid

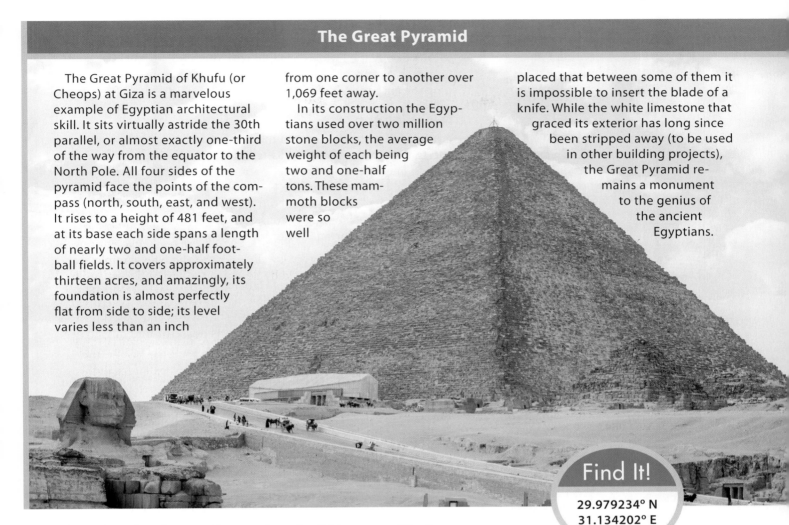

The Great Pyramid of Khufu (or Cheops) at Giza is a marvelous example of Egyptian architectural skill. It sits virtually astride the 30th parallel, or almost exactly one-third of the way from the equator to the North Pole. All four sides of the pyramid face the points of the compass (north, south, east, and west). It rises to a height of 481 feet, and at its base each side spans a length of nearly two and one-half football fields. It covers approximately thirteen acres, and amazingly, its foundation is almost perfectly flat from side to side; its level varies less than an inch

from one corner to another over 1,069 feet away.

In its construction the Egyptians used over two million stone blocks, the average weight of each being two and one-half tons. These mammoth blocks were so well

placed that between some of them it is impossible to insert the blade of a knife. While the white limestone that graced its exterior has long since been stripped away (to be used in other building projects), the Great Pyramid remains a monument to the genius of the ancient Egyptians.

Find It!

29.979234° N
31.134202° E

of the pharaohs. The most famous pharaoh of this age was **Khufu** (KOO foo), or Cheops (KEE ops), who built the Great Pyramid at Giza. Its construction required thousands of men working for twenty years.

Middle Kingdom

After a time of rebellion called "The First Intermediate Period," the Middle Kingdom, also known as "The Age of the People," began (ca. 2040–1650 BC). Aware of the social unrest that preceded them, the Egyptian pharaohs of this period directed their attention to projects that would benefit the country as a whole. As a result, the Middle Kingdom was characterized by peace and construction. For example, the Egyptians built irrigation canals and systems of ponds to store the Nile's waters for use in the dry season.

It was during this time of peace that the Israelites moved to Egypt (Gen. 46–50). God used the influence of Joseph (Abraham's great-grandson) to save the Egyptians from starvation and to provide a haven for the children of Israel during a time of famine (Gen. 47:1–6). The Israelites stayed in the land of Egypt for 430 years, from 1876 to 1446 BC (Exod. 12:40–41). During that time their numbers grew from seventy to over two million.

After the Middle Kingdom, in what has been called "The Second Intermediate Period," a foreign people called the Hyksos (HIK sose) came into the land and eventually became its rulers. It is not

Thutmose III

Golden burial mask of Tutankhamen

known exactly who they were or how they became so powerful. Many believe the Egyptians learned the art of war from the Hyksos. Evidently the Hyksos brought with them horses, chariots, and bronze weapons. The Hyksos may have been responsible for beginning the enslavement of the Hebrews.

New Kingdom

Egypt eventually expelled the Hyksos and restored an Egyptian to the throne. This New Kingdom (ca. 1570–1075 BC) is also called "The Age of the Empire" because it was in this age that Egypt became a great power in the Near East. The pharaohs became "warrior-kings." They extended their control to Palestine, Syria, and the lands of the Nile (that is, to the south). In this age Upper Egypt became more important. As a result, Thebes became the Egyptian capital.

Several pharaohs in this age are of particular interest. An early ruler of the New Kingdom was **Hatshepsut** (hat SHEP soot), one of the rare female rulers of Egypt. She may have been the "daughter of Pharaoh" who discovered Moses in the bulrushes and raised him as her own son (Exod. 2:5–10). Her rule was peaceful, and during her reign Egypt traded extensively with nearby nations. Hatshepsut's reign was followed by that of **Thutmose III** (thoot MO suh), regarded as the greatest Egyptian warrior-king. Under Thutmose, the Egyptian armies conquered Palestine and Syria, extending Egyptian rule all the way to the Euphrates River. One modern historian called Thutmose the "Napoleon of Egypt." Moses, another great leader, lived at this time.

If current Egyptology is correct, Thutmose III was the pharaoh who refused to allow the children of Israel to go. He finally yielded after God sent ten plagues upon the land of Egypt (Exod. 7:8–11:10, 12:29–36). However, Pharaoh changed his mind and pursued the Hebrew people. God overwhelmed Pharaoh's chariots and horsemen by returning the waters of the Red Sea upon them (Exod. 14).

About a century and a half after the Hebrews left Egypt, **Ramses II** came to power. During his long reign, Egypt once again built mammoth temples and monuments. Egypt gradually declined from its rank as a Near Eastern power after his death.

The Culture of Egypt

Egyptian social structure was shaped like a pyramid: at the top was the pharaoh, supremely powerful; below him were the priests and nobles; then came the merchants, the common people, and the foreign slaves, in that order.

Most Egyptians were poor, but anyone from a lower class—even a foreign slave—could rise to a higher class if he gained the pharaoh's favor. This scenario is illustrated by Joseph, a Hebrew slave who became the second most powerful man in Egypt.

Unlike women in other ancient cultures, Egyptian women were especially favored in their society. For example, women could own property and operate a business. They could also occupy religious positions as priestesses. As we have seen, one woman even became a great pharaoh.

The legacy left by the Egyptian civilization is truly great. The Egyptians made important advances in the field of medicine—they increased the knowledge of anatomy and prescribed drugs as remedies for diseases. They also developed a solar calendar, dividing the year into 365 days. They used a form of picture writing called **hieroglyphics** (HY er uh GLIF iks) and developed a type of paper made from reeds of the papyrus plant. They drew upon their understanding of geometry and astronomy to build the pyramids, some of the most amazing architectural achievements of the ancient world.

The Egyptian religion was polytheistic. The people considered the pharaohs to be gods, but there were many other gods as well: animals, natural forces, and especially the Nile itself. The most important gods were Amun and Ra (who later became one god, Amun-Ra, the sun-god), and Osiris and Isis, the husband and wife who ruled the underworld.

The Egyptians believed that after death they would be judged according to their works (their heart). In the afterlife, their heart was placed on a set of scales and weighed against the feather of Maat, the goddess of truth and justice. Egyptians believed that the heart was made heavy by wicked deeds, but if a person's heart was lighter than Maat's feather, he would spend the afterlife in a place of peace—fishing, hunting, and relaxing. The pharaohs' tombs and those of other important men were filled with objects for them to enjoy in the next world. However, the Egyptians believed that these pleasures could not be enjoyed unless the body was preserved. Thus they developed the practice of embalming, or preserving, corpses. Today mummies of the Egyptians lie in museums, preserved by the embalmer's skill and centuries of desert dryness.

Maat, the goddess of truth and justice (the feather represents truth)

The weighing of the heart using the feather of Maat

The greatness of ancient Egypt is no more. After the New Kingdom, Egypt fell successively to the Assyrians, the Persians, the Greeks, and the Romans. God judged the Egyptians for their worship of false gods as well as for their pride, a vice that has often kept people and nations from repenting and trusting the true God: "Thus saith the Lord God; Behold, I am against thee, Pharaoh king of Egypt . . . which hath said, My river is mine own, and I have made it for myself" (Ezek. 29:3). Such arrogance ultimately leads to divine humiliation: "[Egypt] shall be the basest of the kingdoms; neither shall it exalt itself any more above the nations" (v. 15). But in God's judgment He does not forget His mercy. The Bible also speaks of a coming day of blessing for Egypt (Isa. 19:22).

Egypt	
List examples of the features of Egyptian civilization.	
Features	**Examples**
Organized Cities	
Government	
Social Classes	
Job specialization (use your imagination)	
Writing	
Science	
Math	

Section Review

1. To what river was a Greek historian referring when he called Egypt the "gift of the river"?

2–4. List the three major periods of ancient Egyptian history.

5. Who is called the "Napoleon of Egypt"?

6. Who was atop the social structure of ancient Egypt?

✶ Why was preservation of the body following death important to the Egyptians?

✶ Contrast the Egyptian concept of the afterlife with biblical principles found in passages like Ephesians 2:8–9, Luke 16:19–31, 2 Corinthians 5:8, Revelation 4, and Hebrews 9:27.

Guiding Questions

1. What were the key points of the rise and fall of the Assyrian Empire?
2. What characterized the rise and fall of the Chaldean Empire?
3. What were the highlights of the rise and fall of the Persian Empire?
4. How did God use these empires to advance His own purposes?

III. Near Eastern Empires

"The most High ruleth in the kingdom of men, and giveth it to whomsoever he will, and setteth up over it the [humblest] of men" (Dan. 4:17). God uses nations to accomplish His purpose in history. In the ancient world God used the Assyrians and the Chaldeans as instruments of judgment on the Hebrews. In a similar manner God used the Persians to preserve the Jews. Even so, these kingdoms were not excused from the consequences of their own wickedness. God's judgment eventually fell on them too.

The Assyrian Empire

The Assyrians created the largest empire the world had seen prior to 550 BC. For centuries they lived in northern Mesopotamia along the Tigris River, but by the eighth century BC they had built a vast empire that encompassed the Fertile Crescent, Egypt, and part of Asia Minor. Nineveh, the city built by Nimrod shortly after the Flood (Gen. 10:11), became the capital city of the empire.

The Assyrians were indebted to the previous Mesopotamian cultures; their gods, language, art, architecture, science, and literature were in large part adapted from the Sumerian and Amorite cultures. The Assyrians preserved many contributions of the earlier civilizations and spread these accomplishments throughout the ancient world by their military conquests.

Assyrian military might was unmatched by any other civilization of the day. The Assyrian army was equipped with iron weapons, siege towers, battering rams, and war chariots. Its well-trained foot soldiers, spearmen, archers, and cavalry wreaked havoc on the people of the Near East. They terrorized nations with threats of destruction, hoping to gain their submission without the use of force. They earned a reputation for fierceness and cruelty—it was not uncommon for them to butcher, mutilate, burn at the stake, or skin alive their defeated foes. They also practiced mass deportation—removing conquered people from their own land and settling them in a foreign country.

God's Judgment

God used this ungodly, war-loving people to bring judgment against sinful nations and to chasten His disobedient people. In Isaiah 10:5–6 God described Assyria as a rod and staff in His hand that He would use to punish Israel.

Under Tiglath-Pileser (tig lath puh LEE zer), the Assyrians captured the Aramean capital of Damascus. Ten years later, in 722 BC, the Assyrian army led by **Sargon II** destroyed Samaria and took captive the ten northern tribes of Israel (2 Kings 17). Later, Assyrian armies invaded Egypt and seized much of its territory.

Mercy and Judgment

The Assyrians did not acknowledge God and were not aware of His workings. They became arrogant because of their conquests. Under **Sennacherib** (sih NAK er ib) they tried to take Jerusalem during the reign of King Hezekiah. As the Assyrians prepared to take the city, the agents of Sennacherib, standing outside the walls of Jerusalem, boasted of the Assyrian army's conquests and might (2 Kings 18:13–35). But God through His prophet Isaiah declared: "I will punish the fruit of the stout heart of the king of Assyria, and the glory of his high looks. For he saith, By the strength of my hand I have done it, and by my wisdom; for I am prudent" (Isa. 10:12–13). God sent the Angel of the Lord, who killed 185,000 men of Sennacherib's army as they slept (2 Kings 19:35). Sennacherib went home in defeat and was murdered by two of his own sons.

Although the Assyrians were among the most ruthless people of the ancient world, God showed mercy to them. God sent Jonah to Nineveh to preach repentance: "Arise, go to Nineveh, that great city, and cry against it; for their wickedness is come up before me" (Jon. 1:2). As this heathen city "turned from their evil way" (Jon. 3:10), God turned away His wrath. What a great example of God's mercy!

The people of Nineveh, however, eventually returned to their wicked ways, and God's mercy turned to wrath (Nah. 1–3). In 612 BC Chaldean and Median armies destroyed Nineveh and brought the Assyrian Empire to an end.

Assyrian Empire

The Chaldean Empire
Nebuchadnezzar of Babylon

Babylon was one of the oldest and grandest cities of the ancient world. Empires had come and gone, but Babylon had remained. Babylon had been the capital of previous civilizations, but not until the sixth century BC did it reach the height of its glory.

Shortly before 1000 BC a group of Semitic people, the Chaldeans, began to settle around Babylon. Lacking unity, they were constantly subdued by Assyrian kings. Later, however, the Chaldeans allied themselves with the Medes and helped destroy Nineveh in 612 BC. During the reign of **Nebuchadnezzar** (neb uh kud NEZ er), the "New Babylonian" Empire reached it height.

Reconstructed Ishtar Gate of Babylon

The ancient world was amazed at the Chaldeans' sudden rise to power. Jeremiah, the prophet of the Lord, explained that God had given Nebuchadnezzar control over many kingdoms, for a period of time, to accomplish His will (Jer. 27:5–7).

God used Nebuchadnezzar, whom He called His "servant," to punish other nations for their disobedience to Him. For example, in 605 BC Nebuchadnezzar defeated the Egyptian armies under Pharaoh Necho, who tried to conquer Syria and Palestine. Likewise,

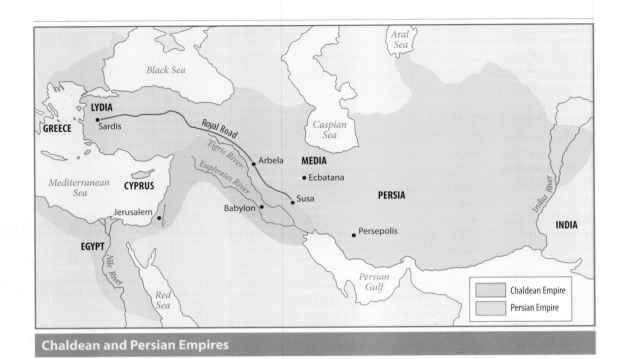

Chaldean and Persian Empires

as previously stated, God allowed Nebuchadnezzar to destroy Jerusalem. The dispersion of the Jewish people is known as the **Diaspora**, or "scattering." Under Nebuchadnezzar, the Chaldeans briefly became the masters of the Fertile Crescent.

Astronomy

The Chaldeans continued the interest in astronomy that had been popular during the Amorite civilization and made additional contributions to the field. They charted the positions of planets and stars, named constellations, and predicted eclipses. As did others who preceded and followed them, they accepted the belief that the position of the sun in relationship to the stars and planets influenced human destiny.

From the book of Daniel, we learn that the "wise men"—astrologers, magicians, and sorcerers—had an important place in Chaldean society. The king often called upon them for advice. Although they claimed the power to interpret dreams and tell the future, these so-called wise men were false prophets. Time and again they proved themselves unable to interpret the king's dreams (Dan. 2:10–11; 5:8). On one occasion Daniel came before King Nebuchadnezzar and said, "The secret which the king hath demanded cannot the wise men, the astrologers, the magicians, the soothsayers, shew unto the king; but there is a God in heaven that revealeth secrets, and maketh known . . . what shall be in the latter days" (Dan. 2:27–28).

God's Wrath

The glories of the Chaldean Empire did not last even a century. Nebuchadnezzar had learned of God's power from the Hebrew captive Daniel. But he viewed his accomplishment out of a heart of pride. Nebuchadnezzar said, "Is not this great Babylon, that I have built for the house of the kingdom by the might of my power, and for the honour of my majesty?" (Dan. 4:30). God judged Nebuchadnezzar for his pride. The Chaldean king temporarily lost his throne and became like a beast of the field until he recognized the folly of his pride and acknowledged the greatness of God (Dan. 4:31–37).

Under Nebuchadnezzar's successors, Babylon—which had been a "golden cup in the Lord's hand" (Jer. 51:7)—became an object of God's wrath. This mighty empire with its seemingly invincible capital fell in one night. The co-ruler of the empire, **Belshazzar**, had made a great feast. He used the golden vessels taken from the temple of God in Jerusalem to drink wine and toast the pagan gods of the Chaldeans. Amidst the drunken revelry, fingers appeared and wrote on the palace wall a cryptic inscription. Daniel was called in; he explained that God had brought Babylon's rule to an end and had given the kingdom to the Medes and Persians (Dan. 5:26–28). On that same night in 539 BC, the conquering Medes and Persians killed Belshazzar. The Chaldean Empire was no more.

The Persian Empire

Out of the land of what is today Iran came an empire which spread across the entire Near Eastern world. At its height the Persian Empire stretched from the coastline of Greece to the Indus River Valley in India and from Egypt to Mesopotamia. The rise of this great empire was hastened in the mid-sixth century BC by the Persian defeat of the Medes, Lydians, and Chaldeans.

Cyrus the Great

The Persian king **Cyrus** was one of the greatest conquerors who ever lived. Cyrus rose to power among the Persian tribes in the

Belshazzar as Co-Ruler

In Daniel 5 we read of the last person to sit on the Chaldean throne—King Belshazzar. Following the writing on the wall, Belshazzar offered to give third place in the kingdom to anyone who could interpret the cryptic message. For many years skeptics pointed to this as an error in the Bible. However, modern research has revealed that Belshazzar was co-ruler with his father, Nabonidus. Thus, the highest position that Belshazzar could offer was the third position of rule over the Chaldean Empire. This is another example of the fact that although the Bible does not provide us with every detail of history, whenever the Bible speaks of a historical event, it is accurate.

Providence

God exercises providential control over all things. He controls the clouds and the wind (Ps. 104:3–4) and ocean waves (Ps. 107:25, 29). When people or even animals eat, God is the one who has provided the food (Ps. 136:25). Children are born according to God's providence (Ps. 113:9). Not even a sparrow dies apart from God's control (Matt. 10:29). God's providence extends to individual lives and the affairs of nations (Prov. 16:1–9, 33). God determines the boundaries of nations (Acts 17:26). He frustrates the plans of nations (Ps. 33:10–11). He shapes the intentions of people's hearts, and when a king is successful in battle, it is not due to his power or superior military equipment. It is due to God (Ps. 33:13–17).

If God is providentially ruling over all things, then everything that happens is providential. The task of the Christian historian is not to discern where God's providence is at work and where it is not at work but rather to discern what God's purposes might be. Often God permits things to happen that seem contrary to the best interests of His people and His kingdom. In fact, sometimes events are so bleak that it would be easy to wonder whether God was in control.

This may well have been a struggle for the Israelites when Jerusalem fell, the temple was destroyed, and the people were exiled to Babylon. It certainly appeared that Nebuchadnezzar was more powerful than God. The book of Daniel, however, lifts the veil. In two visions (Daniel 2 and 7), God revealed the progression of kingdoms that would follow Nebuchadnezzar: Media-Persia (whose king Cyrus would send the Jews back to their homeland to rebuild the temple, as Isaiah had prophesied; Isa. 44:28), Greece, and then Rome. And in the end God's own kingdom would shatter all these empires.

God also brought Nebuchadnezzar, the greatest king in the world at the time, down to the condition of an animal in the field before restoring him to his throne. God did this so "that the living may know that the most High ruleth in the kingdom of men, and giveth it to whomsoever he will, and setteth up over it the [humblest] of men" (Dan. 4:17). After these events Nebuchadnezzar said, "I blessed the most High, and I praised and honoured him that liveth for ever, whose dominion is an everlasting dominion, and his kingdom is from generation to generation. . . . [H]e doeth according to his will in the army of heaven, and among the inhabitants of the earth: and none can stay his hand, or say unto him, What doest thou?" (Dan. 4:34–35).

southern region of the Median Empire (see map on p. 36). After the Assyrian Empire fell in 612 BC, the Medes controlled the land north and east of Mesopotamia. Cyrus took advantage of a rebellion in the Median army and conquered the Median capital of Ecbatana in 549 BC. As he extended his conquests into Asia Minor, he came into contact with the Lydians.

The western region of Asia Minor bordering the Aegean Sea was the homeland of the Lydians. Here rich mineral resources, especially gold, were found in abundance. This land was the supposed home of King Midas, who had the legendary touch of gold. The most important contribution made by the Lydians to the ancient world was the use of coinage as an international medium of exchange. Prior to this time, the barter system (the exchange of one commodity for another) was used. The Persians, Greeks, and Romans later adopted coinage.

The Lydian king Croesus (KREE sus) confronted Cyrus and the advancing Persian army, suffering defeat in 546 BC. Unlike the Assyrians, who had difficulties ruling their vast empire because of their harsh treatment of conquered peoples, Cyrus was a wise and merciful conqueror. He allowed his defeated enemies some measure of self-rule, tolerated their religious beliefs, and restored captive peoples to their homeland. Instead of killing Croesus (according to some accounts), Cyrus took him as a prisoner and allowed him to enjoy the life of the Persian royal court.

Cyrus the Great

Persia and the Nation of Israel

The Bible refers to Cyrus as the "Lord's anointed." Isaiah, a prophet from Judah, some one hundred and fifty years before Cyrus's birth, prophesied Cyrus's rule and impact on Israel (Isa. 45:1, 4). God used Cyrus to free His people from their captivity in Babylon. As God had used the Assyrians and Chaldeans to punish Israel and Judah, He used Persia to reestablish His repentant people in their land. Isaiah 45:13 describes how Cyrus would not only allow the Jews to return to their land but also direct them to rebuild the Temple of God in Jerusalem (see also Ezra 1:2–3).

Through the Persians, God protected and provided for His chosen people. It was through Esther, the Jewish wife of the Persian king Xerxes (ZURK seez), called Ahasuerus (uh HAZ yoo EER us) in the Bible, that God delivered the Jews from the wicked plot of Haman. Later under Artaxerxes I (AR tuh ZURK seez), Nehemiah was allowed to return to Jerusalem to help rebuild the city walls (Neh. 2:1–8).

Persian Government

The Persians developed an effective organization to rule the vast territories that they had conquered. The empire was divided into provinces called **satrapies**. Each province was overseen by a satrap, or governor, who was appointed by the Persian king. It seems that Darius the Mede, an important character in Daniel 5 and 6, was one of these satraps whom Cyrus had appointed to rule for him in the city of Babylon. The king had secret police, known as the "king's eyes," that kept the king informed of matters that took place in each province.

An excellent network of roads facilitated trade and travel throughout the empire. The primary road of the empire—the Royal

Road—ran for 1,677 miles from Susa (one of the Persian capitals) to Sardis near the Aegean Sea. These roads aided the Persian mail service, which was similar to the American pony express. The book of Esther gives us an example of this mail system in action. When Xerxes made the decree to protect the Jews from Haman's evil plot, he sent letters throughout the provinces telling of his decision (Esther 8:3–10).

Persian Culture

Much of Persian culture was adopted from previous civilizations. The Persians borrowed the idea of coinage and gold currency from the Lydians. Their early writing system was a simplified Sumerian cuneiform. Phoenicians and Greeks supplied Persia with its navy. The Persians also popularized the Egyptian calendar.

The religion of ancient Persia was founded by and took its name from the religious leader **Zoroaster** (ZOR oh as ter), who lived during the sixth century BC. Zoroaster rejected the polytheism prevalent in much of the ancient world and instituted the worship of one god, Ahura Mazda. The sacred writings of Zoroastrianism, called the *Avesta*, consist of myths, regulations, and hymns of praise. Zoroaster taught that good and evil are two opposing forces; the world was their battleground. Every man takes part in this struggle, Zoroaster taught, for he serves either the forces of good or the forces of evil. Like so many of the world's false religions, Zoroastrianism held that at the end of life one would be assured of eternal happiness if his good works outweighed his evil.

The Persian Empire continued for about two hundred years after the death of Cyrus. Under Darius the Great, the empire reached its height, expanding all the way to Greece, where the Persian expansion was halted. Although the Greeks stopped the Persian advance, the Persians continued to rule the ancient world until a new conqueror, Alexander the Great, created an even greater empire toward the close of the fourth century BC.

The ruins of the ancient city of Persepolis. It was the residence of the Persian kings from the time of Darius I (521–486 BC) until its destruction by the armies of Alexander the Great in 330 BC.

Section Review

1. What city became the capital of the Assyrian Empire?

2. What prophet was sent by God to Nineveh to preach repentance?

3. What term describes the scattering of the Jewish people by Nebuchadnezzar?

4–5. What was the religion of ancient Persia? What was the name of its sacred writings?

6. Under what ruler did the Persian Empire expand all the way to Greece?

✶ In Daniel 4:22 Nebuchadnezzar's greatness is said to have grown to heaven itself and his "dominion to the end of the earth." He was the most powerful monarch of his day. Yet Daniel counseled him to start acting righteously toward the poor and oppressed in his kingdom (4:27). What does this say about how Nebuchadnezzar had used his power?

✶ How did the Persian Empire benefit from other civilizations? How has our own culture benefited from other civilizations?

Guiding Questions

1. How did geography influence the early development of Indian and Chinese civilizations?
2. How did Hinduism and Buddhism affect Indian culture?
3. What were key elements of early Indian and Chinese civilizations?

IV. Asian Civilizations

India

India is a land of great diversity. In its topography (the physical features of a land), climate, and population, it is a study in contrasts. This triangular subcontinent extends from southern Asia into the Indian Ocean, forming a giant peninsula. Its terrain varies from subtropical rainforest to barren deserts, from low coastal plains to the highest mountain range in the world, the Himalayas. Between the rugged mountain regions in the north and the coastal plains and tropical plateaus of the south lie fertile valleys watered by two great river systems, the Indus and the Ganges. Like the Mesopotamian and Egyptian cultures, the earliest Indian civilization began along riverbanks. The first inhabitants of India probably settled in river valleys along the Indus and Ganges Rivers.

These people must have felt secure from invaders and foreign influences. They were protected by tall mountain ranges in the north and by seas on the east and west. But despite these natural barriers, India did not remain an isolated land. Throughout its history, merchants, foreign invaders, and wandering tribes crossed the mountains along India's northwestern border (through such mountain passes as the Khyber) and settled in the fertile river valleys. As a result, India became a land of many peoples, customs, and languages. From the diverse elements within Indian society, a unique culture developed.

Early Civilization

India derives its name from the Indus River, along whose fertile banks the earliest Indian civilization flourished (ca. 2300 BC). Much of our limited knowledge of this civilization has come from excavations of two of its leading cities: Mohenjo-Daro (moh HEN joh DAH roh) and Harappa (huh RAP uh). These were carefully planned cities with wide, straight streets lined with brick houses. Evidence indicates that these cities had elaborate drainage and sewer systems that were more advanced than those in most modern-day Indian villages. Although a great distance separates India and the Near East, the early inhabitants of India carried on trade with Egypt and Mesopotamia. We know from archaeological evidence that the Indus civilization ended suddenly—perhaps by enemy invasion. It was at this time that a warlike people called the **Aryans** migrated into the Indus Valley.

The Aryans came from central Asia sometime after 1500 BC and subdued the non-Aryan people of northwest India. Many historians believe that the Aryans were related to tribes that were invading the Near East, Greece, and Rome at about the same time. The Aryans were herdsmen; they kept large numbers of cows and horses. Although they left behind no cities as the Indus civilization did, they did establish a new language in India—**Sanskrit**.

Our knowledge of the Aryans and their influence on Indian society comes not from archaeology but from a collection of religious literature known as the *Vedas* (VAY dus), meaning "knowledge." Preserved in the *Vedas* are early traditions and religious beliefs of

Ancient India

the Indians, which were orally passed down from one generation to the next. From Sanskrit literature, we gain insights into the Aryan way of life, which became the basis of Indian culture and tradition. This formative period of Indian history lasted from about 1500 to 500 BC.

Key Features of Indian Society

India has one of the oldest cultures in the modern world. The basic characteristics of Indian society, described in the *Vedas*, have changed little from ancient to modern days.

Joint Family

The family has always been one of the most important social units in India. The extended or **joint family** included the children, grandchildren, wives, and close blood relatives of a common ancestor. The oldest male of the group was the dominant authority over the family. Married sons did not establish their own homes but remained in their father's or grandfather's household. Each family member had duties and obligations, and the interests of the family came before those of the individual. Parents chose the spouses for their children in order to maintain the family's position and honor in society.

Village Life

Unlike the inhabitants of the Indus civilization, who dwelt in cities, the Aryans settled in small rural villages. Family groups living in a village were governed by a headman or a council of village elders. For the most part, the villages were independent and self-governing. Over the centuries village life has remained a vital part of Indian society. Most people in India today live in small villages, much as their ancestors did over two thousand years ago.

Caste

Imagine living in a country in which your status in life was determined the moment you were born. India was, and in some ways still is, such a country. Its population was divided into rigid social groups called **castes**. The Indians formulated strict rules governing the life of the members of each caste group: where they lived, what they did (profession), what they wore, what and with whom they could eat, and whom they could marry. (Marriage was forbidden outside one's own caste.)

There were four major classes within the caste system. The most important group was the priests, called the *Brahmin*. Next in rank were the rulers and warriors, followed by the merchants and traders. The lowest class group was the *Sudras* (SOO dras)—composed of servants and serfs. Outside the caste system and at the bottom of the Indian social ladder were the outcastes, or "untouchables." They performed the most menial tasks in society. Members of the caste structure avoided the "untouchables"; mere contact with them was thought to bring defilement. While anyone could improve his status within his caste, no one could change castes. Thus with the caste system there was little change in the village and family life of India. Over time, the caste system became more complex. Eventually there were hundreds of subdivisions, or sub-castes. This explains in part why Indian society remained virtually unchanged for thousands of years.

Virupaksha Temple (Hindu) at Hampi, India

Religion and the Indian Way of Life

Religion has played a dominant role in shaping Indian culture. From India came two religions that have had a major impact on Asian culture: Hinduism and Buddhism.

Hinduism

Hinduism is ingrained in the way of life for the vast majority of Indians. It developed from India's early culture and traditions: social structure, literature, arts, and customs. It has not only preserved the traditional elements of India's past but also served as a unifying influence in India's diverse society. Because Hinduism has no formal statement of doctrine, it was able to absorb into its system of belief a wide variety of gods and religious concepts found among the many peoples of India. (Hindus believe all religions to be equally true and equally false.) Today, over 80 percent of the people of India are Hindus.

The basic tenets of Hinduism are found in the religious literature of ancient India, namely the *Vedas* and the *Upanishads* (oo PAN uh shadz; philosophical essays elaborating on the teaching of the *Vedas*). Hindus believe that a great god called **Brahman** permeates everything in the universe. The Hindus acknowledge many gods; all deities, however, are considered only manifestations of the eternal, unchanging Brahman. Since Brahman is not a personal being, he is often referred to as the great soul, or world soul. The ultimate purpose and goal of every person, according to the *Vedas*, is to reunite his soul with the world soul. This is done through the process of reincarnation, in which a soul passes through many states (or rebirths) before it escapes the physical world and unites with Brahman. This cycle of rebirths is called the wheel of life.

The Hindu believes that a person's deeds (or **karma**) in this life determine his status in the next. If he has lived a good life (that is, if his good works outweigh his bad), then he may move to a higher caste in the next life. The soul of an evil person may be reborn into a lower caste or even as an animal. By observing the religious rituals prescribed by the Hindu priests and by fulfilling the obligations of his caste, a Hindu believes that he (through repeated rebirths) can ultimately gain release from the wheel of life and attain union with the world soul.

Buddhism

India was also the birthplace of **Buddhism**. The founder of this religion was **Siddhartha Gautama** (sid-DAR-tuh GOU-tuh-muh) (ca. 563–ca. 483 BC), later known as Buddha, the "Enlightened One." At the age of twenty-nine, Gautama became troubled over the misery, poverty, and death that he saw in the world. He became convinced that he should devote all his efforts to finding the way of deliverance from suffering. Therefore, he renounced his life of luxury, gave up his princely heritage, left his wife and child, and set out to find peace and true happiness. After spending six frustrating years living as a hermit in self-sacrifice and meditation, Gautama was at the point of despair. Sitting down under a tree, he vowed that he would not move until the truth came to him. According to

The Great Buddha in Kamakura, Japan

Gautama, he was pondering the questions of life when he realized the truth and attained enlightenment.

Central to Buddha's teaching are his Four Noble Truths: (1) Suffering is part of all existence. (2) Suffering is caused by selfish desires. As long as man craves pleasure, possessions, and power, he will have sorrow and misery. (3) Suffering can be overcome by destroying selfish desires. (4) If a man follows the Eightfold Path, he will destroy selfish desires and end all suffering. This pattern for living includes correct beliefs, intentions, speech, conduct, livelihood, effort, thoughts, and meditations.

Buddha also taught that belief in a soul or a self led to suffering. If there is no soul or self, then a person is less likely to crave things for himself. In Buddhism the "person" is an ever-changing combination of forces that carry the impression of a single person. Though there is no person to be reincarnated according to Buddha, the effects of people's deeds carry on from life to life. Bad actions will have bad effects and good actions good effects. The goal is to achieve **nirvana** (neer VAH nuh), which is changeless reality with no suffering. Since there are no souls and nirvana is not a place, nirvana is not the equivalent to heaven. It does stand in contrast, however, to the present, ever-changing world.

Section Review

1. Along the banks of what river did the earliest Indian civilization begin?

2–3. What were two significant cities in early India?

4–7. List the four broad class groups under the Indian caste system.

8. What is the cycle of rebirths (the process of reincarnation) called?

9–12. What are Buddha's Four Noble Truths?

✯ Evaluate India's caste system in light of Bible passages such as Genesis 1:27; Matthew 22:34–40; Isaiah 55:1; and Revelation 22:17.

China
The Land

At the heart of eastern Asia is the land of China. In ancient days the Chinese called their land the **Middle Kingdom** because they believed China to be the center of the earth. Today more people live in China than in any other country in the world—nearly one-fifth of the world's population. In land size, modern China is slightly smaller than the United States, but China's population is about four times greater.

China is one of the world's oldest civilizations. The earliest Chinese lived in the fertile valleys of China's two major river systems: the Huang He (or Yellow) and the Yangtze (YANG see). In this respect, ancient China was similar to other early river-valley civilizations—Mesopotamia, Egypt, and India. But while these other civilizations were conquered by hostile armies,

Yangtze River in Yunnan Province, China

China during its early history remained relatively free from outside influences.

China was isolated from other centers of civilization for many centuries. The Pacific Ocean, the Himalayan Mountains, and the Gobi Desert protected China from most foreign invasions and influences. Because of the minimal foreign influence, Chinese society remained virtually unchanged from ancient to modern times.

Societal Features

Strong Family Ties

The family was and still is the center of life in Chinese society. Chinese families were large, embracing many generations: parents, children, grandparents, aunts and uncles, nephews and nieces, cousins, and in-laws. Ancestors were also included in the Chinese concept of the family. Many Chinese could trace their family history back hundreds of years.

A major responsibility of every Chinese person was to bring honor to his family. One of the worst offenses a person could commit was to dishonor his ancestors by bringing reproach on the family name. The cult of **ancestor worship** became the leading religion in China. Virtually every Chinese house contained an ancestral altar before which the family burned incense to the spirits of their dead. By caring for their family graves and worshiping before these altars, the Chinese hoped to receive blessings and guidance from their ancestors' spirits.

Language and Learning

The most noticeable feature of China's spoken language is its tonal quality. By varying the tone of voice on a particular syllable, the Chinese can convey more than one meaning. For example, ma may mean "mother," "hemp" (a plant), "horse," or "to scold," depending on the pitch of the voice. Communication is further complicated by the regional variations in the spoken languages. Chinese people from different regions often have trouble understanding each other.

Although the spoken language varies greatly, China does have a common written language. Traditional Chinese writing is not based on a simple alphabet as our English system is; it consists of some sixty-five thousand characters that represent complete ideas, objects, and sounds. For instance, the word for "good" is a combination of the characters for "girl" and "boy." A person has to memorize the characters in order to be able to read—a fact that makes reading and writing extremely difficult. Over the centuries the vast majority of the Chinese people have been illiterate. Even the most literate Chinese know only about four thousand characters. It is little wonder that those who master the written language have always been given a place of distinction in Chinese society.

China has been called a "scholar's world." In most ancient civilizations, soldiers, priests, or merchants held prominent positions in society. But in China no social group exceeded the influence of scholars. For the aspiring scholar, education (consisting mainly of memorizing classical Chinese literature) began at an early age and demanded total dedication of time and energy. The goal of the learned man was a career in government service. Because there were more scholars than government positions, the Chinese developed civil service examinations to choose the best qualified. Those obtaining the highest test scores received the positions.

Chinese Thought and Life

Two native philosophies greatly influenced Chinese life: Confucianism (kun FYOO shun iz um) and Taoism (TOU iz um). These systems of thought became the heart of China's religious beliefs and practices.

Confucianism

K'ung Futzu (KOONG FOO-DZUH) (551–479 BC) is the most honored teacher in Chinese history. The Chinese call him "the Master"; we know him as **Confucius**. Confucius grew up in poverty during a time of social and political unrest in China. Prior to obtaining a political office, he devoted his time to teaching. Confucius believed that a moral government would produce a moral society. He sought to train men who, by entering government service and through proper conduct, would bring about a moral society. His disciples recorded and expanded upon his teaching, developing a system of ethics that became a major influence on Chinese culture.

Fundamental to Confucius's teaching was his belief in five basic human relationships: father and son, elder and younger brothers, husband and wife, friend and friend, and ruler and subjects. Confucius believed that maintaining proper relationships in these five areas would bring harmony and order to society. In addition, he placed great confidence in China's past, trusting it as the basis and guide for human behavior. Since right behavior was found in right relationships, Confucius concluded that the fundamental principle was "What you do not want done to yourself, do not do to others."

Confucius recognized the impossibility of living up to this standard. He observed that it would be difficult to live up to this standard for an entire day. Thus he rightly recognized that no one is truly good. Yet because he did not believe in God who will bring all things into judgment, Confucius counseled his disciples to simply do the best they could.

Confucian Temple in Qufu, Shandong

Taoism

Second in importance to the teaching of Confucius was that of **Taoism**. According to Chinese legend, **Laozi** (also Lao-tzu [LOU DZUH]) taught that tao (meaning "the way") was the pervading force in nature. He encouraged men to find peace and happiness by living in harmony with nature. According to Taoist teaching, men can achieve this harmony by ceasing to strive for power, wealth, and learning; instead they should learn to live with the flow of the natural order. By living in harmony with nature, men can accomplish great things. Taoists illustrated this teaching with the example of water: "There is nothing in the world more soft and weak than water, yet for attacking things that are hard and strong there is nothing that surpasses it. . . . The soft overcomes the hard; the weak overcomes the strong."

Confucianism became the guiding philosophy of China's educational, social, and political systems; Taoism became the basis of mystical, magical, and superstitious elements in Chinese society. In many ways, these two philosophies conflict with one another. Confucianism promotes living an active life and fulfilling one's social obligations. Taoism favors a more passive lifestyle and attempts to free man from the busyness of responsibility. Confucianists strive for improved government, laws, and education, while Taoists minimize external authority and involvement in society.

Dynastic History of China

Many Chinese have had a passion for history. Their interest in antiquity sparked a great tradition of historical writing, much of which traces the history of China's ruling dynasties (or families). From the periods of dynastic rule, historians have established the major divisions of Chinese history.

The Chinese were able to maintain a strong sense of national unity, but they did experience numerous periods of political upheaval and disorder. Each dynasty went through the same cycle: it began, matured, prospered, and then declined. The unrest that ended one dynasty prepared the way for the founding of a new one. While each dynasty had its own special qualities and left its mark on Chinese culture, the fundamental character of society remained essentially the same throughout Chinese history.

Shang Dynasty

The Shang dynasty, one of the earliest known Chinese dynasties, was established along the Yellow River (called Huang He in Chinese) around 1500 BC. The rulers of this dynasty united much of northern China. Archaeologists have unearthed fine examples of Shang bronze work and marble carvings. Much of our knowledge of Shang culture comes from early Chinese writing inscribed on pieces of animal bones and tortoise shells. To obtain answers about the future from their ancestors, the Chinese wrote questions on bones or shells; then they touched them with a hot metal rod, causing them to crack. By "interpreting" the pattern of the cracks, the Chinese believed they could determine the will of their ancestors.

Zhou Dynasty

Shortly before 1000 BC, the people who lived along the Shang's western border overthrew the Shang rulers. The Zhou (JOH) dynasty that they established lasted over eight hundred years—longer than any other dynasty in Chinese history. This period is often called the "classical" or "formative" age of Chinese history. Much of China's culture, such as family life, ancestor worship, the writing system, and Confucian and Taoist thought, became firmly established during this time.

The Zhou government was decentralized. While the Zhou rulers retained the ultimate authority, they allowed powerful nobles great freedom in ruling local territories. However, the Zhou rulers became unable to control the nobles, and sporadic fighting broke out among rival states between the fifth and third centuries BC.

Section Review

1–2. What did the ancient Chinese call their land? Why?

3. What social group held the most esteemed position in Chinese society?

4–8. What five human relationships did Confucius stress?

9–10. What was found in China inscribed on pieces of animal bones and tortoise shells? What was the purpose of these inscriptions?

★ Other than man's relationship with God, what other relationships did Confucius neglect to emphasize?

Making Connections

1. How did the Sumerians and other civilizations carry out aspects of the Creation Mandate?

2–5. What were four major cultural achievements of the civilizations of the Fertile Crescent?

6. How did God use Gentile leaders, including Nebuchadnezzar and Cyrus, to serve Him?

7. Contrast the early cities of India with many modern Indian villages.

8–9. Explain the significance of family in India and China.

Developing History Skills

1. How does the biblical prophecy regarding Cyrus (Isa. 44:28–45:13) demonstrate the accuracy of Scripture? How should this influence our understanding of history in light of Scripture?

2. Read 1 Kings 6:1. Based on this passage and the fact that Solomon's fourth year would have been 966 BC, determine the year of the Exodus of Israel from Egypt.

Thinking Critically

1. Evaluate this statement: "The Bible is not an accurate record of historical events." Provide examples to support your evaluation.

2. Why did God allow wicked nations to conquer His people? Refer to passages such as Isaiah 10:5–6 and 2 Kings 17 in your answer.

Living in God's World

1. The Old Testament provides a behind-the-scenes look at why God ordered certain historical events the way He did. Can Christians discern God's purposes in historical events that are not addressed in Scripture? What are some principles the Christian historian can use in attempting to do this?

2. Confucius believed that by modeling right living those in government could foster a culture in which people lived rightly. Write a brief dialogue between a Christian and a Confucian in which the two discuss the likelihood of the Confucian's efforts succeeding.

People, Places, and Things to Know

Mesopotamia
polytheism
cuneiform
ziggurats
Sargon
empire
Hammurabi
astronomy
astrology
Fertile Crescent
Baal
Abrahamic Covenant
Moses
monotheism
David
Solomon
Babylonian Captivity
Menes
pharaohs
Khufu
Hatshepsut
Thutmose III
Ramses II
hieroglyphics
Sargon II
Sennacherib
Nebuchadnezzar
Diaspora
Belshazzar
Cyrus
satrapies
Zoroaster
Darius the Great
Aryans
Sanskrit
Vedas
joint family
castes
Hinduism
Brahman
karma
Buddhism
Siddhartha Gautama
Four Noble Truths
nirvana
Middle Kingdom
ancestor worship
Confucius
Taoism
Laozi

UNIT

2

ADVANCE OF CIVILIZATION

500 BC–AD 500

3 The Greek Civilization

4 The Roman Civilization

5 Civilizations in Africa and the East

Inside the Colosseum in Rome

700 BC
Kush conquers Egypt

480 BC
Battle of Salamis Bay

460–429 BC
Periclean Age

232 BC
Asoka's death

750–500 BC
Development of Greek city-states

431–404 BC
Peloponnesian War

264–146 BC
Punic Wars

221–206 BC
Qin Dynasty

700 BC	600 BC	500 BC	400 BC	300 BC	200 BC

753 BC
Rome founded

509–31 BC
Roman Republic

336 BC
Alexander the Great becomes king of Macedonia

202 BC–AD 220
Han Dynasty

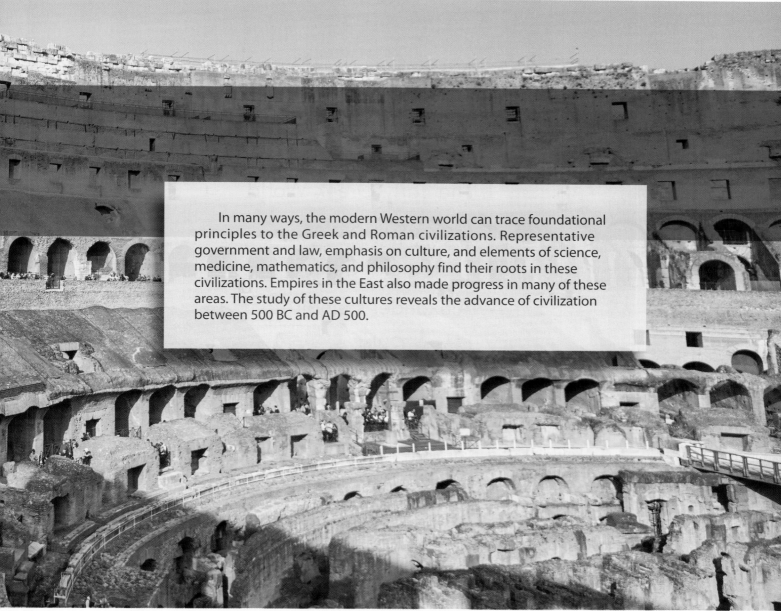

In many ways, the modern Western world can trace foundational principles to the Greek and Roman civilizations. Representative government and law, emphasis on culture, and elements of science, medicine, mathematics, and philosophy find their roots in these civilizations. Empires in the East also made progress in many of these areas. The study of these cultures reveals the advance of civilization between 500 BC and AD 500.

44 BC
Julius Caesar assassinated

31 BC–AD 180
Pax Romana

31 BC
Battle of Actium

31 BC–AD 476
Roman Empire

AD 54
Nero becomes emperor

AD 70
Romans destroy Jerusalem

AD 306
Constantine becomes a co-emperor

AD 313
Edict of Milan

AD 325
Council of Nicaea

| 00 BC | 0 | AD 100 | AD 200 | AD 300 | AD 400 | AD 500 |

AD 30
Crucifixion of Jesus Christ

ca. 6–4 BC
Birth of Jesus Christ

AD 476
Fall of Rome

Acropolis

Big Ideas

1. How did early cultures influence the development of Greek civilization?

2. What forms of government developed in the Greek city-states?

3. What were the main events of the Greek civilization in the 5th century BC?

4. What was the impact of Greek culture on other civilizations?

The Bible states that after the Flood the descendants of Javan (one of Japheth's sons) journeyed westward from Mesopotamia and settled in the islands of the nations (Gen. 10:4–5). This phrase may include the land we now call Greece. This land is a mountainous peninsula in the eastern Mediterranean. Between it and Asia Minor lies the island-dotted Aegean Sea. This land along the Aegean Sea formed the cradle of Greek civilization. Geography influenced Greek history from its very beginning. Mountains made farming difficult, but abundant natural harbors encouraged the Greeks to become seafarers. Furthermore, the rugged terrain hindered communication among the Greek cities, causing them to remain isolated. As a result, the Greeks developed a spirit of independence and local patriotism and became known for their love of individualism and self-sufficiency.

I. The Early Greek World

Aegean Civilizations

Archaeologists have found remains of two remarkable civilizations, the Minoan and Mycenaean, which preceded the Greek civilization in the Aegean region. Although these civilizations did eventually collapse, they left a permanent stamp on later Greek culture.

Crete

The earliest center of civilization in the Aegean region was located on the island of Crete. By 2000 BC the **Minoan civilization** (named after the legendary King Minos) flourished on the island. Through their trade and colonization, the Minoans came into contact with the people of the Fertile Crescent. The Minoans established trade routes with the Egyptians, who desired Cretan olive oil and fine pottery. Many scholars believe that the Philistines, who troubled the Hebrew people in Israel, were colonists from this Cretan civilization.

The grand palace at Knossos, the capital city, gives us an indication of the wealth and achievement of the Minoans. The palace

Guiding Questions

1. What were the notable features of the Minoan and Mycenaean civilizations?
2. What was the influence of Homer's writings?
3. How did Greek mythology affect Greek culture?

Early Greece

had hundreds of rooms and covered several acres. Flush toilets, bathtubs, and piped water were some of the "modern" conveniences found there. The beautiful carvings, pottery, and frescoes (painting done on wet plaster walls) found among the ruins of the palace reflect the Minoan love for beauty.

Mycenae

At Mycenae (my SEE nee) on the mainland of Greece, another center of Aegean culture emerged. The **Mycenaean civilization** was established by invaders from the north. Much of the Mycenaean knowledge of art, building, and commerce came from the Minoan culture. When Knossos was destroyed around 1400 BC (possibly by the Mycenaeans), Mycenae became the leading commercial center of the Aegean region.

While the Minoan culture displayed a love for beauty, the Mycenaean culture reflected the military fervor of its people. Its palaces were built on high hills and fortified with massive walls. Rival kings fought constantly. The Mycenaeans expanded their trade through sea raids, piracy, and colonization.

A major commercial rival of Mycenae was the city of Troy. Located on the western coast of Asia Minor, Troy sat on a hill overlooking the Hellespont (HEL us pahnt), the strait that separates Asia Minor from Europe. (See the map on p. 51.) This strategic site linked the land trade of the Fertile Crescent with the sea trade of the Aegean world.

The Lion Gate entrance into the fortified citadel of Mycenae

According to Greek legend, the Mycenaeans went to war against the city of Troy. After ten years of bitter struggle, Troy finally fell to the Mycenaeans. They had gained entrance to the city by use of the fabled Trojan horse. The glory of Mycenae was short-lived, however. Around 1200 BC, invaders called the **Dorians** came from the north and conquered the main Mycenaean fortresses. The Dorian invasion marked the decline of the Mycenaean civilization and ushered in a new period of Greek history.

The Greek Dark Ages

The period from 1150 to 750 BC is known as the Greek Dark Ages. During this period there were new intruders in the land. These invaders neglected the great palace fortresses, once the centers of culture in the Aegean world. Instead they adopted a simpler life in local villages and had little contact with areas outside the Aegean region. Despite the decline of the Minoan and Mycenaean civilizations, the Greek Dark Ages did witness the blending of the distinctive elements in the Aegean world into a common Greek culture.

Our knowledge of the Greek Dark Ages rests largely on the *Iliad* and the *Odyssey*, epic poems attributed to the blind Greek poet **Homer**. Because Homer's poems provide nearly the only glimpse of the early Greek way of life, historians have also called this period the Homeric Age. With stories of heroic figures, brutal warfare, and adventurous exploits, Homer describes the shaping of Greek culture.

Excerpt from Homer

Tell me, O Muse, of that ingenious hero [Odysseus] who traveled far and wide after he had sacked the famous town of Troy. Many cities did he visit, and many were the nations with whose manners and customs he was acquainted; moreover, he suffered much by sea while trying to save his own life and bring his men safely home.

Homer, Odyssey, 1

The dignity, strength, valor, bravery, generosity, and wisdom seen in Homer's characters are the qualities the Greeks honored most.

Greek Mythology

Greek mythology played a dominant role in shaping Greek culture during the Homeric Age. The Greeks devised stories (myths) to explain their beliefs about life, the world, and their gods. According to Greek mythology, the twelve chief gods and goddesses lived on Mount Olympus, the heaven of the gods. **Zeus**, the "king of gods and man," was the ruler of Mount Olympus. One of his sons, Apollo, was the god of the sun, music, and medicine. **Athena**, patron of the city of Athens, was the goddess of wisdom. Ruling over the sea and earthquakes was the god Poseidon, Zeus's brother. The Greeks believed in many gods, all of whom were endowed with certain human characteristics (**anthropomorphic**, "having human form or attributes"); yet these gods also possessed extraordinary powers and immortality.

According to Greek mythology, the gods had power to both help and harm man. Zeus, for example, often expressed his anger with men by sending lightning bolts to earth. Because these gods were the invention of sinful men, it is not surprising that they exhibited human sins: they were immoral, impatient, whimsical, unjust, and deceitful. The apostle Paul probably had Greek polytheism in mind when he said that the Gentiles had "changed the glory of the uncorruptible God into an image made like to corruptible man" (Rom. 1:23). Even so, the Greeks sought the favor of these gods through prayers and sacrifices.

In honor of Zeus, the Greeks held national religious festivals every four years at Olympia, the site of a temple of Zeus. Physical contests, thought to please the gods, became the chief feature of these festivals. The Olympic Games, as they became known, attracted competitors from all over the Aegean world. Each participant represented his home city. The intense competition indicated the high regard the Greeks had for physical prowess. To attain physical perfection was the ultimate goal of every athlete. The games became so popular that the Olympiad, the four-year interval between the games, became a Greek means of dating historical events. The Olympic Games were a rare example of cooperation between the Greek city-states.

Section Review

1. Where was the earliest center of civilization in the Aegean region located?

2. Which Aegean culture displayed a love for military pursuits?

3–5. From which two epic poems do we get a glimpse of Greek life during the period from 1150 to 750 BC? To whom are these poems attributed?

6. What athletic contests began as an attempt to please the Greek gods through physical prowess?

✶ Why did the isolation of the Greek city-states result in a spirit of independence and a love of individualism?

✶ Contrast the Greek view of work with Genesis 2:15, 3:17–19, and 1 Thessalonians 4:10–12.

Greek View of Work

The Greeks viewed labor as a necessary evil because the gods hid the "means of life" from mankind. This "means of life" referred to men being able to do the minimal amount of work and achieve the maximum amount of benefit. In the *Iliad*, Homer describes ideal conditions as being able to "easily do work enough in a day to supply you for a full year even without working."

Strife in the Greek Mind

The Greek poet Hesiod described two types of strife, one bad and one good. The bad or "harsh" strife "fosters evil war and battle, being cruel." However, the other strife is comparable to our concept of competition. Hesiod noted that this strife motivates lazy men to work and craftsmen to labor to achieve wealth (in competition with other producers).

Statue of Athena

Guiding Questions

1. How did city-states differ from nation-states?
2. How did the government and culture of Sparta and Athens differ?
3. What were the four basic Greek types of government?

II. Greek City-States

Role

Though they shared the same language, customs, and religious beliefs, the Greeks lacked political unity. The Nile River had brought the Egyptian people together and had encouraged their political unification. In sharp contrast, the mountains of Greece isolated the Greek city-states, hindering national unity.

The Greeks usually built their cities at the foot of a hill. For protection, they would construct a fortress at the top of the hill to which they could flee when under attack. They called their city a **polis**, and the fortified hill an acropolis (from *acro*, meaning high).

The polis, or city-state, was the basic political unit of Greece. Although relatively small, Greek city-states exercised powers usually associated with national states. The ultimate source of authority, protection, and livelihood for an individual Greek was his city.

Government

Four forms of government were common in the Greek city-states. The earliest form was a **monarchy**, "rule (*archy*) by one (*mono*)," which was prominent during the Homeric Age. The king often received advice from a council of nobles. Gradually the council of nobles assumed the king's powers and ruled as the privileged class. This "rule of a few," called an **oligarchy** (AHL ih gar kee), produced great tension between the wealthy noble class and the lower classes.

Limited Democracy

While the development of rule by the people in some Greek city-states was remarkable, it needs to be understood in its historical context. Half the population was immediately excluded because only males could vote. The remaining half was reduced considerably by a number of qualifications; for instance, only citizens could vote, and the minimum voting age was typically eighteen to twenty. Other restrictions ensured that only a minority of males in a Greek city-state qualified as citizens. For example, slaves and most of the lower class were not eligible for citizenship. In some cities, having a Greek father and foreign mother disqualified a man from citizenship. In other cities the man had to be the son of a citizen in order to qualify for citizenship. On rare occasions, a man might be granted citizenship by a quorum of citizens as a reward for a major contribution to the city. Therefore, early Greek democracy was clearly a limited democracy with minority participation. Yet it remains a remarkable achievement for this period in history.

The dissatisfaction and unrest of the lower classes often led to **tyranny**. At the head of this government was a tyrant who gained complete control of the government—usually by force. A tyrant was not necessarily a corrupt ruler, as our modern conception of that word implies. Some tyrants were effective rulers who advanced the common good.

A unique political contribution of the Greeks was the development of **democracy**, rule by the people. Under a democratic government, qualified adult male citizens could share in the responsibility of ruling the city.

Development

The period from 750 to 500 BC in Greek history saw the development of the Greek city-states. Important in later Greek history, the city-states of Sparta and Athens represented two opposing political systems and ways of life. Other Greek city-states were to follow the example and leadership of these two.

Sparta

Sparta was located in the southern part of Greece on the peninsula called the Peloponnesus (pel uh puh NEE sus). Conquered by the Dorians, Sparta's inhabitants were made slaves, or **Helots** (HEL uts). The new rulers of Sparta conquered surrounding areas, reducing many of the inhabitants to slave status. In constant fear of an uprising, the rulers created a thoroughly militaristic state.

The way of life at Sparta centered on the training of warriors. The highest goal of any Spartan was to be the best soldier for the Spartan state. Sparta controlled all aspects of its citizens' lives in order to maintain an army ready for battle. Spartan elders determined whether babies were healthy enough to be reared. An unhealthy baby would be left on a hillside to die. When boys reached the age of seven, the state took them from their homes and placed them in army barracks, where they underwent rigorous physical training to make them into fit warriors. They were beaten so that they would learn to endure pain. They were encouraged to steal in order to prove their resourcefulness. At the age of twenty, they became a part of the Spartan army but were not full citizens of the Spartan state until they reached the age of thirty. Even then they had to eat and sleep in the army camp instead of at home; they had to be prepared to fight at all times.

Batsi, a village on the coast of Andros Island. The mountainous terrain of Greece contributed to the political fragmentation of Greek civilization.

Spartan girls went through similar training so that they might learn the same Spartan spirit. Their discipline included running, jumping, and boxing. Their chief goal was to become strong mothers, rearing warriors for the state. Spartan women reportedly sent their sons and husbands off to battle with the words "Return with your shields or on them."

Sparta became the champion of the oligarchical form of government. A board of five Spartan nobles guarded against changes in the Spartan society and any harmful outside influences that would disrupt the status quo (existing state of affairs). To ensure the continuing success of the military state, the Spartans often used force or intimidation to help establish oligarchies in neighboring city-states. These city-states organized the **Peloponnesian League**, with Sparta at its head. This organization was designed to protect against foreign invasion and to prevent tyranny and democracy.

Athens

Life in Athens contrasted sharply with the rigid, disciplined life of Sparta. Sparta became associated with militarism, isolation, oligarchy, and glorification of the state. Athens, however, nurtured creativity, commercial endeavors, democracy, and individualism. The Athenians maintained the creative and intellectual heritage of the Minoan and Mycenaean civilizations.

Like other Greek city-states, Athens was ruled by a king during the Homeric Age. Later the noble class rose in power and established an oligarchy. Power was vested in a council of nobles, with the

Greek Colonization

Greek settlement was not restricted to the land we call Greece. Between 750 and 550 BC, the Greeks established colonies throughout the Mediterranean world. The most important Greek colony in the western Mediterranean was the city of Syracuse on the island of Sicily. In fact, the Greeks established so many colonies on Sicily and in southern Italy that the area became known as Magna Graecia (Great Greece). Some of the colonies were founded to alleviate overcrowding, some were founded as trading posts, and others were founded as places to send the undesirable members of society.

The colonization procedure was as follows: A mother city—called a metropolis—would choose a leader (often a noble) to direct the expedition. After listening to the reports of merchants, the leader then chose a site for the colony. When final preparations had been made, the colonists, taking with them a small amount of soil as well as fire from the altars of the mother city, boarded the ships and set sail.

Once the colonists arrived at their destination, the leader assigned land and established various laws and religious rites. Finally, when the colonists were securely settled, they broke their ties with the metropolis. The new city-state was on its own.

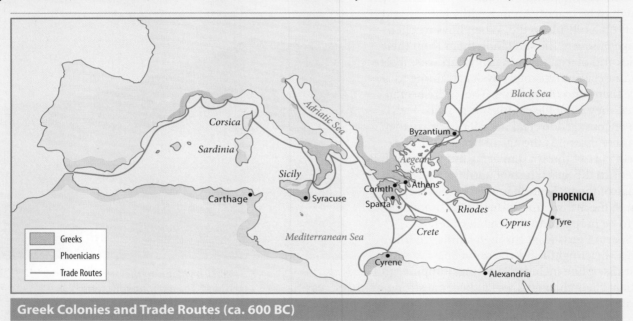

Greek Colonies and Trade Routes (ca. 600 BC)

chief magistrate, or **archon**, being elected from the nobility. As the nobles gained more and more power, hostility arose between them and the common people.

Under the leadership of the statesman **Solon**, Athens took a step toward democracy. Solon assumed the office of archon around 594 BC. Charting a moderate course in Athenian affairs, he provided economic and political stability during a time of tension and hostility. Although Solon was of the noble class, he instituted reforms that helped the common man. For example, he forbade the practice of making debtors into slaves. He also created the Council of Four Hundred, which gave representation to all sections of Athens.

The moderate policies that Solon instituted satisfied neither political side. After Solon's death tension mounted again between the nobles and the common people. Tyrants supporting the cause of the lower classes arose and seized control of the government. They initiated reforms and reorganized the government to allow greater citizen participation. It was not until the fifth century BC under the leadership of Pericles (PARE ih kleez) that Athens established a "rule of the people."

Section Review

1. What was the basic political unit of Greece?

2–5. List and define the four basic forms of government found in the Greek city-states.

6–7. What two Greek city-states represented two opposing ways of life within Greek society?

8. Which Greek city-state was characterized by creativity, commercial endeavors, democracy, and individualism?

★ How did the Spartan system affect family life?

★ Evaluate the strengths and weaknesses of the four basic Greek types of government.

III. The Fateful Century

The Persian Wars

At the outset of the fifth century BC, the westward advance of the Persian Empire threatened Greek independence and isolation. The Persians, expanding into Asia Minor, conquered the Lydians as well as the Greek colonies located along the coast bordering the Aegean Sea. The Greek colonies were treated fairly by the Persians, but the Greeks, who valued independence and self-sufficiency, could not tolerate Persian authority. With the support of Athens, the Greek colonies rebelled and overthrew Persian rule.

Under King **Darius I** the Persians not only crushed the revolt but also sought to punish Athens for its part in the rebellion. (This is the same Darius that is mentioned in Ezra 6:1, 6–12. God used him to aid in the reconstruction of the temple of God at Jerusalem.) In 490 BC a Persian force landed at the Bay of Marathon, about twenty-five miles north of Athens. Though outnumbered and seemingly doomed for destruction, the Athenian army marched to meet the mighty Persian army.

Surprised by the advancing Greek army, the Persians were unable to fully use their cavalry, on which they heavily relied. Instead, they found themselves engaged in hand-to-hand combat; they were no match for the physical strength and battle skill of the Greek soldiers. The Greeks won a decisive victory.

Battle of Thermopylae

Darius organized a full-scale invasion of Greece but died before it could be carried out. **Xerxes**, his son, renewed the struggle. He amassed a great invasion force of men, ships, and supplies. Crossing the Hellespont (see map on p. 58) on a bridge made of boats, the Persian army marched toward Greece.

In 480 BC the Persians, accompanied by their large fleet of ships, made their way down the Greek coast. The Greeks differed on how best to defend their cities. The Spartans suggested that the Greeks mass their forces across the Corinthian isthmus and defend the Peloponnesus. The Athenians objected to this plan because it

Guiding Questions

1. What was the significance of the battles of Thermopylae and Salamis Bay?
2. What role did Pericles play in the development of democracy in Athens?
3. How did the Peloponnesian War affect the course of Greek civilization?

Herodotus's Account of the Battle of Marathon

So when the battle was set in array . . . instantly the Athenians . . . charged the barbarians [Persians] at a run. Now the distance between the two armies was little short of [one mile]. The Persians, therefore, when they saw the Greeks coming on at speed, made ready to receive them, although it seemed to them the Athenians were bereft of their senses, and bent upon their own destruction; for they saw a mere handful of men coming on at a run without either horsemen or archers. Such was the opinion of the barbarians; but the Athenians in close array fell upon them, and fought in a manner worthy of being recorded.

Herodotus, The History of Herodotus, trans. George Rawlinson, 6:112.

Modern view of the pass at Thermopylae. The road on the right was built where the beach would have been at the time of the battle.

would leave Athens exposed to the Persian army. The Greeks finally decided to take their stand at the mountain pass of Thermopylae (thur MOP uh lee), north of most of the city-states. (See the map below.)

At Thermopylae a force of about seven thousand Greeks confronted the advancing Persian army. According to Herodotus, who could never resist improving a story, the Persians numbered about three million. It is more likely that they numbered about two hundred thousand. Though outnumbered, the Greeks had a good position, since only a small number of the Persian army could advance through the narrow pass at one time. The Persians attacked three times but could not take the pass. Then a Greek traitor showed the Persians another way through the mountains. When the Greeks realized that they were almost surrounded, they retreated, but three hundred Spartans along with several hundred Greeks from Thespiae and Thebes remained to hold the pass. All three hundred Spartans fought to the death as well as many of the other Greeks that remained. According to Herodotus "they defended themselves to the last, such as still had swords using them, and the others resisting with their hands and teeth" (Herodotus, 7:225). A monument at the spot bore these words: "Tell them in Sparta, passerby, that here, obedient to their orders, we lie."

Battle of Salamis Bay

Once past the Greek barrier, the Persians swept on to Athens and burned it to the ground. The Athenians had already left the city,

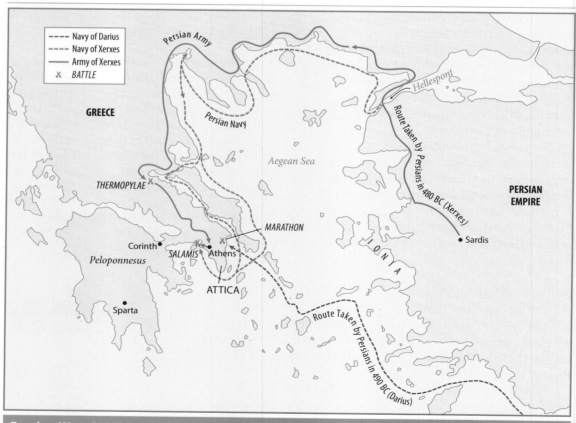

Persian Wars (499–478 BC)

realizing that they would not be able to defend it. They withdrew to an island called Salamis, just off the coast.

Hoping to exploit Xerxes's desire for a quick victory, Themistocles (thuh MIS tuh kleez), the leader of Athens, devised a trap. He sent a trusted slave to Xerxes with the story that the Greeks were frightened and were planning to escape in the morning by sailing northward. The slave also suggested that if Xerxes were to send his ships into the strait between the mainland and Salamis, he would be able to block their escape. The next morning Xerxes ordered his fleet, with many of his soldiers onboard, to attack the Greeks. The Persians entered the strait just as Themistocles had hoped, and the rising morning tide and narrow space made their large ships hard to maneuver. As the Persian sailors struggled to steer their crafts, the Greeks launched their ships from the beaches of Salamis. The small, easily maneuvered Greek crafts created great confusion as they rammed and sank many Persian vessels. From a high vantage point overlooking the bay, Xerxes watched as the Greeks carried the day.

The following year the Greeks, led by Sparta, defeated a sizable Persian army that had remained in northern Greece. Although they had stopped the Persian invasion force, the Greeks did little to weaken the vast Persian Empire. The Persians continued to interfere in Greek affairs for more than a century following the war. Yet the Greeks maintained their hard-fought independence. Freedom bolstered the Greek spirit, furthered the growth of democracy, and encouraged Greek creativity. The way was prepared for the "Golden Age" of Greece—a period of great cultural achievement.

The Periclean Age

Nowhere in Greece following the Persian Wars was the spirit of patriotism and self-confidence stronger than in Athens. It became the leading city-state of Greece; because of its heroic efforts against the Persians, other city-states looked to Athens for protection. The Athenians encouraged the formation of a defensive alliance among the Greek city-states to protect themselves against any further Persian attacks. This alliance became known as the **Delian League**, and Athens became its leader.

The period of Greek history from 460 to 429 BC is often called "The Age of Pericles." For over thirty years **Pericles** was the influential leader of Athens. During his lifetime Athens attained cultural heights unparalleled in the ancient world. Its permissive climate

Pericles on the Athenian Democracy

Our form of government does not enter into rivalry with the institutions of others. We do not copy our neighbors, but are an example to them. It is true that we are called a democracy, for the administration is in the hands of the many and not of the few. But while the law secures equal justice to all alike in their private disputes, the claim of excellence is also recognized; and when a citizen is in any way distinguished, he is preferred to the public service, not as a matter of privilege, but as the reward of merit. Neither is poverty a bar, but a man may benefit his country whatever be the obscurity of his condition.

Thucydides, *trans. Benjamin Jowett, 2:37.*

encouraged advances in thought, art, science, literature, drama, and architecture. So numerous and notable were the Greek accomplishments during this period that special attention will be devoted to them later in this chapter.

Under Pericles's leadership every adult male citizen of Athens gained the privilege and responsibility of sharing in the Athenian government by being able to vote and hold office. No longer was the government controlled only by those of wealth or of noble birth. Now all adult male citizens could participate in government on an equal basis. The majority of the people of Athens, however—the women, slaves, and foreigners—were still excluded from this privilege.

The Peloponnesian War

The Periclean Age came between two violent upheavals in the fifth century BC. The first was the Persian Wars, which temporarily united the Greek city-states in a common defense of their liberty. Following the Golden Age came the **Peloponnesian War** (431–404 BC), a devastating war pitting one alliance of Greek city-states against another. As Athens had grown in influence and wealth, it began to transform the Delian League into an Athenian empire. Sparta became alarmed over the commercial and political power Athens had acquired. The tension between these two rivals and their allies finally flamed into war.

The war has been likened to a struggle between an elephant and a whale. Sparta's strength rested in its land army, whereas Athens and its large fleet reigned supreme on the sea. Early in the war a devastating plague wiped out a large portion of the population of Athens, including its leading citizen, Pericles. Though weakened by these losses, Athens continued to fight. Sparta eventually gained the advantage by forming an alliance with the Persians and was finally able to conquer Athens by destroying the Athenian fleet.

Although Sparta emerged victorious, it had nothing but problems after the war. City-states that had looked to Sparta for deliverance from Athenian domination now found themselves under a greater oppressor. Democratic governments were replaced with oligarchies. The Greeks who had experienced freedom found it difficult to submit to Spartan oligarchical rule. Constant uprisings reduced Sparta's control over the Greek city-states, leaving them disunited once again.

Section Review

1. Which eastern civilization threatened the Greeks at the outset of the fifth century?

2. At which battle did an unorthodox charge by the Greeks help them to win a decisive victory?

3. Where did Xerxes make a bridge of boats to move his army?

4. Who was the influential leader of Athens during its Golden Age?

5. Which group of city-states emerged as victors in the Peloponnesian War?

★ Why did the end of the Peloponnesian War not lead to peace?

★ Analyze Pericles's statement on Athenian democracy.

IV. Alexander's Empire

Rise of Macedonia

North of Greece was Macedonia, inhabited by a people related to the Greeks. King **Philip II** united Macedonia under his rule and extended his kingdom into Greece. Many Greek city-states supported Philip, hoping that he would bring unity to their land. Some resisted him, fearing that their freedom would be lost under Macedonian rule. The weakened and divided Greek city-states were no match for the well-organized army of Philip.

Philip's appreciation for Greek culture led him to treat his many subjects with great tolerance. He hoped to gain Greek support for an invasion of the Persian Empire, the Greeks' constant enemy. But in 336 BC, before he could fulfill his plans, Philip was assassinated. His son **Alexander** assumed the throne at the age of twenty. As a boy, Alexander had been taught by one of the greatest Greek philosophers, Aristotle, who had instilled in him a love for Greek culture. With his conquering armies he carried this culture to the far reaches of the Near Eastern world.

Alexander's Conquests

With amazing speed Alexander led his army across Asia Minor and confronted the Persian army, led by King **Darius III**. In the heat of one battle, Darius fled, leaving behind his wife, mother, and children to be taken captive by Alexander. Alexander took Syria, destroyed the city of Tyre (see p. 26), and marched unopposed into Egypt. The final blow to the Persian Empire came as Alexander, near the Tigris River, defeated the larger army of Darius. Alexander had accomplished what he had set out to do—avenge the Persian invasion of Greece and become the king of Asia.

But his thirst for conquest was not yet satisfied. He marched all the way to India and would have gone beyond, but his weary army refused to go farther. They had fought for eight years and had marched over eleven thousand miles. Alexander sulked over the unwillingness of his army to continue. Although he had conquered almost all the known world of his day, his achievements had not

(see p. 26)

Alexander the Great

Guiding Questions

1. What areas did Alexander conquer, and what was his legacy?
2. What do you find in Daniel 8 that anticipates the conquests of Alexander and the division of his empire?

Empire of Alexander the Great (323 BC)

brought any lasting satisfaction to his heart. How often men have tried to satisfy their soul's desires by seeking the fleeting pleasures of this world. Alexander would not have been satisfied even if he had conquered the whole world. God's Word says, "For what is a man profited, if he shall gain the whole world, and lose his own soul? or what shall a man give in exchange for his soul?" (Matt. 16:26).

Empire Divisions

In 323 BC, at the height of his power, Alexander died of a fever in Bablyon (in Nebuchadnezzar's palace); he had not yet reached his thirty-third birthday. Because Alexander left no plans for a successor to his empire, his chief generals fought among themselves to determine who would rule.

These new kings fought one another as each tried to restore the whole empire under his own rule. From the families of three of Alexander's generals came dynasties that ruled portions of the former empire until the time of the Roman conquests: the Ptolemies (TOL uh meez) in Egypt, the Seleucids (sih LOO sidz) in Syria and Persia, and the Antigonids (an TIG uh nidz) in Macedonia and Greece.

Alexander will be remembered as one of the world's greatest military leaders. His empire spread across the ancient world from Greece to India and included most of the capitals of earlier civilizations. He founded cities that became centers of learning and culture. Some of these he named after himself, such as Alexandria in Egypt. Through his conquests he spread the Greek culture and language to the East. Although his empire split soon after his death, the Greek culture remained a vital force in the ancient world.

Section Review

1. Over what area did Philip II originally rule?
2. Who was Alexander the Great's teacher who instilled in his young pupil a love for Greek culture?
3–5. List three kingdoms that Alexander conquered.
   ✶ Why did Greek culture spread throughout the Middle East, North Africa, and Asia Minor?

V. Greek Culture

The Essence

The culture of a civilization reflects the values and character of its people. The Greeks appreciated beauty, freedom, justice, truth, and knowledge. They exalted the person who had a creative spirit, versatile talents, a thirst for knowledge, physical ability, and a zest for life. The Greek respect for self-control, restraint, balance, and moderation is evident in the Greek motto: "Nothing in excess, and everything in proportion." These qualities characterized much of Hellenic culture.

The term **Hellenic** is used to describe Greek culture. The Greeks called themselves Hellenes and their land Hellas. The height of Hellenic culture occurred during the Golden Age of Athens. The spirit of independence and self-sufficiency, bolstered by the defeat of the Persians, produced the flowering of Hellenic culture in Athens. Most of the Greek men whose achievements history remembers lived in this city.

Ancient Greece has been called the cradle of Western culture. Greek culture left a lasting imprint on the Western world. The Greeks set forth many of the basic concepts of science, mathematics, and philosophy. Greek literature, architecture, and sculpture became models that later civilizations imitated.

Although Alexander's army never conquered the world, Greek culture did subdue a large portion of it. Alexander's conquests spread the Greek language and way of life throughout much of the ancient world. As a result, Hellenic culture mixed with the cultures of the East. A new culture emerged; it was no longer just Hellenic, meaning "Greek," but **Hellenistic**, "like the Greek."

Hellenistic culture permeated the Near East from the time of Alexander until the coming of the Romans in the first century BC. Its influence was so great that this period is known as the Hellenistic Age. This culture united the peoples of the Near East by blending their arts, religions, philosophies, and customs. The Hellenistic Age brought the East and West together in learning, in government, and in trade.

The Expression
Focus on Man

To the Greeks the ability to think and reason made man unique. His humanity was thus worthy of special study. The Greeks were among the first to begin the formal study of human thought and culture, called the **humanities**. Philosophers and scientists praised the human mind and its reasoning powers. Greek literature dealt with how man lives and acts. The goal of physical activity was to develop the human body toward physical perfection. Greek art focused on the human form.

Interest in Philosophy

Throughout history men have looked for answers to the basic questions of life: (1) Where did I come from? (2) Why am I here? (3) Where am I going? and (4) What is the highest good in life? Early in their history the Greeks developed myths to help them answer these questions. Following the sixth century BC, however, many people lost confidence in these myths. Men called **philosophers**, "lovers of wisdom," tried to find the answers to these questions through man's reasoning ability. They believed that the highest good was to seek truth and attain knowledge. This, they hoped, would enable men to live properly.

***Thales of Miletus (ca. 640–546 BC)—*Thales** (THAY leez) is often called the Father of Philosophy. Among the Greeks, Thales was one of the first who sought to explain the origin of the universe in natural terms. He concluded that water was the original substance of all things. He and other early philosophers did not deal with the questions of ethics—what is right and wrong. This was left to later philosophers, the most famous of whom are Socrates, Plato, and Aristotle.

***Socrates (ca. 470–399 BC)—*Socrates** (SAHK ruh teez), a contemporary of Pericles, lived in Athens during its Golden Age. This snub-nosed man with bulging eyes devoted his life to seeking truth and teaching men how to conduct their lives. He took as his motto "Know thyself." According to Socrates, "The unexamined life is not worth living."

Grecian urn

Socrates (left), *Plato* (center), *and Aristotle* (right)

Socrates was not a writer but a teacher. We know what he taught by what his students wrote about him. His method of teaching involved the asking of leading questions followed by the analyzing of the students' answers. Socrates believed that truth (absolutes) could be attained through human reason. To Socrates virtue was knowledge, and ignorance produced evil. Thus reason was the best guide to good behavior.

Many in Athens objected to Socrates's questioning of some of the fundamental institutions of the city. They accused him of corrupting the youth and rejecting the gods of Athens. He was tried and condemned to death. Refusing to flee, Socrates calmly drank the cup of hemlock (poison) by which the sentence of death was to be carried out. He died at the age of seventy surrounded by his followers.

Plato (ca. 427–347 BC)—The most famous pupil of Socrates was **Plato** (PLAY toh). He established a school of philosophy and science called the Academy, located in Athens. In the *Republic*, he devised one of the first plans for an ideal society and government. Although Plato lived in democratic Athens, he realized that too much liberty and freedom without restraint often leads to **anarchy** (the breakdown of government and order). He stated that the "excess of liberty, whether in states or individuals, seems only to pass into excess of slavery."

In his works Plato discussed what he considered to be true reality. He determined that something would have to be permanent (eternal) to be truly real. Since nothing in this world is permanent, Plato concluded that true reality lies outside the physical world. The things on earth are mere shadows, or imperfect reflections, of their eternal counterparts, or "forms," in the unseen realm.

Aristotle (384–322 BC)—The last of the three most famous Greek philosophers was **Aristotle** (EHR uh stot ul). Aristotle was not an Athenian like the other two but came to Athens from northern Greece. At the age of eighteen, he began his study at Plato's Academy. Plato called his most famous student "the mind of the school." Like Plato, Aristotle has had a continuing impact on Western thought through his writings. Aristotle, as we learned earlier, was also the tutor of Alexander the Great, and he instilled in the young prince an appreciation for Greek culture.

Unlike Plato, Aristotle believed that reality was in the physical world. Therefore, he developed wide interests in many fields. He wrote treatises on politics, biology, physics, art, drama, mathematics, and ethics. He is best remembered for his works on logic, which are collectively called the *Organon* ("Instrument"). To aid man's reasoning ability, Aristotle developed the **syllogism**, a three-step logical process of thinking. The following is a good example: (1) All Greeks are human; (2) Aristotle is a Greek; (3) therefore, Aristotle is human.

Epicureans and Stoics—The Epicurean (ep ih kyoo REE un) and Stoic philosophies emerged shortly after the death of Alexander the Great. **Epicurus** believed that great happiness and pleasure could be achieved through the avoidance of pain and fear. Many have thought that this meant that Epicurus thought people should do whatever happens to please them at a given moment. But Epicurus taught that people should take the long view. He counseled a quiet life that avoided the many things in this life that brought pleasure in the short term but would later lead to pain. Epicurus believed that fear of death was the major reason people did not lead happy lives. He argued that when a person dies the atoms of both the body and the soul fall apart, and, since there is no existence after death, there is nothing to fear. **Zeno**, the founder of Stoicism, taught that the affairs of men and the universe were ordered by fixed laws. Man must accept fate and live a life of duty and self-control. These philosophies had greater impact on the Roman world than on the Hellenistic world. (See pp. 99–100.) When the apostle Paul visited Athens in the first century AD, certain Epicurean and Stoic philosophers mocked him because his preaching concerning the resurrection contradicted their teaching (Acts 17:18, 32).

Contributions to Science, Medicine, and Mathematics

The questions raised by the Greek philosophers concerning man and his world encouraged others to seek natural or logical explanations through observation. Even before the Golden Age, **Pythagoras** (pih THAG er us), a philosopher and mathematician of the sixth century BC, had concluded that the universe could be explained in mathematical terms. His geometric theorem, the Pythagorean Theorem, is still studied by students taking geometry.

Hippocrates, (hih PAHK ruh teez) the famed physician of the Golden Age, is known as the Father of Medicine. After studying in Athens, Hippocrates became a wandering physician who traveled throughout Greece and Macedonia. Contrary to common Greek myths which held that disease was the punishment of the gods, Hippocrates taught that every illness has a natural cause. He rejected magic and superstition and instead recommended rest and proper diet as the proper treatments. He wrote manuals that preserved his findings for other physicians.

Euclid (YOO klid) has often been called the Father of Geometry. He founded a school of mathematics in Alexandria, Egypt. His textbook, *Elements*, continues to be the basis for geometry textbooks today. The Greek inventor and mathematician Archimedes (ar kuh MEE deez), born in the Greek colony of Syracuse, was known throughout the Hellenistic world for his many discoveries. One of his discoveries was the principle of the lever, the practical value of which is illustrated today by the raising of a car with a jack. Proud of his discovery of the laws of levers, he once boasted, "Give me a

Greek Philosophers

List key ideas of the following Greek philosophers.

Philosopher	Key ideas
Thales	
Socrates	
Plato	
Aristotle	
Epicurus	
Zeno	

Excerpts from the Hippocratic Oath

I swear . . . that I will carry out, according to my ability and judgment, this oath, and this [written contract]. . . . I will use treatments to help the sick according to my ability and judgment, but never with a view to injury and wrong-doing. Neither will I administer a poison to anybody when asked to do so, nor will I suggest such a course. Similarly I will not give to a woman a pessary to cause an abortion. But I will keep pure and holy both my life and my art. . . . Now if I carry out this oath, and break it not, may I gain forever reputation among all men for my life and for my art; but if I transgress it and [break it], may the opposite befall me.

spot to stand on and a lever long enough, and I will move the earth." The Greek astronomer and geographer **Eratosthenes** (ehr uh TAHS thuh neez) determined the circumference of the globe with amazing accuracy by using the geometry that Euclid popularized. He also formulated the lines of longitude and latitude that are still used today on maps. The belief that the earth is round was advanced by the Greeks some seventeen centuries before Columbus.

Achievement in Literature

History—We get our word *history* from the Greek word meaning "inquiry." The Greeks believed that men could learn lessons from the past to help them live in the present. **Herodotus** (huh ROD uh tus), the Father of History, wrote his history of the Persian Wars in the hope of "preserving from decay the remembrance of what men have done, and of preventing the great and wonderful actions of the Greeks and the Barbarians from losing their due need of glory, and withal to put on record what were their grounds of feud." Although Herodotus tried to be accurate, his work contains many myths and exaggerations as well as an obvious bias toward the Greeks.

Thucydides (thoo SID ih deez), a contemporary of Herodotus, wrote the *History of the Peloponnesian War*, a more accurate and objective record than Herodotus's work. Although Thucydides was an Athenian and fought briefly for Athens during the war with Sparta, he did not let his personal affections influence his account of the war.

Drama—The Greek achievement in literature was unsurpassed in the ancient world. Homer's epic poems are the monuments of early Greek literature. Later the Greeks excelled in poetic drama. An outgrowth of religious festivals, drama became an important part of Greek life. In Athens, for example, several days were set aside each year for the drama festivals. Shops were closed and schools had a holiday as the entire population of the city attended the outdoor performances. The Greeks held contests to determine the best plays and actors.

Greek drama provided more than just entertainment. The plays educated the Greek people in religious beliefs, moral behavior, and civic pride. Both tragedy and comedy were among the favorite forms of Greek drama. **Sophocles** (SAHF uh kleez), a writer of tragedy, and **Aristophanes** (ehr ih STAHF uh neez), a writer of comedy, were among the most famous

Thucydides on the Writing of History

Of the events of the war I have not ventured to speak from any chance information, nor according to any notion of my own; I have described nothing but what I either saw myself, or learned from others of whom I made the most careful and particular inquiry. The task was a laborious one, because eyewitnesses of the same occurrences gave different accounts of them, as they remembered or were interested in the actions of one side or the other. And very likely the strictly historical character of my narrative may be disappointing to the ear. But if he who desires to have before his eyes a true picture of the events which have happened, and of the like events which may be expected to happen hereafter in the order of human things, shall pronounce what I have written to be useful, then I shall be satisfied. My history is an everlasting possession, not a prize composition which is heard and forgotten.

Thucydides, *trans. Benjamin Jowett, 1, 1:22.*

Partially restored ancient Greek amphitheater of the Acropolis of Athens

of the Greek dramatists. Many of the Greek dramas are still enjoyed today; their analysis of human behavior is just as penetrating today as it was in ancient Greece.

Excellence in Art

The Greeks excelled in many forms of art; the most highly prized are their urns, sculptures, and temples. Grecian urns are among the most beautiful ever fashioned. On the exteriors of these graceful forms, the Greeks painted scenes of everyday life, battles, athletic competitions, and activities of their gods.

Greek sculpture falls into three main periods: archaic, classical, and Hellenistic. Pieces from the archaic period show a strong Egyptian influence. Figures stand stiff and expressionless, their fists clenched by their sides. From these somewhat crude forms Greek sculpture gradually became more realistic. During the classical period, Greek sculpture reached its highest achievement. Through their sculpture the Greeks sought to represent the ideal man. In the Hellenistic period Greek sculpture lost its simple beauty. Its calm self-confidence was replaced by a frenzied emotional tone.

The Golden Age of Greek culture (see p. 59) was also the "golden" or "classical" age of Greek architecture. The Greek building style became a standard of excellence that later generations copied. Nothing better reflects the beauty of Greek architecture than the buildings of the Athenian Acropolis. During the Persian Wars, Xerxes had destroyed Athens, but under Pericles new and more beautiful buildings were erected. Formerly a fortress for refuge, the Athenian Acropolis became the site of temples to the Greek gods. The most spectacular of these temples is the **Parthenon**. We can get a glimpse of its former beauty and grandeur today, even in its ruined state.

The Athenians dedicated the Parthenon to the city's patron goddess, Athena. During the days of Pericles, a forty-foot-high gold and ivory statue of Athena stood inside the temple. The building is rectangular in shape and is supported by towering columns in beautiful symmetry. The Greeks gave it the appearance of solidity and symmetry through the subtle use of optical illusions. The steps leading to the entrance are slightly curved at the center; this feature gives the eye the illusion of their being flat. (If they were truly flat, they would appear to dip.) The columns are placed closer together at the

The Porch of Maidens on the Acropolis of Athens, one of the finest examples of Greek statuary

The Parthenon in Athens, a temple dedicated to the Greek goddess Athena

Greek Architectural Orders

From the columns and capitals (the head or top of a column) of Greek buildings, we can distinguish three styles or orders of architecture: (1) the Doric style with solid, strong masculine-looking features; (2) the Ionic style with its splendor and graceful elements and its scroll-shaped capital; and (3) the Corinthian style, whose capitals were richly carved and ornately designed.

Doric

Ionic

Corinthian

sides of the building than at the middle. This spacing gives the appearance of regularity. Likewise, the floor rises gently at the center, giving the whole the appearance of a swelling, living edifice.

The Parthenon symbolizes the cultural achievement of the Greeks. It also symbolizes their spiritual blindness. The apostle Paul visited Athens some five hundred years after its "Golden Age." He preached against the idolatrous practices that the Parthenon and the statue of Athena represented.

Section Review

1. What was the name given to the new culture that emerged in the Near East that mixed Greek culture with the cultures of the East?

2. What philosopher developed the three-step logical process of thinking called a syllogism?

3. Who is known as the Father of Medicine?

4. Who was the more objective historian: Herodotus or Thucydides?

5–7. Identify the three styles of Greek architecture.

★ Why would some modern physicians be opposed to following the principles found in the Hippocratic Oath?

★ How did the Greek advances in science, math, art, literature and architecture influence Western civilization?

Making Connections

1–3. Summarize three differences between the Spartan and Athenian societies.

4–6. What three dynasties emerged following the death of Alexander the Great, and over what regions did they rule?

7. Explain the difference between Hellenic and Hellenistic.

Developing History Skills

1. Why did Athens rather than Sparta become the cultural center of the Greek city-states during the Golden Age?

2. Develop a timeline of Greece that combines its predecessors, significant historical and political events, and a chronology of leading Greek philosophers.

Thinking Critically

1. Use the first chapter of Romans to provide a biblical explanation for the gods worshiped by the Greeks.

2. Use Acts 17:22–34 and 1 Corinthians 1:22–31 to provide a guide for Christians studying Greek philosophy.

3. Propose a system of government based on one or more of the four types of Greek governments.

Living in God's World

1. The Greeks emphasized the need for balance in making ethical distinctions. They also taught that the key to morality was developing character, specifically by using the mind to exercise control over the emotions. What should a Christian think of this approach to morality?

2. Provide biblical answers to the great philosophical questions: (1) Where did I come from? (2) Why am I here? (3) Where am I going? and (4) What is the highest good in life?

People, Places, and Things to Know

Minoan civilization
Mycenaean civilization
Dorians
Homer
Zeus
Athena
anthropomorphic
polis
monarchy
oligarchy
tyranny
democracy
Helots
Peloponnesian League
archon
Solon
Darius I
Xerxes
Delian League
Pericles
Peloponnesian War
Philip II
Alexander
Darius III
Hellenic
Hellenistic
humanities
philosophers
Thales
Socrates
Plato
anarchy
Aristotle
syllogism
Epicurus
Zeno
Pythagoras
Hippocrates
Euclid
Eratosthenes
Herodotus
Thucydides
Sophocles
Aristophanes
Parthenon

CHAPTER

The Roman Civilization

4

Roman aqueduct at Pont du Gard, France

Big Ideas

1. What were the strengths and weaknesses of the Roman Republic?
2. What was the significance of the *Pax Romana*?
3. How was Christ's coming the turning point of history?
4. Why did the Roman Empire decline and collapse?
5. What impact has Roman culture had on modern society?

Today if you were to travel in Spain, France, Britain, Italy, Greece, Asia Minor, Palestine, Egypt, or North Africa, you could find roads built almost two thousand years ago by the Romans. In fact, some of the modern roads in these lands are built on top of the firm and deep base of the old Roman roads. The Romans constructed a network of roads that connected the far corners of their vast empire with their capital city. This led to the saying, "All roads lead to Rome."

In a figurative sense, the road of ancient Western history also leads us to Rome. Rome was the culmination of ancient Western civilization. Despite its power and influence, Rome was deeply bound in spiritual darkness. It readily embraced the pagan gods and false teaching of its many conquered peoples.

The road of God's plan for the ages leads us to Rome as well. God chose to send His Son, Jesus Christ, into the world when the Roman civilization was at its height. God had been at work in history preparing the world for the coming of the Savior. It could be said that the Roman world was the cradle of Christianity. From the Roman province of Judea, the truth of the gospel spread to every part of the empire—on Roman roads.

I. Beginning of Roman Civilization

Geographic Features

The land of Italy, centrally located in the Mediterranean world, was the heart of the Roman Empire. Shaped like a boot, the Italian Peninsula extends into the Mediterranean Sea between the lands of Greece and Spain. At the southern tip of Italy is the island of Sicily, which nearly joins Italy with North Africa.

Geographic obstacles did not hamper the Romans as they did the Greeks. Because of the lack of good soil, the Greeks looked to the sea for their livelihood. However, the soil and climate of Italy were more suitable for farming. The mountains in Greece divided the Greek people and hindered their political unity. The Apennine (AP uh NINE) Mountains, which are located in the middle of the Italian Peninsula, are less rugged than the mountains of Greece and did not hamper the growth of trade and travel among the people of Italy. From the Italian Peninsula, the Romans expanded their territory to include all the land surrounding the Mediterranean Sea. It is little wonder that the Romans would later call the Mediterranean *Mare Nostrum*, which means "our sea."

Early Inhabitants

The earliest inhabitants of the Italian Peninsula had crossed the Alps and had settled in northern Italy. Many of these early settlers—called Latins—moved south and settled in Latium, a plain lying south of the Tiber River near the western coast of Italy. From this region arose a civilization that would one day rule the entire Mediterranean world.

Portions of Italy were also inhabited by the Phoenicians, Greeks, and Etruscans. Both the Phoenicians and the Greeks were known in the ancient world for their sea trade and colonization. Phoenicia established colonies on Sicily and along the coast of North Africa. (The Phoenician colony of Carthage in North Africa later rivaled Rome for mastery of the western Mediterranean world.) The Greeks

Guiding Questions

1. What were important features of early Roman life?
2. What were the strengths and weaknesses of the Roman Republic?
3. Why did Rome become a dictatorship?

Italian Peninsula

established independent colonies on the island of Sicily also, as well as along the coast of southern Italy.

Most people have never heard of the Etruscans. They came to Italy around 800 BC and established one of Italy's earliest civilizations. Little is known of their origin, although some historians believe they came from the East, possibly from Asia Minor. The Etruscans settled along Italy's western coast, just north of the Tiber River. They soon became trade competitors with the Greeks living in Italy. The Etruscans learned much about Greek myths, architecture, sculpture, and language. It is possible that the Etruscans first introduced Greek culture to the Romans. Much of later Roman culture reflected Greek tradition and customs.

The Founding of Rome

The city of Rome began on the banks of the Tiber River, about fifteen miles from the seacoast. Here trade routes that ran along the western coast of Italy crossed the river. At this point the river was easy to ford. People from Latium began to settle on the hills that overlooked this spot. A colony of Latin people established a village on the Palatine Hill near the Tiber. Soon other Latin villages were founded on the surrounding hills. Sometime during the eighth century BC, seven of these villages formed a league—the "**League of the Seven Hills**." This was the beginning of the city of Rome.

Like the Greeks, the Romans developed legends to explain their early history. According to Roman tradition, Rome was founded in 753 BC by the twin brothers **Romulus** and **Remus**. One version of the legend tells how a relative of Romulus and Remus usurped the throne and ordered the two babies, who were of royal descent, to be drowned. The infants were placed in a basket and thrown into the Tiber River to die. But a wolf saved the boys and cared for them until a shepherd found them and took them in. As young men, Romulus and Remus allegedly returned to found a city near the place where the wolf had discovered them. While marking out the boundaries for the city, Romulus killed Remus in a burst of jealous anger. Romulus was said to have founded the city of Rome, named it after himself, and become its first king.

Early Society and Government

The basic unit of early Roman society was the family. The family consisted of a small community—self-sufficient and self-ruled. It included not only the father, wife, and children, but also all the people who lived in the household, such as slaves. (Even property was considered to be part of the family.) The father (*pater* in Latin) was the sole authority over the family, and his control extended to every aspect of family life. He ruled his family without interference from the state.

Romans took great pride in their family heritage. Parents taught their children the values of loyalty, submission to authority, self-control, and duty. Rome's strong families, coupled with the patriotism and hardworking spirit of its people, provided the foundation for its greatness.

The family also provided the basis for larger social groups. A number of families from a common ancestor are called a clan. Likewise, a number of clans united by common beliefs and living in a particular region are called a tribe.

Roman road

Early Roman society consisted of two social classes. They differed greatly from each other in the social and political privileges of their members. The wealthy landholders and noble families made up the aristocratic class (a privileged class) called the **patricians**. They held the highest positions in the early Roman society. The majority of the people, however, belonged to the so-called inferior class called the **plebeians** (plee BEE unz). These were the "common people"—the farmers, traders, and craftsmen.

The early government of Rome was a monarchy. The king served as the chief priest, the commander of the army, and the administrator of justice. The king's authority was called the imperium. A small bundle of rods which enclosed an axe, called the fasces, symbolized his power.

The Early Roman Republic

Establishment

About a century after the founding of Rome, the Etruscans crossed the Tiber River from the north and conquered the Latin villages. During the period of Etruscan rule, Rome grew from a weak league of villages to become the leading Latin city. As the influence of Rome increased, so did the Roman nobility's hatred for the Etruscan monarch. In 509 BC they overthrew the king and established a new form of government called a **republic**. Under the Roman Republic the administration of government was divided among three governing branches: the consuls, the Senate, and the assemblies.

Two elected consuls replaced the king and held the imperium. They supervised the everyday affairs of government, commanded the Roman army, and served as the supreme judges of the land. Power was equally divided between the consuls; one could not act without the consent of the other. Each consul served a one-year term. The shortness of the term prevented a consul from becoming too powerful. From the early years of the republic to 366 BC, members of the patrician class held the office of consul exclusively.

The **Senate** became the most important and most powerful body of the republic. Though the Senate was intended to serve the interests of all the people of Rome, it soon became an aristocratic body that safeguarded the powers of the patrician class. The Senate was composed of three hundred members who were appointed for life by the consuls. The permanency of the Senate resulted in an increase of its powers beyond its early advisory role. It controlled the government's finances, passed laws, and supervised foreign affairs.

The republic also had assemblies through which the people could express their views. Wealth, birth, and the place of one's residence determined the membership and voting procedures of these various assemblies. The chief assembly of the early republic was the **Assembly of Centuries**. This assembly voted on legislation submitted by the consuls, made declarations of war, and elected high-ranking government officials. However, the Senate had veto power over the acts passed by this assembly.

Struggle Within the Republic

The patrician nobles who expelled the Etruscan king took firm control of the government. Patricians held the consulships, controlled the Senate and assemblies, made most of the laws, and controlled the courts. In contrast, the plebeians had few social privileges

Fasces

Citizenship

How can a lack of voice in government result in people suffering injustice?

Power

How might gaining political power address injustice? Does it always?

Justice

How might written and published laws bring about greater justice in society?

and virtually no voice in government. They were excluded from holding public office, and marriage between plebeians and patricians was forbidden. For failing to repay loans, plebeians could lose their property and even be sold into slavery.

For two centuries following the founding of the republic, the plebeians struggled to gain political and social equality. During these two centuries, Rome was constantly waging war against its neighbors in Italy. Because the patricians could not handle the burden of war alone, they had to rely more and more on the common people to help in fighting these wars. As the plebeians shared in the dangers of fighting, they wanted to share in the privilege of governing. By threatening to desert the army, the plebeians gradually gained concessions from the patricians.

One of the first concessions gained by the plebeians was the right to have their own assembly and elected officials. They met as the Council of Plebeians and passed resolutions called plebiscites. These were binding only on the plebeians, however, and not on the patrician class. The Council of Plebeians elected ten men to the office of **tribune**. The tribunes protected the rights and interests of the common people. By crying "Veto!" ("I forbid!"), the tribunes could stop unjust acts of patrician officials.

In the past, patrician judges had taken advantage of the plebeians, who were not familiar with the traditions that made up Rome's unwritten laws. However, continued pressure from the plebeians finally forced the patricians to put the Roman laws into writing. Around 450 BC these laws were written down on twelve tablets and hung in the **Roman Forum**, the section of the city that was the center of government. Now all could know the law. Likewise, the law was to be applied equally to all. These tablets of law, called the **Law of the Twelve Tables**, became the foundation of Roman civil law.

Gradually the plebeians improved their political and social standing in the republic. They gained the right to hold public offices which had previously been held only by the patricians. A few plebeians even became senators. Debtor slavery was abolished, and the law against intermarriage between plebeians and patricians was repealed. In 287 BC the plebeian assembly, now called the **Tribal Assembly**, gained the power to pass laws binding upon all the people of Rome—patricians as well as plebeians. As the distinctions between patricians and plebeians began to disappear, a new class distinction began to develop—the rich versus the poor. Wealthy plebeians and patricians formed a new alliance that maintained control of the Senate and held the reins of power in the republic.

The Roman Forum

Section Review

1. According to tradition, in what year was the city of Rome founded?

2–3. What were the two main social classes of ancient Rome?

4. In what year was the Roman Republic founded?

5. What was the most powerful body within the governmental structure of the republic?

6. What was the name of the Roman law that was written down and placed in the Roman Forum?

7. What was the name of the plebeian assembly that gained the power to pass laws binding on all the people of Rome, regardless of their social class?

✷ How did the family unit play a significant role in the development of early Rome?

✷ Why did the political changes and increased power of some plebeians not end the struggle for power in Rome?

Expansion of the Republic

The Romans had not originally set out to conquer the world. But constant warfare from 509 to 133 BC transformed Rome into the largest empire of its time. How did this expansion take place?

Rome—The Master of Italy

With the expulsion of the Etruscan king in 509 BC, other Latin cities joined with Rome in a defensive alliance for protection against the Etruscans. Just as the members of the Delian League had revolted against the growing power of Athens, so the Latin cities, fearful of the growing power of Rome, revolted. Rome defeated the Latin cities, securing a strong position in central Italy, and later acquired the land to the north by defeating the Etruscans.

Rome soon began expanding into southern Italy, threatening the Greek colonies located there. The Greek colonies feared Roman conquest and appealed to Pyrrhus, a distant relative of Alexander the Great, for help. With the aid of war elephants (the "tanks" of ancient warfare), Pyrrhus defeated the Romans twice. In gaining the second victory, however, Pyrrhus's army suffered such great losses that he reportedly exclaimed, "Another such victory and I shall be ruined." Since that time, a "Pyrrhic victory" has referred to a victory whose costs outweighed any advantage that the winner may have gained. When battle losses forced Pyrrhus to return to Greece, Rome was able to conquer southern Italy.

By 265 BC Rome controlled all of the Italian Peninsula. Its task now was to rule effectively a land that included Latins, Etruscans, and Greeks. Unlike most conquering peoples, the Romans treated their subjects with mercy and fairness instead of force and oppression. As long as they did not rebel, Rome's subjects lived in relative peace. Many conquered subjects in Italy were granted citizenship—the right to vote and hold office. Others enjoyed a great degree of local independence. Although Rome did not demand tribute (payment of money or grain showing submission) from the conquered

Roman Republic to 265 BC

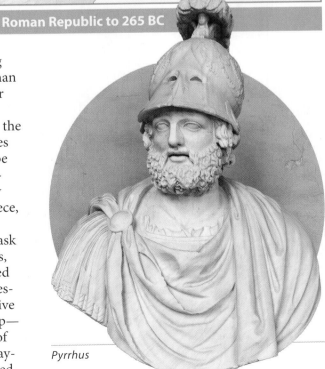

Pyrrhus

states within Italy, it did require them to furnish troops to help Rome fight wars. The protection of Roman law and the stability and prosperity that Rome brought to the Italian Peninsula secured the loyalty of its subjects and allies.

Rome—The Master of the Western Mediterranean

Rome's conquest of the Italian Peninsula brought it into conflict with Carthage, another power in the Western world. Located in North Africa, Carthage possessed good harbors, rich mining resources, and the best navy in the western Mediterranean. While Phoenicia, the mother country of Carthage, grew weak as a result of Assyrian and Chaldean conquests, Carthage built an empire in the West that included the North African coast, southern Spain, the islands of Sardinia and Corsica, and part of the island of Sicily.

Between 264 and 146 BC, Rome and Carthage fought each other in three wars. Both cities controlled much territory in the western Mediterranean. Both were expanding rapidly. In addition, Rome and Carthage were competing for control of trade in the Mediterranean. This rivalry, which was built on both jealousy and fear, led to a series of wars known as the **Punic Wars**.

The First Punic War (264–241 BC)

The First Punic War was fought over control of the island of Sicily. The Romans feared the Carthaginians would become too strong on the island. A powerful rival force could control the waters between Sicily and Italy and thus hinder Roman trade in the Mediterranean. Sicily could also become a base for a Carthaginian attack on southern Italy. The only way Rome could stop Carthage was to break its naval supremacy.

Roman sailors could not match the experience and skill of the Carthaginians. So Rome developed new tactics for fighting at sea. Up to that time, naval battles were won by ramming and sinking the enemy's vessels. Rome substituted soldiers for experienced sailors. When an enemy ship came near, a plank was dropped (like a drawbridge) so that its spiked tip fastened to the deck of the enemy's ship. Armed Roman soldiers then swarmed across and captured the ship. By this method Rome crippled the navy of Carthage. Carthage sued for peace in 241 BC. Terms of the settlement included Roman control of Sicily and the requirement that Carthage pay for Roman losses.

The Second Punic War (218–201 BC)

Carthage recovered from its defeat in the First Punic War and extended its control over much of Spain. In 219 BC Carthage attacked a Roman ally, a Spanish town on the Mediterranean coast. The city fell after an eight-month siege, and a second war broke out between Carthage and Rome. Rome, which now had the superior navy, planned to isolate Carthage's forces in Spain. By sending one army to Spain and another to Carthage, Rome hoped for a quick end to the war against the divided Carthaginian forces. This strategy might have worked had it not been for a young Carthaginian commander named **Hannibal**.

Historians have likened Hannibal to Alexander the Great. His effective leadership and tactical skills won the devotion of his soldiers. This military genius devised strategies that are still being studied by army experts today. (Some of his tactics were used in

Hannibal

tank battles during World War II.) Hannibal believed that his only hope of success was to invade Italy and capture Rome. By invading Italy, he planned to present himself as liberator of Rome's conquered allies and give them an opportunity to break with Rome and gain their freedom. Without the soldiers and resources supplied by its allies, Rome could be conquered—so Hannibal thought.

With cavalry, elephants, and some forty thousand men, Hannibal set out from Spain. He marched his army over the rugged, snow-covered Alps and into northern Italy. The dangerous mountain passes, wintry weather, and attacks from mountain tribes combined to cut his army by about half and left him with only a few supplies and elephants. Nevertheless, he surprised the Romans. They had believed it impossible for any army to cross the Alps—especially during the winter. During the next fifteen years, Hannibal brilliantly led his outnumbered army to many victories in Italy.

Second Punic War

In the spring of 216 BC, the Romans suffered one of the worst defeats in their long history. At Cannae (KAN ee), a small town southeast of Rome, the Roman legions confronted Hannibal's army. Because the Romans outnumbered his army almost two to one, Hannibal had to rely on superior battle tactics. He arranged his forces in the same fashion as the Roman troops—cavalry units on the flanks and infantry at the center. But unlike the Roman line, Hannibal's line bulged forward at the center, inviting the Romans to attack there. The Roman infantry charged the center of Hannibal's line, hoping to break it and divide the Carthaginian forces. While the outside of Hannibal's line held its ground, the center (according to plan) retreated, drawing the advancing Romans into a U-shaped pocket. The Romans soon found themselves hemmed in by the enemy on three sides. Meanwhile, Hannibal's cavalry, which had routed Rome's cavalry, circled around and attacked the rear of the Roman infantry. The surrounded Roman army was almost completely wiped out. Estimates vary, but Hannibal may have lost six thousand men, while the Romans may have lost around sixty thousand men. A generation passed before Rome recovered from this terrible defeat.

To make matters worse, Rome had to contend with a new Carthaginian ally, Macedonia, and suppress Syracuse, a powerful Greek city on Sicily that revolted against Rome. Despite these advantages, Hannibal was unable to conquer the city of Rome. He lacked the heavy siege equipment needed to break down Rome's walls. Furthermore, he gained few recruits from the people he freed from Roman rule. Rome's fair and generous treatment of its subjects encouraged them to remain loyal to Rome.

The turning point in the war came through the daring strategy of a young Roman commander named **Scipio** (SIP ee oh). A member of a powerful family, he became the most famous Roman of his time. After defeating the Carthaginian forces in Spain, he could have moved his army into Italy to take on Hannibal. But instead he crossed over to North Africa and prepared to attack Carthage.

Hannibal, who had not lost a battle in Italy, was ordered back home to defend Carthage. By the time he arrived, it was too late. Not even the leadership of Hannibal could stop Scipio and the Roman legions. At the Battle of Zama (202 BC), the Romans defeated the Carthaginian army. Carthage surrendered and was forced to give up all its territory outside of North Africa, reduce its fleet to only ten vessels, and pay a great sum to Rome for war damages. Rome was now the master of the western Mediterranean world.

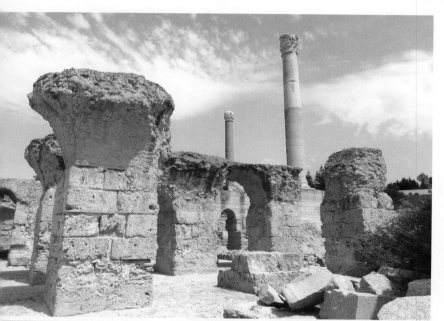

Ruins at Carthage

The Third Punic War (149–146 BC)

Fifty years after the Second Punic War, Carthage broke one of the provisions of its treaty with Rome. In response, Rome harshly demanded that the Carthaginians move their city ten miles inland. Since such a move would mean the death of this commercial center, the citizens decided to fight instead. But the Carthaginians were no match for the Romans. After a three-year siege, the Romans captured the city and destroyed it. They sold the surviving inhabitants into slavery and turned the land around Carthage into a new Roman province called Africa.

Rome—The Master of the Eastern Mediterranean

After the Third Punic War, Rome turned its attention to the eastern portion of the Mediterranean. Here the kingdoms carved out of Alexander the Great's empire—Macedonia, Syria, and Egypt—were engaged in a power struggle of their own. Because Macedonia had joined Carthage against Rome during the Second Punic War, Rome sent its legions to deal with Macedonia after Carthage had been defeated. With Macedonia weakened by its wars with Rome, the king of Syria marched into Asia Minor, crossed the Hellespont, and invaded the kingdom of Macedonia. Rome met this challenge by defeating the Syrian armies. Egypt, the weakest of the three remnants of Alexander's empire, thought it best to make an alliance with Rome. With this completed, Rome became the master of the entire Mediterranean world. The prophet Daniel's visions were fulfilled as the kingdoms of Alexander's generals fell to the Roman Empire (Dan. 7:6–7; 8:8).

At first, Rome allowed its eastern conquests a certain amount of self-government. But because of constant uprisings and petty rivalries, Rome reorganized its Mediterranean holdings into provinces. Governors appointed by the Roman Senate administered these provinces and served as the chief military and civil rulers for each province. The provinces retained local freedom as long as they did not rebel. Their main obligation was to pay tribute—money or grain—to Rome. In return Rome provided order and protection.

Section Review

1. What man led the defense of Greek colonies against Roman expansion in southern Italy?

2. Over what island was the First Punic War fought?

3. What famed Carthaginian leader invaded Rome by an unexpected march over the Alps into northern Italy?

4. At what battle during the Second Punic War did the Roman general Scipio decisively defeat the Carthaginians, making Rome the master of the western Mediterranean world?

✶ Evaluate Roman expansion in the light of justice and power. (See p. 13 in ch. 1.)

II. The Roman Empire Emerges

Decline into a Dictatorship

By the first century BC, Rome was the greatest power in the Mediterranean world. Nevertheless, during the last two centuries before Christ, the very foundation of the republic was shaken—not by any foreign enemy but by problems that arose within the republic as a result of unintended consequences of Roman expansion.

Problems

The economic and military backbone of the early republic was the hardworking citizen-farmer. During the period of Roman expansion, the greatest military burden as well as economic hardships fell on the small farmers. Many of them lost their land. When these citizen-farmers returned from fighting Rome's wars, they faced numerous obstacles. Some of them lacked the money needed to get their land back in shape; others were unable to pay their back taxes and thus lost their farms to the government. Those who were able to grow crops were unable to compete with the large farms of the wealthy aristocrats or with the cheap grain imported from the new Roman territories. In poverty and in debt, small farmers sold their land (usually for a cheap price) and sought jobs in the cities or as tenant farmers. But jobs were hard to find because of the increased number of slaves that were brought into Italy following Rome's conquests. Landless and unemployed, the citizen-farmers became dissatisfied and restless. Their self-reliant spirit broke down, and many turned to the government for help.

But they received no help from the government. Since its early years, the republic had undergone many changes in order to provide equal rights and privileges for all Roman citizens. The Tribal Assembly, which represented the common people, had greatly increased in power. But no sooner had these gains been achieved than the Punic Wars erupted. The common people failed to assume the

Guiding Questions

1. What was the *Pax Romana*?
2. What role did Augustus play in establishing the *Pax Romana*?
3. What rulers followed Augustus during the *Pax Romana*?

Justice and Power

Rome's power led to the unsettling of the social structure in a way that led to injustice for certain Roman citizens. They were called to fight wars which resulted in their being unable to support themselves.

responsibilities they had struggled so long to gain. They relied instead on the more experienced and stronger leadership of the Senate to see them through times of crisis. Thus, during the period of the Roman conquests, the Senate was able to increase its power and again dominate the republic.

The conditions that devastated the poor provided opportunities for increased prosperity for the already wealthy landholders, whose interests the Senate represented. Many of these wealthy landowners expanded their own estates by buying out the small farmers. They also controlled large tracts of land in the new Roman provinces. Many aristocratic senators, once concerned for the best interests of the republic, became selfish and pleasure loving. The pleas for reform from the masses of unemployed and landless went unheeded by the majority in the Senate, whose self-centered interests opposed any change. The Senate was unwilling to address the social and economic problems at home.

The corruption in the government at Rome spread to the Roman provinces. Many of the provincial governors appointed by the Senate used their powers for their own selfish gains. One of the greatest abuses was in the collection of taxes that each province paid to Rome. Roman officials often made agreements with men called publicans to collect taxes in a given province. The publicans would agree to pay a fixed amount to Rome. Whatever they collected above this fixed sum they could keep for themselves. In return for a percentage of the extra money received, some senators and governors made deals to see that certain men were appointed publicans. Soon the publicans were among the most detested people in the Roman territories; they had become rich, but at the expense of the people. These abuses were still part of Roman society during the time of Jesus and His disciples in the first century AD.

Failure of Reform

The poor found champions for their cause in the brothers Tiberius and Gaius Gracchus (GRAK us). The Gracchi (GRAK eye; plural form of Gracchus) were from one of the noble families of Rome. Their father had been a consul, and their grandfather was Scipio, who had led Rome to victory in the Second Punic War. Elected as a tribune in 133 BC, Tiberius strove for reforms in the republic and became the spokesman for the common man.

Tiberius proposed changes in Rome's land policy. For years wealthy aristocrats had monopolized the lands gained through Rome's conquests. Tiberius wanted these "public lands" to be divided among the poor. He also sought to limit the amount of public land controlled by any one person. Although the Tribal Assembly adopted his reforms, his proposals gained him powerful enemies. Wealthy landholders foresaw their own financial ruin, and senators disliked his reviving the powers of the Tribal Assembly. When Tiberius sought reelection as a tribune—an act contrary to Roman tradition at that time—angry senators killed him and three hundred of his followers. The murderers then threw the bodies into the Tiber River.

When Gaius became tribune in 123 BC, he sought to carry on his brother's land reform measures. He also proposed that the government sell grain at low prices to the poor. But the Senate undermined the popular support of Gaius by offering its own programs. (The Senate, however, had no intention of carrying through with

201 BC

133 BC

31 BC

Expansion of the Roman Republic

these reforms.) During a riot carefully planned by his enemies, Gaius lost his life. Some accounts say he committed suicide to keep from falling into the hands of the senatorial forces. Once again the Senate had prevailed.

Civil War

In the early years of the republic, the Senate, in order to preserve the stability of the government, met the challenges of the plebeians by granting concessions. In response to the new challenge of the Gracchi brothers, the Senate abandoned peaceful measures and resorted to violence to preserve the power and wealth of the aristocrats. The failure of the Senate to deal with reform for the poor further weakened the republic. The disorder of the Roman state finally led to civil war.

The First Civil War

In the first century BC, three civil wars shook the very foundations of Rome, exposing the corruption in Roman society. The rivalry between the Tribal Assembly and the Senate gave occasion for the outbreak of the first civil war.

Following the deaths of the Gracchus brothers, the common people found a new champion for their cause in Marius (155?–86 BC). Marius was a well-known military hero who had gained fame for victories in North Africa and Europe. He promised the poor and landless a share in land and money gained in war if they joined the army for long terms of service. This changed the Roman army from a citizen army serving out of loyalty for country to a "professional" army that served for financial gain. Devotion to the commander of the army became greater than devotion to Rome. This shift in loyalty would later be the undoing of Rome.

In 88 BC war broke out in Asia Minor. The Senate appointed Sulla (138–78 BC) to command the Roman army in the east. The Tribal Assembly, however, rejected the Senate's choice and appointed Marius instead. The years that followed saw much bloodshed as the tension between the Tribal Assembly and the Senate, fueled by the rivalry between Marius and Sulla, developed into civil war. In the end Sulla emerged victorious and had himself declared dictator. He then reorganized the Roman government in a way that revived the power of the Senate and removed the influence of the Tribal Assembly and the tribunes. But after Sulla resigned as dictator, the Senate was unable to maintain control of the government.

The Second Civil War

It was now obvious that a powerful man at the head of the army could control the state. Ambitious men sought to gain that control. Crassus and Pompey, two commanders who served in Sulla's army, competed with one another for fame and power after Sulla's death. **Julius Caesar**, nephew of the popular Marius, won greater popular support than either. Caesar (100–44 BC) was a shrewd politician who knew how to sway the common people. Crassus had money, Pompey had the support of the Senate, and Caesar had the favor of the common people. In 60 BC, they formed an alliance called a triumvirate (try UM ver it; "rule of three men") to rule Rome together.

However, each man sought the sole rule of Rome. Caesar built a well-disciplined and loyal army in Gaul. He kept his name before the Roman people by sending written accounts of his military

Pompey

Julius Caesar

accomplishments back to Rome. Pompey sought the help of the Senate to weaken his rival. (Crassus had died in war in Asia.) When the Senate ordered Caesar to return to Rome and disband his army, Caesar crossed the Rubicon (a river in northern Italy) and marched his army toward Rome. By this act Caesar declared war on Pompey and the Senate. In the end, Pompey's armies were no match for Caesar's. After his victory, Caesar had himself proclaimed dictator for life.

As ruler Caesar curbed the corruption of the provincial governments, established colonies for the landless army veterans, granted citizenship to many non-Italians living in Rome's new colonies, and initiated many public works programs. He also established the calendar that is the basis for our modern-day calendar. Although popular with the people, Caesar had enemies among the nobles and senators. On the "Ides" (fifteenth) of March in 44 BC, a group of conspirators assassinated Caesar in the Senate chamber.

The Third Civil War

A third civil war broke out after Caesar's death to determine the next ruler. Caesar's friend and right-hand man, Mark Antony, teamed with Octavian (Caesar's grand-nephew and only male relative) to capture and punish Caesar's murderers. Octavian and Antony then divided the Roman territory in half—Octavian ruling in the west and Antony ruling in the east. Each man, however, was too ambitious to share power with the other. Again war was used to settle the question of who was to be sole ruler of Rome. In **31 BC** Octavian's navy won a decisive victory over Antony at the Battle of Actium. Octavian, only thirty-one years of age, then ruled the entire Roman world.

Section Review

1. What task did the publicans perform in Roman society?

2–3. What were the names of the two brothers who became spokesmen for reform in the later days of the republic?

4–5. Who were the two generals who fought in the first civil war? Which one had the backing of the Senate, and which one the backing of the Tribal Assembly?

6–8. Who were the three rulers of the triumvirate?

9. At what place and in what year did Octavian defeat Antony in the third civil war?

★ Did the three civil wars set a pattern for the duration of the existence of the Roman Empire? Support your answer.

★ Were the concepts of justice and power abused during the Roman civil wars?

Augustus and the *Pax Romana*

Unlike Julius Caesar, who had made himself dictator for life, Octavian announced in 27 BC his desire to restore the republic. He voluntarily chose to share his powers with the Senate. This division of power had existed during the republic. He took the title *princeps* (PRIN keps), or "first citizen." This title was popular among the common people because it conveyed the idea that he was one of them and not a noble. But in fact, the Roman government was a monarchy disguised as a republic. With Octavian, one era of Roman history ended and a new one began. Rome was no longer a republic—a "public matter"—but an empire ruled by an **imperator** (the commander of a victorious army). In his position as the head of the army, Octavian maintained firm control of the government. The Senate conferred the title of **Augustus** on him when he restored the republic. It was a title of divinity, expressing honor and majesty usually associated only with the Roman gods.

Octavian's rule brought a period of peace to the Mediterranean world that lasted from 31 BC to AD 180. During these two centuries the Roman Empire reached its height: its boundaries encircled the Mediterranean Sea and included parts of the old Persian Empire in the east as well as most of western Europe and Britain. In contrast to the period of civil wars that preceded Octavian's reign, the first two centuries of the empire were marked for the most part by internal harmony and unity. Trade prospered, travel and communications improved, and cultural activities flourished. The western ancient world experienced a period of peace and prosperity known as the *Pax Romana* ("Roman Peace"). Nevertheless, this was in a sense an artificial peace. Won by war and maintained by force, it did not long endure. But during the *Pax Romana*, the Author of Peace—Jesus— was born. By His death on the cross, He secured for mankind a true and lasting peace. He said, "Peace I leave with you, my peace I give unto you: not as the world giveth, give I unto you. Let not your heart be troubled, neither let it be afraid" (John 14:27).

During Augustus's reign (27 BC–AD 14), the entire Mediterranean world enjoyed economic prosperity. Agriculture remained the livelihood of most people. But the unity and stability maintained during the *Pax Romana* also encouraged the growth of trade. Rome

Augustus

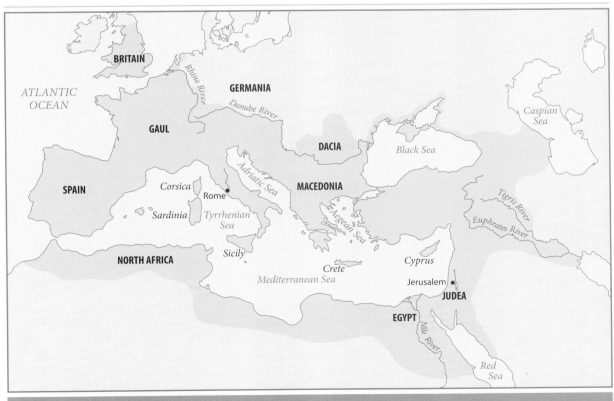

Roman Empire at Its Greatest Extent (ca. AD 117)

established a stable currency of gold and silver coins, which traders could use as a medium of exchange almost anywhere in the empire. Rome reduced piracy on the Mediterranean Sea and provided for safe travel in Roman territory. Ease of communication also aided trade. Greek and later Latin became almost universal languages. Trade not only flourished within the empire but also extended to the world outside the empire. The Romans imported such luxury items as silks, spices, and jewels from India and China; they brought in gold and ivory from Africa. During the *Pax Romana* the material wealth of Rome reached its peak.

In addition to prosperity and peace, Augustus's reign brought stability and order to Roman government and society. Attempting to restore honesty and efficiency in government, Augustus placed ability above social class when selecting government officials. He removed many unqualified, self-seeking men from office and replaced them with well-qualified officials paid by the state. He created a police and fire service for the city of Rome. In addition, he established a postal service and undertook major building programs.

Augustus also sought to abolish corruption in the provincial governments. He reorganized the provinces of the empire, placing some under the supervision of the Senate and others under his own supervision. To provide fairer methods of taxing the provinces, Augustus ordered a census-taking (systematic collection of information about a given people) throughout the empire every fourteen years. From the Scriptures we know that Augustus ordered such a census around the time of the birth of Jesus: "And it came to pass in those days, that there went out a decree from Caesar Augustus, that all the world should be taxed [registered]" (Luke 2:1).

Augustus correctly realized that a civilization is only as strong as the moral character of its people. Therefore, he sought social reforms to revive the traditional Roman virtues of duty, discipline, and hard work. He encouraged the passage of laws that promoted family life and rewarded families that had many children. Other laws punished immorality and placed limits on extravagant living. Despite the laws, Augustus's moral reforms failed.

Successors of Augustus

Though Augustus established an effective and well-organized government, he left no plan for choosing a successor. For nearly a half-century after his death, men who were in some way related to Julius Caesar occupied the imperial office. Most of them led wicked lives and squandered Rome's wealth on their own selfish pleasures. In spite of incompetent leadership, the "Roman peace" continued—it was held intact by the might of the Roman army. Toward the end of the first century, the Roman army began to elevate its favorite generals to the office of emperor. These men of proven ability provided strong leadership for Rome during most of the second century.

Nevertheless, too much power placed in the hands of ambitious and self-seeking men often leads to corruption. The emperors won popular favor by providing "free" grain and amusements for the people of Rome. The Romans failed to realize, however, that these things were not really free. (The necessary funds came from the public treasury.) Civil war often erupted as rival generals fought to gain the emperor's crown. For example, from AD 235 to 285 Rome had twenty-six different emperors. Of these, twenty-five died a violent death.

Section Review

1. What is the name for the period of peace in the Mediterranean world lasting from 31 BC to AD 180?

2–3. List two titles or names by which Octavian was called.

4–5. What did Octavian institute within the empire to provide for fairer taxing of provinces? How often did this take place?

6. How did many of the self-seeking, corrupt emperors of the late empire win the favor of the people?

* Both Augustus and Christ gave moral laws to men. Why were the citizens of Augustus's kingdom unable to obey his law while the citizens of Christ's kingdom were (and are) able to obey His?

* What lessons can we take from this period in Rome's history and apply to our present political system?

III. Rise of the Christian Church

The World Made Ready

God directed the affairs of men and civilizations in ancient times to make the world ready for the coming of His Son and the spread of the gospel. Roman society at the time of Christ was characterized by relatively safe travel and social and political stability. The widely known Greek language made possible the easy exchange of ideas. While these factors aided the spread of Christianity, other factors would encourage the popular acceptance of Christianity. The moral decay throughout the empire demonstrated the inability of human religions and philosophies to satisfy the longings of man's soul and to provide a worthy standard of moral behavior. Into this climate of despair, God sent His Son, who alone could satisfy that hunger and teach people how to live.

After the destruction of Jerusalem and its temple in 586 BC, exiled Jews built new centers of worship called synagogues in the various places to which they were scattered. The spread of Hellenistic culture led many Jews to embrace Greek culture and language. This led to the translation of the Old Testament from Hebrew and Aramaic into Greek. The presence of the Jews and their Scriptures in Greek enabled Gentiles to become acquainted with the revelation that Jesus came to fulfill. The synagogues would later provide the starting place for Christian evangelism in many Greco-Roman cities.

The Life and Message of Jesus

Jesus of Nazareth was born in Judea during the reign of the emperor Caesar Augustus. The events of His earthly life and ministry are recorded in the four Gospels (Matthew, Mark, Luke, and John). At the age of thirty, Jesus began His public ministry—preaching, teaching, and working miracles—demonstrating to all by word and deed that He was the promised Messiah, the Son of God.

The thesis of much of His preaching was the bold statement, "The kingdom of God is at hand: repent ye, and believe the gospel" (Mark 1:15). Jesus also healed the blind and lame and even raised people from the dead. These were visual claims that the kingdom was drawing near. The Old Testament spoke of a Ruler who would

Guiding Questions

1. What was the significance of the life, death, and teachings of Jesus?
2. How did the early church spread throughout the Roman world?
3. How did Christianity influence the Roman Empire?

Modern-day Bethlehem—the birthplace of Christ

reverse injustice and even the effects of sin on nature (Isa. 9:6; 11:6–9). When Jesus announced the kingdom of God, He was teaching that He would establish a kingdom which would reverse all injustice and suffering and set everything right on the earth.

A kingdom that reverses all injustice and suffering certainly sounds like good news. But it is not good news for sinners. It is a message of judgment. Unless the problem of sin is dealt with, no human can be part of the Messiah's kingdom. Jesus said, "Except a man be born again, he cannot see the kingdom of God" (John 3:3). As a result Jesus called for men and women everywhere to admit their sinfulness and follow Him. Jesus also taught that the kingdom would not immediately overthrow oppressors like the Romans. Instead, His followers could expect persecution (Matt. 5:10) and they were to turn the other cheek to their persecutors (Matt. 5:39). As a result, most Jews rejected Jesus as their Messiah. In the words of John's Gospel, "he came unto his own, and his own received him not" (John 1:11).

The religious leaders were offended by such preaching—especially since Christ identified them as hypocrites and called on them

Jesus: The Turning Point of History

Historians may identify certain key events in history as "turning points." For instance, the collapse of the Soviet Union and its satellite nations was a turning point in recent history. It marked the end of a cold war that had lasted for much of the latter part of the twentieth century.

The major turning point in world history is the life, death, and resurrection of Jesus Christ. In His perfect life and death, Jesus provided people with the opportunity to be saved from their sins. His resurrection and ascension came with the promise of His return, at which point Jesus will render judgment on sinners and set to right all injustices and other effects of sin.

Until the ministry of Christ, the message of how God would set the world right and how individuals could be saved from their sins was preserved among the Israelites. But Jesus commissioned his disciples, or followers, to take the gospel message to the ends of the earth.

Providentially, the life of Jesus and the spread of the church occurred at a time in which travel around the Near East, North Africa, and southern Europe was facilitated by Roman rule and the common language of Greek.

Christianity spread and took root in these regions and then spread from there all over the globe. Christ's followers now await the next great turning point in history: His return to set the world right.

to repent. They brought Jesus before the Roman governor **Pontius Pilate**, charging that He was working to overthrow Roman rule. They said that since He claimed to be the Messiah, the King of the Jews, He was opposing the Roman emperor, **Tiberius** (AD 14–37). Although Pilate found no fault in Jesus, he desired to maintain the peace and avoid a possible rebuke from Tiberius (John 19:12–13). Submitting to the Jewish demands, he sentenced Jesus to death by crucifixion.

But three days later, Jesus' tomb was empty. The significance of this event cannot be overstated. When God raised Jesus from the dead, He proved that the life and death of this Man from Nazareth do indeed constitute the turning point of history. With the resurrection, Jesus was exalted to rule from heaven as the Davidic King until the Father subdues all His enemies (Acts 2:30–36). The apostles and early Christians traveled throughout the world preaching the good news of the kingdom of God (Acts 8:4), often referred to as the **gospel**. Those who repented of their sins and submitted to Jesus as Lord and Messiah received forgiveness of sins and were transferred from the kingdom of darkness into the kingdom of Christ (Acts 2:36; Col. 1:13). One day the kingdom of this world will become the kingdom of the Lord and of His Messiah (Rev. 11:15), and Jesus will reign over the world in righteousness from the new Jerusalem forever.

Tarsus Road

The Spread of the Gospel

"Go ye therefore, and teach all nations" (Matt. 28:19). With these words, Jesus Christ charged His disciples to carry the gospel to the world. Conditions in the first century were favorable for the rapid expansion of the Christian faith. It was not until the nineteenth century that the missionary outreach of Christianity again experienced such favorable conditions. The initial spread of Christianity beyond its Jewish cradle was greatly aided by two events: Jewish persecution of Christians and the conversion of Paul.

Jewish Persecution

Jerusalem was the center of the early church. Christ told His disciples, "Ye shall be witnesses unto me both in Jerusalem, and in all Judaea, and in Samaria, and unto the uttermost part of the earth" (Acts 1:8). Through the disciples' preaching, thousands of Jews at Jerusalem turned from their unbelief and trusted in Jesus Christ as their Savior. But as the number of believers grew, so did the opposition of Jewish religious leaders. They began to persecute the Christians, imprisoning many of the disciples and stoning Stephen—making him the first Christian martyr. But the persecution at Jerusalem only served to spread the Christian faith, scattering Christians and their gospel message throughout Judea and Samaria.

The Apostle Paul

Paul (AD ca. 5–ca. 67), originally named Saul, was born into a Jewish home in Tarsus (in present-day Turkey). He inherited Roman citizenship, received one of the best educations a Jew could obtain, and became a Pharisee (one of the strictest of the Jewish religious sects). His religious zeal initially made him a persecutor of the Christian church. But one day on his way to Damascus, Saul, the fervent persecutor, became a zealous Christian (Acts 9:1–6).

Perhaps no person has exceeded Paul in the impact of his work for Christ. The Holy Spirit inspired him, as He also inspired Peter,

Luke, John, and others, to write part of the New Testament Scriptures. Paul wrote more books than any other biblical writer; most of the New Testament epistles (letters) were written by him. Through his missionary endeavors, Paul introduced the gospel to a large portion of the Roman world. He traveled thousands of miles on Roman roads preaching the gospel and establishing churches in Asia Minor, Macedonia, and Greece. The success of Paul's labors among the Gentiles demonstrated that the gospel was for all people—not just for the Jews.

Church Organizational Development

The organization of the early church was very simple. Christians met in private homes for fellowship and worship. They gathered to read portions of God's Word, pray, sing songs of praise, and partake of the Lord's Supper. As the number of believers multiplied, the apostles recognized that they could not minister to all the physical and spiritual needs in the church. Therefore, they appointed "seven men of honest report, full of the Holy Ghost and wisdom" to take care of the daily business of the church. This delegation of responsibility allowed the apostles to devote more time and effort to praying and to the preaching of the Word (Acts 6:1–6).

The earliest leaders of the church were the apostles, who were chosen directly by Christ. As the church spread and the apostles died, Christian leaders chose men of faith and experience to administer the affairs of the local assemblies. When difficult times arose, congregations looked to their pastor-bishops to provide stable leadership in the midst of persecution and protect them from doctrinal error.

Persecution of the Church

Christ told His disciples, "If they have persecuted me, they will also persecute you" (John 15:20). Throughout church history, God's enemies have demonstrated their hatred for God by persecuting Christian people. "All that will live godly in Christ Jesus shall suffer persecution" (2 Tim. 3:12).

One of the most severe periods of persecution of the church occurred during the time of the Roman Empire. The Romans believed that the claims of Christ set Christians at odds with the Roman state and society. They charged that Christians were disloyal citizens because they refused to burn incense on the altars of the emperors, acknowledging Caesar as lord. The Romans, who worshiped many different gods, opposed the exclusive claims of Christians: "Neither is there salvation in any other: for there is none other name under heaven given among men, whereby we must be saved" (Acts 4:12).

The Romans considered Christians "social misfits" and Christianity a threat to their way of life. Christians did not attend the so-called amusements of the arenas, celebrate the pagan festivals, or indulge in the many other vices of the day. Because Christians separated themselves from these public activities, the Romans branded them "haters of humanity." They resented the Christians' fervent desire to tell others about Christ and became alarmed over the rapid growth of the Christian church. Christians became the scapegoats for many of the evils that plagued the empire, from fires to earthquakes.

The first official Roman persecution of Christianity began under the emperor **Nero** (r. 54–68). He accused the Christians of

Nero

The Destruction of Jerusalem (AD 70)

After the destruction of Jerusalem by Nebuchadnezzar in 586 BC, Judea was under the rule of foreign powers—first the Chaldeans, then the Persians, Alexander the Great, the Ptolemies, the Seleucids, and finally the Romans. The Jews tolerated foreign rule as long as they could maintain their religious freedom and administer their own local affairs. But the Jews grew dissatisfied with Roman rule as the Roman governors of Judea gradually became more oppressive and insensitive to the strong religious beliefs of the Jews.

In AD 66 Jewish discontent flared into open rebellion. The Jewish historian Josephus, who later recorded the conflict between the Jews and the Romans, warned the Jews of the folly of armed resistance against the mighty Romans. But the Jews failed to heed his advice. Roman legions were quickly dispatched to suppress the insurrection. In AD 70 the war came to a climax as the Roman legions under their commander Titus breached the walls of Jerusalem, looted the temple, and destroyed the city. God had fulfilled Jesus'

prophecy of Jerusalem's destruction (Matt. 24:2; Luke 19:44) and judged the Jews for their rejection of the Messiah. The Jews lost their homeland and became wanderers among the nations of the earth—objects of ridicule and persecution. Nevertheless, they retained their distinctiveness as a people and the promise in Romans 11 that Israel as a nation will one day be spiritually restored when the Jews accept Jesus as their Messiah.

setting fire to Rome, although he himself may have been responsible. What followed was a hideous display of cruelty and death. The Roman historian Tacitus records that Christians were "torn by dogs, or were nailed to crosses, or were doomed to the flames and burnt, to serve as nightly illumination, when daylight had expired."

From the time of Nero until AD 250, the persecution of Christians was sporadic and confined to small areas across the Roman Empire. However, beginning in 250, persecution became empire-wide. Thousands of Christians—both the young and the old—met death by sword, crucifixion, wild beasts, fire, and burning oil. But they had the steadfast confidence that it is better to "fear him which is able to destroy both soul and body in hell" than to fear "them which kill the body, but are not able to kill the soul" (Matt. 10:28).

The last and most widespread Roman persecution occurred during the reign of the emperor **Diocletian** (r. 284–305). In successive waves of edicts, Diocletian dismissed Christian soldiers from the army and ordered the destruction of Christian churches and the burning of copies of the Scriptures. Later a co-emperor ordered all Christians to sacrifice to the pagan gods under pain of torture and death.

The Romans expected persecution to cause Christians to renounce their faith and deter others from converting to Christianity. Yet the Christian church grew numerically and became spiritually purified. More than a hundred years earlier, one Christian writer had declared, "The blood of the martyrs is the seed of the Church."

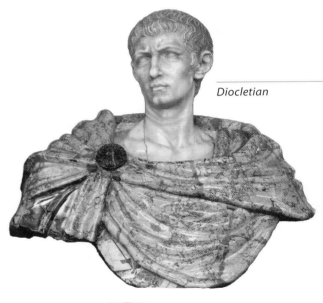

Diocletian

From Imperial Persecution to Acceptance

In 313 one of the most significant events in the history of the Christian church occurred. With the **Edict of Milan**, the Roman emperor **Constantine** (r. 306–37) made Christianity legal, ending almost three centuries of Roman persecution of Christians. Just a year earlier, before a crucial battle with a rival for the emperor's throne, Constantine had claimed to have seen in the sky a vision of a shining cross that bore the inscription "By this sign, conquer!" Upon defeating his foe, Constantine publicly embraced Christianity, attributing his victory to the Christian God. Rome, previously

Constantine

The Spread of Christianity

a persecutor of the church, became the protector and patron of the church. Constantine restored church property that had been confiscated, made Sunday a legal holiday, contributed funds for new church buildings, and encouraged others to embrace Christianity.

Christians now found themselves protected by Roman law, favored by the emperor, and granted privileges by the state. The emperor even tried to help the church sort through a major doctrinal difficulty. When a heretic named **Arius** challenged the deity of Christ, Constantine called for a council of church leaders to settle this doctrinal controversy. In 325, the **Council of Nicaea**, presided over by Constantine, affirmed Christ's deity and the doctrine of the Trinity; it also branded Arianism a heresy. As emperors became more involved in church matters, the church gained more favor and power in the Roman world. At the end of the fourth century, Christianity became the official and exclusive religion of the Roman state by edict of the emperor Theodosius I (r. 379–95).

As a result of the freedom and privileges granted by the Roman government, the church grew rapidly in membership and material prosperity. This position of favor, however, contributed to a decline in the purity of the church's membership, practices, and doctrine. Great numbers of people joined the church—some because they embraced the truth, others because it was the popular thing to do. Some pagan ideas and practices crept into the church. One such practice was monasticism (withdrawing from the world), which exercised a strong influence on the church from the fourth century to the end of the Middle Ages. Roman and Orthodox churches borrowed monasticism from Eastern pagan religions. Because of the moral and economic decay of the Roman Empire and the growing worldliness of the church, many sought escape from the turmoil and evil of the world by living apart from society. Monasteries served as refuge for those who believed that the greatest form of piety was to isolate themselves, practice strict discipline, and carry out religious exercises such as prayer and denial of physical comforts.

Christianity was born in obscurity on the edge of the Roman Empire. Within three hundred years Christianity prevailed and even won the favor of the emperor. With the end of persecution, Christian theologians had the opportunity to defend and define the doctrines of the Trinity and person of Christ. While they did not refute every error, and many false doctrines began to creep into local congregations, God had established His church. Even in the darkest periods, He raised up people who remained faithful to Him.

Section Review

1. What is the term for the centers of worship established by the Jews who were scattered abroad?

2. Why did the Jewish religious leaders reject Jesus as their Messiah?

3. What is the gospel?

4–5. Which emperor made Christianity a legal religion in the empire? Which emperor made Christianity the official religion of the empire?

6–7. What heresy challenged the deity of Christ? At what council in 325 was the truth of Christ's deity affirmed?

✶ How is the message of the coming of Christ's kingdom both bad news and good news?

✶ Arius taught that Christ did not always exist but that He was created by God the Father. Using John 1:1–4 and Colossians 2:8–9, refute this heresy.

IV. Collapse of the Roman Empire

Reason for Decline

In the third century a series of political, economic, and social crises shook the foundations of the empire. Signs of internal weakness and decay were already present. In the fourth and fifth centuries, barbarian invaders entered Roman territory, and Rome was too weak to expel them. What were the reasons for this decline and the eventual collapse of the Roman Empire?

One important reason was Rome's political disorder. By the third century, Rome could no longer boast of a strong and stable government. Inefficiency and waste had accompanied the sharp rise in the size of the government. Rome also suffered from unstable leadership. The Romans had never adopted a definite plan for choosing a successor to the emperor. Hence, ambitious generals plotted and struggled to gain control of the government. As the army became increasingly involved in political affairs, armies were quick to elevate a military leader to emperor to bring stability or to gain rewards. If the army became dissatisfied with an emperor, it could remove him from power and put someone else in his place. In many cases war broke out between different legions as each tried to

Growth of Church Hierarchy

The organization of the church became more complex as the church grew numerically. By the fourth century, the church had a definite hierarchical (hy er AR kih kul) structure—levels of authority among the pastor-bishops and churches in the empire. The organization of the church followed the pattern of the political and geographic divisions of the Roman Empire rather than the example of the early church. The smallest division was the parish, served by a pastor. Next was the diocese (DY uh sis) or district, a territorial division supervised by a bishop and comprising a number of parishes within and around a city. An archbishop administered a number of dioceses called a province. The patriarchates formed the largest administrative districts of the church. The **patriarchs** were the bishops of the most important cities of the empire—Jerusalem, Alexandria, Rome, Antioch, and Constantinople (the new capital founded by Constantine). This position had the most prestige and authority within the church. At first the patriarchs were all of equal rank, but over a period of time the patriarch of Rome began to insist that he be called the "first among equals."

Guiding Questions

1. Why did the Roman Empire experience decline?
2. What attempts were made to reform and reorganize the Roman Empire?
3. What impact did barbarian invasions have on the Roman Empire?
4. What led to the fall of the Roman Empire?

secure the emperor's throne for its own commander. Political turmoil, assassination, and civil war became commonplace. The army, once the protector of the Roman state, now sought to satisfy its own greed.

Closely associated with Rome's political problems were its economic troubles. The cost of maintaining an increasingly large army to defend its extensive borders, as well as the expenses of a huge government bureaucracy, drained the Roman treasury. To solve the economic crisis, the government attempted to raise revenue by increasing the tax burden on the people. In addition, emperors reduced the silver content in the Roman coins, adding cheaper metals instead. As the value of coinage declined, prices rose. This inflation was aggravated by Rome's trade imbalance with India and China, which depleted the empire's gold and silver supplies. Because Roman money became almost worthless, the barter system replaced the use of money. Trade slackened, shops closed, and poverty increased. Confidence in the economic future of Rome all but collapsed.

Moral decay was another factor in the decline of Rome. Rome's strength during its early history was due in large part to the virtues of its citizens—their discipline, patriotism, self-denial, hard work, and respect for authority. However, the moral decay that began during the days of the republic continued during the *Pax Romana*. For many, self-indulgence replaced contentment. Christians' opposition to the violent games and the immorality that engulfed the Roman Empire made them stand out in this increasingly pagan society. People looked to the government to supply free grain and public amusements, which further contributed to the large economic burden on the empire. Family life disintegrated, divorce and immorality abounded, and superstition flourished. Once the backbone of Rome, a hard-working patriotic citizen became difficult to find.

Reform and Reorganization Attempts

By the end of the third century, the Roman Empire was at the point of collapse. But two powerful emperors, Diocletian and Constantine, introduced effective reforms that delayed the fall of the empire for almost two centuries. While earlier emperors tried to work within the framework of the old institutions of the republic, Diocletian and Constantine wielded supreme authority over the state in their attempts to restore order and stability to the empire.

In 284 Diocletian defeated other contenders, and his army proclaimed him emperor of Rome. An able administrator and organizer, Diocletian concluded that the empire was too large for one man to rule effectively. Therefore, he chose a co-emperor, known as an augustus, to rule the western half of the empire while he ruled in the east. Diocletian's plan called for each co-emperor to appoint an assistant, called a caesar, to help the augustus and to become his successor. Diocletian divided the empire into four large administrative divisions, called prefectures, which were to be ruled by the two co-emperors and the two caesars. Through these measures, Diocletian brought temporary stability to the government.

Diocletian also introduced strong measures to combat Rome's economic problems. To curb inflation, he set maximum prices on goods and services. Anyone selling an item above the price limit could be put to death. He tried to revive confidence in Rome's monetary system by introducing new gold and silver coins. He

Ancient Roman coins

also reformed the tax system, but the people still suffered under an excessive tax burden. In each instance, Diocletian's measures to solve Rome's economic worries involved greater government control and regulation. As a result, his measures only added to the problems they were intended to solve.

When Diocletian retired from office in 305, his system of joint rule fell apart. Civil war broke out among those he had appointed to succeed him and his co-emperor. After eight years of struggle, Constantine emerged victorious. He became the sole ruler of the empire and continued Diocletian's economic reforms. Constantine also followed Diocletian's example by ruling from the eastern half of the Roman Empire. He selected the site of the ancient city of Byzantium (bih ZAN shee um) to build his "New Rome," which became known as Constantinople. However, this move to the east only served to weaken the already struggling western half of the empire.

Diocletian and Constantine had prepared the way for the division of the Roman Empire into two empires. This division became permanent in 395 when Emperor Theodosius I divided the empire between his two sons. The Western Roman Empire fell to barbarian invaders soon after this separation. The Eastern Roman Empire, later called the Byzantine Empire, endured for another thousand years, as we shall see in Chapter 6.

Barbarian Invasions

During the latter years of the Roman Republic, growing numbers of Germanic peoples moved down from northern Europe and settled along Rome's borders. These independent tribes included the Angles, Saxons, Franks, Vandals, and Goths. Roman historians described the Germanic tribes as courageous but restless, given to drinking and gambling yet possessing many simple virtues. The Romans called these people "barbarians," a term used to describe all those outside the empire who did not share in the Greek or Roman cultures.

Rome greatly increased the size of its army in an effort to protect its borders from barbarian intruders. At first Rome had a hard time finding recruits for this frontier army. To solve the problem, some emperors allowed the most "Romanized" of the Germanic tribes to settle within Roman territory to serve as a buffer between Rome and other barbarian tribes. Other emperors allowed barbarians to enlist in the army. Gradually, this foreign element in Rome's army became the primary means of protecting the empire against the more restless tribes outside its borders.

Out of the Far East in the late fourth century came a new threat to Rome's security—the **Huns**. This fierce nomadic tribe, which had

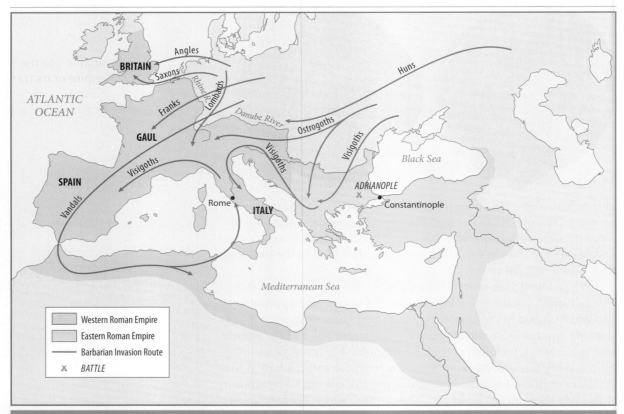

Barbarian Invasions and the Division of the Roman Empire

menaced the Chinese empire for centuries, now moved across Asia into Europe, bringing terror and destruction on all who were in its path. The advance of the dreaded Huns prompted many Germanic tribes to seek refuge in Roman territory.

One such tribe was the **Visigoths**, who crossed the Danube River and settled in the eastern part of the Roman Empire. Following mistreatment by Roman officials, the Visigoths rebelled. In order to put down the revolt, the emperor led the Roman army against the Visigoths. At the Battle of Adrianople in 378, the Visigoths soundly defeated the Roman army and killed the emperor. This was obviously a disaster for Rome: its legions, thought to be invincible, had fallen in defeat before a barbarian people.

The Fall of Rome

In 410, under the leadership of Alaric, the Visigoths moved southwestward into the Italian peninsula and plundered the city of Rome. They eventually settled in what is now Spain. Meanwhile, the Franks moved into northern Gaul, and the Angles and Saxons crossed over into Britain. The Huns, led by their fierce leader **Attila** (r. 433–453; called the "scourge of God" because he was considered to be the instrument of God's wrath on a sinful people), also invaded Roman territory. However, the Romans, with the help of the Germanic peoples, were able to stop the advance of the Huns. Just a few years later, the **Vandals**—a Germanic tribe that established a kingdom in North Africa—raided and pillaged Rome again. To later generations, their name came to mean "a destroyer of property."

With the onslaught of the barbarian invasions, the Western Roman Empire collapsed. Many historians give the date 476 for the

Historical Perspectives

There are a variety of opinions among historians when dealing with the fall of the Roman Empire. Some point to the size of the Roman army or the size of the Roman Empire as a key factor in its collapse. Others insist that the empire did not actually fall, but merely changed or evolved into another form of civilization. What do you think? How would you explain what led to the fall of the Roman Empire or its transition into another form of society? Use the graphic organizer to help formulate your answer.

fall of Rome. In that year, the army ended the long period of Roman rule by placing a non-Roman on the emperor's throne in the west.

Section Review

1–3. List three economic problems troubling Rome in the late days of the empire.

4. Which emperor sought to solve the political problems of the empire by dividing the empire into four administrative divisions called prefectures?

5. Which emperor divided the empire between his two sons, leading to the division of the Roman Empire into two separate empires?

6. What did the Romans call the Germanic peoples who settled along the borders of the empire and threatened the security of the empire?

7. In what year did the Western Roman Empire collapse, when a non-Roman was placed on the imperial throne?

Causes for the Decline and Fall of the Roman Empire

List causes for the decline and fall of the Roman Empire.

V. Roman Culture and Achievement

As Rome expanded into a large empire, it came into contact with a wide variety of people and cultures. Rome borrowed, copied, modified, and preserved many elements of these cultures, blending them with its own values and traditions. Rome, a melting pot of ancient cultures, was able to hold together an empire of diverse peoples.

Greek culture influenced almost every aspect of Roman life. A Roman poet of the first century BC wrote, "Conquered Greece took captive her rude conqueror [Rome] and carried its arts to backward Italy." Rome was actually far from "backward," but the Romans did learn much from the Greeks. The Romans were more practical than the Greeks. While the Greeks built with an eye for beauty, the Romans built with an eye for usefulness. The Greeks made significant contributions in art and philosophy; the Romans, in law and politics.

Contribution to Law

One of Rome's most valuable and enduring achievements was its system of justice. Rome protected the individual rights and property of its citizens. The New Testament records the principle that it was "not the manner of the Romans to deliver any man to die, before that he which is accused have the accusers face to face, and have licence [opportunity] to answer for himself concerning the crime laid against him" (Acts 25:16). The Romans believed that all citizens,

Guiding Questions

1. How did Rome contribute to the concept of law?
2. What Greek achievements were adopted by Rome?
3. What influence did the Roman games have on Roman society?
4. What were the key religious philosophies of Rome?

not just the wealthy and powerful, should have equal rights before the law. Cicero, the famous orator of the republic, wrote: "The legal rights at least of those who are citizens of the same commonwealth ought to be equal. For what is a State except an association or partnership in justice?"

The legal codes of many modern European countries include principles based on Roman law. Even the American system of justice has benefited from Rome's example. Here are some Roman legal principles. Do you notice any similarity between these and America's laws?

- Justice is a constant, unfailing disposition to give everyone his legal due.
- Liberty is a possession on which no evaluation can be placed.
- Freedom is beloved above all things.
- The burden of proof is on the party affirming, not on the party denying.
- In inflicting penalties, the age and inexperience of the guilty party must be taken into account.
- No one [is] to be convicted on suspicion alone . . . [for it is] better for the crime of a guilty person to be left unpunished than for an innocent person to be condemned.
- The credibility of witnesses should be carefully weighed.
- In case of equal [conflicting] claims, the party in possession ought to be considered in the stronger position.
- Every individual is subjected to treatment in accordance with his own action, and no one is made the inheritor of the guilt of another.

Naphtali Lewis and Meyer Reinhold, eds., Roman Civilization: Selected Readings, *2nd ed., vol. 2, 535–50.*

Latin Literature and Language

The Romans modeled their literature after Greek examples but added their own literary ideas and spirit to create a distinct literature of their own. Latin literature expresses the life and history of the Roman people. The greatest Latin literature was produced during the lifetimes of two of Rome's most famous citizens—Cicero and Octavian, who is best remembered by the name Augustus. **Cicero** (106–43 BC) dominated the first half of this literary age. As a leading political figure, author, lawyer, and statesman, he won acclaim as the greatest orator of his day, and he influenced later Roman writers and students of Latin literature.

The peaceful, stable conditions established during Augustus's reign (27 BC–AD 14) fostered another outpouring of literary activity. Optimism, patriotism, and appreciation for traditional Roman values dominated

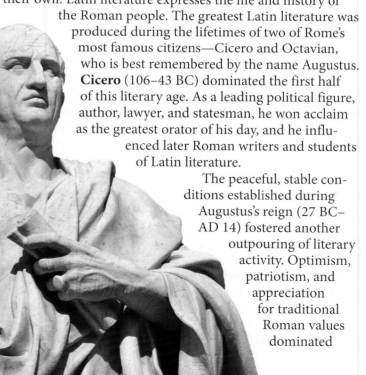

Cicero

this period. Writers of the Augustan Age best expressed these feelings through poetry.

Early Augustan Literature

Often called the "Homer of Rome," Virgil (70–19 BC) is considered the greatest Roman poet. He glorified Rome in his epic poem the *Aeneid* (uh NEE id), one of the most widely read Latin literary works. Virgil modeled the *Aeneid* after Homer's great epic poems, the *Iliad* and the *Odyssey*. But while Homer's works stressed the virtues of the Greek ideal man, Virgil's work exalted Rome as the ideal state.

After the death of Virgil, his close friend Horace (65–8 BC) became the "Poet of the Augustan Age." In a poem written in praise of Augustus, he (like Virgil before him) spoke of the triumph of Rome. Yet Horace did not overlook the seeds of decay in Roman society. He warned of the danger of luxury and ease: "As riches grow, care follows, and a thirst for more and more." Horace praised the simple virtues of morality, justice, courage, and moderation. In his satires (works using ridicule or wit to correct or expose human folly or vice), he described the many follies of contemporary Roman society.

The poetry of Ovid (40 BC–AD 17) is quite different from the poetry of Virgil and Horace. Ovid wrote about mythology and love. His best-known work, *Metamorphoses*, is a collection of over two hundred myths of the ancient world. He skillfully blended these tales to form one continuous story.

The historian **Livy** (59 BC–AD 17), who also lived during the Augustan Age, wrote a lengthy history of Rome. He provided an interesting narrative of the men and events of Roman history from the founding of the city through the end of the republic. Although Livy drew from many unreliable legends, his work offers valuable insight into early Roman customs and history. He saw the traditional virtues and patriotism of the Roman people as the foundation of Rome's greatness.

Later Roman Writers

The mood of Roman writers changed after the death of Augustus. Latin writers of the first century AD were more critical and pessimistic than their predecessors. The poet Juvenal wrote bitter satires on the loose morals and social problems of the empire.

Juvenal longed for a return to the days of the republic. He was not alone. The famed historian **Tacitus** favored the old republic over life under the self-centered emperors. His work *Annals* is a valuable but pessimistic history of Rome from the death of Augustus to the reign of the emperor Nero. In *Germania*, Tacitus gives us a rare glimpse of the lifestyle of the Germanic peoples, who later conquered the Western Roman Empire. He contrasts the simple virtues and customs of the "barbarians" with the corrupt morals of Rome's upper class.

The importance of Latin did not diminish after the collapse of the Roman Empire. Latin continued as the dominant language of medieval learning, government, and religion. From Latin many of the native (or common) languages of Europe arose. Latin was the "parent" of the Romance languages—Italian, French, Spanish, Portuguese, and Romanian. Although English is not a Romance language, thousands of English words are of Latin origin.

Juvenal

And when could you find more vices abounding?
When did the gullet of greed open wider?
When did the dice draw more to the tables?
They don't bring their wallets along,
They bring a whole safety deposit box.

Juvenal, Satires, trans. L. R. Lind, 1.93–96.

Greek Contributions

During the *Pax Romana*, centers of Greek learning, such as Alexandria in Egypt, flourished. Plutarch (AD 45–125) was probably the most famous Greek writer in the Roman Empire. He wrote biographies that compared the lives of important Greek and Roman men. His *Parallel Lives of Illustrious Greeks and Romans* is not only an excellent literary work but also the source of valuable historical information. Advances in medicine continued under the work of the Greek physician Galen. Experimenting with animals, Galen studied the lungs, heart, arteries, and blood. His encyclopedia, a collection of the medical ideas of the ancient world, became the accepted medical authority of the Middle Ages. The Alexandrian astronomer and mathematician **Ptolemy** (ca. AD 85–ca. 165) promoted the theory that the earth was the center of the universe. He taught that the sun, moon, and planets revolved around the earth. Though based on false assumptions, his **geocentric** (earth-centered) **theory** of the universe went unchallenged for almost fourteen centuries.

Art and Architecture

As Roman generals returned from their conquests, they brought captured art and artists back to Rome. Greek art became so popular among the Romans that they commissioned artists to make copies of Greek statues. But not all Roman art was imitative. The Romans excelled in portrait busts (head and shoulder statues). These popular statues portrayed Roman heroes, honored statesmen, and valiant soldiers. Unlike Greek sculpture, most Roman statues are realistic, not idealized. Some even show warts, scars, and wrinkles. The Romans also excelled in relief sculpture (sculpture in which figures project out from a flat background). Realistic reliefs adorned gigantic monuments—triumphal arches and columns—that the Roman emperors built to commemorate their conquests. The reliefs on these monuments gave a visual story of Rome's military exploits.

Even in ruins, these monuments attest to Roman engineering skill. The Romans used new building techniques as well as techniques borrowed from other cultures. Arches and vaults strengthened with concrete enabled Roman engineers to create large indoor spaces enclosed by massive domes. The Romans built **aqueducts** to supply water to many of their cities. Some aqueducts carried over fifty million gallons daily. They also built bridges and an extensive network of roads. Public baths and large amphitheaters provided relaxation and entertainment for many Romans throughout the empire. Unlike Greek buildings, which are known for their simple beauty, Roman buildings are distinguished by their large size, durability, and practicality.

The dome of the Pantheon in Rome, rebuilt by the Emperor Hadrian ca. AD 125

The Roman Games

The Romans flocked to arenas throughout the empire to see their favorite events—chariot races, gladiator contests, and wild beast fights. At the Circus Maximus in Rome, over a quarter of a million people gathered regularly to watch the chariot races. At the Roman Colosseum they delighted in the brutal struggles of the gladiators and wild beasts. The victors in these life-and-death contests became instant public heroes. In many of these arenas, Christians died for their faith as they were slain by the gladiator's sword, thrown to the beasts, or burned at the stake. These bloody "amuse-

Colosseum

ments" were staged by the Roman emperors to win the public's favor and keep the unemployed masses out of mischief.

Religious Beliefs

Roman religious beliefs gradually changed. In the early days of the republic, the Romans worshipped gods of nature. Many of the planets in our solar system bear the names of these Roman gods: Mercury, Venus, Mars, Jupiter, Saturn, and Neptune. As the Romans came into contact with the Greeks, they associated their gods with the mythical gods of Mount Olympus. But like the Greeks, many Romans grew dissatisfied with the old gods and turned to philosophy to find happiness and meaning in life. The Romans had little concern for the abstract ideas of Greek philosophy; but in two Greek philosophies—Epicureanism and Stoicism—they discovered practical guidelines for living.

Epicureanism

The **Epicurean** philosophy may be summed up by the following statements:

> There is nothing to fear in God.
> There is nothing to be alarmed about in death.
> Good is easily obtained.
> Evil is easily endured.

The founder of this philosophy, Epicurus, taught that true happiness comes only as man frees his mind from fear and his body from pain. Epicurus believed happiness rested in the virtues of simple pleasure and peace of mind. He rejected the ideas of an afterlife and divine judgment. For him, happiness was to be found only in this life.

The poet Lucretius (99–55 BC) was probably the greatest expounder of Epicureanism in the Roman world. In his philosophical

---

Seneca's Account of the Roman Games

I chanced to stop in a midday show [of gladiators], expecting fun, wit, and some relaxation, when men's eyes take respite from the slaughter of their fellow men. It was just the reverse. The preceding combats were merciful by comparison; now all the trifling is put aside and it is pure murder. . . . In the morning men are thrown to the lions and the bears, at noon they are thrown to their spectators. "Kill him! Lash him! Burn him! Why does he meet the sword so timidly? Why doesn't he kill boldly? Why doesn't he die game? Whip him to meet his wounds!" And when the show stops for intermission, "Let's have men killed meanwhile! Let's not have nothing going on!"

Lucius Annaeus Seneca, Moral Epistles, *Vol. 1, 31 and 33.*

poem *On the Nature of Things*, Lucretius preserved the teachings of Epicurus. He hoped to reform the declining moral standards of the republic. However, many Romans interpreted the Epicurean teaching "seek happiness as the only good" as meaning they could do anything that would bring them pleasure. What was intended to restore Rome's traditional values became the excuse for the worst excesses of behavior.

Stoicism

The Stoic philosophy had a stronger and more lasting impact on Roman society than Epicureanism. One of the leading Stoics of the Roman Empire was **Seneca** (3 BC–65 AD), the tutor of the emperor Nero and an outstanding writer and thinker. Seneca saw **Stoicism** as the solution to Rome's moral decline.

Stoicism teaches that the highest good is the pursuit of the virtues of courage, dignity, duty, simplicity of life, and service to fellow men. Stoics believed in the brotherhood of man and the moral responsibility of each individual to his society. By proper living, man could bring himself into harmony with the divine law that governs the universe and directs his fate.

Eastern Influence

With the large number of peoples and lands conquered by the Roman Empire came a great variety of religious beliefs and ideas. From the East came the "mystery religions" that won popular acceptance among the Romans. These religions, based on polytheism and mythology, promised immortality to those who performed secret and mysterious ceremonies. Rome tolerated these foreign religious beliefs as long as the people acknowledged that the Roman emperor was a god too.

Also from the East came the practice of emperor-worship. The Roman emperor held the title *pontifex maximus* ("greatest priest"). In this office, he interpreted the will of the gods in the affairs of state. People expressed their loyalty and patriotism to the state by worshiping the emperor.

Section Review

1. What culture greatly influenced Roman culture?

2. Who was called the "Homer of Rome"?

3–4. What was the name of the man who taught that the earth was the center of the universe? What was his theory called?

5–6. Who was a leading Stoic philosopher of the Roman Empire and also tutor to an emperor? Which emperor was his pupil?

＊ Why did Epicurean philosophy fail to raise the declining moral standards of the Roman Empire?

＊ Why did Christians in the Roman Empire take issue with emperor worship? How did the Roman government respond?

Making Connections

1–3. Identify the key players in each of Rome's civil wars, the victor, and the condition of the republic at the end of each.

4–6. Outline three steps by which the plebeians gained a voice in the Roman government.

7–9. How did Octavian seek to improve Roman government and society? List three specific ways.

10–11. Summarize two reasons why the Roman government persecuted Christians.

Developing History Skills

1. What parallels do you see between the conditions contributing to the fall of the Roman Republic and the present conditions in the United States?

2. Based on Acts 16:37–38, 19:38–41, and 25:7–12, what were the rights of a Roman citizen? How do these compare with the rights of an American citizen?

Thinking Critically

1. What made the Roman Republic strong? What made it weak?

2. How did God use the Jews, Greeks, and Romans to prepare the world for the coming of His Son?

Living in God's World

1. Western civilizations in the modern era have often modeled their governments on the Roman Republic. From a Christian perspective, is it wise to imitate a pagan government that had no knowledge of Christ or the gospel?

2. Should civic-minded Christians emphasize virtues and character to hold their own societies together? Explain.

3. Defend the claim that the life, death, and resurrection of Jesus constitute the turning point of human history.

People, Places, and Things to Know

League of the Seven Hills
Romulus
Remus
patricians
plebeians
republic
Senate
Assembly of Centuries
tribune
Roman Forum
Law of the Twelve Tables
Tribal Assembly
Punic Wars
Hannibal
Scipio
Julius Caesar
31 BC
princeps
imperator
Augustus
Pax Romana
Jesus of Nazareth
Pontius Pilate
Tiberius
gospel
Paul
Nero
Diocletian
Edict of Milan
Constantine
Arius
Council of Nicaea
patriarchs
Huns
Visigoths
Attila
Vandals
Cicero
Livy
Tacitus
Ptolemy
geocentric theory
aqueducts
Epicurean
Seneca
Stoicism

The Civilizations in Africa and the East

5

I. Africa

II. India

III. China

Family of elephants in Tarangire National Park, Tanzania

Big Ideas

1. How did civilizations in Africa, India, and China develop during this period?

2. What were key cultural features of ancient Africa?

3. What were the political and cultural features of the Mauryan and Gupta Empires?

4. What were the political and cultural developments of China in this period?

The historical books of the Bible center on the nations of Israel, Egypt, Babylon, Persia, Greece, and Rome. However, at the same time that these civilizations flourished, other equally splendid civilizations developed in Africa, India, and China. In the centuries following the ministry of the apostles, the gospel also spread to these parts of the world. There is little evidence that Christianity thrived initially in these regions. Recently, however, Christianity has begun to grow in Africa and Asia more quickly than in many other regions of the globe. Therefore, understanding the history of these cultures is important for Christians.

I. Africa

The second largest continent, Africa covers over one-fifth of the earth's land surface. It is nearly four times the size of the continental United States. Although much of the continent is a large plateau, its mountains, deserts, grassy flatlands, and jungles give Africa a unique beauty.

We have studied some of Africa's history in earlier chapters. The Egyptians established on the banks of the Nile the earliest recorded civilization in Africa. Carthage built a thriving civilization in North Africa in the days of the Roman Republic, and the Romans later made the area part of their empire.

As important as these events are, they involve only a portion of that great continent. The history of the rest of Africa, known as **sub-Saharan Africa** (so named because it is south of the Sahara), is not as well known but is nonetheless important.

African Migration

While secular historians assume that mankind and his predecessors inhabited Africa for many thousands of years, the first trace of people in Africa may be found in what anthropologists refer to as the **Bantu migration**. The people who took part in this migration are known by little more than a family of languages that became known as the Bantu languages. Given the speculative nature of this information, it should not be surprising that scholars vary on how many African languages fit under the Bantu heading and that lists vary from 300 to 600 languages. Theories about the origin of this migration suggest dates as far back as 3000 BC. If this time frame is correct, it would roughly correspond with the dispersion of the people at the Tower of Babel and might tie the migration of people to Africa to the biblical account in Genesis 11. However, if this migration was more recent, then it would have affected people living in central and southern Africa at that time. Possible changes could have included intermarriage, conquest where the immigrants found resistance, and pressure on original residents to move to unpopulated regions.

Ancient African Civilizations
Eastern Africa

Centuries before Europeans penetrated sub-Saharan Africa, several African civilizations flourished. In ancient times, two important kingdoms arose in northeast Africa, south of the Egyptian civilization. The earliest was the kingdom of Kush in what is today northern Sudan. (Ruins of its capital, Meroë, still exist near the modern city of Khartoum.)

Guiding Questions

1. How did the Bantu migration influence sub-Saharan Africa?
2. What were key cultural and geographic features of the Kushite civilization?
3. What led to the rise and fall of the kingdom of Aksum?
4. What were key features of Western African culture?
5. Where did Christianity appear in Africa?

Kush and Aksum

Pyramids of the northern cemetery of Meroë, Nubia

Kush

For nearly two thousand years **Kush** served as a province of Egypt. The Egyptians valued the gold, granite, slaves, and other resources that were abundant in Kush and passed through this region in trade. To maintain and protect this commerce, the Egyptians constructed and occupied several forts along the Nile River, which served as the focal point that united Egypt and parts of eastern Africa.

Over time, Egypt's power declined and it could no longer dominate this region. By 1000 BC Kush had won its independence from a weakened Egypt and began to seize territory previously controlled by the pharaohs. Kush continued to grow in power until 700 BC, when it had not only overthrown Egyptian rule but also conquered all of Egypt and established its own dynasty of pharaohs. (The Tirhakah of Ethiopia mentioned in 2 Kings 19:9 is one such Kushite ruler, Taharqa.) Kushite control of Egypt was brief. The invading Assyrians drove the Kushites out of Egypt in the mid-600s BC. Yet the Kushite kingdom continued for nearly another thousand years.

Aksum

Kush eventually fell to a kingdom to its south and east known as **Aksum** (or "Axum"). The ruler of Aksum recorded the shattering defeat he inflicted on the Kushites around AD 330:

> I made war on them. . . . They fled without making a stand, and I pursued them . . . killing some and capturing others. . . . I burnt their towns, both those built of bricks and those built of reeds, and my army carried off their food and copper and iron . . . and destroyed the statues in their temples, their granaries, and cotton trees and cast them into the [Nile].
>
> Robert W. July, A History of the African People, 38.

Aksum was unusual among the early African kingdoms in that it embraced a form of Christianity. Later tradition claimed that the rulers of Aksum were descendants of King Solomon and the Queen of Sheba. However, the kingdom's conversion to Christianity was believed to be the work of a Syrian Christian named **Frumentius**. Aksum's conversion intensified its already extensive trade with the Roman Empire. Later Muslim invasions in North Africa cut off Aksum from almost all European contact. The civilization nonetheless continued to exist and became the nucleus of the modern state of Ethiopia.

Frumentius, "Apostle to the Abyssinians"

The conversion of Aksum (sometimes known as "Abyssinia") is believed to be the result of the ministry of an unlikely missionary named Frumentius. We have little information about his early years. We know that he was a professing Christian and a Roman citizen, probably from Tyre, who was born around AD 300. While still a young man, he and his brother were traveling abroad with a relative. Pirates attacked their ship, massacring most of the crew and passengers. The pirates spared the brothers, however, and sold them into slavery in Aksum. Frumentius and his brother, like Joseph in Egypt, rose to high positions in government because of their abilities. As treasurer and secretary to the king of Aksum, Frumentius earned the trust of high officials in government. When the king died, the queen asked Frumentius to help administer the government until the young prince was old enough to rule on his own.

While serving the kingdom, Frumentius also promoted his Christian faith. He encouraged Christian merchants from the Roman Empire to hold private services during their visits to Aksum. Under Frumentius's preaching and guidance, the citizens of Aksum also began to convert to Christianity. The young prince whom Frumentius served was probably Ezana, the king who won the great victory over Kush in 330. Ezana seems to have accepted Christianity later in life. Historians note that he did not credit his victory over Kush to pagan gods, as he had done with victories earlier in his reign, but "by the might of the Lord of Heaven Who in heaven and upon earth is mightier than everything which exists." He also praised the "Lord of Heaven, Who . . . to all eternity reigns the Perfect One." Ezana's conversion was perhaps the crowning work of Frumentius, a man since remembered as the "Apostle to the Abyssinians."

Achievements—Aksum demonstrated significant accomplishments in the advance of their culture. For example, Aksum possessed the only known written language in this period of African history. The kingdom also minted coins from bronze, silver, and gold to serve as currency. Agricultural advances included terrace farming that compensated for the lack of flat farm land. This technique transformed hilly regions into productive soil capable of growing abundant crops. To supply a steady source of water, Aksum also constructed canals and reservoirs to channel and collect water.

Perhaps the most enduring achievement was the development of commemorative stone pillars or steles (STEE leez). The Aksum stele was constructed from stone cut miles from the eventual site, and carved with images including false doors, wooden beams, and windows.

(top left) *Aksum coin, obverse with gold central cross*

(middle left) *gold coin of Ezana (ca. AD 340)*

(right) *King Ezana stele in the Northern Stelea Park in Aksum, North Ethiopia; erected in the fourth century AD; stands 24.6 meters high and weighs approximately 150 tons*

Nok

Nok head, Nigeria

Rather than bond the stones with mortar, craftsmen designed the stones to fit tightly together once assembled. The tallest of these structures was probably about 100 feet tall, and the tallest surviving stele is 60 feet tall.

Decline—Muslim invasions of Eastern Africa beginning in the seventh century weakened Aksum. While Aksum resisted invading forces, lands surrounding this kingdom fell to Muslim assaults. As a result, Aksum's trade was hindered and its power declined. The rulers of Aksum responded by moving the capital to a more secure mountain location. By the middle of the tenth century, this kingdom fell to foreign invasion.

Western Africa

The earliest evidence for civilization in West Africa appears to be the **Nok** culture, located in modern Nigeria. These people were named after a village where archaeologists discovered the first artifacts of this culture. They used stone tools, engaged in farming of typical African crops, including pearl millet and cowpeas, and made terracotta statues. The Nok culture smelted iron and formed tools and weapons.

Given the limited amount of evidence available, estimates on the formation of this culture vary from 1000 BC to 500 BC, and its demise is dated from AD 200 to 300. Artifacts of their culture have been found as far as three hundred miles away, thus indicating significant trade in this part of Africa.

Perhap the oldest city in West Africa, **Djenné-Djeno** (jeh NAY jeh NOH) was located on a tributary of the Niger River in West Africa. Artifacts include pottery, copper ornaments, glass beads, stone bracelets, and iron tools. At its zenith this city may have supported a population of fifty thousand people. Dates for this city vary, but occupation may have begun around 250 BC and continued until as late as AD 1400 (some sources say 900).

Archaeologists believe the inhabitants of this city initially built reed houses plastered with mud. Later, the people constructed homes with mud brick. The location near a river made fishing and growing rice natural sources of food. Trade appears to have been extensive and would have included exchanging rice, cattle, and fish for copper, gold, and salt that was abundant in other regions. Evidence of iron production and terracotta statues was also discovered in this city.

African Culture
Daily Life

Daily life for most Africans centered less on kingdoms and empires than on smaller social organizations. Many Africans concerned themselves with little more than life as it existed in their villages. The family was foundational. Since **polygamy** (marrying more than one spouse) was common in many tribes, families were large and complex. Several families with a common ancestor formed a clan. A group of two or more clans, in turn, formed a tribe. The tribe was perhaps the most important cultural organization, and an African kingdom was typically dominated by a single tribe.

Religious beliefs in Africa were diverse. Some regions, such as Aksum, embraced a form of Christianity. Islam later claimed a large number of converts, but Islamic visitors from the Middle East often complained that Africans combined folk religion with Islam. Muslim patterns often influenced African kingdoms in structuring their governments, organizing their systems of education, and establishing their currency.

The majority of the people in sub-Saharan Africa held to traditional tribal religions. In general, these traditional religions taught that there was a high god who created the universe and below him were a number of lesser gods and the spirits of dead ancestors. Prayers and sacrifices were offered to these gods to ward off illnesses and increase crop yields.

Agriculture

Most Africans relied on farming or herding to sustain themselves and their families. Improved methods of farming resulted in an abundance of food. Trade resulted as regions with surplus food interacted with cultures rich in other natural resources. In addition to food grains (including flaxseed and millet), gold, salt, ivory, iron, and animal skins became valued products for trade.

Ironworking

Processing of iron ore and other metals predated the Flood (Gen. 4:22), and this knowledge may have been passed down through Noah's sons to succeeding generations. Evidence of the refining of iron ore in Africa may be traced back to approximately 1000 BC. African workers heated the ore in a charcoal-fueled stone furnace and used a type of bellows to add air that raised the operating temperature of the furnace to about 2,000 degrees. Craftsmen fashioned the smelted iron into tools and weapons. Iron bars even served as a form of currency, much like gold.

Artist's concept of African iron weapons

Section Review

1–3. Name three religions found in sub-Saharan Africa.

4. What ancient African civilization conquered the Egyptians for a time?

5. What ancient African civilization converted to Christianity?

6. What is the name of perhaps the oldest city in West Africa?

7–9. Name three items that were important goods in African trade.

★ What aspects of civilization were evident in ancient Africa?

II. India

In Chapter 2 we examined the early culture and features of Indian society. We also looked at the influence of Hinduism and Buddhism on Indian culture. In this chapter we will study the political, cultural, and religious elements of India between 500 BC and AD 500.

Lack of Political Unity

While many aspects of Indian society have remained the same for centuries, the political history of India has been one of frequent change. Through much of its history, India has been little more than a patchwork of small rival kingdoms. Successive waves of foreign invaders streamed into the Indian subcontinent. The powerful

Guiding Questions

1. What led to the rise and fall of the Mauryan and Gupta Empires?
2. How did Hinduism and Buddhism in India change during this period?
3. How did Christianity influence India?

empires established by these invaders provided brief periods of unity and stability for the Indian peoples.

Mauryan Empire

In 326 BC Alexander the Great threatened India. His armies crossed the Indus River and conquered many small kingdoms in India's northwestern region. Alexander intended to advance farther into India, but when his army refused to continue, he had to turn back. According to traditional accounts, he met a young man named **Chandragupta Maurya** (CHUN-druh-GOOP-tuh MAH-oor-yuh) while in India. As Alexander's empire began to disintegrate after his death, Chandragupta conquered the disorganized and weak kingdoms in the north and created the first strong empire of India—the Mauryan Empire.

The most famous of the Mauryan rulers was Chandragupta's grandson **Asoka**. He extended the Mauryan Empire to include all but the southern tip of India. Sickened by the results of his own bloody conquests, Asoka renounced war and converted to Buddhism. He spent much of his reign promoting the Buddhist religion. Asoka is credited with building thousands of Buddhist shrines called stupas (STOO puz). He also had Buddhist teachings inscribed on stone pillars throughout the empire. Many of these stone pillars still stand, providing valuable information concerning Asoka's reign. One of his most far-reaching acts was the sending of Buddhist missionaries abroad. Buddhism soon spread across much of Southeast Asia, where it became a powerful force in other Asian cultures. It did not gain a wide following in India, however. Hindu priests viewed Buddhist teaching as dangerous to the caste system. Fearing

Justice, Power, and Citizenship

Asoka's injustices early in his reign led him to reconsider his ways and rule with more concern for his subjects later in his reign. But because Asoka did not give his subjects the rights of citizenship or limit the power of rulers, his reforms did not continue beyond his lifetime.

Mauryan Empire (250 BC)

that they might lose their prestige and rank in society, they worked against the acceptance of Buddhist beliefs.

Gupta Empire

The first great period of Indian unity was short-lived. Not long after Asoka's death (232 BC), the Mauryan Empire collapsed. The years between the second century BC and the third century AD witnessed multiple invasions and the rise of small competing kingdoms. During this time of turmoil, India did enjoy a profitable trade with Rome and China. Even so, it was not until the fourth century AD, with the rise of the **Gupta** (GOOP tuh) **Empire**, that India entered a new, and perhaps its greatest, era of prosperity and achievement.

One historian has stated that "at the time India was perhaps the happiest and most civilized region of the world." The rulers of the Gupta dynasty reunited northern India under a strong and effective government. Trade routes connected India with Southeast Asia and China to the east, and Persia, the Middle East, and Aksum to the west. The Silk Road also developed during this period and enabled merchants to carry on trade from China to Rome.

India's culture spread throughout Southeast Asia. India's universities attracted students from all over the continent, and its people made great strides in the fields of textiles and ironwork. The Gupta Age was also one of the finest periods of Indian art, architecture, literature, and science.

Gupta literature became renowned for its adventurous and imaginative fables and fairy tales. The foremost Indian poet and dramatist of this period was **Kalidasa** (kah lih DAH suh), whose

Gupta Empire (AD 400)

plays have earned him the title "the Indian Shakespeare." The popularity of various Indian stories soon spread outside India, where many of them found their way into the literature of other lands. (Western authors such as the brothers Grimm and Rudyard Kipling drew upon Indian stories for ideas for their writing.)

This was also an age of advance in mathematics, science, and medicine. Our so-called Arabic numerals originally came from India. Indian mathematicians were among the first to use negative numbers, the decimal, and the zero. Centuries before Isaac Newton, Indian scientists developed their own theories of gravity. Indian astronomers knew that the earth was round and that it rotated on its axis. If in need of medical attention, the people of the Gupta Empire went to free hospitals where Indian physicians performed many surgical procedures.

During the sixth century the Gupta Empire collapsed under the repeated attacks of the so-called White Huns (perhaps related to the Huns who plagued the Roman Empire during the fifth century). India again entered a period of political disorder; the country became divided into small warring kingdoms. Waves of foreign invaders again entered the land; but as in the past, Hinduism absorbed the culture of these foreign elements into Indian society. The history of India took a dramatic turn when northern India fell under the domination of Muslims, who brought with them an ideology as all-encompassing as Hinduism.

Decline in Buddhism and Changes in Hinduism

During the Mauryan dynasty, Buddhism split into two philosophical schools. The Theravada Buddhists continued to hold to the original teachings of Buddha and emphasized his humanity. Mahayana Buddhists transformed Buddha into a supernatural being. They also gained support among the common people by teaching that anyone could become enlightened. Buddhism grew under Asoka and enjoyed royal support. During the Gupta Empire, Buddhism lost royal support but was sustained by the merchant class. During this period, worship of images of the Buddha became common.

Pandu Leni caves in Nashik, Maharashtra, India; ca. 3rd century BC

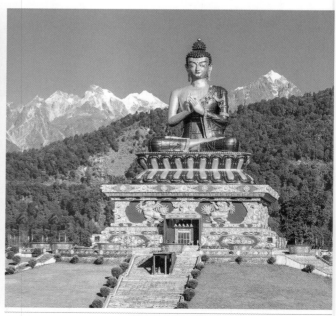

Gautama Buddha statue in South Sikkim, India

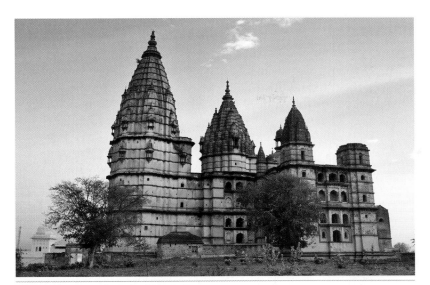

Chaturbhuj Temple in Orchha, India

Despite commercial support, Buddhism declined during the Gupta Empire as the rulers tended to support Hinduism. In addition, Hinduism experienced a revival during this period by reinventing its teachings. Hindu priests adopted some Buddhist ideas that made Hinduism more attractive to the Indian people and eroded popular support for Buddhism. Hinduism de-emphasized the thousands of Hindu gods and offered a simplified version that centered on Brahma (creator of the world), Vishnu (preserver of the world), and Shiva (destroyer of the world). The reformation of Hinduism into a more personal religion resulted in great popular appeal in India. As a result, Buddhism ceased to be a significant religious force in India.

Spread of the Gospel to India

According to tradition, the apostle Thomas brought the gospel to India. Whether this tradition is accurate or not, travel between the Roman Empire and India was common in the first century. It is likely that early in the church's history Christians did bring the gospel to India. The church historian Eusebius recorded that a man named Pantaenus traveled as a missionary to India. When he arrived he found Christians there already, and they had copies of the Gospel of Matthew. By the fourth century, Christians in Persia had made contact with the Christians in India. The Indians sent their leaders to schools in Persia for training until the Muslims conquered Persia. The scattered communities of Indian Christians were never very large, but they were still in existence when the Portuguese landed in India in the fifteenth century to open trade between India and Europe.

Section Review

1–2. Identify the two empires that temporarily brought national unity to India.

3. What famous Indian poet earned the title of "the Indian Shakespeare"?

4. Who is traditionally believed to have brought Christianity to India?

★ Why did the Hindu priests in India resist Buddhism?

★ What was notable about the culture of the Gupta Empire?

Guiding Questions

1. How did the Qin dynasty influence China?
2. What were significant features of the Han dynasty?
3. What were key cultural achievements of China during this period?

III. China

Qin Dynasty

In chapter 2, we saw that China fell into disorder and anarchy between the fifth and third centuries BC. Order was restored by Zheng, who took the name Qin Shi Huang (r. 247–210 BC). Zheng

Qin Shi Huang

became the founder of the short-lived but memorable Qin (sometimes spelled Chin) dynasty—the dynasty from which China may have derived its name. **Qin Shi Huang** (CHIN SHEE HWAHNG), which means "First Emperor of the Qin," was the first to unite the provinces of China under one strong centralized government. He standardized the Chinese weight, measurement, and coinage systems and brought

The Tomb and Terracotta Army of Qin Shi Huang

Qin Shi Huang, the first emperor of China, died in 210 BC. His body was entombed in an elaborate mausoleum that had taken workers his entire reign to construct. (Thirty-six years before his death, he drafted nearly a million Chinese laborers for the project.) According to contemporary Chinese historians, the tomb contained a model of his palaces and various government buildings. It also housed a replica of his empire complete with rivers and seas of mercury, which actually flowed by mechanical means.

To protect his grave, the Chinese installed crossbows that would release automatically if an intruder entered the tomb. According to the custom of the day, Shi Huang's son ordered his father's concubines who had not borne him sons to be buried with the emperor. He also ordered that those who had worked on the safety devices in the tomb be buried too. Once the emperor was interred, the Chinese covered the mausoleum with earth and planted trees over

it to give the appearance of a hill. Today it is called Mount Li. It stands fifteen stories high in the midst of a plain.

In 1974 a group of Chinese farmers, while digging a well in the Mount Li area, unearthed a subterranean passageway. Inside were huge terracotta statues (made of hard, waterproof ceramic clay) of ancient Chinese soldiers. In the years since the discovery, Chinese archaeologists have uncovered about six thousand soldiers—life-size replicas of the men in Qin Shi Huang's army. No two statues are alike. Some are old with wrinkles, and others are young and fair. Some are smiling, and some are serious. In addition to the soldiers, archaeologists found clay horses and chariots. Because the ceiling of the tomb had collapsed and crushed many of the terracotta statues, the task of excavating was a difficult one. When the work of the excavators was completed, the Chinese created a museum on the site.

Chinese Characters

When God scattered Noah's descendants throughout the world (Gen. 11:1–9), they carried with them a knowledge of man's earliest history. They knew of Creation, the Fall, and the Flood. Those who migrated to China seem to have preserved some of these truths in their writing system. Since most Chinese characters tell a story, we can break down the more complex characters into simpler ones and discover the meaning of each part.

to forbid

wood/tree

God

For example, the Chinese character for "to forbid" tells the story of God's command to Adam in Genesis 2:16–17. God planted two special trees in the Garden of Eden: the tree of life and the tree of knowledge of good and evil. God commanded Adam not to eat of the tree of the knowledge of good and evil but gave him permission to eat fruit from any other tree in the garden. It is interesting to note, therefore, that the character "to forbid" is made up of the symbol for "wood" or "tree" (notice that two are indicated) and

sacrifice

ox/cattle

sheep

beautiful

spear

righteous

one of the basic Chinese symbols for God. (This character for God also had the idea of "to command" or "to express.")

The scriptural idea of sacrifice (the killing of a spotless animal) is also found in Chinese writing. The word "to sacrifice" is made up of four major parts: "ox" or "cattle," "sheep," "beautiful" or "unblemished," and "spear" (the weapon by which the animal was killed).

Closely associated with the idea of sacrifice is the concept of righteousness. The character that means "righteous" or "righteousness" is made up of the symbol for "lamb" and the symbol for "me." Notice

lamb

me

that when the two characters are combined to create the word *righteous*(ness), the lamb is placed over the person. In the same manner, Christ, who is the perfect Lamb of God, covers our sins with His blood.

boat

small vessel

eight

person

Another interesting study is the character for "boat" or "ship." It is made up of the symbol for "small vessel," the symbol for the number eight, and the symbol that means "person," "population," or "mouth." The largest boat built in antiquity (as far as we know) was the ark. It saved Noah and his family—a total of eight persons.

The written Chinese language indicates that at some time in the past the Chinese knew God's truth. Although most Chinese people today do not have access to the Scriptures, the written language preserves not only the truth of man's sin but also the wonderful fact of God's saving grace.

---

uniformity to China's writing system. Perhaps the most remarkable achievement of the Qin dynasty was the beginning of construction of the Great Wall. The wall was twenty-five to thirty feet high and fifteen feet wide. A road ran along its top, providing for rapid movement of troops and swift communication. A consolidation of existing structures, the Great Wall eventually covered over 1,400 miles of often-rugged terrain. The wall served as a defensive barrier against the invasions of the barbaric Huns (whose descendants later invaded the Roman Empire). Although Qin Shi Huang brought order and protection to China, he did so through harsh and ruthless measures. Soon after his death, the people revolted, ending the Qin dynasty.

Han Dynasty

The next dynasty to rule China was the Han dynasty, established in 202 BC by rebel leader Liu Bang. The Chinese later called him Emperor Gaozu of Han. This dynasty became so popular that to this day some Chinese call themselves the "sons of Han." The

Description of a Chinese Civil Service Examination

"The candidates had to get up in the middle of the night and come to the palace at dawn, bringing their cold meals with them, for they would not be able to leave until the examinations were over. During the examinations they were shut up in cubicles under the supervision of palace guards. There was a rigorous system to prevent bribery or favoritism. . . . While the candidates were let out after the examinations, the judges themselves were shut up within the palace, usually from late January [until] early March, until the papers were properly graded and submitted to the emperor. The candidates were examined first on questions of history or principles of government. There was a second examination on the classics, and finally, after the successful ones had been graded, there was one—under the direct supervision of the emperor—on lyrics, descriptive poetry, and again essays on politics."

Lin Yu-t'ang, The Gay Genius, 38.

most famous Han ruler was **Wu Ti** (r. 140–87 BC). He drove back the Huns and extended China's territory. To meet the growing need for well-trained government officials, the Han rulers introduced a civil service system in which competitive public examinations determined appointments to government posts. The Han established the **Pax Sinica** ("Chinese Peace") throughout China and much of central Asia. During this period trade routes were opened with the West. Over the "Silk Road"—named for China's chief export—traders brought China into direct contact with the Greek and Roman civilizations. The Han period also marked the entrance of Buddhism into China. It soon became one of China's leading religions.

Han Dynasty (202 BC–AD 220)

Political Decline

In AD 220, revolts overthrew the last of the Han rulers. For the next four centuries China suffered from internal wars and barbarian invasions. During this period attempts to establish a lasting central government were unsuccessful. Chinese history records political efforts to centralize power under headings including the "Period of the Three Kingdoms" (220–280) and "Northern Wei" (386–534) or "Period of Division" (316–588).

Contributions

Despite periods of political decline, the Chinese made several important technological contributions to human history. For example, the Chinese developed a method called block printing in which they carved raised characters on a block of wood. By inking the block and pressing it on paper, the Chinese were able to print multiple copies. However, the printing of different pages involved the slow process of carving another block of wood. To speed up this process, the Chinese invented movable type—that is, they carved smaller separate blocks for each Chinese character. The blocks could then be rearranged and reused. However, because there were thousands of characters, movable type was not widely used in China, nor was it practical.

The Importance of the Chinese Family

"The family had functions which in the modern West are commonly assumed by the state. It educated its youth, cared for its unemployed, disciplined its erring members, and supported its aged. In turn, the state held the family accountable for the misdeeds of its members. . . . The individual was of far less importance than the family. The individual member was to make his earnings available to his less fortunate relatives. . . . Marriage was primarily not for the happiness of those who entered into that relationship, but for the purpose of continuing the family line. No sin was greater than that of dying without leaving male issue to revere the memory of one's ancestors."

Kenneth Scott Latourette, A Short History of the Far East, *158.*

The Sayings of Confucius

We studied Confucius in chapter 2. His teachings influenced China and other regions of Asia for centuries after his death. The philosophy of Confucius is contained in a collection of his sayings and activities called the *Analects*. Some of what Confucius said is remarkably sound advice. This demonstrates how the image of God in fallen man still enables him to discern a certain amount of wisdom in how to live. However, those who try to live wisely apart from God cannot achieve this goal to the degree that God intended.

- It does not greatly concern me . . . that men do not know me; my great concern is my not knowing them.
- To go beyond is as wrong as to fall short.
- It is moral cowardice to leave undone what one perceives to be right to do.
- Learn as if never overtaking your object, and yet as if apprehensive of losing it.

- Impatience over little things introduces confusion into great schemes.
- They who care not for the morrow will the sooner have their sorrows.

- The nobler-minded man . . . will be agreeable even when he disagrees; the small-minded man will agree and be disagreeable.
- The cautious seldom err.
- Faults in a superior man are like eclipses of the sun and moon: when he is guilty of a trespass, men all see it; and when he is himself again, all look up to him.
- When you meet with men of worth, think how you may attain to their level; when you see others of an opposite character, look within and examine yourself.
- Learning without thought is a snare; thought without learning is a danger.
- With a meal of coarse rice . . . and water to drink, and my bent arm for a pillow—even thus I find happiness. Riches and honors without righteousness are to me as fleeting clouds.
- Where there is habitual going after gain, there is much ill-will.

Many other products associated with the Western world originated in China. Can you imagine a classroom without paper or an ink pen? The Chinese were the first to develop paper (as we know it) and one of the first peoples to use ink. Think of what navigation would be like without the Chinese invention of the magnetic compass. Another important Chinese discovery was gunpowder; this substance was first used in the manufacturing of fireworks. The Chinese were remarkably ahead of the West with regard to many discoveries and inventions.

Section Review

1. What Chinese philosopher is known for his collection of wise sayings?

2. What is perhaps the most remarkable building achievement that occurred under the Qin dynasty?

3–7. List five specific contributions that China made to the Western world.

★ Evaluate Qin Shi Huang's rule in China.

★ Contrast the Qin and the Han dynasties.

Making Connections

1–2. Describe the significance of family in Africa. What role did polygamy play?

3. Who was influential in bringing Christianity to the African kingdom of Aksum?

4. Why did Hinduism regain its popularity during the Gupta period?

5. Why did China remain largely protected from foreign invasions while India was frequently invaded?

Developing History Skills

1. Compare and contrast Hinduism and Buddhism in this period with earlier forms of these religions.

2. Compare and contrast justice, power, and citizenship in Han China and the Roman Empire.

Thinking Critically

1. How do the Eastern religions mentioned in this chapter rely on human works to find happiness in this life and in the life to come? (You might want to also refer to chapter 2 in answering this question.)

Living in God's World

1. How could Asoka have made his efforts to ensure justice for his subjects more enduring?

2. What are possible responses to Christianity being marginalized by other religions (as happened geographically with Aksum)? Evaluate these possible responses.

People, Places, and Things to Know

sub-Saharan Africa
Bantu migration
Kush
Aksum
Frumentius
Nok
Djenné-Djeno
polygamy
Chandragupta Maurya
Asoka
Gupta Empire
Kalidasa
Qin Shi Huang
Wu Ti
Pax Sinica

3

CULTURES OF THE WORLD
500–1100

Great Wall of China

ca. 250–900
Classic period in Mayan history

618–907
Tang Dynasty

732
Battle of Tours

622
Muhammad flees to Medina

661–750
Umayyad Caliphate

500

600

700

476–1453
Byzantine Empire

Development of the Eastern Woodlands Indian culture

ca. 700

750–1000
Abbasid Caliphate

ca. 700–1200
Ghana Empire

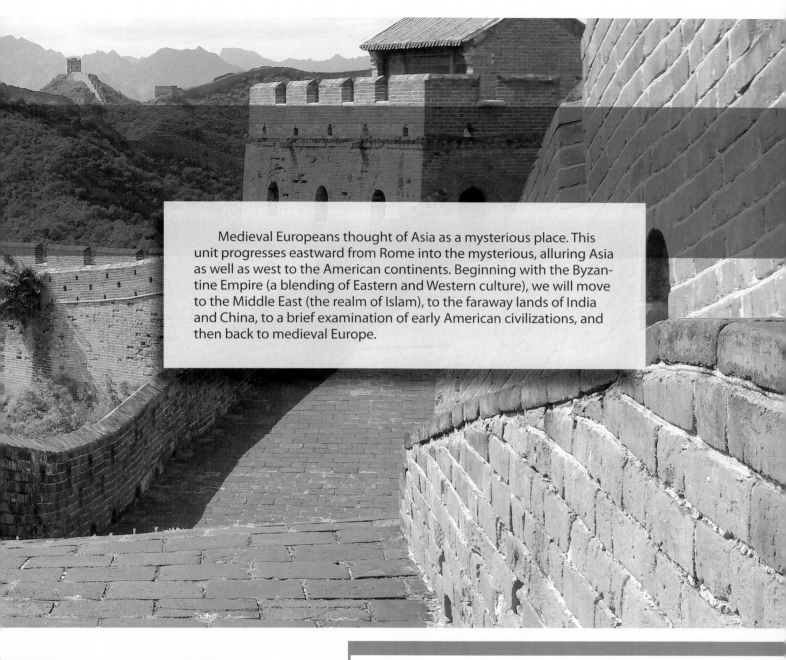

Medieval Europeans thought of Asia as a mysterious place. This unit progresses eastward from Rome into the mysterious, alluring Asia as well as west to the American continents. Beginning with the Byzantine Empire (a blending of Eastern and Western culture), we will move to the Middle East (the realm of Islam), to the faraway lands of India and China, to a brief examination of early American civilizations, and then back to medieval Europe.

ca. 950–1539
Postclassic period in Mayan history

960–1279
Song dynasty

1059
The College of Cardinals created

1066
William of Normandy conquers England

ca. 1200 ▶
The Aztecs settle in the Valley of Mexico

800
Crowning of Charlemagne by the pope

ca. 800–1600
Mississippian Indian culture

800 | **900** | **1000** | **1100**

ca. 916
Koryŏ dynasty established in Korea (lasts until 14th century)

1077
Henry IV forced to go before Pope Gregory VII at Canossa

CHAPTER

The Byzantine & Islamic Empires

6

I. The Byzantine Civilization

II. Early Russia

III. The Islamic Civilization

Hagia Sophia in Istanbul, Turkey

Big Ideas

1. What cultural contributions did the Byzantine Empire make to other civilizations?

2. What characterized the early history of Russia?

3. What religious and cultural contributions did Islamic civilizations make to other civilizations?

In 476 the Roman Empire collapsed in the West. It endured in the East, however, for another thousand years. This Eastern Roman Empire became known as the **Byzantine** (BIZ un teen) **Empire**. The Byzantine civilization was a blending of the cultural heritage of ancient Greece and the cultures of the Near East. Byzantine culture strongly influenced the people of Russia and southeastern Europe.

The growth of Christ's kingdom continued here in the East as it did in the West. And the spiritual contamination that was common in the West was also common in the East. Christ had promised that His kingdom would grow in this manner. He taught His disciples that the kingdom of heaven would be like a mustard seed once it is planted. It would begin very small but would experience amazing growth (Matt. 13:31–32). Christ also revealed that this kingdom would be like a field of wheat into which an enemy plants many weeds (Matt. 13:24–30). Much of the story of the human race from the Resurrection of Christ to the present is the working out of these two truths. God is at work in the earth growing the kingdom of His Son, and this kingdom is constantly being corrupted by people whose faith in Christ is counterfeit.

But God allows more than just artificiality to challenge Christ's kingdom. He also allows the development of rival movements. During the seventh century, Islam arose in the desert land of Arabia. Its zealous followers, Muslims, spread their faith through military conquest; they built an empire that stretched from Spain to India. At the same time, they forged a remarkable civilization by combining their own customs and traditions with the arts and learning of the people they conquered. This chapter will trace the beginnings, growth, and interaction of the Byzantine and Islamic civilizations.

I. The Byzantine Civilization

The Rise of "New Rome"

In 330 the emperor Constantine formally dedicated a new capital for the Roman Empire. He called the city "**New Rome**," but it became more widely known as Constantinople, "Constantine's City." This "second Rome" was ideally located on a peninsula that juts out into the waters of the Bosporus, a narrow strait that separates southeastern Europe from Asia Minor. Constantinople was the meeting place of East and West, the vital link in both land and sea trade routes. Wealth from all over the world passed through its port.

In addition to being a flourishing commercial center, Constantinople also became an important political and religious center. After the days of Constantine, Roman emperors continued to live there. When the emperor Theodosius formally divided the empire into two parts (see p. 93), the city became the permanent capital of the Eastern Roman Empire. It was also recognized as one of the five major patriarchates of the Christian church.

While the Eastern Roman Empire continued to prosper, conditions in the western empire steadily declined. During the fourth and fifth centuries, barbarian tribes threatened Rome's borders. The weak western empire crumbled under the onslaught, but the richer and stronger eastern empire was able to withstand the attacks. Constantinople, the "queen of the Mediterranean," became the foremost city of the empire.

The Byzantine Empire took its name from the ancient Greek city Byzantium, on which Constantinople was built. Inhabitants

(see p. 93)

Guiding Questions

1. What led to the split between Eastern Orthodox and Roman Catholic churches?
2. What caused the Byzantine Empire to fall?
3. What were the main cultural contributions of the Byzantine Empire?
4. Did Justinian ensure justice and use his power wisely?

of this empire still considered themselves Romans, and in many respects their civilization was a continuation of the Roman Empire. In addition to having many of the same customs and traditions, the eastern empire retained the political and legal structures of ancient Rome. But Byzantine culture was influenced even more by the Hellenistic culture that still permeated the region; it was more Greek than Roman, more Asiatic than European. While a more civilized way of life declined in the West, it endured and flourished in the East under the Byzantine Empire.

The Reign of Justinian

The first great period of Byzantine history and culture came during the reign of **Justinian** (juh STIN ee un; r. 527–65). He rose from humble origins to become one of the most famous Byzantine emperors. However, he owed much of his success to the timely counsel and strong will of his wife, **Theodora**. In 532 a riot erupted in Constantinople, threatening to topple Justinian from power. This riot flamed into a popular uprising, named the **Nika Revolt** after the people's battle cry: "Nika!" ("Conquer!"). Justinian was about to flee the capital and admit defeat when Theodora's bold advice encouraged him to stay:

> My opinion then is that the present time, above all others, is inopportune for flight, even though it bring safety. . . . For one who has been an emperor it is unendurable to be a fugitive. May I never be separated from this purple [sign of royalty]. . . . If, now, it is your wish to save yourself, O Emperor, there is no difficulty. For we have much money, and there is the sea, here the boats. However consider whether it will not come about after you have been saved that you would gladly exchange that safety for death. For as for myself, I approve a certain ancient saying that royalty is a good burial-shroud.
>
> *Procopius,* History of the Wars, *trans. H. B. Dewing, 1.24.*

This was the turning point in Justinian's reign. He remained in the capital, used loyal members of the army to kill thousands of insurrectionists, and crushed the revolt. In this manner Justinian firmly established himself as emperor.

Justinian then turned his attention to his chief objective: restoring the greatness of the Roman Empire. To accomplish this goal, he sought to recover the Roman territory in the West that had fallen into the hands of barbarian tribes. For over two decades Justinian's generals led military campaigns throughout the Mediterranean world. His forces defeated the Vandals in North Africa, captured Italy from the Ostrogoths, and penetrated the southern portion of the Visigoth kingdom in Spain. Justinian's conquests extended the boundaries of the Byzantine Empire to their greatest extent; nevertheless, he was unable to recover all the land once held by Rome.

One of the most enduring achievements of the Byzantine Empire was the preservation of Roman law. By the sixth century, the reliable Roman legal system had become a complex and disorganized mass of legal opinions. Its many laws were often confusing and contradictory. The Romans had created so many regulations that they almost forgot the foundational concepts of truth and justice. Justinian appointed a commission of ten scholars to compile, reorganize, and condense the vast body of law that had accumulated

Justinian and Theodora

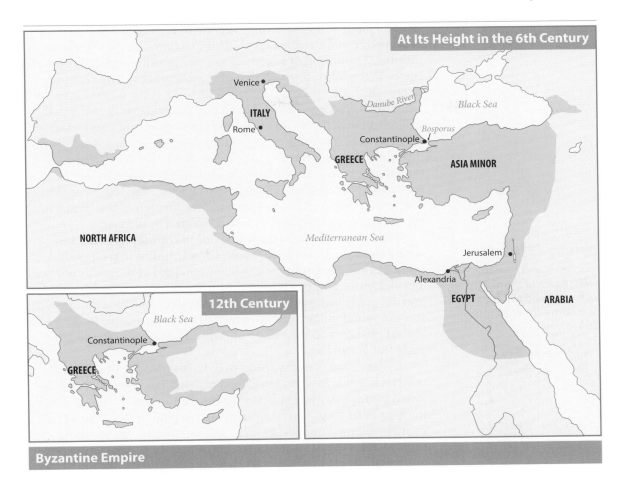

At Its Height in the 6th Century

12th Century

Byzantine Empire

from the days of ancient Rome. Their work resulted in the **Justinian Code**, a systematic arrangement of laws that clarified Roman legal principles. This code preserved the heritage of the Roman legal system, which was to provide a foundation on which most modern European nations would build their political and legal systems.

Justinian's reign marked a golden age of Byzantine culture. Like Constantine, he desired to restore the grandeur of ancient Rome. Sparing no expense, he initiated an extensive building program to construct churches, public buildings, aqueducts, and roads both in the capital city and throughout the empire. He also patronized Byzantine art. From this period comes the finest example of Byzantine architecture, the Church of **Hagia Sophia** (HAH-juh so-FEE-uh), meaning "Holy Wisdom."

Even so, Justinian left his successors with an empire beset by many problems. In his attempts to reclaim the West, he had neglected the defense of the empire's eastern and northern borders. Likewise, his costly military campaigns, coupled with his massive building program, left the empire financially drained. Thus it may be said that Justinian took the Byzantine Empire to the height of glory but left it at the brink of ruin.

Eastern and Western Churches Separate

When Constantine founded "New Rome," he established not only a new political capital but also a new religious center. He desired Constantinople to be a Christian city, a "new Jerusalem." Under his influence, Christianity became the favored religion of the Roman Empire. It was quite natural for "Constantine's City" to rise to a place of honor in the structure of the organized church; it became one of the five patriarchal cities, second only to Rome in prestige. The bishop of Rome became the most important religious leader in the West; the patriarch of Constantinople held that position in the East.

The churches of East and West had participated in councils that defended the deity of Christ and the Holy Spirit. They agreed about the Trinity. Both church organizations developed into a structure that included bishops, priests, and deacons. Both also developed a sacramental approach to religion. Yet, despite the shared foundation, each church developed a distinctive character. This led eventually to the division between the Roman Catholic Church in the West and the Byzantine or **Eastern Orthodox Church** in the East.

The church in the East became one of the most powerful institutions in the Byzantine Empire. Closely linked to the political framework of the empire, it gradually emerged as the state church. The Byzantine emperor was at the same time the head of the state and the protector of the church and its teachings. This relationship was not found in the West after the fall of Rome. People in the West looked primarily to the bishop of Rome, instead of a king or emperor, for leadership.

Other differences existed as well. East and West also differed over such issues as when to celebrate Easter. The eastern church allowed parish priests to marry, whereas the Roman Church gradually forbad priests from marrying. The eastern church used **icons** (EYE kahnz)—painted images of Christ and the saints—in their worship, whereas the Roman Church permitted the use of statues and more realistic art in worship. Perhaps most significantly, the western church made an addition to a creed without consulting with the eastern churches. In addition, the leaders of the Byzantine church resented the interference of the bishop of Rome in the religious affairs of the East. They refused to acknowledge the bishop of Rome's growing claim that his authority was supreme over all churches (see p. 91).

As a result, a bitter rivalry developed between the eastern and western churches. Tensions culminated in 1054 when the pope sent a delegation to Constantinople stating that the pope was assuming authority over the churches in southern Italy that had been under the patriarch's authority. When the patriarch refused to accept the pope's actions, the pope's representatives **excommunicated** him

Justinian and Eastern Orthodoxy

In addition to organizing laws and constructing architectural marvels, Justinian sent missionaries from the Eastern Orthodox Church to other lands. Kush, a country located south of Egypt, was one of those lands.

The Eastern Orthodox Church

The churches in the eastern Mediterranean that refused to recognize Rome's control over them became known as the Eastern Orthodox. The word *orthodox* comes from two Greek words that together mean "straight (*orthos*) opinion (*doxa*)." During the early days of the Eastern churches, the leaders played an active role in the defense of the Trinity and the person of Christ as the Son of God. However, the Eastern Orthodox Church also includes teaching and practices that many Protestants do not consider orthodox, including baptismal regeneration, a sacramental approach to religion, and the veneration of icons.

The Eastern Orthodox Church consists of various national churches. Today, for example, there is a Russian Orthodox Church, a Greek Orthodox Church, and a Romanian Orthodox Church, among others. In addition, the Orthodox churches do not recognize one man as their leader as the Roman Catholics recognize the pope. Each patriarch exercises authority over his own national church and is equal in position to every other patriarch.

The Meaning of Icons

A characteristic feature of Eastern Orthodoxy is its use of icons. They occupy prominent places in churches and homes and are held in great reverence by the Orthodox faithful. Scripture does not forbid religious art—as evidenced by the art utilized in the Tabernacle and the Temple—but it does forbid using images to represent God or worshiping images.

Although we frequently speak about looking at a painting, the Orthodox believe that one should not merely look at icons. Instead, the viewer should direct his mind beyond the icon to the heavenly reality it represents. For example, one viewing a picture of the apostle Peter should not see a painted figure but should see in his mind's eye the real Peter in heaven.

In an effort to make the painted figures appear otherworldly, the artists, who were usually monks, developed several techniques that remained unchanged for many centuries. For example, there are no shadows in icons because the shadows imply something material and earthly. Second, historical scenes that occurred inside a building are often shown outside with the building in the background. In this way, the painters hoped to elevate the event beyond its historical context and give it universal meaning. Third, the figures in icons are portrayed unrealistically with very thin noses, small mouths, and large eyes. This illustrates the fact that the figures supposedly conquered their five senses (their earthly selves) and lived in holiness according to their spiritual nature.

Even the colors used by the icon painters had special meaning. For example, the monks usually portrayed Christ wearing garments of red, blue, and gold. The red symbolized love, and the blue and gold represented truth and heaven. In pictures of the transfiguration, Christ is usually shown wearing white—a symbol of light and holiness.

(depriving an individual of the sacraments and excluding him from the fellowship of the church). Then, in retaliation, the patriarch excommunicated the pope.

The Empire Under Siege

The Byzantine Empire experienced both success and failure during the period from the sixth to the fifteenth centuries. It enlarged its empire repeatedly, only to see the gains erased by outside forces. During the fourth and fifth centuries, it endured strong barbarian attacks. After Justinian's reign in the sixth century, the empire was besieged on almost every side for several hundred years. From the West came the Lombards, a Germanic tribe that conquered most of Italy. From the North came the Slavs and the Bulgars, who settled in the Balkan Peninsula. Out of the East came the Sassanids, who sought to restore the glory of the Persian Empire. Although often weak and on the brink of collapse, the Byzantines managed to drive out all these foreign invaders.

In the seventh century the Byzantine Empire had to reckon with a new and energetic force—the Arab Muslims. The Muslims, advancing from the Arabian Peninsula, smashed the Byzantine defenses both on land and at sea. Soon they threatened Constantinople itself. But the "city protected by God" (as it was called) withstood the Arab attacks.

Constantinople was aided by its defensible location, its strong fortifications, and a new secret weapon called "Greek fire." Though the Byzantines stopped the Muslim expansion into southeastern Europe, they lost Syria, Palestine, Egypt, and North Africa. The Byzantine Empire at one time encompassed the Mediterranean Sea; by the eighth century its territory had been greatly reduced.

Between 850 and 1050 the Byzantine Empire gradually recovered its former strength and prosperity. No longer did it remain on the defensive; it pushed back the Muslims and reasserted itself as

East Meets West

List characteristics for each group and differences or questions that arose.

Eastern Church Characteristics	Differences/ Questions	Western Church Characteristics

Greek Fire

One reason Constantinople was able to withstand enemy sieges was its secret weapon known as "Greek fire." This weapon, which the Byzantines developed in the seventh century, was an explosive mixture of chemicals possibly including quicklime, sulfur, naphtha, and potassium nitrate. Soldiers squirted it from tubes or launched it in jars from catapults at the enemy. Greek fire ignited spontaneously and burned even under water. This weapon proved to be particularly effective against wooden ships and enabled the Byzantines to control the Mediterranean Sea for many centuries.

the dominant power in the Mediterranean. This period of military success reached its height under **Basil II** (r. 976–1025). Known as the "Bulgar Slayer," Basil crushed the Bulgars in the Balkan region and added their kingdoms to the empire. The Byzantines not only reclaimed some of the territory they held during Justinian's day but also revived their commercial and cultural interests. Constantinople abounded with the riches of trade, art, and architecture. Merchants and missionaries carried these achievements to other lands; many of these lands still bear the marks of Byzantine culture.

After two centuries of expansion, new obstacles confronted the empire. The growth of commercial rivals—especially the city of Venice in Italy—challenged Byzantine trade supremacy in the eastern Mediterranean. Competition from Venetian merchants cost the empire sorely needed resources and markets. At the same time, the **Seljuk Turks** emerged as a powerful force in the East. These Turks, originally nomadic tribes from central Asia, had adopted Arab culture and Islam. The important Byzantine territory of Asia Minor fell to these fierce warriors in 1071, when they annihilated the Byzantine army at the Battle of Manzikert (MAN zih kurt). Fearful that Constantinople would fall, the desperate Byzantine emperor appealed to the Christians in the West for aid. The West responded by sending several military expeditions, known as the **Crusades**, to free the East—especially the Holy Land—from these Muslim invaders.

One tragic episode occurred in 1204 as an invading army breached the defenses of Constantinople. The invaders captured and looted the city, slaughtering both young and old. Shockingly, these soldiers were not Muslims, but warriors from the West on a "holy" Crusade. Unscrupulous Venetian merchants had enlisted the aid of these crusaders and used them to destroy Constantinople—Venice's commercial rival. Neither their cause nor their conduct was holy. In fact, they returned to Europe without even attempting to carry out their original mission of freeing the Holy Land. Although Byzantine forces later recaptured Constantinople, the Byzantine Empire never fully recovered from the destruction it suffered.

Massive siege cannon possibly used in 1453 against the walls surrounding Constantinople

For two centuries the empire continued to exist, but it was in a state of steady decline. The empire finally came to an end in 1453, when a new wave of Muslim invaders, the **Ottoman Turks**, blasted through the city's massive walls with cannons, slaughtered its inhabitants, and sacked Constantinople.

Byzantine Civilization Contributions

When the Turks brought an end to the Byzantine Empire, they destroyed the protective barrier that for hundreds of years had shielded the West against the spread of Islam. This protection had given the West time to recover from the long period of chaos that followed the collapse of Rome. In addition, Byzantine civilization was important in its own right. It was the means by which the classical heritage of Greece and Rome was preserved and transmitted to the West.

Although the size of the Byzantine Empire had gradually diminished from its peak under Justinian, the influence of the Byzantine civilization had expanded. Its many achievements had attracted the less civilized peoples who came into contact with the empire. They marveled at the material wealth that abounded at Constantinople and tried to copy the effective governmental system that the Byzantines had adapted from ancient Rome.

Furthermore, many of the pagan peoples of eastern Europe had embraced Eastern Orthodoxy along with Byzantine culture. Two Byzantine missionaries, the brothers Cyril and Methodius (muh THO dee us), had gone to the Slavic peoples. Their work eventually reached Russia and southeastern Europe. The Slavic tribes did not have a written language, so Cyril and Methodius developed one for them. Their system, a modification of the Greek alphabet, became the foundation of the Slavic written language.

Byzantine art and architecture demonstrated the wealth and splendor of this once-mighty empire. The art was primarily intended to glorify God; it adorned the interiors of churches. Craftsmen excelled in wall paintings, carved ivory, illuminated manuscripts (manuscripts decorated with ornate letters or designs in bright colors or precious metals), and marble and metal work. A favorite decorative art—the **mosaic**—graced the walls and ceilings of the churches. By inlaying tiny pieces of glass or stone in wet cement or plaster, artists could form beautiful patterns and pictures.

The churches housed some of the best examples of Byzantine art, and they were in themselves the best examples of Byzantine architecture. The architects demonstrated a mastery of design and engineering skill. They especially excelled in domed structures. The most famous of these structures is the beautiful Hagia Sophia, sometimes called the Santa Sophia. In size and rich adornment, no other church in the empire could equal it. It became a model of architectural design that was copied in other cities and lands. Still standing today, its great dome reaches a height of 180 feet and has a diameter of 108 feet. Procopius, a sixth-century historian, described the splendor of the Hagia Sophia as "a spectacle of marvellous beauty, overwhelming to those who see it, . . . for it soars to a height to match the sky, and as if surging up amongst the other buildings it stands on high and looks down upon the remainder of the city, adorning it. . . . It exults in an indescribable beauty."

Mosaic of Christ from the Hagia Sophia

Section Review

1. What Byzantine emperor sought to restore the greatness of the Roman Empire by enlarging the boundaries of the Byzantine Empire to their greatest extent?

2. What is the name of the organized church that developed within the Byzantine Empire?

3. What decorative art did Byzantine artists create by inlaying tiny pieces of glass or stone in wet cement or plaster?

4. What is the name of the most famous Byzantine architectural structure?

5–6. List two causes for the fall of the Byzantine Empire.

★ In what ways did the Byzantine Empire advance culture?

★ Why did aspects of Byzantine civilization continue to spread even as the empire declined?

Guiding Questions

1. What characterized the development of early Russian civilization?
2. How did Byzantium influence Russia?
3. What led to the rise and fall of Kiev?

II. Early Russia

Beginnings

Looking at a map of the modern world, one cannot help noticing the enormous size of the land of Russia. Covering about one-sixth of the land mass, it is the world's largest country. Russia occupies a large portion of two continents—Europe and Asia. Within its borders is a population composed of people of many different ethnic and linguistic backgrounds. The largest group is the **Slavs**, whose ancestors played a major role in establishing the early Russian state.

No one knows for sure where the Slavs first lived. They moved into eastern Europe as the Germanic tribes there migrated farther westward. Eventually three groups emerged: the West Slavs—the Poles and Czechs—settled in the Danube region; the Yugo-Slavs, or "South Slavs," moved down into the Balkan area; and the East Slavs, the ancestors of the Russians, occupied the territory between the Baltic and Black Seas. Running through the land of the East Slavs is a network of rivers along which they built their village communities. The Slavs participated in the prosperous trade that flourished along these river highways.

During the eighth and ninth centuries, bands of Swedish Norsemen, known to the Slavs and Byzantines as **Varangians** (vuh RAN jee unz), sailed south from the Baltic Sea using the waterways. Like the Vikings who terrorized western Europe (see p. 182), the Varangians plundered Slavic villages along the rivers. Attracted by the possibilities of opening trade routes with the Byzantine and Muslim civilizations, many Varangian warriors settled along the inland waterways. Slavic settlements often hired these warriors to protect their villages from other raiding tribesmen.

In the city of Novgorod (NAWV guh rawt), according to a traditional account, the Slavs invited Varangian rule: "Our whole land is great and rich, but there is not order in it. Come to rule and reign over us." Whether by invitation or by force, the Varangian warrior **Rurik** gained control of Novgorod about 862. That year is the traditional date for the beginning of Russian history. Rurik established the first ruling dynasty of Russia. His successors captured and ruled other cities in the region, the most important of these being Kiev (KEE ef). Yet despite their military superiority, the Varangians were greatly outnumbered by the Slavs and were soon absorbed by the populace.

Shortly after Rurik's death, Kiev became the center of the early Russian state. This city was located on the shores of the Dnieper (NEE pur) River, the major route for trade with the Byzantine Empire. For three centuries Kiev held the prominent position in a loose confederation of city-states. Established by Varangian princes, this confederation sought to further the region's common commercial interests and protect important trade routes. The area under Kievan influence became known as Russia, perhaps deriving its name from the Slavic designation of the Norsemen, **Rus**, meaning, "rowers" or "seafarers."

Byzantine Cultural Influences

Russian culture bears a strong Byzantine imprint. Because of early commercial contacts, Kiev and Constantinople developed close cultural ties. A significant event in Russian history was the adoption of Eastern Orthodoxy by the Kievan ruler **Vladimir I** in

Russia About 1000

988. He ordered the destruction of pagan idols and temples and established Orthodox Christianity as the official state religion. By adopting Eastern Orthodoxy rather than Roman Catholicism, Russia cut itself off from the mainstream of Western thought and instead came under the influences of the Eastern church and Byzantine culture.

Russian Orthodox Church

The influence of the Orthodox church upon Russia was great. The Russian language profited from the Slavic alphabet, which the Byzantine missionaries Cyril and Methodius had adapted from the Greek alphabet. The Slavic alphabet enabled the Russians to translate Greek works into their Slavic language. It also prompted the growth of native Russian literature. Russian artists made beautiful icons like those adorning Byzantine churches. The Russians even patterned their cathedrals after Byzantine models. One feature of their cathedrals, however, is uniquely Russian—the onion-shaped dome.

Height of Kievan Russia

Kiev reached the zenith of its power and prestige during the reign of Yaroslav (yuh ruh SLAHV) "the Wise" (r. 1036–1054). Yaroslav greatly strengthened the city's position of leadership; Kiev became known as the "Mother of Russian cities." His reign saw the greatest territorial expansion of the early Russian state. He gained international recognition by negotiating marriage alliances between his princely house and the royal families of France, Sweden, Norway, Poland, Hungary, and the Byzantine Empire. He also sponsored the earliest known Russian code of laws, which combined Slavic tribal law and Byzantine law.

Yaroslav desired to make Kiev a rival of Constantinople. In size, wealth, and culture, Kiev became one of the leading cities of its day. It was a prosperous center of commerce—a meeting place of the world's merchants. Yaroslav's patronage of art, education, and the church attracted Byzantine painters, architects, teachers, and priests. With the aid of Byzantines, the Russians constructed their own cathedral of Hagia Sophia. Kiev also boasted schools, libraries, monasteries, cathedrals, and fortifications that Yaroslav built.

After the death of Yaroslav, Kiev lost its prominence among the Russian cities when his heirs fought to determine who would succeed him on the throne. Cities that had formerly looked to the Kievan rulers as the Grand Princes of Russia began to assert their independence. New trade routes and commercial centers drew away much of Kiev's wealth and population. Kiev's declining influence suffered a deathblow in the thirteenth century, when the Tartars—fierce Mongolian warriors from central Asia—swept into Russia (see ch. 12). They destroyed Kiev in 1240 and ruled Russia until the late 1400s. After the decline of Mongol power, a new center of Russian society—Moscow—arose in the north.

Vladimir and the Orthodox Church

According to legend, the Russian ruler Vladimir decided that he would establish a monotheistic religion among his people to replace their polytheistic, pagan beliefs. Before he decided what that new religion would be, he investigated what the world had to offer. He summoned representatives of Islam, Judaism, Roman Catholicism, and Eastern Orthodoxy and had each of them explain why their particular religion was best. After listening to the claims of each, Vladimir sent out envoys to observe these religions on a firsthand basis. When they returned, he made his decision.

First of all, Vladimir rejected Islam because the Qur'an forbade the drinking of alcoholic beverages. Second, he rejected Judaism because the Jewish people had been defeated and scattered across the world. Since their God did not seem strong enough to protect them, He could not be counted on to protect the Russian people, thought Vladimir. Third, the king rejected Roman Catholicism because the Catholic churches were dark and damp and the services were dull. Vladimir chose Eastern Orthodoxy.

The reason for his choice was simple. When his envoys returned from Constantinople, they enthusiastically described a service they had attended at the Hagia Sophia. They told him how the whole church seemed to shine as the mosaics reflected the light of the burning candles. They told him of the beautiful music, the clouds of incense, and the gorgeous robes of the patriarch who led the service. Impressed by what he heard, Vladimir adopted Eastern Orthodoxy. The Russian Orthodox Church was established.

Section Review

1. What ethnic group played a major role in establishing the early Russian state?

2. What city became the center of the early Russian state?

3. What Russian ruler adopted the Eastern Orthodox Church as the official religion of the Russian state?

4–5. What two Byzantine missionaries developed a written language for the Slavic people of Russia?

6. Under whose leadership did the city of Kiev and the early Russian state reach the height of its power and prestige?

✵ According to legend, why did Vladimir choose Eastern Orthodoxy over other religions?

✵ What contributed to the rise and fall of the city of Kiev?

Guiding Questions

1. What were key events in Muhammad's life and the beginning of Islam?
2. What are the basic teachings of Islam?
3. What cultural contributions did Islamic states make?

Arabian Peninsula

III. The Islamic Civilization

The Land of Arabia

The cradle of Islam was Arabia—a large peninsula that extends south of the Fertile Crescent in the Middle East. This peninsula lies between Asia and Africa, bounded by the Persian Gulf in the East and the Red Sea in the West. In land area, it is about one-third the size of the United States. Much of the land is a barren wilderness of deserts and stony plains. Vegetation is sparse, and agriculture is limited because of the extreme heat and lack of adequate rainfall. This uninviting environment kept most of Arabia in relative isolation until the birth of Islam in the seventh century.

The land of Arabia is also adjacent to the Bible lands. As do the Hebrews, Arabs trace their beginnings back to Abraham: the Hebrews, through his son Isaac; the Arabs, through his son **Ishmael**. Although Ishmael was not the child of God's special promise (Gal. 4:22–23), God blessed him: "I have blessed him, and will make him fruitful, . . . and I will make him a great nation" (Gen. 17:20). Ishmael's descendants dwelt in the Arabian Peninsula and became a numerous people, just as God had foretold.

Because they had no organized government, the Arab people had little unity before the advent of Islam. Each Arab was loyal to his own tribe, and warfare among the tribes was frequent.

In addition, there were two distinct lifestyles among the people of Arabia. Many of the Arabs traveled through the harsh desert wilderness in independent bands. These nomads, called **Bedouins** (BED oo inz), roamed the desert in search of pastureland and water for their herds of goats, sheep, and camels. Over the centuries the Bedouin way of life has remained relatively unchanged; today they can be seen traveling from oasis to oasis across the desert land.

Not all Arabs were desert nomads, however; some lived a more settled life along the outer rim of the peninsula. They established cities along important trade routes or along the coast, where rainfall was more abundant and the land was more fertile. A few of these cities became important trade centers for camel caravans, which carried goods across the desert to and from other lands. Out of one of these cities arose a leader who united the people of Arabia.

The Founding of Islam

Muhammad

Shortly after the death of the Byzantine emperor Justinian in 565, **Muhammad** (moo HAHM id) was born in Arabia. Muhammad (570–632) claimed to be the last and greatest of the prophets of the god **Allah** (AH luh). His teaching became the basis for a new religious movement known as **Islam** (is LAHM), meaning "submission" (to the will of Allah). His followers are known as **Muslims** ("submitters to Allah").

Muhammad, whose name means "highly praised," was born to a poor family in the city of Mecca, in western Arabia. Little is known of his early life except that he became an orphan at the age of six and was reared by his grandfather and uncle. As a young man he entered the employment of Khadijah, a wealthy merchant and widow. At the age of twenty-five, he married her. For the first time in his life he enjoyed financial security. He spent much of his leisure time in a cave near Mecca meditating on religion and struggling with the polytheism of his people. During his travels he had encountered many religions, and he borrowed from them to form a new religious movement that would govern every aspect of life.

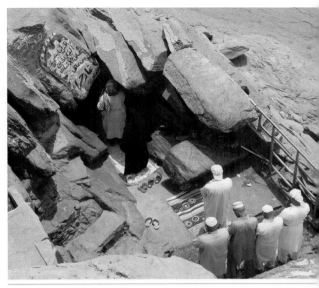

Cave Hira in Mecca, Saudi Arabia

The Messenger of Allah

Muslim historians record that in his fortieth year, Muhammad received a vision in which the angel Gabriel gave him a divine revelation to "Recite!"

> RECITE in the name of your Lord who created—created man from clots of blood.

> Recite! Your Lord is the Most Bountiful One, who by the pen taught man what he did not know. (Sura 96:1)

According to Muslim teaching, these revelations continued throughout Muhammad's lifetime. Initially he feared that these messages might be from Satan. However, Muhammad's wife and a trusted friend convinced him that he was the messenger of God entrusted with a new revelation for man. Muhammad began preaching that there was only one god, Allah, and that he, Muhammad, was Allah's prophet.

He had little success in gaining converts at first. Muhammad's early followers were family members and close friends. Most of the people of Mecca ridiculed him, viewing his teaching as contrary to their religious beliefs and a threat to the city's commercial interests. Mecca had become a leading trade center, situated at the crossroads of trade routes in western Arabia. It had also developed into a center of religious worship because the **Ka'bah** was located at Mecca. This stone building served as a sacred shrine that housed hundreds of idols. People from across Arabia made pilgrimages to this shrine. Meccan merchants profited from this pagan worship. The principal attraction was the famous Black Stone, possibly a meteorite, set into the wall of the Ka'bah. For centuries Arabs had walked around the Ka'bah and kissed the Stone as a form of worship. According to Muslim tradition, the angel Gabriel sent the stone to Abraham, who, along with his son Ishmael, built the Ka'bah. Rejecting Muhammad's

The Ka'bah

monotheism and fearing it would hinder their profitable business, the leaders of Mecca persecuted Muhammad and his followers.

The Flight to Medina

In 622 Muhammad made a historic decision. He and his followers decided to flee Mecca and accept an invitation to move to Medina (mih DEE nuh), a city about two hundred miles to the north. This move is known as the **Hegira** (hih JIE ruh), or "flight." (It is celebrated as year 1 on the Muslim calendar.) At Medina, Muhammad's following grew rapidly. The Arabs there not only accepted Muhammad as their spiritual leader but made him their political and military leader as well. Once in power, Muhammad the persecuted became Muhammad the persecutor. While in the minority, he had presented his cause peaceably through preaching, but now he advanced it by force and military conquest. With an army of militant Muslim followers, he slaughtered any who opposed him. A bitter struggle with the rival city of Mecca ended in 630 when Muhammad violated a truce and reentered the city of his birth in triumph. He destroyed all the idols of the Ka'bah—except the Black Stone—and turned the Ka'bah into the center of Islamic worship. Mecca became the "holy city" of this new religious system.

The Teachings of Islam

The Qur'an

Page from the Qur'an

The heart of Islam is the **Qur'an** ("recitations"), the sacred book of the Muslims. Muslims believe that the archangel Gabriel revealed the words of Allah to Muhammad through numerous dreams and visions. These revelations formed the basis of his teaching. Many of his followers committed his teachings to memory; others wrote them down on anything they could find. After Muhammad's death, they compiled his teachings into the Qur'an. Composed of 114 chapters, or suras, the Qur'an is the primary authority on Muslim belief and practice. Dedicated Muslims memorize the entire Qur'an, which is about the same length as the New Testament.

The central doctrine taught by the Qur'an (kuh RAHN) is the belief in one god, Allah (al, "the"; Ilah, "god"). According to the Qur'an,

> He is God, besides whom there is no other deity. He knows the unknown and the manifest. He is the Compassionate, the Merciful.

> He is God beside whom there is no other deity. He is the Sovereign Lord, the Holy One, the Giver of Peace, the Keeper of Faith; the Guardian, the Mighty One, the All-powerful, the Most High! Exalted be God above their idols! (Sura 59:22–23)

Muslims believe that Allah sent more than one hundred thousand prophets to reveal his will to man. However, Islam reveres Muhammad as the last and greatest of Allah's prophets and the Qur'an as Allah's final revelation, superseding all others.

The moral teaching of the Qur'an serves as a guide for the conduct of its believers. Some passages in the Qur'an encourage Muslims to cultivate humility, duty, kindness, and benevolence. Others condemn idolatry, murder, gambling, drinking of wine, and adultery, although Muslim men are allowed to have up to four wives and may arrange temporary marriages. Muslims are taught to fear Allah because, while he may or may not reward good works, he will definitely punish evil in the life to come. The Qur'an gives a description of this day of judgment:

> He that comes before his Lord laden with sin shall be consigned to Hell, where he shall neither die nor live. But he that comes before Him with true faith, having done good works, shall be exalted to the highest ranks. He shall abide forever in the gardens of Eden, in gardens watered by running streams. Such shall be the recompense of those that keep themselves pure. (Sura 20:74–76)

The Qur'an reflects many ideas that Muhammad drew from Jewish and Christian sources. It mentions several stories and characters from the Old and New Testaments. The Qur'an honors Noah, Abraham, David, and even Jesus as prophets of Allah. Likewise, the Qur'an echoes many concepts found in the Bible. It emphasizes prayer, moral conduct, a coming day of resurrection and judgment, and the existence of heaven (paradise) and hell. Islam also stresses the worship of one god and regards the Bible as a holy book.

But while Muhammad used many biblical terms in his teaching, he distorted biblical truth. Muhammad claimed to worship the same God as the Christians, but the god of the Qur'an is not the God of the Bible. For example, Muhammad rejected the doctrine of the Trinity and denied that Christ is the Son of God (see 1 John 4:2–3). In reference to Christians, the Qur'an says:

> People of the Book, do not transgress the bounds of your religion. Speak nothing but the truth about God. The Messiah, Jesus, son of Mary, was no more than God's apostle. . . . So believe in God and his apostles, and do not say: 'Three' [there is a Trinity]. Forbear, and it shall be better for you. God is but one God. God forbid that He should have a son! (Sura 4:171)

The Five Pillars

The Qur'an teaches about a paradise in which faithful Muslim men will enjoy gardens of delight, rivers of wine, and the company of beautiful women. To have any hope of entering this paradise, a Muslim must perform certain religious duties. The Qur'an teaches Muslims to fear Allah's punishment if these basic religious practices are not observed. These rituals are called the **Five Pillars of Islam**:

1. Shahadah: The shahadah is the confession of Islam and must be sincerely believed and recited regularly: "There is no God but Allah, and Muhammad is his prophet."

2. Salat: This word means "prayers." Every Muslim must recite prayers up to five times a day while facing Mecca.

3. Zakat: This word means "purification," and it refers to alms (money) that the devout are to give to the poor.

4. Sawm: The sawm is a required fast that all Muslims are to observe from sunrise to sunset during the sacred month of Ramadan (ram uh DAHN).

5. Hajj: The hajj is a pilgrimage to Mecca. Every Muslim who is physically and financially able is commanded to make at least one trip to Mecca in his lifetime.

Pilgrims circling the Ka'bah

The Spread of Islam

By the time of his death in 632, Muhammad had united the Arabian peninsula under Islam. But he died without having appointed a successor. This presented a serious problem for Islam and the Arab people. Who should succeed Muhammad as the rightful leader of Islam and the emerging Arab state? The closest friends of Muhammad chose his first four successors from among themselves. These men, who were called **caliphs** (KAY lifs; "successors"), directed the affairs of Islam, exercising spiritual, political, and military authority. The first caliph was **Abu Bakr** (AH-boo BAH-kur; r. 632–34), early convert of Muhammad and father of one of Muhammad's wives. He and the three caliphs who followed him (Umar r. 634–44, Uthman r. 644–56, and Ali r. 656–61) initiated a policy of military conquest that led to the creation of a vast Arab empire founded upon Islam.

With amazing speed, Arab warriors burst forth from their desert homeland, conquering Palestine, Syria, Egypt, Iraq, and Persia. Many factors contributed to this rapid expansion:

1. The Arabs sought an escape from the poverty of the barren Arabian peninsula. Tremendous wealth could be gained through conquest.

2. The Byzantine and Persian (Sassanid) Empires had become weak by the seventh century. Years of constant warfare had left those two rivals exhausted and their territories vulnerable to attack.

3. Islam united the warring Arab tribes around a common cause. The Arabs viewed each conquest as a **jihad** (jih HAHD; "holy war"), and they defended the honor of Islam with their swords. Their religious zeal was intensified by the promise that a Muslim's death in battle assured him entrance to paradise.

Umayyad Caliphate (661–750)

In 661 a Muslim general proclaimed himself caliph. He moved the political capital of the empire from Medina to Damascus and established the rule of the **Umayyads** (oo MY yadz). The Umayyads created a hereditary dynasty, ending the practice of selecting the caliph from among the close friends and relatives of Muhammad.

The Umayyads continued Arab expansion. Muslim forces pushed eastward into India, laid siege to Constantinople, and advanced across North Africa. In 711 they crossed the Mediterranean and invaded Spain. They pressed on into southern France until they were stopped by the Franks at the **Battle of Tours** (see p. 178). The year of this battle was 732, one hundred years after the death of Muhammad. Although the Muslim advance into Europe was stopped, the Arabs could boast of an empire that stretched from Spain to India.

Abbasid Caliphate (750–ca. 1000)

Discontent over Umayyad rule soon mounted. A growing number of non-Arab Muslims were dissatisfied with being treated as second-class citizens by Arab rulers. In addition, many Arab Muslims did not consider the Umayyads the rightful successors of Muhammad. Abbas, a descendant of Muhammad's uncle, overthrew the Umayyad caliph in 750 and founded the **Abbasid** (AB uh sid)

Sunni vs. Shia Islam

Initially the key difference between Sunni and Shia Islam was their beliefs on who should succeed Muhammad. Sunnis believed that since Muhammad did not appoint a successor, any worthy Muslim could be appointed to lead Islam. As a result, the caliphate was established. The caliph was a political leader who served as judge, administrator, and general, but he was not the Muslims' spiritual leader.

Shia Muslims believed that Muhammad intended Ali, his son-in-law, to be his successor with authority over political and spiritual matters. Shia Muslims called their leader imam rather than caliph.

Today, Sunnis use the term imam to refer only to the leader of worship in a mosque, while Shiites claim an unbroken succession of imams from Ali to the present.

caliphate. Under the Abbasids, Arab supremacy within the Muslim empire gradually declined as many non-Arabs were appointed to high government positions. Also, non-Arabs became increasingly influential in Islamic society.

The Abbasid caliphate marks the peak of the Muslim empire. The Muslims controlled more territory than had the ancient Romans. The new capital, Baghdad, became one of the world's leading commercial centers, rivaling Constantinople. In addition, during the Abbasid rule, Islamic culture flourished.

The Turks and the Crusades

The Arabs had been the primary agents in the early spread of Islam. Their military conquests had created the expansive Muslim empire. But during the Abbasid dynasty, the political unity of the Muslim world began to crumble. Disputes over the succession to the caliphate broke out among rival Muslim factions. Soon independent dynasties appeared, each proclaiming its own caliph. Meanwhile, the Seljuk Turks entered the territory of the weakened Abbasids. These fierce and aggressive warriors accepted Islam and led a new wave of Islamic expansion. The Seljuks not only reunited much of the former Arab empire but also took control of Asia Minor, which had been under Byzantine control. Muslim forces destroyed churches and monasteries and attacked Christian pilgrims as they passed through Asia Minor on their way to visit the Holy Land.

The revived aggressiveness of the Muslim empire and reports of the brutal attacks on Christians caused great alarm among the Christian peoples of western Europe. As a result, the West assembled a series of armies to free the birthplace of Christendom from the Muslim Turks (see p. 217). The Crusades did little to remove the Muslims from Palestine, but they did succeed in weakening the power of the Seljuks. In the thirteenth century the Seljuk Empire came to a violent end when the Mongols swept into the Muslim world. At the beginning of the fourteenth century, the Ottoman

Panorama overlooking the Old City of Jerusalem, Israel, including the Dome of the Rock

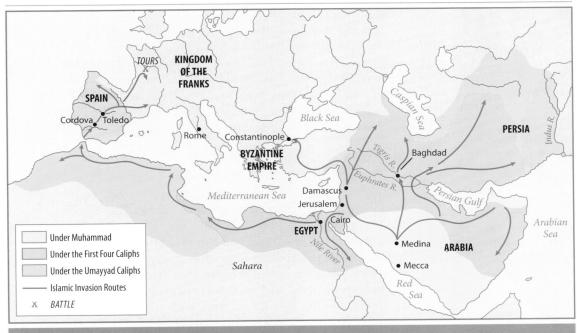

Expansion of Islam

Turks, former subjects of the Seljuks, restored Turkish rule. Once again Muslim forces built a vast empire. The Ottoman Empire stretched across North Africa, over much of the Middle East, and into southeastern Europe. For a time, the Ottoman navy even controlled the Mediterranean Sea and the Black Sea.

Muslim Cultural Contributions

The Arabs built the Muslim empire through conquest. Then they borrowed, embraced, and added to the rich cultural heritage of the peoples with whom they came into contact—the Persians, the Byzantines, the Egyptians, and the Syrians. By blending the many cultural influences within the empire with Islam, the Muslims developed a prosperous civilization.

As previously stated, by the middle of the eighth century, the Muslim empire was no longer predominantly Arab. As a result, Muslim leaders moved the capital from Damascus to Baghdad, and Islam demonstrated a more Persian influence. As the empire continued to expand, so did its trade routes. Now Muslim merchants traveled to China, India, and East Africa, bringing back new products and ideas (such as paper from China and mathematics from India). These products and ideas, as well as the achievements of Muslim culture, later found their way to the West as European merchants opened up trade routes to the Middle East. In addition to trade, these routes also enabled Persian Christians to take the gospel to China.

As the crusaders came to Muslim lands, they were astounded to find silk, muslin (fine cotton), linen, and damask (cloth woven with silver and gold thread). They admired magnificently woven carpets ("Persian" or "Oriental" rugs), finely tooled leather, delicate filigree jewelry (ornamental work done with fine wire), engraved silver and gold, and exquisite knives and swords. Ships that had carried crusading forces to the Holy Land returned to Europe loaded with these treasures in addition to dates, oranges, lemons, apricots, peaches, and melons, all of which were previously unknown in the West during this period.

An important way the Muslims gained knowledge was to translate manuscripts from other lands into Arabic. They translated the writings of Aristotle, Plato, Galen, Hippocrates, Archimedes, Euclid, Ptolemy, and others. They also translated important works from Persia and India. Many of these manuscripts might have been lost had they not been preserved by Muslim scholars, who built great libraries to house these manuscripts and their Arabic translations.

Medicine

In the field of medicine, the Muslims profited from the Greek writings of Galen and Hippocrates. Muslim doctors put into practical use what they learned from the classics and developed new medical procedures. Two of the most famous Muslim physicians were **al-Rāzi** (AL RAY-zee) and **Ibn Sina** (IB-un SEE-nuh; also known as Avicenna). Both men wrote many medical books in which they recorded their practical experience in identifying and treating various diseases. Al-Rāzi is best remembered for his work with smallpox, and Ibn Sina for his work with tuberculosis.

Muslim doctors developed amazing surgical skills. They performed such delicate operations as removing cancer from the body and cataracts from the eye. The Muslims also built hospitals

al-Rāzi (top) *and Ibn Sina, or Avicenna* (bottom)

throughout the empire. Although they did not know about germs, they suspected that dirt led to disease. Therefore, they tried to keep their patients and hospitals as clean as possible. In addition, Muslims had something similar to modern pharmacies that filled prescriptions. Government inspectors supervised these merchants to ensure the purity of the medicines.

Literature

In addition to their religious, scientific, and medical writings, the Muslims produced rich and colorful imagery in both their poetry and their prose. Perhaps the most renowned Muslim poet (also a famed mathematician) was **Omar Khayyam** (OH-mar kie-YAHM). His *Rubaiyat* (roo by YAHT; a poem with verses of four lines) remains quite popular in the West. Like most Muslim poetry it is very picturesque. Better known to both young and old is *The Thousand and One Nights* (popularly known as *The Arabian Nights*), telling the tales of Sinbad the sailor, Aladdin and his wonderful lamp, and other exotic stories.

Mathematics

The Muslims borrowed much of their basic mathematical knowledge from India. The so-called Arabic numerals are of Hindu origin. So are the decimal system and the concept of zero, which the Muslims popularized. The Muslims studied and improved algebra, which came from India, as well as the geometry and trigonometry of the Greeks.

Art and Architecture

Religion plays an important part in Muslim art. Muhammad is said to have forbidden the representation of men and animals in art. He feared that the people might worship statues or paintings of living things. Therefore, Muslim artists developed decorative designs that are more abstract than representational. The most common patterns found in Muslim art are abstract designs of stems and leaves and geometric figures. Muslim artists also excelled in **calligraphy**, the art of beautiful writing. They adorned the walls of buildings with verses from the Qur'an written in beautiful Arabic

Muslim artists creating Qur'an verses using calligraphy

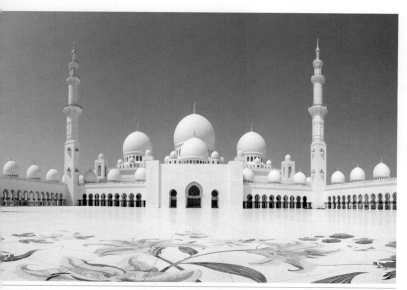

Sheik Zayed mosque in Abu Dhabi

script. One of the most honored forms of Islamic art was manuscript illumination; Muslim artists used miniature paintings and decorative colors and ornamentation to illustrate or "illuminate" their books—especially the Qur'an.

In architecture, however, Muslim art reached its highest achievement. The Muslims drew from the architectural styles of Persia and Byzantium but gradually produced their own unique style. The best examples of Muslim architecture are the **mosques** (MAHSKS; places of Muslim worship). Muhammad did not believe Muslims should build elaborate mosques since these buildings were only places of prayer. Nevertheless, many of his followers spent fortunes on their houses of worship.

The typical features of a mosque are its courtyard, minaret, and dome. In the courtyard is a pool for ceremonial washing before prayer. Either as part of the mosque or adjacent to it is a tall minaret (or tower). From this tower the muezzin (myoo EZ in; "crier") calls the faithful to prayer five times a day. One of the characteristic features of Muslim architecture is the dome, which usually covers the main portion of the mosque. Inside, the walls are generally white and inscribed with quotations from the Qur'an. Some walls, however, are highly decorated with tile and mosaic designs. In one wall of each mosque is a niche that indicates the direction of Mecca, toward which a Muslim prays.

Section Review

1. What name is given to the Arab nomads who roam the desert in search of pastureland and water?

2. Who claimed to be the last and greatest of the prophets of Allah?

3–4. What became the holy city of the Islamic faith? What is the most sacred shrine in that city?

5. What is the name of the holy book of Islam?

6. What is the name for the local Muslim place of worship?

7-9. List three cultural contributions of Islam.

✶ Evaluate the Muslim description of Jesus as an honored prophet and of Muhammad as the ultimate spokesman for divine truth (from John 1:1–3, 18; Heb. 1:1–5).

✶ Contrast the teaching of some Muslim scholars that jihad is merely an inner struggle with the historic practice of jihad.

Making Connections

1–3. How did the reign of Justinian affect the Byzantine Empire? (List three things.)

4–5. How did the Byzantine civilization influence early Russia? (List two things.)

6. How did Islam unite the Arabs?

7–8. At what battle was the European invasion of Islam halted? In what country?

Developing History Skills

1. Islam does honor Jesus as a good man and an important prophet, but it vehemently rejects the Bible's teaching that Jesus is God the Son or that God would allow his prophet to be crucified (Sura 4:157). What contradictions does this lead to within Islamic teaching?

2. What might have happened if the Franks had lost the Battle of Tours?

Thinking Critically

1. Why did a split occur between the Roman Catholic Church and the Eastern Orthodox Church? What could have prevented that split?

2. Based on what you have read in this chapter, do Christians and Muslims worship the same God? Explain your answer.

Living in God's World

1. Imagine that you are an emperor who wishes to create just laws for his people. Write a brief law code that deals with some of the areas found in Justinian's law code: protection of property, slavery and freedom, marriage, wills, and commerce. Remember that the Bible provides standards of justice to which all laws ought to conform.

2. Write a paragraph evaluating the use of icons in Orthodox churches in light of Exodus 20:4 and Deuteronomy 4:12–24.

People, Places, and Things to Know

Byzantine Empire
New Rome
Justinian
Theodora
Nika Revolt
Justinian Code
Hagia Sophia
Eastern Orthodox Church
icons
excommunicated
Basil II
Seljuk Turks
Crusades
Ottoman Turks
mosaic
Slavs
Varangians
Rurik
Rus
Vladimir I
Ishmael
Bedouins
Muhammad
Allah
Islam
Muslims
Ka'bah
Hegira
Qur'an
Five Pillars of Islam
caliphs
Abu Bakr
jihad
Umayyads
Battle of Tours
Abbasid
al-Rāzi
Ibn Sina
Omar Khayyam
calligraphy
mosques

CHAPTER

The Civilizations of Asia

7

Zhouzhuang, ancient town near Shanghai

Big Ideas

1. What were the cultural achievements of Chinese dynasties during this period?

2. How did geography influence East Asian cultures?

3. How were Southeast Asian civilizations influenced by Chinese empires?

4. What characterized the people groups later known as the Mongols?

The historical books of the Bible center on the nations of Israel, Egypt, Babylon, Persia, Greece, and Rome. However, at the same time that these empires flourished, other civilizations developed in Asia. In the centuries following the ministry of the apostles, the gospel spread to these parts of the world. There is little evidence that Christianity thrived initially in these regions. Recently, however, Christianity has begun to grow in parts of Asia more quickly than in many other regions of the globe. Therefore, understanding the history of these cultures is important for Christians.

I. China

In 220, revolts overthrew the last of the Han rulers. For the next four centuries China suffered from internal wars and barbarian invasions. During this period attempts to establish a lasting central government were unsuccessful. However, one dynasty did briefly unite China through marriage alliances and military expansion. The **Sui** (SWAY) dynasty emerged under the leadership of Yang Jian (r. 581–604) and his son, Yangdi (r. 604–618). Yangdi conscripted workers to complete the **Grand Canal**, begun by his father, that connected the Yellow and Yangtze Rivers. The Sui reorganized the Chinese government and used examinations to recruit qualified government workers. Unfortunately, Yangdi's extravagant building projects and repeated attempts to conquer Koguryo (northern Korea) proved unsuccessful, resulting in the deaths of hundreds of thousands of Chinese, and turned the people against this ruling family. Insurrection and rebellion followed. Emperor Yangdi sent general Li Yuan to suppress the rebellions, but the general chose to form his own dynasty when Yangdi was assassinated.

Tang Dynasty

In 618, beginning with Li Yuan, rulers restored unity and prosperity to China. The **Tang dynasty** became a second golden age in Chinese history (the Han dynasty was the first golden age). The people enjoyed a stable government, an expanding empire, and increased trade.

By the early 700s China had become perhaps the wealthiest kingdom in the world at that time. The Silk Road ended at the capital city, Chang'an, and vast wealth poured into this city from all over Eurasia. Chang'an was carefully planned and occupied around thirty square miles, enclosed by a wall. The city was divided into rectangular sections, each one divided by walls, with access through a single gate. The design of the city resembled a single home, and each section was an enlarged version of a room in the home. Absent from the city were any public buildings such as forums or stadiums, which were popular in other cultures. This city was the home of the emperor, and its occupants were his subjects.

Culture

In Tang China many foreign types of music, food, and culture became popular. People from as far away as India, Iran, Syria, and Arabia were welcome in China. Thousands of foreigners lived

Guiding Questions

1. What were the cultural achievements of the Tang and Song dynasties?
2. What role did religion play in these dynasties?
3. What prompted the decline of these dynasties?

Tang Dynasty (ca. 750)

in the capital city alone, including eight thousand Korean students. (Although the Tang could not conquer Korea militarily, they did significantly influence Korean culture through education.) Many of the non-Chinese visitors were merchants who traded their nation's products for Chinese commodities.

The Chinese enjoyed many advances in learning, art, and literature. For example, the Tang era was one of the finest periods of Chinese poetry. The most popular and prolific poet was **Li Po**, who wrote thousands of poems expressing emotional and sentimental themes.

While some Chinese cultures built great stone monuments, the Tang placed great value on the written word. As a result they developed calligraphy and woodblock printing as a means of preserving Chinese writings. They also developed a growing list of substances from which medicines could be produced. These items included certain stones, minerals, metals, plants, animals, and cereal crops.

Woodblock for printing

Chinese medicine ingredients

Religion

Taoism was the official religion of the Tang dynasty, but Buddhism also flourished. During this period of openness to foreign influence, the Tang court also welcomed representatives of the Nestorian Christian Church. Some members of the royal family are believed to have embraced this form of Christianity.

In Tang China, Buddhism and Taoism competed for popular support. The following chart shows some of the ways these two religions vied for the hearts of the Chinese.

Tricolor glazed pottery of the Tang dynasty

Competing Chinese Philosophies	
Buddhism	**Taoism**
Claimed to have loftier principles	Claimed to have better spells to ward off evil or misfortune
Claimed to have better techniques to help deceased loved ones achieve better rebirths	Claimed to have more control over malevolent local gods
Widely circulated Buddhist scripture	Reserved Taoist scripture for religious elites
Accepted local deities	

Early Christianity in China

History is silent regarding the first Christian missionaries to China. However, there is evidence that a form of Christianity surfaced in China by the 600s. The first Tang emperor had recently established himself. He loved books, and he had built a library with thousands of volumes. When Christian missionaries from Persia arrived with a religion that centered on a holy book, he was very interested, and he asked them to translate the Bible into Chinese.

Later explorers discovered Christian writings in China from this time period. These writings teach that Jesus was born of a virgin, that He died on the cross in the place of sinners, that salvation is by faith and not by works, and that a Christian must love his neighbor and submit to the emperor.

By the early 900s the Tang dynasty had ended. The new Chinese government attacked foreign religions and attempted to eliminate Christianity. In the thirteenth century, with the rise of Mongol rule, Christians from Persia were again able to renew missionary work in China.

Nestorian stele containing Christian teaching

Decline

The glory of the Tang lasted about three centuries. As self-seeking rulers began squandering much of the country's wealth, the Tang dynasty lost both prosperity and power. A serious rebellion threatened the stability of China in the middle of the eighth century, and the Tang dynasty never regained full control. During the final fifty years, conflict increased and bandit gangs arose from the growing ranks of the poor and displaced. These gangs formed confederations and developed into a full-scale rebellion. The weakened dynasty collapsed shortly after 900.

Song Dynasty

Fifty years later a new dynasty—the **Song**—restored order under emperor Taizu (r. 960–976). Compared to the other dynasties of China's past, however, the Song dynasty was politically weak. A significant cause for this weakness was the presence of non-Chinese people, known as the Khitan, in northern China. Since neither group could subdue the other, Song leaders chose to accept political weakness in exchange for stability. One of the ways the Song maintained stability was by dividing power between civilian and military forces and placing military power in civilian hands. Using strategies that included rotation of troops and frequent changes of command, Song leaders prevented generals from accumulating enough power to pose a threat to the Song government.

At the same time, China maintained a large army and equipped it with advanced weaponry primarily based on improved use of an earlier invention, gunpowder. Chinese scientists developed a crude flamethrower, a precursor of grenades, cannons, and rockets.

Even with these advances, China was unable to prevent the northern portions of China from falling under barbarian control. As a result, China was divided into the

Emperor Taizu

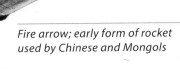

Fire arrow; early form of rocket used by Chinese and Mongols

Northern Song (960–1127) and the Southern Song (1127–1279). Mongolian forces finally overcame Chinese resistance and conquered all of China by 1279.

Despite these problems, the Song dynasty carried on active trade, and the Chinese culture flourished. Population doubled to about 100 million; production of rice, wheat, and other crops increased to support the growing population. During this period the Chinese also excelled in landscape painting, printing, and porcelain.

Northern Song Dynasty (ca. 1050)

Southern Song Dynasty (ca. 1150)

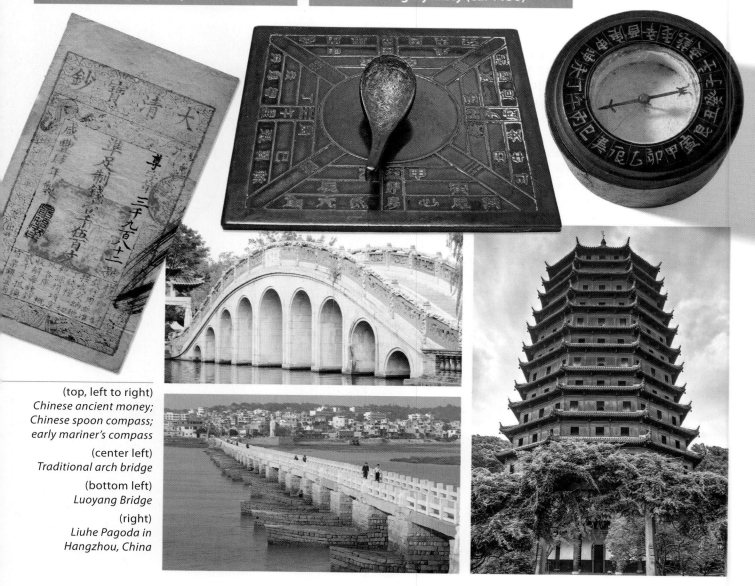

(top, left to right)
*Chinese ancient money;
Chinese spoon compass;
early mariner's compass*

(center left)
Traditional arch bridge

(bottom left)
Luoyang Bridge

(right)
*Liuhe Pagoda in
Hangzhou, China*

Role of Women

Little is known about the status of women in China prior to the Song dynasty. With the advent of printing, however, much literature about women was preserved from this period. This provides insight into the role of women in Song China. For most women who lived in villages, life remained unchanged, as did their opportunities. Women labored long hours rearing children, growing and harvesting crops, and doing the basic tasks required to survive. Among the elite and the fortunate few, women perhaps had new opportunities in business ventures, reading and writing poetry, and exerting influence on Chinese society.

However, the practice of **footbinding** of women is believed to have started during this dynasty. Mothers would break most of the toes and bind the feet of their young daughters to prevent the feet from growing normally. Tiny, narrow feet were considered beautiful and supportive of dainty movements. This practice continued until Christian missionaries and reform-minded Chinese leaders during the nineteenth century called for its end.

Chinese shoe for bound foot

Examination System

Examinations had been used by previous Chinese dynasties to recruit the best candidates for government service. However, during the Song dynasty, the system was reformed and became the primary means of staffing the growing Song bureaucracy. The Song instituted new safeguards to ensure impartiality and make cheating much more difficult. Candidates were required to have a mastery of Chinese literature, and examinations occurred at the local level, continued in the capital city, and culminated in the palace under the watchful eyes of the emperor. Successful candidates often worked until their mid-thirties to receive the coveted *jinshi* ("presented") degree. The emperor awarded key government positions to recipients of this degree, and many of them became leading statesmen during the Song dynasty and beyond, until this system was abolished at the beginning of the twentieth century.

Palace examination of Kaifeng during the Song dynasty

Section Review

1. What massive construction project was completed during the Sui dynasty?

2. During what dynasty did China enjoy an important period of Chinese poetry?

3. In what way did the Tang dynasty demonstrate the importance of the written word?

4. What foreign religion came into prominence during the Tang dynasty?

5. What was the key ingredient in Song military weapons?

6. What led to the decline of the Tang and Song dynasties?

✶ Contrast the key points of Buddhism and Taoism with Nestorian Christianity.

✶ Evaluate the role of women in the Song dynasty.

Guiding Questions

1. How did geography shape the Japanese and Korean cultures?
2. How did Chinese culture influence Japan and Korea?
3. What were Japanese and Korean religious beliefs and practices?

Ancient Japan

Shimogamo (Shinto) Shrine in Kyoto, Japan

II. East Asia

Japan

Over one hundred miles off the coast of Asia—opposite China, Korea, and Siberia (Russia)—is the island nation of Japan. Japan consists of four main islands and hundreds of lesser ones. If placed alongside the Atlantic coast of the United States, Japan would stretch from Maine to Florida. In land area Japan is about the size of the state of California. Most of this land, however, is mountainous; less than 20 percent of it is suitable for farming. Through much of its history, Japan was more geographically remote than China; for centuries it remained isolated from the mainstream of the world's civilizations. It was not until the late nineteenth century that Japan made its presence felt in the arena of world affairs.

Early History

Although Japan is younger than most Asian civilizations, little is known about its early history. Instead of keeping historical records as the Chinese did, the early Japanese passed down myths and legends, many of which played an influential role in shaping Japanese culture. According to Japanese mythology, the god Izanagi and goddess Izanami, while standing on the rainbow bridge of heaven, dipped a jeweled spear into the ocean. Drops falling from the tip of the spear formed the islands of Japan. The god and goddess descended to live on the islands. Their offspring were the Japanese people.

Our first historical glimpse of ancient Japan finds the land divided by a number of warring clans. In early Japanese society, the clan—a group of families claiming descent from a common ancestor—was the basic unit of social, religious, and political organization. Each clan had its own land, its own god, and its own chieftain. The chieftain served as both political and religious leader. By the fifth century AD, one clan had risen in power and prestige over rival clans. Centered on the island of Honshu (the main Japanese island), the **Yamato clan** extended its authority and forged a unified Japanese state.

The leaders of the Yamato clan used Japanese mythology to secure the loyalty of other clan chieftains. According to legend the first emperor of Japan, **Jimmu Tenno** (tenno, "heavenly prince"), was a direct descendant of the sun goddess. The Yamato clan claimed that its rulers were descendants of Jimmu Tenno; they were, therefore, believed to be divine. From this clan arose the imperial family of Japan. Subsequent Japanese emperors all claimed Jimmu Tenno as their divine ancestor. Unlike China, which has had many ruling families or dynasties, Japan has had but one imperial family in its history. For this reason, the imperial family has served as a symbol of unity and continuity in Japanese society.

Supporting the belief in the divine origin of the emperor was Japan's native religion, **Shintoism** ("the way of the gods"). Shintoism was originally a form of nature worship that attributed deity to anything in nature that was awe-inspiring or extraordinary, such as fire, a waterfall, or a high mountain. However, Shintoism also stressed the supremacy of the sun goddess and the divine descent of the emperor. In many respects it became a religion of feeling, inspiring love for one's homeland, loyalty to one's clan, and reverence for one's emperor.

Shintoism

While a thorough examination of Shintoism requires extensive study, there are some basic concepts that will explain this Japanese religion. The goal of Shintoism is to achieve harmony with nature, which is animated by *kami* (gods or spirits).

Shintoism also teaches that there are three kinds of gods (*kami*)—ancestors, powers of nature, and departed rulers/heroes. Its followers believe that humans are basically good because they are potential *kami*. Shintoists also believe that

man's problem is alienation from the balance of nature. They believe this problem can be resolved by performing Shinto rituals. This will bring order and restore harmony with nature.

Influence of China

As previously stated, Japan remained in relative isolation during its early history. In the fifth to the eighth centuries, however, the Chinese invaded the Japanese islands. This was not a military invasion by soldiers but a cultural invasion of ideas, learning, and art. China was experiencing the golden age of the Tang dynasty, and the Japanese welcomed the influx of what they considered the superior Chinese culture.

There were two important vehicles that transmitted Chinese culture to Japan. The first was the Chinese writing system, which the Japanese adopted and later adapted to complement their spoken language. For the first time, the Japanese were able to keep written records and produce their own literature. From an understanding of Chinese characters, they were also able to read and study Chinese literature and learn of the life and thought of the Chinese people.

Secondly, Chinese culture flowed into Japan through Buddhism. The Japanese learned much about the Chinese way of life from Buddhist monks who came from China. For example, the Japanese learned to appreciate Chinese art and architecture from the numerous Buddhist temples built in Japan. Buddhism became firmly established in Japan during the seventh century when **Prince Shotoku** made Buddhism the favored national religion, while retaining Shinto concepts that he found useful. He had many Buddhist temples, hospitals, and schools built. He also sent many young men to China to study Chinese ways: agriculture, science, architecture, law, government, philosophy, and religion. Japan borrowed not only Chinese writing, literature, and religion but also China's system of weights and measurements, medical practices, calendar, styles of furniture and dress, and methods of building roads and bridges.

In the mid-seventh century, the leaders of Japan sought to weaken the influence of the local clan chieftains and extend the power of the emperor to all of Japan. They modeled their government after the strong centralized bureaucracy of the Tang dynasty. This turnabout in the Japanese political and economic structure became known as the "Great Change" or **Taika** (tie EE kuh) **Reform**. Like the Chinese, the Japanese established civil service examinations, granting government posts to men of ability. A new judicial code and tax system came into existence, and at Nara the Japanese established their first permanent capital, which was modeled after the main city of China. (Later the capital was moved to Kyoto, where the Japanese emperors maintained their court until 1868.)

The Taika Reform changed the nature of Japan's political structure from semi-independent clans to a centralized government

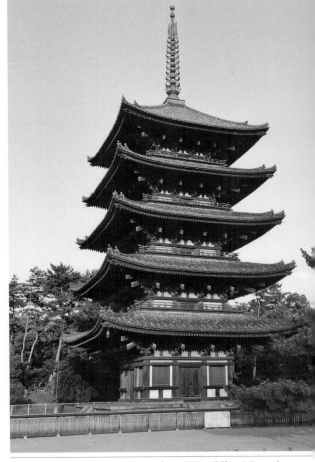

Five-storied pagoda of the Kofuku-ji (Buddhist) Temple in Nara, Japan

headed by the emperor, at least in theory. In reality, government authority rested in the hands of powerful families who controlled the key posts of government. One such family, the **Fujiwara**, had married their daughters to the sons of the imperial family. When a male child was born, they forced the ruling emperor to abdicate. The Fujiwara elders then ruled Japan as regents of the infant emperor.

Rise of the Samurai

The Fujiwaras enjoyed the wealth and extravagance of the imperial city. However, the luxurious life of the royal court brought corruption and bankruptcy to the government. Disorder followed as the central government was no longer able to provide protection for outlying provinces. Many provincial governors began to rely on strong military clans for protection. Soon power struggles erupted among rival military families. In the twelfth century **Yoritomo**, the leader of the Minamoto clan, became the supreme military leader of Japan when he defeated the only remaining powerful clan. The powerless emperor granted Yoritomo the title of **shogun** ("great general"). Yoritomo created a warrior state, ruled by military rather than civilian officials. Although the line of the imperial family continued, powerful shoguns held the real power over the Japanese government from 1192 to 1868.

With the rise of the office of shogun, the warrior class became the leading class in Japanese society. The Japanese warrior was called **samurai** or bushi. Besides mastering the military skills of horsemanship, fencing, archery, and jujitsu (a form of martial arts), the samurai studied history, literature, and the art of writing. He used these skills in providing protection for his master and lord. An unwritten military code known as the **Bushido** (BOOSH ih doh; "the way of the warrior") governed the conduct of the samurai. It demanded that he live by loyalty, honor, duty, justice, courage, sincerity, and politeness. To avoid the disgrace of capture, atone for deeds of misconduct, or resolve questions regarding his loyalty to his master, a warrior could end his life with honor by committing suicide according to the ceremonial practice of hara-kiri.

The Way of the Warrior

A Japanese warrior learned Bushido almost from birth. One authority on Bushido describes the early training this way: "Does a little [baby] cry for any ache? The mother scolds him in this fashion: 'What will you do when your arm is cut off in battle? What [will you do] when you are called upon to commit *hara-kiri?*'"

Section Review

1. How did geography shape Japanese culture?

2. What was the basic social, religious, and political unit in early Japanese society?

3–4. According to legend, who was the first Japanese emperor? What do the Japanese believe about his ancestry?

5. The culture of what foreign civilization had a profound effect on Japan's history?

6. What was the name of the reform movement that sought to weaken the influence of local clan leaders while strengthening the authority of the emperor and the central government?

7–8. What were Japanese warriors called? What was the unwritten military code that governed their conduct?

★ How did Shintoism contribute to the power of the government in Japan?

★ Evaluate the practices of the samurai, such as hara-kiri, from a biblical worldview.

Korea
Geography

The Korean peninsula has many natural borders that aided its isolation, including the Yellow Sea to the west, the East Sea (also known as the Sea of Japan) to the east, the East China Sea to the South, and the Yalu River on the border with China in the north. The southern and western regions are plains, while the eastern and northern regions are mountainous. (About 70 percent of Korea is covered by mountains.) Several Korean rivers have large flood plains that are suitable for growing rice.

Early Civilization

Korea's early history is one of competing clans and frequent struggle for control of the peninsula. There was also an early Chinese influence when the Han dynasty conquered Korea in 108 BC. As Han influence declined, tribes formed federations, from which three rival kingdoms (Koguryŏ, Paekche, and Silla) developed. During the mid-seventh century, the Silla kingdom conquered the other two kingdoms and united the Korean peninsula. Buddhism thrived under this kingdom, and the Silla adopted Chinese characters to develop a Korean written language.

Koryŏ Dynasty

In AD 935 a Korean general who took the name T'aejo (Grand Progenitor) secured the submission of the last Silla king and established the Koryŏ dynasty (an abbreviated form of Koguryŏ). Given the strong Chinese influence, the Koryŏ embraced the Tang system of political administration based on Confucian and Buddhist teachings. They also adopted the civil service examination system to recruit qualified scholars for government service. Ownership of Korean land resided with the government, and the state granted tracts of land for families to use during their lifetime. After death, the land would be returned to the state.

Korea's social structure had six levels during this period, with the royal caste being the highest. The next three levels of society were composed of government officials, and peasants were near the bottom. The lowest class in Korea was the outcasts—composed of criminals, immigrants, and prisoners of war. They labored under the close scrutiny of the state and were restricted to their assigned community. Jobs that were considered to be defiling based on Buddhist teachings, such as killing and processing of animals, were reserved for outcasts. The government controlled manufacturing and used a variety of people to produce or process raw materials including gold, silver, iron, silks, paper, salt, ink, and ceramics.

In addition to influencing Korean laws, Buddhism also played a key role in Korean culture. Having been introduced to this peninsula around 372, Buddhism gained strong support and avoided conflict with Korean shamanism, which had been practiced in Korea since its earliest history. **Shamanism** is based on the belief that a gifted person can interact with spirits. Shamans claimed to have power to cure illness, drive away evil spirits, make predictions, and interpret visions and dreams. Korean Buddhists adopted aspects of shamanism and added them to their teaching. During the Koryŏ dynasty Buddhism enjoyed royal support, and the three Buddhist holidays became celebrated occasions throughout Korea. During

Ancient Korea (5th century)

later Korean dynasties, Buddhists were persecuted and struggled to regain acceptance.

The Koryŏ dynasty endured many external threats and internal struggles. However, by the end of the fourteenth century a group of Korean scholars and government officials overthrew this dynasty and replaced it with a new government.

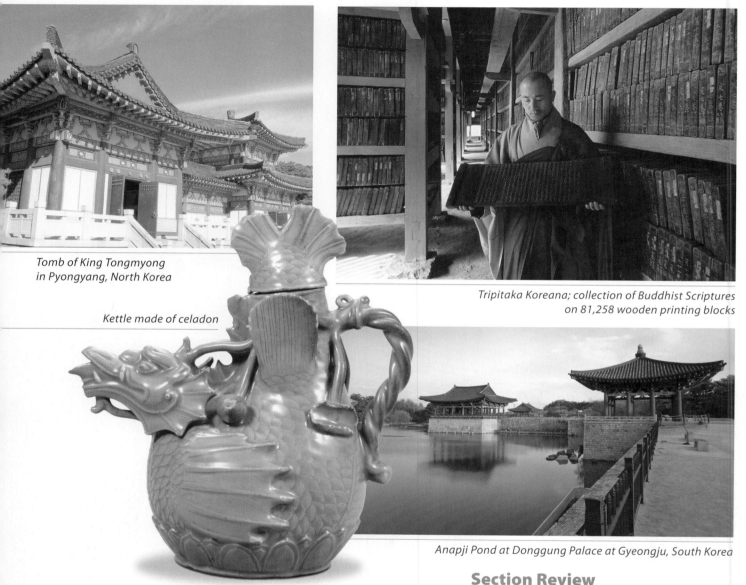

Tomb of King Tongmyong in Pyongyang, North Korea

Kettle made of celadon

Tripitaka Koreana; collection of Buddhist Scriptures on 81,258 wooden printing blocks

Anapji Pond at Donggung Palace at Gyeongju, South Korea

Section Review

1. How did geography influence the development of Korean culture?

2. What Chinese dynasty exerted influence over Korea during this period?

3. Which kingdom first united the Korean peninsula?

4. What was the name of Korea's first dynasty?

5–6. In the Korean social structure, which group was highest? Which group was lowest?

★ Evaluate Korea's social structure.

★ Evaluate the relationship between religion and government in Korea.

III. Southeast Asia

This region lay between India and China and had contact with both cultures. India's interaction with Southeast Asia was limited to trade and the spread of religions, including Hinduism and Buddhism. China maintained extensive trade with this region but also exerted military force during the expansive periods of Chinese dynasties. Many ideas and skills spread to Southeast Asia from China, including a written language, metallurgy, and ceramic production.

Vietnam

Geography

Vietnam is located on the eastern Indochina Peninsula and has a coastline that stretches over 2,100 miles. At some points Vietnam narrows to 31 miles wide; the widest point spreads to 370 miles in the north. Most of the land is hilly and densely forested, with level land composing around 20 percent, mountains 40 percent, and tropical forests covering 40 percent.

The north region has a humid, subtropical climate with highlands and the Red River delta. Central Vietnam has a monsoon climate and large annual rainfall. The southern region of Vietnam has a tropical savanna climate with coastal lowlands, mountains, and large forests. The geography and climates contributed to a variety of cultural developments.

(top) *Women working in a rice field*

(middle) *Karst landscape in Halong Bay*

(bottom) *Vietnamese farmers rowing across a flooded rice field in Mekong delta, Vietnam*

(background) *Terraced rice field landscape of Mu Cang Chai in Yenbai, Northern Vietnam*

Southeast Asia (ca. 1200)

Early Civilization

The Han Dynasty conquered northern Vietnam around 100 BC and controlled this region until the early tenth century. With the collapse of the Tang dynasty, the Vietnamese broke from Chinese domination and formed the kingdom of **Dai Viet**. Buddhism flourished and became the state religion.

A separate kingdom, **Champa**, thrived in central and southern Vietnam during this period. Between the tenth and fourteenth centuries, forces from Dai Viet slowly expanded southward and took control of central Vietnam. By the end of the fifteenth century, the kingdom of Champa had been overrun, and the Dai Vet gained control of the territory that constitutes modern Vietnam.

Angkor (Cambodia)
Geography

Located west of Vietnam is the country of Cambodia, known in the ancient world as Angkor. This region is composed of low-lying plains surrounded by uplands and small mountains. The Mekong River flows through this land. This region also has a massive lake called Tonle Sap (literally "large river") that measures about 1,000

Satellite image of Tonle Sap

Stilt houses on a river near Siem Reap, Cambodia

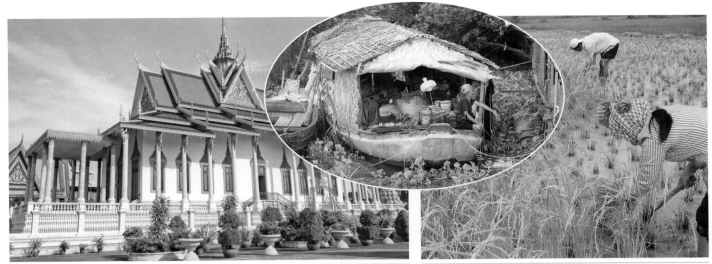

(left) *Ancient Silver Pagoda in Phnom Penh, Cambodia*
(middle) *Woman sitting in a houseboat*
(right) *Cambodian farmers cutting rice*

square miles during the dry season and expands to 9,500 square miles during the rainy seaon. Early Cambodian civilizations formed along these bodies of water and learned to adapt to the drastic seasonal changes.

Early Civilization

Cambodia's long history can be traced back to 1000 BC. Beginning in the third century AD, India and China influenced this region. The **Khmer** (kuh MEHR) empire developed some time between the ninth and the thirteenth centuries. The city of Angkor became Khmer's center of power. Angkor Wat was the largest of one thousand Buddhist temples built in Cambodia.

A series of wars with Cambodia's neighbors resulted in the decline of the Khmer empire. The Thai and Vietnamese gained control of this region in the fifteenth century and dominated it for the next four hundred years.

Angkor Wat; aerial view

Find It!

**13.413° N
103.867° E**

Angkor Wat

Section Review

1. Which culture affected Vietnam more, India or China?

2–3. What two kingdoms developed on the eastern Indochina Peninsula?

4. What religion became dominant in this region?

5. What huge temple was built in the Khmer Empire's capital city?

★ How would the extensive expansion and contraction of bodies of water like the Tonle Sap affect the lives of the Cambodian people?

Guiding Questions

1. How did geography shape the development of Mongol culture?
2. How did the Mongols adapt to their environment?

IV. Mongolia

Geography and Environment

This high-altitude region averages nearly 5,200 feet above sea level. It is landlocked and bounded by Russia, China, and the Gobi Desert. The land is covered in vast plains and ringed with mountains. The humans and animals who thrive in this region have historically been strong, self-sufficient, and resourceful. Frequent migration became necessary in order to sustain the herds of sheep, camels, horses, and other animals. Mongolia is a land of long, cold winters with a very short growing season for grasses and wildflowers. Rainfall is limited in Mongolia and typically varies between 4 and 14 inches per year. Sources of water include over one thousand

Mongolia

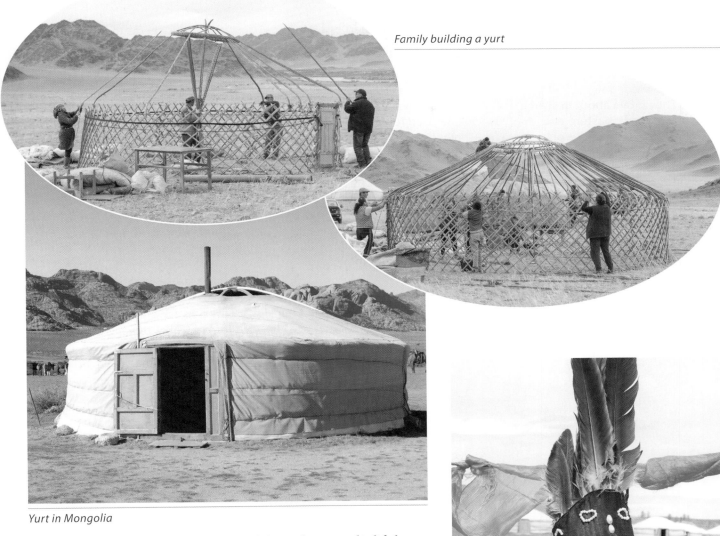

Family building a yurt

Yurt in Mongolia

rivers and around four thousand small lakes. The nomadic life became virtually the only way to survive in this difficult region.

Religion

The tribes who inhabited this harsh region typically practiced shamanism. Shamans decided when a tribe should go to battle or break camp and move to their next grazing area. They were consulted on virtually every important decision that affected the people of that tribe.

Superstitions also abounded, and the people used charms and magic to ensure good fortune and ward off evil spirits. They placed great importance on sacred animals, such as a feather from a peacock, the flight of a crow, or the good luck that results from owning geese.

Early Civilization

Since ancient days, central Asia has been the homeland of many nomadic peoples. Vast, grassy plains called steppes stretch from western China to eastern Europe. This pastureland was a highway along which roving tribes sought food for their flocks and herds.

Mongolian Shaman

Asian Nomads from a Chinese Perspective

Chinese historian Sima Qian recorded the following observations about the Xiongnu (Huns). This would also reflect Chinese thinking about the Mongols.

They move about in search of water and pasture and have no walled cities or fixed dwellings, nor do they engage in any kind of agriculture. Their lands, however, are divided into regions under the control of various leaders. They have no writing, and even promises and agreements are only verbal.

The little boys start out by learning to ride sheep and shoot birds and rats with a bow and arrow, and when they get a little older they shoot foxes and hares, which are used for food. Thus all the young men are able to use a bow and act as armed cavalry in time of war. It is their custom to herd their flocks in times of peace and make their living by hunting, but in periods of crisis they take up arms and go off on plundering and marauding expedi-

tions. This seems to be their inborn nature. For long-range weapons they use bows and arrows, and swords and spears at close range. If the battle is going well for them they will advance, but if not, they will retreat, for they do not consider it a disgrace to run away. Their only concern is self-advantage, and they know nothing of propriety or righteousness.

Burton Watson, Records of the Grand Historian: Han Dynasty, II, 129.

Illustration of Mongol soldiers on horseback shooting arrows

These tribes included the Huns, Turks, Avars, and Mongols. Over time several of these groups vied for control of this region (later called Mongolia). During the Han dynasty, the Huns dominated this area and posed a serious threat to northern China. During the Tang dynasty, Turks tried to invade China. Other tribes integrated with the Chinese and adopted their ways.

These central Asian tribes made effective use of a device developed by the Chinese—the stirrup. This addition to a saddle enabled the rider to maintain stability when riding a horse, and the Asian warriors became highly skilled at firing arrows with lethal accuracy while riding a horse at a full gallop. The Mongols used the short, sturdy horses native to this region for hunting, herding, and war. Each Mongol warrior had several horses and switched mounts several times a day on a long march. The skills developed by the Mongols made them a formidable force, and the birth of a great leader (Genghis Khan) in the twelveth century would transform the potential of these Asian tribes into an unstoppable empire.

Section Review

1. What name is given to the vast, grassy plains that stretch from western China to eastern Europe?

2. How would you describe the geography and environment of this region?

3–5. Name three groups that lived in Mongolia.

6. What Chinese invention was very useful to Mongol warriors?

☆ Why do you think shamanism held such power over the tribes in Mongolia?

☆ Discuss the reasons frequent fighting occurred in Central Asia.

Making Connections

1–3. List three cultural achievements of the Tang dynasty.

4. What painful cultural practice was believed to have been started during the Song dynasty?

5–6. How important was the concept of loyalty to the samurai warrior? How might he resolve any question of his loyalty?

7–10. List four ways that Southeast Asian civilizations were influenced by Chinese empires.

11. What countries discussed in this chapter are considered part of Southeast Asia?

12. What animal was most important for the Mongols for hunting, herding, and war?

Developing History Skills

1. Contrast the levels of trade in Asian countries with western Europe during this period. (You may need to consult Chapters 9 and 10 for more information about western Europe.)

2. What period of Japanese history do historians know the least about? What information would historians find useful to know?

Thinking Critically

1. Evaluate Japanese culture and religion from Scripture.

2. Evaluate justice, power, and citizenship in the Japanese and Korean cultures.

Living in God's World

1. If you were a missionary to China in the seventh century, what obstacles would you have had to overcome? Outline a plan for evangelism that addresses these obstacles.

2. Explain in a brief paragraph the difference between a biblical worldview and the worldview encapsulated in Japanese myths as described in the following quotation: "But what is quite distinctive about the Japanese myths is an avoidance of moral judgment as to good and evil. Certain acts bring censure and punishment, but no moral sermonizing. Behavior is accepted or rejected depending on the situation, not according to any obvious set of universal principles. This is exactly what many commentators remark upon in present-day Japanese behavior. The roots of such behavior clearly run deep."

Kenneth Henshaw, A History of Japan: From Stone Age to Superpower, 7.

People, Places, and Things to Know
Sui (dynasty)
Grand Canal
Tang dynasty
Li Po
Song (dynasty)
footbinding
Yamato clan
Jimmu Tenno
Shintoism
Prince Shotoku
Taika Reform
Fujiwara
Yoritomo
shogun
samurai
Bushido
Shamanism
Dai Viet
Champa
Khmer

CHAPTER

Civilizations of the Americas

8

I. North American Civilizations

II. Middle American Civilizations

III. South American Civilizations

Cliff Palace at Mesa Verde in Colorado

Big Ideas

1. How did American civilizations develop?

2. How did the American civilizations differ from one another?

3. What characterized the religions of the early American civilizations?

While civilizations were developing in Europe, Asia, India, and Africa, people were migrating to what is now known as the Americas and establishing civilizations with varying degrees of sophistication. Just as Africa experienced the Bantu migration, so families migrated to North America and expanded throughout what we know as North, Middle or Meso, and South America over many generations. How they arrived in North America is still open for discussion, but our knowledge of these civilizations once they settled on this continent continues to expand as archaeologists and scientists make new discoveries about these fascinating people.

I. North American Civilizations

Unanswered Questions

Where did the original inhabitants of North America come from, and by what route did they migrate? These questions have yet to be definitively answered, and opinions vary widely. A popular theory is that they came from Asia via the Bering Strait, crossing the ice or a land bridge (called **Beringia**). Those who believe that human life began in Africa might suggest a crossing of the Atlantic Ocean as the most viable avenue of travel. Others believe people from Europe came by sea and inhabited this land thousands of years before Columbus's famous journey. Still others support multiple origins and routes whereby several people groups migrated to the Americas over many centuries.

Another question historians must consider is how to classify the Indian groups. Linguists have attempted to classify North American Indians into **tribes** (several families sharing common customs) and **language families** (groups of Indian languages that are believed to have had a single ancestral language). Others classify Indian groups based on **culture areas**, in which several tribes lived near each other and shared similar customs, means of livelihood, and level of civilization.

Similarities

Many of the Indian tribes lived in villages, although these varied in size and complexity. Families that included several generations tended to live together and provided an extended support system to face the challenges of neighboring tribes or changing conditions.

The Indians developed very effective hunting methods, using the bow and arrow, thrusting lance, spear, and drives to trap and kill game. They drove game into confined areas using fire (on the prairies, plains, and desert) or noise produced by members of the tribe. In open areas they chased animals into nets or across concealed pits. They also trapped game using snares, traps, and nooses.

Guiding Questions

1. What role did geography play in the development of early North American civilizations?

2. What were some of the religious beliefs of early North American civilizations?

3. How did early North American civilizations develop and expand?

Beringia

Prickly pear cactus and fruit

Agave

Amaranthus

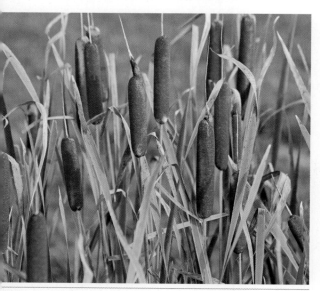

Cattails

They became skilled farmers and grew maize (corn), beans, pumpkins, and squashes. The Indians tended to farm in wooded areas rather than open meadows because of the limitations of their wooden tools and because the soil tended to be softer in the woods than in open areas. They cleared areas of forests by killing trees (by removing a ring of bark around a tree) and by burning vegetation. In certain regions they also harvested food from cacti and a variety of other plants, including agave, amaranthus, and cattails.

The Indians prepared food by different means depending on available resources. When Indians had the materials to make a pot that could be set over a fire, the food was cooked in a heated pot. When a basket or other utensil that could not withstand fire was the only option, stone boiling was used (where heated stones were placed in a container to bring the liquid to a boil).

The American Indians possessed deep faith in the supernatural and shared several common beliefs about religion and life in general. All natural objects—from animals to rocks and trees—had their own spirits. Yet the Indians believed in one "Great Spirit." They placed much emphasis on dreams and visions and actively sought them. They also had shamans, or medicine men (or women), who they believed had supernatural powers over sickness, enemies, and harvests. They also shared a belief in an afterlife; death was not an end but only one step in a long journey. Many tribes passed creation, flood, and other stories orally to the next generation. These accounts attempted to answer fundamental questions about the origins of mankind and of their ancestors in particular.

Differences

The various American Indian groups spoke different languages. Historians estimate that as many as 2,200 different languages were being spoken by the time Europeans first encountered the Indian groups. Communication between neighboring tribes was probably made possible by a common sign language.

Various Indian groups lived in different types of houses, depending on their geographic environment. Some lived in rectangular longhouses. Some lived in tepees. Others lived in domed, wood-framed homes covered with bark or fur. Still others lived in baked clay (adobe) buildings. And still others lived in caves in the sides of cliffs.

Although warfare was a way of life for some of the tribes, many tribes were peaceful and fought only to protect their territory or retaliate for attacks from others. Indian warfare was often sporadic and involved swift raids, with few protracted battles. One tribe in the Southwest was called the **Hopi** (abbreviated from *Hopituh Shi-nu-mu*, which means "the peaceful people") because of its peaceful culture. More warlike tribes included the Iroquois, the Apache, and the Comanche.

West

Indians of the West Coast are remembered for their totem poles, which they carved out of tree trunks to depict their local gods. Several tribes in this area had access to the Pacific Ocean or rivers and thrived by hunting whales or salmon, which were abundant in this region. Forested lands provided rich soil for raising various crops commonly grown by American Indians.

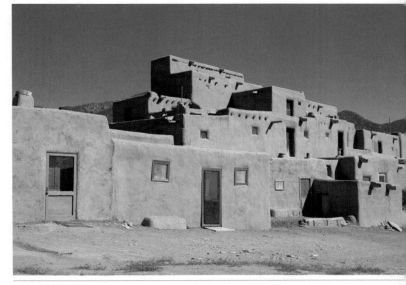
Taos Pueblo in New Mexico

The Indians of the Southwest built villages, called *pueblos* ("towns"), out of adobe, or sun-dried brick. The **Pueblo Indians** often lived in small villages consisting of two or three family groups or clans. Some of the Pueblo Indians lived in caves along the rims or under ledges of canyons and became known as cliff dwellers. Some of the tribes among the Pueblos were the Zuni, the Hopi, the Ute, the Paiute, the Navajo, the Apache, and the Havasupai ("blue-green water people"), who lived in the bottom of the Grand Canyon.

The pueblos were independent of each other, and each town was ruled by a council of elected elders. The villages probably were not able to develop into cities because of the scarcity of food in this arid region. When a young man married, he moved into his wife's clan and built a new room onto or above the existing adobe house. One result of this tradition was the decline of families with sons and the expansion of families with daughters.

Navajo hogan

Pueblo Indians were farmers. They also made baskets and pottery. They tended to be a stationary people but were sometimes forced to move because their water source became insufficient or because of threats by other tribes. Historians believe the Pueblos thrived until around AD 1000. By the end of the thirteenth century, water shortages and raids by other Indian tribes led to the decline of the Pueblo civilization.

Plains

The Plains Indians were skilled at subsisting in a region that offered minimal resources and required frequent relocation in order to survive. Transportation prior to the arrival of horses (brought

Herd of bison, Yellowstone

Sioux tepees

Serpent Mound in Peebles, Ohio

by the Spanish) was on foot, and dogs were often used as pack animals. The Indians who roamed these grasslands combined great bison-hunting skills with a knowledge of edible plants and roots to provide food for their families. Bison were tracked and approached by Indians hiding under animal skins to get within killing range with arrows or lances. Another technique was to drive the bison over a cliff or chase them into a canyon where they could be killed. The Indians utilized every part of the bison, and successful hunters were expected to share with everyone in the tribe. Meat was cut into strips and preserved by being dried in the sun. The bison's hide provided clothing and shelter, as Plains Indians lived in tepees made from poles up to eighteen feet long and covered with bison skins.

Mound Builders

Three successive cultures developed in what is now called the Midwest. The civilizations developed along the Ohio River Valley and later spread eastward to the Chesapeake Bay area, New York, and New England. These people lived in fixed agricultural settlements where they grew squash, gourds, and sunflowers. They even grew tobacco. They produced bountiful harvests that supported significant population growth.

These Indians were noted for the hundreds of large burial mounds and effigy mounds they built; as a result, they were called the **Mound Builders**. The Indians buried their dead with elaborate detail reminiscent of the tombs of Egyptian pharaohs. The burial mounds measured up to thirty feet in height and two hundred feet in circumference. One of the most famous effigy mounds is the **Great Serpent Mound** in southern Ohio. It portrays a slithering snake more than 1,300 feet long. Although many items were buried in the mounds, most of them rotted in the damp soil. Only objects made of clay, stone, or metal (such as copper) have survived.

The Mound Builders developed an extensive, nearly continental trading network. They traded for copper from Indians in the Great Lakes area, seashells and shark teeth from Indians along the Atlantic and Gulf coasts, quartz and grizzly bear teeth from the Rocky Mountains, and freshwater pearls from surrounding rivers.

Adena (ca. 1000–200 BC)

While some believe that **Adena** mounds (named after a large mound on a nineteenth-century estate in Ohio called "Adena") may have numbered in the thousands, only around two hundred can still be located. The Adena people

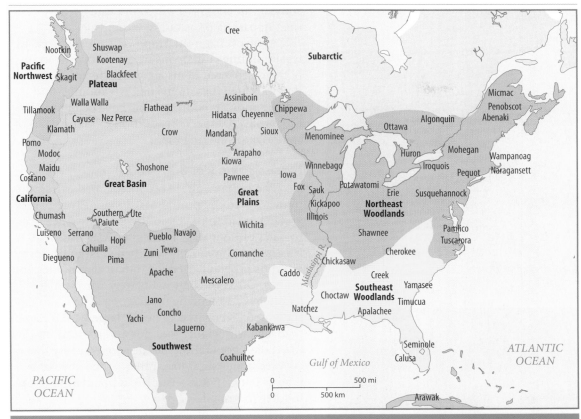

North American Indian Culture Groups Before European Contact

lived in large dome-shaped structures up to forty-five feet in circumference. The roof was supported by wood posts that were covered with bark or skins. Bark or woven material may have been used to form the walls.

Archaeologists have discovered artifacts that have representations of humans being transformed into animals and then back into human form. These were possibly used by shamans who would have claimed to have such magical powers. Small stone tablets about four inches by four inches were found that might have been used to stamp designs on cloth or animal hides or on the Indians themselves. Pottery found in these mounds was tempered with grit or small pieces of limestone and was often plain.

Hopewell (ca. 200 BC–AD 500)

This Indian culture developed along rivers in the northeastern and midwestern regions of the country. Historians assigned the name **Hopewell** based on an Ohio family that owned land containing a mound group in Ross County, Ohio, in the 1890s, centuries after the demise of the Indian tribes. Rather than being a single culture or society, the Hopewell tradition was followed by a wide and dispersed group of related Indian populations. It is believed that a network of trade routes united these Indian tribes.

The purpose of the mounds constructed by this culture is difficult to ascertain. The huge works made of soil took the form of geometric shapes or animals and may have had some religious significance. Some speculate that the geometric mounds were used to observe lunar activity or to mark seasonal changes such as the summer solstice. Archaeologists have also found human remains at

Artist's conception of a mound village

Monks Mound

Iroquois longhouse

some of the mounds, which indicate they were, at least in part, used as burial mounds.

Artifacts from the Hopewell culture reveal a wealth of fine craftsmanship and artwork. Many of the discovered items appear to be linked to religious activities. Items made from mica and copper and carved from bone have been found in the burial chambers, in addition to many types of statues and smoking pipes.

Mississippian (ca. 800–1600)

The Indian culture broadly named **Mississippian** covered the central Mississippi River Valley and extended to the Ohio River Valley and south to parts of Kentucky, Tennessee, Alabama, and Mississippi. Indian sites contained large platform mounds probably used for Indian ceremonies and homes. Often these mounds were surrounded by ditches and fencing for security. The Cahokia settlement is believed to be the largest Mississippian site, with eighty mounds and indications that the Indian population had developed a city that covered about six square miles. Some have estimated that Cahokia sustained a population of up to forty thousand.

Eastern Woodlands

Another diverse American Indian civilization developed in the Southeast and along the Atlantic coast into the Northeast. These tribes were called the **Eastern Woodlands Indians**. The civilization may have developed around AD 700 and spread throughout the Southeast, especially after 1200. They tended to settle along the rich bottomlands of the Mississippi, Ohio, and Tennessee Rivers and developed tight-knit agricultural communities. The women grew crops while the men hunted and served as warriors when necessary. These Indians had a matriarchal society, meaning that the women held an unusual degree of power in the social structure and political decision-making. They were politically engaged and developed a high level of civilization among the Indian tribes.

Section Review

1. What is the name of the possible land bridge that many believe was the migration route to America?

2. Whom did the Indians look to as religious leaders?

3–4. List the names of two Native American groups.

5. What type of burial did many Indians along the Ohio River Valley use?

★ Why do you think many tribes passed down creation and flood stories?

★ How did geography influence the North American Indians?

II. Middle American Civilizations

Historians estimate that Indians in this region spoke about 350 different languages. There may well have been as many cultures. Rather than uniformity, great diversity was more likely the norm in early Central America.

Mayas

Geography

Three environmental zones make up this region. The highlands divide the narrow Pacific coastal plain from the extensive plain that covers the Yucatán Peninsula. The terrain varies from rugged mountains to level plains, and the climate varies from desert to dense forests. Indian farmers grew plentiful harvests in regions with rich volcanic or alluvial soil, whereas areas with poor soil needed greater attention in order to produce crops.

History

Preclassic Period (ca. 2000 BC–AD 250)

According to some historians the first signs of civilization in Mesoamerica appeared as early as 2600 BC. From the limited information gleaned from artifacts, it appears that the people grew crops of maize, beans, squash, and chili peppers. They established communities and manufactured items including pottery and baked clay figures. Gradually the villages expanded into cities, and signs of developing civilization appeared. The oldest known Mayan **stele** (an upright stone slab or column carved with inscriptions) was created around 400 BC. These complex columns continued to be carved for the next several centuries, containing dates and images of important rulers. The Aztecs, another Mesoamerican civilization, also developed a writing system based on a form of hieroglyphics that is often found on surviving steles.

Classic Period (ca. 250–900)

This period of Mayan history was characterized by large, independent city-states. Each city-state was ruled by a god-king. Many had large pyramids, temples, and palaces. Many of these cities formed complex alliances in an effort to protect against other

Guiding Questions

1. How did the Middle American civilizations develop and expand?
2. Why did the Mayan civilization experience decline?
3. What were the religious beliefs of the Middle American civilizations?

Mayan Civilization

Teotihuacan influenced later Mayan and Aztec civilizations.

Chichén Itzá Pyramid
(insets) *The Great Ball Court of Chichén Itzá and a close-up view of a ring in the ball court*

Mayan stele

Calakmul Mayan temple engulfed by the jungle

city-states. Cities that endeavored to become the center of power and influence included **Tikal** (tee KAHL) and **Chichén Itzá** (chee-CHEHN ee-TSAH). Despite many conflicts, no city-state or alliance of city-states was able to maintain control over the others for a long period.

During the ninth century the political system in many of these city-states appears to have collapsed for some unknown reason. Cities were abandoned, dynasties collapsed, and power shifted from the southern lowlands to the northern Yucatán Peninsula. Despite this political collapse, trade appears to have flourished, and life for the average Mayan Indian continued as before. When the Spanish arrived centuries later, they marveled at the wealth and level of trade among the Mayan Indians.

Postclassic Period (ca. 950–1539)

This was a period of decline for the Mayan civilization. Historians theorize that the Mayan population migrated to areas where water was abundant and new cities were built for ease of defense rather than easy access. The role of the Mayan leader as a ritual authority rather than an effective leader proved to be a serious weakness of the Mayan system of government. This made the Mayan rulers ill equipped to adapt to changing conditions. As a result, prolonged warfare, disease, and natural disasters continued to weaken the Mayan civilization.

Religion and Culture

The Mayas' culture centered on their religious beliefs. They believed there were gods of corn, death, rain, and war. They developed a precise calendar, known as the **Long Count** calendar. They did this in part because they believed each day was a living god and the god's actions could be predicted by a system of calendars.

They constructed massive stone temples for worship and aligned them based on solar or lunar events. Even the directions had religious significance for the Mayas. They considered the center to be a position that represented the significance of the **ceiba tree**, which the Mayas believed supported the sky. Since the sun appeared in the East each morning, this direction symbolized rebirth. The West represented death, as the sun was believed to have fallen into the Mayan underworld, *Xibalba* (si BAL ba), each evening. North was considered straight up, like the apex of the sun at noon. The Mayas believed that South was straight down and pointed to the underworld. In *Xibalba* the dead sun fought the gods of the underworld in order to attain rebirth the next morning. The Mayas also believed that caves were entrances to this underworld.

Two groups of Mayas directed worship of the gods: shamans and priests. Mayas believed these religious leaders had the ability to communicate with the gods and provide vital information about the

Ceiba pentandra tree with a close-up of the thorny trunk of a young ceiba tree; sacred tree of the Mayas

Six sheets of the Mayan codex

0	**1**	**2**	**3**	**4**
5	**6**	**7**	**8**	**9**
10	**11**	**12**	**13**	**14**
15	**16**	**17**	**18**	**19**

Mayan Counting System

world. Shamans were typically recruited from the common people, while priests tended to be selected from the elite class.

Mayan worship included prayers and offerings of food, flowers, incense, human blood (from cutting or piercing), and even human sacrifice (usually prisoners of war). The offering of human sacrifice was not a daily event, but Mayan priests performed this gruesome task for special events, such as the inauguration of a new ruler or the dedication of a new temple or ball court. The most prized human sacrifice was another king who had been captured in war.

Aztecs
Geography

Mesoamerica is a mountainous area with steep wooded slopes. Early human habitation was concentrated on large highland valleys composed of large, internally-drained basins ringed by volcanic mountains. The valleys were full of rich soil and shallow, swampy, saline lakes. During Aztec rule, freshwater swamps were turned into raised fields that enabled the growing of crops to support the large Aztec population.

Precursors

Several civilizations inhabited Mesoamerica prior to the arrival of the Aztec people. While little is known of them, stone construction and early forms of counting seem to have been present when the Aztec people migrated to this area.

Olmecs

This early civilization was located in present-day Guatemala and Mexico. There are many unknowns due to various interpretations of the artifacts. Art from this period includes colossal heads, jade face masks, and statues. The ruins of altars and other stone carvings suggest an early form of writing (glyphs) and possible development

Olmec pyramid

of the long method of counting used by the Mayas. This culture is thought to have emerged from previous cultures in this region around 1500 BC and prospered until around 400 BC. A pyramid in La Venta, Tabasco (Mexico), rises about 112 feet above the flat terrain, and there archaeologists have discovered about a thousand tons of smooth serpentine stone, large mosaic pavements, nearly fifty polished jade tools, and other items believed to have been given as offerings.

Serpentine stone

Zapotecs

This civilization lived in the valley of Oaxaca (wuh HAH kuh; present-day Mexico). Archaeological finds include buildings, ball courts, tombs, and evidence of polytheistic religious practices. The Zapotecs appear to have developed as early as the sixth century BC and survived in some form as late as the sixteenth century AD, although their influence may have diminished as early as AD 200.

Civilization

The Aztecs settled north of the Mayan civilization in the Valley of Mexico around 1200. Initially insignificant and poor, the Aztecs demonstrated ambition and persistence. About 1345 the Aztecs built the city of **Tenochtitlán** (tay NAWCH tee TLAHN; present-day Mexico City) on an island in the middle of a lake in central Mexico. This walled city, connected to the mainland by several long bridges and causeways, had a huge pyramid temple as well as several other beautiful temples and palaces. Describing the network of canals throughout the city, a visitor from Europe called Tenochtitlán "the Venice of the New World."

Around 1428 the Aztecs allied with the city-states of Texcoco and Tlacopan to form the **Triple Alliance**; by the 1500s this alliance had conquered a region encompassing eighty thousand square miles. The Aztecs and their allies demanded tribute in the form of

---

Quetzalcoatl

Around 1000, a leader of a Mesoamerican tribe called the Toltecs encouraged his people to worship a god named **Quetzalcoatl** (keht SAHL koh AHT uhl; "feathered serpent"). However, the Toltecs rejected this new god and exiled their ruler. He then spread the myth of this god to other people in the Valley of Mexico. While there are many versions of this myth, according to one account, Quetzalcoatl had been exiled and traveled east, crossing the sea. His worshipers believed he would return one day and usher in a new day of light and peace.

Pyramid of the Sun in Teotihuacan (ca. AD 100)

Mesoamerica

Obsidian

gold, maize, cacao beans, cotton, and jade. Failure to pay tribute resulted in brutal destruction of the offending village.

The social structure of the Aztec culture resembled a pyramid, with the emperor at the top of the Aztec class system. Government officials, priests, and military leaders formed the nobility in the Aztec empire. The common people and slaves formed the base of this social pyramid.

Trade in the Aztec empire was extensive and based on a barter system rather than on money. Items traded included beans, corn, pears, squash, tobacco, cotton, tomatoes, peppers, turkeys, feathers, and blankets. Obsidian, a form of volcanic glass, was considered an especially valuable trade item. It could be fashioned into plates and a variety of tools, including sharp knives and arrowheads. Obsidian knives were used in the human sacrifices that frequently occurred in the Aztec religion.

The Aztecs probably borrowed much from other Mesoamerican cultures. This borrowing would include a form of writing that included complex pictures and glyphs. The Aztec calendars were also very similar to those developed by the Mayas. Aztec scholars monitored the movement of planets and stars. They carefully recorded these movements and even built some temples to align with

Aztec pictographs

the sun and the spring equinox (March 21). They used astronomical information to predict solar and lunar eclipses. Perhaps adding to what they had learned from other cultures, the Aztecs developed hundreds of medicinal herbs, set broken bones, covered injured limbs with plaster casts, and treated wounds with ointments, herbs, and bandages.

The Aztecs were fighters, and they required every able-bodied Aztec man to serve in the army. With an aggressive and well-trained force, they conquered more than five million people and collected tribute from them all. The army often took prisoners of war to sacrifice to their gods. Sometimes Aztec priests even ate the flesh of their human sacrifices. The Aztecs proved to be better fighters than governors, however, and failed to develop a lasting or cohesive empire. Many conquered Mesoamerican cultures resented the oppressive rule of the Aztec rulers.

According to various Aztec myths, the gods sacrificed themselves to create the world and the sun, and they used their own blood to create mankind. Humans therefore owed the gods a great debt that could only be repaid by frequent offerings of blood through autosacrifice (giving some of one's own blood) or human sacrifice. The Aztecs built temples in Tenochtitlán in which they worshiped many gods. However, the sun god appeared to gain preeminence, and Aztec priests regularly sacrificed human victims to ensure that the sun would rise each day. Thousands of slaves, criminals, and war captives perished at the top of the great temple pyramid as their hearts were cut out with obsidian knives.

Section Review

1. During which period of Mayan history were city-states prominent?

2. What Mesoamerican culture developed a precise calendar?

3–5. What were the three major components of Mayan worship?

6. Name the god that some Aztecs worshiped thinking he would return someday.

7. What Aztec city was named "the Venice of the New World" by a European visitor?

★ Why did the Mayan civilization decline?

★ Evaluate the Aztec religion.

III. South American Civilizations

As many as one thousand languages may have been spoken in South America, a vast region composed of diverse climates and varying natural resources. Yet great civilizations developed that overcame natural barriers in the quest to build empires.

Geography

The western border of South America is composed of steep mountains, valleys at various altitudes, and desert. While the area may seem inhospitable, it became the home of several early civilizations that built villages in this region. Indians developed terraced farming methods to grow the needed crops and thrive in this challenging climate.

Guiding Questions

1. How did the Incan civilization develop and expand?

2. What were some unique elements of Incan culture?

3. What were the religious beliefs of the Incan civilization?

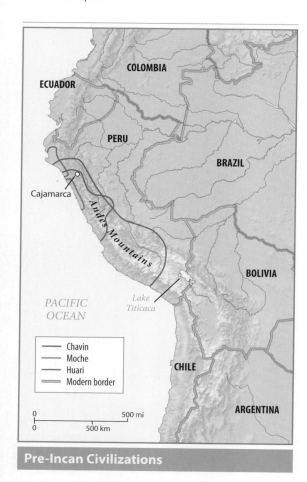

Pre-Incan Civilizations

Civilization

The Incas lived in a high plateau of the Andes and eventually settled in the Valley of Cuzco. They established a kingdom by the thirteenth century, when the powerful leader Pachacuti (PAH chah KOO tee) began the conquest of Peru and neighboring lands. By 1500 the Incan empire stretched about 2,500 miles along the western coast of South America.

To maintain their empire, the Incas developed an extensive road system consisting of up to 14,000 miles of roads and bridges. These roads were restricted for use by the ruler ("Inca"), his entourage, the army, and government officials. In some areas the roads were wide enough for eight horsemen to ride abreast (as noted by the Spanish conquerors). In many areas the road was paved with blocks of stone, with trees to shade the travelers. However, in remote regions the road may have been little more than gravel, with short walls on each side to mark the path. The Incas constructed shelters in the form of a single shed or a group of buildings every eight to fifteen miles along the road. Local Incas kept these buildings supplied with fuel and provisions for the Inca, his officials, and the army.

To communicate across their empire, the Incas developed a system of runners (*chasqui*) who would carry an important message for about one mile and then hand it off to the next runner. In this way a message could be carried about 150 miles per day. A message could

Peruvian and Bolivian civilizations that preceded the Incas	
Civilization	Years
Chavin	900–200 BC
Nazca	100 BC–AD 800
Moche	100–800
Huari	500–1000

Machu Picchu

travel from one end of the Incan Empire to the other in about five days. This system alerted officials of danger, rebellion, or other time-sensitive information.

Incan engineers constructed bridges that spanned deep gorges and swift-flowing rivers. They built these suspended bridges out of cables (as thick as a man's thigh) woven from cabuya fiber, fixed to wooden beams, and anchored to stone pylons. Once the major cables had been secured, workers tied a network of finer cords to form the sides and floor. Following initial construction, locals were responsible to keep these bridges in good repair.

(top and bottom) *Incan suspension bridge made of woven grass over the Apurimac River in southern Peru*

Quipu

Strings spun from cotton or perhaps llama hair were used by the Incas to record and store a wide assortment of information. The **quipu** (or **khipu**) were collections of knotted strings used for accounting and recording data; different-colored strings indicated different sets of numbers, and each quipu could have up to two thousand cords.

Rather than collect taxes to maintain the Incan empire, the government operated a

Llamas

The llama is one of the four types of "camels of the Andes" (the other three are the guanaco, the vicuña, and the alpaca). The llama is well suited for mountain life. Its lungs are effective in the thin air, and it has a much greater concentration of oxygen-carrying red blood cells than other mammals. It can survive on the sparse grasses and shrubs on the mountain slopes. The llama is a sure-footed pack animal and is able to travel up to eighteen miles per day while carrying a load of up to 130 pounds. Because llamas were indispensable for transporting people and their goods, they played a key role in the Incan economy and culture.

Incan Empire

system in which the Incas paid in labor to build roads, graineries, bridges, and other structures. The men also served in the army as a form of payment.

The Incan empire, which reached its zenith between 1380 and 1570, flourished along the western coast of South America where Peru is today. Incan families lived in tightly organized communes in which several families shared possessions. Most Incas were farmers and grew crops common to the Indian cultures. All the communes were closely controlled by the Inca, whom the people worshiped as a god.

Religion

Incan religion has been described as a combination of nature worship, primitive fetishism, animism, and magic. The number of gods worshiped by the Incas increased as they conquered new lands. If they were impressed with, or afraid of offending, a local god, the Incas would add it to their list of gods. Oracles, who claimed to know the future, also played an important role in Incan worship. Ancestors received veneration as well. However, as in other Indian cultures, worship of the sun god became preeminent. Since the people believed that the reigning Incan king descended from and was the manifestation of the sun, worship of the sun was the most important aspect of Incan religion and frequently involved human sacrifice.

Section Review

1. Name the Indian civilization that settled in the Valley of Cuzco.

2–3. What message-carrying system did the Incas use? About how far could a message be carried in one day?

4. What system did the Incas use to record data?

5–6. Name two ways the Incan civilization developed and expanded?

7–8. What were two aspects of the Incan religion?

★ Evaluate the Incan system that replaced the paying of taxes.

★ What were some elements of the Incan culture that differed from other Indian cultures?

Making Connections

1. What term is used to describe a group of languages that are believed to have had a single ancestral language?

2. What group of Indians was known for hunting bison?

3. What is the name for a Mayan upright stone slab or column carved with inscriptions?

4. What system was used for trade in the Aztec empire?

5. What was the main transportation network used by the Incas?

6–8. What were three distinct elements of Incan culture?

9. Describe the development of early American civilizations.

Developing History Skills

1. What are possible historical explanations for the similarities of the religions discussed in this chapter with many other world religions?

2. Compare and contrast the role of shamans in this chapter with that of the shamans in chapter 7.

Thinking Critically

1. How did the civilizations discussed in this chapter differ from each other?

2. What were the primary characteristics of religion among the Indian civilizations?

Living in God's World

1. Document the primary ways you see the Creation Mandate demonstrated in early American civilizations.

2. Imagine that you are an advisor to an Aztec ruler charged with reforming the empire to ensure that power is used wisely and that justice is carried out for all citizens. What reforms would you recommend? Present your counsel as one informed by a Christian worldview.

People, Places, and Things to Know

Beringia
tribes
language families
culture areas
Hopi
Pueblo Indians
Mound Builders
Great Serpent Mound
Adena
Hopewell
Mississippian
Eastern Woodlands Indians
stele
Tikal
Chichén Itzá
Long Count
ceiba tree
Quetzalcoatl
Tenochtitlán
Triple Alliance
quipu (khipu)

CHAPTER

9

The Making of Medieval Europe

I. Early Medieval History

II. Early Medieval Culture

III. Early Medieval Church

Reenactment of a knight holding his sword

Big Ideas

1. What characterized the culture of the early Middle Ages?

2. What were the components of the feudal system?

3. How did the medieval church develop?

During the Middle Ages, European society was composed primarily of three classes of people: the clergy, the nobility, and the peasants. Each played an important part in shaping European life and culture. Their roles in society have been described simply: the clergy were called to pray; the nobility, to fight; and the peasants, to work. Accordingly, each group represented an institution of medieval Europe—the church, the feudal system, and the manor.

I. Early Medieval History

At the beginning of the Middle Ages, western Europe faced widespread invasions, social unrest, and political disorder. The kingdoms established by leaders of Germanic tribes were often small and lacked strong central governments. Gradually the **Franks** became the most powerful of the Germanic peoples. They established many independent kingdoms in Gaul (modern-day France). From these Frankish kingdoms arose a new empire that temporarily reunited much of western Europe.

Clovis and the Franks

In 481 **Clovis** became the head of a Frankish tribe in northern Gaul. Through treachery and exceptional military ability, he conquered other Frankish tribes, uniting them into one kingdom. He soon became known as "king of the Franks." Once Clovis pushed the Visigoths out of southern Gaul, his territory included most of the area of present-day France (which takes its name from the Franks).

Important to the history of both western Europe and the Frankish kingdom was Clovis's outward conversion to Christianity. Like the emperor Constantine, Clovis was in danger of being defeated in battle when he cried out to God for help. He vowed to believe in God and be baptized in His name if granted the victory. Emerging victorious in battle, Clovis remained true to his vow. He even required three thousand of his soldiers to be baptized into the church. As a result, Clovis gained the support of the Roman Catholic Church, which found him to be a powerful champion for its cause. Thus began an alliance between the Frankish rulers and the Church of Rome that lasted for centuries. The so-called conversions of Clovis and his men were typical of many medieval conversions made for convenience or by coercion.

The Mayors of the Palace

Clovis died in 511, having established a strong, unified kingdom. In accordance with Frankish custom, the kingdom was divided among his four sons. Their descendants continued to reign over the Franks well into the eighth century. This royal family line was known as the **Merovingian House**, taking its name from an ancestor of Clovis named Merovech. However, the Merovingian family was plagued by quarrels. Clovis's sons became rivals. Each sought to gain the others' territory, using murder and treachery when necessary. Yet despite the domestic feuds and confusion under the Merovingian kings, Frankish rulers remained in power.

Even so, by the seventh century, they had lost much of their prestige and effectiveness through drunkenness, immoral living, and family strife. They became known as the "do-nothing kings." They reigned, but they did not rule. The principal palace official (called the major-domo, or the mayor of the palace) became the real

Guiding Questions

1. How did Charlemagne's empire and the Holy Roman Empire develop?
2. What were the chief political achievements of the early English and French kingdoms?
3. Should this period be described as the Dark Ages?

power behind the throne. Originally, the mayor of the palace supervised only the king's household, but succeeding mayors extended their authority over the financial, military, and administrative functions of government.

Near the end of the seventh century, **Pepin II** became the mayor of one of the stronger Frankish states. He defeated all rival mayors and reunited almost all of the Frankish territories under one rule. The Merovingians still occupied the throne, but they were mere puppets of the mayors. Probably the best remembered of all the mayors of the palace is **Charles Martel**, son of Pepin II. In 732 Charles won his fame by defeating the Muslims at the Battle of Tours in western France. This feat earned him the title Martel, or "the Hammer."

Pepin the Short (r. 751–768), like his father Charles Martel, served as mayor of the palace. He possessed all the powers of the king, but he wished to have the title as well. Pepin appealed to the pope, asking him to decide whether he, Pepin, or the "do-nothing" Merovingian king should be the rightful ruler of the Franks. The pope replied that the one who wielded the power should be king. Pepin promptly deposed the king and seized the throne in 752. Two years later the pope traveled to France and sealed the change in ruling families by anointing Pepin "by the grace of God king of the Franks." The Carolingian House—named after its most illustrious member, Charlemagne—now officially ruled the Franks.

In return for his support, the pope asked Pepin to protect him against the Lombards. They were a Germanic people who through conquest had moved into northern Italy (a region still known today as Lombardy). In the first half of the eighth century, the Lombards had invaded central Italy and now threatened the city of Rome. Coming to the pope's aid, Pepin defeated the Lombards and gave their lands to the pope. These lands eventually became the Papal States. The pope, head of the Roman Church, became a ruler involved in European politics. His successors continued to rule as kings over this region for the next one thousand years.

The Empire of Charlemagne

When Pepin died in 768, his sons Carloman and Charles succeeded him as corulers. After only a few years, Carloman died, and Charles became the sole ruler of the Frankish kingdom. Charles was not only the greatest Carolingian king but also one of the outstanding figures of the Middle Ages. His accomplishments won him the title **Charlemagne** (SHAR luh mane), or "Charles the Great."

Conquests

The Frankish kingdom reached its peak under Charlemagne's rule (768–814). As his father had done, Charlemagne rescued Rome, which had again been invaded by Lombards. With this foe subdued, he directed his military campaigns against the Saxons, a Germanic tribe in northern Europe. After thirty-three years of bitter struggle, he conquered this people also. Near the Danube River in central Europe, he defeated the Avars, a nomadic people similar to the Huns. And in the south, he drove the Spanish Muslims back across the Pyrenees. By the time of his death, Charlemagne had created an empire that stretched over most of western Europe. He laid the foundation for the modern European nations of France, Germany, and Italy.

Charlemagne's Empire

Charlemagne divided his empire into hundreds of administrative districts, or counties. He appointed counts to supervise each district. They administered justice, maintained the peace, and raised an army in times of war. To ensure the enforcement of his policies on the local level, Charlemagne sent pairs of royal messengers into the districts to investigate local conditions and to hear complaints leveled against any of the local officials. These envoys then sent back written reports to Charlemagne.

Crowning

Since the days of the Roman emperors, no one man in the West had ruled as much territory as Charlemagne. Western Europe looked upon him as another Constantine, ruling and protecting both church and state. As a result, while Charlemagne was attending a church service in Rome on Christmas Day, 800, Leo III, a grateful pope, placed a crown on his head and proclaimed him Roman emperor. The assembly present cried out, "To Charles Augustus, crowned by God, the great and pacific [peaceful] emperor of the Romans, life and victory."

Although the title "emperor" did nothing to increase the actual power of Charlemagne, it did have an important impact upon later medieval history. His empire eventually collapsed in the years after his death, but Charlemagne's crowning had revived the idea of a restored Roman Empire that would again unite the territories of western Europe. This crowning also raised a serious question: whose authority is supreme—the state's or the church's? Though Charlemagne's authority was unquestioned in his day, popes later

Throne of Charlemagne, Palatine Chapel, Aachen, Germany

insisted that their authority superseded that of kings, noting that a pope had crowned Charlemagne. Some popes even claimed the power not only to confirm kings but also to depose them. This struggle for supremacy between popes and kings intensified during the late Middle Ages.

Revival of Learning

Charlemagne's love of learning prompted him to promote education throughout his empire. His royal court at Aachen, (also known by its French name, Aix-la-Chapelle; AYKS lah shah PEL) became the leading center of learning in the realm. There he assembled the best scholars of western Europe. The most distinguished of these was Alcuin (AL kwin) from York, England. He took charge of the palace school and trained the king's children as well as the children of other noble families. Alcuin also taught the king. Einhard, Charlemagne's biographer, wrote of Charlemagne's education:

> The King spent much time and labor with [Alcuin] studying rhetoric, dialectics, and especially astronomy; he learned to reckon [calculate], and used to investigate the motion of the heavenly bodies most curiously, with an intelligent scrutiny. He also tried to write, and used to keep tablets and blanks in bed under his pillow, that at leisure hours he might accustom his hand to form the letters; however, as he did not begin his efforts in due season, but late in life, they met with ill success.
>
> Einhard, The Life of Charlemagne, trans. Samuel Epes Turner, 54.

Perhaps it was under Alcuin's influence that Charlemagne developed his deep concern for a better-educated clergy. He encouraged the church to establish schools to upgrade the literacy of the priests and monks. In a letter to church leaders, Charlemagne set forth what has been called the charter of education for the Middle Ages. In it, he said:

> And hence we have begun to fear that, if [the clergy's] skill in writing is so small, so also their power of rightly comprehending the Holy Scriptures may be far less than is befitting; and it is known to all that, if verbal errors are dangerous, errors of interpretation are still more so. We exhort you, therefore, not only not to neglect the study of letters but to apply yourselves thereto with that humble perseverance which is well-pleasing to God, that so you may be able with greater ease and accuracy to search into the mysteries of the Holy Scriptures.
>
> Donald A. White, Medieval History: A Sourcebook, 239.

Charlemagne's educational reforms renewed interest in the Bible and the works of classical writers. For several centuries in western Europe there had been little opportunity for an education; as a result, few people could read or write. During that time many ancient manuscripts were lost or damaged; others were full of copyists' mistakes. One of the most important contributions of Charlemagne's reign was the rediscovery and preservation of these ancient works. In addition, God used the Carolingian scholars to preserve copies of the Bible.

Monasteries became the primary centers for studying, copying, and preserving ancient manuscripts; they were the "printing houses" and libraries of the Middle Ages. Monks undertook the painstaking process of making handwritten copies of earlier works. During this period, they developed a new and beautiful style of handwriting known as the Carolingian minuscule. This clean and simple writing style became the model for much of our lowercase writing today. Many manuscripts were "illuminated" with colorful illustrations.

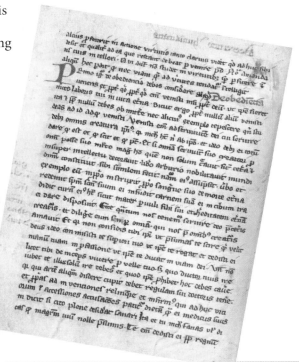

Examples of Carolingian minuscule

Successors

Although the effects of this renewed interest in learning lasted for centuries, Charlemagne's impressive empire deteriorated rapidly. Within a century after his death, the Carolingian Empire had collapsed, torn by civil war and pillaged by foreign invaders.

When Charlemagne died in 814, his empire passed to his only surviving son, Louis the Pious. During Louis's reign, a bitter rivalry developed among his sons concerning which portion of the empire each would inherit. Even before Louis's death this rivalry led to war. After years of fighting, the brothers met at the city of Verdun to settle their differences. In the **Treaty of Verdun** (843), they agreed to split the empire into three separate kingdoms: **Charles the Bald** received West Frankland; **Louis the German**, East Frankland; and the eldest brother, **Lothair**, retained the title of emperor and ruled the land between his brother's kingdoms. (See map to the right.) Notice how closely the modern countries of France, Germany, and Italy correspond to these divisions.

During the ninth and tenth centuries, the Carolingian Empire offered little resistance to the foreign invaders that beset it on every side. From North Africa came Muslim raiders, who devastated the Mediterranean coast of Europe and seized many prisoners to be sold into slavery. They captured Sardinia, Corsica, and Sicily and pillaged southern Italy with similar tragic results. From the East came a group of Asiatic nomads who later became known as the Hungarians. They swept into the Danube region of southeastern Europe, where they ravaged the eastern borders of the empire.

Treaty of Verdun (843)

However, the most feared invaders were the **Vikings**, or Norsemen. These Germanic tribes swooped down from the lands known today as Norway, Sweden, and Denmark. Fearless warriors, skilled seamen, and daring adventurers, Viking sailors eventually braved the waters of the Atlantic to sail to Iceland, Greenland, and North America. Some sailed down the rivers of Russia, while others sailed along the European coast and into the Mediterranean, plundering coastal villages and towns. The Vikings struck terror into the hearts of the people of Europe; their swift raids left villages aflame, homes and crops destroyed, and churches and monasteries ransacked. Few in Europe felt safe from these attacks. "From the fury of the Northmen, O Lord deliver us" was a prayer offered in churches across western Europe.

Section Review

1. What man united the Frankish tribes and became known as "King of the Franks"?

2. What palace official became the real power behind the Frankish throne?

3–4. At what battle and in what year did Charles Martel defeat the Muslims?

5. Under whose rule did the Frankish empire reach its peak?

6–9. Name the treaty that split the Carolingian Empire into three parts, and identify the brothers and the portion of the kingdom each received.

★ Evaluate Clovis's approach to Christianizing his kingdom.

★ What was a major cultural achievement during the reign of Charlemagne, and how was it significant?

The Holy Roman Empire

In East Frankland, the weak descendants of the ruler Louis the German offered little protection against the Magyars—savage horsemen who were terrorizing southeastern Europe. Local tribal leaders called dukes assumed the role of protectors.

German nobles selected the Saxon duke **Henry the Fowler** to be the first of the Saxon line of German kings. According to tradition, Henry was called "the Fowler" because the messengers who brought him the news of his election found him enjoying his favorite pastime—hunting game with hawks. As king, Henry I (r. 919–36) forced the other dukes to acknowledge his royal status, but he permitted them to guide the internal affairs of their own territories.

Henry's son **Otto I** (r. 936–73), often called "the Great," became one of the strongest German kings. Unlike his father, he was not content with the mere title of king but sought to actually assert his royal authority over the other duchies. In his struggles against rival dukes, he relied on the support of high-ranking church officials, many of whom he had appointed to office. These powerful bishops and abbots pledged their allegiance to Otto and supplied soldiers for his army.

Establishment of the Empire

Tenth-century Italy was divided into many warring factions. Fearing that a rival duke would seize northern Italy and threaten his

Crown of the Holy Roman Empire (962) made for Emperor Otto (r. 936–73)

monarchy, Otto crossed the Alps, took possession of Lombardy, and proclaimed himself king of Italy. Ten years later, in 962, he crossed the Alps again, this time marching his army into Rome. The pope, who had appealed to Otto for protection against the Roman nobles, crowned Otto emperor. Like Charlemagne, he had come to the pope's rescue and in return had received the emperor's crown. Otto believed that his new role as protector made him superior to the pope, a claim disputed, of course, by the papacy.

The conquests and coronation of Otto revived the memory of the Carolingian and Roman empires. Later German kings considered themselves the successors of Charlemagne and the Roman caesars. Because of its alliance with the Roman Church and its symbolic association with the empire of ancient Rome, the German empire became known as the **Holy Roman Empire**. But as the eighteenth-century French author and philosopher Voltaire observed, it was "neither holy, nor Roman, nor an empire." The empire was built on the union of Germany and Italy and on the alliance of the church and state, neither of which could provide a strong foundation.

Conflict Within the Empire

Although the Holy Roman Empire, founded by Otto I, became the most powerful state in Europe, it experienced many internal conflicts. The first was a conflict of interest. The German rulers often intervened in Italian affairs. Otto's grandson, Otto III, built a palace in Rome and planned to make Rome the capital of the empire. But in focusing on Italy's welfare, Otto III and other German rulers neglected the affairs of their homeland. This lack of attention gave the German nobles an opportunity to increase their power. The divided interests of the Holy Roman emperors ultimately weakened their authority and hindered efforts to create a unified Italy and a unified Germany.

Another conflict that plagued the empire was the struggle between the emperors and the popes. Beginning with Otto I, the emperors actively intervened in papal affairs. They even began choosing the popes. In addition, they continued the longstanding practice of appointing important church officials within their realm (a situation later to be resolved by the Concordat of Worms in 1122; see p. 198). As reform spread throughout the Roman Church, the popes began to challenge the emperor's authority to appoint church officials.

The third and perhaps most damaging conflict was the one between the German nobles and the Holy Roman emperors. For almost a century while the emperors had been preoccupied with Italian affairs, the German nobles had enjoyed great independence. The situation began to change, however, when a new royal line, the Salian House (1024–1125), succeeded the Saxon kings. The Salian kings, including Henry IV, attempted, unsuccessfully, to establish a strong centralized monarchy that would weaken the power of the great nobles. After Henry's son died without an heir, civil war broke out among rival noble families competing for the crown.

The civil wars further weakened the German monarchy and led to the development of feudalism throughout the empire. The large regions in Italy and Germany broke up into many small states. Powerful nobles became feudal lords, forcing lesser nobles to become their vassals. During this period, several of the strongest nobles

Holy Roman Empire (ca. 1100)

firmly established the practice of electing the German monarch. The power of the nobles became supreme in the land.

Empire Under the Hohenstaufens

In 1152 the German princes hoped to end the civil wars by choosing as ruler a member of the Hohenstaufen (HO un SHTOU fun) family, **Frederick I**, also called Barbarossa ("Red Beard"). Frederick (r. 1152–90) sought to restore the glory and stability of what he termed the "holy empire." Like previous German kings, Frederick meddled in Italian affairs. His expeditions brought strong papal opposition. Though most of Frederick's advances into Italy ended in failure, he was successful in forming a marriage alliance between his son and the heiress of the kingdom of Sicily.

The last notable Hohenstaufen ruler was **Frederick II** (r. 1215–50), the grandson of Frederick I. Frederick was heir not only to the German throne but also to the throne of Sicily. The latter kingdom was established by the Normans in the eleventh century and included all of southern Italy. Frederick II grew up in Sicily, where he became acquainted with the Greek and Arab cultures. Later his court would become a leading center of culture. One of the most learned men of his day, he also distinguished himself as a patron of artists and scholars.

As a boy, Frederick became the ward of Pope Innocent III, the most powerful man in Europe. Innocent recognized the threat of having Hohenstaufen possessions encircling the Papal States. Therefore, he secured the German throne for Frederick in return for his promise to give up the throne of Sicily. Shortly after Innocent's death, however, Frederick broke his promise. He devoted almost all his attention to Sicily and Italy, leaving the feudal princes of Germany relatively free from imperial interference. Frederick expanded his Italian holdings and might have united all of Italy under his control had it not been for the resistance of the papacy.

The death of Frederick II in 1250 marked the decline of the Holy Roman Empire. German kings continued to call themselves Holy Roman emperors, but their contact with Italy was minimal. The attempts of the German emperors to unite Germany and Italy ended in failure. Their lack of success marked the beginning of a long period of disunity for the two countries. Not until the late nineteenth century did Italy and Germany become unified national states.

Feudal Monarchs in England

The Anglo-Saxons Settle England

Roman authority over the Celts in Britain came to an end in the early fifth century. After nearly four hundred years as an occupying force, the Roman legions had to withdraw from the island in order to protect Roman territory on the Continent. Soon afterwards, Germanic tribes from northern Europe, including the Angles and the Saxons, invaded Britain. They established their own independent kingdoms and transformed "Roman" Britain into England (or "Angle land," meaning the "land of the Angles").

During the ninth century, the Danes (Scandinavian Vikings) began to raid the land. The petty kingdoms of the Angles and Saxons had little success in resisting the Danes—that is, until the time of King **Alfred the Great** (r. 871–899). Alfred, the ruler of the impor-

Alfred the Great

tant Saxon kingdom of Wessex, defeated the Danes and pushed them back into northeastern England. He extended his rule over the south of England, laying the foundation for a unified English monarchy.

Alfred's success was not confined to the battlefield. He was an able ruler and a patron of learning. He built a navy to repel future Danish invasions—an undertaking that earned him the title "founder of the English navy." He strengthened the Anglo-Saxon practice of local government. His realm was divided into many local districts, governed by officials called shire-reeves (from which we get our word *sheriff*). He built churches, founded schools, and invited foreign scholars to his court. During his reign, scholars began to translate important literary works into the common language of the people. In addition, monks began to compile the **Anglo-Saxon Chronicle**, which traces the history of England from Roman times to Alfred's day. The *Chronicle* was continued after Alfred; monks added current events and revised older passages.

Alfred was a man of strong character. He won the love and respect of his people as well as the admiration of later generations. Unlike many of the men who have been highly praised by historians, Alfred truly deserved the title "the Great." His life demonstrated that true greatness lies not in wealth or worldly fame but in a man's character—not necessarily in what a man does but in what he is.

Less than a century after Alfred's death, the Danes renewed their attacks. England fell to the Danish ruler Canute, who made England part of the Danish Empire, which also included Norway. Although Canute ruled England well, his successors were weak. The Anglo-Saxons eventually drove out the Danish rulers and placed Edward the Confessor on the throne.

William of Normandy Conquers England

Edward (r. 1042–66) was a descendant of Alfred. He was called "the Confessor" because of his devotion to God. In January of 1066, he died without a direct heir. His cousin William, the French duke of Normandy, claimed the throne, asserting that Edward had promised it to him. The English nobles, however, refused to grant William the crown. Instead they elected Harold, the powerful earl of Wessex, king. William refused to be deprived of what he thought was rightfully his. Obtaining the blessing of the pope, he raised a large army, crossed the English Channel, and invaded England.

On October 14, 1066, the armies of William, duke of Normandy, and Harold, earl of Wessex, met in the **Battle of Hastings**. Much more was at stake than the English throne; the outcome of this battle altered the course of English history. Before the day ended, Harold had been killed and the Anglo-Saxons defeated. William, known as "the Conqueror," established a new line of English kings, the Norman dynasty.

William brought to England the centralized feudalism of Normandy and established himself as feudal lord over the entire country, which, in theory, was now his by right of conquest. He divided his holdings among his military followers. To maintain his power over all the feudal nobles, he required them to swear allegiance to him as their lord. He also extended his authority over the English church; William—not the pope—appointed the bishops of his kingdom.

England in the Time of Alfred the Great

Were the Middle Ages Dark?

"The . . . Greek intellectual tradition did not simply lose vigour and disappear. (Its survival and continued progress in the Arab world is testimony to that.) Rather, in the fourth and fifth century A.D. it was destroyed by the political and religious forces which made up the highly authoritarian government of the late Roman empire. . . . So one finds a combination of factors behind 'the closing of the Western mind': the attack on Greek philosophy by Paul, the adoption of Platonism by Christian theologians and the enforcement of orthodoxy by emperors desperate to keep good order. The imposition of orthodoxy went hand in hand with a stifling of any form of independent reasoning. By the fifth century, not only has rational thought been suppressed, but there has been a substitution which drew heavily on irrational elements of pagan society that had never been extinguished."

Charles Freeman, The Closing of the Western Mind: The Rise of Faith and the Fall of Reason, *xvii–xix.*

"Charlemagne and his innovations did not appear suddenly at the end of the eighth century. They were part of a whole series of economic, social, and political developments from the fifth century on that archaeological evidence reveals to us even when written sources say little about them.

· · · · · · · · · ·

"Charlemagne brought great scholars and teachers to create the lively artistic and intellectual environment known as the Carolingian Renaissance. How did this development come about? . . . [F]rom the fifth century on major new developments in the arts, architecture, scholarship, writing and education took place in Europe. A few major centers of learning and culture emerged, such as Wearmouth and Jarrow, in Northumbria, England, in the seventh century and Charlemagne's Aachen in the late eighth century. But many of these changes took place at different locations throughout the continent and happened during all four centuries between 400 and 800."

Peter S. Wells, Barbarians to Angels: The Dark Ages Reconsidered, *186–88.*

1. What does Wells give as evidence that the early Middle Ages were not a dark age?

2. What causes does Freeman give for the disappearance that he notes?

3. How would you go about evaluating these sources?

To determine the taxable resources that belonged to him as king, William commissioned a great survey. His royal officials traveled throughout the country gathering detailed information about property holders and their belongings. According to the *Anglo-Saxon Chronicle*, "there was not a single hide or rood [1/4 acre] of land, nor even was there an ox or a cow or a pig left that was not set down in his writings." The findings of the survey were collected in a record known as the ***Domesday Book***.

Feudal Monarchs in France

The Capetians and Their Royal House

The kingdom of West Frankland, once the heart of the Carolingian Empire, broke up into many kingdoms soon after the death of Charlemagne in 814. In 987 the great lords chose the count of Paris, **Hugh Capet** (kah PAY; r. 987–96), as their king, thus ending the rule of the Carolingian monarchs, which had become weak. Hugh Capet founded a new royal line, the Capetian (kuh PEE shun) House, whose members built a strong monarchy in France.

Many factors helped the Capetian kings to steadily increase their power over the feudal lords. For instance, for more than three hundred years every Capetian king had a son to succeed him. There were therefore no wars of succession to threaten the stability and continuity of royal power. This power gradually increased as the size of the royal domain increased. Capetian rulers enlarged their royal possessions by conquest and through marriage alliances. They also developed an effective system of centralized government, which laid the foundation for the French national state. Furthermore, the Capetians found valuable allies in the Roman Church and townspeople. By tapping the wealth of the towns and the church, the Capetians won financial independence from the great lords.

Philip II and Royal Expansion

Although the early Capetians bore the title of king, they actually ruled only a small area around Paris, known as the **Île-de-France** (eel duh FRAHNS). Like an island, it was surrounded by lands ruled by the king's nobles. Many of these were powerful lords possessing more land and authority than the French king. (William, duke of Normandy, and Henry Plantagenet are noted examples.)

The early Capetian kings were constantly struggling to maintain control of their holdings. Not until the reign of the fifth Capetian king, Louis VI (r. 1108–37), did the French king become master of his royal domain. For the first time the Capetians had a strong and solid base from which they would extend their royal power over the rest of the kingdom. It was **Philip II** "Augustus" (r. 1180–1223), however, who became known as the real founder of France. By enlarging the territory under his rule and by increasing his power over his vassals, he began a period of Capetian predominance.

The chief obstacle to the expansion of royal power in France was the large amount of land held by the English kings. Although the Plantagenet monarchs that ruled England were servants of the French king, their landholdings in France far exceeded those ruled directly by the French king. Philip II attempted to deprive the English kings Henry II and Richard the Lion-Hearted of their continental holdings but met with little success. He found King John easier to deal with. A controversy broke out between John and one of his French vassals. When John refused to stand trial in Philip's court as the French monarch's vassal, Philip declared John's French lands forfeited. Because John had lost the support of his French nobles and had alienated the English nobles, he lost Normandy, Anjou, Maine, and Touraine to Philip. The French king had broken the power of

French Royal Domain | Controlled by French Nobles | Controlled by English

Growth of France (11th–12th Century)

King John in France and, in doing so, had tripled the size of his own royal domain.

Philip also increased the effectiveness of royal government. He replaced local feudal officials with new royal ones called baillis (bah YEE), or bailiffs, whom the king appointed and paid. Similar to Henry II's itinerant justices, these bailiffs collected royal taxes, enforced feudal rights, and administered justice, reinforcing the king's authority throughout his realm.

Section Review

1–2. What German king founded the Holy Roman Empire? In what year did this take place?

3. What conflict of interest did many of the German emperors have?

4–6. From what family did the German princes choose a king in hopes of ending the period of civil war? List two emperors who belonged to this family.

7. What man defeated the Danes and laid the foundation for a unified English monarchy?

8–11. What two men struggled for the English throne in 1066? What was the name of the battle where this issue was settled? Who won?

⭒ Why did the Holy Roman Empire prove to be an inaccurate name?

⭒ What was the chief political achievement of the French kingdom?

Guiding Questions

1. What were the major elements of the feudal system?

2. What were postive and negative aspects of the feudal system?

3. How were justice, power, and citizenship reflected in the feudal system?

Elements of the Feudal System

The feudal system was characterized by a political system managed by local rulers. During this period, land was valued as a measure of wealth, and the land belonged to the king. The king would grant use of his land to lords in exchange for a portion of the crops and service in the king's army. The lords served as the king's vassals. Ranks in the feudal system included nobility, clergy, freemen, and serfs. During this time, life centered on the manor.

II. Early Medieval Culture
Development of the Feudal System

As Charlemagne's empire disintegrated, powerful nobles replaced the weak Carolingian kings. There arose a new political system in which local rulers offered the people protection in return for their services. This system, known as **feudalism**, was the form of government prevalent in western Europe from the ninth to the thirteenth centuries. It provided relative order and security until more centralized governments emerged.

Land was the basis of wealth and power during the Feudal Age. Governing power formerly exercised by a central government gradually passed into the hands of land-holding nobles, or **lords**. In theory, the king was the supreme lord, holding all the land in the kingdom by right of conquest or inheritance. But when foreign raiders threatened his territory, the king had to rely on the help of powerful nobles. In return for their services (usually military aid), the king granted them the use of landed estates. The land grants became known as **fiefs**, or in Latin, *feudum*, from which our word *feudal* comes.

A fief could be extremely large or very small. The recipient of such an estate became the king's **vassal** (servant). A vassal did not own the land, or fief, but held it as payment for service rendered to the king. Originally, the king granted his vassal the use of a fief for as long as the vassal lived. When the vassal died, the fief reverted to the king. Later, however, many fiefs became hereditary, remaining in the hands of the vassal's eldest son upon payment of a fee. Often a vassal parceled out portions of his fief to gain the services of lesser nobles, who became his vassals, and he, in turn, their lord. Each new vassal could likewise partition his fief and become a lord. This process could continue until a fief was too small to subdivide any further.

Relationships and Obligations

At the heart of feudalism was the relationship between a lord and his vassal. Solemn ceremonies symbolized the agreement entered into by these two nobles. Homage was the ceremony by which a man became a vassal and thus eligible for a fief. This ceremony usually took place in the lord's court with many witnesses present. The would-be vassal knelt before the lord and placed his hands between his lord's hands; he then professed himself to be the "lord's man." With a ceremonial kiss, the lord recognized him as his vassal. After performing homage, the vassal took an oath of fealty (fidelity), pledging faithfulness and loyalty to his lord. In turn, the lord handed to the vassal a small stick, lance, or clod of earth. By this symbolic act, known as **investiture**, the lord gave to the vassal the right of use of a fief.

In addition to the grant of a fief, the lord guaranteed his vassal protection and justice. The vassal's primary duty was to provide military service for his lord. He was expected to furnish a specified number of knights (for at least forty days a year) to assist the lord in his battles. Not all of the vassal's responsibilities were military, however. A vassal also agreed to supply financial payments on special occasions, such as when his lord's eldest son became a knight or when the lord's eldest daughter was married. Vassals attended the lord's court to give counsel and to assist in the administration of justice. In addition, the vassal was obligated to pay a ransom if his lord were captured in war.

Painting depicting medieval homage. The vassal on the left is placing his hands between the lord's hands. The man in the middle is the witness.

Life of the Nobility

The castle was the center of life for the nobility. It was not only the lord's home but also the local jail, the treasury, the armory, the court, and the seat of government. Modern books and films have romanticized daily life in the medieval castle. Yet as impressive as feudal castles may have appeared from a distance, they were often damp, cold, musty, and dark. Tapestries and flowers were used to add warmth and cheer to the otherwise bleak surroundings. Feudal castles had few of the comforts and luxuries that we associate with the elegant, aristocratic palaces of a later day.

Castles were built primarily for defensive purposes. The word *castle* comes from the Latin word *castellum,* meaning "fort" or "fortress." At first castles were often just wooden blockhouses set on high mounds surrounded by a stockade and a ditch (moat). It was not until about the tenth century that castles assumed the features that most people think of today: massive stone walls, towering battlements, wide moats, and wooden drawbridges. It was the lord's responsibility to protect the inhabitants of the surrounding countryside. When invaders threatened the land, the local villagers fled into the safe confines of their lord's castle. High atop the castle's battlement, defenders could repel an attack with spears and arrows or by pouring molten metal or dropping large boulders on the heads of attackers.

Reenactment of a knight on a horse during a jousting tournament

Reenactment of knights jousting

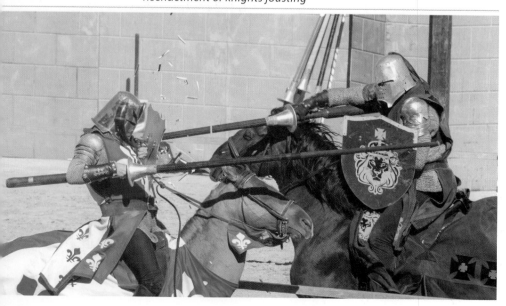

Also important to the protection of life and property during the Middle Ages was the **knight**. In the early Middle Ages, anyone brave and strong enough could become one. Later, however, knighthood was restricted to the nobility.

The preparation for knighthood was long and hard. At age seven, a boy's initiation formally began. At that time his parents placed him in the care of a knight (often an uncle) for special training. For the next several years, the youth, or **page**, developed both his mind and body. He studied religion, science, and history. He also learned to fence (fight with a sword), ride a horse, and hunt with falcons and dogs. In his midteens, the page became a **squire**, the personal servant of a knight. His training intensified, and his responsibilities increased. The squire cared for the knight's armor, weapons, and horse. He helped dress his knight each morning and waited on him, his family, and guests as they ate.

When he was about twenty-one, a squire became eligible for knighthood. Occasionally a man was knighted instantly on the battlefield in recognition of unusual bravery. More often, however, a squire received knighthood in a special religious ceremony. The knight promised to live by a strict code of behavior, called the "code of chivalry." The word *chivalry* comes from the French word for *horseman* (i.e., a knight). It is closely related to the English word *cavalry*. A true knight was expected to be brave in battle, skillful with his weapons, honest, generous, and loyal to his lord. He never attacked an unarmed knight but gave him the opportunity to put on his armor before engaging him in battle. Likewise, it was improper for an entire company of knights to attack a single knight; they were to fight him one at a time.

The Roman Catholic Church gradually influenced the knightly code. According to the twelfth-century philosopher John of Salisbury, knights were to "defend the Church, assail infidelity, honor the priesthood, protect the poor from injuries, pacify the province, pour out their blood for their brothers, and if need be lay down their lives." The church not only tried to improve the conduct of the knights but also attempted to place limitations on feudal warfare through decrees known as the **Peace of God** and the **Truce of God**. By the Peace of God, the church forbade the pillaging of church property and extended protection to all noncombatants in society. The Truce of God sought to limit fighting to specified weekdays by forbidding combat from Wednesday evening to Monday morning. Although often unable to enforce these decrees, the church did strive to improve some of the harsh and brutal conditions of the feudal period.

Even in times of peace, the knight was expected to maintain his skills. He often went hunting and fishing, but his real love was fighting. When peaceful conditions kept him at home, he sometimes kept fit by staging a mock war, called a tournament. The typical tournament included two types of contests: the joust and the melee. Jousting was a competition between two knights on horseback who charged at each other, carrying lances with which each tried to unseat his opponent. The melee was a team competition. At a signal, the two sides rushed at each other on horseback and fought what amounted to a full-scale battle. Often they fought within a fenced area so that the battle would remain compact and thus more intense and exciting to watch.

The Manor

The manor was home for the majority of people living in medieval Europe. It was the center of medieval society, a self-contained farming community controlled by a lord and farmed by peasants. The manorial system arose out of the economic and social conditions of the early medieval period, since during that time trade decreased, the size and number of towns diminished, and money was rarely used as a medium of exchange. Most Europeans lived on estates, where they labored to provide for their daily needs.

Because of the decline of trade, the manor had to be largely self-sufficient. Each manor usually had its own priest and skilled workers. Craftsmen made such items as furniture, shoes, tools, and woven cloth. The laborers on each manor produced their own food, built their own homes, and made their own clothing. They grew crops and raised cattle, sheep, and pigs; they constructed bridges and roads. About the only items the manor could not provide were salt, iron, and tar, all of which had to be imported unless available locally.

The center of a typical manor was the village, usually located near a stream or at a crossroad. Here peasants lived in clusters of cottages, which were often one- or two-room huts with thatched roofs and walls made of various materials, including dried mud and straw. The peasants enjoyed few comforts or possessions and had meager furnishings. Nearby was a small plot on which a peasant family could plant a vegetable garden and build a stable to house any livestock it might own. It was not uncommon for some of the livestock to be housed inside the cottage.

Artist's conception of a typical medieval village with a blacksmith, a grist mill, and a village oven

Two buildings dominated the manor: the lord's residence and the village church. Depending on the size of the manor, the lord's dwelling might be a castle or a simple wooden building known as the manor house. In either case, it was often situated on a high hill or some other defensible site. Usually the village was close by; when enemies attacked, the villagers sought refuge inside the fortified walls of the lord's house. Not far from the manor house stood the village church and the priest's home. The church steeple towered above the manor, directing the villagers' gaze heavenward. The church was not only the place of worship but also the place for village meetings, court sessions, and social gatherings.

Activities were not confined to the village. Villagers obtained building material and firewood from nearby forests and grazed their livestock in the pastures. They fished in streams and ponds and hunted for game in the manor's woodlands. The lord and villagers

Grist mill

Blacksmith

Water wheel

divided the cultivated fields on the manor. One-sixth to one-third of the farmland was set apart as the lord's; the rest was allotted to the villagers. The village peasants often worked together to plow the land, sow the seed, and harvest the crops, since no one peasant had enough equipment or oxen to do the job alone. The open fields were divided into long, narrow strips. In each field, a villager farmed one or more of these strips. Often the lord's land was not a separate field but rather the most fertile strips in each open field.

The population on even the smallest manors reflected the medieval class structure: clergy, nobility, and peasantry. While throughout the Middle Ages the highest social status belonged to the clergy and the nobility, every person on the manor had specific duties. The parish priest cared for the religious needs of the villagers, while the local lord provided protection and justice. The peasants worked to provide for the physical and nutritional needs of everyone on the manor.

A small percentage of the people on the manor were **freemen**. These were the more privileged peasants who served as manorial officials or skilled laborers, such as blacksmiths, millers, and carpenters. Some freemen owned their own land, but others rented land from the lord. Freemen did not have the same obligations as the average peasant. For example, freemen were often exempt from laboring in the lord's fields. They also had the freedom to leave the manor. Although they had greater privileges, the freemen's living conditions differed little from those of average peasants.

The majority of those living on a manor were peasants known as **serfs**. The status of the serf was midway between the ancient slave and the medieval freeman. He had the use of a small portion of land and had opportunity to provide for himself and his family. Unlike the freeman, the serf was bound to the land on which he was born and was not free to leave the manor without the lord's permission.

In return for the use of the lord's land and his protection, the serfs owed the lord various services and payments. These services often took the form of labor; serfs were bound to work on the lord's land. They plowed his fields, sowed and harvested his crops, gathered his hay, and cared for his livestock. The lord might call on them to build fences, clear woodland, or dig a moat for his castle. Usually the serfs devoted two or three days a week to working for their lord.

Serfs also had to pay the lord—usually in produce—for the use of his land and its resources. Serfs gave the lord a portion of their crops, a share of the fish caught in the village stream, cheese in exchange for pasturing their cattle in the lord's fields, and a share of the firewood cut. In addition, the serfs were obligated to use the village mill and bakery owned by the lord. They paid to use these facilities with a portion of their grain and flour.

The only world most peasants ever knew was the manor on which they were born. It was their home—the place of their work, their worship, and their death—just as it had been for their ancestors before them. In fact, a peasant seldom traveled more than twenty miles from the place where he was born.

Each year there were two major holy days (holidays)—Easter and Christmas. Christmas brought a two-week celebration (alluded to in our carol "The Twelve Days of Christmas") and a great banquet at the lord's house. There were also other holidays, such as May Day (in the spring) and Harvest Day (much like our Thanksgiving).

Even with the holidays, life was hard for the peasant on the manor. He worked from sunrise to sunset but barely managed to subsist. What little income he earned usually went either to the lord in rent and fees or to the church in tithes. Famines also plagued the land, and frequent feudal wars ruined crops and killed livestock. Strenuous labor, filthy living conditions, poor diet, and lack of medical care combined to give the average peasant a short lifespan.

Section Review

1–4. What were four major elements of the feudal system?

5. What place was the center of life for the nobility?

6–7. What two stages of preparation did a young man go through to become a knight?

8–11. What were two positive and two negative aspects of the feudal system?

★ How did chivalry promote justice during the Middle Ages?

★ How did the vassal relationship affect ideas about citizenship?

III. The Early Medieval Church

Outwardly, things looked bleak for western Europe at the outset of the Middle Ages. Rome had fallen; the order and stability the empire had once provided were gone. Barbarian tribes began to carve out their own kingdoms from the territory once held by the caesars. Monuments of Rome's former grandeur—its aqueducts, amphitheaters, public baths, and roads—were in disrepair. Productivity and trade, as well as education, were on the decline. The lifestyle of the barbarians gradually replaced Greco-Roman culture.

Amidst the confusion and change, one stable institution remained. It represented order and authority and preserved elements

Guiding Questions

1. What was the structure of the Roman Catholic Church?

2. Why did lay investiture lead to controversy?

3. How do the seven sacraments compare with Scripture?

of classical culture. This institution became known as the Roman Catholic Church. It served as the heart of medieval society, influencing almost every aspect of life. The Roman Church cared for the poor, sick, and aged and took the leading role in education. (There was little literacy and learning outside of monasteries during the medieval period.) As the church absorbed almost all of the people in western Europe, it amassed great power, prestige, and wealth. Gradually, the church assumed leadership in political as well as religious matters.

To fully understand the Roman Church, one must examine Christianity and its development in the days of the Roman Empire. At that time (and still today) the word *church* had two different meanings. Specifically, it referred to a local assembly of believers. There were many such local churches scattered throughout the Roman world. The word also had a universal meaning, namely, the "body of Christ." In this sense, *church* referred to the spiritual body composed of all true believers everywhere who were united by faith in Christ. Scripture presents Jesus as "the head over all things to the church, which is his body, the fullness of him that filleth all in all" (Eph. 1:22–23). Recognizing the unity of their faith, the early Christians described this church as **catholic**, a word meaning simply "universal" or "encompassing all."

As mentioned in chapter 4, a bishop oversaw a collection of local assemblies and answered to an archbishop. Over time the bishop of Rome exercised rule over all western churches. As a result, the universal body of Christ came to be understood as an outward, visible institution that became known as the Catholic Church.

Head of the Church

The church and the bishop of the city of Rome played key roles in the development of the Roman Church. As discussed earlier (see p. 91), the church had been organized according to the political and geographical divisions of the Roman Empire. The Church of Rome administered one of the five patriarchates, the highest-ranking divisions within the church. (Jerusalem, Antioch, Alexandria, and Constantinople administered the other four.) At first the patriarchates were equal in rank and authority; however, the Church of Rome gradually rose to a place of preeminence. Its bishop began to assume sole authority over the church in the West.

There were many reasons for this rise in power and prestige. The bishop of Rome presided over the largest and wealthiest city in the western empire. As the people of the Mediterranean world looked to Rome for political and economic leadership, it was natural for them to look to Rome for spiritual guidance as well. Furthermore, all the other patriarchal bishops were located in the East. With the collapse of the western empire in the fifth century, the Roman bishop became one of the few remaining sources of stability in the West. Under Bishop **Leo I** of Rome, the prestige of the office was further enhanced in 452, when the barbarian Huns threatened the city of Rome and Leo persuaded their leader, Attila, to spare the city. Leo was hailed as *papa*, or pope ("Father-Protector"). This title had been applied to other bishops in both the East and the West. By the sixth century, however, it referred almost exclusively to the bishop of Rome.

During the fifth and sixth centuries, the bishops of Rome began to translate their prestige into authority over all churches. For the

Bishop Leo I

most part they were successful. By the end of the sixth century, the bishop of Rome was generally regarded as the pope, the head of the visible church in the West.

To support their claim of primacy ("first in rank"), the bishops of Rome advanced the **Petrine theory**. This theory, based on Matthew 16:18–19, holds that Christ made Peter the first pope and gave him supreme authority over the church on earth. According to this theory, Peter became the vicar, or substitute, of Christ on earth. As the first bishop of Rome, he supposedly transferred his office with all its authority to those who succeeded him.

Perhaps the best representative of the early medieval popes was **Gregory I** (r. 590–604), called "the Great." As bishop of Rome, he greatly expanded the power and authority of his office by defending its supremacy. In fact, Gregory is commonly recognized as the first true pope—a title which he, however, disclaimed. Gregory preferred the title "servant of the servants of God." He was a man of deep devotion and fervent piety who exercised episcopal care over the churches of Gaul, Spain, Britain, Northern Africa, and Italy. Yet Gregory also promoted many unbiblical doctrines that the Roman Catholic Church later officially embraced: the mass, the equal authority of tradition and Scripture, and the sacrament of penance. He also promoted the existence of **purgatory** (a place of temporary punishment where souls bound for heaven must go after death to pay for minor unconfessed sins).

Teaching of the Church

The Middle Ages are often called an "age of faith." Religion dominated society, and nearly every aspect of a person's life was influenced by the Roman Catholic Church. The power of the Roman bishops grew greater than that of monarchs. And the few bright spots of culture that existed at this time were made possible by the church.

As previously mentioned, one significant contribution of the Middle Ages was the continued copying of the Bible in monasteries. Those who could read and had access to manuscripts continued to study the Bible in the Middle Ages. Also, the method of interpreting the Bible improved as the allegorical approach of seeing symbols and pictures of truth in historical passages of the Bible slowly gave way to a more literal approach. But access to Scripture also revealed many practices that had developed over time but could not be found in the Bible. In response, some argued that church tradition had the same authority as the Scriptures. As a result, the doctrine and practice of the Roman Catholic Church became a dangerous mixture of truth and error.

The Roman sacramental system developed, in part, from misinterpretations of Scripture texts about baptism and the Lord's Supper. By the second century the idea that baptism regenerates and cleanses from sin gained acceptance. Baptism, and then the other sacraments, became defined as "the visible sign of an invisible grace." The Roman Catholic Church defines a sacrament as a religious act that grants grace (spiritual benefit) based on the recipient's right intentions. Rome teaches that the sacraments are the core of worship and doctrine in the church.

Through the sacraments, the Roman Catholic Church wielded great power over the Western world because the church claimed that no one could be saved without receiving the sacraments.

Pope Gregory I

Jerome and the Vulgate

Because most people in the Roman Empire spoke Latin, there was a great need for a Latin translation of the Bible. From the earliest days of the church, many people had attempted to meet that need. By the fourth century there had been so many mistakes in translating and copying the Scripture that most Latin manuscripts were no longer reliable. To correct the problem, the Bishop of Rome asked a scholar named Jerome (340–420) to revise the Latin text. Jerome agreed to do so and worked for over twenty years, revising existing translations of portions of the Bible and making original translations of other portions. The result of his labor is a translation that came to be called the Latin Vulgate—a name which means "common" or "well-known." Although Jerome's work also contained some inaccuracies, the Vulgate became the most widely-used Bible of the Middle Ages. Later it became the official Bible of the Roman Catholic Church.

The Sacraments

By the beginning of the thirteenth century, the Roman Catholic Church recognized **seven sacraments** and taught the following regarding them:

1. Baptism initiates one into the church by washing away original sin.
2. Confirmation brings one into full fellowship with the church and confers on him the Holy Spirit to strengthen his spiritual life.
3. Through penance a church member merits forgiveness for sin committed after baptism. Penance includes contrition (sorrow), confession (to a priest), satisfaction (actions done to make amends for sins), and absolution (forgiveness by a priest of the guilt of sins).
4. The Holy Eucharist (YOO kur ist), or Holy Communion, is both a sacrament and a sacrifice. During this service, known as the **mass**, the priest claims to transform the bread and the wine into the actual body and blood of Christ. The Eucharist is intended to restore the recipient spiritually.
5. Matrimony unites a man and a woman as husband and wife. It confers grace on the couple to strengthen their union and make it permanent.
6. Holy Orders sets an individual apart for the service of the church by ordaining him into the priesthood. It confers power to absolve sin and consecrate the bread and wine of the Eucharist.
7. Extreme Unction, sometimes called the last rites, gives an anointing or blessing to a seriously ill or dying person. Its purpose is to grant absolution from any remaining sin and to offer spiritual comfort.

Furthermore, they could be administered only by the church. Thus, it maintained that there was no salvation outside the one visible catholic church.

Leaders of the Church

There gradually arose a sharp distinction between the common church parishioners and those who entered (through Holy Orders) the special service of the church. The leaders of the church were called **clergy**; the parishioners were called the **laity**. Only the clergy were members of the church. Thus, in the medieval mind, only the clergy were servants of the church.

The clergy of the Roman Church were organized into different branches of service. One branch was called the **secular clergy** (from *seculum*, Latin for "world"). These men conducted religious services, administered the sacraments to the laity, and supervised the business and property of the church.

The **regular clergy** renounced the things of this world. Some sacrificed their own personal ambitions in order to maintain an active mission of social service. Most retired to a life of solitude and study. They lived in monastic communities under strict regulations. (The word *regular* comes from the Latin *regula*, meaning "rule.")

The most popular system of rules in medieval Europe came from Benedict of Nursia (480–547), often called the "Father of

Benedict of Nursia

Western Monasticism." Characterized by discipline and order, the **Benedictine Rule** strictly regulated the lives of monks. They engaged in such daily activities as manual labor, study, religious services, and prayer. Monks entering this order took vows of poverty, chastity (celibacy), and obedience to the abbot, the leader of the monastery.

The regular clergy, or monks, played an important role in the growth of the medieval church and in the progress of Western society. Some became missionaries of the medieval church. Two of the most renowned medieval missionaries were English monks: **Patrick** (ca. 387–ca. 460), who took the gospel to Ireland, and **Boniface** (ca. 672–754), who was known as the "Apostle of the Germans." Monks also developed new farming techniques.

Reforms in the Church

By placing a crown on Charlemagne's head and declaring him emperor, Pope Leo III unintentionally established a precedent. Later popes claimed that this practice demonstrated their superiority over civil rulers. In Charlemagne's day no such claim of supremacy existed. During the political disorder that followed the collapse of Charlemagne's empire, however, the papacy had opportunity to establish its claim of supreme political power. Yet the church's assertion of supremacy came gradually and experienced many setbacks. Corrupt popes and worldly clergy cost the Roman Church much of its prestige and influence. However, the reforms of the eleventh through the thirteenth centuries restored much of the church's prestige and elevated the papacy to the height of its power.

Need for Reform

During the ninth century and the early part of the tenth, much of the Roman Church had sunk deep in moral corruption. It amassed great wealth as many churchmen neglected their religious duties for temporal gain. When the political conditions in Europe became more unstable, the church needed protection for its large landholdings. The greatest threat to the church's possessions was the Viking raiders. Churchmen secured protection from these and other enemies by entering into feudal relationships. They became vassals, and their loyalties were divided between the church and feudal lords. Some kings and nobles began to claim the right not only to appoint church officials but also to invest them with their religious authority—a practice known as **lay investiture**.

Soon it became commonplace for lay lords to appoint men with few spiritual qualifications to church offices in return for their political loyalty and financial favors. Unscrupulous men, enticed by the wealth and power of high church office, bought and sold church positions. The condition of the papacy was little better. Inept and immoral men filled the office and brought disgrace upon the church. In addition, striving factions of nobles in Rome struggled over the appointment of popes.

The scandalous conditions in the Roman Church prompted a reform movement. It began in 910 at a monastery in Cluny, France, and spread quickly throughout the church. Members of this movement exposed and sought to remedy abuses within the Roman Church. They introduced measures to forbid simony (the buying and selling of religious goods, which at the time extended to the selling of church offices), to free the church from secular control resulting from lay investiture, and to restore the dignity and authority of the papacy.

One of the most influential of the reforming monastic orders was the Cistercians (sih STUR shunz). Monks of this order adopted lives of seclusion and strict discipline. They wore rough garments, abstained from meats, and worked hard in the fields. This order was made popular by its most zealous member, Bernard of Clairvaux (klare VOH; 1091–1153). A man of deep piety and sincere devotion, Bernard demonstrated by his life the genuineness of his religious convictions. He was an outspoken critic of worldliness in the Roman Church and in society.

Rivalry Between Pope and Emperor

A primary goal of church reform was to rescue the papacy from the state of weakness and corruption into which it had fallen. In 1059, the **College of Cardinals** was created to ensure that churchmen rather than Roman nobles or German kings would choose the popes. After almost two centuries of worthless popes, men of moral strength and able leadership restored dignity to, and increased the power of, the papal office. In fact, the papacy soon became the driving force of the reform movement.

King Henry IV submitting to Pope Gregory VII at Canossa

Probably the greatest of the reforming popes was **Gregory VII** (r. 1073–85). As a Benedictine monk, Gregory had been a leading advocate of papal reform. He used his influence as pope to curb other abuses in the church and to strengthen his office. Gregory believed that the Roman Church was superior to the state; therefore, he wanted to free the church from secular control. This meant doing away with lay investiture.

In 1075 Gregory formally prohibited (on penalty of excommunication) any layman from appointing a person to church office or investing a person with spiritual authority. The German emperor Henry IV refused to obey, insisting on his right to appoint the bishops in his realm. He declared that Gregory was not pope but a "false monk." In retaliation, Gregory excommunicated him and freed Henry's subjects from their oaths of loyalty. The struggle between the two might have continued, but growing discontent among the German nobles prompted Henry to seek the pope's forgiveness. In the winter of 1077 at Canossa (a castle in northern Italy), the desperate Henry was said to have stood barefoot in the snow for three days, waiting for the pope to speak to him. Gregory had temporarily won a great victory for the papacy.

The struggle over lay investiture did not end with Gregory and Henry. It continued until 1122, when another pope and another German emperor reached a compromise. At the city of Worms, they signed an agreement—the Concordat of Worms—that recognized the right of the church to elect its own bishops and abbots and to invest them with spiritual authority. These elections, however, had to be held in the presence of the emperor or his representatives. In addition, the emperor retained the right to invest church officials with secular authority.

Section Review

1–2. List two reasons for the rise of the bishop of Rome to prominence over other bishops.

3. What term is defined by the Roman Church as a religious act (necessary for salvation) that grants spiritual benefit to the one who does it?

4. Which religious act brings one into full fellowship with the Roman Catholic Church and confers the Holy Spirit to strengthen one's spiritual life?

5–6. Members of what group were considered members of the Roman Catholic Church? What are the parishoners of the Roman Catholic Church called?

7–8. Name the two English monks who were known for their missionary activity.

9–10. What pope and emperor had a showdown at Canossa in 1077? Which man initially won?

✶ Evaluate the claim that the bishop of Rome has supremacy over all other bishops based on Matthew 16.

✶ Why did lay investiture lead to controversy?

Making Connections

1. From a practical standpoint, what official actually ruled during the time of the Merovingian House?

2. Under what system did fiefs, lords, and vassals become commonplace?

3–5. List three contributions made by monasteries during the Middle Ages.

6–7. What were the roles of the secular and regular clergy?

8. How did Philip II strengthen royal authority in France?

9. What organization was created to ensure churchmen would choose the popes?

10. Who was known as the greatest reforming pope?

Developing History Skills

1. Develop a basic timeline showing the development of the medieval church based on information found in this chapter.

2. Develop a family tree covering four generations of the Carolingian House.

Thinking Critically

1. Evaluate each of the seven sacraments from Scripture.

2. Summarize the relation of church and state in the medieval world. What should be the proper relationship between church and state?

Living in God's World

1. Imagine that you are a Christian king in medieval Europe. Write a list of laws concerning the practice of religion in your nation.

2. Evaluate the feudal system from a biblical point of view. Describe an economic system for an agrarian culture that is consistent with biblical teaching.

People, Places, and Things to Know

Franks
Clovis
Merovingian House
Pepin II
Charles Martel
Charlemagne
Treaty of Verdun
Charles the Bald
Louis the German
Lothair
Vikings
Henry the Fowler
Otto I
Holy Roman Empire
Frederick I
Frederick II
Alfred the Great
Anglo-Saxon Chronicle
Battle of Hastings
Domesday Book
Hugh Capet
Île-de-France
Philip II
feudalism
lords
fiefs
vassal
investiture
knight
page
squire
chivalry
Peace of God
Truce of God
freemen
serfs
catholic
Leo I
Petrine theory
Gregory I
purgatory
seven sacraments
mass
clergy
laity
secular clergy
regular clergy
Benedictine Rule
Patrick
Boniface
lay investiture
College of Cardinals
Gregory VII

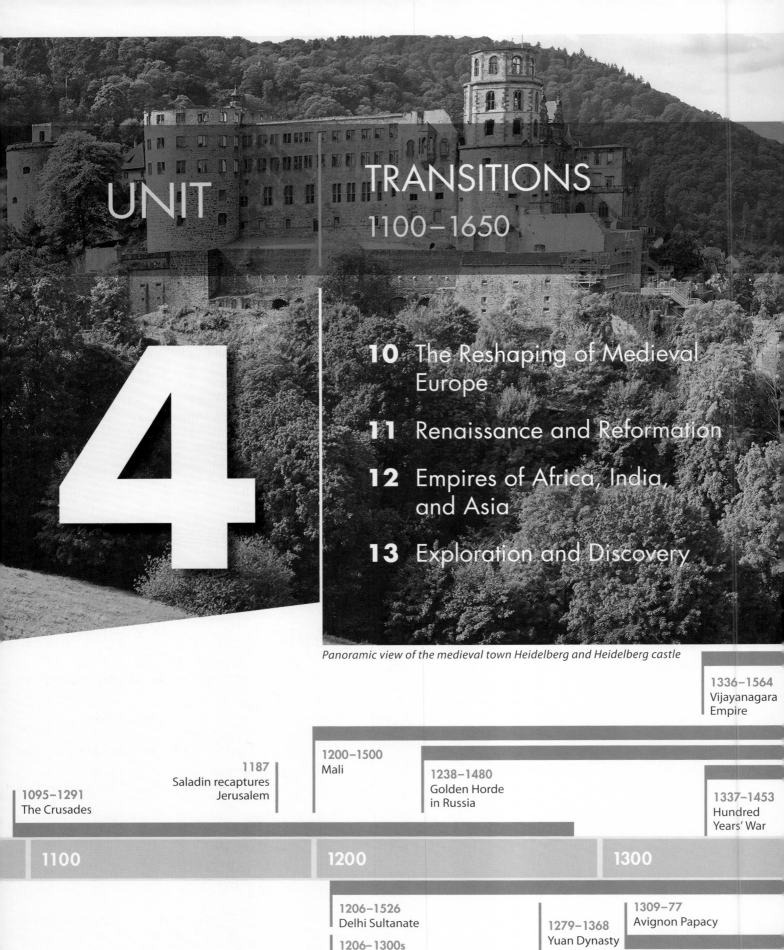

UNIT

TRANSITIONS
1100–1650

4

10 The Reshaping of Medieval Europe

11 Renaissance and Reformation

12 Empires of Africa, India, and Asia

13 Exploration and Discovery

Panoramic view of the medieval town Heidelberg and Heidelberg castle

1336–1564
Vijayanagara Empire

1200–1500
Mali

1238–1480
Golden Horde in Russia

1187
Saladin recaptures Jerusalem

1095–1291
The Crusades

1337–1453
Hundred Years' War

1100

1200

1300

1206–1526
Delhi Sultanate

1206–1300s
Mongol Empire

1279–1368
Yuan Dynasty

1309–77
Avignon Papacy

The five centuries beginning with 1100 can be described in many ways, but the era definitely encompassed noteworthy transition. This unit progresses in European history from the late Middle Ages to the period of European exploration and discovery. During this period Europe experienced momentous change due to the Renaissance and Reformation. At the same time, African, Indian, and Asian states developed significant empires that controlled a large part of their respective continents. These empires built vast trade industries and accumulated massive riches that would become the envy of European states, thus triggering the aforementioned age of exploration.

1572
St. Bartholomew's Day Massacre

1485
Henry VII becomes king

1492
Ferdinand and Isabella expel Moors
Columbus sails to the Americas

1588
Spanish Armada

1534
Henry VIII becomes head of the English Church

1493
Line of Demar-cation

1516
Erasmus publishes Greek NT

1607
Jamestown founded

1440–1897
Benin

1545–63
Council of Trent

1400

1500

1600

1450s
Gutenberg Bible printed

1517
Ninety-Five Theses

1517–1648
Reformation

1598
Edict of Nantes

1608
Quebec founded

1453
Fall of Constantinople

1470–1591
Songhai Empire

The Reshaping of Medieval Europe

10

The growth of towns dramatically changed the social structure of medieval Europe.

Big Ideas

1. How did the growth of trade influence the growth of towns in medieval Europe?

2. What were key achievements of medieval learning and art?

3. What characterized the Roman Church in this period?

4. How did nation-states develop in Europe?

In the previous chapter, we began discussing the political and religious life of people in the Middle Ages. This chapter expands that discussion to include the economic and social developments of the Middle Ages, which reveal the beginnings of modern Western society. All of these aspects are intertwined. During the late medieval period (1200–1500), Europe experienced significant changes. Merchants pursued trade with renewed vigor, towns grew in size and importance, and a new social class emerged. Contact with other cultures sparked interest in learning and the arts, and nations began to appear. At the same time, the feudal and manorial systems weakened, and the Roman Church, once the dominant force in Europe, declined in strength and influence.

I. Revival of Trade and Growth of Towns

During the early Middle Ages, trade activity sharply declined in Europe. Money was in short supply. Travel was often treacherous since roads were poor, and robbers and pirates often threatened merchants on the trade routes. Towns, which were once the heart of economic activity, declined in size. The manors became the new economic centers of medieval Europe. Unlike towns and cities, manors depended less on trade and were virtually self-sufficient. The few items that could not be made or grown on a particular manor could be obtained by barter—exchanging goods for goods. For the most part, trade remained localized and relatively insignificant. This began to change gradually beginning in the thirteenth century.

Towns, like trade, did not entirely disappear in the West during the Middle Ages. Even so, Europe could boast few cities that could compare in size and population to the many bustling cities of the Roman Empire or other parts of the world. Renewed trade, however, stimulated the growth of towns. Towns provided needed markets and were important centers of exchange.

Revival of Trade

Trade Routes

The reopening of trade routes between western Europe and the East became a major factor in the revival of European commerce. During the early Middle Ages, Byzantine and Muslim merchants had dominated trade in the Mediterranean region. Later, however, enterprising Italian merchants, with their large fleets, began to secure trade rights in the Near East. Soon Italian cities such as Venice, Pisa, and Genoa gained a virtual monopoly on Mediterranean trade.

European commerce expanded as the Italian merchants became middlemen in trade between Europe and the Orient. Once goods from the Far East reached the Mediterranean, Italian merchants transported them to Europe, where they were distributed to European markets. Traders who brought goods from the Orient reached the Mediterranean by three principal routes.

1. The southern route was almost entirely on water. Ships laden with goods from India and China sailed across the Arabian Sea and northward up the Red Sea. The goods were then hauled overland to the Nile River and transported to the Mediterranean.

2. The central route combined land and sea travel. Ships from the Far East carried goods to the Persian Gulf,

Guiding Questions

1. What encouraged the revival of trade in Europe?
2. How did trade influence medieval life?
3. What caused the growth of towns in medieval Europe?
4. How did the rise of towns affect justice, power, and citizenship in medieval Europe?

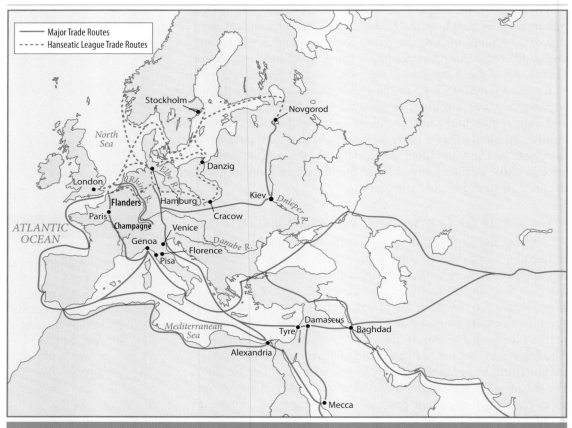

Medieval Trade Routes

where caravans transported the merchandise to Baghdad or Damascus. Other traders then brought the goods to port cities along the Mediterranean and Black Seas.

3. The northern route, known as the "Silk Road," was an overland route across central Asia. It connected Beijing and Constantinople.

Italy controlled Mediterranean trade, but Flanders was the marketplace of northern Europe. The region of Flanders (which included parts of present-day Belgium, France, and Holland) lay at the crossroads of northern European trade routes. The Flemish, who were makers of fine cloth, had easy access to the markets of Europe.

Markets and Fairs

As trade activity increased, so did the need for places where merchants could meet and exchange their goods. On the local level, markets became the primary centers for trade. Once a week traders met along important highways, in church courtyards, or in village squares. The goods sold there benefited both the people on the manor and those in the towns. The market offered incentive for the laboring serfs to produce more because at the market they could sell their surplus produce. Many serfs saved their money, desiring to buy goods or hoping one day to be able to buy their freedom from the manor. The market also offered craftsmen and merchants an opportunity to sell their goods. Thus these places of trade met the demands of the local population. Townspeople obtained surplus food from the manors, and the people of the manor acquired articles made and sold by local craftsmen and merchants.

Trade fairs operated on a larger scale than local markets and attracted merchants from all over Europe as well as many foreign countries. These fairs were sometimes great regional or international events. Merchants assembled annually, and the fairs could last from several days to several weeks. Because they were held in nearly every part of Europe, fairs were often scheduled in sequence so that merchants could attend one after the other.

Fairs provided a meeting place for East–West trade. Italian middlemen and foreign merchants from Constantinople, Damascus, and Alexandria brought spices, silks, precious gems, cotton, linen, rugs, and dyes from the East. Peddlers and town merchants bought these luxury items and distributed them locally. In return, foreign merchants purchased local products such as wool, grain, timber, and fish.

One of the most famous and important of the medieval fairs was held in Champagne, a region in northeastern France. This province became an important trade center for merchants traveling between Flanders and Italy. At almost any time during the year, fairs were being held in the towns of this region, each one lasting about six weeks.

Money and Banking

The barter system in use during the early Middle Ages could not meet the expanding demands of the trade fairs. Therefore, money gained wider use as a means of exchange. This development helped trade and provided a standard of value for the purchase and sale of goods. Feudal lords and commercial towns began minting their own coins. Their values varied greatly, depending on the amount and purity of the metal contained in them. Certain coins of high quality became widely accepted as mediums of exchange.

Because most merchants did not know the value of coins minted outside their own region, **moneychangers** grew in importance at the markets and trade fairs throughout Europe. These men were experienced in judging the approximate value of coins, discovering counterfeit currency, and determining one currency's value in relation to another. Merchants could be assured of the value of a foreign currency that they accepted for their goods. If the merchants then wanted that currency exchanged into their own, moneychangers were also ready to perform that service—for a fee.

Moneychangers did more, however, than just evaluate and exchange money for merchants. They provided many other services that we commonly associate with modern banks. Since they dealt constantly with money, moneychangers went to great lengths to protect their own funds. Realizing this, merchants began entrusting their surplus cash to the moneychangers for safekeeping. Over time, moneychangers also became moneylenders. Kings, nobles, and even popes borrowed from them to finance their activities. For example, a king might borrow money to finance a Crusade to the Holy Land. He risked great danger, however, by carrying large sums on his journey. It was much safer and more convenient to obtain a letter of credit in Europe. (Letters of credit were much like our modern checks.) Once the king reached the Holy Land, he could present the letter of credit to another moneychanger and receive cash in return.

The Medieval Church and Business Practices

There was little economic freedom in Europe during much of the medieval period. Most people had little opportunity or incentive

Medieval Fairs

Fairs such as the ones at Champagne were more than just places to exchange goods; they were festive occasions.

> The neighboring lords and their families came to see and to buy and to enjoy the diversions of the fair. The monks from the abbey and the secular clergy mingled with the throng. No doubt many an artisan and many a runaway serf from the neighboring manors [were] drawn hither by the strange sights and sounds and the gay-colored crowd. Mountebanks [sellers of "medicine"], jugglers, and musicians of every description vied in their efforts to attract the crowd, men with trained monkeys, dogs, or dancing bears, wrestlers, wandering minstrels singing ancient lays, fakers [magicians] without number were there to entertain and astonish the populace. There were gathered as in modern fairs the thief, the pick-pocket, the cutpurse, the thug, the prostitute, beggars. Often the sergeants were hard pressed to maintain order in this heterogeneous mob.

James Thompson, An Economic and Social History of the Middle Ages, *602.*

Gold Florin coin

Banks

It should not be surprising to learn that our word *bank* comes from the Italian **banca**, which means "bench," referring to the table of the moneychangers.

to improve their way of life. Feudal lords held virtual monopolies over the economic life on the manors. In addition, some of the teachings of the Roman Church tended to discourage economic activity.

In a day when religion dominated society, it was natural for the church to shape the economic ideas. The Bible teaches, "Lay not up for yourselves treasures upon earth, . . . for where your treasure is, there will your heart be also" (Matt. 6:19, 21). As a result, the church said that a seller must not take advantage of the buyer simply to gain more wealth for himself. Instead, the seller must charge a **just price** for goods sold—a price that included the cost of materials, a fair return for labor expended, and a reasonable profit. If any man received a profit greater than his needs, he was expected to give it to charity.

Furthermore, the Roman Church prohibited usury—the practice of charging interest for the use of lent money. Based on passages from the Mosaic law, usury was considered a sin (Exod. 22:25; Lev. 25:35–37; Deut. 23:19–20). The church assumed that anyone who borrowed money was in great need. Therefore, it was wrong for someone to profit from a loan made to a brother in need. Such a loan should be an act of charity, not a moneymaking venture. The revival of trade made this church teaching obsolete. Merchants borrowed money not because of poverty but for business investment. Soon it became acceptable to charge interest on loans made for investment purposes. Profit made on such loans was considered a fitting reward for the risk taken, since loss was an equal possibility.

The revival of trade and changes in business methods brought new opportunities and incentives to much of Europe's population. Sound economic principles made Europe prosperous: the dignity of labor, the legitimacy of profit, freedom of exchange, and individual responsibility for economic matters. More and more people in Europe were gaining financial independence.

Growth of Towns

By the eleventh century, forces at work in Europe began to give shape to the forerunners of the modern city. Improved farming methods led to increased agricultural production. Townspeople who wished to devote their full energy to a specific trade or craft could depend on others to produce surplus food. An increased food supply encouraged families to have more children and boosted Europe's population. As Europe's population grew, so did its towns. Some towns revived within the decayed walls of old Roman cities, while others sprang up at locations important to trade: crossroads, bridges, fords, river deltas, and harbors.

Townsmen Gain Basic Freedoms

Merchants and craftsmen, who lived in the growing urban centers, did not fit into the medieval class structure. They were not lords, vassals, or serfs. And their labor contributed little to the agricultural output of the local manor. Nevertheless, nearly every town was initially subject to some feudal lord.

Townsmen with common interests soon banded together to gain freedom from feudal interference and to secure local self-government. They achieved this independence in a variety of ways. Some towns bought privileges from feudal lords who were willing to grant certain liberties in exchange for large sums of money. Other

Quentin Matsys, The Moneylender and His Wife

lords bestowed these privileges freely, since a thriving town meant greater revenues from sales taxes and tolls. However, some lords did not want to relinquish control under any circumstances. In such cases, towns might support a king who would grant them freedom in exchange for payment of taxes.

The privileges granted to a town by a feudal lord or king were usually written down in a legal document called a **charter**. This document outlined the rights and freedoms of the townspeople. The more favorable the charter, the greater the number of people attracted to settle in the town. While liberties varied from town to town, most townsmen shared certain basic freedoms:

1. *Free Status.* The most important privilege enjoyed by a townsman was that of being a freeman. No matter what his previous status, a man who lived in a town for a year and a day gained his freedom. A serf, for example, who ran away from his manor and managed to escape capture by living in a town for one year broke all ties with his manor. An old German proverb said, "Town air makes one free."

2. *Exemption from Manorial Obligations.* Town charters usually exempted townsmen from laboring for the lord of the manor. The townsmen as a group, not as individuals, owed service to the lord. This service was usually rendered in the form of a cash payment.

3. *Town Justice.* Townsmen also won the privilege of administering their own justice. Instead of being tried in a feudal court and judged by feudal customs, a townsman was tried in the court of his town and was judged by townspeople and town customs.

4. *Commercial Privileges.* The chief commercial freedom granted to townsmen was the right to buy and sell freely in the town market. The merchants were free from feudal interference and were protected from competition by outside merchants.

Merchants and Craftsmen Establish Guilds

Merchants and craftsmen in growing towns banded together to protect their common commercial interests. They formed organizations called **guilds**, whose primary function was to regulate the business activity of a given town. By acting together, town merchants gained greater security, discouraged outside competition, and increased profits. Guilds also provided aid to members in need. They established schools and cared for the poor, widows, and orphans. Powerful guilds helped towns obtain favorable charters and played an important role in town governments.

There were two types of guilds: merchant and craft. The earlier type was the merchant guild. It guarded the trade interests of merchants by giving them a monopoly of a town's trade. The guild restricted outsiders from doing business in town except upon payment of a heavy fee. The guild also fixed prices at which goods could be bought and sold in the town market.

At first each town had only one guild. But as a town's trade grew and became more specialized, each merchant guild divided into many craft guilds. There were guilds for the town's bakers,

Guild halls in Antwerp, Belgium

tanners, shoemakers, butchers, wheelwrights, and other craftsmen. Each craft guild regulated the hours its members worked, the wages earned, and the number of employees hired. Members of a particular guild guaranteed the quality of their products. They punished members who used shoddy materials, dealt dishonestly, or sold goods cheaper than the established price.

Within each craft guild there were three classes of members: apprentices, journeymen, and masters. A young boy began his training as an **apprentice**. He entered the home of a master craftsman and was expected to work hard in return for his food, lodging, and training. It was the master's responsibility to teach the young apprentice not only the skills of the trade but also proper conduct. At the end of his apprenticeship—a period varying from two to seven years—the young man became a **journeyman**, or "day laborer." He could then seek employment and earn wages as a skilled worker. Usually a journeyman remained at the home of his master and worked at his master's shop.

Every journeyman looked forward to the day when he could become a master himself. This required years of experience, as well as funds to open a shop. To become a **master**, a journeyman had to undergo an oral examination, present an example of his workmanship (called a "master piece"), and take an oath to conduct himself according to the regulations of the guild. Once approved by the other masters of the guild, the new master could open his own shop and take on his own apprentices and journeymen.

Sometimes towns formed associations with other towns to promote and protect their mutual commercial interests. The most famous of these was the **Hanseatic League**, composed of more than seventy German cities in northwestern Europe. The Hanse (German for "guild") sought to organize and control trade in Sweden, Russia, Flanders, and England. Although the Hanse primarily sought commercial privileges, it also became a powerful political force. The Hanse negotiated treaties, maintained its own navy, and even waged war against other countries.

A New Social Class Emerges

In early feudal society, a great social and economic gulf had separated the nobility and the peasants. With the growth of towns during the eleventh and twelfth centuries, however, a new social class arose, commonly referred to as the **middle class**. It was composed of merchants, bankers, craftsmen, and skilled laborers. These were the "men of the town" known as burgesses in England, *bourgeois* in France, and *burgers* in Germany. (The word *burg* means "a walled town.") The members of this new class had freedom and money. They were energetic, independent, mobile, and growing in number and power. Their world was the town market, and their livelihood was trade. The middle class contributed to the decline of feudalism and helped shape modern society.

Most noblemen considered the middle class a threat to their position in society. Social ranking, formerly determined by birth or landholding, had gradually shifted toward those who possessed the greatest amounts of money and goods. A nobleman's wealth was in his land; a merchant's wealth was his money or goods. While the nobleman usually spent the money he derived from his land, the merchant invested his money, often at great risk, to gain more wealth. Soon many merchants, bankers, and master craftsmen possessed more goods, fine clothes, and comfortable dwellings than the feudal lords.

By challenging the nobility's social position, the middle class also weakened the nobility's political authority. By the twelfth century, most towns had gained some degree of self-government. Although townsmen were able to regulate trade within their own town, they realized that the sectionalism produced by feudalism and the tolls and sales taxes levied by feudal lords hindered widespread trade. As a result, the middle class desired the stable and uniform government a national king could offer rather than the localism of feudal lords. Kings, who had previously relied on nobles to supply revenue and soldiers, now could draw upon the rich resources of the towns and the middle class, usually in the form of taxes.

Town Life

Medieval towns were small. By the thirteenth century, only a few, such as Paris, Rome, Venice, and Florence, had populations of over fifty thousand. The typical town averaged only about five thousand people. Most towns were enclosed by thick walls for protection. As the population of the town grew, conditions became overcrowded. Old walls had to be torn down and new ones built to create more room. Because land space within walled towns was limited, houses were crowded together along narrow streets. It was not uncommon for houses to be four or five stories high. The upper stories of houses often extended out over the streets.

The streets below were dark, crooked, and filthy. The townspeople tossed their garbage into open gutters lining the roads. According to medieval writers, the stench from some towns could be smelled miles away. Poor sanitation caused disease, and epidemics spread rapidly, carried throughout the town by the pigs, rats, and dogs that roamed the streets.

Although town life was not easy or comfortable, it was often exciting. During the day the streets hummed with the noise of merchants and peddlers selling their wares, of craftsmen plying their

Narrow street in Italy

trades, and of children playing in the streets. The center of activity was the town square. Here visiting merchants displayed dazzling items from foreign lands. Within the square's large open space, the town's militia drilled, boys played, and actors performed. Lining the square were the town hall, various guild halls, and the towering cathedral.

Section Review

1–2. List two factors that led to the revival of trade in Europe.

3–4. List two factors that contributed to the growth of towns in medieval Europe.

5–6. List two basic freedoms shared by most townspeople.

7. What was the primary function of a guild?

8–9. What new social class arose with the rise of towns in the eleventh and twelfth centuries? What were the chief occupations of the people of this class?

★ How did trade change life in medieval Europe?

★ How did the rise of towns affect justice, power, and citizenship in medieval Europe?

Guiding Questions

1. What were the key achievements of medieval culture?
2. How did the rise of universities affect medieval Europe?
3. What were the strengths and weaknesses of Scholasticism?
4. How did medieval science lay the groundwork for scientific accomplishments?

II. Advance of Medieval Learning and Art

The Middle Ages is often considered a period of ignorance and superstition—a "dark age" for learning. While there was little formal education of the masses throughout much of this period, education never completely died out. Learning continued, primarily under the influence of the Roman Church. The monks constituted the vast majority of the educated. The primary centers of education were the monasteries and cathedrals.

A basic part of medieval education was the liberal arts curriculum, which was divided into two groups of studies: the trivium, consisting of grammar (Latin), rhetoric (effective speaking), and logic; and the quadrivium, consisting of arithmetic, geometry, astronomy, and music. A medieval bishop and historian described his own education:

> [I was taught] by means of grammar to read, by dialectic [logic] to apprehend the arguments in disputes, by rhetoric to recognize the different meters, by geometry to comprehend the measurement of the earth and of lines, by [astronomy] to contemplate the paths of the heavenly bodies, by arithmetic to understand the parts of numbers, by harmony to fit the modulated voice to the sweet accent of the verse.
>
> Gregory of Tours, History of the Franks, trans. Ernest Brehaut, 248.

During the twelfth century, a revival of learning began to sweep across Europe. It was brought about by several factors:

1. Political and economic conditions in Europe were improving, producing a climate more favorable for intellectual and cultural pursuits.

2. Europe's contact with the Byzantine and Arab civilizations through the Crusades exposed Europe to ancient documents and new ideas. These cultures transmitted to Europe not only their own knowledge but also the

preserved learning of ancient Greece and Rome. New avenues of study opened as Justinian's code of laws, the works of Aristotle, copies of the Bible in Greek, and medical writings in Greek and Arabic became available in Europe.

3. As towns grew and the functions of government expanded, there was an increasing need for education. A theological training was no longer sufficient to meet all the needs of law and business. Greater numbers of people—including many from the rising middle class—were seeking to enter the ranks of the educated.

Universities

One of the most important developments during this period was the rise of universities. These new centers of learning gradually replaced most of the old monastery and cathedral schools of the Roman Church. During this period, students had little concern about the town or school in which they studied. They were more interested in the qualifications of their teacher. Students traveled all over Europe to find the best instructor in their subject area. A master teacher attracted many students, who paid him a fee to teach them. As the number of teachers and students grew in a given locality, the students and scholars—like craftsmen—formed educational guilds for privileges and protection. Initially, any association of people, such as a guild, was called a ***universitas***. But gradually the term came to designate only those people united for the common purpose of education.

Two of the earliest universities were at Bologna in northern Italy and at Paris. Each school offered training in specialized areas of study. Bologna became a leading center for the study of law. Paris became the center for the study of theology. Another early university, in Salerno, Italy, specialized in the study of medicine. These schools served as models for other universities.

Great Hall of Study at the University of Bologna

Philosophy and Theology

The schools and universities of twelfth-century Europe provided a home for a new intellectual movement known as **Scholasticism.** Scholasticism finds its roots in Bible study. The scholar began by reading the Bible. He outlined the book he was reading and then reread the book in sections. As he read these sections, the scholar would note the doctrines discussed by those parts of the Bible, and he would write down questions that the Bible brought to mind. He then would think through all the possible answers to the questions he had recorded in an attempt to discern the right answers. After many years, the questions were removed from the commentaries on the biblical text and organized logically in categories, such as God, angels, man, and the sacraments. The Scholastic method raised the question of how knowledge gained by revelation and knowledge gained by reason fit together. In general, Scholastic theologians believed that revelation was more important and that reason served to help Christians understand revelation.

Three of the most significant Scholastic thinkers were Anselm, Peter Abelard (AB uh lard), and Thomas Aquinas (uh KWY nus). In their writings, these men wrestled with the relationship between revelation and reason. The earliest of these was Anselm (1033–1109),

Statue of Anselm

the archbishop of Canterbury, whose view of the relationship between reason and revelation may be summed up by the following statement:

> I do not try, Lord, to attain Your lofty heights, because my understanding is in no way equal to it. But I do desire to understand Your truth a little, that truth that my heart believes and loves. For I do not seek to understand so that I may believe; but I believe so that I may understand. For I believe this also, that "unless I believe, I shall not understand."

Charlesworth, M. J. Trans., St. Anselm's Proslogian, 1.

Anselm realized that faith in God's revelation is essential to proper understanding. Nevertheless, he did not reject the use of reason. Anselm believed Christians should use reason to better understand God's revelation. He is best remembered for his use of logical arguments to support two major doctrines of the Christian faith: the existence of God and the satisfaction concept of the atonement (that Christ's death on the cross satisfied God's holiness and justice and redeemed fallen man).

Peter Abelard (1079–1141) advocated the frequent asking of questions as the "first key to wisdom." Abelard, a popular teacher of philosophy and theology at Paris, governed his studies by the following principle: "By doubting we arrive at inquiry [asking critical questions], and through inquiry we perceive the truth." In his most famous work, *Sic et Non* ("Yes and No"), Abelard listed 158 questions concerning important articles of faith. With each question he presented pro-and-con statements made by earlier church scholars. He thereby demonstrated that seemingly contradictory

Thomas Aquinas

views existed. Abelard expected his students to use critical reasoning to harmonize the seemingly contradictory statements of the earlier scholars. When statements could not be harmonized, they were to settle on the view that had the greatest authority supporting it. However, some church leaders viewed his emphasis on reason as dangerous to the teachings of the Roman Church.

Scholasticism reached its height under Thomas Aquinas (c. 1225–74), called "the Prince of the Schoolmen." Aquinas faced a new challenge. Until his time reason was used by the Schoolmen to help in formulating theology. But once the philosophy of Aristotle was rediscovered, the Schoolmen wondered if an entire philosophical system, especially a pagan one, could serve as an aid to theology. Some theologians said no, and they rejected Aristotle altogether. Other theologians said yes, and where theology and philosophy disagreed, they said there could be two different truths: something could be true in philosophy and false in theology or true in theology and false in philosophy. Aquinas rejected both of these views. He said that Aristotle's philosophy could be used to help understand theological ideas, but he also said that when the church's teaching and Aristotle disagreed, the church's teaching was right and Aristotle was wrong. Aquinas's book *Summa Theologiae* followed this approach to theology and philosophy.

The Scholastics were the first systematic theologians, and much of the theology they developed was believed by later Roman Catholics as well as Protestants. But the Scholastics also experienced a serious problem. In studying men's answers to biblical questions, they moved further and further away from Scripture, and reason began to take center stage instead of revelation. This departure resulted in a reaction against Scholasticism that eventually bore fruit in the Protestant Reformation.

Medieval Science

Much of the knowledge that led to the development of science in Europe resulted from access to documents that Muslim scholars had preserved from Greek and Roman scientific writings. Albert the Great, a Dominican friar, played an important role in introducing the documents to medieval universities. Robert Grosseteste, bishop of London, also proved to be a central character in advancing medieval science. Grosseteste influenced one of his students, **Roger Bacon** (c. 1214–94), in the areas of optics and astronomy. Bacon made significant contributions in the areas of physics, geography, and optics. He also advocated observation and experimentation as tests for scientific conclusions.

Roger Bacon

The scientific thinking of medieval scholars was shaped by the writings of Aristotle. But these scholars knew that Aristotle was not right about everything. For instance, Aristotle taught that the world was eternal. Medieval scholars, however, believed the Bible's teaching that God created the world from nothing. In this and other areas, these scholars modified Aristotle's thought. Some of their work prepared the way for the Scientific Revolution. However, the development of the university as a place where people learned and wrote about the natural world may have been the most important contribution to future generations.

Language and Literature

As previously mentioned, the language of the learned during the Middle Ages was Latin. It was firmly established in the universities and governments throughout Europe and was the official language of the Roman Catholic Church. It was not the spoken language of the common people, however. The common tongue varied from region to region; French, German, Italian, Spanish, and English were among those spoken. By the twelfth century, writers began to use the common spoken language, or **vernacular**, in literature.

Among the earliest forms of vernacular literature was the heroic epic—a long narrative poem that celebrated the adventures of legendary heroes. Many of these epics have become national treasures: England's *Beowulf*, France's *Song of Roland*, Germany's *Song of Nibelungs*, and Spain's poem "The Lay of the Cid" about El Cid. Wandering minstrels popularized the vernacular in lyric poetry. They traveled from castle to castle singing their songs of love and adventure to noblemen and their ladies. They also popularized stories about knights, chivalry, and love. Probably the best known of these medieval romances are the tales of King Arthur and the Knights of the Round Table.

The two greatest writers of the late medieval period were Dante and Chaucer. **Dante Alighieri** (DAHN-tay ah-lee-GYEH-ree; 1265–1321) was an Italian poet. His *Divine Comedy* ranks as one of the most brilliant works in all literature. In this long poem Dante takes an imaginary journey through hell, purgatory, and paradise. His work reflects the religious beliefs, social order, and political turbulence of the late Middle Ages.

Geoffrey Chaucer (CHAW sur; c. 1343–1400) was a prominent English poet. His masterpiece, *The Canterbury Tales*, presents a collection of stories told by pilgrims on their way to visit the tomb of Thomas à Becket at Canterbury (see p. 220). Chaucer used his skill as a storyteller and his insight into human behavior to depict English life and customs. By their masterful use of the vernacular in literature, both Dante and Chaucer aided the development of their native languages.

Art and Architecture

The art of the Middle Ages was primarily religious. Since most Europeans were illiterate, the church used the visual arts to teach Bible stories. Artists depicted Bible characters and popular "saints" of the church with certain characteristics. These symbols helped the observer identify the painted or sculptured figures. For example, John the Baptist is always shown wearing an animal skin and carrying a staff with a cross on top. The skin illustrates the fact that "John was clothed with camel's hair" (Mark 1:6). The cross symbolizes his message: "Behold the Lamb of God, which taketh away the sin of the world" (John 1:29).

The most prominent form of medieval art was religious architecture. The people of Europe poured much of their wealth and energy into building impressive cathedrals. From 1050 to about 1150, the prevalent architectural style in Europe was **Romanesque** (roh muh NESK), which means "Roman-like." Romanesque builders modified the rectangular Roman basilica (which earlier church architects had copied) and constructed churches in the shape of a Latin cross. Thick walls supported the tremendous weight of stone vaults and ceilings. Other features included rounded arches, heavy columns, and small doors and windows. The interiors of these churches were dark and gloomy.

Beginning about the thirteenth century, architects devised a way to support stone vaults and ceilings by the use of "flying," or external, buttresses. These supports made it possible for cathedrals to have higher ceilings, thinner walls, and larger windows and doors. This new style was called **Gothic**. In contrast to the dark and heavy elements of the Romanesque, Gothic architecture was light and delicate. The spacious and lofty Gothic cathedrals

Medieval church in Poitiers, France

Cathedral of Notre Dame in Paris, an example of Gothic architecture

created an atmosphere of dignity and serenity. Their high towers and pointed arches soared toward heaven, inviting people to turn their thoughts toward God. Another feature of Gothic architecture was stained-glass windows. They added beauty, light, and color to the interior of churches. They also served as a type of visual Bible. By arranging the glass pieces, artists illustrated biblical stories in vivid colors.

Section Review

1–3. List three key achievements of medieval culture.

4–5. What were two of the earliest universities begun in Europe?

6–9. What were two strengths and two weaknesses of Scholasticism?

10. How did medieval science lay the groundwork for scientific accomplishment in the early modern period?

11–12. Who were the two greatest writers of the late Middle Ages?

 ★ How did the rise of universities affect medieval Europe?

 ★ How is the debate over the relation between Aristotle and theology similar to modern controversies between science and theology?

III. Rise and Fall of the Roman Church

Zenith

The years of reform (discussed in chapter 9) restored the church's prestige, tightened its hold over its members, and broadened its influence on medieval society. Nowhere was this power more evident than in the papacy. For centuries popes had contended that their power exceeded that of kings; the reality of that claim was now established. The battle over lay investiture and the formation of new religious orders had resulted in increased papal authority throughout Europe.

Innocent III

Papal power and prestige reached its zenith under Pope **Innocent III** (1198–1216). No pope before or after him exercised such

Guiding Questions

1. How did the Roman Catholic Church enjoy a rise and suffer a fall in this era?
2. What were central aspects of the medieval church during this period?
3. What resulted from the decline of the Roman Catholic Church?

Innocent III

extensive authority over both church and state. Innocent likened his authority to the sun, and that of kings, to the moon:

> The Creator of the universe set up two great luminaries [sources of light] in the firmament of heaven; the greater light to rule the day, the lesser light to rule the night. In the same way . . . he appointed two great dignities; the greater to bear rule over souls (these being, as it were, days), the lesser to bear rule over bodies (these being, as it were, nights). These dignities are the [papal] authority and the royal power. Furthermore, the moon derives her light from the sun, and is in truth inferior to the sun in both size and quality, in position as well as effect. In the same way the royal power derives its dignity from the [papal] authority.
>
> Henry Bettenson, ed., Documents of the Christian Church, 157–58.

How was Innocent III able to enforce this claim when earlier popes had failed? A large measure of his success was due to the strength of the Roman Catholic Church over which he ruled. By the thirteenth century the Roman Church had matured into a large, wealthy, and powerful organization. By summoning the vast resources of the church that were at his disposal and by taking advantage of its strong influence on society, Innocent established his authority over all of Europe.

Papal Weapons

It was difficult for anyone to resist the ecclesiastical weapons that popes directed against those who offended the Roman Church. The primary weapons in the church's arsenal were the following:

1. *Excommunication*—the punishment of an individual by depriving him of the sacraments and excluding him from the fellowship of the Roman Church. This was an especially powerful weapon in the hands of the pope because churchmen believed that a pope controlled access to heaven and could through excommunication deprive an individual of any hope of eternal salvation.

2. *Interdict*—the suspension of public church services and of the administration of all sacraments (except baptism and extreme unction) in a given location. Popes often used this weapon against disobedient kings. By placing a king's realm under an interdict, the pope hoped that the suspension of spiritual blessings from the church would bring about a public outcry that would force the erring king to submit.

3. *Inquisition*—a special church court commissioned by the pope to stamp out heresy. Heresy, which the Roman Church defined as the holding of beliefs contrary to its teaching, was considered to be the greatest of medieval crimes. Therefore, popes granted inquisitors special powers to seek out and judge alleged heretics. Inquisitors often used torture to make the accused admit to heresy; under such torture, even many innocent people "confessed." Those who would not bend, even under torture, often faced death as punishment. Over time, even those who did confess faced the possibility of death by burning at the stake.

The Crusades

During the eleventh century, the Seljuk Turks advanced into Palestine and seized the holy places of Christendom, making it almost impossible for European pilgrims to travel to the sacred sites. They also invaded Asia Minor and threatened the security of Constantinople. Seeing his land in peril, the Byzantine emperor appealed to Christians in the West for help against the Turks. Pilgrims returning from the Holy Land also described the atrocities committed by the Muslim Turks against churches, monasteries, and groups of pilgrims.

In 1095 Pope Urban II addressed a council of church leaders and French noblemen at Clermont, France, calling for a holy crusade to free the Holy Land from the Turks. He urged them to avenge the wrongs done by Muslim forces and challenged them to take control of this region.

There were eight major Crusades between 1095 and 1291, although only the First Crusade was anything close to a successful military campaign. Some crusaders traveled alone or in small bands; most, however, joined the large organized expeditions. The Fourth Crusade proved disastrous for the Byzantines when the crusaders attacked and plundered Constantinople. Subsequent crusades also failed to defeat Muslim forces in the Holy Land.

Despite their failures, the Crusades had far-reaching consequences. In the Middle East the Seljuk Empire declined and eventually came under Ottoman domination. However, Islam remained dominant in the region. In addition, Muslim traders sold goods at exorbitant prices to Europeans, who had come to place a great value on the spices, fruits, and other commodities brought back to Europe by the crusaders and European merchants. This led to a rush for European nations to find alternate routes to the East in order to bypass the Muslim middlemen.

Although it is impossible to fully measure the effects of the Crusades on western Europe, several profound changes can be identified:

1. The Crusades weakened the feudal structure of Europe. Feudal nobles, seeking to raise money to go on Crusades, allowed the serfs to buy their freedom. Freed serfs left the manors with hopes of finding new opportunities in the growing towns. With the decline of feudalism came the emergence of strong nations ruled by kings. Under the pretext of financing the Crusades, several European kings gained the power to tax. Taxation provided badly needed revenues, which monarchs used to extend their powers.

2. The Crusades expanded the commercial activity of Europe. The crusaders were amazed at the riches they found in the East. They came to know and desire such luxuries as sugar, spices, fruits, silks, cotton, and glass mirrors (which Middle Eastern countries obtained through trade with the Orient). The heightened demand for these goods in Europe led enterprising individuals to import them. The increase in trade prompted the renewal of a money economy (as opposed to a barter system) and the need for banking services. It also motivated Europeans to search for even greater profits by finding new routes to the East.

3. The early Crusades strengthened the papacy. By calling for the Crusades and collecting taxes or tithes to finance them, popes extended their powers in both secular and sacred matters. As most of the Crusades failed, however, people became disillusioned and began to disregard the continued calls for new Crusades. Respect for the crusading ideals and the papacy continued to diminish as popes called for Crusades to seek out and kill so-called heretics in Europe and battle with unruly German kings.

4. The Crusades opened new horizons to the people of medieval Europe. Contact with the East changed their attitudes and introduced them to Byzantine and Muslim culture. In addition, the Crusades renewed interest in the knowledge of ancient Greece and Rome—knowledge that had been preserved by the civilizations in the East. Furthermore, the Europeans' travel experiences and increased understanding of world geography gave impetus to the later period of exploration.

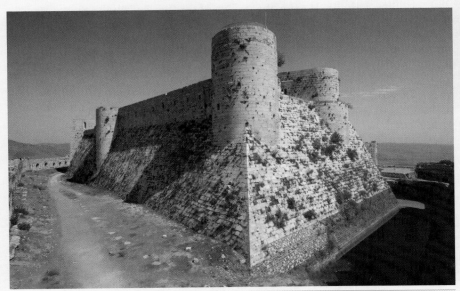

Crusader castle

Decline

The reign of the Roman Catholic Church, however, was brief. After reaching its zenith under Innocent III, the papacy fell into disgrace in less than a century. It lost not only its hold on the kings of Europe but also its position of leadership in the church. The church lost power and prestige, not only because of the growing moral corruption of the clergy but also because of the shifting loyalties in European society. With the rise of strong states, national loyalties began to overshadow church loyalty. Many kings no longer tolerated papal interference in their lands. Furthermore, the expansion of knowledge challenged the traditions of the Roman Church, and a critical spirit of inquiry gradually replaced the passive acceptance of the church's teachings. In addition, the steady growth of wealth in European society turned people's attention from spiritual concerns to earthly gain.

Papal Humiliation

The declining power of the papacy became apparent during the administration of Pope **Boniface VIII** (r. 1294–1303). He sought to control Europe the same way that Innocent III had. However, conditions had changed, and the demands of Boniface met with stiff resistance.

Trouble began when the French king Philip IV decided to levy a tax on the French clergy. The pope denounced this act, but his words went unheeded. The conflict intensified when Philip arrested a bishop who was accused of violating French law and brought him before a royal court to stand trial. Boniface ordered Philip to release the bishop. When Philip refused, Boniface issued the famous papal document ***Unam Sanctam*** (1302). In this strong statement of papal supremacy, Boniface asserted that "it is altogether necessary to salvation for every human being to be subject to the Roman pontiff."

Philip, supported by the French people, defied the pope. He accused Boniface of heresy and sought to bring him to trial. Philip's agents, accompanied by a band of soldiers, traveled to the papal residence and took the pope captive. Boniface was severely beaten and nearly died. After three days of captivity, Philip's agents freed the feeble pope. He died a few weeks later.

Papal Exile

National awareness and royal power triumphed over the demands of the papacy. A short time after the death of Boniface, Philip pressured the College of Cardinals to elect a Frenchman to the papal office. The new pope moved the papal capital from Rome to Avignon (AH vee nyawn), a city on the border of France. From 1309 to 1377 the popes—all Frenchmen—resided at Avignon. This period is known as the **Babylonian Captivity** of the church, or the Avignon Exile. Although the popes were not actually held captive, they did remain under the influence of the French kings.

During the Avignon years, the power of the papacy declined even further. The rising tide of nationalism caused the English, Germans, and Italians to resent a French-controlled papacy. In addition, critics of the Roman Church denounced the wealth and corruption that marked the Avignon court. Some of the popes raised new church taxes and sold church offices to maintain their lives of luxury. While the Avignon popes were able administrators of

Boniface VIII

the church bureaucracy, they appeared to show little concern for spiritual matters. Once again calls for reform echoed across Europe.

Papal Schism

Pope Gregory XI (r. 1370–78) returned to Rome in 1377 but died soon after taking up residence in the city. The French-dominated College of Cardinals, threatened by a Roman mob, elected an Italian as pope. Several months later, the cardinals declared the election invalid and elected a new pope, who ruled from Avignon. The Roman Church now had two popes—one in Rome and one in Avignon. Both men claimed to be the rightful pope, and each excommunicated the other. For forty years this **Great Schism** divided the allegiance of the nations of Europe.

In 1409 church leaders met at Pisa to resolve the schism within the Roman Church. The council deposed both popes and appointed a new one. However, the other two refused to relinquish their office, so the church now had three popes. The matter was finally settled at the **Council of Constance** (1414–18). This large gathering of church leaders succeeded in deposing the other claimants to the papal office and secured the election of Martin V as the sole pope. The council healed the schism and restored the papacy to Rome. But because it was unwilling to enact any meaningful reforms, the council failed to stop the growing criticism of the church's doctrine and practice. As a result, the Babylonian Captivity and the Great Schism added more fuel to the smoldering discontent that would soon flame into the Protestant Reformation.

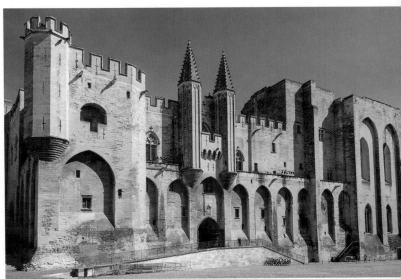

The papal palace at Avignon

Section Review

1–5. Summarize the rise and decline of the Roman Catholic Church during this period, beginning with Innocent III and ending with the Council of Constance.

6. Why was the French king Philip IV able to ignore the pope's demands and decrees?

★ Was the Roman Catholic Church's exercise of political power during this period just? Why or why not?

★ What resulted from the decline of the Roman Catholic Church?

IV. Emergence of National States

Nation-states developed in the late Middle Ages as people in certain regions became more fully aware of their common traditions and language. This awareness became the foundation of nationalism. Accompanying the growth of nation-states was the rise of national monarchies. The monarchy served as the symbol of national pride. The independent king ruling a group of people with common interests formed the basis of early nation-states. Royal power steadily increased in the fourteenth and fifteenth centuries while feudalism gradually declined. As differences among the various people in Europe became more distinct, boundaries between nation-states

Guiding Questions

1. What was the impact of military conflicts in this period?
2. What European nations developed during this period?
3. Why did Italy and the German states fail to achieve national unity?

began to solidify. By 1500 the major states of Europe were established. The medieval age was passing; the modern age was at hand.

England
Reforms Strengthen Royal Authority

When William's sons William II and Henry I died without a male heir, the Norman line came to an end. After a period of dispute over rightful succession, the crown passed to the Plantagenet (or Angevin) family, founded by Henry II (r. 1154–89), the great-grandson of William the Conqueror. A Frenchman, Henry possessed more wealth and territory outside England than within. Through inheritance and marriage, he had gained landholdings in France that far surpassed those ruled directly by his feudal lord, the French king. This situation provoked jealous rivalry between the French and English thrones.

Henry strengthened royal authority in England by expanding the jurisdiction of the royal courts. Before this time, each lord had his own court for deciding cases concerning his vassals and serfs. Henry established circuit courts with justices who traveled throughout the land hearing cases. During Henry's time, the circuit courts usually heard only cases involving land disputes, but later other cases were handled also.

Before the circuit justices arrived in a shire, a jury composed of men of that district would make a list of **indictments** (accusations) of what crimes had been committed and who the suspected offenders were. (From this practice arose the modern-day grand jury, which decides whether there is sufficient evidence to hold an accused person for trial.) When the justice heard a case, he often relied on information supplied by a smaller jury of men acquainted with the facts of the case. Gradually, it became the accepted practice to have "twelve good and truthful men" serve on this jury, the forerunner of trial juries in America. Unlike their modern counterparts, however, these men gave evidence upon which the justice could render a verdict, instead of being the ones to hear the evidence and give the verdict.

As a result of Henry's judicial reforms, more cases were tried in the royal courts than in the feudal ones. The decisions of Henry's justices provided uniform laws for all of England and thus superseded the local feudal laws. This **common law** not only helped ensure justice but also helped to draw the English people together into a unified nation.

Henry hoped to strengthen his authority over the church by appointing his friend Thomas à Becket archbishop of Canterbury, the highest church office in England. Once in office, however, Becket became a bitter opponent of Henry's interference in church matters. The controversy reached a climax when Henry attempted to bring clerics accused of committing grave crimes to trial in royal, instead of church, courts. Becket resisted. Outraged by his opposition, Henry reportedly exclaimed, "What a pack of fools and cowards I have nourished in my house, that not one of them will avenge me of this turbulent priest!" Four knights, hearing the king's rash words, traveled to Canterbury and murdered the archbishop at his altar. Because of the popular uproar over Becket's death in 1170, the king abandoned his plans to control the clergy. Becket became a martyr and his tomb a popular shrine.

Henry II

Magna Carta Limits Royal Power

After Henry's death his oldest son, Richard I (r. 1189–99), became king. Richard, known as "the Lion-Hearted," was an able warrior and an admired crusader. Nevertheless, he contributed little to the English crown. He spent less than six months of his ten-year reign in England. His participation in the Third Crusade and the defense of his French holdings from the king of France occupied most of his reign. While he was absent from England, his brother John and the king of France plotted to overthrow him. His reign provides the setting for the adventures of the legendary English hero Robin Hood.

The death of Richard elevated John (r. 1199–1216) to the English throne. John was a competent ruler, but he lacked the strong personal qualities that had won Richard the trust and admiration of the people. John's weak will and cruel, unscrupulous ways brought him nothing but trouble. John's reign was marked by continual conflict with three formidable opponents: the French king, the pope, and the English nobles—all of whom got the better of him. The French king Philip II took advantage of John's weakness and extended his royal control over many of John's French possessions.

In the meantime, John clashed with Pope Innocent III over who would be the next archbishop of Canterbury. When the archbishop of Canterbury died in 1206 and John failed to appoint a new one, the monks at Canterbury decided that they would choose a new archbishop. (This choice was usually made with the approval of the king and the English bishops.) The monks sent the man of their choice to Rome to be confirmed by the pope. When John heard of this, he was outraged and had the bishops choose another man, who was also sent to Rome. When both men arrived in Rome, Innocent III refused to confirm either. Instead he selected a friend of his, an English cardinal named Stephen Langton, to be archbishop. When John refused to allow Stephen into England (he had been out of the country for several years), trouble broke out.

Innocent placed England under an interdict and excommunicated the king. Having no allies and threatened by a French invasion, John submitted to the pope, even to the point of becoming the pope's vassal and making England a fief of the papacy. Restored to the pope's graces, John was able to avert Philip's invasion of England. However, he was not able to put down a rebellion of the English barons (nobles).

The English barons were dissatisfied with John's reign. They resented his excessive taxes and his disregard for their feudal privileges. In 1215 the infuriated nobles revolted. At Runnymede, a meadow near London, they forced John to set his seal to the **Magna Carta** (Latin for "Great Charter"). Originally intended as a guarantee of feudal rights, the Magna Carta became one of the most important documents in English history. Later Englishmen looked to the Magna Carta as establishing the principle that the king's power is limited: the king is not above the law and can be removed for refusing to obey it.

Magna Carta Memorial

Parliament Becomes an Important Institution

One of England's most gifted medieval kings was **Edward I** (r. 1272–1307). He attempted to extend English rule over all of Britain—Wales, Scotland, and England. He conquered Wales and made

Louis IX

Saint Louis

Louis IX's character is demonstrated in the instruction he gave to his son and heir:

> Fair son, the first thing I would teach thee is to set thine heart to love God; for unless he love God none can be saved. . . .
>
> If God send thee adversity, receive it in patience, and give thanks to our Saviour, and bethink thee that thou hast deserved it, and that He will make it turn to thine advantage. If he send thee prosperity, then thank Him humbly, so that thou become not worse from pride. . . .
>
> Maintain the good customs of thy realm, and abolish the bad. Be not covetous against thy people; and do not burden them with taxes and imposts save when thou art in great need. . . .
>
> See that thou hast in thy company men, whether religious or lay, who are right worthy, and loyal, and not full of covetousness, and confer with them oft: and fly and eschew the company of the wicked. Hearken willingly to the Word of God and keep it in thine heart. . . .
>
> Give often thanks to God for all the good things He has bestowed upon thee, so that thou be accounted worthy to receive more.
>
> In order to do justice and right to thy subjects, be upright and firm, turning neither to the right hand nor to the left, but always to what is just.

Sir Frank Marzials, Memoirs of the Crusades, *321–22.*

his son Prince of Wales. (Since that time, it has been customary to confer the title "Prince of Wales" on the eldest male heir to the English throne.) Edward's attempts to subdue Scotland, however, met with fierce resistance.

Probably the most important and enduring contribution of Edward's reign was the development of **Parliament**. It had always been the custom of English kings to seek counsel from a group of advisers. The Anglo-Saxon kings had the witan, an assembly of the great men of the kingdom. William the Conqueror established the Great Council—also known as the *curia regis* (king's council)—a feudal body composed of his chief vassals.

When Edward became king, he enlarged the membership of the Great Council to include representative knights from every shire and representative burgesses (citizens) from every town. The word *parliament* (from a French word meaning "to speak" or "to discuss") came to designate this expanded assembly. The meeting of Parliament during Edward's reign has been called the "Model Parliament" because it had the basic features of later Parliaments.

In the fourteenth century, members of Parliament began to meet in two separate groups: the chief vassals in one, and the knights and burgesses in another. The members of the latter group were called the "Commons" because they represented the community. Their assembly became known as the House of Commons, and that of the chief feudal lords became known as the House of Lords.

Over the centuries Parliament became more and more powerful. Edward had acknowledged that the king could not propose new taxes without the consent of Parliament. Therefore he, as well as his successors, had to summon Parliament regularly in order to obtain needed revenue. The members of Parliament soon discovered that by withholding their approval of new taxes, they could force the king to hear their grievances. This "power of the purse," as it came to be called, gradually transformed Parliament from an advisory body into a legislative body. The rise of Parliament served as a check on the king's power and in later centuries helped to convert English government into a limited monarchy.

France
Louis IX and Royal Dignity

Philip II's grandson, **King Louis IX** (r. 1226–70), has been called the ideal medieval king. He combined sincere piety and just rule to build respect and loyalty for the French throne. Concerned about the welfare of his subjects, Louis IX made peace and justice the primary goals of his reign. He sought to protect the rights of all, regardless of their rank in society. Louis further expanded the jurisdiction of the royal courts over the feudal courts. He also established a permanent royal court at Paris, which served as the supreme court of the land. Fearful that his royal agents (the bailiffs) might infringe the feudal rights of his subjects, he appointed special men to search out abuses in the royal government. He was also the first French king to issue ordinances (i.e., legislation) without first consulting his chief vassals. His efforts at judicial reform earned him the title "the French Justinian."

Louis IX led two crusades against the Muslims in North Africa. Although he was a zealous warrior, both campaigns failed. While on his second crusade, he contracted a disease and died. He is remembered in history as "Saint Louis."

Philip IV and Royal Strength

The climax of Capetian rule came during the reign of **Philip IV** (r. 1285–1314). Known as "the Fair" (because of his handsome features), Philip IV further expanded royal power in France. He strengthened the organization and authority of the central government. As the royal government increased in size, the king needed greater revenue. Philip therefore taxed the French people as no French king before him had done.

As was discussed earlier in the chapter, Philip even levied taxes against the French clergy (see p. 218). Pope Boniface VIII objected strongly, but Philip succeeded in defying the papacy because he had the support of the French people. Their loyalty was gradually shifting away from the Roman Church and the papacy to the state and the French king.

To strengthen popular support for his policies, Philip summoned representatives from the church, the nobility, and the townspeople to meet at Paris. The meetings of these three estates (or classes) became known as the **Estates-General**. The king sought advice from this representative body, but he did not wait for its consent to enforce legislation or raise taxes. Thus the power of the French monarch grew without restraints such as those the English Parliament imposed on the English kings. This trend partly explains why the French government developed into an absolute monarchy while the English government became a limited monarchy.

Growth of France (1328)

French Royal Domain

Controlled by French Nobles

Controlled by the English

War Between England and France

During the fourteenth and fifteenth centuries, England and France became embroiled in a long struggle known as the **Hundred Years' War**. Intermittent battles and broken truces spanned the years from 1337 to 1453. What began as a conflict between feudal lords ended as a rivalry between two emerging nation-states. The war contributed to the decline of feudalism in England and France while stimulating the growth of national identity in both countries.

Causes

For centuries English and French monarchs had confronted one another over the matter of English holdings in France. Although Philip II had drastically reduced the size of the English possessions, the king of England still held the duchy of Aquitaine. More fuel was added to this flame of discord when the French monarch attempted to take possession of the rich commercial territory of Flanders. This act threatened England's profitable wool trade. War finally erupted after the last Capetian king died without a male heir. The English king, **Edward III**, whose mother was the sister of the three previous French kings, claimed to be the rightful heir to the French throne. But the French nobles were unwilling to give the crown to the long-time rival of the French monarchs. Instead, they chose Philip VI of the house of Valois (vah LWAH) as king.

A skilled longbow archer could send an arrow a distance of 270 yards.

Conflict

English forces crossed the Channel and won several major victories over the French—at Crécy (kray SEE) in 1346, at Poitiers (pwah TYAY) in 1356, and at Agincourt (AJ in kort) in 1415. Their success was due in large part to new battle tactics and weapons. The English relied on archers armed with longbows. Some

Joan of Arc

Henry VII has a red rose in his hand for the house of Lancaster.

arrows shot by these powerful weapons could penetrate certain types of armor. The longbow gave English archers greater range and accuracy than their French counterparts, who used the conventional crossbow. Through the strategic deployment of bowmen and knights in battle, the outnumbered English routed the French.

The English nonetheless had little to show from their victories over the French. Decades of skirmishes had left them drained of resources. Political unrest at home decreased their zeal for fighting a foreign war. For the French, the war was one of humiliation and destruction. They not only suffered one defeat after another but also saw their countryside pillaged by the English knights.

Even though the English won most of the battles, the French eventually won the war. What turned the tide for the French was a surge of nationalism inspired by a simple peasant girl named **Joan of Arc**. Believing that heavenly voices had directed her to drive the English out of France, she roused the weak French king to action, rallied the dispirited French troops, and accompanied the French army into battle. Although English forces captured Joan and burned her at the stake in 1431, her example stirred the French army to achieve victory over the English.

Consequences

The English defeat became a blessing in disguise. No longer did the English kings concentrate their efforts on holding on to their French possessions. Instead they began to build a strong nation-state at home. The war also furthered the cause of nation making in France. The rivalry over the English presence in France had stirred French nationalism. This bolstered the cause of the French kings as they continued to increase their royal powers.

In England—After a century of fighting on French soil, the English troops returned home only to become involved in a civil war. Two rival families, the houses of York and Lancaster, fought for the English throne. The series of conflicts between these noble families became known as the **Wars of the Roses**. (The emblem of the House of York was a white rose; the emblem of the House of Lancaster, a red rose.) After thirty years of intermittent conflict, the struggle ended when Henry Tudor defeated Richard III at the battle of Bosworth Field. Henry was crowned King **Henry VII** (r. 1485–1509). He founded the powerful Tudor dynasty. During the sixteenth century, the Tudors firmly established the power of the English monarchy and built the English nation into a major European power—a position England held for over four hundred years.

In France—Weary of the death and destruction, the Estates-General had, during the war, allowed the French king to levy a royal land tax called a *taille* (TAH yuh) with which he could maintain a strong army and thereby defeat the English. The eventual success over the English greatly increased the power of the French king. Unlike the English king, who had to depend on Parliament for funds, the French king could raise money without consent of the Estates-General. There was no check on his growing power.

Reconquista in Spain and Portugal

Nation-states did not develop as quickly in the Iberian Peninsula as they had in England and France. For three centuries, most of the peninsula had remained under Muslim control. In the eleventh century a few small non-Muslim states in the north began a concerted effort to drive out the Moors (Spanish Muslims). By the late thirteenth century, warriors of the ***Reconquista*** ("reconquest") had successfully reclaimed the entire peninsula except for the kingdom of Granada.

As European forces drove the Moors out, the small northern states expanded into the reclaimed land. Three principal kingdoms emerged: Portugal, Castile, and Aragon. Like most other European states, these kingdoms experienced struggles between a developing monarchy and feudal nobles. There arose in each kingdom the equivalent to an Estates-General or Parliament—the Cortes, a council composed of nobles, clergy, and representatives of the cities. The expulsion of the Moors, together with the support from the growing towns and the decline of feudalism, increased the power of each king above that of his feudal nobles and the Cortes.

The nation of Spain was created when **Ferdinand**, heir to the throne of Aragon, married **Isabella**, heir to the throne of Castile. (The kingdom of Portugal remained independent.) Ferdinand and Isabella firmly established their royal power in the new nation. They authorized the Spanish Inquisition, a systematic persecution of Muslims and Jews. Inquisitors later directed their attacks against Christians who opposed the Roman Catholic Church. Ferdinand and Isabella completed the reconquest by driving the Moors out of Granada in **1492**, the same year that Christopher Columbus, under Spanish sponsorship, landed in the New World.

Disunity in Italy and Germany

In contrast to the rising tide of nationalism and strong monarchies elsewhere in Europe, Germany and Italy remained divided into many small regional states. "Germany" and "Italy" were geographic expressions, not unified nations.

The collapse of the Hohenstaufen house in the thirteenth century brought an end to German influence in Italy. Italy was left divided among the kingdom of Naples, the Papal States, and powerful northern cities such as Florence, Venice, Genoa, and Milan. There was little opportunity for national unity while each region struggled to prevent the others from becoming too powerful. Despite its political turmoil and disunity, Italy prospered commercially and later gave birth to the period of cultural achievement known as the Renaissance (see chapter 11).

During this period, imperial authority declined in Germany and small territorial states emerged. The office of emperor remained, but the real power of government passed into the hands of the great nobles. By the middle of the fourteenth century, a written constitution known as the **Golden Bull** established the **Diet** of the Holy Roman Empire. The Diet was the German equivalent of the English Parliament and the French Estates-General. The most important members of the Diet were the seven electors (three archbishops and four noble princes) who selected the German emperors. The electors generally chose weak men as emperors in order to protect the power of the German nobility. In addition, they passed the imperial crown from one family to another so that no single family would

Iberian Peninsula

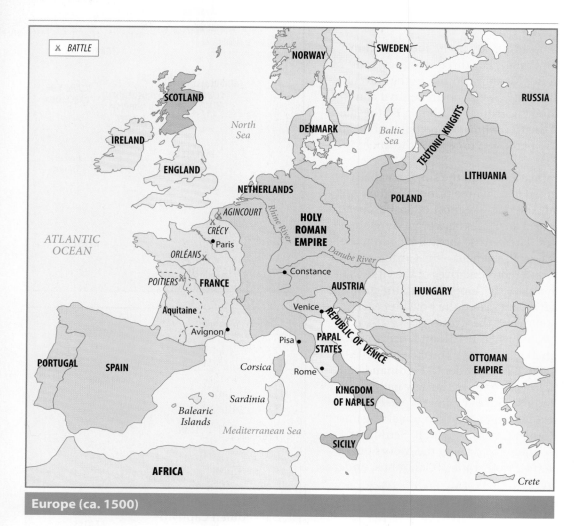

Europe (ca. 1500)

become too powerful. While other lands were striving toward national unity, the German electors sought to avoid it.

Despite the efforts of the German nobles, the **Habsburg** family built a strong base of power among the southern German states. These states became known collectively as Austria. (Members of the Habsburg family ruled from the city of Vienna until after World War I.) After 1438 only members of this family were elected to the German throne. Emperor **Maximilian I** (r. 1493–1519) greatly enlarged the Habsburg possessions through marriage. His first marriage brought the rich region of the Low Countries (modern Belgium and Holland) under his rule. His second marriage brought him Milan. He also formed a marriage alliance between his son and the daughter of Ferdinand and Isabella of Spain. In this way Spain, the Low Countries, the Holy Roman Empire, and territory in the New World (the Spanish possessions) came under Habsburg rule.

Section Review

1–2. What two nations fought during the Hundred Years' War?

3–4. Which side won most of the battles of the Hundred Years? What side won the war?

5–6. What people did the Spanish and Portuguese seek to drive out of the Iberian Peninsula? What was this effort called?

7–8. What was the German constitution called? What assembly did it establish?

★ What was the impact of military conflicts in this period? What European nations developed during this period?

★ Why were Italian and German efforts to achieve national unity unsuccessful?

Making Connections

1. Why was the consistent quality of coinage important?

2. How did moneychangers make traveling less dangerous?

3–4. What parts of a "just price" are good? What part is flawed?

5. How did guilds protect the consumer?

6–11. What papal weapons were used to ensure a favorable outcome for the Roman Catholic Church in any controversy? How did these affect citizenship, power, and justice?

12–13. How did Henry II of England and Philip IV of France strengthen royal authority in their respective countries?

Developing History Skills

1. Beginning with one of the consequences of the Crusades, make a list of historical events or developments that proceeded from this consequence.

2. Compare and contrast the development of nations in western Europe and central Europe.

Thinking Critically

1. Contrast the use of power by John of England and Louis IX of France in light of scriptural passages including Proverbs 16:5–7, 12, 18–19.

2. In the *Divine Comedy*, Dante describes a trip to hell and speaks of clergy, popes, and cardinals residing in the fourth ring of hell because of their greed (*Inferno*, Canto VII, lines 46–48). Based on the information in this chapter and other sources, explain why Dante was able to make such statements without fear of punishment by civil authorities or the Roman Church.

Living in God's World

1. If you were a Christian magistrate during the Middle Ages, what regulations would you impose on the town fairs to remove some of the abuses noted in the quotation on page 205?

2. If you were a leader in a church, what Scripture should guide you in the kind of art that is used in church?

People, Places, and Things to Know

moneychangers
banca
just price
charter
guilds
apprentice
journeyman
master
Hanseatic League
middle class
universitas
Scholasticism
Anselm
Peter Abelard
Thomas Aquinas
Roger Bacon
vernacular
Dante Alighieri
Geoffrey Chaucer
Romanesque
Gothic
Innocent III
Boniface VIII
Unam Sanctam
Babylonian Captivity
Great Schism
Council of Constance
nation-states
indictments
common law
Magna Carta
Edward I
Parliament
Louis IX
Philip IV
Estates-General
Hundred Years' War
Edward III
Joan of Arc
Wars of the Roses
Henry VII
Reconquista
Ferdinand
Isabella
1492
Golden Bull
Diet
Habsburg
Maximilian I

11

I. The Renaissance

II. The Reformation

Santa Maria del Fiore in Florence

Big Ideas

1. Was the Renaissance worldview scriptural?
2. How did the Reformation affect Western civilization?

A new age was dawning in Europe beginning in the fourteenth century. The Western world was on the threshold of a widespread revival in learning and of a brilliant flowering of the arts. This period of change in Europe from the fourteenth century through the sixteenth century is known as the **Renaissance** (REN uh sahns), a French word meaning "rebirth." During the sixteenth century, a protest against the corruption in the Roman Catholic Church developed into the **Reformation**. Luther and the other Protestant reformers soon realized that the corruption of the Roman Catholic Church resulted from false doctrines that had developed during the Middle Ages. Reform of corrupt practices would need to go hand in hand with doctrinal reform. People needed to recognize the Bible as the sole authority for Christian life and belief. They also needed to understand that salvation was through Christ and His work alone and not through the sacraments of the Roman Church. From this return to biblical Christianity, many Protestant denominations developed.

I. Renaissance

For many people in Europe, the Renaissance became a cultural bridge from the art, literature, and thinking of the Middle Ages to the beginnings of modern history.

Characteristics of the Renaissance

Contrast with the Middle Ages

The Renaissance man considered the time in which he lived a sharp break from the ignorance and superstition of the Middle Ages. To him the medieval period was merely a backward, unimportant interval between the achievement of classical culture and the glory of his own "modern" age. He failed to realize that the Renaissance was the culmination of gradual changes that had begun during the Middle Ages.

The Renaissance attitude toward life differed sharply from the medieval outlook. A hearty zest for living replaced the sober, otherworldly concerns of earlier generations, who were consumed with the welfare of their souls and with the work of the church. People during the Middle Ages fixed their thoughts on the future joys of heaven. The dusty past and the troubled present were of little interest or importance. The Renaissance man, on the other hand, gloried in the past and lived with enthusiasm in the present. The future could take care of itself, or so he thought.

Focus on Man

The Renaissance emphasized human individuality, ability, and dignity. In medieval times the group—not the individual—had been all-important (for example, the church, a guild, or a particular social class). During the Renaissance, however, people praised the wonders of human achievement. They conceived of the ideal man as one with diverse interests and talents.

This renewed focus on man's capacities is called **humanism**. Unlike modern secular humanism, Renaissance humanism did not abandon belief in God. Nevertheless, like every movement that puts undue emphasis on human ability, it led to the false assumption that man is basically good. "There is nothing to be seen more wonderful than man," wrote an Italian humanist. Shakespeare's immortal character Hamlet exclaims, "What a piece of work is a man! How noble

Guiding Questions

1. What were the basic components of a Renaissance worldview?

2. What were the major cultural contributions of the Renaissance?

Humanism

Humanism is an overemphasis on human worth and ability, leading man to glorify himself instead of God. There have been many historical expressions of humanism. The Greek humanists, for example, emphasized man's uniqueness above the animals; they taught that man's reason was the standard of truth. Likewise the Renaissance humanists praised human accomplishment and talent. Although most were church members and acknowledged the existence of God, they were primarily interested in classical learning.

Humanists understood the truth that man, created in God's image, is the apex of God's creation. However, because it tends to minimize or reject man's submission to God, humanism tends to lead people away from God and spiritual concerns. It promotes the false idea that man is good and that he is independent of or superior to God. The secular humanism of the twenty-first century rejects belief in God altogether and worships man as god.

in reason! how infinite in faculty! in form and moving how express and admirable! in action how like an angel!"

Created in God's image and given dominion over creation, man does possess a unique position in God's universe. But God's image in man was badly marred by the Fall in the Garden of Eden. Because of Adam's disobedience man is a sinner in need of the Savior. Because many people in Renaissance society denied man's true nature, much of their culture was devoid of eternal values, biblical ethics, and godly living.

Revival of Learning

The expansion of trade and the growth of town and national governments during the later Middle Ages increased the need for well-educated laymen with professional skills. Merchants, bankers, lawyers, clerks, and diplomats—to name a few—needed a well-rounded education to meet the demands of an increasingly complex society.

Soon a new course of study became popular in the West. The humanities, also known as the liberal arts, included the study of history, science, and grammar, as well as classical literature and philosophy. Those who studied the liberal arts were known as humanists. Unlike the Scholastics of the Middle Ages, most Renaissance humanists prepared themselves for life in the secular world rather than for service in the Roman Church.

The goal of Renaissance education was to develop well-rounded individuals. Humanists, who considered ignorance the source of evil, looked to education as the remedy for sin. They criticized medieval man for being ignorant and narrow-minded, and they praised men of their own day for their wide interests and quest for knowledge. They scorned the medieval practice of passively accepting ideas without question. Renaissance man examined established ideas to discern their trustworthiness.

Renaissance humanists greatly admired the classical age of ancient Greece and Rome. They praised the amazing versatility that the ancients had possessed. Cicero received special honor because he was not only a renowned scholar, lawyer, and statesman but also an eloquent orator and master of literary expression.

This fascination with classical culture led to an intense search for ancient manuscripts. Men went to great lengths and spent vast fortunes to obtain classical works. They found many Latin manuscripts in the libraries of monasteries, where they had lain neglected and forgotten for centuries. Although Greek works were rare in the West, many had been preserved in the East by the Byzantine and Muslim civilizations. As the humanists recovered these precious works, they examined them to determine their accuracy and authenticity. Essential to such an investigation, of course, was a thorough knowledge of the classical languages. This need gave rise to the renewed study of Greek and classical Latin during the Renaissance period.

Course of the Renaissance

The Renaissance began in Italy. This land had been the center of the ancient Roman Empire, and even in the fourteenth century, the Italians still thought of themselves as Romans. In their long history Italians had also come into close contact with the Byzantine and Islamic civilizations. Several cities in northern Italy had maintained trade and cultural ties with the East during the Middle Ages. When commerce began to revive throughout Europe during the eleventh and twelfth centuries, the Italian cities rose to prominence. Their control of the Mediterranean trade routes to the East brought them great riches. To display their newly acquired wealth, these cities commissioned talented artists to design buildings, decorate churches, and carve statues for public squares. Affluent bankers and merchants became sponsors or patrons of these artists. No longer were artists dependent solely on the Roman Church for support.

Perhaps the most famous of the Renaissance patrons, besides the Roman Church, were the members of the **Medici** (MED uh chee) **family**. The Medici had become enormously wealthy through commerce and banking. They used their riches and prominence to gain political control of the city of Florence and also used their financial resources to promote learning and the arts. They sponsored searches for manuscripts, established a public library (one of the first in Europe), and commissioned great works of painting, sculpture, and architecture. The most notable and most generous patron of the Medici family was **Lorenzo de Medici** (1449–1492), called *Il Magnifico* ("The Magnificent"). During his rule the city of Florence became the most influential city of the Renaissance movement.

Until about 1500 the Renaissance remained primarily an Italian movement. During the sixteenth century, however, enthusiasm for art and learning spread throughout Europe. It was carried abroad, in part, by students who had studied in Italy and merchants who traded with Italian cities. The Renaissance took hold in England, France, Germany, and the Netherlands. At first the people of these lands copied the Italians, but before long they developed their own ideas and styles.

Thought and Literature
Italian Humanist Writers

Most of the writers, painters, sculptors, and architects of the early Renaissance lived in Florence. At the beginning of the fourteenth century, Florentine writers gave expression to the growing secular attitudes. They looked to the literature of ancient Greece and Rome for inspiration. Their study of the classics stirred an increased emphasis on education in Europe.

The pioneer of Renaissance humanism and one of the most important figures in Italian literature was Francesco Petrarch (1304–1374), the son of a Florentine merchant. As a youth he followed his father's wishes and entered law school. But his real love was the classical writings of Greece and Rome.

After his father's death, Petrarch gave up his study of law and devoted his life to classical literature. He searched monastic and church libraries to find ancient manuscripts, which he collected and studied. He composed his own Latin poems, modeling them after classical poetry. These he considered his best works. Later generations, however, remember him best for his vernacular writings. In sonnets (fourteen-line poems) and letters to his friends, Petrarch wrote about nature, his pride in his homeland, and his love for Laura (the woman he idealized). His love of poetry had an immense influence on later writers.

In letters addressed to his heroes of the past—Cicero, Virgil, and Livy—Petrarch placed his own day on an equal plane with the days of ancient Rome. Because Petrarch led the way in reviving interest

Lorenzo de Medici

Renaissance

Niccolò Machiavelli

and study in classical literature, he is known as the Father of Humanism.

Another Italian, Baldassare Castiglione (cahs tee LYOH nay; 1478–1529), wrote one of the most famous books on etiquette (social behavior) published during the Renaissance. *The Courtier* quickly became a bestseller and was translated into many different languages. It set the standard for courtly behavior all over Europe.

One of the most influential Renaissance writers was the Florentine public official and political thinker **Niccolò Machiavelli** (mah kyah VEL ee; 1469–1527). From 1489 to 1512 Machiavelli worked as a diplomat for the Florentine Republic. During these years he was able to observe firsthand various political developments in Europe.

Machiavelli wrote several important and influential works on government. The most important and controversial of these is an essay titled *The Prince*. In this work Machiavelli reflects on the political conditions of his day and tells readers that the successful ruler must do what is expedient and not be governed by Christian principles of right and wrong. Such a man uses force when necessary since "it is much safer to be feared than loved." Later rulers took his advice to cast aside virtue and embraced this amoral system as an ideal political philosophy.

Northern Humanist Writers

While the Italian Renaissance initially influenced the Renaissance in northern Europe, the northern humanists generally had a greater interest in religious matters than the Italian humanists did. These religious concerns often led to a greater emphasis on church reform in the North. Accordingly, several northern humanists gave more attention to Christian than to classical sources. They placed the study of the Hebrew Old Testament and the Greek New Testament above the writings of Cicero, Virgil, and other ancients.

Perhaps the most honored and influential scholar of the Renaissance was **Erasmus** of Rotterdam (1466–1536). As a young man he entered a monastery, but his stay was brief. Soon he began to travel throughout Europe and obtained an education in Latin and Greek. Erasmus quickly distinguished himself as the foremost scholar of Europe and became widely acclaimed as the Prince of Humanists. In his most famous work, *In Praise of Folly*, Erasmus uses satire to point out the evils and follies of Renaissance society.

Erasmus became a leading advocate of church reform and was an outspoken critic of monasticism, the ignorance and worldliness of many of the clergy, and the Roman Church's empty ritualism. Yet he refused to break with the Roman Catholic Church.

Erasmus capitalized on his skill in biblical languages and became the first to publish a Greek New Testament in 1516. Martin Luther used Erasmus's Greek New Testament to make a German translation of the New Testament. Many others, including the translators of the King James Version, also used revised editions of Erasmus's text as the basis for translating the New Testament into the common languages of the people.

A close friend of Erasmus was the English humanist Sir **Thomas More** (1478–1535). More devoted much of his life to the service of his country. His interest in social and political matters prompted him to write a book setting forth his views on the ideal government. This work, titled *Utopia* (meaning "nowhere"), is the story of an imaginary state built on Christian principles and Plato's philosophy.

Scripture in the Vernacular

In the preface of his Greek New Testament, Erasmus explains to readers his position on translating Scripture:

> I strongly dissent from those who are unwilling to have the Scriptures translated into the vernacular and read by the ignorant, as if Christ taught so complicated a doctrine that it can hardly be understood even by a handful of theologians. . . . It is perhaps reasonable to conceal the mysteries of kings, but Christ seeks to divulge his mysteries as much as possible. I should like to have even the most humble women read the [Gospels] and the Epistles of St. Paul. . . . Would that the plowboy recited something from them at his plowshare, that the weaver sang from them at his shuttle, and that the traveler whiled away the tedium of his journey with their tales.

The Renaissance: Maker of Modern Man, National Geographic Society, 300.

More believed that if men would govern themselves by a sense of community and brotherly love, they could achieve political, social, and economic equality. According to More, the three deadliest sins of the English community were laziness, greed, and pride. In *Utopia*, all men would be compelled to work. Thus everyone would have economic security, eliminating all laziness and greed. All pride would be centered in the state.

The foremost Spanish writer of the late Renaissance was **Miguel de Cervantes** (sur VAN tez; 1547–1616). His novel *Don Quixote* (DAHN kee-HO-tay) satirizes chivalry and the chivalric literature that was popular in Cervantes's day. The main character, Don Quixote, imagining himself to be a knight, puts on a suit of armor, mounts an old horse, and gallops around the Spanish countryside seeking to right the world's wrongs. In doing so, he makes a fool of himself. Through this work Cervantes pokes fun at outdated medieval ideas while vividly portraying life in sixteenth-century Spain.

Renaissance literature reached its peak in the works of **William Shakespeare** (1564–1616), who is generally considered the greatest playwright of all time and the finest poet in the English language. Shakespeare's lifework includes 154 sonnets and at least thirty-seven plays. His dramatic works are classified into histories, comedies, and tragedies. The tragedies, including *Hamlet*, *Othello*, *King Lear*, and *Macbeth*, are generally recognized as his greatest works. Fourteen of his plays are set in Italy. This delighted English audiences, because in true Renaissance spirit they looked to Italy as the birthplace of learning. Several of Shakespeare's plays reflect the surge of national pride in England.

Shakespeare left an indelible imprint on Western culture through his writings. Shakespeare's poems and plays have been the object of careful study by scholars in every generation since his death. His literary genius enriched the English language and influenced its development. Many of the phrases and expressions that he coined are part of everyday speech in modern society.

Gutenberg

A resourceful German named Johannes Gutenberg helped to change the course of history. He is recognized as the man who developed movable-type printing in Europe. The Chinese had already developed movable-type printing, but there is no evidence that Europeans were aware of this accomplishment. Gutenberg achieved his goal of printing the Bible, and that edition was later named after him.

The advent of movable-type printing is a milestone in the history of the Western world. The cost of books dropped steadily because copyists no longer had to produce books by hand. In addition, mass production continued to bring down the price of printed books. The printing press also paved the way for the rapid spread of ideas, including humanist works of the Renaissance and Protestant works of the Reformation.

William Shakespeare

Section Review

1. Define *humanism*.

2–3. In addition to the Roman Church, what family became the most famous patron (sponsor) of Renaissance learning and art? Who was the most noted patron of this family?

4. Who is called the Father of Humanism because he led the way in reviving interest and study in classical literature?

5. What work of Erasmus did later reformers and Bible translators use?

6. What contribution did Johannes Gutenberg make to European history?

7. What Englishman is generally considered the greatest playwright of all time?

✳ Why did Renaissance scholars seek ancient manuscripts? How would the discovery of discrepancies between the Greek and Latin texts of the Bible have helped prepare the way for the Reformation?

✳ In *The Prince*, what was Machiavelli subtly denying or disregarding?

The Visual Arts

Renaissance artists rightly presented man as the greatest of God's creatures in a good creation rather than directing all attention to an otherworldly realm. Sadly, Renaissance humanism exalted man to a position independent of God instead of arriving at a biblical balance.

Renaissance artists drew their inspiration and ideas from the classical world. They broke with the artistic traditions of the Middle Ages in the following ways:

1. Renaissance art emphasized the present physical world. Medieval art had emphasized the spiritual realm and the life to come.

2. Secular patrons often supported the Renaissance artists. During the Middle Ages, the Church of Rome had almost exclusively patronized the artists.

3. Most Renaissance artists were extremely proud of their work and wanted their names known and their works praised. Medieval artists, on the other hand, had worked primarily for the glory of God and the church and usually did not gain any personal recognition.

4. Renaissance art was realistic and three-dimensional. Medieval art was flat and two-dimensional.

5. Most Renaissance portrait painters frequently painted kings, merchants, and other important secular individuals. Medieval painters usually portrayed church leaders, biblical characters, or saints of the Roman Church.

6. Painting and sculpture were the most popular media during the Renaissance. The glory of medieval art was its architecture.

Early Italian Painters

Giotto di Bondone (JAWT-toh DEE bone-DOH-nay; c. 1267–1337) is the most famous painter of the early Italian Renaissance. He is often called the Father of Renaissance Painting. He opened a new era in Western art by seeking to make his paintings more natural. His figures exhibited human feelings, unlike the stiff expressionless figures portrayed in medieval art. Giotto is famous for his frescoes (paintings on wet plaster) on the walls of the church at Padua.

In the late fifteenth century, **Sandro Botticelli** (bot ih CHEL ee; c. 1444–1510) added another dimension to Renaissance art: movement. He depicted forms with bold lines and gave clarity and a sense of activity to his characters. With their flowing hair and wispy garments, his painted figures seemed to move and sway. Botticelli's early paintings reflected the humanistic spirit prevalent in the Medici court. He painted pagan themes of classical mythology. But when the Medici family was expelled from Florence, Botticelli came under the influence of the preaching of the monk Girolamo Savonarola. He became one of Savonarola's converts, and his painting, as a result, took on a more religious and moral outlook.

High Renaissance Painters

The artistic achievement of the Italian Renaissance culminated in the early sixteenth century. During this period, known as the

High Renaissance, the center of culture shifted from Florence to Rome, and the papacy became the major patron of Italian artists. High Renaissance artists mastered the painting techniques that the Italian artists of the fifteenth century had pioneered. The most famous High Renaissance painters are Leonardo da Vinci, Raphael, and Michelangelo.

Leonardo da Vinci (duh VIN-chee; 1452–1519) is probably the best example of the so-called Renaissance man. He displayed interests in a wide range of fields. Leonardo was an accomplished sculptor, architect, painter, and musician. He also studied anatomy, botany, geology, astronomy, engineering, and mathematics.

As a young man Leonardo demonstrated extraordinary skill in painting and sculpture. He was admitted into the Florentine painter's guild, but he believed that the restrictions of the guild stifled his creative talents. Therefore, in 1482 he sought a position in Milan. While in Milan, Leonardo painted his famous mural *The Last Supper* on a wall in a monastery. The painting illustrates his mastery of perspective and exemplifies the Renaissance love for balance. He vividly depicts the intense feelings of the disciples when Christ announced that one of them would betray Him.

Raffaello Sanzio (1483–1520), better known as **Raphael** (RAF ee el), completed an enormous number of paintings and frescoes in his short lifetime. His interest in painting undoubtedly began at home because his father was a painter. As a young man Raphael studied the works of the masters in order to perfect his own technique. He soon became one of the most beloved painters of his time. *The School of Athens* is an excellent example of his work; it displays balance, harmony, and perspective. In this painting he creates a spacious setting in which are gathered the great philosophers and scientists of the classical world.

Raphael

This painting is an excellent example of perspective. Perspective appears to show three dimensions. It is based on an optical illusion where parallel lines appear to meet a spot on the horizon called a vanishing point.

The School of Athens *by Raphael*

Michelangelo Buonarroti (my-kul-AN-juh-lo bwawn-uh-RAW-tee; 1475–1564) is one of the most famous artists in all of history. His contemporaries praised his artistic masterpieces. As a young boy he exhibited unusual skill in sculpting, and his father apprenticed him to a leading Florentine artist. While an apprentice, the talented youth caught the eye of Lorenzo de Medici, who took Michelangelo into his household as his adopted son.

Michelangelo, Creation of the Sun, Moon and Plants, from the Sistine Chapel in the Vatican

In 1508 Pope Julius II commissioned Michelangelo to paint the ceiling of the **Sistine Chapel** in the Vatican (the papal residence in Rome). Protesting that he was a sculptor and not a painter, Michelangelo began the mammoth project reluctantly. After four years of working on scaffolds nearly seventy feet above the floor, he finished painting the 5,800-square-foot ceiling. The original plan had called for only twelve figures; however, when Michelangelo finished the project, he had painted over three hundred figures, most of which were ten to eighteen feet tall. This magnificent fresco depicts the stories of Creation, the Fall, the Flood, and the redemption of man as prophesied by the Old Testament prophets.

Venetian Painters

During the late Renaissance, the city of Venice became a leading center of culture as a result of its economic prosperity. Wealthy merchants built grand palaces and commissioned artists to adorn the city with great works of art. The beautiful, wealthy, and proud city of Venice became known as the Queen of the Adriatic.

Tiziano Vecelli (c. 1488–1576), known as Titian (TISH un), was the leading figure of the Venetian school of painting. He ranks with Michelangelo as one of the foremost painters of the Renaissance. A prolific painter known for his rich use of color, Titian is especially remembered for his portraits.

Tintoretto (1518–1594) was the last of the great sixteenth-century Venetian painters. He was born Jacopo Robusti but is known by the nickname Tintoretto (Italian for "little dyer") because his father was a dyer by profession. In his paintings he sought to combine the bright colors of Titian and the masterful drawing of Michelangelo.

Northern European Artists

The German painter **Albrecht Dürer** (DOOR ur; 1471–1528) was sometimes called the Leonardo of the North. Like Leonardo, he was accomplished in many different fields: writing, designing, engraving, and painting. He had a high regard for Italian art and was the first northern artist to travel to Italy for the express purpose of studying art. Although Dürer is a celebrated painter, he is best remembered for his woodcarvings and engravings, which were used to illustrate printed books.

Another celebrated German painter was **Hans Holbein** (HOHL bine) the Younger (c. 1497–1543). He is considered the finest portrait painter of the Northern Renaissance. He traveled throughout

Europe working in many countries—especially England. Holbein became the official court painter of Henry VIII, the king of England. This German master also painted the portraits of leading figures of the Northern Renaissance, such as Erasmus and Sir Thomas More.

Architects and Sculptors

Renaissance architecture and sculpture also reflected the new secular concerns of the Renaissance Age. In the medieval period the primary function of architecture had been to glorify God through the building of magnificent cathedrals. During the Renaissance, however, architects also designed and built spacious palaces and comfortable villas for powerful princes and wealthy merchants. Similarly, sculpture, which had been used during the Middle Ages to decorate churches, now graced town squares and homes of the wealthy.

Around 1401 the leading men of Florence held a contest to select an artist to design a set of bronze doors for one of the entrances to the baptistery of Florence. Among the many artists who entered the competition were Lorenzo Ghiberti (gee BEHR tee; 1378–1455) and Filippo Brunelleschi (broo nuh LES kee; 1377–1446). According to the contest rules, each participant had to present a sculptured relief depicting the story of the sacrifice of Isaac. Ghiberti's work was judged the best.

Ghiberti's ten-panel doors depicting scenes from the Old Testament

Disgusted with losing the competition to design the doors of the baptistery in Florence, Brunelleschi turned from sculpture to architecture. He traveled to Rome where he studied Roman monuments. He later returned to Florence and defeated Ghiberti in a competition to design and construct a dome for the cathedral of Florence. Brunelleschi's dome became the crowning glory of the Florence cathedral. Most of the domes designed during the Renaissance conformed to his model.

Donatello (c. 1386–1466) was the leading sculptor of the early Renaissance. He mastered the art of sculpting freestanding statues. One of his most famous works was his statue of David, whom he depicted as a young Florentine shepherd boy. Donatello also cast the first full-scale equestrian statue (man on horseback) since Roman times. His realistic, freestanding statues later inspired the most outstanding sculptor of the Renaissance—Michelangelo.

Michelangelo was a man of many talents. He was a noted painter, sculptor, architect, engineer, and poet. While in his early twenties, he completed one of his most famous masterpieces, the *Pietà* (pyay TAH; Italian term meaning "pity" or "compassion"). It depicts the virgin Mary mourning over the crucified Christ. Another famous work by Michelangelo is his marble statue of David. Like many other Renaissance artists, Michelangelo glorified the human body. His *David*, standing eighteen feet high, is the embodiment of Michelangelo's vision of a perfect specimen of young manhood.

Consequences of the Renaissance

The Renaissance and the Reformation that followed it are in many respects exact opposites. The Renaissance was a secular age; men placed confidence in human ability and gloried in human achievement. Artists and scholars, who looked to classical Greece and Rome for inspiration and authority, helped stir a revival in

The Florence Cathedral featuring Brunelleschi's dome

classical learning and the arts. The Reformation was a religious age; the Scripture led men to place confidence in God and to glory in God's salvation. Men of God, who looked to the Bible as the sole authority, helped stir a great spiritual revival.

Despite these differences, it would be wrong to assume that there was no connection between the Renaissance and the Reformation. Every period of history is preparatory to the age that follows. In God's providence, the Renaissance prepared western Europe for the coming Reformation.

Positive

The Renaissance provided the tools that shaped the Reformation movement. In this sense the Renaissance made the Reformation possible.

First, the Renaissance provoked a spirit of inquiry. People became more critical in their evaluation of the Roman Catholic Church's teachings. This analytical spirit encouraged some to examine the Scriptures to see which teachings were scriptural and which needed to be discarded.

Second, it revived interest in the literature and languages of antiquity. In their search for classical sources, Renaissance humanists recovered many Christian sources—manuscripts of the Old and New Testaments. The discovery of these manuscripts led to a renewed interest in the biblical languages (Greek and Hebrew) and in the study of the Bible itself.

Third, it developed movable-type printing. The new publishing industry made possible the mass production of written material. The printed page would be instrumental in spreading the ideas of the reformers throughout Europe.

Fourth, it made education more widely available to the middle class. More people were now able to read what was being printed.

Fifth, it stressed the importance of the individual, thus restoring the proper emphasis on individual responsibility—the obligation each man has to God and to his fellow man.

Negative

First, the Renaissance's secular emphasis helped weaken moral restraints and thereby made the need for reform more readily apparent. The Roman Church, which should have been the example of moral righteousness, was caught up in worldliness and wickedness as many church leaders lived openly in luxury and immorality.

Second, the humanists, who sought to imitate the best of the classical world, often embraced its evils. The revival of classical literature and art carried with it the danger of a revival of heathenism in religion and morality.

Third, the worship of classical forms often led to the worship of classical ideas. Some humanists and artists combined culture with Christian faith and devoted their genius to the cause of truth and virtue, but many effectively worshiped the ideals of Greece and Rome rather than the God of the Bible.

Fourth, as educational opportunities improved, many embraced the error that ignorance is the source of evil and that education would solve man's spiritual problems.

Fifth, many who embraced the Renaissance supported the lie that man is, by nature, good and capable of achievement apart from God.

Section Review

1. During the High Renaissance, what city became the cultural center of Italy?

2–7. List the three most famous painters of the High Renaissance period; beside each, give the title of one of his masterpieces.

8–10. What were three cultural contributions of the Renaissance?

* What were the basic components of a Renaissance worldview?

* Analyze major contributions of the Renaissance in terms of this worldview.

II. Reformation

Forerunners

The spiritual awakening that swept across Europe during the sixteenth century was the culmination of centuries of activity. For many generations men had attempted to curb the abuses in the church. Most reforming efforts, however, were directed only against its most visible evils. Many had failed to recognize the need for doctrinal purity and genuine moral reform. Attempting to stir inward reform, godly reformers attacked the church's corrupt teaching as well as its corrupt practices. These brave men held to the Bible as the sole authority for the Christian faith. Asserting that Christ was the only Head of the church, they rejected the authority of the pope. God used these godly men to prepare the way for the later reformers of the Reformation Era.

John Wycliffe

One of the strongest voices of protest against the wickedness in the Roman Church came from the Englishman **John Wycliffe** (WIK lif; c. 1328–84). Wycliffe was a fearless preacher, a distinguished scholar and lecturer, and a patriotic leader. Because many of his convictions and teachings were later embraced by the sixteenth-century reformers, he has been called the "Morning Star of the Reformation."

From his study of the Bible, Wycliffe became convinced that the church had strayed from its original purity both in doctrine and practice. Through sermons, lectures, and writings, he opposed the temporal power and wealth of the Roman Church. Wycliffe sought to purge the church of its corrupt clergy. He denounced monastic orders, criticized the practice of confessing sins to a priest, and rejected the teaching about the mass. He, as well as other Englishmen of his day, resented the claims of the papacy upon the church in England. But Wycliffe went a step further than his countrymen when he proclaimed the papacy to be an institution "full of poison." He preached Christ as the only Head of the church.

Wycliffe upheld the Bible as the supreme authority for all believers, clergy as well as laity. He believed that every Christian should study the Bible and that God's Word is the only source of spiritual truth and the only accurate presentation of the way of salvation. Wycliffe contended that a knowledge of Scripture would expose the error in the practice and teaching of the Roman Catholic Church and would start true reform. For this reason, he initiated the translation of the Bible from Latin into English so that more people could discover the truths found in Scripture. This first complete English

Guiding Questions

1. What conditions led to the Reformation?

2. How did the Reformation spread throughout western Europe?

3. What were the teachings of key figures of the Reformation and Counter Reformation?

4. How did the Reformation affect Europe?

John Wycliffe

John Huss

Martin Luther

translation of the Bible—known as the Wycliffe Bible—was finished in 1382.

Wycliffe's reforming efforts met with stiff opposition. Church leaders sought to suppress his teaching, which they condemned as heretical. In 1384 Wycliffe died from a stroke, but his death did not end the persecution. For more than a century after his death, the church attempted to eradicate his teaching and followers in England. Many of his followers were imprisoned, tortured, and burned at the stake. However, the flame of truth could not be extinguished.

John Huss

Wycliffe's views soon spread to the Continent (mainland Europe), where they influenced the Bohemian reformer **John Huss** (c. 1369–1415). From the city of Prague, Huss challenged the Bohemian people to oppose the worldliness in the church. Huss, who taught and defended many of Wycliffe's beliefs, was accused by church leaders of spreading heresy. Though excommunicated, he remained steadfast in his beliefs and continued to be a popular preacher.

In 1414 church leaders met in the city of Constance to settle the pressing disputes over the papal schism (see p. 219) and church reform. Sigismund, the Holy Roman emperor, wishing to settle the question of heresy in Bohemia, summoned Huss to the Council of Constance, promising him imperial protection. Huss traveled to Constance expecting to have an opportunity to defend his teaching from the Word of God. But soon after his arrival, church leaders had him imprisoned and placed on trial for teaching heresy. When the officials could not show from God's Word that he was in error, Huss refused to renounce his beliefs. Despite the emperor's promise of protection, the council condemned him to die at the stake.

The day of execution came, and Huss was led to the stake. Moments before the fire was kindled, he was asked to renounce his beliefs and thereby save his life. He responded, "I shall die with joy today in the faith of the gospel which I have preached." Although the flames ended his earthly life, his influence remained strong, and the work for reform continued.

The council that condemned Huss to death also reexamined the writings of Wycliffe. The Roman Church formally condemned Wycliffe as a heretic on 260 different counts and ordered his writings to be burned. His enemies at the council also ordered his body to be dug up and burned—an act that supposedly signified his condemnation to hell. More than a decade passed, however, before this order was carried out. In 1428, forty-four years after his death, Wycliffe's bones were dug up and burned. His ashes were thrown into a nearby stream.

The Roman Church seemingly triumphed over Wycliffe and Huss. Nevertheless, these "reformers before the Reformation" faithfully stood for truth and boldly opposed the errors of Roman Catholicism. In doing so, they prepared the way for the Protestant Reformation.

Beginning

The name **Martin Luther** is inseparably linked to the Reformation period. His courageous stand against the Roman Catholic Church sparked the religious awakening known as the Protestant Reformation.

Luther's Early Life

Strict discipline characterized Martin Luther's early training both at home and at school. At the age of eighteen, he entered the University of Erfurt, where he became acquainted with both Scholastic and classical studies. It was also at the university that he saw a complete Bible for the first time.

After graduation Luther planned to obey the wishes of his father and prepare for a legal career. But these plans changed suddenly during the summer of 1505. While returning to Erfurt after a visit with his parents, Luther was caught outside in a violent thunderstorm. When a lightning bolt struck nearby, Luther, thinking himself near death, cried out in terror, "Saint Anne, help me! I will become a monk." To the shock of his parents and friends, Luther remained true to his vow and entered an Augustinian monastery.

Luther spent his days in the monastery zealously performing good works, which he hoped would earn him salvation. In 1507 he was ordained a priest. A few years later he was made professor of Bible at the newly formed university at Wittenberg and became a pastor of the town church. Though a respected monk, pastor, and teacher, he was filled with doubt and despair over his own salvation. How could he, a sinner, stand before a just and holy God? His good works offered no relief from his burden of guilt and sin. Through his study of Scripture, however, Luther soon discovered that no amount of good works could justify a sinner before God; justification was by faith alone. This doctrine transformed Luther's life, and to the day of his death, it was the heart of his preaching. *Sola fide* (justification by faith alone) became the rallying cry of the Reformation movement.

Controversy

In 1514 Pope **Leo X** (1513–21) launched a campaign to complete the rebuilding of St. Peter's Basilica in Rome. Because of the lavish spending of the Renaissance popes, the papal treasury had been drained of funds. In order to raise the needed money, Leo sent out agents to sell **indulgences**, certificates which, according to Catholicism, granted pardon from the punishment of certain sins. In 1517 one of these agents, a Dominican friar named Johann Tetzel, began selling indulgences near Luther's parish at Wittenberg. People flocked to see Tetzel, believing they could purchase forgiveness for sins. He told them that by buying an indulgence a person could free a relative from suffering in purgatory. He is said to have preached, "As soon as a coin in the coffer rings, the soul from purgatory springs." Martin Luther had concluded that salvation was God's gift and detested the exploitation of his people in the name of religion. From his pulpit he preached against the abuses accompanying the sale of indulgences.

Leo X's issuance of indulgences was nothing new for the Roman Church. For centuries, popes had granted certificates of pardon. It was the position of the Roman Church that although Christ died to save men from hell, they still had to do penance or suffer in purgatory as punishment for their individual sins. The popes maintained that they had the power to suspend these punishments for specific individuals. This practice rested in the theory that the saints did more good works than necessary to get themselves into heaven. Their so-called excess works, along with the merits of Christ's

> ### *Luther's Spiritual Awakening*
> Night and day I pondered until I saw the connection between the justice of God and the statement that "the just shall live by faith" [Rom. 1:17]. Then I grasped that the justice of God is that righteousness by which through grace and sheer mercy God justifies us through faith. Thereupon I felt myself to be reborn and to have gone through open doors into paradise. The whole of Scripture took on a new meaning, and whereas before the "justice of God" had filled me with hate, now it became to me inexpressibly sweet in greater love. This passage of Paul became to me a gate to heaven.
>
> *Roland H. Bainton,* Here I Stand: A Life of Martin Luther, *49–50.*

Pope Leo X

perfect life, were to be collected in a type of spiritual bank, known as the treasury of saints. According to this theory, the pope served as treasurer and could dispense these extra good works. At first, popes granted indulgences only to people who performed some special work, such as giving money to charity or fighting on a crusade. However, by the time of the Renaissance, popes often sold indulgences to raise money for church projects. This is one of the abuses that drove Luther to produce his Ninety-Five Theses, or questions for Rome to answer.

While Tetzel's methods were scandalous, his cash boxes overflowed with money for Leo's building program. However, some sincere church members wondered why the pope, if he were truly the keeper of the treasury of saints, did not give these merits out freely to all, or why, if he could pardon one soul from purgatory, he did not pardon everyone. Luther raised these same questions. His opposition to the sale of indulgences ultimately shook all of Western Christendom.

Luther's Break with Rome
The Ninety-Five Theses

On October 31, 1517, Luther posted a list of grievances that later became known as his **Ninety-Five Theses**. Luther's document challenged the sale of indulgences, and he wrote these talking points in Latin for a scholarly debate. Little did he realize he would stir up a great controversy. Almost overnight Luther's document became a symbol of defiance against the corruption and hypocrisy of Rome. By questioning indulgences, Luther inadvertently—but providentially—challenged the whole system of Roman Catholicism.

Within weeks, copies of his Ninety-Five Theses, printed in German, circulated widely in Germany and received a sympathetic response among the people. Many Germans were disgusted with indulgence salesmen such as Tetzel; others looked for an occasion to stop the flow of German money into the papal coffers at Rome. Indulgence sales soon dropped off sharply—angering Tetzel and other church officials. They denounced Luther as a heretic and urged leaders of the Roman Church to take action against him. At first Pope Leo X refused to get involved in what he considered a minor quarrel among monks. But when funds from parts of Germany stopped flowing into the papal treasury, the pope reacted.

The Leipzig Debate

Opponents of Luther, thinking him to be nothing more than an ignorant and misguided monk, sought to engage him in debates in order to show him the error of his ways. But Luther, armed by years of diligent study of the Scriptures and guided by the Spirit of God, proved to be more than their match. The climax of this confrontation occurred in the debate at Leipzig (LIPE sig) during the summer of 1519. Here Luther met the formidable scholar Johann Eck, a champion of Catholicism. The debate occurred over three weeks, and centered on the question of authority in the church. Luther asserted that the pope had human rather than divine authority and that he could err just as any other man. The great reformer insisted that Scripture was the only reliable authority. (Thus the principle of *sola scriptura* became foundational to the Reformation.) Eck charged that Luther's views were similar to those of John Huss, who had been burned as a heretic a century earlier. In response Luther maintained that not all of Huss's teachings were heretical—a position that led him to conclude that even church councils might err.

The Leipzig debate only widened the breach between Luther and Rome. Luther had entered the debate believing himself to be a good Roman Catholic who had called attention to a few corrupt practices. But because he renounced the authority of popes and councils, he was driven to the Scriptures for guidance. He soon became even more firmly convinced that the Bible alone is the sole authority for the Christian faith.

In the months that followed, Luther wrote a series of pamphlets intended to rouse the German people to action. He wanted them to take a stand against the corrupt Roman system. Because the papacy failed to take the initiative, he called on civil rulers to reform the church. He attacked the sacramental system of the church, stating that it distorted the true meaning of salvation. He maintained that every believer was a priest and that each had the freedom to approach God personally through faith (Eph. 2:18; 1 Pet. 2:9).

The Road to Worms

The pope was unable to take serious action against Luther. One reason for this was that Luther was the subject of one of the most respected and powerful territorial princes in all of Germany, Frederick the Wise, Elector of Saxony. Frederick opposed the idea of having any of his subjects stand trial outside of Germany—especially if that trial were to take place in Italy.

In June of 1520, the pope finally heeded the counsel of his advisers. He issued a papal bull that condemned Luther for advancing heretical doctrines and gave him sixty days to recant. If Luther did not submit, he would be excommunicated. At a public gathering near the city gate of Wittenberg, Luther responded by ceremoniously tossing the papal bull into a bonfire, sealing his separation from Rome. As expected, a few weeks later he was formally excommunicated from the Roman Church.

The newly crowned German emperor, **Charles V**, sensing Luther's strong public support, refused to condemn him without a hearing. In the spring of 1521 he summoned Luther to the city of Worms to appear before the German Diet. The emperor gave Luther the promise of imperial protection to and from Worms, but Luther's friends reminded him of what had happened to John Huss in a similar situation. Despite their warnings, Luther proceeded to Worms to defend the truth before the imperial Diet.

On the afternoon of April 17, 1521, Luther stood before the emperor, princes, and bishops of the Holy Roman Empire at the **Diet of Worms**. He was given no chance to defend his teaching. Instead he was simply asked whether a number of books lying on a table in front of him were his writings and whether he would recant the heresy contained in them. To the first question Luther answered yes; to the second, he asked for time to consider his answer. The next day the questions were again put to him, and he was asked to give a clear and simple reply. With firmness of conviction, he gave his memorable declaration:

> Unless I am convicted of error by the testimony of Scripture or (since I put no trust in the unsupported authority of pope or of councils, since it is plain that they have often

Charles V

erred and often contradicted themselves) by clear reason I stand convicted by the Scriptures to which I have appealed, and my conscience is taken captive by God's word, I cannot and will not recant anything, for it is neither safe nor right to act against the conscience. Here I stand. I can do no other. God help me! Amen.

Luther left the city. The emperor soon afterwards issued an edict declaring Luther an outlaw of the empire. He banned Luther's writings, forbade anyone to give him aid, and demanded that he be seized and turned over to the authorities. If captured, Luther was to suffer the fate of a condemned heretic—death. God, however, was not through with this man. Luther lived for twenty-five years under the imperial edict and died a natural death in 1546. During these years the truth of God's Word, which he so boldly defended, took root in the hearts and lives of men and women all over Europe.

Progress in Germany
Continuation of Luther's Work

Despite the Edict of Worms, the doctrines of the Reformation continued to spread rapidly. They were proclaimed from pulpits, heralded from street corners, and circulated in printed pamphlets. Perhaps the greatest help to the reforming cause in Germany was Luther's translation of the New Testament (and later the whole Bible) into German. This work, based on Erasmus's Greek New Testament, created widespread enthusiasm for the Bible among all classes of German people. The power and beauty of its expression helped to create a standard German language for all of Germany.

Luther's work did not end with his translation of the Bible. In order to make the principles of the Reformation so clear that even a child could understand them, he wrote his *Shorter Catechism*. In question-and-answer form, this catechism gives instruction in the fundamental doctrines of Scripture. Luther also used music as a means of teaching the gospel. He urged the people to sing doctrinal hymns at home, work, and church. His own hymn, "A Mighty Fortress Is Our God," called the "victory hymn of the Reformation," is one of the best-known and most-loved hymns of the Christian church.

As the followers of Luther's teaching increased in number, it soon became necessary to frame an official statement of Lutheran beliefs. In 1530 **Philipp Melanchthon**, Luther's close friend and co-worker, drew up the Augsburg Confession, which clearly sets forth the chief doctrines for which Luther and his followers contended. This document became the doctrinal standard for the Lutheran Church and has remained that denomination's most highly respected statement of faith.

Preoccupation of Charles V

One reason for the rapid spread of Lutheran doctrine was Charles V's preoccupation with the political affairs of Europe. Charles, the crowned ruler of the Holy Roman Empire, was also the ruler by inheritance of the Habsburg possessions of Spain, Sicily, Naples, the Netherlands, and Austria, plus territory in the New World. His vast holdings gave him great power but many problems as well. He was constantly defending the borders of his far-flung possessions, putting down revolts, and repelling invasions.

Philipp Melanchthon

Between the years 1522 and 1546, Charles fought several wars with his chief rival, **Francis I**, the king of France. The French king was particularly concerned that his country was encircled by Charles's possessions. Meanwhile, Charles was faced with another threat. The Ottoman Turks, led by **Suleiman** (r. 1520–66), invaded the eastern portion of the Holy Roman Empire. By the early 1540s Charles had halted the Turkish advance and had signed a truce with the French king. He could now turn his attention to the religious situation in the German states. But over twenty years had elapsed since the Diet of Worms. Lutheranism was firmly established.

In 1546, the year of Luther's death, Charles began his attack on the German Protestants. For nearly nine years his imperial and pro-Catholic forces waged war against the anti-imperial and Protestant forces of German princes. In 1555 the warring parties agreed to a compromise settlement known as the **Peace of Augsburg** that allowed each prince the right to choose whether his territory would be Lutheran or Roman Catholic. The people within a given territory had to either accept the choice of their prince or move elsewhere. The compromise only postponed the religious and political problems in Germany; in 1618 war would break out once again.

Section Review

1–4. Summarize the rise and decline of the Roman Church during this period, beginning with Innocent III and ending with the Council of Constance.

5–6. What did men like Tetzel sell to raise funds for the rebuilding of St. Peter's Basilica? How did this contribute to the Reformation?

7. At the Leipzig debate, Eck charged that Luther was holding views similar to what earlier reformer?

8. What doctrine did Luther discover that transformed his life?

9–10. What settlement ended the civil war that broke out among the Catholic and Protestant princes of Germany? What compromise was reached by this settlement?

✷ How did those who preceded the Reformation pave the way for it? Provide two examples.

✷ Evaluate the positive and negative aspects of the Peace of Augsburg.

Spread

The Protestant Reformation was not confined to the land of Germany. Nor was Luther its only leader. God raised up reformers in many lands who protested the abuses of Roman Catholicism and sought to restore biblical Christianity. Though the reformers often differed on matters of biblical interpretation, they were in agreement with the key doctrines of the Reformation movement: Scripture alone, faith alone, grace alone.

Switzerland

Switzerland was one of the first places outside Germany to feel the influence of the Protestant Reformation. The Swiss Confederation began in 1291 when three cantons (or states) banded together for mutual defense. By the time of the Reformation, the number of cantons had grown to thirteen. Switzerland enjoyed a remarkable degree of independence even though in theory it was still part of the Holy Roman Empire.

Zwingli in Zurich

An early leader of the Swiss Reformation was **Ulrich Zwingli** (ZWING lee). He was born in 1484 in a small village in the northern German-speaking region of Switzerland. He studied at several leading universities, where he developed a keen interest in the classics. His training acquainted him with Erasmus, under whose influence he began to study the Bible. As a young man, Zwingli was ordained a Roman Catholic priest. Early in his ministry, however, he realized that there was corruption in the Roman Church. He soon became an outspoken critic of its abusive practices. In 1519 Zwingli became the priest of the largest church in Zurich, one of the leading towns in the Swiss Confederation.

While in Zurich, Zwingli was exposed to Luther's writings, and through them he came to understand that salvation comes only by the grace of God through faith. With the support of the Zurich city council, Zwingli began to make significant changes in his church. These changes aroused Roman Catholic opposition, but Zwingli ably defended his position in several public debates. For one such occasion, he drew up his Sixty-Seven Conclusions. These articles, similar in style to Luther's Ninety-Five Theses, set forth Zwingli's belief in the Bible as the sole rule of faith. He rejected Roman Catholic teaching concerning the mass, the celibacy of priests, purgatory, and the primacy of the pope. He declared that Christ is the only way to salvation—that He alone is the eternal High Priest, the only mediator between God and man.

Civil war broke out in Switzerland between the cantons that embraced Protestantism and those that remained Roman Catholic. In 1531 Zurich went to war against some neighboring Catholic districts. Zwingli accompanied the troops as a chaplain and was killed at the Battle of Kappel as he sought to aid a wounded soldier. Others carried on Zwingli's reforms in Zurich. Some of his followers joined the ranks of the Lutherans, while others merged with the followers of another famous reformer, John Calvin.

The Anabaptists

Although Zwingli and his followers dominated the religious and political life of Zurich, there were those who were not satisfied with the pace or restraint of his reforms. Some of them met together in 1525 and organized their own congregation, calling themselves the Swiss Brethren. Among other things, these men opposed the practice of infant baptism in favor of believer's baptism. As a result, those who joined their ranks and had been baptized as infants were rebaptized. For this reason their enemies called them **Anabaptists** (from a Greek word that means "baptize again"). The Swiss Brethren did not call themselves "rebaptizers" because they did not find support for infant baptism in Scripture. When the city council tried to force the Swiss Brethren in Zurich to present their children for infant baptism, they refused to comply. As the number of Anabaptists continued to increase, officials responded with persecution. Some of the leaders were imprisoned, others were compelled to flee the city, and one was martyred by drowning.

Ulrich Zwingli

Other groups that opposed the Catholic Church and some practices of Lutherans and other magisterial reformers (reformers who worked with secular authorities) continued to spring up in Europe. These varied religious bodies were grouped together under the common title "Anabaptist" even though on many issues they were in sharp disagreement. Some so-called Anabaptists had revolutionary ideas or advocated heresy and twisted Scripture to support their false doctrines. However, most wanted nothing more than to be left in peace to worship God freely and to study His Word. Nevertheless, because of the wrongdoing of a few, all who were labeled Anabaptists were persecuted, and many suffered martyrdom.

In spite of their geographic isolation, most Anabaptists held certain beliefs in common. For instance, in addition to believer's baptism, they believed that only true believers should be members in the local church. This was considered a radical position since all the inhabitants of a particular community in most areas of Europe were automatically church members regardless of their spiritual condition. Second, most Anabaptists believed in the separation of church and state—that is, they rejected state interference in their affairs. In addition, many of them believed it was wrong for Christians to hold political office. (This seemed logical to them since those in political office were often their persecutors.) Third, many Anabaptists believed that a Christian should not take up arms against anyone, even in time of war. This belief is called pacifism.

Most of the groups labeled as Anabaptists either disappeared or merged with the Mennonites. This group of Anabaptists was labeled, by their enemies, after one of their founders, Menno Simons. In the seventeenth century, a Mennonite named Jacob Amman split from the Mennonites over matters of discipline, and his followers became known as the Amish. Both groups have continued to the present day.

Calvin at Geneva

John Calvin became one of the most famous and influential magisterial Protestant reformers after Martin Luther. Born in 1509 in northwestern France, he studied both law and theology at the universities of Orléans, Bourges, and Paris. The Reformation was in full swing during his student days: Luther's ideas were undoubtedly being discussed at the French universities. Calvin diligently searched the Scriptures during these years to determine the validity of Reformation doctrine. Sometime around 1533 Calvin was converted and joined the Protestant movement.

About a year after Calvin's conversion, the king of France intensified persecution of French Protestants. Calvin fled his native land and sought refuge in the Swiss city of Basel, where he wrote the first edition of one of the most significant and influential books on theology ever written. The first edition of *The Institutes of the Christian Religion* was published in 1536 when Calvin was just twenty-six. It was revised and expanded throughout Calvin's life. Calvin had two purposes in writing the *Institutes*: to teach the basics of the Christian religion so that people might live godly lives and to defend the teachings of the Reformation in the face of persecution.

In 1536, while returning from a visit to France, Calvin stopped for the night in Geneva, Switzerland. The Protestants of Geneva asked Calvin to stay and become their pastor and teacher. Though

John Calvin

Calvin's Theology

The heart of Calvin's system of theology can be found in the first section of Calvin's 1538 catechism: "The chief concern and care of our life ought to be to seek God, to aspire to him with our whole heart, and to rest nowhere else but in him." This goal Calvin called piety or godliness. He observed that everybody has the urge to show piety to something, but the fallen human heart does not worship God. Instead, the human heart is an idol factory. Because of this, Calvin said that theology must teach us to know God and to know ourselves. When humans come to know themselves and God, they find that they are slaves to sin who cannot do right. God's law shows the standard of God's righteousness, and nobody is able to meet that standard. This should cause people to look to God for salvation. The main goal of salvation is godliness or piety. The law continues to play its role in showing people what God's standard of righteousness is, but the Christian now has the indwelling Holy Spirit, who gives Christians a love for God's law and the ability to obey it.

Wall of the Reformers Monument, Geneva, Switzerland

hesitant at first, he finally agreed, taking up the work of the Reformation that others had already begun in the city. The relationship with the city leaders did not begin well. Calvin wanted all the citizens to subscribe to a confession of faith. He also wanted the church to have freedom to deny the Lord's Supper to those the pastors deemed unfit to receive it. However, the city council insisted that it had the right to determine who could partake of the Lord's Supper. When Calvin would not budge on these issues, he was ordered to leave the city. Calvin traveled to Strasbourg and became the pastor of a group of French refugees. However, in 1541 Geneva called him to return, and he remained there until his death in 1564.

Calvin sought to build a Christian community based on the Word of God. While he stressed the independence of church and state, he believed that both were subject to the rule of God. Calvin asserted, as did many in this era, that the duty of the state was to promote piety, punish evildoers, and assist the church by providing an atmosphere that would encourage godliness in the lives of church members. Under Calvin's leadership, the city of Geneva became a leading center of the Protestant Reformation.

Section Review

1. What city and country are associated with the ministry of the reformer Ulrich Zwingli?

2–3. List two beliefs that most of the early Anabaptists held.

4–5. What influential work on theology did John Calvin write? What city associated with his ministry became a leading center of the Protestant Reformation?

★ Evaluate Calvin's influence on European society.

England

Cries for reform had echoed in England since the days of John Wycliffe. His persecuted followers, the Lollards, opposed papal tyranny and preached the authority of the Word of God. During the sixteenth century, efforts for reform intensified in England as Luther's writings were widely circulated and read. The English Reformation, which did not have a dominant leader like Luther or Calvin, was influenced by two important factors.

The first factor was the publication of English translations of the Bible. The importance of the Word of God in bringing about spiritual revival in Europe cannot be overemphasized. The Bible itself instructs us that "faith cometh by hearing, and hearing by the word of God" (Rom. 10:17). During the late fifteenth and early sixteenth centuries, the Bible was translated and printed in the native languages of almost every European country. In England a number of versions of the Bible were published and distributed. These were translated from the ancient tongues into the common language of the English people. A readable, understandable Bible helped increase the knowledge of God's Word and revealed the extrabiblical teaching of the Roman Catholic Church.

The second factor was the involvement of the English rulers. The English Reformation began as a political movement under the direction of the English Crown. During the sixteenth century, members of the Tudor family occupied the throne. There were five Tudor rulers in all: Henry VII, the founder of this royal line; his son Henry VIII; and Henry VIII's three children—Edward VI, Mary I, and Elizabeth I. Under most of the Tudors, England broke with the papacy, and the claim of papal authority over the church in England was rejected. Most of the English people supported the Crown. They were filled with national pride and resented the claims of a foreign pope on their land. At first the majority of Englishmen remained in the Roman Church. However, a growing number became increasingly dissatisfied with Rome and embraced Protestantism. Political motives gradually gave way to spiritual concerns as the truth of God's Word found acceptance in people's hearts.

The Break with Rome Under Henry VIII

King **Henry VIII** (r. 1509–47) was on the throne of England when the Protestant Reformation began in Germany. He branded Martin Luther a heretic and wrote a book attacking Luther's teaching. The pope promptly proclaimed Henry "Defender of the Faith." Nevertheless, Henry later broke with Rome also, though not for the same reasons that motivated Luther. Henry wanted to divorce his wife, Catherine of Aragon, the daughter of Ferdinand and Isabella of Spain. The pope, not wishing to offend Catherine's nephew, the powerful emperor Charles V, refused to grant Henry the divorce. Therefore, Henry decided to take matters into his own hands. He appointed a new archbishop of Canterbury, **Thomas Cranmer**, who declared Henry's marriage to Catherine invalid and legalized his new marriage to Anne Boleyn. In 1534, Henry had Parliament pass the Act of Supremacy, which made the king the "supreme head" of the church in England. This act completed the break between England and the papacy. It also placed the English church under the direct control of the state. Even so, during Henry's day, the English church remained generally true to Roman teaching and practice.

Protestant Gains Under Edward VI

When Henry VIII died in 1547, his son **Edward VI** succeeded him to the throne. Edward, a frail boy, was only nine years old when he became king. He was strongly influenced by his advisers, who were sympathetic to the Protestant Reformation. As a result, sweeping changes were made in the English church. Parliamentary acts legalized the marriage of clergymen, abolished many Catholic ceremonies, and required church services to be in English rather than in Latin. In addition, the clergy were required to use the *Book of Common Prayer* in their churches. This prayer book was drawn up by Cranmer, who had become a leading voice of Protestantism in England. It contains Bible readings and prayers for special occasions and prescribes orders of worship for various church services.

The statement of faith known as the Forty-Two Articles reveals the extent of Protestant gains during Edward's reign. Formulated by Cranmer and issued by Edward, it became the official creed of the English church. The document sets forth the major Protestant doctrines of justification by faith alone and the sole authority of

Henry VIII

the Bible. It renounces transubstantiation and recognizes only two sacraments—baptism and the Lord's Supper.

Catholic Reaction Under Mary I

The sickly Edward died of tuberculosis at the age of sixteen (1553). His half sister Mary succeeded him to the throne. **Mary I**, the daughter of Henry VIII by Catherine of Aragon, was a devout Roman Catholic. She sought to restore Roman Catholicism to England by compelling Parliament to repeal the religious laws passed during Edward's reign. She removed from office thousands of clergymen who had Protestant sympathies or who had married.

As political and religious opposition mounted against Mary's pro-Catholic policies, she revived laws against heresy and began to persecute the Protestants. Hundreds of Englishmen fled to Germany and Switzerland. Many of those who remained in England were imprisoned; some became martyrs at the stake. Two famous victims of Mary's persecution were bishops Hugh Latimer and Nicholas Ridley. They were condemned to be burned at the stake. Mary next turned her fury on Thomas Cranmer, the man who had declared her mother's marriage invalid. Charged with heresy, imprisoned, interrogated, and facing death, Cranmer weakened. He signed statements renouncing his Protestant beliefs and acknowledging the authority of the pope over the church in England. Yet Mary and the papal representatives sentenced Cranmer to die at the stake. On the day of his execution, he publicly condemned his previous weakness and boldly reaffirmed his Protestant convictions.

Persecution continued until Mary's death in 1558. During her five-year reign, Mary ordered the execution of nearly three hundred leaders—earning her the nickname "Bloody Mary." However, her actions only strengthened English Protestantism and increased anti-Catholic sentiment.

Break with Rome Confirmed Under Elizabeth

When Mary I died, her half sister **Elizabeth I** (1558–1603) became queen. Her forty-five-year reign marks one of the greatest periods in English history. A strong and determined woman, Elizabeth ruled England effectively during a crucial period of its history. During her long reign she was a symbol of stability and strength. The English people affectionately called her "Good Queen Bess."

The Church of England—Though reared a Protestant, Elizabeth favored a compromise solution to England's religious problems. She restored Protestantism to England; yet she tried to avoid alienating the English Roman Catholics. Like her father, she had Parliament pass an Act of Supremacy (1559), which rejected papal authority and affirmed her position over the Church of England; however, it changed her title from "Supreme Head" to "Supreme Governor" in order to be less offensive to Roman Catholics. Under Elizabeth, Cranmer's Forty-Two Articles were revised to become the Thirty-Nine Articles—another Protestant statement of faith.

The attempt by Elizabeth to settle England's religious problems through compromise laid the foundation for the Church of England, also known as the **Anglican Church**. This institution became the established state church of England and took as its creed the Thirty-Nine Articles. While the Anglican Church embraced Protestant doctrines, it did not alter its church government, nor did it abolish certain established rituals that were not expressly forbidden

Elizabeth I

in Scripture, such as clerical vestments (robes) and candles on the communion table.

War with Spain—England's shift toward Protestantism did not go unopposed by Roman Catholics outside of England. England's most formidable Catholic opponent was King Philip of Spain. **Philip II** (r. 1556–98) was the son of Habsburg emperor Charles V. When Charles abdicated in 1556, Philip became the ruler of the Habsburg territories in Spain, the Netherlands, and the New World. One of the strongest defenders of the Roman Catholic Church, he worked hard to stamp out Protestantism. He attempted to prevent the spread of the Reformation in his realm by turning the Spanish Inquisition against the Protestants. As leader of the strongest Catholic country in the world, Philip sought to bring Protestant England back into the fold of the Roman Catholic Church.

Shortly before becoming king, Philip had married Mary I, the Roman Catholic queen of England. A child born of that union would no doubt have been reared a Roman Catholic and would have been by right the next ruler of England and Spain. But in God's providence Mary died childless, and her Protestant sister Elizabeth became queen. Philip sought to marry Elizabeth. But while he was wooing her, Elizabeth was secretly working against Spain. She encouraged her sea captains (men such as Francis Drake) to plunder Spanish ships returning with treasure from the New World. She also aided the Dutch in their revolt against the Spanish ruler.

Because Elizabeth opposed Philip's political and religious involvement in various parts of Europe, he began plotting her overthrow. He conspired to have Elizabeth killed and have her cousin Mary Stuart—the former queen of Scotland—crowned queen of England. The plot was discovered, however, and Elizabeth had Mary put in prison and later executed.

Exasperated and angry, Philip decided to invade England. He amassed a great fleet of 130 ships which was to sail to the Netherlands, pick up a large Spanish army, and transport the invasion force to England. In 1588 this fleet, called by some the "Invincible Armada," set sail from Spain with the pope's blessing. However, the large, unwieldy Spanish galleons were no match for the smaller, more maneuverable English ships. The battered Spanish fleet turned north only to be overtaken by fierce storms that wrecked many Spanish vessels along the coast of Scotland and Ireland. The "Invincible Armada" limped back to Spain with only about half the number of ships it had set out with.

The defeat of the **Spanish Armada** had a significant impact on world history. First, it preserved England from both Spanish and Roman Catholic domination. Second, it accelerated the decline of Spain, which during the period of exploration had been one of the richest and strongest European countries. The battle weakened Spanish sea power and as a result weakened Spain's position in the New World. Finally, it established England as a sea power at the very time English colonial expansion was under way. The way was opened for English Protestants, instead of Spanish Catholics, to settle in North America.

English Protestants acknowledged God's help in their victory. They had no doubt that the "Protestant wind" that had wrecked the Spanish fleet came from God, for "the Lord hath his way in the whirlwind and in the storm, and the clouds are the dust of his feet" (Nah. 1:3).

Philip II

John Knox

William of Orange

The Puritans—Though Protestantism had triumphed in England, not all Protestants were in agreement with the Church of England. Many believed that the Anglican Church retained too many of the "trappings of popery." They wished to "purify" the church of those practices that reminded them of Roman Catholicism. Thus originated their nickname—the **Puritans**. Other Englishmen saw no hope of bringing about change in the English Church. Those who removed themselves from the church were known as **Separatists**. Englishmen with Catholic leanings, however, were not satisfied. They hoped to bring the Church of England back in line with Roman Catholicism.

Scotland

John Knox (1505–72) became the leader of the Protestant Reformation in Scotland. Having been a noted preacher in England during the reign of Edward VI, he fled to Geneva when Mary I came to the throne. There he was greatly influenced by John Calvin.

He returned to Scotland in 1559. Through fiery preaching, he attacked the evils of Roman Catholicism. Under his leadership Scotland became a Protestant nation. The Scottish parliament rejected papal authority, abolished the mass, and adopted a Calvinistic statement of faith drawn up by Knox. They established the Presbyterian Church in Scotland.

The Reformation in Scotland flourished even though Scotland had a Catholic queen, Mary Stuart (r. 1542–87). Mary was less than a week old when her father, King James V, died and she was proclaimed queen of Scotland. She grew up in France, however, the homeland of her mother, while her mother acted as her regent in Scotland. In 1561 the young queen returned to Scotland only to find that her Catholic and French upbringing alienated the nationalistic Scottish Protestants.

Her downfall came when she was implicated in plotting her husband's death. To make matters worse, she married her husband's suspected murderer. Forced to abdicate, she fled to England, leaving behind her infant son James VI, the next king of Scotland. When Elizabeth I died in 1601, James VI was invited to assume the English throne; he was crowned King James I of England.

The Netherlands

The Netherlands was one of the many territories ruled by Charles V. When Charles abdicated, this territory came under the control of his son, Philip II. Because Philip was both Spanish and Catholic, many of his subjects disliked him. Not long after he became king, Protestant unrest in the Netherlands prompted him to send troops to put down the trouble. His troops severely persecuted the Protestants there, causing them to break out in armed revolt in 1568. The Protestants fought under their leader William of Orange, and for a time even many of the Roman Catholics living in the southern part of the Netherlands turned against Spanish rule.

The war dragged on for years, but the Netherlands, aided by the English, managed to hold off the Spanish troops. In 1581 the Protestant areas of the Netherlands declared their independence from Spain. The Roman Catholic area (modern Belgium) remained under Spanish control. William was murdered a few years later. However, the Dutch Protestants continued their struggle and won a truce with Spain in the early seventeenth century.

France

The writings of Luther flowed into France, arousing widespread interest in the Reformation. The works of John Calvin also had a strong influence there. By the middle of the sixteenth century, there were over two thousand Protestant congregations in France, and perhaps as many as one-half of the nobility had become Protestants. Despite these gains, France remained a thoroughly Catholic country. The government, fearful of the growing political and religious power of Protestantism, fiercely persecuted the **Huguenots** (French Protestants).

St. Bartholomew's Day Massacre

One of the most shocking incidents occurred in 1572. Catherine de Medici, the mother of the French king and the real power behind the throne, instigated a massacre of the Huguenots in Paris. Catherine planned this attack and lured many Huguenot leaders to Paris under the guise of attending a marriage that would end the conflict. Early on the morning of August 27 (St. Bartholomew's Day), bands of Roman Catholics began roving the city, breaking into homes and murdering the unsuspecting and unarmed Protestants. Coordinated massacres occurred throughout France.

By the time the massacre had ended, an estimated twenty thousand Huguenots had been murdered. The **St. Bartholomew's Day Massacre**, needless to say, increased the tension between the French Roman Catholics and the Protestants, whose differences had already led to war. Conflict broke out once again, this time over the question of who would rule France. The Valois family, which had ruled France since the fourteenth century, was dying out. Two other families were seeking the throne. The Guise family was Roman Catholic and traced its line back to Charlemagne. The other family, the Bourbon, was Huguenot and traced its ancestry back to Louis IX.

Henry of Navarre, the head of the Bourbon family and the leader of the Huguenots, emerged victorious in the struggle for the throne. He declared himself to be Henry IV (r. 1589–1610), the king of France. However, there was one serious problem. The majority of Frenchmen were Roman Catholic and would not allow a Protestant to become king. To please the people and secure the throne

Henry IV

Providence

God is actively working out His purposes in history, and He has revealed some of those purposes to us in the Bible. Christian historians can humbly seek to discern this working out of God's plan in history. The Spanish Armada and the "Protestant wind" are a famous example of how God allowed the English, through the combination of a storm and the English's superior firepower, to decisively defeat the Catholic Spanish Armada. As a result, Protestantism persisted in England, paving the way for England's later role in global missions.

However, victory does not always imply God's approval, nor does defeat mean His displeasure. France's massacre of French Huguenots during the St. Bartholomew's Day Massacre was certainly not out of God's control. It was not a sign of Catholic France's righteousness before God. God's will includes the suffering of His people (2 Tim. 3:12), and this massacre is part of the working out of this purpose.

he had so eagerly sought, Henry IV became a Roman Catholic. He supposedly remarked, "Paris is well worth a mass." Although Henry IV deserted his Huguenot followers, he did grant them a certain amount of religious toleration in the famous **Edict of Nantes** (1598). However, as we shall see in chapter 14, this period of toleration was brief.

Section Review

1–2. What two factors resulted in the spread of the Reformation to England?

3. Which English ruler earned the title "Defender of the Faith" from the pope but later broke with Rome?

4. Which English king, though frail in health, approved sweeping changes to the English church?

5–6. Who was the fiery Scottish preacher who advanced the cause of the Reformation in Scotland? What Protestant church became the state church in Scotland?

✭ How did the Reformation spread throughout western Europe?

✭ How did Henry IV provide temporary relief for the Huguenots? Why would it be temporary?

The Counter Reformation

In the early stages of the Reformation, it seemed as if the Roman Catholic Church was fading because of the efforts of the reformers. Northern Europe as well as many areas of eastern Europe had rejected the Roman Church. A strong Protestant movement was underway in France. There were even small Protestant groups in such Catholic strongholds as Spain and Italy. In an effort to prevent further losses to the Protestants, the Roman Catholic Church promoted reforms of its own.

The Catholic Reformation is often called the **Counter Reformation**. (The word *counter* means "to oppose".) The Protestant leaders had directed their efforts primarily against false doctrine. Most Catholic reformers, however, attempted to clean up the church by correcting some of the outward moral problems. They failed to see that the root of their problems was doctrinal error.

Jesuits

The Society of Jesus, or the **Jesuits**, became instrumental in promoting the Counter Reformation. This new religious order was founded by the Spanish soldier Ignatius of Loyola (loy OH luh; c. 1491–1556). While recovering from a battle injury, Ignatius underwent a religious experience in which he determined to devote his life to the Roman Church. In 1540 the Jesuit order officially came into existence. Unlike those in other religious orders, the Jesuits took a special vow of absolute obedience to the pope.

From its beginnings the purpose of the Jesuit order was to suppress heresy and to promote Roman Catholic education. The Jesuits realized the importance of careful training. Those who wanted to become members of the organization had to undergo a two-year period of probation. During that time the prospective member studied the *Spiritual Exercises* written by Ignatius and learned to be completely submissive to those in authority. "We ought always to be

Ignatius of Loyola

ready to believe that what seems to us white is black if the hierarchical Church so defines it," Ignatius once said. If the two-year probation period ended successfully, the individual became a member of the Jesuits. He usually continued his studies, sometimes spending a total of fifteen years in preparation for his work.

The Jesuits used every means available to promote their own order and to turn people back to the Roman Church. They believed it was proper to do wrong in order to accomplish something good. For example, some Jesuits taught that it was acceptable to murder someone—even a ruler—if that death furthered Catholic purposes. They exercised great influence in schools and governments, attacking Protestantism and spreading the Counter Reformation wherever they went. Many Jesuits were also zealous missionaries. Francis Xavier (1506–52) became the best-known Jesuit missionary. He served in India, China, and Japan.

Inquisition

To stop the spread of Protestantism, Pope Paul III (r. 1534–49) reorganized the Inquisition that brought terror and death to Protestants in countries where Roman Catholicism was dominant. As in previous centuries, the Inquisition operated on the assumption that anyone accused of heresy was guilty until proved innocent. After being arrested, often at night, the accused would stand before an inquisitor. Without knowing what charges had been brought against him or who had brought them, the accused person would be asked to confess his wrong. If mild methods of persuasion failed to produce a confession, the inquisitors often used torture. Many, whether or not they had confessed, were turned over to secular authorities to be burned at the stake. The family of the accused often suffered as well, through arrest or loss of property.

Index of Prohibited Books

When Gutenberg introduced movable-type printing in Europe, the price of books and pamphlets dropped sharply. Previously only the rich could afford books, but by the sixteenth century many people could purchase printed material. Printed copies of the Bible and books written by the reformers circulated throughout Europe. Realizing the impact that the printed page was having on the spread of the Reformation, the Roman Church tried to regulate what its members read. In 1559 the Roman Catholic Church established the *Index of Prohibited Books*, which condemned, among other things, forty-eight allegedly heretical editions or versions of the Bible. Only those books that received an ecclesiastical license had official church approval. Even today, books officially sanctioned by the Roman Church contain inside the front cover the Latin words *imprimatur* ("let it be printed") and *nihil obstat* ("nothing hinders").

Council of Trent

Twenty-five years after the beginning of the Protestant Reformation, Pope Paul III called a church council to discuss doctrinal questions and to propose needed reform. Charles V, the Holy Roman emperor, had demanded such a council because the religious division in Germany was increasing. He wanted to end the division

Title page of the Index of Prohibited Books

and to restore unity to his land. Fearful of what a general church council might do, Pope Paul III structured it in such a way that the pope's representatives, as well as the other Italian delegates, controlled the proceedings. The outcome was predetermined. In 1545 the council held its first meeting in Trent, a city of northern Italy. Church leaders did not meet on a continuous basis but gathered for an extended period of time on three separate occasions. In 1563 the Council of Trent held its last session.

The Council of Trent is significant for two major reasons. First, it explicitly condemned many of the biblical principles that Protestantism is based on. Most importantly, it rejected the doctrines of justification by faith alone and the sole authority of Scripture. This sealed the break between Protestant and Roman Catholic churches. Second, the council set forth a complete doctrinal position of the Roman Church and made its position binding for all Roman Catholics. No deviation from the council's decrees would be tolerated.

Section Review

1. What was the name for the Catholic Reformation that sought to stop the spread of the Protestant movement?

2–3. What new religious order was formed to suppress heresy and promote Roman Catholic education? Who was the founder of this order?

4. What court of the Roman Church focused its attention on finding and punishing those accused of holding Protestant beliefs?

5. What did the Roman Church issue to regulate what its members could read?

6–7. At what council did the Roman Church set forth its doctrinal position? Which pope called for this council?

★ How did the Counter Reformation respond to the concepts of *sola scriptura* and *sola fide*, and what impact did the Council of Trent have on the Roman Church?

Making Connections

1–3. Contrast the attitudes of the Renaissance man and the medieval man toward life. (List three.)

4–5. Contrast Renaissance and medieval art. (List two.)

6–8. For what teachings did the Roman Church condemn Wycliffe and Huss as heretics? (List three concepts they taught or opposed.)

9–10. Briefly describe the teachings of two key figures of the Reformation.

11–12. How did the Roman Church respond to the Protestant Reformation? (List two aspects of the Counter Reformation.)

Developing History Skills

1. Assess the influences of previous and current empires on Italy, as well as other advantages that resulted in this peninsula becoming the home of the early Renaissance.

2. What conditions led to the Reformation?

Thinking Critically

1. Evaluate from the Bible the shift of Renaissance paintings from an otherworldly emphasis to a focus on the goodness of creation. (Considering the opening and closing chapters of the Bible might be helpful.)

2. Assess the impact of the Reformation on Europe.

Living in God's World

1. Imagine you are an author, painter, or composer. You meet a Catholic priest one day. He tells you that if you really want to serve God you must take holy orders. How would you respond?

2. At the heart of the Reformation is the doctrine of justification. Research this biblical topic and write a brief paragraph explaining the doctrine of justification by faith alone.

People, Places, and Things to Know

Renaissance
Reformation
humanism
Medici family
Lorenzo de Medici
Niccolò Machiavelli
Erasmus
Thomas More
Miguel de Cervantes
William Shakespeare
Sandro Botticelli
Leonardo da Vinci
Raphael
Michelangelo
Sistine Chapel
Albrecht Dürer
Hans Holbein
Donatello
John Wycliffe
John Huss
Martin Luther
sola fide
Leo X
indulgences
Ninety-Five Theses
sola scriptura
Charles V
Diet of Worms
Philipp Melanchthon
Francis I
Suleiman
Peace of Augsburg
Ulrich Zwingli
Anabaptists
John Calvin
Henry VIII
Thomas Cranmer
Edward VI
Mary I
Elizabeth I
Anglican Church
Philip II
Spanish Armada
Puritans
Separatists
John Knox
Huguenots
St. Bartholomew's Day Massacre
Henry of Navarre
Edict of Nantes
Counter Reformation
Jesuits

Empires of Africa, India, and Asia

I. Africa

II. India

III. Asia

Sikh Golden Temple in Amritsar, Punjab, India

Big Ideas

1. What characterized the history and culture of African civilizations during this period?

2. What characterized Indian culture?

3. How did the Mongols affect Asian civilizations?

Between 1100 and 1650, while Europe was transitioning from the Middle Ages to laying the foundation for the modern world, civilizations thrived in Africa, India, and Asia. These regions experienced sustained trade from the time of the Roman Empire, and city-states and empires enjoyed vast wealth and luxury that Europeans could only dream of. Toward the end of this period, many of these thriving civilizations declined, even as Europe became ascendant and would soon threaten the sovereignty of these kingdoms.

I. Africa

East African City-States

Along the eastern coast of Africa lay a series of important trading ports, each an independent city-state. These trading ports had existed as early as the days of the Roman Empire, and after the collapse of Rome, they continued to flourish as outlets for gold, iron, ivory, and animal skins to the Arabs and Persians. Prosperous city-states such as **Kilwa** (in what is today Tanzania) received goods from the tribes and kingdoms in the interior and sold them to Arab sea traders. As a result of this profitable trade, as well as a temperate climate, the seaside city-states attained wealth and a more refined culture. In the fourteenth century a Muslim visitor wrote, "Kilwa is one of the most beautiful and well-constructed towns in the world." A European visiting in 1500 wrote, "In this land there are rich merchants, and there is much gold and silver and amber and musk and pearls. Those of the land wear clothes of fine cotton and of silk and many fine things."

Although they were independent of each other, these coastal city-states shared a common culture, one that was a mixture of Arab, Persian, and African elements. The architecture, for example, was predominantly Arab. The language of the city-states, **Swahili**, was primarily native African but also contained elements of Arabic, Persian, and Indian dialects.

Central and Western Africa

During Europe's Middle Ages several important kingdoms arose in central and western Africa. Our knowledge of these civilizations is limited because most of their histories were not written down but were passed on orally. However, oral tradition, archaeology, and some accounts written by non-Africans provide us with a general picture of these cultures. In central Africa, for example, the kingdoms of Kanem (ca. 700–1376) and Bornu (1380–1893) thrived on the shores of Lake Chad. These successive kingdoms derived their profits from the camel-caravan trade and built strong military forces.

Also important were the three kingdoms of western Africa—Ghana, Mali, and Songhai, each progressively larger than the previous. All three built prosperous civilizations whose wealth derived from gold mines within their empires and the camel caravan trade in gold, salt, and other precious items that crossed the Sahara. The Niger (NYE jur) River in particular provided a lifeline for these empires, as its waters drew travelers crossing the desert.

Camels were the perfect means of transportation to carry precious cargo across the Sahara.

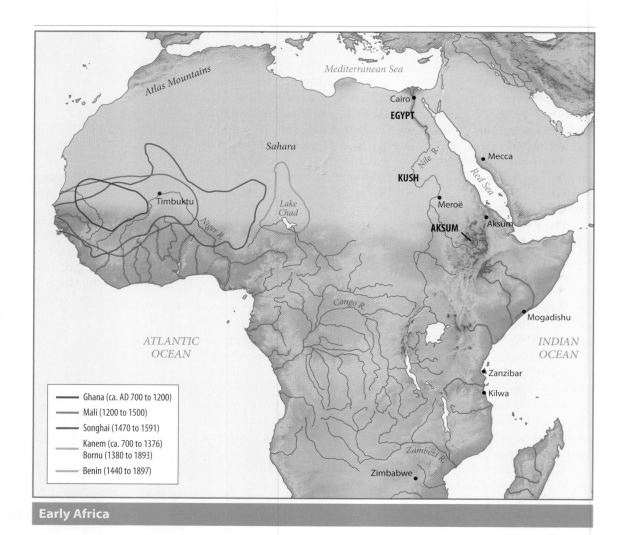

Early Africa

The kingdom of **Ghana** rose to prominence from about 700 to 1200. Ghana became a major destination for commercial caravans crossing Africa. The most important commodities included gold and salt. The rulers of Ghana received a tariff on all goods passing through Ghana, and the royal treasury overflowed with wealth. At the kingdom's highest point, the king of Ghana was considered one of the richest monarchs in the world. Ghana's prominence ended following an Islamic revival in the 11th century and the launching of jihad against Ghana. The capital was destroyed in 1203, and the kingdom of Ghana collapsed.

In its place rose the kingdom of **Mali**, dominating western Africa from 1200 to 1500. This kingdom became noted for its agricultural productivity as well as its transdesert trade in gold, salt, and copper. The capital, **Timbuktu**, became an important center of trade. **Mansa Musa** (r. 1312–ca. 1337), the most famous ruler of Mali, made a pilgrimage to Mecca in 1324. So splendid was his traveling party that it caught the attention of the non-African world. Musa took with him sixty thousand men and several thousand pounds of gold on one hundred camels. He astonished even the Egyptians with his wealth during a stay in Cairo. It was said that he spent so much gold in Cairo that he temporarily depreciated the value of the precious metal. He also encouraged learning in his realm, attracting so many scholars to Timbuktu that it is said books began to rival gold as an item for trade.

Following the death of Musa, the kingdom of Mali lacked effective leadership and declined. Frequent quarrels among the leadership in the palace continued to weaken the kingdom and invited outside attack.

In the fifteenth century, the **Songhai Empire** overthrew the Mali Empire and began to gain control of territory formerly held by Mali. Under the leadership of Sunni Ali (r. 1464–1492) this kingdom extended farther than either Ghana or Mali, stretching to the Atlantic in the west and pressing the kingdom of Bornu on Lake Chad in the east. After Sunni Ali drowned in 1492, the next ruler secured the trade routes and gained control of the salt and gold trade in the western Sudan. However, the empire's wealth proved more attractive than its power proved fearsome. Armed with muzzle-loading guns, invading Moroccan forces brought an end to the Songhai Empire in 1591 and, with it, an end to the western African empires.

Forest Kingdoms

Providing the goods for the eastern city-states to sell were the "forest kingdoms" of the interior of Africa. Records of these kingdoms are even more scarce than those of the central and western empires to the north. The best-known forest kingdoms are those with which Europeans came into contact right after the close of the Middle Ages. Perhaps the most important was the kingdom of **Benin** in western Africa (today's southern Nigeria). It arose in 1440 and lasted until 1897.

In addition to being a center for trade, Benin produced fine statues and relief sculptures in bronze. The metalworking of Benin became a significant artistic accomplishment of early African history.

Beginning late in the Middle Ages, African trade began to change. As Europeans began sailing to African ports, the camel-caravan trade became less important. Tragically, a new trade opened with Arabs and later with Europeans—the slave trade. Although slavery had existed in Africa for centuries, demand for slaves increased as Islam became dominant in many regions. In addition, this traffic in human lives unfortunately became one of the main points of contact for African-European relations after 1500, leading to terrible suffering and exploitation of the African people.

Benin relief sculpture

Section Review

1–2. What language developed in East Africa from African, Arabic, Persian, and Indian dialects? What role did it play in the development of African empires and city-states?

3–5. What three successive empires developed in western Africa?

6. What role did trade have in the development of these African civilizations?

7–8. What two items were considered valuable and became an essential part of African trade?

✴ What role did geography play in these African civilizations?

✴ Why did the demand for slaves increase? What two groups played a role in this increase?

Guiding Questions

1. What contributed to the rise and fall of the Indian empires?
2. What were the key features of Indian cultures?
3. Why did India continue to be overrun by foreign invaders?

II. India

After years of constant raids by Muslim forces, Islamic warriors conquered much of northern India, where they established a kingdom. Almost immediately a conflict arose between the Muslim and Hindu elements within Indian society. For example, the Hindus believed in many gods, while the Muslims acknowledged only one. The Hindus followed the rigid caste system, while the Muslims believed in the equality of all men before their god, Allah. Although Muslim control of northern India ended at the close of the fourteenth century, their rulers left India scarred from the brutal execution of vast numbers of Hindus. As a result, the hostilities between Hindus and Muslims in Indian society have continued to the present.

Delhi Sultanate

The first of five successive Muslim dynasties seized power in 1206 and ruled in northern India near the city of Delhi. When a ruling dynasty failed to produce a strong leader, a cycle of instability and struggle would ensue until another effective ruler emerged. The **Delhi Sultanate** was one of the few kingdoms in Asia to successfully repel a full-scale Mongol invasion for nearly three hundred years. The Delhi Sultanate reached its greatest geographic footprint during the third dynasty and controlled most of the Indian subcontinent briefly. One of the common practices of this Islamic kingdom was to destroy Hindu temples and then replace them with new structures based on Indo-Islamic architecture. During the span of this kingdom, Buddhism virtually disappeared from India. Hinduism survived in this Muslim-dominated civilization by adapting its teachings and practices, including absorbing popular tribal beliefs. In the sixteenth century the Delhi Sultanate finally collapsed due to the advance of Mongol forces.

Vijayanagara Empire

The city of **Vijayanagara** (from *Vijaya Nagara*, "city of victory"), from which an empire by the same name emerged, was established in 1336 when Delhi Sultanate forces were pushed out of the Deccan Plateau. Gradually, leaders of this city-state expanded their control and ultimately claimed sovereignty over India south of the Krishna River. The rulers sought to gain legitimacy for their seizure of power by protecting Hinduism and its shrines against Muslim desecration. Thus the leaders used the promotion of Hinduism to expand the territory under their control and bring about a measure of unity. To grow sufficient food for the growing empire, engineers developed "tank-irrigated agriculture" (systems of reservoirs) in higher lands to supply a consistent water supply. Merchants developed coastal regions into centers of trade between Europe and Southeast Asia and brought great wealth to central and southern India. This kingdom also developed a distinct architecture, and the rulers patronized fine arts and literature in several prominent Indian languages.

Mamluk dynasty (1206–90)
Tughlaq dynasty (1320–1414)
Lodi dynasty (1451–1526) (fifth and last dynasty)

Delhi Sultanate

Vijayanagara Empire

Defensive wall and water reservoir near Jaipur, Rajasthan, India

The Vijayanagara Empire thrived for two centuries despite ongoing internal and external threats. The military repelled frequent foreign attacks by recruiting Muslim soldiers and adopting Muslim military tactics, including the use of cavalry and forts. In order to retain power, rulers attacked Hindus as well as Muslims, when it suited their purposes. Rulers even allied with Muslims against other Hindus to maintain control of the loose confederation of states that composed the empire. In 1564, competing regions briefly united to break the power of the ruler of Vijayanagara. Their military alliance succeeded in killing the ruler and defeating his army. Victorious forces looted the capital city and seriously weakened the empire, although it survived for another century.

Lotus Temple in Hampi, India

Section Review

1–2. What was the fate of Buddhism and Hinduism in India during this period?

3. Name one of the few kingdoms in Asia to successfully repel a full-scale Mongol invasion.

4. What did the Vijayanagaran rulers use as a means of unifying their empire?

5. How did the Vijayanagara Empire feed people as it expanded?

∗ What were key features of Indian cultures during this period?

∗ Why did India continue to be overrun by foreign invaders during this period?

Guiding Questions

1. What led to the rise and fall of the Mongol Empire and the Yuan and Ming dynasties?
2. What were the cultural accomplishments of the Mongols and the Chinese during this period?
3. What role did justice, power, and citizenship play in these empires?

III. Asia

The Mongols

You first read about the inhabitants of Mongolia in chapter 7. During this period a Mongol teenager harnessed their vast numbers and great potential and turned them into an unstoppable military force. From an obscure land and humble beginnings, this youth conquered or influenced a large percentage of the world's population and built a vast empire spanning thousands of miles.

Building the Mongol Empire

The Mongol people arose north of China, in the land known today as Mongolia. Their round felt tents dotted the eastern portion of the Asiatic grasslands. They raised sheep, goats, and horses. They had no central government and were divided into small tribes. In approximately 1162, **Temujin** (TEM yoo jin) was born to the family of a tribal chief. Overcoming many hardships in his youth, Temujin succeeded his father as leader of his tribe at the age of thirteen. He gradually united all the Mongol tribes under his authority and established an empire in Mongolia. He became "lord of all the people dwelling in felt tents." In 1206 the Mongols gave him the title "**Genghis Khan**" (GENG-gis KAHN), meaning "universal ruler."

Genghis Khan was one of the greatest conquerors in history. He believed that he had a divine commission to conquer the world. Having organized the Mongols into a well-disciplined fighting force, he conquered northern China. He then turned his army westward. The Mongols overran central Asia, advanced to the banks of the Indus River, pushed into Persia, and crossed into southern Russia. Returning from his western conquests, Genghis Khan renewed his campaign against China. His death in 1227, however, prevented him from seeing the whole of China fall under Mongol control.

Much of Genghis Khan's success lay in the organization and mobility of his army. He skillfully deployed his forces in battle. His army, which he divided into groups of tens, hundreds, and thousands, could strike with great speed. In addition, the Mongols were expert horsemen. Riding into battle on horseback, they had a distinct advantage over the armies of other civilizations. Like the ancient Assyrians, the

Genghis Khan

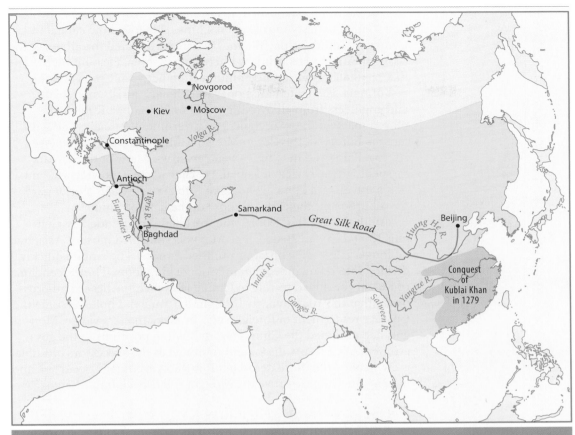

Mongol Empire (1279)

Mongols gained a reputation for terrorizing the peoples they were about to conquer. They sometimes massacred the entire population of a city to teach others the futility of resistance. The Mongol conquests left fear, destruction, and death in their wake.

Mongol expansion did not cease with the death of Genghis. His sons and grandsons enlarged his empire. Their armies completed the conquest of China, swept farther into Russia, and overran the Muslim states in central and southwestern Asia. They sacked Baghdad, brought an end to the Abbasid dynasty, and broke the power of the Seljuk Turks.

The Mongols chose one of Genghis Khan's sons to succeed him as the Great Khan, the ruler of the entire Mongol Empire. But the empire eventually became too large for one man to rule effectively. By the time of the fifth ruler, the empire had already begun to fragment into many separate Mongol states in China, Russia, central Asia, and India.

The Yuan Dynasty in China (1279–1368)

The Mongol attack came as no surprise to the Chinese. For hundreds of years the Chinese had defended their borders against the attacks of central Asian nomads. But none of the previous invaders had possessed the military strength of the Mongols. Not even the Great Wall could stop their advance. The conquest of China begun by Genghis Khan was completed by his grandson **Kublai Khan** (KOO-blye KAHN). Kublai was the last of the Great Khans. After a long campaign, he succeeded in conquering southern China, the stronghold of the ruling Song dynasty.

Kublai Khan

Kublai Khan established the Mongol (or Yuan) dynasty, the first foreign dynasty to rule all of China. He moved the capital to Cambaluc (modern-day Beijing), where he directed the affairs of the Mongol Empire. His primary interest was China. He built highways that facilitated trade and communication between China and the rest of Asia. He invited missionaries, scholars, artists, merchants, and engineers from all over the world to his capital. Kublai employed many of these foreigners as government officials. The most famous European traveler to Mongol China was Marco Polo (see ch. 13). Polo lived in China seventeen years. Many of those years he spent in the service of Kublai. He later wrote a glowing account of his travels and of the wonders of Kublai's court. His stories gave most Europeans their first glimpse of the land of China.

With the death of Kublai, the world empire founded by Genghis Khan came to an end. The Mongols still ruled most of Asia, but no longer could they boast of a unified empire. The empire quickly divided into many independent Mongol kingdoms. The descendants of Kublai continued to rule in China. However, the peace and prosperity that the Yuan dynasty brought to China did not overcome the Chinese resentment of foreign rule. To make matters worse, Mongols had excluded the Chinese from holding positions in the government. As a result, discontent mounted as the successors of Kublai grew weaker and more decadent. Rebellion eventually occurred, and in 1368 the Chinese drove the Mongol rulers back into Mongolia.

The Golden Horde in Russia

While Kublai was occupied with the conquest of China, another grandson of Genghis, **Batu Khan**, led the Mongols into Europe. Between 1238 and 1242, the Mongols—or **Tartars**, as the Europeans called them—crushed the Russian defenses and penetrated Hungary and Poland. Western Europe now lay vulnerable to Mongol attack. But Batu stopped his advance and consolidated his conquests in central Asia and Russia. His realm, the strongest Mongol state in Western Asia, became known as the "**Golden Horde**." (The word *horde* comes from the Mongol *ordu*, which means "camp.")

For nearly two hundred and fifty years, Russia remained under the yoke of the Golden Horde. The Mongols not only exacted tribute from the Russian cities but also gathered recruits for their army from among the Russian people. During the period of Mongol domination, Russian ties with western Europe and the Byzantine Empire weakened as Asian influences grew stronger.

During this period Moscow transformed from an insignificant town to the capital of the budding Russian nation. Many factors aided Moscow's rise. Moscow stood at the center of Russia's inland waterways. Its location was advantageous for both trade and defense. Furthermore, the leaders of Moscow cooperated with the khans of the Golden Horde. They served as the khans' tax collectors. In return, the khans recognized the prince of Moscow as the Grand Prince of Russia. The Russian church also enhanced the prestige of Moscow. When the head of the Russian Orthodox Church moved from Kiev to Moscow, Moscow became Russia's religious center.

While Moscow grew strong and prosperous, the Golden Horde weakened. By the late fourteenth century, the grand princes openly challenged their Mongol overlords. Under **Ivan III**, who was the Grand Prince from 1462 to 1505, Moscow refused to pay further

Ivan III

tribute to the Mongols. By 1480 Moscow had freed itself from the Mongol yoke and had become the political and religious capital of the new state. Ivan extended his control over much of northern Russia. He laid the foundation for an independent Russian state and emerged as its autocratic (ruling with unlimited authority) leader. After the collapse of Constantinople in 1453, many people considered Moscow the "'Third Rome,' the defender of the Orthodox faith."

Later Mongol Empires

Tamerlane's Empire

In the late fourteenth century, there arose a central Asian conqueror who attempted to rebuild Genghis Khan's empire. His name was Timur the Lame; he was known to the Europeans as **Tamerlane**. Tamerlane belonged to a Mongol-Turkish tribe and claimed to have descended from Genghis Khan.

Having established his power in central Asia, Tamerlane raised an army and began a new wave of Mongol invasions. His army swept over the Muslim lands in southwestern Asia, capturing Baghdad and Damascus and defeating the Ottoman Turks in Asia Minor. His march into southern Russia weakened the Golden Horde and indirectly aided the Russian princes in their struggle to gain freedom from Mongol control. Turning to the East, Tamerlane led his army into India, where in 1398 he reduced the city of Delhi to ruins and slaughtered an estimated one hundred thousand so-called infidels in a single day. He died in 1405 while planning an invasion of China.

Tamerlane was a capable but cruel conqueror. He left a trail of merciless plundering, destruction, and massacres. His conquests reached from India to Asia Minor. But his empire was much smaller than the earlier Mongol Empire, and it collapsed shortly after his death.

Tamerlane

Mughal Empire

As previously mentioned, Mongol forces frequently attacked India. From the time of Genghis Khan up to the invasion of Tamerlane, Mongol raiders had often terrorized the people of northern India. But unlike other Asian lands, much of India resisted Mongol rule until the seventeenth century, when Mongol armies overwhelmed Indian forces and dominated nearly all of India. This process began under **Babur** ("tiger"; r. 1495–1530), who was a descendant of the two greatest Asian conquerors, Genghis Khan and Tamerlane. At the age of twelve, he became the leader of the Turkish-Mongol tribes in what today is Afghanistan. Following several failed attempts to build a kingdom in Afghanistan, he turned his attention to India. With an army of about twelve thousand men, Babur crossed the mountain passes and invaded northern India. After capturing the capital city of Delhi, he slaughtered or enslaved the Hindu inhabitants and established the Mughal dynasty in 1526. ("Mughal" is the name given to the Mongols in India.) Later Mughal rulers extended the empire and tried to impose Islam over all of India.

Under the Mughals, Indian civilization was transformed. While the cruel destruction inflicted by Tamerlane continued, the Mughal rulers eventually established law and order that made possible a

Mongols and Islam

Initially, the Mongols killed and conquered without regard to a nation's religion. However, over time, Mongol leaders converted to Islam and added *jihad* (holy war) to their motives for conquest and brutality. Tamerlane is the first known Mongol leader who clearly sought to carry out *jihad* and mercilessly slaughtered Hindus by the hundreds of thousands because of their polytheism. He also killed many Christians in campaigns against India and Armenia by burying them alive, in addition to other brutal forms of execution.

Babur and Akbar continued to carry out *jihad* against the Hindus of India. This resulted in an enormous loss of life.

Andrew G. Bostom, ed., The Legacy of Jihad, 77–78, 459.

Sikhism

Sikhism (from the Punjabi term meaning "disciple" or "learner") was founded around 1500 by a Hindu man named Nanak (1469-1539) in the Punjab region of India. Sikhs retained ideas of reincarnation and karma but rejected the caste system. Nanak and ten other successive leaders were known as *gurus* (teachers or experts). The tenth successor of Nanak declared himself the final *guru* and placed his authority in the Sikh scriptures, *Granth Sahib*, composed of hymns. These scriptures also contain the traditions and teachings of several Hindu Bhakti saints.

Sikhs meditate on the words of the Sikh scriptures through music or by silently repeating their god's name. They believe that this enables the disciple to sense their god's presence and maintain control over the "Five Thieves"—lust, rage, greed, attachment, and conceit. Positive Sikh attributes include being truthful, faithful, self-controlled, and pure.

This religion formed in a region of India controlled by the Mughal Empire and experienced treatment varying from patronization (during Akbar's reign) to violent persecution (during Aurangzeb's reign). Mughal rulers executed two of the ten *gurus* who succeeded Nanak, and many Sikhs became skilled warriors to preserve their way of life. One of the desired qualities of a Sikh was to become a "sant-Sipahi," a saint-soldier. Members of the *khalsa* (army of the pure) distinguished their appearance by refraining from cutting their beards or their hair, wearing a steel bracelet on the right wrist, and carrying a sword.

Sikh guard near the Golden Temple

period of achievement in art and architecture. The most successful Mughal ruler was Babur's grandson **Akbar** (r. 1556–1605). He became ruler around the age of thirteen and ruled the Mughal Empire under the watchful eye of a regent. Akbar proved to be a brilliant military strategist and expanded the empire to include all of northern and central India north of the Krishna River.

Initially Akbar was a dedicated Muslim and approved the slaughter of nearly half a million Hindus and the enslavement of many women and children in the name of Islam. Gradually he interacted with other religions and concluded that Islam did not possess exclusive truth. This abandonment of Islam alienated many Muslim clerics and threatened Akbar's rule. Akbar protected himself by removing Muslim clerics from places of influence, by ending the collection of the tax on non-Muslims (*jizya*), and by promoting many Hindus to key positions in his government. He restricted access to the empire's wealth to those who could pose no political threat and gave political power to those who had no access to soldiers or the empire's wealth. Akbar also encouraged emperor worship and initiated the adding of haloes to the paintings of the royal family.

Akbar's grandson, Shah Jahan (r. 1627–1658), is best remembered for commissioning the construction of a mausoleum for his

Shah Jahan (with halo)

Taj Mahal

Red Fort in Delhi, India

favorite wife. Known as the **Taj Mahal**, it became a stunning example of Mughal architecture. Shah Jahan became ill in 1658, and his eldest son tried to assume control of the empire. However, Jahan's third son, **Aurangzeb** (r. 1658–1707), quickly seized power, had his brother executed, and imprisoned his father. Under Aurangzeb's leadership the Mughal Empire briefly doubled in size and nearly encompassed all of India.

The Mughal Empire

Aurangzeb was a dedicated Muslim who ended the emperor cult originated by Akbar. He restored collection of the *jizya* and had newly constructed or remodeled churches and temples destroyed. Aurangzeb restricted royal support of architecture and intellectual work to projects compatible with Islam.

Aurangzeb spent the first thirty years consolidating Islamic influence in his empire. A failed revolt in 1681 motivated Aurangzeb to march south to seize control of independent kingdoms in southern India. However, despite a vast army and twenty years of military victories, Aurangzeb found that Hindu forces refused to surrender, and Hindu peasants seized many of the supplies meant for his forces. Ill health forced Aurangzeb to abandon the struggle and return home. Following Aurangzeb's death, weak successors were unable to maintain stability, and the empire descended into chaos.

Ming Dynasty in China

Following the expulsion of the Mongols, a new Chinese dynasty, the **Ming** ("brilliant") **dynasty**, restored Chinese rule and reestablished Chinese ways. Reacting to years of Mongol rule, the Chinese adopted an antiforeigner spirit that led to the closing of China to outside influences for nearly three centuries (1368–1644).

They established a highly structured government and organized the population into social classes, which led to a period of social stability but also social rigidity. This was the last imperial dynasty in China ruled by ethnic Han Chinese.

The first Ming ruler, Emperor Hongwu (r. 1368–98), organized rural communities into self-sufficient centers that maintained a rigid system designed to support a stable class of soldiers for his kingdom. He developed a standing army that exceeded one million

Emperor Hongwu

Emperor Yongle

men and built navy dockyards in Nanjing that were possibly the largest in the world at that time.

Following Emperor Hongwu's death, his teenage son was quickly deposed and replaced by the prince of the city of Yan, who became Emperor Yongle (r. 1402–24). He moved the capital of China to the city of Beiping (modern Beijing). His building projects included the Forbidden City as a royal residence and the restoration of the Great Canal. Emperior Yongle also restored the use of imperial examinations to select government officials. He provided funds for one of his favorite officers, Zheng He, to make seven voyages abroad in massive ships. This Chinese fleet traveled as far as Arabia and the Eastern coast of Africa, bringing back many exotic animals to China. Succeeding emperors abandoned the large naval enterprises and concentrated their efforts on repairing the Great Wall and expanding it to its modern form.

During the Ming dynasty, attempts were made to take a regular census of the Chinese population, and the estimated population during the late Ming dynasty varied from 160 to 200 million. The numbers varied greatly, in part, because many farmers found ways to avoid being counted in the census and circumvented the resulting tax. Others "donated" their land to tax-exempt officials or to temples and thus evaded being counted and taxed.

The Ming dynasty experienced gradual decline. Political decline resulted, in part, from the growing isolation of rulers from the

Chinese population, and frequent palace intrigue. Economic decline accelerated following crop failures, floods, and epidemics. A weakened Ming dynasty collapsed following a rebellion led by a group that would form the Qing dynasty.

Ming China

Ming porcelain featuring carp in a lotus pond

Cultural contributions of the Ming dynasty include literature, painting, and ceramics. Chinese writers began to write vernacular novels. This added to existing Chinese literature that had been written in the classical Chinese language. Writing in the vernacular made Chinese literature available to average Chinese readers and became very popular. Informal essay writing and travel writing also gained wide acceptance. Chinese painting during this period continued the style developed during the Song dynasty, with subtle Ming adaptations. The Ming dynasty also developed distinct works in ceramic and porcelain.

Section Review

1. What was Genghis Khan's original name?

2. Which Chinese dynasty fell to the Mongols?

3. What was the European name for the Mongols?

4. Who tried to rebuild Genghis Khan's empire?

5. How did the Russians break free from Mongol control?

✶ How did Akbar protect his rule after his acceptance of religions other than Islam?

✶ What were key cultural achievements of the Yuan and Ming dynasties?

Making Connections

1. Name the prosperous East African city-state that was located in what is now Tanzania.
2. Explain the longevity of the kingdom of Benin.
3. What was the predominant religion of conquered India?
4. What helped Genghis Khan achieve success?
5. Who was the last of the great khans, the heir to the Mongol world?
6. What name was given to the strongest Mongol state in western Asia?
7. What Chinese dynasty restored the Grand Canal and was the first to use the Forbidden City as a royal residence?

Developing History Skills

1. How did African and European civilizations differ during this period?
2. Analyze common reasons for the rise and fall of empires in this chapter.

Thinking Critically

1. Compare and contrast Sikhism with Hinduism.
2. What role did justice, power, and citizenship play in these civilizations?

Living in God's World

1. Analyze the role of trade in spreading religion in Africa during this time. Apply your knowledge to ways Christianity could spread into otherwise closed countries.
2. If you were a Christian missionary who was invited to participate in the government of the Yuan dynasty, what reforms would you seek to undertake in the government?

People, Places, and Things to Know

Kilwa
Swahili
Ghana
Mali
Timbuktu
Mansa Musa
Songhai Empire
Benin
Delhi Sultanate
Vijayanagara
Temujin
Genghis Khan
Kublai Khan
Batu Khan
Tartars
Golden Horde
Ivan III
Tamerlane
Babur
Sikhism
Akbar
Taj Mahal
Aurangzeb
Ming dynasty

Exploration and Discovery

13

I. Preparation for Discovery

II. Process of Discovery

III. The Commercial Revolution

Replica of Henry Hudson's ship, the Half Moon

Big Ideas

1. What changes in the Old World led to exploration of the New World?
2. How did European nations engage in exploration?
3. What were the strengths and weaknesses of mercantilism and capitalism?

The two hundred years from 1450 to 1650 marked the great age of European exploration and discovery. Men crossed uncharted waters, braved violent storms, and suffered starvation and disease as they sailed to distant parts of the globe. What prompted these explorers to face untold perils? Most desired wealth; some sought adventure and fame; others sought to spread the gospel to other lands. But whether motivated by greed, pride, or compassion, these explorers opened the continents of North and South America, the coast of Africa, and part of Asia to European trade and colonization.

I. Preparation for Discovery

Several developments in Europe gave rise to this Age of Exploration. The Crusades awakened interest in lands beyond Europe's borders. Travelers such as **Marco Polo** stirred the popular imagination with tales of strange customs and unbelievable riches in the Far East. The Renaissance provided western Europe with the means, namely navigational equipment and finances, to reach Asia. In the endeavor to reach the East, Europeans discovered the New World.

Motives for Exploration
Search for New Trade Routes

Spurred by the stories of fabulous wealth, Europeans reopened trade routes with the East. They imported numerous luxury items from China, India, and the Spice Islands (located north of Australia). Merchants traded for precious gems, silk, and expensive porcelain (china). Spices, such as cloves and cinnamon, were in great demand. Europeans used them to flavor and preserve food and as ingredients in medicines and perfumes.

All these items came across Asia to Europe by way of the Middle East. But there were many problems for traders along this long route. Much of the terrain was rugged and difficult to cross. In addition, Muslim rulers charged trading caravans for the privilege of passing through their territory; taxes and tolls drove up the prices of the products. Furthermore, the Italians held a monopoly on Asian trade. Merchants from Genoa controlled the northern routes that came overland from Asia, and merchants from Venice controlled the southern routes that ran along the coast of India, up the Persian Gulf, and across the desert to Palestine. (See map on p. 204.) Not only were Italians draining gold from the rest of Europe, but they were also keeping traders from other European countries from sharing in the profits.

In the 1400s these problems became more acute when the Ottoman Turks seized power in the Middle East. These recent converts to Islam attacked caravans and destroyed trading posts. The Europeans, who still craved Eastern luxuries, needed to find a new route to Asia. Some wondered if it might be possible to get to the East entirely by sea, avoiding the Turks, the Italian traders, and all the tolls and taxes. The quest began in earnest in the late fifteenth century. Early European adventurers sailed south and east around Africa, others sailed west across the Atlantic, and some even tried to find a Northwest Passage through Arctic ice.

Quest for Gold

For many years there had been stories circulating in Europe that there was gold—lots of gold—somewhere in Africa. Europeans,

Guiding Questions

1. What motivated the Europeans to explore other lands?
2. How did new tools make exploration possible?

Marco Polo and the Awakening of Curiosity

Marco Polo was only seventeen when he set off on a journey that would revolutionize the world. He was accompanying his father and his uncle, both Venetian traders, on their second voyage to the little-known kingdom of Cathay (China). The year was 1271.

For four years the three men traveled eastward, finally reaching the city of Cambaluc (Beijing), the capital of Cathay. Young Marco Polo quickly became a favorite of the ruler, Kublai Khan. He learned the languages of the court and by the age of twenty-three became the Khan's adviser. The Polos lived in Cathay for seventeen years, traveling and seeing sights that few Europeans ever imagined. In 1292 they began the long journey home. When they arrived in Venice, their old friends did not recognize them; most at first refused to believe their stories, but the travelers convinced them by producing a wealth of gems that they had received in Cathay.

Three years after his return to Italy, Marco was captured while fighting in a local war and jailed in Genoa. To pass the time, he recounted his adventures to a fellow prisoner, who recorded them in what was soon to become a very popular book: *The Book of Sir Marco Polo Concerning the Kingdoms and Marvels of the East*. The work was far more accurate than the few other books about Cathay that were available in Europe at that time. Its readers were astonished by the tales of a strange black rock (coal) that the Mongols burned. They thrilled to hear the description of fantastic riches in gold, spices, and many other luxuries. They wondered about the islands of "Cipango" (Japan) that Polo described. More importantly, they learned of the great sea (the Pacific) that lay beyond Asia.

Nearly two centuries after Polo, a man from Genoa read this book and wondered if the ocean to the west—the Atlantic—might be the same one that Polo saw. This man's name was Christopher Columbus.

however, knew very little about this huge continent. While the northern coast was well known to travelers, few Europeans had traveled south into the heart of the continent. Occasionally African traders arrived in Mediterranean ports, bringing gold from the interior, but no European knew the exact origin of this gold. Not surprisingly, many wanted to find it. Explorers were willing to take great risks to obtain wealth but often suffered great losses instead.

Desire for Adventure and Glory

While some explorers craved great riches, others sought the thrill of adventure and the praise of men. The Renaissance, which encouraged a spirit of curiosity and emphasized individual achievement, may have played a part in these desires. Men risked their lives, sailing through unknown waters and traveling to distant lands. Through their daring adventures, they hoped to achieve worldly fame. While several explorers did become famous for their exploits, many others died in the quest for glory.

Religious Concerns

Though overlooked or neglected by some historians, religious concern also motivated many explorers. The crusading spirit was alive in Europe because the Muslim threat was still very real. Even as late as the fifteenth century, the Moors still controlled the southern portion of the Iberian Peninsula. After the fall of Constantinople to the Ottoman Turks in 1453, Europeans feared a full-scale Muslim invasion of eastern Europe. European rulers searched for ways to stop further Muslim victories.

There were rumors of a king in Africa named **Prester John**, supposedly a wealthy and powerful Christian who wanted to help the Europeans fight the Muslims. During the fifteenth century, explorers sailed along the west coast of Africa searching for this mythical kingdom. They hoped to enlist his help; by attacking from both the north and south, their combined forces could defeat the Muslims. However, Prester John was never found.

Not all of Europe's religious zeal was directed against the Muslims. Some explorers sought to spread the gospel to people of other cultures. However, most of the early explorers were Roman Catholics who won converts to the Roman Church rather than to Christ.

Competition Among European Nations

Exploration was also sparked by the commercial rivalry among the nations of Europe. As Italian merchants brought precious gems, spices, and silks from the East, Europeans were filled with great excitement—but also with great envy. Non-Italian merchants wanted to profit from the Asian trade, and kings wanted to increase their own countries' wealth and power. As the explorers traveled to unknown regions, they claimed their discoveries for the country for which they sailed. European countries were eager to trade with newly discovered lands. Nations established trade settlements and encouraged colonization to protect their commercial interests. Little thought was given to those who already lived in these regions.

Tools for Exploration
Navigational Aids

Three things became very important to explorers: accurate maps to guide them to their destination, a compass to tell them what direction they were going, and some kind of "locator" instrument to tell them their position. On a trackless and featureless ocean, they needed accurate and trustworthy instruments.

Maps

Maps of the known world became much more accurate beginning in the fifteenth century as Italian mapmakers updated sailing charts based on the reports of traders and fishermen. These maps were fairly reliable guides for sailing in the Mediterranean Sea or along the European coast, but they were of little help to the explorers, who sailed in uncharted waters. As explorers returned from their voyages, they updated their maps to include their discoveries. With the invention of printing, these updated maps were widely distributed, encouraging further exploration.

Instruments

The **compass** greatly aided sailors in navigation and mapmaking. Invented by the Chinese, the early compass was a magnetized needle floating in a bowl of water on a piece of reed or cork. In the late 1300s, Europeans mounted the compass on a stiff card marked with the cardinal points (north, south, east, and west). This small improvement made a great difference to sailors, who could now use the instrument easily on a moving ship. The compass became an invaluable tool; it helped sailors determine direction and follow a definite course.

Sailors also relied on more complicated instruments to determine their position on an unmarked ocean. The three most common instruments—the astrolabe, the quadrant, and the cross-staff—measured the angle between the sun or a star (usually the North Star) and the horizon. From this information the sailor could determine his **latitude**, or distance from the equator. With any one of these instruments, the captain of a ship, even though out of sight of land, could compute his position with a limited degree of accuracy. The instruments did have two major drawbacks, however. They were useless in cloudy weather, and they were not very accurate when used on the rolling deck of a ship.

Early navigational instruments

Seagoing Vessels

Around 1400, Europeans began to build ships to sail long distances over wide and sometimes stormy seas. Early ships used to cross the Mediterranean Sea had made great use of oars. However, an oar-powered ship would need such a large crew to travel the ocean that it could not carry enough supplies to feed the crew. Oceangoing vessels, therefore, needed to use sails. However, of the two types of sails in use, triangular and square, neither was satisfactory for a long ocean voyage.

The Arabs used triangular sails, which made their boats easily maneuverable, even when the wind changed directions. This kind of sail, however, could power only a relatively small craft. Such vessels would not be big enough to carry the needed supplies and then return with enough spices to make a trip profitable.

Northern sailors, such as the Vikings, used square sails, which could power a larger ship and required a smaller crew. They could carry enough supplies and had room for a large quantity of spices. However, these ships were not very maneuverable.

Caravel

The solution came in the middle of the fifteenth century with the development of a versatile ship called a **caravel**. This light, fast vessel was popular with the early explorers. It had several masts on which were mounted large square sails to provide power and smaller triangular sails to provide maneuverability. The caravel's high sides and its broad and deep construction made it suitable for ocean travel.

Section Review

1–4. List four motives that prompted European explorers to "seek out and discover."

5–6. What man's account of his travels awakened European curiosity about Asia? In what Eastern land did he spend seventeen years?

7. What light, fast vessel was popular with the early explorers of the late fifteenth century?

★ Why were early maps of limited help as explorers ventured farther in search of new lands and new trade routes?

★ How did new tools make exploration possible?

Guiding Questions

1. Who were the major explorers, and what regions did they explore?

2. How were American Indian populations treated by European explorers?

3. How did motives differ among the major countries during the Age of Exploration?

II. Process of Discovery

The early European explorers were pioneers. They set sail across vast, unexplored oceans with uncertain prospects of ever returning home. While some never returned, others brought back the exciting news of their discoveries. They told of new routes to Asia, of great riches to be gained, of new lands to be explored, and of people who needed to be evangelized. Europe eagerly responded to the challenge. Merchants, soldiers, settlers, and missionaries followed the explorers. Through trade along the African coast and in Asia and through colonization in the New World, Europe rapidly extended its influence to many regions of the world.

Portugal and Spain

Portugal and Spain were the leading nations of the Age of Exploration. Several factors accounted for their early success. Shipping had long been a principal industry in these lands; Portugal and Spain were bounded by the waters of the Atlantic Ocean and the Mediterranean Sea. Because the Italians had gained a monopoly on trade in the Mediterranean, sailors from the Iberian Peninsula turned southward to the coast of Africa and westward across the Atlantic in search of new trade routes to the East. Furthermore, the experienced Portuguese and Spanish sailors were greatly aided by the navigational and mapmaking skills they had learned from the Moors. A strong motivating force behind their drive for discovery was the crusading spirit, which was very much alive in the peninsula. (The last Muslim stronghold in the Iberian Peninsula was not conquered until 1492.) Many Portuguese and Spanish sailors initially set sail to spread Roman Catholicism and battle Muslims.

Portugal Rounds Africa

Prince Henry (1394–1460), called "The Navigator," was largely responsible for Portugal's early success in exploration. Although he never went on an expedition, he has been called "the greatest figure in the history of exploration." As a youth, he was fascinated with the

Prince Henry, "The Navigator"

great land of Africa to the south. How big was it? Where was the source of the gold that came from its interior? Where was Prester John's kingdom? These questions led Prince Henry to start a school of navigation on the coast of Portugal. It was not a *school* in our sense of the word; it was more like a *storehouse* of knowledge about navigation. He attracted to his palace geographers, astronomers, mapmakers, and sea captains. Under his sponsorship, these men improved navigational instruments, drew up more accurate maps, and developed the caravel. Henry sent sailors out to explore the coast of Africa and to bring back all the information they could find. On each voyage, Henry's sailors went farther south along Africa's coast. They had not yet reached the equator when he died in 1460, but his accomplishments laid the foundation for the achievements of two other men who would finish the job that he had begun.

In 1487, nearly thirty years after Prince Henry's death, the king of Portugal sent **Bartolomeu Dias** down the coast of Africa to find a sea route to India. As he neared the southern tip of the continent, a fierce storm blew his ships out of sight of land for thirteen days. When he finally sighted land again, he noticed that the sun rose on the ship's right instead of its left; he was therefore heading north. He rightly concluded that he had rounded the tip of Africa during the storm and that indeed there might be an all-water route to Asia. When his men refused to go any farther, he turned and headed back to Portugal. As he rounded the tip of Africa again, he sighted a huge rocky cape, which he named "The Cape of Storms." The king later changed its name to "The Cape of Good Hope" because he hoped that Dias had finally found a direct water route to India.

Ten years after Dias's discovery, the king of Portugal selected **Vasco da Gama** to lead an expedition around the Cape of Good Hope to India. In 1497, with a fleet of four ships, da Gama set sail from Lisbon, Portugal. He did not follow the African coast all the way to the Cape of Good Hope as Dias had done. Instead, he made a great westward sweep to gain more favorable winds and currents. At one point he was actually closer to South America than to Africa. He stayed out of sight of land for fourteen weeks before reaching the tip of Africa.

Nearly a year after leaving Portugal, da Gama arrived in India. He was the first European to reach the great subcontinent by sailing around Africa. He told those who met him, "We have come to seek Christians and spices." But he found Muslim merchants living there who controlled trade in the region and opposed his efforts to trade with the Indians. Despite much opposition, he was able to trade for spices—enough to pay for the voyage sixty times over!

Vasco da Gama

The Portuguese swiftly took advantage of da Gama's discovery of the ocean route to India. They soon not only controlled this water route but also broke the Muslim trade monopoly in the Indian Ocean. The Muslim fleet was no match for the heavy artillery on the Portuguese ships. It was not long before ships loaded with spices were a familiar sight in Portuguese ports.

Spain Sails Westward

When Dias returned from his voyage around the Cape of Good Hope, an Italian named **Christopher Columbus** heard his report: India could be reached by sailing around the tip of Africa. But Columbus, who had studied the writings of the ancient geographer Ptolemy and the traveler Marco Polo, believed that he could reach

The Naming of America

When Columbus landed on an island in the Caribbean in 1492, he mistakenly assumed that he had succeeded in reaching Asia. Upon his return, most Europeans believed his reports, but when later expeditions failed to bring back any riches, doubts began to arise. An Italian merchant named Amerigo Vespucci sailed west to settle the uncertainty. What he found was not a water route to the Orient but a new continent. He was the first known European to reach and explore the landmass that now bears his name—South America.

Hearing of Amerigo Vespucci's discovery, a German mapmaker named Martin Waldsee-müller began to sell maps of the new continent. Proposing that the land be named after its discoverer, he referred to it as "America." The name was accepted, and before long people applied it to the large landmass to the north of the Spanish possessions as well. They called it "North America."

Japan and China by sailing west—that Japan was perhaps as close as three thousand miles from Portugal. For many years he tried to persuade the king of Portugal to finance his voyage westward. But the king's advisers declared the undertaking to be impossible. In Spain Columbus was finally able to secure support for his voyage from King Ferdinand and Queen Isabella. In August of 1492 he set sail from Spain with three ships: the *Niña*, the *Pinta*, and the *Santa Maria*.

Columbus wrote that he believed he was commissioned by God to spread the Catholic faith in distant lands. He was confident that his voyage would be a success. His men, however, did not share his optimism. After weeks of being out of sight of land, they demanded that the ships turn back. Columbus was able to persuade them to continue for two or three more days. Two days later, on the morning of October 12, he sighted land and named it San Salvador ("Holy Savior"). Columbus thought that he was near the East Indies; actually, he was in the Bahamas. He sailed south to Cuba, which he thought was Marco Polo's Cathay, and to Hispaniola, which he identified as Cipango (Japan).

In three later voyages Columbus explored further in the Caribbean and landed on the South American continent in what is now Venezuela. He never found the great riches he was seeking, and he continued to believe that he had reached Asia. Although Columbus was mistaken regarding where his voyages had taken him, his discovery was nonetheless of great importance. He opened up a "New World" that attracted European exploration and colonization for

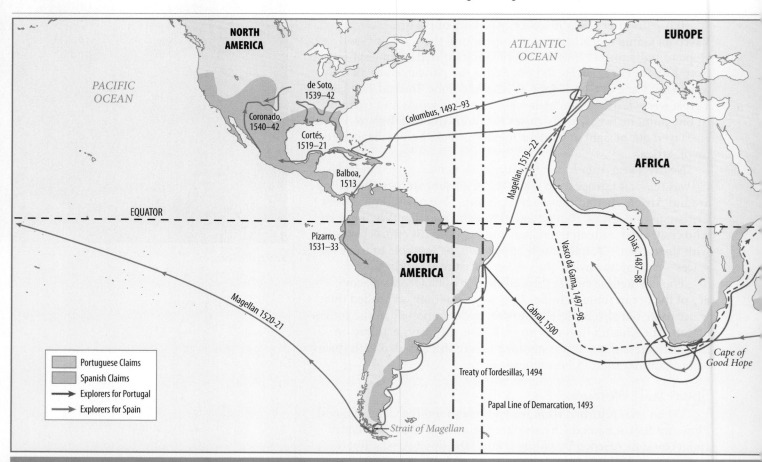

Early Explorers

centuries following. Sadly, Columbus also prepared the way for an Indian slave trade.

As a result of Columbus's discoveries, Spain began to compete with Portugal for trade rights and new territory. To avoid disputes with Portugal, Spain asked Pope Alexander VI to divide the world between the two countries. In 1493 he issued a document that drew a **Line of Demarcation** running north and south down the middle of the Atlantic Ocean. (See map on p. 280.) Portugal, he said, could claim lands to the east of the line, while Spain could claim those to the west. After negotiations between Spain and Portugal, it was agreed the following year to move the line farther to the west.

This agreement between Spain and Portugal had several important results.

1. It encouraged Portugal to colonize in Africa and the East Indies, which were east of the line.

2. It gave Spain the right to nearly all of the New World with one exception—the line cut across present-day Brazil, giving that land to the Portuguese, who later explored and settled there. That is why even today the language of Brazil is Portuguese, while almost all of the remainder of South America speaks Spanish.

3. It prohibited Spain from sailing around Africa to get to India and China. To remain competitive, Spain had to find a westward route. It was not long before the Spanish found a sailor who would do it.

Providence

Columbus was not the first to discover the New World. The Vikings made the voyage from Europe in the tenth and eleventh centuries. A few historians even think that the ancient Phoenicians landed in South America before the time of Christ. But in God's plan, the lands of the New World remained virtually unknown to Europe until the sixteenth century—a time when Europeans were also rediscovering the truth of God's Word. During the seventeenth century, the New World, especially North America, became a haven for Christians and others who fled from political and religious persecution in Europe. However, the colonization of Central and South America by the Spanish and Portuguese resulted in long-term obstacles in those regions.

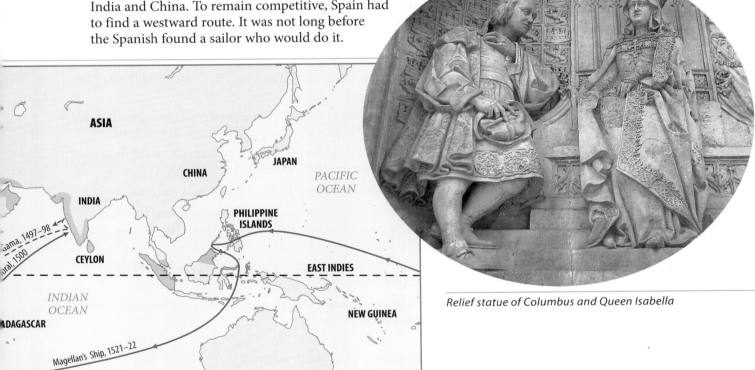

Relief statue of Columbus and Queen Isabella

Ferdinand Magellan

Life at Sea

Life at sea was full of hardships during the Age of Exploration. In return for their hard labor, sailors were paid very little and were fed the worst sorts of food imaginable. Since many ships remained at sea for long periods of time, the sailors often had to live for months on a dreary diet of biscuits (hardtack), salt beef, salt fish, and beer. The salted meat was tough, usually stank, and often had maggots in it. The biscuits were usually of poor quality. Some sailors jokingly refused to eat those biscuits that were not infested with maggots, stating that they did not want to eat something that even the maggots had refused. All ships carried barrels of water, but within a short time the water became stagnant and undrinkable. It became discolored, gave off a terrible odor, and was full of tiny organisms. Unfortunately, the only thing onboard that did not spoil was the liquor.

One disease that plagued sailors and brought death to many was a vitamin C deficiency called scurvy. It caused the gums to become swollen and bloody (loosening the teeth in the process) and caused the limbs to become swollen and discolored. Although no one knew about vitamin C at the time, various sea captains stumbled upon a cure for scurvy, finding that sauerkraut, fresh fruit, and vegetables stopped it. Since fresh produce could not be carried on long sea voyages, the British navy made it compulsory in 1798 for their ships to carry lime juice. Because of this practice, British sailors acquired the nickname "limeys."

In September of 1519 **Ferdinand Magellan** set out with a fleet of five ships to do what Columbus had failed to accomplish. By this time he knew that Columbus had found not Asia but an intervening landmass. He thought that he could sail around its southern end and then get to the Spice Islands. He sailed from Spain to the coast of South America, where he spent the winter. There he saw natives who were so large that he named them Patagonians ("Big Feet"). He then sailed around the southern tip of South America through what we now call the Strait of Magellan. There one of his five ships deserted, and he lost a second in a severe storm. When he finally reached the ocean to the west, he appreciated its calmness so much that he named it *Pacific* ("peaceful").

As the three ships sailed westward across the Pacific, they ran out of supplies, and many sailors starved to death. Finally they reached the Philippines, but Magellan was killed when he tried to help a local ruler in a tribal war. Magellan's crew continued and reached the Spice Islands, where they took on a large cargo of spices. With only one ship left, they sailed around Africa and back to Spain. The ship returned with only eighteen of the more than two hundred men who had started the trip. This three-year-long, tragic voyage, the first **circumnavigation** of the earth, has been called "the greatest single human achievement on sea." It demonstrated that one great body of water covered the earth. Magellan's voyage also made it clear to Europeans that the discoveries of Columbus were not as near to Asia as Columbus had hoped.

Section Review

1. What two European nations led the way during the Age of Exploration?

2–3. What member of the Portuguese ruling family greatly aided the Age of Exploration? What nickname did he earn?

4. Da Gama's discovery led to the Portuguese establishment of an all-water route to what land?

5. For whom are North and South America named?

6–7. Who settled the trade disputes between Spain and Portugal by dividing the world between the two countries? What was the dividing line called?

★ How did Henry's interest in navigation promote European exploration?

★ How did Columbus's discovery of America impact the people who already lived there?

Europe and the New World

When Columbus landed in the Bahamas, he thought he had reached the East Indies. He thus called the native peoples whom he found there "Indians." As you learned in chapter 8, these peoples had lived in North, Central, and South America for several thousand years before the Europeans arrived.

Spanish Exploration

The early Spanish explorers who came to the New World found that the Indian civilizations could be conquered. Spain, which claimed rights to this land, sent **conquistadors** ("conquerors") to search for riches, to convert the Indians to Catholicism, and to establish Spanish authority. By using their firearms and horses, which the terrified Indians had never seen, small bands of Spanish soldiers were able to subdue entire Indian tribes and empires.

But the conquistadors were often cruel to the Indians they had come to convert. Many of these men used the same ruthless methods to gain both riches and converts. They apparently saw no conflict in their quest for both. However, their desire for wealth and fame often overshadowed their religious zeal, making their religious efforts a poor reflection of the gospel.

Vasco Núñez de Balboa

One notable conquistador was **Vasco Núñez de Balboa**. He came to the New World in search of adventure but soon found himself working on a farm on the island of Hispaniola. Dissatisfied and heavily in debt, he stowed away aboard a ship bound for the mainland, where a new colony was to be established. Balboa joined the colony as a soldier, but by plotting against those in charge, he was able to win control of it. Under his leadership the colony moved to a new site on the coast of Panama.

Balboa knew that complaints had been lodged against him before the king of Spain. The only way to gain royal favor, he decided, would be to find gold or make some striking discovery. Balboa heard rumors of a great ocean to the west and of a people wealthy with gold. In 1513, with a force of some two hundred men, he began cutting his way westward across what is today Panama, making his way through the heavy jungle of the isthmus (a narrow strip of land connecting two larger landmasses). After three weeks Balboa and his men neared the western coast. Wanting to be the first European to see the new ocean, Balboa ordered his men to wait while he walked to the crest of a small mountain. There he saw a great body of water, which he named the "South Sea"; Magellan renamed it "Pacific" seven years later.

Balboa sent word of his discovery back to Spain, hoping to receive a royal commendation. However, in the meantime, authorities arrested him on false charges made by a jealous rival and beheaded him.

In 1519 **Hernando Cortés** landed on the shore of Mexico. After sinking his ships so that none of his soldiers would desert, he moved his army inland toward the Aztec capital. When the Aztec king, **Montezuma**, heard of their approach, he thought that Cortés might be the returning god *Quetzalcoatl* (ket SAHL koh AH t'l), or at least his representative. (An Aztec god, *Quetzalcoatl*, was supposed to return someday from across the sea.) Instead of fighting Cortés, Montezuma welcomed him with gifts of gold and jewels, which only intensified the Spaniard's greed. Cortés himself had said, "We Spaniards suffer from a disease that only gold can cure."

The Requirement

Before the conquistadors attacked the Indians, they were required to read to the Indians a document issued by the king of Spain. The statement, known as the *requerimiento*, informed the Indians that the eternal God gave the pope in Rome authority over all men. Pope Alexander VI in turn had given Spain authority over the New World. This document invited the Indians to embrace the Roman Catholic religion and to become loyal subjects under Spanish rule. If they refused, the document warned that "with the help of God, we [the Spanish] shall powerfully enter into your country and shall make war against you in all ways and manners that we can, and shall subject you to the yoke and obedience of the Church and of Their Highnesses. We shall take you and your wives and your children, and shall make slaves of them, and as such shall sell and dispose of them as Their Highnesses may command. And we shall take your goods, and shall do you all the mischief and damage that we can, as to vassals who do not obey and refuse to receive their Lord and resist and contradict him." The *requerimiento* effectively gave legal justification to those Spaniards who enslaved or massacred Indians who would not submit. To make matters worse, conquistadors often read the Spanish document to the Indians without a translator to enable the Indians to understand the demands made upon them. At other times conquistadors read the document when no Indians were present to hear it or after they had already imprisoned the Indians. While the ruler of Spain did abolish use of the *requerimiento* in 1556, brutal treatment of Indians by Spanish forces continued.

Hernando Cortés

Cortés and Montezuma at a Mexican temple

After a time of uneasy peace, war broke out. The Spanish guns took their toll as the Spaniards massacred thousands of Aztecs. According to the Spanish, Montezuma's own people stoned him to death as a traitor. In 1521, after a four-month siege, Cortés finally defeated the Aztecs and destroyed the city. On its ruins he began to build what is now Mexico City. This city later became one of the capitals of New Spain. One of the several *viceroys,* or "assistant kings," appointed by the Spanish king, lived there.

Cortés and his men were not satisfied with their successes. Some soldiers headed north, still lusting for gold. Others fought over their newly acquired treasures. Cortés finally returned to Spain in 1541 and died six years later, a discouraged and frustrated man.

Francisco Pizarro (pih ZAHR oh) was possibly the cruelest of all the conquistadors. He came to the New World for one reason: to find gold. He accompanied Balboa in his march across the Isthmus of Panama. After Balboa's execution, he decided to find the people to the south—the Incas—who were rumored to be very wealthy. In 1531 he and his men set out for Peru. After landing by ship on the coast, they marched through jungles for six months, plundering villages as they went. Raiding the Inca Empire, they captured **Atahualpa** (AH tah WAHL pah), the Inca ruler, and held him for ransom. Atahualpa promised to fill a room with gold and silver to buy his release. After receiving the promised ransom of gold and silver, Pizarro broke his promise and executed Atahualpa. With only a handful of men, he completed the conquest of the Inca Empire.

Two years later Pizarro founded the city of Lima, which is today the capital of Peru. Soon afterwards, other Spaniards, as greedy as Pizarro and jealous of his gold, attacked and killed him in his home. Pizarro had found more gold in the New World than anyone else, but greed—his own greed and that of others—prevented anyone from enjoying it. Like Pizarro, many other conquistadors died violently, fighting to keep the gold which they thought would help them enjoy life.

Not all Spaniards who came to the New World were seeking gold. In 1502 **Bartolomé de las Casas** (1474–1566), a Roman Catholic friar, arrived in the Americas as a missionary to the Indians. Deeply distressed over the cruelty of his countrymen, he wrote several works decrying the abuse of the Indians in the New World. He described, for example, the death of one Indian chief who was being burned at the stake. A priest told him to become a Christian so he could go to heaven. The man refused, saying that he did not want to go to any place where there were Christians. Unfortunately, the Indians, like many people today, rejected the gospel because of the lives of people who claimed to be Christians.

Las Casas devoted his life to improving the plight of the Indians in the New World. In 1542 he helped pass the "New Laws," which protected the Indians from being made slaves. Previously, the Spanish had forced the natives to labor on plantations where they were overworked and mistreated. These new laws forbade this practice. Las Casas also opposed the common Roman Catholic practice of

Bartolomé de las Casas

giving people the choice of converting to Catholicism and being allowed to live as slaves or rejecting the Roman Church and being killed. No man, he said, could be converted by force; real conversion comes only to those who are persuaded gently.

Spanish exploration was not confined to Latin America. Rumors of "a land of gold" to the north enticed other explorers to the regions of what is now the United States. In 1539 **Hernando de Soto**, who served with Pizarro in Peru, landed near Tampa Bay, Florida, in search of "golden" cities. In his exploration of the southeastern United States, he discovered the great Mississippi River. Though he did not find gold, his expedition led the way for further exploration of the North American continent.

Another explorer of the lands to the north was **Francisco Vásquez de Coronado** (KOR uh NAH doh). He set out from Mexico in 1540 to find the "Seven Cities of Cíbola," which were reportedly rich in gold. He led his expedition into what is now New Mexico and Arizona and then through what is now Kansas and Texas. Some of his men went westward and discovered the Grand Canyon.

Neither de Soto nor Coronado realized the value of the lands they explored. Since they found no gold, they concluded it to be a waste of time to explore further. Because of these two expeditions, the Spaniards decided to concentrate their efforts on the land they already held, leaving most of North America open for other European nations to explore.

French, Dutch, and English Exploration

When the pope gave Spain and Portugal rights to all newly discovered lands in 1493, the other nations of Europe objected. King Francis I of France commented sarcastically, "I should like to see Adam's will, wherein he divided the earth between Spain and Portugal." After Magellan's voyage, most Europeans realized that the land to the west was not Asia, but a new world; and the French, Dutch, and English sought to claim some of it for themselves.

French Explorers

The first great French explorer in the New World was **Jacques Cartier** (kar TYAY), who made three voyages to what is now eastern Canada. In 1534 he sailed to Newfoundland and Labrador, which was so desolate that he remarked, "I am rather inclined to believe that this is the land God gave to Cain."

On his second voyage (1535) he sailed up the St. Lawrence River to an Iroquois Indian village. The view from a nearby mountain was so impressive that Cartier named the site "Mount Royal" (in French, "Montreal"). Today one of the largest cities in Canada stands there. Like many other explorers of his day, Cartier was certain that there existed a water route—the so-called Northwest Passage—which would take him to the Pacific Ocean and from there to the Orient, but he was unsuccessful in finding it.

Some seventy years after Cartier, Samuel de Champlain (sham PLANE), the "Father of New France," explored and colonized the area around the St. Lawrence River. In 1608 he founded the city of Quebec. He worked closely with the local Indians, who led him to two of the Great Lakes (Ontario and Huron) and to what we now call Lake Champlain. Like Cartier, he was seeking a route west to China.

Another noted French explorer was the Jesuit missionary **Jacques Marquette** (mar KET). In 1673 he and a friend, **Louis Joliet**

Hernando de Soto

Jacques Cartier

Samuel de Champlain

Henry Hudson landing on the shores of Delaware Bay

John Smith

(JOH lee ET), explored the Mississippi River. They paddled canoes downstream to a point in southern Arkansas before turning back. In 1682 Sieur de La Salle (luh SAL) traveled to the mouth of the Mississippi River and claimed the entire Mississippi Valley for France. He called it "Louisiana" in honor of King Louis XIV of France.

Dutch Explorers

The most famous explorer for the Netherlands was the Englishman **Henry Hudson**, whom the Dutch hired to find a shorter route to the East. He explored the northeastern coast of America in his ship the *Half Moon*. In 1609 he entered the Hudson River, thinking it might be the Northwest Passage. He continued upriver to where Albany, New York, now stands. His exploration gave the Dutch a claim to the region. In 1621 the Dutch founded the city of New Amsterdam, which is today New York City.

English Explorers

The English began exploring the New World soon after Columbus's first voyage. They hired an Italian sailor named **John Cabot** to lead the first English expedition to North America. After a six-week voyage across the Atlantic, Cabot dropped anchor off the coast of Canada. The first European after the Vikings to set foot on the North American mainland, he returned to England and was rewarded by King Henry VII. In 1498 Cabot made a second voyage to the New World, this time accompanied by his son Sebastian. They explored the northern coast of North America. Though they did not find gold or spices, they found rich fisheries off the Newfoundland coast. These two expeditions to the New World were the basis for England's claim on America. The Cabots paved the way for the founding of English colonies on the North American continent a century later.

Like the Spanish, the English also sought gold. But they went about obtaining it very differently. For the most part, the English did not engage in the extreme cruelty to the Indians that was typical of the Spaniards. The English brought their families and sought to develop the land, not exploit it. Their first permanent settlement was **Jamestown**, founded in 1607 near the mouth of Chesapeake Bay. Under the leadership of Captain **John Smith**, the settlers built a village and began to explore the land. In 1608 much of the village burned, and the few remaining settlers had almost given up when a new governor, Lord de la Warr, arrived. The influx of new settlers and fresh supplies gave new life to the struggling colony.

This English settlement, the first of many in the New World, was the beginning of what would later become the United States of America. Most of the freedoms that Americans have enjoyed—freedom of religion, freedom of speech, and many others—resulted, in part, from the influence of Protestant settlers who traveled to North America during the seventeenth century.

Europe and Asia
The West Reaches the East

Europe's exploration efforts were not limited to the New World; it also had interests on the other side of the world in Asia. Spain was largely excluded from this area by treaty with Portugal (although Spain did colonize the Philippines). Portugal, the Netherlands, and England, however, traded and colonized extensively in the East.

The Portuguese

Soon after da Gama returned from his historic voyage, the Portuguese, under the leadership of **Pedro Cabral**, established a trading post in India. From this small beginning they were able to establish numerous trading posts throughout the Indian Ocean. Their fully armed ships gave them an insurmountable advantage over Muslim and native traders in the region.

In 1506 **Afonso de Albuquerque** (AL buh KUR kee) was named the viceroy of Portuguese holdings in the East. He discouraged cruelty to the natives and led his men in establishing trading posts and plantations along the trade routes to support and protect Portuguese traders. Under his leadership the Portuguese began to build a vast commercial empire. They captured and controlled the entrances to the Persian Gulf and the Red Sea. After Albuquerque's death they pushed farther eastward. By 1520 they had taken Ceylon (present-day Sri Lanka) and the town of Banten on the island of Java. The latter controlled one of the two water entrances to the Far East. Since the Portuguese already controlled the other entrance at the Strait of Malacca, they were able to dominate all the sea trade between Europe and Asia. In 1542 they began trading with Japan, and in 1557 they founded the colony of Macao on the Chinese mainland.

However, the Portuguese "eastern empire" had some fatal weaknesses. It was spread too widely for the little country of Portugal to administer and defend effectively. Furthermore, since many sailors died at sea, Portugal's manpower was drained to a critical point. (About one voyage in seven ended in disaster.) Finally, the cruelty of the traders—despite Albuquerque's reforms—caused the Asians to hate them. With the lack of cooperation essential for successful trading, Portuguese commercial interests were hampered. When other European nations began to compete for business in the East, the Asians granted it to them.

The Dutch

The Dutch were not a wealthy people in the sixteenth century, but they were experienced sailors. When prices soared under the Portuguese monopoly, the Dutch decided to go directly to the source for their Asian goods. In 1596 they settled on Java and Sumatra and expelled the Portuguese from the key city of Banten. They later captured the main Spice Islands and founded the city of Batavia, which became a key port and trading post in the East Indies. They soon became the only nation with which Japan would trade. They also began trading with Formosa (modern Taiwan) and seized the island of Ceylon. By the middle of the seventeenth century, Dutch control extended from Persia to Japan.

In order to provide fresh water, vegetables, and meat for ships making the long voyage around Africa to the Indies, the Dutch in 1652 established a settlement at the Cape of Good Hope at what is now Cape Town, South Africa. The mild climate of the cape attracted many settlers; before long it became a sizable colony.

The English

When England defeated the Spanish Armada in 1588, the English realized that they had enough sea power to carry on a busy trade with the East. In 1591, almost a century after da Gama, English merchant-seamen made a trading voyage to India. Although they started late, the English far surpassed the Portuguese in long-

Pedro Cabral

Afonso de Albuquerque

range influence in Asia. They followed the Dutch into the East Indies, trading alongside them for several years. Soon, however, they turned their main attention to India. England seized control of the Persian Gulf and opened trade on both the east and west coasts of India. This was the beginning of England's influence in India—an influence that continued into the twentieth century.

The East Responds to the West

China and Japan resented Western intervention in their affairs. The same insular attitude that had kept them from exploring other lands for most of their history also kept them from welcoming traders to their lands. They had been secure in their traditions, and they did not take kindly to European sailors who attempted to claim their properties for unknown kings and their souls for Roman popes. The Portuguese, who were the first to come to the East, were especially tactless and cruel, and by 1550 there had already been several bloody battles between Chinese and Portuguese soldiers. The people of China resisted the European way of life as well as Christianity. They wanted to be left alone. The Chinese did allow the Portuguese to colonize the port city of Macao, but for this privilege the Portuguese had to pay $30,000 per year in tribute. Except for isolated instances, there was no direct trade between China and the European countries for many years.

Japan at first was more friendly to the Europeans than China. The Japanese welcomed **Francis Xavier**, the famous Jesuit missionary. Later, however, the government, influenced by Buddhism, expelled the foreign missionaries who had followed Xavier to Japan. Those who stayed were severely persecuted. More trouble occurred in 1639 when the Japanese shogun learned that Portuguese trading ships were smuggling in Catholic missionaries disguised as merchants. Furious, he commanded that any Portuguese who came to Japan be killed on sight. Some traders who did not think the shogun was serious learned otherwise and paid with their lives. The Japanese did allow a few Dutch ships to trade in their ports, but for the most part, Japan, like China, remained closed to European travelers.

Francis Xavier

Section Review

1–3. After crossing the Isthmus of Panama, Balboa saw what body of water? What did he call it? Who gave it its present name?

4–6. Compare and contrast the motives of three major European countries during this period.

✶ Evaluate the treatment of Indian populations by European explorers.

✶ Why were European missionaries forbidden in China and Japan?

Guiding Questions

1. What are mercantilism and capitalism?
2. How is wealth produced in mercantilism and capitalism?
3. Which system was better?

III. The Commercial Revolution

During the fifteenth and sixteenth centuries, Europe underwent many political, social, religious, and economic changes. Ownership of land was no longer considered the primary basis of wealth. Money became the medium of exchange in trade. As new sources of gold and spices were discovered in distant lands, wealth became redefined. Soon after the earliest explorers had returned home, commercial ventures were organized to establish trade ties with newly found peoples across the seas. Great wealth quickly began to flow into Europe from around the world. Europe's business thinking and practice changed. These changes became known as the **Commercial Revolution**.

Mercantilism: Nations Acquiring Wealth

The dominant economic system practiced during the Age of Exploration is called **mercantilism**. Mercantilists believed that the newly found wealth should benefit the mother country. A nation's strength and greatness was believed to rest upon the amount of gold and silver it possessed. For this reason, the goal of nations governed by mercantilism became obtaining as much precious metal as possible. To achieve this goal, nations acquired colonies, sought to become self-sufficient, and worked to maintain a favorable balance of trade by exporting more than they imported.

Under mercantilism, colonies existed to supply the mother country with raw materials and to provide markets where goods from the mother country could be sold. To prevent competition, the colonies were not allowed to produce anything that the mother country produced. Nor were the colonies allowed to trade with any other country. Mexico, for example, had to buy everything it needed from Spain, and whatever it produced had to be sold to Spain. Likewise, it was not allowed to trade directly with other Spanish colonies; for Mexican products to reach Peru, for example, they had to be shipped across the ocean to Spain and then back again to Peru. As a result of mercantilism, the mother countries became wealthy.

Under this system the government regulated a nation's economic activity, creating national monopolies that deterred competition. More often than not, the interests of the government superseded the interests and welfare of the people—especially those in the colonies—and the colonies usually suffered.

Mercantilists did not view trade as a "two-way street" benefiting both buyer and seller. They thought of it only in terms of the seller, who obtained gold and silver for his product. This one-sided foreign trade, in which goods went out of a country and gold and silver came in, was a detriment to a country's agriculture and industry. The goods and crops a nation produced were deemed important only if they could be traded abroad for gold and silver. Once gold and silver were obtained by a mercantilist country, the wealth was seldom used to benefit the people. Instead, these precious metals were hoarded in royal treasuries.

Capitalism: Individuals Advancing Wealth

The opportunity for acquiring great wealth also became open to individuals. During this period another economic system—**capitalism**—developed alongside mercantilism. Unlike mercantilism, the goal of capitalism was not simply to acquire wealth but to advance wealth. Enterprising individuals used the money they had to make more money. They invested their wealth, often at great risk, in hopes of making a profit.

Many of the early capitalists were bankers. They made money by buying and selling bills of exchange, by safeguarding money for others, and by exchanging money. They often invested their own resources in business ventures, such as financing trade voyages. But

Spanish gold doubloons and pieces of eight salvaged from a 1715 wreck; the pieces of eight are cut from an eight-ounce piece of molten silver and stamped with the shield of Philip V of Spain and the cross.

sea travel at this time was perilous: it was not uncommon for the stormy seas to sink ships or for pirates to seize a ship's cargo. Such disasters could bring financial ruin to an individual. To spread the risk, men organized **companies** in which they pooled their resources; they shared the gains as well as the losses.

From this practice arose the **joint-stock company**. People invested money in such companies, and in return they were issued stock certificates showing the amount of money they invested. The invested money became part of the company's **capital**, or supply of money. The company then used this capital to finance a business venture. If the company made a profit, the stockholders received payment in the form of **dividends**.

There were many joint-stock companies during the Age of Exploration. Three are especially important. The English East India Company, founded in 1600 with only a small amount of capital, began trading primarily in India. It was astonishingly successful. Profits for the years 1609–13, for example, averaged almost 300 percent each year (that is, investors received back every year dividends three times their original investment). The Dutch East India Company, founded in 1602, traded in the East Indies (such as Java and Sumatra). It too made great profits, paying dividends of 18 percent each year for many years. The French Company of New France traded in Canada, mainly for furs. These companies did more than just trade, however. They also set up bases, or settlements, to make their work more permanent.

A fleet of East Indiamen at Sea

Another method of attracting financial support for an enterprise was to post in a public place a prospectus—details of a proposed business venture. People wrote their names below the prospectus, stating that they would help share the cost of the enterprise. If it was a success, they would share in the profits; if it was a failure, they agreed to sustain the loss. It is from this practice that we get the word **underwriter**, which today we use to describe an insurance company. One of the earliest insurance companies was Lloyds of London. It was founded in 1688 by a group of men who underwrote voyages to the New World.

Section Review

1. What are the changes in Europe's business thinking and practice during the fifteenth and sixteenth centuries called?

2. What was the dominant economic policy of most European nations during the Age of Exploration?

3. What was the purpose of colonies under this economic policy?

4. The use of wealth to make more wealth defines what economic policy?

5. Contrast the mercantilist view of wealth with the capitalist view of wealth.

★ Which economic policy (mercantilism or capitalism) provided the greatest long-term benefits for a country? Why?

Making Connections

1–2. How did the Renaissance (ch. 11) influence the Age of Discovery? (List two ways.)

3–8. Define and distinguish the economic policies of mercantilism and capitalism. (List three distinctions for each.)

Developing History Skills

1. What were the long-term results of Portuguese and British colonization?

2. What effect did the defeat of the Spanish Armada in 1588 (see chapter 11) have on the early history of the English colonies in North America?

Thinking Critically

1. Evaluate the motives of many of the explorers in light of 1 Timothy 6:9–10.

2. If a Christian ruler had to choose between adopting a mercantilist approach or a capitalist approach, which should he choose? Why?

Living in God's World

1. Recently historians have emphasized that Europeans were wrong to force the native peoples to submit to them and to adopt European cultures. Some have even declared that Christian missions is wrong. They claim that missions is simply another way of replacing a native culture with a Western culture. Respond to this claim.

2. Choose a land explored by the Europeans and research its religious beliefs. Did the country have a form of Christianity in which the people already believed? Did it have a form of morality by which people lived? If so, explain what they believed from a Christian perspective.

People, Places, and Things to Know

Marco Polo
Prester John
compass
latitude
caravel
Prince Henry
Bartolomeu Dias
Vasco da Gama
Christopher Columbus
Line of Demarcation
Ferdinand Magellan
circumnavigation
conquistadors
Vasco Núñez de Balboa
Hernando Cortés
Montezuma
Francisco Pizarro
Atahualpa
Bartolomé de las Casas
Hernando de Soto
Franciso Vásquez de Coronado
Jacques Cartier
Samuel de Champlain
Jacques Marquette
Louis Joliet
Henry Hudson
John Cabot
Jamestown
John Smith
Pedro Cabral
Afonso de Albuquerque
Francis Xavier
Commercial Revolution
mercantilism
capitalism
companies
joint-stock company
capital
dividends
underwriter

UNIT

5

THE ENLIGHTENED WORLD
1600–1800

14 Pursuit of Power in Europe

15 Age of Reason

16 Attempts at Liberty

Statue at Versailles

1611
King James Version

1618–48
Thirty Years' War

1649
Execution of Charles I

1660
Restoration

1685
Revocation of the Edict of Nantes

1688
Glorious Revolution

1689
English Bill of Rights

1600

1650

170

1649–60
Protectorate

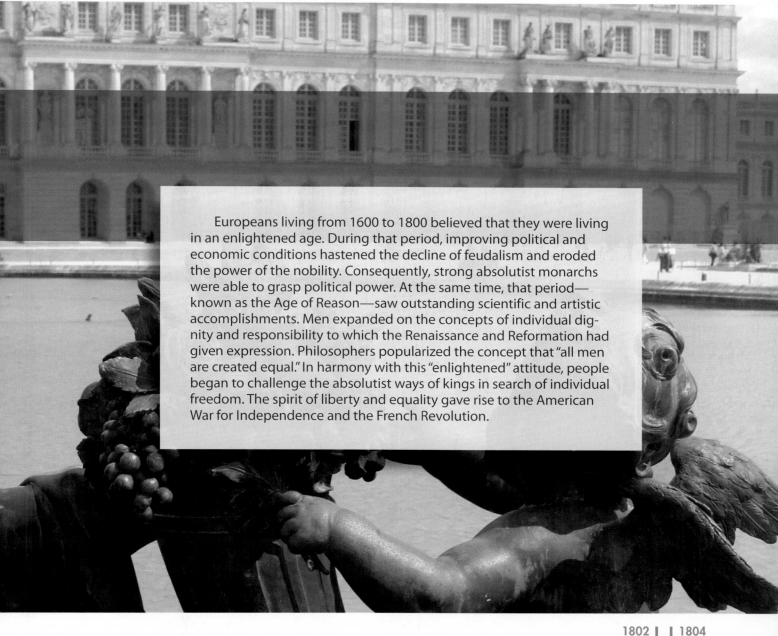

Europeans living from 1600 to 1800 believed that they were living in an enlightened age. During that period, improving political and economic conditions hastened the decline of feudalism and eroded the power of the nobility. Consequently, strong absolutist monarchs were able to grasp political power. At the same time, that period—known as the Age of Reason—saw outstanding scientific and artistic accomplishments. Men expanded on the concepts of individual dignity and responsibility to which the Renaissance and Reformation had given expression. Philosophers popularized the concept that "all men are created equal." In harmony with this "enlightened" attitude, people began to challenge the absolutist ways of kings in search of individual freedom. The spirit of liberty and equality gave rise to the American War for Independence and the French Revolution.

1763
Treaty of Paris ending the Seven Years' War

1802
Napoleon named First Consul for Life

1804
Napoleon crowned Emperor

1799 BC
Directory founded by Napoleon

1805
Napoleon victorious at Austerlitz

1756–63
Seven Years' War

1775–83
American War for Independence

1799–1815
Napoleonic Era

1750

1800

1720–90
Great Awakening

July 14, 1789
French National Day/Bastille Day

1813
Napoleon defeated at Leipzig

1815
Napoleon defeated at Waterloo

CHAPTER

Pursuit of Power in Europe

14

I. Absolutism Triumphs in France
II. Absolutism Spreads in Europe
III. Absolutism Defeated in England
IV. Balance of Power

Louis XIV

Big Ideas

1. What was the significance of the Peace of Westphalia on the history of Europe?
2. How did justice, power, and citizenship vary in European nations?
3. How did absolutism differ in England and France?
4. How did the role of power develop in Europe in this period?

During the Middle Ages, royal power in Europe remained limited for several reasons. Popes struggled with kings over the question of whose authority was greater. Strong feudal nobles competed with kings for power within a territory. But with the papacy's decline in power and the passing of feudalism, royal power began to increase.

During the seventeenth and eighteenth centuries, European rulers worked to make their political power **absolute** (unlimited and unrestrained). They sought to increase their royal authority by (1) increasing their control over their nation's finances, religion, and nobility; (2) increasing the size of the standing army or developing a strong navy; (3) increasing the size of the government bureaucracy and making it an instrument of their royal will; and (4) increasing the size of their territory—through war if necessary. They justified the extension of their power on religious grounds. They asserted that God had established their authority; therefore, they ruled by **divine right**. This right, they said, gave them absolute authority: they were not bound by any manmade laws but were responsible only to God for their actions.

Absolutist rule was accepted by most Europeans, who believed that a strong ruler was the best way to ensure security, order, and prosperity. Nevertheless, some people recognized the danger of an unrestrained increase in royal power. In some nations, representative assemblies that had developed alongside growing monarchies championed the opposition to absolute royal power. However, with the exception of the English Parliament, these assemblies had little success in restraining royal control. Most absolutist kings were able to crush any opposition to their authority.

I. Absolutism Triumphs in France

France became the leading absolutist nation in Europe during the seventeenth century. Two chief advisers to the French throne, Cardinals Richelieu and Mazarin, secured much of the power wielded by French kings. For several decades, Richelieu and then Mazarin guided both French policy and French kings. They increased their personal power by strengthening royal power in France and French power in Europe. Their efforts encouraged the growth of absolutism in France, and King Louis XIV (r. 1643–1715) became the ultimate beneficiary of their labors. For more than seventy years, he reigned in France with unparalleled pomp and power, becoming the leading absolutist ruler of Europe.

Growth of Absolutism: Richelieu and Mazarin

Bourbon king **Henry IV** (r. 1589–1610) helped lay the foundation for absolutism in France. After his victory in the French civil wars (see p. 253), Henry worked to strengthen royal power. He reduced the privileges of the nobility and increased government control of the economy. However, he was assassinated by a Catholic extremist in 1610, and his nine-year-old son, Louis XIII (r. 1610–43), came to the throne. During the years of Louis's youth, his mother, Marie de Medici, ruled France. But in 1624 the Duc de Richelieu (RISH uh loo)—better known as **Cardinal Richelieu**—became Louis XIII's chief minister.

Richelieu strengthened the power of the king by destroying the Huguenots (French Protestants), whom he viewed as a danger to the state. He also wanted to weaken the great nobles and prevent them

Religious Defense of Absolutism

A staunch defender of political absolutism was the French Catholic Bishop Bossuet (baw SWAY), whom King Louis XIV chose to tutor his son. He wrote the following:

> The royal power is absolute. With the aim of making this truth hateful and insufferable, many writers have tried to confound absolute government with arbitrary government. But no two things could be more unlike. . . . The prince need render an account of his acts to no one. . . . Without this absolute authority the king could neither do good nor repress evil. . . . God is infinite, God is all. The prince, as prince, is not regarded as a private person: he is a public personage, all the state is in him; the will of the people is included in his.

But Bossuet also warned kings:

> Kings, although their power comes from on high, . . . should not regard themselves as masters of that power to use it at their pleasure. . . . They must employ it with fear and self-restraint, as a thing coming from God and of which God will demand an account. . . . Kings should tremble then as they use the power God has granted them; and let them think how horrible is the sacrilege if they use for evil a power which comes from God.

James Harvey Robinson and Charles A. Beard, *Readings in Modern European History*, 1:6–7.

Guiding Questions

1. How did the theory of divine right support absolutism?
2. How did absolutism develop in France?
3. How did the Thirty Years' War and the Peace of Westphalia influence Europe?

Cardinal Richelieu

from regaining their lost power. Richelieu sought to accomplish the first of his policies by putting extraordinary burdens on the Huguenots. For example, he forced them to house French soldiers but exempted Roman Catholics from such obligations. Richelieu ordered that Huguenot children be taken from their homes and be reared by Roman Catholics. He also sent spies to Huguenot churches to listen for any criticism of the government. Critics were either arrested or heavily fined.

Richelieu made progress toward accomplishing his second objective—weakening the nobility—by removing nobles from positions of authority in local government. He replaced them with officials directly responsible to the king. In addition, Richelieu destroyed many of the castles of the nobility. He imprisoned those who defied him and executed those he considered to be a threat.

To increase the prestige and power of France, Richelieu brought France into the **Thirty Years' War** (1618–48), the last great religious war fought in Europe. It began in Bohemia, the land of John Huss, when Protestant Bohemian nobles revolted against the newly crowned Catholic emperor, who had revoked their religious freedoms. The emperor sent his troops into the region and ruthlessly crushed all Protestant resistance. Soon, the war had spread to other parts of the Holy Roman Empire; Protestantism seemed to be on the verge of collapse.

Gustavus Adolphus (gus-TAY-vus uh-DAHL-fuss; r. 1611–32), king of Sweden, rescued the Protestant cause. With a small band of troops, Gustavus landed in northern Germany, recruited additional soldiers, and marched against the emperor's pro-Catholic, pro-imperial forces. Gustavus won several important victories but then was killed in battle. Soon after his death, France entered the war—on the side of the Protestants.

Although France was a Roman Catholic country, Richelieu feared what would happen if the Holy Roman emperor solidified his power by subduing all his Protestant opponents. France would then be surrounded by two strong Habsburg powers—Spain and the Holy Roman Empire. For this reason, Richelieu joined the Protestant cause in 1635, making the war more a political than a religious conflict.

After several more years of fighting, the war finally ended in 1648 with a Protestant-French victory. The peace treaties, collectively known as the **Peace of Westphalia**, contained two important provisions. (1) The treaties recognized the independence of the Protestant provinces of the Netherlands and the Swiss confederacy. (2) The treaties recognized more than three hundred independent German states and reaffirmed the principle that each prince would determine the religion of his territory. For all practical purposes, this resulted in a more politically fragmented Germany and delayed German unification. France emerged as the strongest nation on the continent of Europe.

Richelieu died in 1642. King Louis XIII died only five months later, and the crown of France passed to Louis's five-year-old son, **Louis XIV** (r. 1643–1715). During Louis XIV's youth, the government was controlled by a new chief minister, **Jules Mazarin**. Mazarin (maz uh RAN) maintained the absolutist policies of his predecessor, Richelieu. Shortly after the wily Cardinal Mazarin and the young king came to power, Mazarin imposed new taxes, and France

The Peace of Westphalia

The Thirty Years' War brought great devastation to many regions of Europe, and German territories suffered most of all. The Peace of Westphalia ended this terrible conflict and resulted in lasting changes for Europe. This agreement marked a turning point in which Roman Catholic forces recognized they could not stamp out Protestantism, and more Europeans enjoyed limited religious toleration. It confirmed the Peace of Augsburg that gave German princes the right to determine the religion of their subjects. Reformed Christianity also gained acceptance alongside Lutheranism. This agreement also led to independent sovereign states rather than a single entity under the umbrella of the Holy Roman Empire.

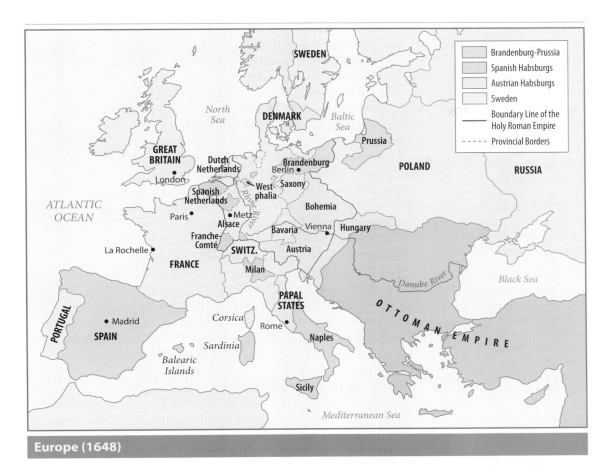

Europe (1648)

begin to experience unrest. Those who opposed the growing power of the crown participated in a series of riots, civil wars, and anti-government plots. These upheavals forced Louis XIV to leave Paris for a time, but they were unsuccessful in destroying French absolutism and ended in 1653. They were the last serious attempt to limit the power of the king until the outbreak of the French Revolution in 1789. (See chapter 16.)

Epitome of Absolutism: Louis XIV

When Mazarin died in 1661, Louis XIV decided against appointing a replacement. Instead, Louis became his own chief minister. He told his advisers, "You will assist me with your counsels when I ask for them." Louis believed in "one king, one law, and one faith." These three were wrapped up in the person of the king and his power over the state. Although he may never have said, "*L'état, c'est moi*" ("I am the state"), these words reflect Louis's view of himself. From 1661 until his death in 1715, Louis dominated European affairs to such an extent that historians sometimes call these years "the Age of Louis XIV."

Financial and Military Policies

One of the first things Louis did after the death of Mazarin was to set French finances in order. The French government was near bankruptcy because it was spending money faster than it took it in. To remedy this dangerous situation, Louis appointed **Jean-Baptiste Colbert** (kohl BEHR; 1619–83) as his minister of finance. Colbert brought temporary fiscal order to France by tighter government

Jules Mazarin

Louis XIV's Vanity

A nobleman who lived in the royal palace described Louis's vanity:

[It was] without limit or restraint; it colored everything and convinced him that no one even approached him in military talents, in plans and enterprises, in government. Hence those pictures and inscriptions in the gallery at Versailles which disgust every foreigner; those opera prologues that he himself tried to sing; that flood of prose and verse in his praise for which his appetite was insatiable; those dedications of statues copied from pagan sculpture, and the insipid and sickening compliments that were continually offered to him in person and which he swallowed with unfailing relish; hence his distaste for all merit, intelligence, education, and most of all, for all independence of character and sentiment in others; his mistakes of judgment in matters of importance; his familiarity and favor reserved entirely for those to whom he felt himself superior in acquirements and ability; and, above everything else, a jealousy of his authority which determined and took precedence of every other sort of justice, reason, and consideration whatever.

James Harvey Robinson and Charles A. Beard, *Readings in Modern European History*, 1:10.

control of the French economy. He encouraged commercial activity and economic self-sufficiency. A proponent of mercantilism, Colbert favored limiting imports and increasing exports. He also encouraged constructing a navy to protect French trade abroad.

Louis also set about to reorganize the French army so that the soldiers would owe their loyalty to him rather than to the colonel of their regiment. To weaken the influence of the nobility over the troops, Louis placed lieutenant colonels over each regiment. Through these lieutenants, who were responsible to the king, Louis gained control of the army. He required his troops to wear identical uniforms rather than allowing them to wear the colors of their colonels. His well-trained, well-paid, and loyal troops became the finest soldiers in seventeenth-century Europe.

Revocation of the Edict of Nantes

In his efforts to create religious uniformity in France, Louis XIV revoked the Edict of Nantes in 1685. Since 1598, this edict had guaranteed religious toleration of French Protestants. As a result of its revocation, Huguenots lost any remaining freedom to worship. Louis also forbade all Protestant education, demolished Huguenot churches, and forced some Huguenots to serve as galley slaves on French ships.

Although Louis may have believed that such persecution was for the good of France, his revocation of the Edict of Nantes had the opposite effect. Between 250,000 and 500,000 Huguenots—many of them merchants, small businessmen, and craftsmen—left France. Since they comprised much of the spiritual, moral, and economic backbone of the country, their departure had a devastating effect on the French nation. The nations in which the Huguenots settled benefited from their spiritual fervor and productive skills. Some of these lands were rivals of France; thus Louis unintentionally strengthened his enemies.

Life at Versailles

Louis XIV took the sun as the symbol of his reign. As the "Sun King," he considered himself the center of European life, with everyone else "revolving" around him. Louis was a proud man who loved to glorify himself and his own accomplishments. He loved luxury and the attention of the people of his court.

To show his power and splendor, Louis had a great palace built about twelve miles southwest of Paris. When completed, the palace of **Versailles** (vehr SYE) was an awesome sight. Around the palace were elaborate formal gardens. The building itself was nearly a half mile long and contained hundreds of grandly decorated rooms. Dazzling works of art adorned the palace's interior. To maintain the building's symmetrical appearance, Louis refused to allow chimneys to be seen from the front of the palace, even though their shortness meant smoky rooms. Elegance and grandeur were important, not utility.

Louis used his palace to impress his subjects. He also used it to keep the nobility subservient to him. He required nobles to live at Versailles for at least part of each year. While they were there, Louis kept them so busy that they did not have time to plot against him. There were plays, balls, and frivolous activities that kept their minds distracted from the affairs of state.

From the time Louis rose in the morning until he went to bed at night, the nobility flocked around him. They vied with one another for the privilege of performing some small task, such as handing him his shirt in the morning or bringing him a cup of hot chocolate at night. Everything in Louis's life became a pompous ritual designed to make the king the absolute center of attention.

In spite of all its grandeur, Versailles was the center for all that was base and immoral. Adultery and homosexuality were openly embraced. Gambling was commonplace. Every sort of vice could be found in the king's palace.

(above) *Versailles chapel;* (below) *Versailles*

Foreign Policy

To expand French territory and increase his influence in Europe, Louis XIV engaged in numerous wars. He tried to extend French borders to what he said were their natural boundaries: the Rhine, the Alps, and the Pyrenees. Although he did gain some territory, these wars brought much harm to France. Their cost, in addition to Louis's extensive building programs, brought France to the edge of bankruptcy. On his deathbed, Louis said to his heir, "Try to remain at peace with your neighbors. I have loved war too much. Do not copy me in that, or in my overspending."

Louis died in 1715. He reigned longer than any other European king. Louis had outlived both his son and grandson, who were heirs to the throne. His great-grandson **Louis XV** (r. 1715–74), who was five years old when Louis XIV died, succeeded him. During the early years of the young king's reign, capable regents kept France out of war and rebuilt its economy. But Louis XV, following the example of Louis XIV, later involved France in disastrous and humiliating wars, which once again drained the royal treasury. This near bankruptcy played a decisive role in the eventual overthrow of the French monarchy.

Section Review

1. Explain how the divine-right theory supported absolutism.

2–3. What two chief advisors to the French kings Louis XIII and Louis XIV helped strengthen the power of France and the French monarchy?

4. What major event in Europe did the Peace of Wesphalia resolve?

5–7. Who epitomized absolutism in France? Why? What was the name of his palace?

8–9. What did the French king revoke in 1685? What group was persecuted as a result?

★ How was French support for Protestants during the Thirty Years' War inconsistent with French treatment of Protestants in France?

★ Evaluate the theory of divine right in light of Deuteronomy 17:18–20.

Guiding Questions

1. How did absolutism develop in continental Europe?
2. How were justice, power, and citizenship characterized in continental Europe?

II. Absolutism Spreads in Europe

French absolutism influenced other European monarchs, who gradually embraced not only absolutism but also France's language, fashions, and morals. Three territories in particular came under the rule of absolutist monarchs: Brandenburg-Prussia, Austria, and Russia. Following the example of Louis XIV, known as the "Grand Monarch," the rulers of these territories increased their personal and national power.

Absolutism in Prussia

After the Thirty Years' War, Germany remained a fragmented land consisting of small, weak states. One of these, Brandenburg-Prussia, gradually obtained enough power and territory to become the strongest of the German states. Brandenburg-Prussia (later simply called Prussia) was an unlikely candidate to become a major

European power. Prussia's soil was poor, its economic resources were few, and its territories were scattered. Prussia had no natural frontiers such as mountains or rivers to provide protection. Yet it did have energetic and capable rulers (called electors) who used any means necessary to increase their power and the size of their territory. These rulers built a large standing army and established an efficient bureaucracy. They also gained the cooperation of the Prussian nobility, who worked closely with the electors in governing the country and serving as officers in the Prussian army.

The first important Prussian ruler, **Frederick William** (r. 1640–88), was called "the Great Elector" because he became the most powerful of the German princes, who elected the emperor. He forged Prussia's scattered territories into a unified state. Frederick William's chief source of power was the standing Prussian army, which numbered about thirty thousand men. He increased taxes to support such a large army; in fact, Prussians paid twice as much in taxes as French citizens did during this period. The army became a chief instrument by which Prussian rulers obtained and demonstrated their absolute power. During the next two centuries, militarism played a major role in creating and shaping a German national state.

Under Frederick William's successor, Frederick I (r. 1688–1713), the army continued to grow. Frederick I, however, was more interested in the arts than in warfare. He sought to imitate Louis XIV in as many ways as possible. Frederick had a new palace built for himself and beautified Berlin, the capital of Prussia, with many new public buildings.

Although Frederick I did little to increase the actual power of Prussia, he did increase Prussia's prestige among the other German states. After the War of the Spanish Succession (see p. 311), Frederick acquired for his successors the title of "King in Prussia." (The title "King *of* Prussia" would have been unacceptable to the Holy Roman emperor, who officially ruled all the German states.) This royal title helped to enhance the Prussian rulers' prestige among the nations of Europe.

Building upon the foundation of his predecessors, Frederick William I (r. 1713–40) firmly established Prussian absolutism. He was a violent-tempered man who believed in discipline and routine. He not only reduced court luxury and created a strong centralized bureaucracy but also demanded absolute obedience from all citizens. "Salvation belongs to the Lord," he said. "Everything else is my business."

Frederick William I spent most of his time enlarging Prussia's military forces. During his reign, the army grew to 83,000 men. It was a highly trained and battle-ready force, but Frederick William was not eager for war. He had spent so much money and energy on the military that he could not bear to see his men killed in battle. At the end of his life, Frederick William had built one of the five largest armies in Europe, despite the fact that Prussia did not rank in even the top ten in population. "Prussia," said one of his contemporaries, "is not a state with an army but an army with a state."

Although Frederick William I loved military life, his son **Frederick II** (r. 1740–86) seemed to have no interest in the army. As a young man, Frederick II loved to compose music, play the flute, write French poetry, and follow French fashions. His father opposed such pursuits, and the two quarreled constantly. Though Frederick II

Citizenship
How do you think Frederick William I's manner of rule affected the lives of his people? Would you like to live under such a ruler?

Frederick II

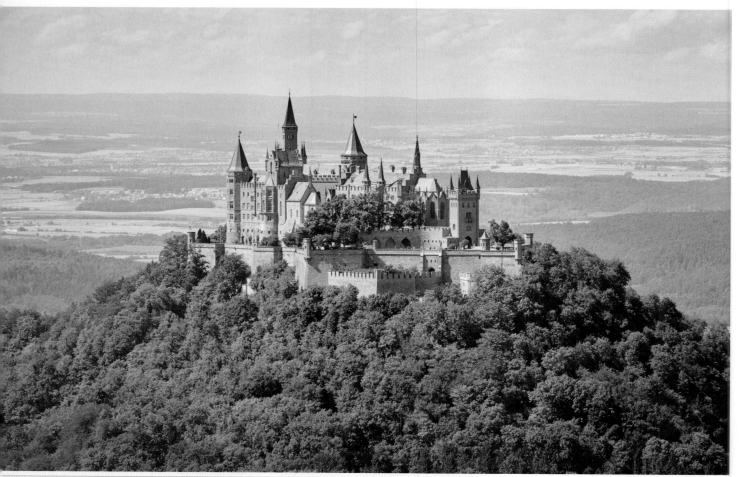

This home of the Hohenzollern kings was rebuilt in the nineteenth century; Frederick William I and Frederick the Great are buried here.

never abandoned his interest in culture, he did become one of Prussia's greatest military heroes. He became known as Frederick "the Great," the greatest soldier of his day. During his reign, he tripled the size of the Prussian state. Frederick also strengthened Prussia's economy by establishing a silk industry and by stabilizing grain prices. He enacted a wide variety of political and social reforms. For example, he abolished the torture of prisoners and granted religious freedom to Roman Catholics and Jews. Yet despite these and other reforms, Frederick remained firmly dedicated to the principle of absolutism.

By Frederick II's day, Prussia was a strong rival to the Habsburg rulers of Austria. The **Hohenzollern** (HO uhn ZAHL urn) rulers built Prussia into a first-class European power. This provided an advantage for Prussia as it competed with Austria for control of the many German states. Eventually, Prussia won the struggle, and the Hohenzollern rulers united the German states into one country during the nineteenth century.

Absolutism in Austria

By the beginning of the eighteenth century, the Habsburg rulers of Austria not only controlled a large amount of territory but also held the title of Holy Roman emperor. Although this title gave them no additional power, it did give them an added measure of prestige.

Despite these advantages, Habsburg rulers were unable to create a strong absolutist state. Many obstacles hindered them. (1) The

Roman Catholic Church and the nobility held great power and opposed any limitation of their traditional rights. (2) Austria was surrounded by aggressive neighbors (particularly France and later Prussia) who desired to seize Habsburg territories that bordered on their own. Since the Austrian rulers needed the support of the nobles to defend the country, the rulers dared not upset them by increasing their own royal power. (3) The Habsburgs ruled so many different nationalities that it was almost impossible to create a strong, unified government. The Hungarians especially resented Austrian control and did not willingly cooperate with their Habsburg rulers.

During the eighteenth century, the emperor Joseph II (r. 1765–90) made a strong effort to create an absolutist state in Austria. He began his reign as coruler with his mother, Maria Theresa (r. 1740–80). During the years of joint rule, Maria Theresa made gradual and careful changes. After her death, Joseph II embarked on a bolder course of action, directing his efforts against the power of the nobility and the Roman Catholic Church. He forced both groups to pay higher taxes, while reducing the tax burden on the peasants. At the same time, he made the government more centralized by weakening local authority.

Many of Joseph's actions were directed specifically against the Roman Catholic Church. For example, he dissolved hundreds of monasteries, allowing to remain only those that performed what he termed a useful service, such as teaching or ministering to the sick. He altered the church's organization and in 1781 granted religious freedom to non-Catholics. Since many of Joseph's changes were both sudden and drastic, few of them continued after his death. In fact, the nobility and the Roman Catholic Church regained many of their former privileges and reasserted their authority. Absolutism was never as strong in Austria as it was in many other European nations.

Absolutism in Russia

Soon after Russia gained its independence from the Mongols (see ch. 12), **Ivan IV** (r. 1533–84), called Ivan "the Terrible," became the ruler. He expanded Russian territory and built the beautiful St. Basil's Cathedral in Moscow. A cruel tyrant, Ivan had many of the Russian nobility murdered. In a fit of rage, he even murdered his own son. Ivan also oppressively taxed his people, treating them like slaves of the state. To glorify himself and his position, Ivan took the title of **czar**, a term that comes from the word *Caesar*.

After Ivan's death, Russia underwent a period of upheaval. Rival groups fought for control of the government, while bands of peasants roamed across Russia, killing and plundering. This turmoil finally ended in 1613, when the **Romanov** family came to the throne. (This dynasty ruled Russia until it was overthrown by the revolution of 1917.) **Peter I** (r. 1682–1725), one of the early Romanovs, did much to continue Russia's transformation into an absolutist state.

When Peter became czar, Russia was out of step with the rest of Europe. It was isolated and backward; Russia's economy was weak, and its government was disorganized. He determined that if Russia were to become a great power, it would have to adopt Western ways. Therefore, in 1697 Peter traveled in western Europe and learned all that he could. He visited Holland, France, and England, and when Peter returned to Russia to crush a revolution, he brought back

Joseph II

Peter I

more than seven hundred western Europeans. Many of them were shipbuilders, mathematicians, and engineers.

With this outside help, Peter began a westernization and modernization program in Russia. The Russians, with the help of these Western experts, worked to improve the Russian economy; they encouraged production of consumer goods such as paper products and textiles. They also began building a navy and a new capital, which they called St. Petersburg.

Peter tried to force Western ways upon his people. He outlawed long beards and oriental costumes such as long robes on men. In 1699, Peter introduced the Western calendar, which ended the Russian tradition of celebrating New Year's Day on the first of September (a date the Russians believed marked the first day of Creation). However, many Russians resented these changes.

In addition to his westernization program, Peter had another major goal: to expand Russian territory and acquire warm-water ports. In the **Great Northern War** (1700–1721) the Russians defeated Sweden and won additional territory along the Baltic Sea. Because of this victory, the Russians gave Peter the title "the Great."

Peter strengthened his power in Russia by seizing greater control of the Russian Orthodox Church. When the head of the church (the patriarch) died, Peter did not allow anyone to fill the vacancy. Instead, he created the Holy Synod, which governed the church like a board of directors. Peter and his successors controlled the Synod, ensuring that the Orthodox Church remained in line with the policies of the czar.

After the death of Peter (d. 1725), Russia endured a period of weaker leadership. Absolutism resumed in Russia under Empress **Catherine II** (r. 1762–96), who also came to be called "Catherine the Great." Catherine was a hardworking and very capable ruler, but she was driven by uncontrolled ambition. For example, shortly after her marriage to Peter III she gained the trust of those in power and may have been responsible for her husband's murder. Like Peter I, she sought to increase the authority of the monarchy. She allowed the nobles to retain their privileged positions as long as they served the state. In 1766, Catherine gave the nobles the right to exile rebellious peasants to Siberia (an extremely cold region in northern Russia). This harsh treatment produced several violent uprisings during her reign, and her government savagely suppressed them.

Catherine seemed to be an enlightened reformer. She encouraged education and corresponded with some of the notable scholars of her day. However, though she supported certain social reforms, she was an absolute monarch at heart. Catherine demonstrated this motivation by being the first Russian monarch to formally institute government censorship. She also weakened the Russian Orthodox Church by transferring church property to the government. In addition, Catherine forced Russians to westernize, following the example of Peter the Great.

In foreign affairs, Catherine continued Russia's expansion program, particularly at the expense of the Poles and the Turks. One of her major territorial goals was to secure additional seaports. During Catherine's reign, the Russians seized some territory on the north shore of the Black Sea from the Turks. The goal of later Russian czars to control the Black Sea and compete in Mediterranean trade became an important issue in international diplomacy.

Catherine II

Section Review

1–3. What three countries followed the example of France and came under absolutist rule?

4. What Austrian ruler sought to create an absolutist state by attacking the church and nobility?

5. How did Peter the Great propose to get Russia in step with the rest of Europe?

6. Why did Russia seek to control territory along the Black Sea?

★ Appraise Frederick William I's absolutist view of his power, as exhibited in his statement "Salvation belongs to the Lord; everything else is my business."

★ How did Catherine the Great uphold or violate biblical standards of justice? Evaluate her use of power.

III. Absolutism Defeated in England

Unlike the other countries, England did not become an absolutist state. English kings had to contend with Parliament, which over the centuries gradually increased its power and refused to surrender its hard-won rights. Of special significance was its right to grant or deny a king's request for additional revenue.

During the sixteenth century, the Tudors worked with Parliament to gain their desired goals. They relied on skillful politicians to advise them, and they remained sensitive to public opinion. As a result, they were able to control parliamentary legislation. During the last years of Queen Elizabeth's reign, however, tension began to grow between Elizabeth and Parliament. At issue was whether the crown or Parliament should have the ultimate responsibility for directing government policy.

Since Elizabeth was the last surviving member of the Tudor dynasty, she made sure to name a successor. Her choice was King James VI of Scotland, the son of Mary Stuart. Although Elizabeth had ordered Mary to be beheaded for treason (see p. 251), her selection of the Stuart family to take the throne of England was not surprising. James was Elizabeth's cousin and her closest living relative. Parliament, therefore, invited James to become the king of England after Elizabeth's death. When James (r. 1603–25) became the king of England, he took the title **James I** because England had never had a king by that name.

James made very clear from the beginning of his reign that he expected everyone to conform to the Anglican Church. On one occasion, he told the Puritans that if they did not cooperate, he would "harry them out of the land." True to his threat, James harassed those who refused to compromise their religious convictions. However, a small group of Separatists escaped James's persecution. Known as the Pilgrims, they settled in Holland for several years then sailed to the New World in search of a land where they could practice their religious beliefs without government opposition.

Not all of James's problems were religious. In addition to leading a scandalous private life, he spent government money extravagantly and relied on personal favorites rather than veteran politicians to give him political advice. James believed he was king by "divine right"—a fact that Parliament did not dispute. But Parliament did

Guiding Questions

1. How was absolutism rejected in England?
2. How did governmental power differ in France and England?

James I

Charles I

question the extent of his authority and was angered by the high-handed manner in which he governed the kingdom.

Since James had financial problems, he was forced to call Parliament into session and ask for additional funds. But each time Parliament met, it debated James's foreign and domestic policies. This so infuriated him that he dismissed the House of Commons time after time. "That which concerns the mystery of the King's power is not lawful to be disputed," James had said. The only thing that his hasty actions accomplished, however, was to unite his opponents against him.

James's son, **Charles I** (r. 1625–49), inherited his father's views. Charles's policies intensified the tension between the king and Parliament. During his reign, the persecution of the Puritans became more severe, causing thousands of them to leave the country and sail to the American colonies.

Like his father, Charles wanted to be an absolute ruler but did not have the army or the bureaucracy to enforce his will. When he convened Parliament, many of its members proved to be quite uncooperative. They demanded that the king recognize their rights to free speech and freedom from arrest. Charles responded to their request by dismissing them. Later, he reconvened Parliament, but when they repeated their demands, he dismissed them once again.

In need of funds, Charles was forced to recall Parliament a third time. Angry with the king, members of Parliament devised a document called the **Petition of Right** (1628). Among other things, it stated that the king did not have the right to make people pay taxes without Parliamentary consent and that Parliament would not tolerate arbitrary imprisonment of any subjects. They informed Charles that if he refused to sign the document, they would not grant him any additional funds. Charles signed the petition, but when Parliament made further demands, he dismissed them once again. From 1629 to 1640 he sought to govern England without calling Parliament into session by using every means possible to raise money apart from Parliament. Charles sold knighthoods, forced various individuals to lend him funds, and established high taxes on shipping. In the process, however, he succeeded in alienating merchants and landowners.

In spite of everything Charles tried to do, he had to recall Parliament when Scotland rebelled against him. His agents had tried to force the Scottish church to use the Anglican prayer book, and the Scots responded by raising an army to defend their religious liberties. In a very weak position, Charles was ready to make concessions to Parliament. He was forced by financial necessity to sign various acts that greatly strengthened Parliament's power. These acts guaranteed (1) that Parliament would meet every three years, even without royal permission; (2) that Parliament could not be dissolved without its own consent; and (3) that no taxes were legal except those passed by Parliament. In addition, Parliament abolished those royal courts that had become tools of Charles's absolutist policy.

In the following months, the Puritans in Parliament also demanded an end to episcopal church government and criticized the formalism of the Anglican prayer book. At the same time, Parliament extended its political power by placing the military under its control. Realizing that his power was slipping away, Charles decided to act.

In January 1642, he marched into the House of Commons with four hundred armed men. Charles demanded that five of his harshest critics be arrested. These men, however, could not be found. They had escaped from the chamber only minutes before. Charles's rash behavior in this regard only further antagonized Parliament.

Each side began gathering an army, and before the year was over, war had erupted. The Puritans, the lesser gentry, and the merchants supported Parliament's cause. Their opponents called them **Roundheads** because most of them had short hair. Most members of the nobility as well as the Anglicans supported the king. The Roundheads called them **Cavaliers**—a reference to the Spanish soldiers, the *cavaliero*, who had killed many Protestants in Europe.

Initially, the king's forces were victorious. But when Parliament reorganized its army and removed incompetent leaders, the New Model Army, as it was called, gained the upper hand. Under the able leadership of **Oliver Cromwell** (1599–1658), the Roundheads defeated Charles at the Battle of Naseby (1645). This defeat proved to be the deathblow to the Royalist cause, and Charles surrendered eleven months later.

The victory of Parliament's forces did not bring an immediate end to England's problems. The leaders of Parliament and the commanders of the army disagreed over how the new government should be run. Not all who had opposed the king wanted to destroy the monarchy; many simply wanted to limit the king's power. Leaders of the parliamentary army, however, envisioned a republic where every man would have equal opportunities and privileges. They saw nothing wrong with replacing England's longstanding political traditions to attain that end.

When the conservatives (those who wanted only to curb Charles's power) in Parliament realized that the war had gone further than they had intended, they tried to dissolve the army. The army, however, refused to disband. Its forces occupied London and expelled several conservatives from the House of Commons. In 1648, the conservatives who remained in Parliament made an alliance with Charles, who had just escaped from captivity and was willing to make several concessions to regain his throne. However, Cromwell's army easily put down all resistance. Cromwell's forces recaptured Charles and expelled some 140 conservative members from the House of Commons, leaving a governing body of less than one hundred men. (At the beginning of the civil war, the House of Commons had more than five hundred members.) The remaining members, together known as the Rump Parliament, set up a special court that tried and condemned the king for treason. On January 30, 1649, officials beheaded Charles I.

The next eleven years (1649–60) were a time of experimentation in new forms of government in England. Cromwell, the leader of the army, had no program for governing the country. Consequently, he ruled by trial and error. At first, he and the "Rump" governed jointly, but problems soon arose. Cromwell found, just as Charles I had before him, that it was very difficult to rule with an independent-minded Parliament. So Cromwell dissolved Parliament and ruled without it until his death in 1658.

Taking the title Lord Protector, Cromwell established what is called the **Protectorate**. He ruled in accordance with a written constitution, the Instrument of Government. Although his rule was sometimes arbitrary, he was a man of deep religious conviction who

A cavalier

Oliver Cromwell

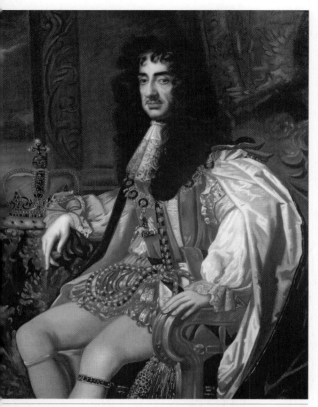

Charles II

tried to do what he thought was best for the people. Nevertheless, the Protectorate came to an end soon after Cromwell's death. His son Richard succeeded him as Lord Protector, but he did not have the same forceful personality or leadership ability that his father had. In addition, most Englishmen were dissatisfied with the country's political condition. They wanted the Stuart monarchs to return to the throne.

Sensing the sentiment of the people, Richard allowed the Parliament that Charles I had called in 1640 to reconvene. The members in turn asked Charles's son to take the throne. He accepted their offer, and in 1660 England had a new king—**Charles II** (r. 1660–85).

The reestablishment of the Stuart monarchy is called the **Restoration**. In reality, the old monarchy was not restored because Parliament retained much of the power it had won earlier. In 1679, for example, Parliament again passed the **Habeas Corpus Act** (first passed under Charles I), which made it illegal for the government to arbitrarily hold someone in jail. By obtaining a writ of habeas corpus, a prisoner could force the government to officially charge him with a crime or release him. This act meant that English monarchs could no longer imprison a person simply for being critical of their policies. Juries could issue verdicts without fear of being imprisoned for rendering unpopular decisions, and the press could openly criticize royal policy.

Although his power was limited, Charles II did his best to remain financially independent of Parliament. He received monetary grants from Louis XIV in return for promises to support the objectives of French foreign policy. Charles also told Louis that he would publicly declare himself a Roman Catholic. But despite his promises, Charles did very little that really helped France, and he did not profess Roman Catholicism until he was on his deathbed.

The Whigs and the Tories

As the English Parliament grew in power and influence, factions developed within its ranks. These competing groups became the forerunners of Britain's first political parties—Whigs and Tories.

Following the Restoration, Parliament became sharply divided over the policies of Charles II. Some members disliked the favoritism he showed toward the Roman Catholics and France. Others were opposed to the idea of having the throne pass to the Roman Catholic James, duke of York. The leader of this opposition, the Earl of Shaftesbury, realized that if he could influence a majority of votes in Parliament he could control the government and the king. His group became known as the Country Party.

Another group consisted of those who considered the person of the king and his rightful heir to be sacred. Led by the king himself, this group became known as the Court Party. It came into open conflict with the Country Party when Charles did not produce a legitimate son. Those opposing the succession of James introduced a bill into Parliament excluding him from the throne.

The fight over this bill became intense, with the Court Party defeating its passage. In the debates, each side called the other side names. Those against James were called "Whigs"—a name applied to Scottish robbers who killed their victims before plundering them. Those supporting James were called "Tories"—a name applied to Irish rebels. Soon

the opposing parties adopted these nicknames as their official titles.

Once the matter of Protestant succession to the throne had been settled by an act of Parliament, the two parties shifted their attention to other issues. The divisions between them were never as sharp again. The Tory Party continued to favor the king and the Anglican Church and to oppose great change in the status quo. The Whigs were now willing to support the king, but they favored a policy of religious toleration and were eager to see certain changes made in government policy. Although the Whig Party faded away, the Tory Party has continued to the present.

Since Charles II had no legitimate children, he was succeeded by his brother **James II** (r. 1685–88). James was an ardent Roman Catholic and a firm believer in absolutism. In spite of his tactless actions, Parliament decided to tolerate him since he was old and his only heirs were two Protestant daughters. But the political picture changed dramatically in 1688, when James's second wife, a Roman Catholic, gave birth to a son. Members of Parliament feared that absolutism would be reestablished and England would be forced back into the Roman Catholic Church.

In June 1688, leaders of Parliament invited William of Orange (the Protestant leader of the Netherlands and husband of James's daughter Mary) to come to England and take the throne. William accepted the invitation and landed in England with a small Dutch army. Many Englishmen rallied to support him. When James tried to send his troops against William, he found that even his officers had deserted to the other side. Having no other recourse, James fled to France with his wife and son. The House of Commons declared that "King James II, having endeavored to subvert the constitution of the kingdom by breaking the original contract between king and people, and by the advice of Jesuits and other wicked persons having violated the fundamental laws, and having withdrawn himself out of the kingdom, has abdicated the government, and that the throne is vacant." The House added that "it hath been found by experience to be inconsistent with the safety and welfare of this Protestant kingdom to be governed by a popish prince."

William III

Mary II

The Bill of Rights

The English struggle for rights and liberties goes all the way back to 1215 when King John signed the Magna Carta at Runnymede. The Bill of Rights (1689) is a landmark of English constitutional history. It marked the first time that the demands on the monarch were made on behalf of a representative assembly. Among the ancient rights and liberties declared in the Bill of Rights are the following:

That the pretended power of suspending of laws or the execution of laws by regal authority without consent of Parliament is illegal.

That it is the right of the subjects to petition the king, and all commitments and prosecutions for such petitioning are illegal.

That the raising or keeping a standing army within the kingdom in time of peace unless it be with consent of Parliament is against law.

That the subjects which are Protestants may have arms for their defence suitable to their conditions and as allowed by law.

That election of members of Parliament ought to be free.

That the freedom of speech and debates or proceedings in Parliament ought not to be impeached or questioned in any court or place out of Parliament.

That excessive bail ought not to be required, nor excessive fines imposed, nor cruel and unusual punishments inflicted.

England had undergone a "bloodless" or **Glorious Revolution** when Parliament dethroned James II. Parliament then invited **William and Mary** to become joint rulers of England. Their reign marked the only time in England's history that the country had corulers.

However, before Parliament officially granted the throne to William and Mary, it established a set of conditions that had to be met. Those conditions were embodied in a document called the **Bill of Rights** (1689), which limited royal power, established certain civil liberties, and forbade future kings or queens from being Roman Catholics. William and Mary accepted Parliament's conditions and were crowned William III (r. 1689–1702) and Mary II (r. 1689–94).

In 1701, Parliament passed the **Act of Settlement**, which had far-reaching consequences for the English crown. By this act, Parliament decided who could occupy the throne. The concept of kings ruling by divine right had passed away. England had become a nation ruled by constitutional law—that is, law established by tradition and acts of Parliament.

After the reign of Mary's sister, Queen Anne (r. 1702–14), the throne passed to a German, George of Hanover (a descendant of James I). Because the new king, who took the title of George I (r. 1714–27), could not speak English, he had to rely on others to carry out many of the responsibilities of government. During his reign and the reign of his successor, George II (r. 1727–60), the cabinet system of government developed in England.

Cabinet government first began during the reign of Charles II, who often called his closest advisers to his office—called a "cabinet"—to discuss matters of state. George I, who had little interest in political matters, did not attend cabinet meetings. He left the affairs of government in the hands of his chief minister, Robert Walpole, whom historians consider to be the first prime minister of England. Executive powers gradually shifted from the king to the chief ministers of the king's cabinet. Later, the prime minister and the cabinet, who were originally responsible only to the king, became accountable to Parliament.

Robert Walpole

Section Review

1–2. What body in England competed with the monarchy for authority? What special privilege did that body hold over the monarchy?

3–4. Contrast the Tudors' and the Stuarts' relationship with Parliament.

5–6. What English king was beheaded during the English Civil War? Who was the leader of the Roundheads, the parliamentary forces?

7. Who came to the English throne as a result of a "bloodless" revolution?

8. What did the English Bill of Rights accomplish?

★ Why was England able to reject royal absolutism?

IV. Balance of Power

To increase their power on the Continent, some European monarchs used their armies to seize the territories of weaker nations. Each ruler watched his neighbors closely, ensuring that they did not become too strong. Nations formed alliances in an effort to preserve the balance of power, thereby hoping to ensure that no one nation would dominate the other countries of Europe. When they felt it was necessary, they went to war to maintain this balance. Because war often demonstrated new strengths and weaknesses in nations, many shifts in diplomatic alliances resulted. Countries that had previously been enemies often became friends, and nations that were once allied squared off against each other. Despite the many changes in alliances during the eighteenth century, Prussia remained the constant foe of Austria, and England was always aligned against France. The three major wars of this period demonstrated the workings of this system of alliances.

War of the Spanish Succession (1702–13)

In 1700, the Habsburg king of Spain died, leaving no direct heir to the Spanish throne. In his will he granted the throne to his young grandnephew Philip, who was also the grandson of Louis XIV of France. Louis, seeing an opportunity to make political and territorial gains, claimed the Spanish throne for Philip. Other nations in Europe—especially England and the Netherlands—feared what the union of France and Spain might bring. They formed the **Grand Alliance** to block Louis's actions.

The armies of the Grand Alliance won many victories on the European continent. At Blenheim in 1704, they almost wiped out the French force. In 1705, England captured Gibraltar, a post on the southern tip of Spain. The English also fought the French in North America in what was called Queen Anne's War. The war ended in 1713 with the signing of a series of agreements called the **Treaty of Utrecht**, which included the following provisions:

1. Philip was allowed to retain the throne of Spain as long as the crowns of France and Spain were not united.

2. Spain had to surrender its possessions in the Netherlands and in the Mediterranean area to Austria.

3. Britain won various Canadian territories from France: Newfoundland, Nova Scotia, and the Hudson Bay territory. In

Guiding Questions

1. What was the significance of the balance of power in Europe?

2. What were the outcomes of the War of the Spanish Succession and the War of the Austrian Succession?

3. What caused the Seven Years' War, and what was the result?

addition, Britain kept the strategic Mediterranean port of Gibraltar. (During the war, England and Scotland were united into a single kingdom called Great Britain. From that time, it has been proper to speak of Britain rather than England.)

War of the Austrian Succession (1740–48)

"Because a Monarch robbed a neighbor he had promised to defend, red men scalped each other by the Great Lakes of America, while black men fought on the [Indian] coast of Coromandel." Thus did British historian Thomas Macaulay describe the War of the Austrian Succession—a conflict that spread to three continents.

In 1713, the emperor of Austria, Charles VI, wrote a document called the **Pragmatic Sanction**. It was designed to prevent Austria's neighbors from taking advantage of his daughter, **Maria Theresa**, once she came to the Austrian throne. The rulers who signed the document agreed to respect the territorial boundaries of Austria, allowing Maria Theresa to rule in peace.

One ruler who had no intention of honoring the agreement that his father had signed was Frederick II of Prussia. He desired the rich mining area of Silesia, which belonged to Austria, and decided to seize it. In August 1740, after Maria Theresa had been empress for only two months, Frederick invaded the province. By the following year, Prussia had firmly established its hold on Silesia and had signed a peace treaty with Austria.

The situation in Europe became more complicated when France entered the war against Austria, hoping to gain territory at Austria's expense. Spain also entered the war to retrieve the Italian lands it had lost to Austria in 1713. Britain then entered the war on the side of Austria to neutralize French power and the Prussian threat to George II's Hanoverian domains.

Maria Theresa

The war was not confined to the European continent, however. It spread to North America, where the British defeated the French, and to India, where the French defeated the British. Weary of war, the nations of Europe finally decided to end the conflict and signed the **Treaty of Aix-la-Chapelle** in 1748. This treaty did not settle the differences among the nations; it merely ended the fighting temporarily. Except for Silesia, which Frederick was allowed to keep, the treaty restored the *status quo ante bellum* (how things were before the war).

Seven Years' War (1756–63)

A complex series of events in several countries expanded into what became known as the Seven Years' War. In 1754, fighting (called the French and Indian War) erupted between France and Britain in the New World as forces representing these two nations began to struggle for control of key trade areas. At the same time, Frederick II decided to take some more of Austria's territory. He assumed that France would not interfere, because France and Austria had been bitter enemies for centuries. Neither did he fear British reprisals since he had just signed a defensive alliance with Britain in January 1756. But Frederick miscalculated. France unexpectedly reversed its foreign policy. Fearing the growing threat of Prussia's might, France put aside its old antagonism for the Austrian Habsburgs and joined Austria to stop Prussian expansion. This radical change in alliances, called the **Diplomatic Revolution**, set the stage for the **Seven Years' War**.

Soon after the fighting broke out, the British statesman **William Pitt** the Elder devised a system for winning the war. His strategy called for supplying Prussia financial aid and using that nation to keep French troops preoccupied in Europe. Meanwhile, Britain would attempt to destroy French sea power, making it easier to defeat the French in North America and India.

Britain had tremendous success with its part of the plan. In North America, it had more than forty thousand regular and colonial troops. By the end of the war, these troops had seized many French forts and had captured the key French city of Quebec. In India, British forces under the leadership of Robert Clive defeated the French and the Indian princes who had allied with them.

On the continent of Europe, however, Prussia ran into difficulties. Open hostilities began when Frederick II invaded the neighboring kingdom of Saxony. He soon found himself surrounded by enemies. Russia, Sweden, most of the German states, and Spain had joined France and Austria in opposing Prussia. At first, Frederick's superior army and his brilliant leadership kept his enemies at bay. But his opponents outnumbered him, and although he won battles, he despaired of ever winning the war. In addition, when George III became the new British monarch in 1760, he eliminated all subsidies to Prussia. By the end of that year, the Russian army had burned Berlin, and all seemed lost. Frederick and Prussia, nevertheless, survived the conflict because Russia dropped out of the war. In 1762, a new czar who greatly admired Frederick II came to the throne. He withdrew his troops from Prussian territory and signed an agreement with Frederick. Unable to continue without Russian support, Frederick's other opponents withdrew from the conflict one by one.

William Pitt the Elder

Europe (1763)

The Treaty of Hubertusburg (1763) brought the war to a close on the continent of Europe and allowed Frederick to maintain his hold on Silesia.

In that same year, France, Britain, and Spain signed the **Treaty of Paris**. This settlement had a number of important consequences.

1. France lost all territory on the mainland of North America. Britain acquired all of Canada and French territory east of the Mississippi.

2. France lost most of its commercial holdings in India. The Battle of Plassey (ch. 19) paved the way for the British East India Company to eventually take over all of India.

3. Spain lost Florida to Great Britain but received New Orleans and Louisiana from France in return.

As a result of the Seven Years' War, Great Britain became not only the leading European power but also a world power.

The Partition of Poland

The balance of power was not always maintained by war; sometimes diplomatic negotiations proved to be more effective. One such case in the eighteenth century involved Poland, which was a large, independent nation that lacked natural boundaries by which its people could easily defend their territory. In addition, the Polish government was weak and inefficient. Neighboring countries—Prussia, Russia, and Austria—plotted to gain parts of Poland, but each ruler knew that the moment he tried to seize the territory he wanted, the others would step in to stop him. So through secret negotiation, these countries agreed to partition Poland among themselves. On three separate occasions during 1772–95, Prussia, Russia, and Austria seized Polish territory until Poland finally disappeared from the map of Europe. Not until after World War I did Poland again exist as an independent nation.

Partition of Poland

Section Review

1. What did European monarchs seek to preserve to ensure that their neighbors did not become strong enough to threaten their borders?

2–3. What two major events led to the War of the Spanish Succession?

4–5. What country and monarch was the Pragmatic Sanction designed to protect?

6. What is the dramatic change in alliances among the major European powers before the Seven Years' War called?

7–9. List the three countries that divided defenseless Poland.

 ★ Why was the Pragmatic Sanction unsuccessful?

 ★ Analyze Louis XIV's decision to claim the Spanish throne.

Making Connections

1–2. How did Cardinal Richelieu strengthen the power of the French king? (Give two ways.)

3–4. How did Peter I and Catherine II strengthen their authority at the expense of the Russian Orthodox Church?

5–7. Give the name of the ruling family in each of the following countries: Prussia, Austria, and Russia.

8. Why did the English people restore the monarchy following the death of Cromwell?

Developing History Skills

1. Assess the significance of the Peace of Westphalia on the history of Europe.

2. Evaluate the historical significance for France of the Revocation of the Edict of Nantes.

Thinking Critically

1. Assess the rule of Louis XIV in light of Proverbs 16:12.

2. Contrast the governmental development in France and England during this period.

Living in God's World

1. Aristotle lists three forms of government: monarchy (rule by one), aristocracy (rule by several of the best men), and polity (rule by the many under a constitution) along with their perversions—tyranny, oligarchy, and democracy. Of these three forms he says monarchy is the best and constitutional government the worst, but of the perversions he says democracy is the least evil and tyranny the most. Do Aristotle's observations align with Scripture? Explain.

2. If you were the tutor for one of the young absolute monarchs mentioned in this chapter, what form of government would you advocate as the best? Base your answer on Scripture and on your answer to the previous question.

People, Places, and Things to Know

absolute
divine right
Henry IV
Cardinal Richelieu
Thirty Years' War
Gustavus Adolphus
Peace of Westphalia
Louis XIV
Jules Mazarin
Jean-Baptiste Colbert
Versailles
Louis XV
Frederick William
Frederick II
Hohenzollern
Joseph II
Ivan IV
czar
Romanov
Peter I
Great Northern War
Catherine II
James I
Charles I
Petition of Right
Roundheads
Cavaliers
Oliver Cromwell
Protectorate
Charles II
Restoration
Habeas Corpus Act
James II
Glorious Revolution
William and Mary
Bill of Rights
Act of Settlement
cabinet government
Grand Alliance
Treaty of Utrecht
Pragmatic Sanction
Maria Theresa
Treaty of Aix-la-Chapelle
Diplomatic Revolution
Seven Years' War
William Pitt
Treaty of Paris

15

Galileo Galilei before the Holy Office in the Vatican

Big Ideas

1. What was the significance of the Scientific Revolution?

2. Is Enlightenment thought biblical?

3. What role did religion play in the Enlightenment?

4. How did the arts reflect the Age of Reason?

When God created man in His image, He gave him (among other things) the gift of reason. Because of sin, however, man's understanding is darkened, and he is filled with spiritual blindness (Eph. 4:18). Only by the entrance of God's Word into the heart can a person receive light and understanding (Ps. 119:130). During the seventeenth and eighteenth centuries (known as the **Age of Reason**), some individuals used reason under the authority of Scripture to expose errors in theology and philosophy while defending biblical truth. But for many, this era marked a shift. Rather than using reason as a help to understand God's Word and His world, people tended to view reason as the supreme authority by which everything, including God's Word, must be tested. In this chapter we will examine the effects of these two attitudes on science, philosophy, religion, and the arts.

I. Scientific Revolution

Causes of the Scientific Revolution

During the Middle Ages, most Europeans relied on two principal authorities for their understanding of the universe: ancient philosophers and church tradition. The tendency was to passively accept the validity of what the ancient philosophers or the Roman Church taught, rather than seek to uncover new knowledge about God's world. However, a growing number of scholars advocated experimentation and observation. As a result, some medieval scientists made careful annotations and conducted experiments that led to the development of new technologies, including the magnetic compass, mechanical clocks, and lenses. These scientific advances prepared the way for the greater scientific discoveries that would follow.

The intellectual atmosphere in Europe continued to develop during the sixteenth century. The Renaissance had rekindled a desire for learning, and the Reformation had reasserted the Bible as the trustworthy authority for man's understanding. Thoughtful individuals had discovered errors in church tradition and in the writings of ancient philosophers. Realizing they could no longer accept blindly what the Roman Catholic Church had to say about the Bible, these individuals searched out the truths of God's Word for themselves. Similarly, since they could no longer depend on what ancient philosophers taught about God's universe, scientists sought out the laws of nature for themselves. In coming years some men would seek to pit science and reason against Scripture, but others would find in science a means of glorifying God: they would examine the handiwork of His creation and find practical knowledge to help their fellow man.

Scientific Advancements

From the Renaissance to the eighteenth century, scientific inquiry and achievement advanced so rapidly that historians often speak of a scientific revolution. This "revolution" greatly increased man's knowledge of the physical universe. Old myths and legends were discarded as men discovered the principles that God established to govern His creation.

Astronomy

Astronomy, the study of celestial bodies, is an ancient science. The magi of Matthew 2:1–12 might have been astronomers. Until

Guiding Questions

1. What were the key causes of the Scientific Revolution?
2. Who were the significant figures of the Scientific Revolution, and what were their contributions?
3. How did medieval scientific thinking compare with early modern scientific thinking?

Nicolaus Copernicus

the sixteenth century, astronomers usually relied on the theories of the ancient Greek geographer Ptolemy. He taught that the entire universe revolves around the earth—a theory known as the geocentric, or "earth-centered," theory. The changes that came with the Scientific Revolution transformed astronomy, radically altering it as a science.

The Polish astronomer Nicolaus **Copernicus** (kuh PUR nih kus; 1473–1543) questioned Ptolemy's theory of the universe. Copernicus, who did not have a telescope to study the heavens, used instruments such as the astrolabe to measure the position of stars and planets in the skies. He found that the movements of heavenly bodies would be difficult to explain if the earth were the center of the universe. Therefore, he concluded that the sun is the center and that the earth and other planets orbit around it. This view is called the **heliocentric** (sun-centered) **theory**. While many Roman Catholic churchmen embraced the geocentric (earth-centered) theory, others encouraged Copernicus to publish his findings. However, Copernicus's work convinced few to abandon the geocentric theory in his lifetime.

The noted German astronomer **Johannes Kepler** (1571–1630), a Lutheran, did not fear the threats of the Roman Catholic Church. Although he agreed with Copernicus that the earth revolves around the sun, he disagreed with him on the nature of the orbit. Copernicus had taught that the orbits of the planets are circular. Kepler, however, found that the orbits are elliptical (oval-shaped). A devout Christian, Kepler prayed that God would keep his investigations free from personal bias: "I ask God to make my spirit strong so that I direct my glance at the pure truth, from whichever side it should be presented, and do not let myself be misled, as so often happens today, by the admiration or contempt of persons or sides."

The best-known astronomer in history is probably the Italian **Galileo Galilei** (GAL-uh-LAY-oh GAL-uh-LAY-ee; 1564–1642). Galileo made important contributions to other scientific fields as well—notably physics. As a young man, he observed a lamp swinging in the Pisa cathedral. As he watched, he wondered if there was a regular rhythm to the swing. After repeated experiments with pendulums, he found that though he increased the size of the arc, the pendulum still swung in rhythm; therefore, he suggested the use of the pendulum to measure time. The results of his work can be seen today in timepieces such as the grandfather clock.

(above) *Galileo Galilei;* (right) *Galileo's telescope*

Galileo improved on a Dutch invention, the telescope, and used it in his own work. He confirmed the heliocentric theory and agreed with Kepler that the planets move in elliptical orbits. When Galileo published his findings, however, he came into conflict with some of the hierarchy in the Roman

Comets

Until well into the sixteenth century, most people had a superstitious fear of comets. In fact, from ancient times people viewed them as evil omens. Even as late as 1556, Thomas Digges, an English mathematician and astronomer, wrote, "Comets signify corruption of the stars. They are signs of earthquakes, of wars, of changing of kingdoms, great dearth of corn, yea, a common death of man and beast."

Since disastrous events sometimes coincided with the appearance of a comet, such superstitions persisted. The Roman emperor Vespasian believed that a comet seen in AD 79 was an evil sign, but he supposedly remarked, "This hairy star does not concern me; it menaces the king of the Parthians [Rome's enemy], for he is hairy and I am bald." Yet it was Vespasian who died in AD 79, and in that same year an eruption of Mount Vesuvius buried the cities of Pompeii and Herculaneum. Thus, the course of events reinforced some people's fear.

In 1066, another comet appeared in the sky, greatly alarming the English Saxons. They had just experienced the death of their king, Edward the Confessor, and wondered what else the year had in store for them. In October, the Saxons were defeated at the Battle of Hastings, and King Harold was killed. William of Normandy became the new ruler of England.

The comet that had appeared in 1066 was the same one that Englishman Edmund Halley viewed in 1682. Halley's observation and study indicated that the comet moved around the sun in an elliptical orbit. He further calculated that it appeared regularly, approximately every seventy-five years. When the comet appeared again in 1758 as Halley had predicted, astronomers appropriately named it Halley's Comet. It reappeared in 1835, 1910, and 1986; its next appearance should be in 2061.

Catholic Church. This conflict was due to many factors, including political intrigue and competing church factions. To end this controversy, church officials told Galileo that he would be excommunicated if he did not retract his contention that the earth moved. Kneeling before the inquisitors, he publicly retracted, but according to legend, as he rose from his knees he muttered, "But it does move!"

The same year that Galileo died, **Isaac Newton** (1642–1727) was born in England. Like Galileo, he was an astronomer who also contributed to several other fields, such as physics and mathematics. For example, he demonstrated with a prism that "white light" is actually composed of many different colors. With his invention of the reflecting telescope and his development of calculus, Newton was able to make more accurate observations and to apply mathematics to the study of the universe.

We remember Newton best for his discovery of the laws of gravity. According to a story related by the French philosopher Voltaire, Newton once observed an apple falling from a tree. Intrigued, he wondered why objects fall. From his observation and experimentation, he formulated his famous theory of gravitation. He explained not only why objects fall to the ground but also how planets are held in their orbits by the pull of gravity. Newton expressed these ideas in his greatest work, *Principia*, published in 1687. His contributions won him the esteem of his day; English poet Alexander Pope praised his achievements: "Nature and nature's Laws lay hid in Night: / God said, 'Let Newton be!' and all was light."

Isaac Newton

Medicine

While astronomy led the way for scientific development in the Age of Reason, there were also many important discoveries in other fields. The study of medicine, which involved the practical application of many discoveries, was greatly affected by the Scientific Revolution.

Andreas Vesalius

In 1543, **Andreas Vesalius** (vuh SAY lee us; 1514–1564) of Flanders published his great treatise on human anatomy, *On the Fabric of the Human Body*. He gained information for this monumental work from the dissection of cadavers (corpses). By examining the actual structure of the human body, Vesalius disproved many ridiculous ancient theories, such as the idea that the heart contained a bone. With a clearer understanding of how the human body functions, doctors were better able to treat illness and disease. For his contribution to science, Vesalius has been called the Father of Anatomy.

Swiss-born P. A. T. Bombast von Hohenheim (1493–1541) made the first clinical study of disease and established the use of chemicals in the treatment of illness. He became better known by his self-given name, **Paracelsus** (PEHR uh SEL sus), which means "better than Celsus," a famous Roman physician. Paracelsus suggested that since the human body is chemical in nature, chemicals should be used to treat disease. Although not all of his prescriptions were safe or effective, he advanced the science of medicine.

The Englishman **William Harvey** (1578–1657), called the Father of Experimental Biology, also prepared the way for modern medicine. He carefully studied the heart and the circulation of blood. Ancient theory held that both the heart and the liver prepared different kinds of blood, which were sent to the different parts of the body to be consumed. Harvey discovered that the heart alone acts as a pump, pushing blood through the arteries and the veins; thus, blood is not "consumed" but constantly circulated.

Another Englishman, **Edward Jenner** (1749–1823), developed the smallpox vaccine. Jenner's work is a model of the scientific method. First, he observed that milkmaids who contracted the disease cowpox did not contract smallpox, a dreaded disease that kills or horribly disfigures its victims. Jenner speculated that if a person

Edward Jenner inoculating his child

were inoculated with the fluid from a cowpox sore, he would then become immune to smallpox. Jenner tested his theory by inoculating a boy with cowpox, from which the child contracted only a mild case. Later, he inoculated the same boy with smallpox. The child did not contract that disease. Jenner called his method of inoculation against disease "vaccination" after the Latin word *vaccinia*, meaning "cowpox." Today, because of Jenner's work, smallpox has been nearly wiped out.

Chemistry

The modern concepts of chemistry developed from the medieval so-called science of alchemy. Despite some abuses, alchemists handed down a legacy of lab techniques and functional equipment with which to conduct experiments. The alchemists' approach to experimentation also laid the foundation for the modern scientific method. In their day, Newton, Boyle, and Francis Bacon would have been considered alchemists. However, these men and many others made significant scientific contributions.

Irishman **Robert Boyle** (1627–91) was the first to publish the law of inverse gas pressure. Boyle found that increasing pressure on a gas reduces its volume whereas decreasing the pressure causes the volume to expand. Scientists call this principle Boyle's law. In addition to studying chemistry, Boyle, who was a dedicated Christian, diligently studied the Bible. He lectured in defense of Christianity and sought to refute those he termed "notorious infidels." He even left money in his will so that these lectures could be continued after his death.

English Unitarian minister and chemist **Joseph Priestley** (1733–1804) discovered several important chemical substances: ammonia, oxygen, nitrous oxide (better known as "laughing gas"), hydrochloric acid, and carbon dioxide, among others. Modern carbonated beverages owe their existence to his work with carbon dioxide.

Robert Boyle

Priestley, who was influenced by his friend Benjamin Franklin, also performed experiments with electricity.

The Father of Modern Chemistry was Frenchman **Antoine Laurent Lavoisier** (luh VWAH zee ay; 1743–94). He used logical rather than fanciful terminology for chemicals. For example, he named one substance *hydrogen* ("water former") because it forms water vapor when

Joseph Priestley

Antoine Laurent Lavoisier and his wife

mixed with air. Lavoisier also formulated the law of conservation of matter, which states that matter cannot be created or destroyed; it only changes form.

Contributions in Other Scientific Fields

Many other scientists contributed to the Scientific Revolution. Anton van Leeuwenhoek (LAY vun hook; 1632–1723) of the Netherlands greatly improved the microscope by making lenses that could magnify up to 160 times. With such lenses he discovered the existence of microbes and bacteria. Gerhardus Mercator (mur KAY tur; 1512–94) from Flanders devised a way to map the earth on a flat surface. Today the Mercator projection, as it is called, is still a standard pattern for mapmaking.

Effects of the Scientific Revolution

The Scientific Revolution resulted in a dramatically improved understanding of the natural world, and researchers discovered how to develop many natural resources. This resulted in improved medicines, a healthier society, and an improved quality of life for an increasing number of people.

Attitudes during this period reflected a decline of respect for the past and previous learning. Instead, many assumed an attitude of superiority, given the newfound discoveries and significant advances in many areas.

Many academic and scientific leaders also moved away from accepting the Bible as a valid source of knowledge and wisdom. In its place they promoted the false premise that human problems were largely technical in nature and solvable through science and technology alone.

Section Review

1–2. What were the two principal authorities for truth during the Middle Ages?

3–4. What Polish astronomer challenged the theory of an earth-centered universe? What is his view called?

5. What contribution did Edward Jenner make to the field of medicine?

6. Who is the Father of Modern Chemistry?

✶ How did alchemy contribute to the development of modern chemistry?

✶ Compare and contrast medieval and early modern scientific thinking.

II. The Enlightenment

Scientific discoveries prompted philosophers to apply the scientific method to both their study of mankind and their search for truth. In doing so, they placed such a strong emphasis on the power of human reason that this period of history is known as the Age of Reason. It culminated in an eighteenth-century intellectual movement called the **Enlightenment**.

Philosophers of the Enlightenment looked to human reason as the solution for all of life's problems. They praised reason for making possible the achievements of science and providing new approaches to learning. Reason, they believed, was the gateway to human progress. No longer was reason considered just a method of gaining knowledge; these philosophers believed it was the only sure source of knowledge and truth—an attitude known as **rationalism**.

Enlightenment View of Reason

Approaches to Learning

New approaches to learning aided the expansion of knowledge during the seventeenth century. Two methods of reasoning—the inductive and the deductive—assisted scientists in their investigation of the physical world and aided philosophers in their quest to understand that world.

Inductive Reasoning

One of the leading advocates of the inductive method of reasoning was English philosopher Sir **Francis Bacon** (1561–1626). In his important work *Novum Organum*, he criticized the manner in which many ancient and medieval philosophers arrived at their conclusions about the natural world. Their hasty generalizations, he asserted, created great obstacles for later generations. Believing that people must get rid of all false ideas before they can arrive at truth, Bacon questioned all existing knowledge. He advocated the use of careful observation and experimentation before arriving at general conclusions. Scientists, he asserted, should form tentative conclusions and then gather more information to verify their results. Such reasoning—from specific cases to a general conclusion—is called the **inductive method**.

Bacon believed that man, using this rational approach, could discover and understand truth. Likewise, he could dispel superstition and error. Many of Bacon's contemporaries, however, objected to his insistence that all knowledge should be questioned. They considered his method an assault on religion. Bacon answered this charge: "If the matter be truly considered, natural philosophy is, after the word of God, at once the surest medicine against superstition and the most approved nourishment for faith; and therefore she is rightly given to religion as her most faithful handmaid, since the one displays the will of God, the other is his power." Sadly, less than a century later, people exalted reason as the highest authority, placing it above faith in God and His Word.

Deductive Reasoning

Another method of gaining knowledge was advanced by the French philosopher and mathematician **René Descartes** (day KART; 1596–1650). He feared that people could be deceived by their senses and that observation and experimentation were therefore unreliable. While Bacon let observation and experience guide his reason, Descartes relied on reason aided by the methods of mathematics. Like Bacon, however, Descartes believed that every false idea and prejudice had to be discarded before one could arrive at truth. This led him to doubt everything. The first step in his system of thought was to find some truth or idea that could not be doubted. No one, he believed, could doubt that man is a thinking being, capable of understanding truth. Thus he began his quest for truth with the premise, "I doubt, therefore I think; I think, therefore I am." On this premise he built his system of thought. He taught that

Sir Francis Bacon

René Descartes

John Locke

Baruch Spinoza

Pantheism and the Word of God

The Bible teaches that God is everywhere (Ps. 139:7–10; Jer. 23:24), but it also teaches that God is distinct from His creation (Col. 1:17; 3:1–2). However, pantheists do not recognize God as a personal being. Instead, they think of Him as an abstract system of truths. As a result, pantheists reject, among many truths revealed in God's Word, the biblical concept of God as a heavenly Father.

by starting with such a simple premise, through careful logic, people could arrive at another, more complex truth. This system is called the **deductive method** of reasoning.

Another influential philosophy of the seventeenth century was empiricism. Empiricism—the idea that all knowledge comes through experience—was the philosophy of Englishman **John Locke** (1632–1704). Locke rejected the idea that God has implanted certain truths within each person from birth. Instead, he maintained that the mind of a baby is like a blank tablet on which the experiences of life are written. Thus Locke argued that given the right experiences and education, a child would grow into the right kind of person. He rejected the doctrine of original sin, choosing to believe that humans are basically good. Locke agreed that divine revelation is vital but denied that it could contradict man's reason.

The questions that these philosophers were raising were not new. They had been discussed by philosophers and theologians throughout the Middle Ages. The difference was that these philosophers now believed that their own reason or their own experience carried more authority than Scripture.

Enlightenment View of Reality

Inductive and deductive reasoning were vital elements of the scientific method, helping scientists to understand the natural world. But could these same reasoning processes be applied to the study of man and society? Through reason, could man comprehend the spiritual realm? And what was the relationship between the physical and spiritual worlds? Philosophers of the seventeenth century sought answers to these questions.

From a man-centered perspective, Descartes constructed a system of philosophy known as *dualism* (*dual* meaning "two"). According to Descartes, there are two types of reality: mind (the spiritual world) and matter (the physical world). While Descartes admitted that there are certain spiritual truths (such as the existence of God) that reason cannot discover, he taught that people can discover truths about the physical world only by using reason. In fact, Descartes emphasized reason so strongly that he stated, "We should never allow ourselves to be persuaded of anything except by the evidence of our reason."

Another philosopher who emphasized the importance of reason was **Baruch Spinoza** (spih NO zah; 1632–77). Spinoza was one of the first Bible interpreters to demand that reason judge whether Scripture passages are true or not. He also taught that the Bible was a historical book without relevance to the present. Instead of the biblical distinction between God and His creation, Spinoza taught that everything in the universe, whether spiritual or physical, is all part of one great substance called "god." This view is called *pantheism*.

Enlightenment View of Government

The scientific discoveries and philosophic ideas of the seventeenth century gave rise to a spirit of optimism in the eighteenth century as men looked to their own reason as the hope for the future. The eighteenth-century French writers and social critics known as the *philosophes* (FIL uh SOFS) became the most prominent spokesmen of the so-called enlightened attitude. These men were more than mere thinkers; they were social reformers. They openly challenged established values and institutions in hope of conforming society to their ideas. They contended that certain religious beliefs restricted a person's freedom to think and express himself. They championed a secular society, religious toleration, freedom of speech, and the natural rights of all people. The *philosophes* mistakenly believed that the right philosophy could solve society's problems and that perfectibility was attainable for both society and man.

Locke

Political reform became one of the chief concerns of the eighteenth-century *philosophes.* Many of the French writers were influenced by the political ideas of John Locke. He advanced the idea that people possess certain natural and unalienable rights—rights that cannot be transferred or surrendered. In his *Two Treatises of Government*, Locke stated that the basis of government is the consent of the governed. People enter into a social contract with government; if government violates the people's trust, the people have a right to change their government.

Montesquieu

Locke's ideas, which were advanced as a justification of the Glorious Revolution in England, inspired the *philosophes.* Among those influenced by his rational defense of natural rights and his promotion of the idea that men could change their government was the Frenchman Baron de **Montesquieu** (MAHN tes kyoo; 1689–1755). He believed that England symbolized political freedom. The liberty of the English, he concluded, resulted from the separation of the three powers of government: the executive, the legislative, and the judicial. Montesquieu's political theory had a great impact on the framers of the Constitution of the United States.

Montesquieu

Voltaire

The leading figure of the Enlightenment was François-Marie Arouet, better known as **Voltaire** (vawl TEHR; 1694–1778). He used his clever wit to criticize other people. As a young man, Voltaire was thrown into prison for insulting a French noble. Later he was banished from France. He went to England, where he became an admirer of the ideas of Isaac Newton and John Locke. The atmosphere of intellectual freedom that he found in English society made a strong impression on him.

Voltaire became an outspoken critic of the abuses in society, especially political and religious intolerance. As a result, he learned to hate organized religion and advocated deism. Voltaire was also a popular champion of freedom of the press. His cutting wit made him a favorite in many aristocratic and scholarly circles. However, Voltaire's scathing attacks on the arbitrary rule of kings and nobles resulted in his being forced to flee country after country.

Voltaire

Rousseau

Another *philosophe*, **Jean-Jacques Rousseau** (roo SOH; 1712–78), was a friend to the other philosophes but was out of step with most of them because he favored emotion and sentiment above reason. He has often been called the Father of Romanticism. Rousseau's slogan "back to nature" also set the pattern of thought for the

Jean-Jacques Rousseau

Mary Wollstonecraft: Enlightenment Thinker

In her most famous work, *A Vindication of the Rights of Woman*, Mary Wollstonecraft proposed an Enlightenment solution to the mistreatment of women in eighteenth-century England. She correctly identified many societal problems stemming from unbiblical views of women and male/female relationships, but her solution was also unbiblical: the elevation of reason. Her work, in large part, was a critique of Rousseau's *Emile*. Rousseau described his view of the proper role of women: to be taught by men and to be useful to them. Wollstonecraft vehemently disagreed, arguing that reason elevates humans above the animal kingdom. Therefore, to expect women to be silly and uneducated except in the art of flirtation is to degrade them to the level of an animal. Though Wollstonecraft was correct in her critique and correct in promoting the education of women, her solution was too closely tied to Enlightenment rationalism.

first half of the nineteenth century, which was called the Romantic Age (see chapter 17).

Rousseau also became an influential political writer. He believed people are born free and should be able to do whatever is in line with the general will. Rousseau also believed in the basic goodness of humanity. Personal liberty and order in society, he contended, would come as people freely obeyed the laws of society. In his work *The Social Contract*, he maintained that government should be built on and should carry out the "general will" of the people. By "general will" Rousseau meant majority rule. Unlike most political thinkers of his day, he favored a democracy rather than a representative government or an absolute monarchy. Rousseau's political ideas influenced leaders of the nineteenth-century political movements that advocated popular participation in government.

Section Review

1. Which English philosopher was one of the leading advocates of the inductive method of reasoning?

2–3. What name is given to the idea that everything in the universe is part of one substance called "god"? Who was the leading advocate of that philosophy?

4–5. What were the most prominent spokesmen of the "enlightened" attitude called? What country were they from?

6. What aspect of English government did the French philosopher Montesquieu credit as aiding political liberty?

★ How did Enlightenment proponents view reason, reality, and government?

★ Assess John Locke's view of mankind in light of Romans 3:23.

III. Religion and the Enlightenment
Enlightenment View of Religion

Many scientists and philosophers of the Enlightenment put their faith in reason instead of in God's revelation, the Bible. Though they did not deny the existence of God, they refused to accept orthodox Christianity because it did not conform to their new ideas. They tended to reject the supernatural, ridiculing both the miraculous and prophetic elements in Scripture. They also denied the fact that humans are born in sin, believing instead that they are basically good. Reason was their standard of truth: it was their guide to understanding the universe and the proper way to worship God. On other points their views differed significantly, but they are generally called **deists**.

Differences Among Deists

"The term 'deist' had a wide application, and scholars have frequently disputed the definition of the term. Perhaps it would be best to speak of 'deisms,' since [there was great diversity of views]. Despite family resemblances, their views diverged significantly. Some deists . . . doubted the immortality of the soul, but others . . . considered this essential. [Some] thought that rewards and punishments in a future life were fundamental to faith, while [others] regarded them as dubious. Most deists believed that moral principles could be derived from abstract reasoning, but [other deists] scoffed at this notion. [Some] held that people were innately benevolent, while [others were] just as convinced that they were controlled by self-interest. [Some deists were] materialist while . . . most other deists believed in a soul. Most deists believed in human free will, though [some] denied it. It is not surprising that some refer to the 'elusiveness of deism' and regarded the word as a label of convenience rather than a precise term of analysis. According to one interpretation, the decline of the deists' influence was due to this very diversity and the conspicuous failure to arrive at a consensus in identifying the 'rational' or 'self-evident' principles of religion."

McClymond and McDermott, The Theology of Jonathan Edwards, *52–53.*

Many deists viewed the universe as a machine. God was its First Cause, or Grand Architect. They believed that He designed the universe as a self-sustaining mechanism and established the natural laws by which it operates. Most deists asserted that once God had finished Creation, He no longer intervened in human affairs. To many deists, God was merely an impersonal being, much like a clockmaker who, having made a clock and wound its spring, sat back and let it run.

Most deists had little use for a personal God or His salvation. They asserted that the truths of religion could be discovered naturally. They believed that a virtuous life guided by human reason would be rewarded in the life to come. Despite these boastful claims, deism was built on mere human wisdom. The Bible warns against such error in 1 Corinthians 2:5, 14, and 16.

Rise of the Evangelical Movement

Not everyone living in the Age of Reason trusted in human wisdom as the only way to find truth. Many people realized that although science could improve man's standard of living, it could not improve man; neither could man through his own wisdom understand the things of God. Genuine enlightenment came as men discovered the truth of God's Word and submitted to it.

Guiding Questions

1. What was the Enlightenment view of religion?
2. How did the evangelical movement develop?
3. How did the evangelical movement differ from the Enlightenment view of religion?

This spiritual enlightenment produced several revivals that changed the lives of men and women and altered the moral climate of the countries where these revivals occurred. As a result, Christian groups in parts of Europe and the American colonies rejected the false premise that a purely intellectual knowledge of Christ or simply belonging to a church resulted in salvation. Instead, they proclaimed that true repentance of sin and faith in Christ alone made one a child of God. These believers emphasized that Christians should live holy lives in conformity to God's Word while also seeking earnestly to bring others to salvation.

Pietism in Germany

In the seventeenth century, a movement known as **Pietism** arose in Germany. (The word *pietism* originated in 1689 as a term of ridicule for those who gathered for Bible study.) By the middle of the century, much of the Lutheran Church had experienced significant spiritual decline. Although there were exceptions, many of the clergy, often poorly trained and sometimes unconverted, neglected the spiritual needs of their people. Their dull, lifeless sermons produced no change in the unconcerned attitudes of many church members.

In the midst of this spiritual decline, a Lutheran minister in Frankfurt named **Philipp Spener** (SHPAY nur; 1635–1705) became burdened for his congregation. Realizing that those who had experienced personal conversion needed close Christian fellowship, Spener organized special meetings in his home for Bible study and prayer. In addition, he published his famous work *Pia Desideria* ("Pious Wishes"), in which he outlined the failures of the church and issued a call for spiritual renewal. Though many church officials attacked his ideas, concerned Christians throughout Germany followed his example and organized themselves into groups known as *collegia pietatis* ("assemblies of piety").

As the movement continued to grow, **August Francke** (FRAHNG keh; 1663–1727), a professor at the University of Halle, became a leader in the training of Pietist pastors and missionaries. Through his efforts, student lay preachers carried the gospel throughout Germany, and mission works were established in the American colonies and India. In addition to his teaching responsibilities, Francke helped establish and supervise an orphanage, elementary and secondary schools, and a Bible-printing organization. In all, he established twenty-one different types of educational institutions that emphasized godliness and Christian wisdom. Though persecuted by various civil and religious authorities, he temporarily turned Halle into the most influential center of German Pietism.

Count **Nikolaus von Zinzendorf** (TSIN tsen DORF; 1700–1760) was a student under Francke at Halle. Later, Zinzendorf left the Lutheran Church and became the leader of the Moravians. This group, which began in Bohemia and Moravia during the time of John Huss, had almost disappeared by the eighteenth century. In 1722, however, a small group of Bohemian refugees settled on Zinzendorf's estate in Germany and established a religious community which they called Herrnhut ("Lord's Lodge"). From this humble beginning, the movement grew as zealous Moravian missionaries traveled around the world, not only preaching the gospel but also seeking to unite all Christians. It was through the Moravians that John Wesley came to a personal assurance of salvation.

Nikolaus von Zinzendorf

The Moravians became one of the first Protestant movements to stress missions. When there were no more than three hundred occupants of Herrnhut, the Moravians began to send out missionaries. As their group increased, they continued to send as many as one quarter of their members as missionaries to North America (to the Indians), the Caribbean islands, Greenland, South Africa, and as far as Australia.

The Pietists did much good work for the Lord, but they also had a significant weakness. They elevated personal experience over sound doctrine as found in Scripture. At first they simply assumed sound doctrine, but the next generation emphasized experience without teaching doctrine. The third generation then followed the spirit of the age in looking to their own experience and reason as authorities since scriptural doctrinal authority had been minimized. This led to the confusing situation of many liberals who descended from Pietists but denied key beliefs of the Christian faith that were characteristic of early Pietists.

Methodism in England

By the eighteenth century, interest in spiritual matters had almost disappeared in England. Throughout the country, most Anglican clergy sought personal comfort and ease and seemed interested primarily in secular pursuits. Smaller denominations also became complacent. As a result, few pastors preached salvation by grace through faith, and moral corruption seemed to worsen with every passing year. Nevertheless, during the eighteenth century a mighty spiritual awakening shook Great Britain as God blessed the preaching of faithful men.

John Wesley

Probably the best known of these preachers is **John Wesley** (1703–91). During his lifetime, he traveled about 250,000 miles on horseback and preached approximately 42,000 sermons. Ordained as an Anglican minister in 1728, Wesley returned to Oxford University as a student and joined a club that his brother Charles had helped to establish. Although many of this "Holy Club" were unconverted at the time, they tried to live righteous lives. They met often for mutual encouragement. Many students mocked their methodical lifestyle and often referred to them derisively as "Methodists"—a term that Wesley's converts later gladly accepted.

Conversion—In 1735 Wesley sailed to the American colony of Georgia to be a missionary to the Indians and to serve as pastor in the town of Savannah. During the voyage and then later in Savannah, however, Wesley came into contact with some Moravians, who impressed upon him his own spiritual need. Though he had tried to live a good life, he realized that something was lacking. Wesley records in his journal that soon after he arrived in Georgia, the head of the Moravian settlement there spoke to him:

> "Do you know Jesus Christ?" I paused, and said, "I know He is the Saviour of the world." "True," replied he; "but do you know He has saved you?" I answered, "I hope He has died to save me." He only added, "Do you know yourself?" I said, "I do." But I fear they were vain words.

Because of conflicts with some of the colonists, his ministry in America soon failed. As he returned to Great Britain, he wrote in

John Wesley

Susanna Wesley (1669–1742)

Susanna Ann Wesley was born in London on January 20, 1669. Although her father was a Nonconformist minister (Protestant who did not conform to the governance of the Church of England), Susanna later joined the Anglican Church. Samuel Wesley, whom she married in 1689, was also reared in the home of a Nonconformist minister. Later, however, he too joined the established church and became an Anglican minister.

For almost forty years, Samuel and Susanna served the rural parish of Epworth in Lincolnshire. Samuel devoted his time to scholarly pursuits while Susanna managed the household and reared the children. (She had nineteen children, nine of whom died in childhood.) Although she carefully budgeted the family's meager income, the Wesleys were always poor and often in debt. Furthermore, their house burned twice and had to be rebuilt.

Since poverty prevented her sons from attending school until they

were about twelve years old (there were no schools for girls), Susanna taught all of her children at home. As soon as a child could talk, she taught him to pray and to memorize Scripture. Realizing that her busy schedule made it difficult to spend sufficient time with each child individually, Susanna set aside a special time in the evenings for each of them. After he had left home, John Wesley wrote to his mother that he would give anything to be able to spend Thursday evenings (his special time) with her again.

Though Susanna Wesley never achieved earthly wealth or fame, she reared two sons who by God's grace brought revival to eighteenth-century Great Britain. She said of her life, "I am content to fill a little space if God be glorified." The space she filled as a dedicated Christian mother was certainly glorifying to God.

his journal, "I went to convert the Indians; but O! who shall convert me?" Back in London, he contacted some Moravians, and on May 24, 1738, "went very unwillingly" to one of their meetings on Aldersgate Street

> where one was reading Luther's preface to the Epistle to the Romans. About a quarter before nine, while he was describing the change which God works in the heart through faith in Christ, I felt my heart strangely warmed. I felt I did trust in Christ, Christ alone, for salvation; and an assurance was given me that He had taken away my sins, even mine, and saved me from the law of sin and death.

Ministry—After his conversion, Wesley began to travel throughout the British Isles, preaching as often as four times a day. He once wrote, "I look on all the world as my parish." Since most Anglican churches soon closed their doors to him, he began to preach to large crowds in the open air and saw many conversions. Opposition to his preaching increased, however, and on numerous occasions he faced stone-throwing mobs, hostile clergymen, and unsympathetic civil officials. Yet his ministry never faltered. He rose daily at 4:00 a.m. and often preached his first sermon of the day as early as 5:00 a.m. On one occasion when he was seventy, he spoke to thirty thousand people, and all heard him clearly. At eighty, he still traveled four to five thousand miles a year to meet his preaching responsibilities.

Although Wesley did not intend to leave the Anglican Church, he is considered the founder of the Methodist Church. He originally planned for the Methodist societies, which his converts had organized, to remain within the church like the *collegia pietatis* in Germany had remained within the Lutheran Church. The Anglican hierarchy, however, refused to ordain Wesley's lay preachers. Ultimately, the Methodist societies were forced to leave the Anglican Church. When Wesley died, the Methodists had 630 lay preachers and about 175,000 members.

The work of Wesley and others like him had a tremendous impact on Great Britain. Spiritual revival broke the apathetic attitudes among professing Christians and led to domestic reform and foreign missions. The revival also improved the nation's moral condition—helping to restrain the type of social upheaval that soon engulfed France (see chapter 16). In addition, the spiritual awakening stimulated an interest in Christian education, led to the establishment of the first Sunday schools, and encouraged the production of good Christian literature and music.

George Whitefield

One of John Wesley's contemporaries was a dynamic evangelist named **George Whitefield** (WHIT feeld; 1714–70). The son of a tavern keeper, Whitefield had played a leading role at Oxford, along with Charles Wesley, in founding the group that became known as the Methodists. Whitefield was converted in 1735 and was ordained an Anglican minister the following year. Whitefield also traveled constantly and preached the gospel wherever he went. When he and the Wesleys were excluded from preaching in Anglican churches, Whitefield encouraged the Wesleys to follow his example and preach wherever people tended to gather. He not only preached throughout Great Britain with great results but also crossed the Atlantic seven times on preaching tours in the American colonies. Whitefield was used of God to play a substantial role in the Great Awakening in America.

George Whitefield

Awakening in the American Colonies

During the first half of the seventeenth century, many Puritans fled Great Britain and settled in the American colonies. For several years, the spiritual zeal of these colonists remained strong, but by the end of the seventeenth century their descendants were no longer fervent for the Lord. During the eighteenth century, George Whitefield summarized the condition of the American churches this way: "I am verily persuaded, the generality of preachers talk of an unknown, unfelt Christ. And the reason why congregations have been so dead, is because dead men preach to them."

During 1740–42, as the Methodist revival progressed in the British Isles, America experienced the climax of a tremendous spiritual harvest known as the **Great Awakening**. Through the preaching of Whitefield and other traveling evangelists, thousands of people heard the message of salvation. The real key to the long-term spiritual success of the Great Awakening, however, lay with local pastors who ministered faithfully to the needs of their own congregations.

One such pastor, whose name is inseparably linked with the Great Awakening, is **Jonathan Edwards** (1703–58). A brilliant young man who graduated from Yale at the age of seventeen, Edwards used his considerable talents to further the cause of Christ.

Jonathan Edwards

Foundations for Modern Hymnody

From the Reformation until the eighteenth century, English Protestants did not use hymns in their church services. Instead, they sang rhymed settings of the Psalms, believing that church music should be drawn directly from Scripture. Many of these psalm settings, however, were poorly written and hard to sing. Determined to improve the music in his own congregation, a minister named Isaac Watts (1674–1748) began to write hymns. Although at first many Protestants of all denominations rejected this "innovation," Watts persevered in his efforts. He is known today as the Father of English Hymnody.

Watts believed that hymns should be doctrinally sound and easily understood. Sometimes he paraphrased a psalm; for example, "O God, Our Help in Ages Past" is based on Psalm 90, and "From All that Dwell Below the Skies" is based on Psalm 117. On other occasions, he composed hymns that were based upon a particular scriptural theme, such as "When I Survey the Wondrous Cross." In everything he wrote, Watts tried to direct the worshipers' attention to Christ.

Churchgoers in the early eighteenth century did not have hymnals; therefore, the pastor or someone else had to read the lines of the psalm or hymn aloud. After each line was read, the congregation would sing it, and then the reader would proceed to the next line. Therefore, Watts ensured that each line of his hymns made sense when read by itself.

Joy to the world! the Lord is come;
Let earth receive her King;
Let every heart prepare him room,
And heaven and nature sing.

Although Watts laid the foundation for English hymnody, Charles Wesley (1707–88) popularized hymn singing in Great Britain. Like his brother John, Charles traveled as an evangelist, but his health forced him to retire early. He settled down to a pastoral ministry and continued to write hymns; by the time he died, he had written more than six thousand.

Charles Wesley is considered the greatest English hymn writer. With his hymns, he sang the Methodist revival into the hearts of the people and helped strengthen them in Christian doctrine. Whereas Watts's

hymns are formal and reserved (reflecting the age in which he lived), Wesley's are filled with emotion. For example, Watts wrote,

Come, sound his praise abroad
And hymns of glory sing;
Jehovah is the sovereign God,
The universal King.

Wesley, on the other hand, penned the following words on the first anniversary of his conversion:

O for a thousand tongues to sing
My dear Redeemer's praise,
The glories of my God and King,
The triumphs of His grace!

Wesley wrote hymns to fit every occasion, including Christmas hymns ("Hark! the Herald Angels Sing"), Easter hymns ("Christ the Lord is Ris'n Today"), and communion hymns. He also wrote hymns of praise, comfort, and contemplation. In all of his compositions, however, he emphasized primarily the theme of love. For example, "Jesus, Lover of My Soul" and "Love Divine, All Loves Excelling" proclaim the love of Christ. Many of Wesley's hymns also highlight the themes of grace, light, and joy.

In 1729 he succeeded his grandfather as pastor of the Congregational Church in Northampton, Massachusetts. Through his sermons and books, he advocated the need for personal conversion. He was a diligent lifelong student, often studying thirteen hours a day and writing works of great theological and philosophical depth.

Probably the most famous sermon Edwards preached was "Sinners in the Hands of an Angry God," delivered in 1741 at Enfield, Connecticut. Basing his sermon on the phrase "their foot shall slide in due time" (Deut. 32:35), Edwards warned his unrepentant hearers that only God's mercy kept them from instantly plunging into hell:

O sinner! consider the fearful danger you are in. . . . Are there not many here who have lived long in the world, and are not to this day born again? . . . Therefore, let every one that is out of Christ now awake and fly from the wrath to come.

As Edwards preached, the Spirit of God brought such conviction on the congregation that people began to cry out, "What shall I do to be saved?" Many people began to weep. In fact, the noise became so loud that Edwards had to stop preaching several times and urge the people to be quiet that he might continue his sermon. As a result of that sermon, many of the unsaved in Enfield came to salvation.

This incident is only one example of the spiritual awakening that swept through the American colonies. Although many political and social benefits derived from the Great Awakening, the most significant results were spiritual. A large number of the colonists were converted. For example, in New England alone, which had a population of 300,000, between 25,000 and 50,000 people were converted, and 150 new churches were established. Christians became concerned about mission work and made renewed efforts to reach the American Indians with the gospel. In addition, several groups established schools for the training of Christian ministers. The Presbyterians, for example, established the College of New Jersey, which later became Princeton University. In spite of several denominational splits, the revival also helped to draw together Christians of various denominations in a bond of fellowship and cooperation in winning the lost. This Great Awakening was the first of several revivals that were to come to America over the next two centuries.

Section Review

1–2. What aspects of biblical Christianity did some Enlightenment philosophers and scientists reject? What became the new religion of the Age of Reason?

3–5. List three major Pietist leaders in Germany.

6–7. Name two men who founded the Methodists.

8. What was the name of the spiritual revival in America that climaxed in the 1740s?

✷ Why do deists reject miracles?

✷ How could Pietism lead to rationalism? How can truly pious people avoid following the same dangerous path?

IV. Artistic Reflection

Between the Renaissance and the Enlightenment, Europe underwent great social, political, religious, and intellectual changes. These changes produced tension and restlessness among the people of Europe. But with the coming of the Enlightenment, doubt and uncertainty gave way to an emphasis on order and restraint. The values, attitudes, and concerns of these historical periods are reflected in their architecture, painting, music, and literature.

The Baroque Age in Art

The doubts and contradictions of the sixteenth century and the new ideas and discoveries of the seventeenth century found expression in two styles of art: mannerism and baroque. These styles illustrate different aspects or moods of the troubled and changing times.

Mannerism was the artistic style that was prevalent throughout much of the sixteenth century. It reflected the political and religious tension of the Reformation era. Unlike Renaissance artists, mannerist artists did not strive for realism and balance. Instead, their works are filled with distortions and exaggerations: colors are often unnatural or clashing, and the human form is often distorted. An

Guiding Questions

1. What characterizes the baroque and neoclassical styles?
2. Who were significant artists and musicians during the classical and neoclassical periods?

outstanding painter in this style was El Greco (1541–1614), a Greek who settled in Spain. His figures have elongated bodies and limbs. He often created a mystical atmosphere with dramatic and sharply contrasting colors.

The art of the seventeenth century captured the mood of the time and is as varied as the personalities of the artists who created it. This new style was called baroque, a term probably originating from a Portuguese word meaning "an irregularly shaped pearl." The term, originally used in a negative sense, refers to the period in art history that stretches from 1600 to about 1750. (Nineteenth-century art critics regarded the art of the seventeenth century as theatrical, deformed, and too ornamental.)

The Agony in the Garden of Gethsemane *by El Greco*

Left wing of St. Peter's Square at the Vatican, designed by the architect Bernini.

The Hippopotamus and Crocodile Hunt *by Rubens*

The baroque style is grand, dynamic, heroic, active, swirling, sensual, and emotional. It engages the complete attention of the viewer. It includes everything from the ornate façades (fronts) of buildings to beautiful fountains; from gigantic canvases that seem to reach out and include the viewer to arrogant portraits; and from dazzling church domes to lofty, painted ceilings that seem to reveal views of paradise. The baroque style originated primarily as an architectural style and soon spread to painting, sculpture, and music.

Christ in the Storm on the Lake of Galilee *by Rembrandt*

The Baroque Age in Music

Like baroque art, baroque music expresses the vigor of the seventeenth and early eighteenth centuries. Many of the adjectives that describe baroque art apply to baroque music, which broke with

Claudio Monteverdi
(opera)

George Frideric Handel
(opera, oratorio)

Johann Sebastian Bach
(religious music)

past tradition, initiating a radical departure from the music of the fifteenth and sixteenth centuries.

The Classical Age in Music

The classical age in music covers the period from 1750 to the early 1800s. Classical music turned from the elaborate style of J. S. Bach to an elegant style that showed precision, clarity of composition, and emotional restraint. The main types of compositions—sonatas, concertos, string quartets, and symphonies—reflected the order and balance of the Enlightenment. This music became a popular pastime among the aristocracy and the rich middle class. In addition, a new instrument, the piano, became a favorite, and many wealthy people even had one in their homes.

Franz Joseph Haydn   *Wolfgang Amadeus Mozart*

Section Review

1. What artistic age spanning from 1600 to 1750 is characterized by its grand, heroic, sensual, and emotional style?

2. Who designed the colonnades at St. Peter's Square?

✶ Contrast baroque art with mannerist art.

✶ Contrast baroque and classical music.

Making Connections

1–2. Distinguish between inductive and deductive reasoning.

3–5. How did the Wesley/Whitefield revivals positively impact Britain and the American colonies? (List three.)

Developing History Skills

1. Evaluate the spiritual impact of the tiny Moravian movement on many areas of the world.

2. Summarize the political ideas of the Enlightenment that influenced the formation of government in the United States following the War for Independence. Include the source of each idea.

Thinking Critically

1. Assess the accuracy of the following statement: "Science is a trustworthy method for gaining knowledge."

2. Hymns, such as those written by Watts or Wesley, play what role in a church service?

Living in God's World

1. How should you as a Christian respond to someone who puts his own reason or his own experience in the place of final judge of what is true and false?

2. Choose a biblical doctrine (look at a basic theology book), do some reading and Bible study about it, and pray about the doctrine. Thank God for it (be specific). Confess any sins that you have done related to it. Make requests to God based on that doctrine. Then write a brief paragraph describing how meditating on a doctrine has affected your relationship with God.

People, Places, and Things to Know

Age of Reason
Copernicus
heliocentric theory
Johannes Kepler
Galileo Galilei
Isaac Newton
Andreas Vesalius
Paracelsus
William Harvey
Edward Jenner
Robert Boyle
Joseph Priestley
Antoine Laurent Lavoisier
Enlightenment
rationalism
Francis Bacon
inductive method
René Descartes
deductive method
John Locke
Baruch Spinoza
Montesquieu
Voltaire
Jean-Jacques Rousseau
deists
Pietism
Philipp Spener
August Francke
Nikolaus von Zinzendorf
John Wesley
George Whitefield
Great Awakening
Jonathan Edwards

Coronation of Napoleon and Joséphine

Big Ideas

1. What was the outcome of the American struggle for liberty?

2. What led to the destruction of the Old Regime in France?

3. What contributed to the rise and fall of Napoleon?

During the Enlightenment, men asserted that God had provided political liberty. Thomas Jefferson stated, "The God who gave us life gave us liberty at the same time." Enlightenment philosophers claimed that man was endowed with certain "natural rights," the most cherished being the rights to life, liberty, and personal property. But in the eighteenth century, few people enjoyed these rights; ecclesiastical and political absolutism was the order of the day. The desire for personal and political liberty, however, prompted a series of revolutions.

This chapter contrasts two eighteenth-century revolutions: the American and the French. While both were influenced by the Enlightenment, the American Revolution was a conservative movement tempered by the Protestant background of many of the colonists. Americans attempted to preserve time-honored traditions of religious and political liberty. The French Revolution, on the other hand, became radical. The French sought to overthrow the power of a corrupt monarchy, aristocracy, and church. Like many later revolutions, the French Revolution did not establish liberty but led to social upheaval and dictatorship.

I. American Struggle to Preserve Liberty
Colonial Liberties

Unlike the French and Spanish settlements in the New World, English settlements were primarily formed by individuals and groups seeking freedom. These people sought to escape oppression, poverty, and absolutist governments. Some people, of course, sought adventure; others sought wealth. Many of the early settlers, however, came to the New World seeking a haven from religious persecution in Europe. At great personal cost, they left their homelands for a wilderness where they hoped to begin a new life—a life grounded in religious and political liberty.

In 1620, a group of English Separatists called **Pilgrims** set sail for America. They sought a land where they would be free to worship God without government opposition. Though they had been granted permission to settle in the Virginia Colony, navigational errors and storms forced them north to Massachusetts. There they settled and founded the Plymouth Colony. From the outset, the Pilgrim leaders realized the need for discipline to maintain order among themselves because they knew that unrestrained liberty leads to anarchy. While still aboard the *Mayflower*, they drafted a temporary agreement called the **Mayflower Compact**, establishing civil authority for the Plymouth Colony.

> Having undertaken, for the glory of God, and advancement of the Christian faith, and honor of our king and country, a voyage to plant the first colony in the northern parts of Virginia, [we] do by these presents [witnesses] solemnly and mutually in the presence of God, and of one another, covenant and combine ourselves together into a civil body politic, for our better ordering and preservation and furtherance of the ends aforesaid; and by virtue hereof to enact, constitute, and frame such just and equal laws, ordinances, acts, constitutions, and offices, from time to time, as shall be thought most meet and convenient for the general good of the colony, unto which we promise all due submission and obedience.

Guiding Questions

1. Why did Europeans come to the New World?
2. How did the American colonies gain independence from Great Britain?
3. What is the significance of federalism and popular sovereignty?

The United States (1775–1800)

Legend:
- Original Thirteen States
- Territories and Added States
- British (after 1783)
- Spanish (after 1783)
- Disputed Territory
- X BATTLES

Ten years after the Pilgrims landed at Plymouth, a steady migration of Puritans crossed the Atlantic. They too longed for a land where they could freely practice their religion. In 1630, under the leadership of Governor John Winthrop, more than one thousand Puritan men and women settled in New England—most in Boston. Like the Pilgrims, these Puritans believed that they had been sent on a divine mission. They sought to establish an ideal state based on biblical principles. The purpose of government, they believed, was to promote piety and restrain evildoers. The state was to assist (not interfere with) the church in molding godly character in the community. But their ideal society eventually failed as later Puritan generations professed but did not possess the Christian faith of their parents and grandparents. Nevertheless, Puritan morality and theology had a great impact on the culture of the American colonies.

In addition to the Pilgrims and Puritans, other Englishmen settled along the North American coastline. They were joined by Irish, Scottish, German, Dutch, Swedish, and French settlers. As the number of colonies grew, so did their differences. Distinctions developed—the natural result of the wide variety of geographic and climatic conditions within the colonies. Each section—from the New England colonies to the middle colonies and down to the southern colonies—developed its own lifestyle and trade pattern; each had a unique appeal for immigrants of different religious and vocational backgrounds.

Even with their diversity, many American colonists shared a common European background and a Protestant heritage. In spite of the colonies' different types of organization, their forms of government were remarkably similar. That similarity often resulted from a common respect for English law and a desire for local self-government.

British Restrictions

Until 1763, English colonists living in America under the authority of the British crown and Parliament enjoyed great freedom and prosperity. But after a series of wars that culminated in the French and Indian War (see chapter 14), the direction of Britain's policy toward its colonies changed. Britain was faced with the development of a worldwide empire that was neither planned nor organized. Furthermore, it was nearly bankrupt because of the cost of the wars with France. Britain therefore expected its colonies to "pay their own way" by making financial contributions to the mother country in exchange for the benefits Britain provided.

Between 1763 and 1774, Parliament passed a series of new laws placing restrictions on colonial trade. The colonists protested while remaining loyal to both king and country. They recognized that Britain provided a bulwark of defense against French and Spanish designs on the West and unfriendly Indians on their frontiers. Furthermore, their objections were not primarily related to the amount of taxes they had to pay because they paid very little in comparison to their English relatives. So what was the cause of their protest? After enjoying nearly 150 years of noninterference, the American colonists resented the new parliamentary measures as an invasion of their internal affairs. They believed that Parliament had overstepped its authority and had violated the colonial charters. These charters specified that all powers of taxation rested with the colonial assemblies, not with the houses of Parliament. Thus the issue was not the amount of the taxes but who should levy and collect taxes. "No taxation without representation" became a popular rallying cry in the colonies.

In December 1773, colonial opposition to parliamentary acts escalated to action. Under the cover of night, a group of colonials dressed as Indians dumped a shipload of tea into Boston Harbor to protest a new tax on tea. In response to the Boston Tea Party, Parliament closed the port of that vital colonial city to all shipping. Other laws reduced colonial liberties in Massachusetts. Martial law was imposed, and the colonists were forced to house and financially support the British troops sent to enforce the unwanted edicts of **George III**, their monarch, and Parliament. The colonials viewed such acts as intolerable.

Another act that alarmed the colonists was the Quebec Act. Parliament extended special privileges to the territory of Quebec, a former French colony, by granting favored status to Roman Catholicism and reinstating French law. The colonists perceived this act as a dangerous precedent that could pose a threat to their religious and political freedom.

The American colonists protested these acts and expected to see these new laws repealed since previously Parliament had backed down after firm colonial resistance. But now the louder the colonial protest grew, the more British troops arrived to enforce the decrees of the king and Parliament. A growing number of colonists viewed armed resistance as the only option to defend their homes from the British troops sent to oppress them. They began to stockpile munitions in the event that such resistance proved necessary. When the British learned of one such stockpile, they sent troops to destroy it. Along the way, these troops encountered colonial militiamen, and two skirmishes ensued at Lexington and Concord near Boston in April 1775. Thus began a war that neither side had planned or desired.

American Independence

Attitude Toward War

Colonists who resisted the British did so reluctantly, reservedly, but purposefully. Many did not seek a rebellion or a war. Nevertheless, they believed that their English rights had been violated, and many refused to bow to parliamentary pressure, despite the threat of military force. But not all colonists favored armed resistance against Britain. Though they disliked British interference in colonial matters, these colonists remained loyal subjects.

The Christians in the colonies were also divided in their views of resistance. Many believed that they should be loyal to their elected representatives in the colonial legislatures. Therefore, when their elected representatives called for opposition to the edicts of Parliament and king, those Christians were able to support the colonial cause in good conscience. Other Christians, however, believed that their first loyalty lay with the British government in London. When war began, many of them sided with Britain.

Before fighting erupted, few colonists had thoughts of separating from Britain. But as fighting continued, the mood among the colonists gradually changed. Their cause became a struggle to preserve their freedom and to secure independence from Britain. This spirit was clearly stated on July 4, 1776, in the **Declaration of**

Forcing Colonists to House British Troops

To punish the people of Massachusetts for the Boston Tea Party, the British government forced the colonists to quarter (house) British troops in their homes. This was a violation of the English Bill of Rights, which complained about the king "raising and keeping a standing army within this kingdom in time of peace, without consent of Parliament, and quartering of soldiers contrary to law." Thus the British government was placing an intolerable burden on the colonists in Massachusetts that the British people themselves had refused to endure.

The first shots of the American War for Independence were fired on this bridge in Concord, Massachusetts.

Preparing American Colonists for Independence

One might think that colonists with a religious background and a Bible that told them, "Let every soul be subject unto the higher powers," (Rom. 13:1) would be the last people to fight for independence from their lawful government. However, various influences on colonial thought prepared the way for the American Revolution. Some of the influences were religious. Though he opposed rebellion, John Calvin had pointed out that in some governments lesser magistrates had the responsibility to oppose the tyranny of greater magistrates. Other influences came from the English Civil War. Certain writers from that time became popular among American colonists. They pointed out the dangers of government power and the importance of giving people representatives in government. From the Enlightenment came an emphasis on rights and the idea that government was formed as a contract with the people. Enlightenment writers claimed this contract could be dissolved if the people's rights were not being upheld. This mixture of ideas provided the soil from which the American Revolution would grow.

Independence. That document, written primarily by Thomas Jefferson and adopted by the Continental Congress, declared firmly,

> That these United Colonies are, and of Right ought to be, Free and Independent States; that they are Absolved from all Allegiance to the British Crown, and that all political connection between them and the State of Great Britain, is and ought to be totally dissolved; and that as Free and Independent States, they have full power to levy War, conclude Peace, contract Alliances, establish Commerce, and to do all other Acts and things which Independent States may of right do.

Course of the War

The fighting, which started more than a year before the signing of the Declaration of Independence, dragged on for seven years. During the early years of the conflict, it seemed as though Britain would crush American resistance. The small and poorly-equipped American army suffered great hardships and often had to retreat from the more numerous British forces. The American cause, however, was strengthened by the determined leadership of General **George Washington**. Also, the American soldiers were fighting for their homes and freedom. These proved to be strong personal motivations that the British troops, many of whom were German mercenaries, could not match.

The turning point in the war came in October 1777, when the American forces won a major victory over the British at Saratoga, New York. After hearing of that victory, France openly declared its support for the American cause and provided the colonies with badly needed aid. (Later, Spain and the Netherlands also entered the war against Britain.) At

Washington Crossing the Delaware, a painting by Emanuel Leutze

Reenactment of the Battle of Monmouth, originally fought on June 28, 1778

Yorktown, Virginia, in 1781, the combined French and American forces forced the British army commanded by Lord Cornwallis to surrender. When news of the surrender reached London, the British government, which was involved in a struggle with the French, Dutch, and Spanish around the world, was willing to bring the war to an end.

After two years of negotiations, the **Treaty of Paris** (1783) was signed. The British made many concessions to the Americans—many more than the British could have anticipated. Most importantly, though, they officially acknowledged the independence of the American colonies. The Americans had won their war for independence. Its success was due in large part to its defensive nature. Its protest was not against government as such but against a government that had violated its own rules. The colonists did not fight an offensive war; they simply defended their homeland and fought to preserve the freedoms they had enjoyed for more than a century.

Republic

After the war, the American colonists had their independence, but they lacked a strong national government. At first, they organized themselves as independent states in a weak confederation. Under the Articles of Confederation, however, the states had so much power that the central government was ineffective. In 1787, delegates from the various states met to amend the Articles. Instead, they adopted a new constitution.

After carefully examining the strengths and weaknesses of governments throughout history, the delegates to the Constitutional Convention chose a republican form of government modeled after the Roman Republic. They divided the powers of government among three branches: executive, legislative, and judicial. To ensure that no one branch became too powerful, they gave each branch specific functions and specific checks on the other branches.

To remedy the problems they experienced under the Articles, the convention established the principle of **federalism**, delegating specified powers to the national government and reserving all other powers for the state governments or the people. They sought to give the central government sufficient power to function on behalf of the mutual interests of the states. At the same time, they left to the states the freedom to act in matters affecting their individual interests.

The framers of the Constitution stressed such concepts as **popular sovereignty** (government based on the consent of the governed) and the "natural rights" of all men. In this regard, they reflected the influence of the Enlightenment. But while Enlightenment philosophy taught that man was essentially good, the constitutional fathers had a healthy fear of fallen human nature, which led them to limit both the power of government and the power of the people. Their Protestant-Puritan heritage taught them that man could not be trusted.

Although the new Constitution placed checks and balances on the federal government, it contained no specific guarantees that government would protect the personal and religious liberties for which the Americans had fought so valiantly. Many leaders refused to support ratification of the new Constitution unless such provisions were added. Therefore, the constitutional leaders promised that among the first acts of the new Congress would be the introduction of several amendments to the Constitution. The first ten

Independence Hall, Philadelphia

amendments, called the **Bill of Rights**, clearly defined these liberties and placed restraints on governmental interference. The most cherished personal liberties were listed in the first amendment:

> Congress shall make no law respecting an establishment of religion, or prohibiting the free exercise thereof; or abridging the freedom of speech or of the press; or the right of the people peaceably to assemble and to petition the government for redress of grievances.

The Constitution, formally adopted in 1789, established a new nation—the United States of America. Under this constitution, American citizens enjoyed greater freedom and prosperity than any other people on earth. From the days of their early settlement, through their difficult years of war, in the framing of their government, and in the developing of their new nation, many Americans looked to God for guidance, deliverance, and strength.

Section Review

1. Following the French and Indian War, what did England expect from its colonies in exchange for the benefits England provided?

2. What was at the root of the colonial protest against the actions of Parliament?

3–4. What battle fought in October 1777 was the turning point in the War for Independence? What European country openly supported the American cause as a result of this victory?

5. Briefly define *federalism*.

★ How did the British actions threaten colonial access to justice and impact American citizenship (cf. p. 13 in ch. 1)?

★ Evaluate whether popular sovereignty is consistent with a biblical worldview.

Guiding Questions

1. What were the social classes in the French regime?
2. What political and economic factors contributed to the French Revolution?
3. How did the French Revolution decline into the Reign of Terror?

II. French Destruction of the Old Regime

During most of the eighteenth century, France was the cultural center of Europe. European monarchs imitated the French absolutist government; they fashioned their royal courts after Versailles. French fashion, art, and learning became the envy of Europe. France had one of the largest populations and one of the most active trade economies in Europe. But beneath the surface of this seeming prosperity were roots of unrest and turmoil. French *philosophes* had espoused the ideas of personal rights and liberties. However, under the authority of an absolute monarch and the domination of the Roman Catholic Church, few Frenchmen enjoyed such freedom.

The Enlightenment had raised expectations of reform in French government and society. The American War for Independence gave hope to Frenchmen who desired the same freedoms for themselves. Yet the French political and social order remained the same. In addition, extravagant government spending and oppressive taxation brought the country to the brink of economic collapse. Such were the conditions in France on the eve of the French Revolution.

Reasons for Discontent

Of the many factors that contributed to the French Revolution, none by itself was sufficient motivation for revolt. But when linked together, they stirred widespread discontent with the **Old Regime** (the name given to the political and social order in France before the French Revolution). Revolution was only a short step away.

Social Inequality

As late as 1789, French society was still organized according to the old feudal class divisions of estates. The inequality of social privileges and taxation, which were determined by one's social class, caused deep-seated resentment among the underprivileged.

The **First Estate** consisted of the clergy of the Roman Catholic Church. (Since the revocation of the Edict of Nantes in 1685, the Roman Catholic Church had been the only recognized church in France.) The church had great wealth: it controlled vast land estates and was exempt from taxation. It used part of that wealth to provide education and to care for the sick and needy; yet many of the upper clergy (such as the bishops) considered the church's wealth to be their own. The wealthy clergy made up part of the aristocratic group that often advised the king in state matters. However, the lower clergy (the parish priests) were poor or, in some cases, destitute.

The nobility made up the **Second Estate**. They too were a privileged class. Nobles were exempt from many of the taxes levied by the French king. They also held some of the highest positions in government and society. In addition, the nobility owned vast estates, amounting to an estimated 40 percent of the land in France. Most of the nobles, however, were not interested in improving their land but were concerned only with exploiting it. Many nobles lived extravagantly at Versailles and paid agents to extract as much as they could from the impoverished tenants who lived on their estates. Because nobles could lose their titles for participating in trade, they sought to increase their income by assuming the best and most financially rewarding posts in the army, church, and legal professions. Many of the nobles who took such posts did not do any of the work that their positions demanded; they let others do the work while they drew the income.

The **Third Estate** was by far the largest class, comprising 98 percent of the French population. Of the three estates, this class had the greatest social and economic diversity among its members. It was subdivided into three groups. At the top were the lawyers, doctors, bankers, and wealthy businessmen. Below them came the workers in the cities and towns. At the bottom of the social structure were the peasants, who comprised about 80 percent of the population. Although some of the peasants owned their land, the majority were extremely poor, working as tenants on the large estates of the wealthy. Although their wages were low and they generally had few material possessions, the peasants bore the heaviest tax burden. In addition, the peasants suffered under lingering feudal obligations. They were required to do the following:

1. Pay an annual fee to the noble who owned the land on which they lived and worked.

2. Pay a fee to the former owner when the land changed hands.

3. Pay an annual fee for the use of mills, ovens, and winepresses, even if they did not use them.

4. Perform the *corvée*—a system of forced labor. During the Middle Ages, the peasants had performed the *corvée* for their feudal lord. In eighteenth-century France, the peasants

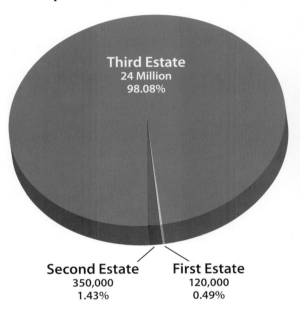

Population of France in 1789

Third Estate
24 Million
98.08%

Second Estate
350,000
1.43%

First Estate
120,000
0.49%

worked for the government, building and maintaining roads and canals.

5. Respect the nobles' hunting privileges. From ancient times, the nobles had been allowed unlimited freedom to hunt, unhindered by property rights. Peasants, however, were forbidden to kill rabbits, crows, or foxes even if these animals ruined their crops.

Political Inefficiency

Neither King Louis XV (r. 1715–74) nor King **Louis XVI** (r. 1774–92) had the character or inclination to rule France in the absolute fashion of Louis XIV. They were indifferent to the affairs of government. They had little sense of responsibility, being more interested in the frivolous pleasures of life at Versailles. When they did turn their attention to matters of state, they often followed the capricious advice of their mistresses or fell prey to the intriguing schemes of the nobles in their court. Local rulers still imposed old feudal obligations, increasing their power while further restricting the freedom of the French people. The central government, which should have been a unifying force, was thus incompetent and inefficient.

The different social groups, hoping to take advantage of this confused situation, were eager to assume political power. The nobles thought that Louis XIV had unlawfully deprived their ancestors of their positions of authority. The middle class, well versed in Enlightenment thinking, wanted political power equal to their economic wealth. The lower classes resented their unfair burden of oppressive taxation in addition to numerous outdated feudal obligations.

Economic Irresponsibility

Unbalanced Tax System

As previously mentioned, the French system of taxation was grossly out of balance. The privileged classes were exempt from most taxation. Those who had the least—the peasants—bore the greatest part of the tax burden. The peasants resented not only the unequal assessment of tax obligations but also the wasteful manner in which the tax money was used.

The most common and important taxes levied by the French government were the *taille*, the *capitation*, and the *vingtième*. The *taille*, originally levied for military purposes, was a tax on real and personal property; the *capitation*, or poll tax, was a tax on each person; and the *vingtième* was an income tax. Some of the nobles, clergy, and wealthy middle class either purchased or were granted exemptions from many of these taxes. Others, because of their privileged status, evaded their tax responsibilities altogether. Their failure to share the tax burden not only increased the financial strain on the peasants but also reduced the income the government received and thus contributed to the national debt.

Virtual Bankruptcy

Despite levying heavy taxes, the French government continued to sink deeper into debt. The successors of King Louis XIV continued to wage war and spend extravagantly. Louis XV plunged France into the Seven Years' War, which cost France most of its colonies and overseas trade. Louis XVI, who had no sympathy for the Ameri-

Louis XVI

can colonists' cause, nevertheless aided the Americans in hopes of weakening Britain. In addition, both monarchs continued to spend money from the public treasury for their personal luxuries at Versailles.

To reduce the national debt, the French government levied more taxes, debased the French currency, and borrowed more money from private banks. But these steps only increased the financial problems. To make matters worse, no one knew exactly how much money the government actually needed to pay its bills since France did not have a budget. Finally, in 1787, the private banks refused to extend any more credit to the French government. This financial crisis paved the way for the outbreak of the revolution.

Beginning of the Revolution

Calling of the Estates-General

From the beginning of Louis XVI's reign, able finance ministers had tried to solve France's economic problems. They told Louis that no money remained in the treasury and urged him to tax those who were paying no taxes. Louis, however, was a weak king who did not wish to offend anyone. Therefore, when the economic proposals of his finance ministers proved to be highly unpopular with the nobility, Louis dismissed his ministers. The nobles accused Louis of mismanagement and said that only the Estates-General could change the tax laws. That representative body, however, had not met since 1614. Desperate to find a solution to France's economic problems, Louis sent out a decree instructing the people to choose representatives for a meeting at Versailles in May 1789. He told the people to give their deputies lists of grievances (called **cahiers**) that they wanted the king to consider. Little did he realize what trouble he had invited.

In towns and villages across France, the people met to choose deputies to represent them at Versailles. Excitement ran high at the meetings of the Third Estate. Led by the educated middle class, the people drew up their *cahiers*. Their lists of grievances were similar from province to province; most called for a written constitution, equal taxation, equal justice, and the destruction of the remnants of feudalism. The First and Second Estates chose deputies too. For the most part, their *cahiers* contained ideas different from those of the Third Estate. They did, however, call for a constitution that would stop the king from infringing on their rights and privileges.

Convening of the Estates-General

The deputies made their way to Versailles in late April 1789. They arrived armed with their *cahiers*, fully expecting the king to listen carefully to their complaints and to right the wrongs so readily apparent in French society. The deputies of the Third Estate, however, were soon disillusioned. At the formal reception given by the king, he kept them waiting for hours. Unlike the richly attired nobles and clergy, they had to dress in black, keep their hats off, and enter the hall through a side door. When they were finally presented to the king, Louis XVI stood in silence as they filed by.

The opening meeting on May 5 was also a disappointment. Louis XVI, instead of assuring the deputies that he would be interested in their ideas for reform, was noncommittal. His only instructions were that they should meet as estates and vote as estates—each estate receiving one vote.

The Opening of the Estates-General at Versailles, May 5, 1789

The deputies of the Third Estate objected. They wanted each delegate's vote to be counted separately, regardless of his estate. They would thus have the majority vote because the deputies of the Third Estate outnumbered those of the First Estate 578 to 291; the Second Estate had only 270 deputies. They realized that if each estate received only one vote, their reforms had little chance of passing. The First and Second Estates were not interested in the grievances of the Third Estate; thus the Third Estate could be outvoted two to one.

Forming of the National Assembly

The disagreement over voting continued until June 17, when the delegates of the Third Estate proclaimed themselves the National Assembly. Since they were sent by the people, they claimed to speak for the people. These delegates asserted the principle of popular sovereignty and denounced the unfair social order of France. They invited the members of the other estates to join them, and a few did.

On June 20, when the members of the Third Estate arrived at their assembly room, they found the doors locked. Undaunted, the deputies gathered in the nearby royal indoor tennis court. There they adopted the famous **Tennis Court Oath**, declaring that they would not disband until a written constitution was established.

Three days later, at a joint meeting of the Estates-General, Louis again stated his opposition to a meeting of the three estates as a group unless it was for the purpose of raising taxes. While he made some reforming concessions, he insisted that the old distinction between the estates be maintained. He then dismissed the deputies

The Tennis Court Oath

The National Assembly, considering that it has been summoned to establish the constitution of the kingdom, to effect the regeneration of public order, and to maintain the true principles of monarchy; that nothing can prevent it from continuing its deliberations in whatever place it may be forced to establish itself; and, finally that wheresoever its members are assembled, there is the National Assembly; decrees that all members of this assembly shall immediately take a solemn oath not to separate, and to reassemble wherever circumstances require, until the constitution of the kingdom is established and consolidated upon firm foundations.

John H. Stewart, A Documentary Survey of the French Revolution, 88.

Meeting of the representatives of the Third Estate in the royal tennis court

and left. Most of the members of the First and Second Estates left with him, but the deputies of the Third Estate remained. By then, they were defiant.

When the king's messenger returned to tell them to go home, one of their leaders said, "Go and tell those who sent you that we are here by the will of the people and that we will go only if we are driven at the point of the bayonet!" When this message was conveyed to the king, he responded, "Well, let them stay."

On June 27, Louis ordered the First and Second Estates to join the National Assembly, which now called itself the National Constituent Assembly. The Assembly immediately set about to draw up a constitution. For a while it looked as if the king had surrendered to the Third Estate. However, he had not. On the advice of some members of his court, he ordered troops to Versailles and Paris, supposedly for protection. What he actually had in mind was to close down the Assembly. This double-mindedness was typical of Louis. He did not hesitate to change his mind to keep the peace or avoid offending someone. Like the "double minded man" of James 1:8, Louis was foolishly indecisive.

Storming of the Bastille

On July 12, Paris became the scene of rioting and looting by angry mobs. Angered by both high prices for bread and rumors that Louis's troops intended to murder them, the Parisians began searching for weapons to defend themselves. The disturbance lasted well into the next day, when the mob heard that arms were stored at the Hôtel des Invalides (a hospital for soldiers) and the Bastille (a royal prison for political prisoners). On the morning of July 14, 1789, part of the mob stormed the Invalides; others laid siege to and captured the Bastille. When the gates to the Bastille were opened, the mob stormed in and murdered the governor of the prison and his men.

The storming of the Bastille was the action of a frenzied mob. Yet it came to symbolize the downfall of the Old Regime. When Louis heard of the incident, he said, "This is a revolt." His aide replied, "No, Sire. This is a revolution!"

An artist's rendering of the storming of the Bastille, July 14, 1789

Phases of the Revolution
Destruction of the Old Regime

The storming of the Bastille intensified uprisings throughout the French countryside. Peasants unleashed their frustration by plundering the homes of the nobility and destroying the feudal records that obligated them to service. In hope of stemming fear and halting the increasing violence, the National Constituent Assembly passed legislation that made sweeping changes in French society, bringing the Old Regime to an end. From 1789 to 1791 the Assembly passed more than two thousand laws. One of the first steps it took was to abolish feudalism. Many of the nobles in the Assembly, frightened by the peasant uprisings, renounced their feudal rights and privileges.

Most prominent among the Assembly's early actions was the adoption of the **Declaration of the Rights of Man** on August 27, 1789. This declaration derived its ideas partly from the English Bill of Rights; partly from the ideas of Montesquieu, Locke, and Rousseau; and partly from the American Declaration of Independence. In the Declaration of the Rights of Man, the Assembly listed what it considered to be the natural rights of all people and the rights that they possessed as citizens.

> Men are born and remain free and equal in rights. Social distinctions can be based only on public utility.

> The aim of every political association is the preservation of the natural and imprescriptible rights of man [rights that cannot be taken away]. These rights are liberty, property, security, and resistance to oppression. . . .

> Liberty consists in the power to do anything that does not injure others. . . .

> Law is the expression of the general will. All citizens have the right to take part personally or by their representatives in its formation. It must be the same for all, whether it protects or punishes. . . .

> Every individual [is] presumed innocent until he has been proved guilty.

> No one should be disturbed because of his opinions, even in religion.

Louis, however, refused to give his consent to the recent legislation passed by the Assembly. His refusal, added to continued food shortages in Paris, brought mobs out into the streets once more. When a crowd of women could not get bread at a bakery, they decided to march the ten miles to Versailles to protest their plight. Their number swelled to several thousand. En route, they were joined by many French soldiers. On reaching Versailles, they burst into the meeting of the Assembly and demanded bread. Getting little satisfaction there, a group of the marchers broke into the royal palace the next day and murdered two of the king's guards. They insisted that the royal family accompany them back to Paris. The king gave in, and he and his family traveled back to Paris. A few days later, the delegates of the Assembly moved to Paris as well.

In response to this latest uprising, Louis gave his approval to the decrees of the Assembly. But the problem that had ignited the Revolution—France's bankruptcy—had not been solved. In fact, it had become worse. The people refused to pay the king's tax collectors, and the Assembly had not devised any new system of tax collection. Finally, the Assembly came up with a solution. Since the Roman Catholic Church possessed great quantities of land, the Assembly confiscated the land. The Assembly then issued paper money, called *assignats*, which was backed by the value of that land. They used these *assignats* to pay off the debts of the government.

In addition to seizing the Roman Church's lands, the Assembly passed the **Civil Constitution of the Clergy** (July 1790). This bill placed the church under state control, provided for the election of all the clergy by the people, and required the clergy to take an oath of loyalty to the state. When the pope condemned the constitution, many clergy refused to take the oath. As a result, two groups of

Roman Catholic clergy arose in France: juring clergy (those who took the oath) and nonjuring clergy (those who did not take the oath). In many areas of France, the people would not recognize the juring clergy. Thus, while the Assembly had weakened the influence of the Roman Catholic Church in France, it had antagonized many of the French Roman Catholics, creating yet another problem.

Overthrow of the Monarchy

Although 1790 was a rather peaceful year by revolutionary standards, 1791 proved to be another turbulent year. The king, seeing his powers being taken away and fearing for his life, tried to escape from France. Once out of the country, he hoped to enlist the aid of foreign monarchs and restore his power in France. He and his family disguised themselves and slipped out of the palace on the night of June 20, 1791. Their carriage was almost to the border when they were recognized by a postmaster. They were captured and escorted back to Paris by an armed guard.

In September, the National Constituent Assembly completed the constitution over which it had labored for two years. The document restructured the French government. The king's power, formerly absolute, was now limited by a constitution. The constitution also guaranteed equal taxes, ended special privileges, created a balanced system of justice, and established a new governing body called the Legislative Assembly. Louis was compelled to agree to this constitution, and he issued a proclamation calling on all Frenchmen to support it.

Problems of the Legislative Assembly

In October 1791, the Legislative Assembly convened for the first time. Its newly elected members had no experience in governing France. In addition, the body was divided into several factions. One group of legislators wanted to maintain the limited monarchy as established by the constitution. Because they were satisfied with the accomplishments of the Revolution and sought no further changes, they were known as the conservatives. Another group wished to rid France of the monarchy completely and to establish a republic in its place. These radicals advocated sweeping changes in the government. The third group, the moderates, sided with the conservatives on some issues and with the radicals on others.

Few Frenchmen supported the new government. The king and some of the nobility and clergy hoped to restore the Old Regime. Other Frenchmen, however, believed that the Revolution had not gone far enough. They wanted even more reforms. Some of them wanted to abolish the monarchy. The **Jacobins** advocated the most radical changes. (They took their name from an empty Jacobin convent that they used for meetings.) Although the Jacobins gathered followers from all over France, the group in Paris became the most influential. Its most prominent leaders were **Jean-Paul Marat** (mah RAH), **George-Jacques Danton**, and **Maximilien de Robespierre** (ROHBZ pee EHR).

To achieve their radical goals, the Jacobins often stirred up mobs in the cities, especially in Paris. Jacobin rabble-rousers appealed to Paris workers known as the *sans-culottes*—literally, "without breeches." (Unlike the men of the upper and middle classes, the men of these lower classes did not wear fashionable knee breeches but full-length trousers.) The Jacobins believed that the new

The Death of Marat *by Jacques-Louis David; Marat was viewed as a hero of the Revolution after his assassination.*

constitution favored only the middle class. They wanted a greater share of French wealth for themselves and more power in the French government.

War with Austria and Prussia

In April 1792, the Legislative Assembly, backed by the king, declared war on Austria. (From this time until the final defeat of Napoleon in 1815, there was almost constant war in Europe.) Each political faction within France had a different reason for wanting war. The king, for example, hoped that Austria would defeat the Assembly's forces and come to his rescue.

The Assembly hoped that a quick defeat of Austria would gain the French people's support for their government. The Jacobins, however, did not want war; they feared that a French victory would end their hopes of seizing power. Therefore, Marat and Danton deliberately sabotaged the war effort by delaying requests for army supplies.

Things did not go well for France early in the war. Prussia soon joined with Austria. The Austrian and Prussian armies, under the leadership of the Duke of Brunswick, invaded France. In July 1792, the Duke issued the **Brunswick Manifesto**, calling on the French people to rally behind their king and protect him from the leaders of the Revolution. He threatened to punish those who harmed the king and promised that he would restore Louis XVI to authority when Paris was captured.

Execution of the King

The Brunswick Manifesto, along with early military defeats, made the people of Paris distrustful of Louis. On August 10, 1792, a mob under the leadership of Danton invaded the palace and murdered the king's Swiss guards. (Louis temporarily found refuge with the Assembly.) The mob demanded that the Legislative Assembly call for another convention to write a new constitution for France. Facing tremendous pressure from the radicals, the Assembly called for elections to a new body that was to be called the National Convention.

In August and September, while new deputies were being chosen, Danton became the virtual dictator of France. During this time, many supporters of the monarchy met violent deaths by the radical mobs. In September, widespread massacres took place. Mobs emptied the prisons of nobles and nonjuring clergy who were suspected of working against the Revolution—mercilessly slaughtering them.

On September 22, the newly elected National Convention abolished the monarchy and proclaimed 1792 to be Year One of the French Republic. The new government, faced with internal disorder and foreign invasion, took action against Louis XVI. Tried and found guilty of treason, the king was sentenced to death. On January 21, 1793, Louis XVI, who had once been called "Good King Louis," was taken by coach to a square in the middle of Paris, where he was led to the guillotine. He was allowed a few last words: "I die innocent," he said; "I pardon those who have occasioned my death."

Louis XVI en route to his execution by beheading

As drums rolled, the blade did its work, and the head of the former king was held up for the crowd to see. The people threw their hats into the air and shouted, *"Vive la nation!"* ("Long live the nation!")

The Reign of Terror

The French Revolution now took an even more destructive and bloody turn. The rebellion and violence in French society were not without their consequences—national suffering was sure to follow.

The Committee of Public Safety

Faced with unrest at home and a critical situation on the battlefront, the National Convention appointed twelve men to take over the everyday affairs of government, particularly the war. With Robespierre as their leader, these men made up the **Committee of Public Safety**. They set about to create a new order in France.

This Committee gave the Revolutionary Tribunal orders to suppress opposition to the Revolution. Anyone suspected of being an "enemy of the people" was arrested. Most suspects, regardless of whether they were guilty, were hastily tried and executed—some were drowned, others were shot, and many more were guillotined. An estimated twenty to forty thousand people died at the hands of the Tribunal. Surprisingly, the largest percentage of those executed were peasants or *sans-culottes*. The slogan of the Revolution— "Liberty, Equality, and Fraternity (brotherhood)"—had become virtually meaningless.

The Committee responded to the looming threat of foreign invaders by mobilizing the entire nation into a unified effort to defeat its enemies. In August 1793 the Committee issued a decree of ***levée en masse***, stating that "the young men shall go to battle; the married men shall forge arms and transport provisions; the women shall make tents and clothes, and shall serve in the hospitals; the children shall turn old linen into lint; the old men shall [go] to the public places to stimulate the courage of the warriors and preach the unity of the Republic and the hatred of kings." This was one of the first instances of a nation calling on all of its citizens to take an active part in the war effort.

Model of a guillotine

The Guillotine

During a debate in the National Assembly about the equality of all Frenchmen, a man named Dr. Joseph Guillotin rose to express his views on capital punishment. Under the Old Regime, he said, nobles received special treatment. When the situation called for their execution, they were decapitated by ax or sword, whereas the common man suffered execution by hanging or burning at the stake. If all Frenchmen were equal, Dr. Guillotin pointed out, all of the condemned should be given a humane means of execution. The Assembly agreed and appointed Dr. Antoine Louis to develop an instrument of execution. After much research and experimentation on sheep and cadavers, he developed the guillotine, which was named for Dr. Guillotin. (The guillotine was not a new instrument. It had been used in Scotland, Germany, and Italy; Dr. Louis just developed a new, streamlined model.) In March 1792 the National Assembly adopted the guillotine as the official instrument of execution in France. In later years of the Revolution, thousands of "equal" Frenchmen mounted the scaffolds to be "shaved by the national barber."

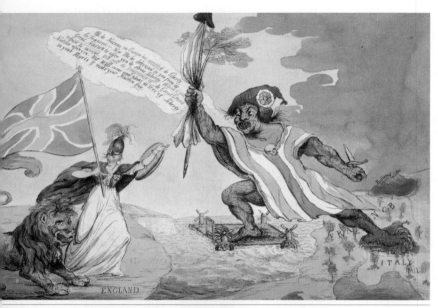

A British cartoon from 1798 portrays the French Revolution as a devouring monster who, having ravaged the Continent, is attempting to take Britain as well.

The citizen army won a series of victories over the forces of the European **coalition** (a temporary alliance of nations), which was determined to prevent the Revolution from spreading throughout Europe. News of the victories reduced the tension back in Paris. Danton and others no longer felt that the Reign of Terror was necessary. Danton appealed to Robespierre to stop the bloodshed, but Robespierre had him arrested as a traitor and guillotined. Members of the Convention became alarmed when Robespierre stood in the assembly and declared that many traitors were still in their own ranks. "These must be weeded out," he said, "to save the Republic." Fearful for their own lives and weary of the Reign of Terror, the Convention had Robespierre and his followers arrested and sent to the guillotine. Like so many other revolutions, the French Revolution illustrates the saying that "a revolution devours its own." Proverbs 11:5 states, "The wicked shall fall by his own wickedness."

The End of the National Convention

In 1795, a new constitution was enacted, bringing an end to the Convention and establishing the **Directory**. This new government provided for a two-chamber legislature: the Council of Five Hundred and the Council of Ancients. The executive branch was a group of five men called the Directors, who were to be nominated by the Council of Five Hundred and elected by the Council of Ancients.

The Directory inherited many problems. Constant warfare had brought France once more to the edge of bankruptcy. Internal unrest was threatening to cause another revolution. As before, various groups worked to overthrow the new government to gain their selfish ends. Although Prussia had made peace with France in 1795, France still faced the threat of Austrian and British forces. The Directory placed the hopes of the defense of France in the hands of a young general named Napoleon Bonaparte.

Section Review

1–2. List two elements of Enlightenment thought that influenced the French Revolution.

3. Who bore the greatest tax burden under the French system of taxation?

4. What is the name for the list of grievances that the delegates took to the convening of the Estates-General?

5. List one of the most common grievances listed by the delegates of the Third Estate.

6. What action of the Parisian mob is considered the beginning of the French Revolution?

✱ Why did the phrase "Liberty, Equality, and Fraternity" become an empty promise to the average French citizen during the Revolution?

✱ Contrast the French and American Revolutions in their foundations and consequences.

III. The Napoleonic Era

Few individuals have so influenced and dominated the continent of Europe as did **Napoleon Bonaparte** (1769–1821). So strongly did he make his presence felt in Europe that the period from 1796 to 1815 is often called "the Napoleonic Era."

Napoleon was born on the island of Corsica. He attended a military academy in France, and he spent many hours during his early career in the army studying military strategy. He served in the revolutionary army and later distinguished himself when he suppressed a Paris riot in 1795, helping to pave the way for the establishment of the Directory. As a result, the Directors of the new government chose him to lead the French forces against the Austrians. Instead of directly attacking Austria, however, Napoleon launched a campaign in northern Italy, which was under Austrian domination. Fighting by what his opponents called "new rules"—marching at night, fighting on Sundays, and fighting in the rain—he won victory after victory. He exacted a heavy toll on his defeated foes, allowing his poorly equipped soldiers to take booty. In 1797, Austria made peace with France, and Napoleon returned to Paris a hero.

Members of the Directory were jealous and fearful of Napoleon's popularity. To get him out of Paris, they directed him to invade England. Rejecting this idea, he decided instead to attack Egypt to cut off Britain's trade with the Near East. In 1798, he invaded Egypt with an army of some thirty-five thousand men. After some early victories by Napoleon, the British fleet under the command of Lord Nelson destroyed the French fleet anchored at Alexandria. The British then blockaded Napoleon and his troops in Egypt, cutting them off from needed supplies. In this desperate situation, Napoleon received word that a new European coalition composed of Britain, Russia, Austria, and the Ottoman Turks had been formed to renew the war against France. Leaving his army in Egypt, Napoleon made his way back to France.

Overthrow of the Directory

Napoleon landed in southern France, where crowds welcomed him as a new caesar returning in triumph. (They did not know of his defeats or of the fate of his army in Egypt.) Declaring that he had come to save France, he triumphantly made his way to Paris. Once there, he and his supporters staged a successful *coup d'état* (KOO day TAH), a sudden and illegal seizure of power. By the end of 1799, a new government, called the Consulate, was formed under yet another constitution. When Napoleon submitted the constitution to the people for confirmation in a vote called a plebiscite, they overwhelmingly approved. The constitution established a three-man Consulate modeled after the Roman government. The real power, however, was concentrated in the First Consul, Napoleon.

Promising peace and the restoration of internal order, Napoleon first worked to establish peace with France's external foes. After long negotiations, France signed peace treaties with Austria (1800) and Britain (1802).

Napoleon Bonaparte; (inset) *Lord Nelson*

Meanwhile, Napoleon initiated many domestic reforms. He began public works programs (constructing roads, bridges, and canals) and founded the Bank of France, which standardized the monetary system. Napoleon also set up an equitable tax system, which helped to stabilize the national debt. He established a system of public education supervised by an agency called the University of France. Perhaps his most famous accomplishment was the codification of French laws, later to be named the **Code Napoleon**. Napoleon appointed a commission to systematize the various laws that came out of the Revolution. This code established the civil, criminal, and commercial laws of France, many of which still exist today.

Since most Frenchmen remained loyal Roman Catholics, Napoleon realized that he could increase his popularity and influence by restoring certain privileges to the Roman Catholic Church. Therefore, in 1801 he reached an accord with the pope that returned certain lands to the church, allowed seminaries to operate, and permitted church services to be held openly. In addition, the agreement specified that the state would nominate the bishops and pay the salaries of all the clergy. Although Napoleon appeared to restore the role of the Roman Catholic Church in France, he undermined this agreement with other laws that were hostile to the church.

Creation of Napoleon's Empire
Napoleon's Crowning

After seizing the French government in 1799, Napoleon worked to increase his personal power. In 1802, he held a plebiscite in which the people overwhelmingly agreed to make him First Consul for life. Then, in 1804, the Senate proclaimed Napoleon the emperor of France. In a spectacular ceremony in Notre Dame Cathedral on December 2, 1804, Napoleon took the imperial crown from the hands of the pope and placed it on his own head. Napoleon's assumption of imperial power officially brought the Republic to an end. France, which had begun the Revolution with the weak rule of an absolute king, now had an ambitious emperor who ruled with absolute power.

Napoleon's Conquests

Napoleon's unbridled ambition would not be satisfied until he became master of all Europe. His chief obstacle, however, was Great Britain. Napoleon began planning an invasion of Britain, but his plans were thwarted by a decisive naval battle in 1805. The British fleet, under the leadership of Admiral Lord Nelson, encountered the French fleet off the Cape of Trafalgar on the southern coast of Spain. Nelson was killed in the ensuing battle, but his fleet ensured Britain's control of the seas by soundly defeating the French.

The Battle of Trafalgar

Abandoning his English invasion, Napoleon launched an all-out campaign against British allies on the Continent. Austria, Russia, and Sweden had joined with Great Britain in 1805 to form the Third Coalition against France. Although outnumbered, Napoleon's army crushed the combined armies of Austria and Russia at Austerlitz. Then, in 1806, Napoleon dissolved the Holy Roman Empire and set

Austerlitz—Napoleon's Greatest Triumph

A French general with outstretched arm presents the standards of the enemy to Napoleon at Austerlitz.

Napoleon Bonaparte was the greatest military commander of his day. He consistently defeated opponent after opponent for almost twenty years. Napoleon's method was to move with speed and flexibility, keeping his forces spread out for easy movement yet close enough to join quickly for battle. Napoleon believed that by concentrating on a single weak point in the enemy's position, he could defeat his opponent. Above all, he planned his campaigns in a daring manner that confused and frustrated his opponents. No battle illustrates Napoleon's military genius more clearly than the Battle of Austerlitz.

In 1805, the French faced the combined armies of Austria and Russia, called the Allies. Napoleon responded by suddenly invading Austria with seventy thousand French troops. He surrounded and captured thirty thousand stunned Austrian troops at Ulm and then turned northward to face the Russians and remaining Austrians. He decided to bait a trap for them. First, Napoleon selected a

site near the town of Austerlitz for the battle. Then he made his army appear smaller by sending twenty thousand men one day's march behind him. He ordered his main forces to fall back slowly, luring the Allies forward to the chosen battlefield. Finally, he tempted the Allies to attack the right end of his line by crowding his troops at the foot of a plateau and exposing his line of retreat to the enemy.

Czar Alexander I arrived in the Allied camp and took command of the forces. Seeing the apparently weak French position, he assumed that Napoleon had blundered and ordered an attack. On December 2, the Russian and Austrian forces rolled forward. They planned to swing around the southern end of the French line, cut off Napoleon's retreat, and then crush the French emperor's force—which was exactly what Bonaparte expected.

Napoleon was ready. He had already called back the twenty thousand men he had hidden. As the Allies moved forward, the French

retreated from the heights. Meanwhile, an early morning fog covered the movements of the other French forces as they prepared a surprise blow. When the Allies were halfway down the slope chasing the "retreating" French, Napoleon sent his other forces forward in a sharp counterattack. Surprised and confused, the Allies began to give way. The center of the Allied line broke, and the French swept south, "rolling up" the enemy's line and driving them back. Thousands of panicking Russian troops had to flee across frozen lakes whose icy surfaces cracked and broke under their weight. By the end of the day, thousands of prisoners had fallen into French hands, and the Allied armies fell back in disorganized retreat.

up the Confederation of the Rhine, composed of western German states under Napoleon's protection. When Prussia entered the war against France, its armies were likewise defeated.

By 1808, Napoleon had truly become the master of the mainland of Europe, and his personal power was at its height. Nevertheless, Great Britain still controlled the seas. Thus Napoleon could not directly attack the British Isles. Instead, he devised a plan of attack that became known as the **Continental System**. Using his superior land forces, Napoleon attempted to close Europe's ports to British ships. He hoped that such a blockade of British trade would cause the British economy to collapse.

Napoleon's Downfall

As Napoleon's armies swept through Europe, many Europeans initially welcomed the French troops as liberators who had come to free them from the oppression of their absolute rulers. They soon found, however, that Napoleon had merely replaced one form of oppression with another. In many European countries, Napoleon replaced the national rulers with his relatives and demanded that these subject lands furnish him with soldiers and supplies. Napoleon also looted many lands of their national art treasures, which he took back to France. Overall, he showed little concern for their national feelings or interests.

Nationalistic pride soon began to stir across Europe, and people began to seek freedom from French domination. Furthermore, they resisted the Continental System because even though it was aimed at destroying the British economy, they too were suffering from the loss of British trade.

Conflict broke out in the Iberian Peninsula when Portugal violated the blockade against British trade and Spain revolted against the rule of Napoleon's brother. French troops were sent to crush the uprisings, but they met with fierce resistance from small bands of Spanish troops who attacked the French garrisons and then retreated into the hills. These attacks were called *guerrillas* (Spanish for "little wars"). In addition, British troops soon landed in Portugal and began a campaign that eventually drove the French out of the peninsula.

Disaster in Russia

The Portuguese were not the only ones who refused to cooperate with the Continental System. In 1810, Russia broke with the system too. When Czar Alexander I refused to suppress British trade, Napoleon declared war on Russia. He amassed a huge army, called the Grand Army, totaling about six hundred thousand men (including many non-French soldiers), and in 1812 invaded Russia.

Napoleon planned to engage the Russians in one decisive battle near their western border. But when the Russians realized that their forces were outnumbered, they slowly retreated, drawing the Grand Army deeper and deeper into Russia. As the Russian army retreated, they burned everything that might be of value to the enemy and left nothing. (This strategy is called the **scorched-earth policy**.)

Napoleon continued to press on, hoping that if he could capture Moscow, the czar would come to terms. He won several battles along the way, but he could not destroy the Russian army, which kept retreating. Finally, in September 1812, his army reached Moscow. When Napoleon entered the city, he found it abandoned. That

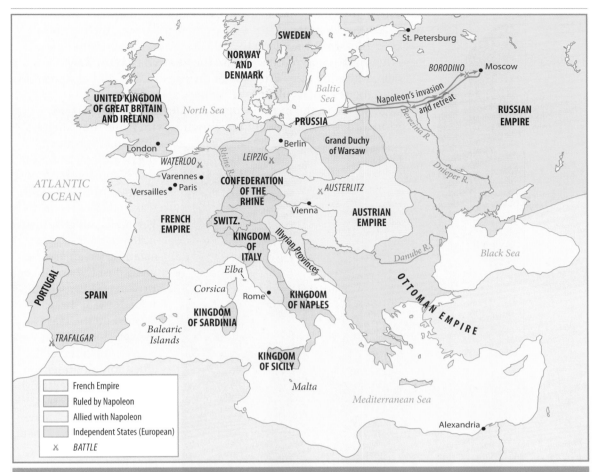

Napoleon's Empire

Map labels:
SWEDEN
St. Petersburg
NORWAY AND DENMARK
Baltic Sea
BORODINO Moscow
Napoleon's invasion and retreat
UNITED KINGDOM OF GREAT BRITAIN AND IRELAND
North Sea
PRUSSIA
RUSSIAN EMPIRE
Berezina R.
London
Berlin
Grand Duchy of Warsaw
WATERLOO
Rhine R.
LEIPZIG
Varennes
Dnieper R.
ATLANTIC OCEAN
Versailles
Paris
CONFEDERATION OF THE RHINE
AUSTERLITZ
FRENCH EMPIRE
SWITZ.
Vienna
AUSTRIAN EMPIRE
KINGDOM OF ITALY
Illyrian Provinces
Danube R.
Black Sea
Elba
PORTUGAL
Corsica
Rome
KINGDOM OF NAPLES
OTTOMAN EMPIRE
SPAIN
KINGDOM OF SARDINIA
TRAFALGAR
Balearic Islands
KINGDOM OF SICILY
Malta
Mediterranean Sea
Alexandria

Legend:
French Empire
Ruled by Napoleon
Allied with Napoleon
Independent States (European)
× BATTLE

night fire swept through the city, destroying most of it. Napoleon remained in Moscow more than a month, thinking that the czar might still surrender. Winter was approaching, however, and Napoleon knew that his troops were clad only in summer uniforms and did not have enough supplies to spend the winter in Moscow. Frustrated, he finally ordered retreat.

As the Grand Army made its way back across the Russian plains, the bitter cold and snow of the Russian winter set in. The Russians, like packs of wolves, picked off the stragglers one by one. At the Berezina River, they burned the bridges, further delaying the French retreat until new bridges could be built. Some Frenchmen tried to swim across the river but froze to death. Napoleon abandoned his army there and sped on to Paris to maintain control of the government before the people heard the dreadful news. In the end, fewer than one hundred thousand of his soldiers returned safely from Russia.

Napoleon's retreat from Russia

Defeat and Exile

The following year, Napoleon once more persuaded the French people to raise an army to defend his empire against a new coalition of European powers. In a long campaign in 1813, Napoleon's forces

Duke of Wellington and scene from the Battle of Waterloo

were finally defeated at Leipzig, Germany, in what was later called the Battle of Nations. After a series of negotiations, the European Coalition forced Napoleon to abdicate. They allowed him to go to the small island of Elba just off the western coast of Italy. They granted him the title "Emperor of the Isle of Elba," and he agreed to spend the rest of his life on the island.

Meanwhile, the European powers met in Vienna to try to restore order to Europe. But in February 1815, while the Congress of Vienna was meeting, word reached them that Napoleon had escaped from Elba and was making his way to Paris. He entered Paris in triumph and once again raised an army to go against the armies of Britain and Prussia. On June 8, 1815, the armies clashed on the plains of Waterloo in what is today Belgium. The allied forces, under the leadership of the British **Duke of Wellington**, won a decisive victory. Napoleon was banished to St. Helena, a little island in the middle of the South Atlantic, where he lived out his days under guard. He died on May 5, 1821, and was buried on the island. In 1840, his body was moved to Paris. Napoleon had said in 1804, "Death is nothing; but to live defeated and inglorious is to die daily." How he must have "died" during those six years on St. Helena!

Section Review

1. What is the period of European history from 1796 to 1815 often called?

2–3. What event officially brought an end to the French Republic? In what year did it occur?

4. What battle illustrates the military genius of Napoleon and is often called his greatest triumph?

5–6. What country did Napoleon invade in 1812? What policy did that country practice to impede the French invasion?

7–8. In what battle was Napoleon defeated for the final time? Who led the allied forces?

★ Assess Napoleon's reforms.

★ Analyze Napoleon's defeat.

Defeated Napoleon in exile

Making Connections

1–2. Why did Europeans settle in the American colonies? (List two reasons.)

3. Why were those citizens in France who were least able to pay taxes burdened with the most taxes?

4–5. What factors combined to bring France to the point of revolution? (List two.)

6. Why were French leaders unable to prevent a revolution?

Developing History Skills

1. Summarize the course of the American War for Independence and its potential impact on the United States for the next two centuries. (You may want to look at chapters 20 and 22 to help develop your answer.)

2. Summarize the course of the French Revolution and its potential impact on the nation for the next two centuries. (You may want to look at chapters 17 and 21 to help develop your answer.)

Thinking Critically

1. Compare and contrast the contributing factors leading to the American and French Revolutions.

2. Evaluate Napoleon's rule of France. Provide both positive and negative aspects of his rule.

Living in God's World

1. Imagine you are a member of the legislature of France at the time of the French Revolution. Which statements from the Declaration of the Rights of Man would you, as a Christian, need to dissent from? Why?

2. Do you think the current American view of popular sovereignty aligns with the Founders' viewpoint? Which viewpoint is more biblical? Outline ways to maintain or revert to a more biblical approach.

People, Places, and Things to Know

Pilgrims
Mayflower Compact
George III
Declaration of Independence
George Washington
Treaty of Paris
federalism
popular sovereignty
Bill of Rights
Old Regime
First Estate
Second Estate
Third Estate
Louis XVI
cahiers
Tennis Court Oath
Declaration of the Rights of Man
Civil Constitution of the Clergy
Jacobins
Jean-Paul Marat
George-Jacques Danton
Maximilien de Robespierre
Brunswick Manifesto
Committee of Public Safety
levée en masse
coalition
Directory
Napoleon Bonaparte
Lord Nelson
coup d'état
Code Napoleon
Continental System
guerrillas
scorched-earth policy
Duke of Wellington

UNIT

THE EUROPEAN WORLD
1800–1914

6

17 Reaction and Revolution

18 Industrial Revolution and European Society

19 European Expansion

Steam train in North Norfolk, England

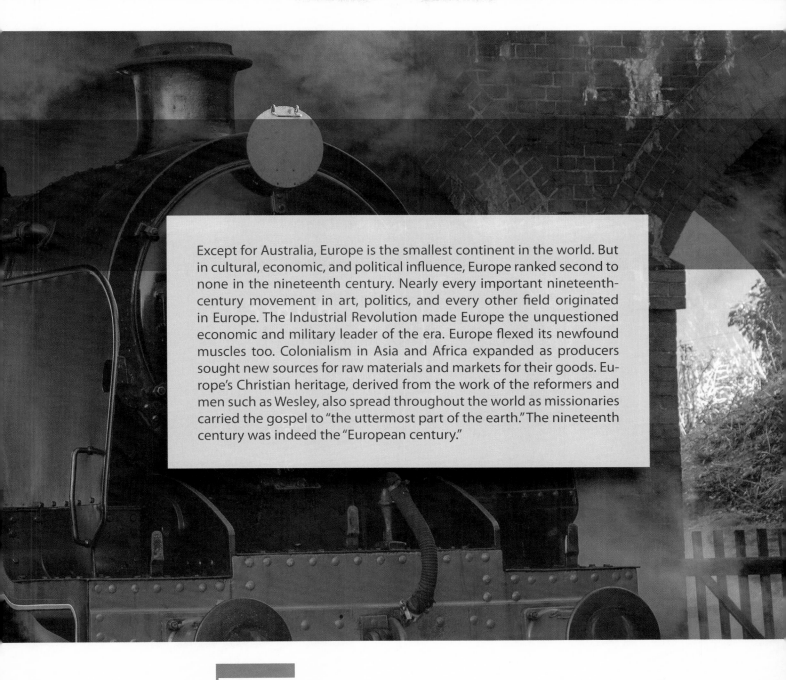

Except for Australia, Europe is the smallest continent in the world. But in cultural, economic, and political influence, Europe ranked second to none in the nineteenth century. Nearly every important nineteenth-century movement in art, politics, and every other field originated in Europe. The Industrial Revolution made Europe the unquestioned economic and military leader of the era. Europe flexed its newfound muscles too. Colonialism in Asia and Africa expanded as producers sought new sources for raw materials and markets for their goods. Europe's Christian heritage, derived from the work of the reformers and men such as Wesley, also spread throughout the world as missionaries carried the gospel to "the uttermost part of the earth." The nineteenth century was indeed the "European century."

1864–71
Austro-Prussian War

1894
Sino-Japanese War

1866–71
Unification of Germany

1899
Boxer Rebellion

1856–60
Second Opium War

1870–71
Franco-Prussian War

1904–5
Russo-Japanese War

1850

1875

1900

1854–56
Crimean War

1859–70
Unification of Italy

1869
Suez Canal opened

1899–1902
Boer War

Reaction and Revolution

France's tricolor flag, adopted during the French Revolution, became a symbol of revolutionary ideas not only in France but also all across Europe.

Big Ideas

1. How did Europeans strive to maintain stability?
2. What were the leading political philosophies of early nineteenth-century Europe?
3. How did nationalism develop in early nineteenth-century Europe?
4. What impact did romanticism have on early nineteenth-century Europe?

The spirit of revolution did not cease with the defeat of Napoleon. From 1815 to 1848, violent uprisings continued to break out on the streets of Paris and spread like a virus all over Europe, causing one European statesman to remark, "When France sneezes, all Europe catches cold." The "cold" to which he referred was the desire for freedom that was being stirred by liberalism and nationalism, the longing for independence and local autonomy.

Conservative elements, however, opposed these forces of change. The rulers of Europe reacted by attempting to repress reform and restore the social and political order present in Europe before 1789. But their task was not easy. Rulers tried to suppress revolts with their armies; for the most part, they were successful in the early part of the nineteenth century. But they could not stamp out revolutionary ideas. Such ideas found expression in virtually every aspect of European culture—especially in the literature, art, and music of the romantic movement. As a result, the second half of the nineteenth century saw the forces of liberalism and nationalism triumphing over the forces of conservatism.

I. Search for Stability

Napoleon had produced a new Europe. His conquests had shattered existing national boundaries and had overthrown ruling families. His military campaigns had unleashed nationalism and liberalism all across Europe. But with his downfall in 1814, Europe was ready for peace; there had been almost continuous fighting for twenty-five years. The victorious nations of the Grand Alliance—Britain, Austria, Prussia, and Russia—were now faced with restoring order and stability in Europe. They decided to convene a congress of European leaders to draw up a settlement.

Congress of Vienna: Restoration of the Old Order

In September 1814, the leading statesmen of Europe gathered in Vienna, Austria. Many European rulers were present, and hundreds of diplomats and their wives from nearly every European country crowded into the city. The **Congress of Vienna** was a glittering social occasion. When the delegates were not involved in the difficult negotiations, they and their wives spent much time at lavish parties, festive balls, and musical performances.

The delegates did not meet in large formal sessions. Most of the negotiations were conducted in small, informal, and often secret gatherings dominated by the spokesmen for the great powers: **Lord Castlereagh** (KASS ul ray), the foreign minister of Britain; Czar **Alexander I** of Russia; and **Prince Klemens von Metternich**, the Austrian minister of foreign affairs.

Metternich (1773–1859) was the leading figure at the Congress. He attempted to reverse the trends begun by the French Revolution and restore Europe to its pre-Revolution conditions. So strong was his influence over the congress and later European politics that the period from 1815 to 1848 is called the "Age of Metternich."

Another important figure at Vienna was **Charles Maurice de Talleyrand** (1754–1838). Talleyrand, the representative of defeated France, was a shrewd and opportunistic politician. He had been a delegate to the Estates-General in 1789, a prominent figure in the National Assembly, and later foreign minister under the Directory and Napoleon. He attended the congress as the new foreign minister

Guiding Questions

1. What were the outcomes of the Congress of Vienna?
2. What were the challenges posed to the Concert of Europe?
3. What were the weaknesses of the alliance system?
4. What was the impact of colonial revolts on Latin America?

Alexander I

Charles Maurice de Talleyrand

of the French king Louis XVIII, the restored Bourbon monarch. Talleyrand took advantage of the disagreement among the great powers at the Congress to secure a favorable settlement for France.

Redrawing the Map of Europe

Many Europeans hoped that the Vienna peace settlement would support some of the rights and freedoms championed by the French Revolution. But the leading diplomats at Vienna were more concerned about restoring order to Europe. They sought to reestablish political stability, maintain the balance of power among the leading European nations, and respond to the revolutionary ideas spread by France.

Safeguards Against France

In dealing with defeated France, the Congress was fairly lenient. Members feared that harsh punishment would only infuriate the French and thus hinder any chances of achieving a lasting peace in Europe. The Congress did, however, strip France of its conquests, reducing its territory to its 1792 borders. In addition, France had to pay indemnities—compensation to other nations for war damages.

Although the members of the Congress agreed to this moderate settlement, they still feared the French. To prevent any further acts of French aggression, they sought to encircle France with a buffer of strong powers. They united the Austrian Netherlands (Belgium) with the Dutch Netherlands to form a protective barrier to the north. To the east, they gave Prussia territory along the Rhine River and retained the Confederation of German States established by Napoleon. On France's southern border, they enlarged the Kingdom of Sardinia. (See map on p. 367.)

Restoration of Legitimate Rulers

During his conquests, Napoleon had deposed many European rulers, placing his relatives on their thrones. The congress removed these rulers and, where possible, restored those whom Napoleon had unseated. In France, for example, the monarchy was reestablished, and Louis XVIII was invited to assume the throne of his brother Louis XVI. (Louis XVI's young son, considered "Louis XVII" even though he did not rule, died in prison during the French Revolution.)

Grants of Compensation

Delegates to the Congress of Vienna; Talleyrand is seated on the right with his arm resting on the table. Metternich, in white breeches, is standing on the left.

The victors of the Napoleonic Wars and those nations that lost territory in the encirclement of France were compensated with additional territory. In return for relinquishing its holdings in the Netherlands, Austria received territory in northern Italy. Sweden allowed Russia to keep Finland and received Norway in return. (Norway was taken from Denmark, which had sided with Napoleon.) Although Great Britain did not receive any territory on the Continent, it retained control of some French and Dutch colonies seized during recent wars.

Balance of Power

Another chief concern of the Congress of Vienna was to maintain the balance of power in Europe. The delegates wanted to prevent any nation from becoming so strong that it could threaten the security of Europe as France had done. This concern was increased by jealous rivalries among the major European powers. Metternich, for example, was especially fearful of the growing power of Prussia, which threatened Austria's domination over the German Confederation. In addition, the ambition of Czar Alexander I, who claimed the remnants of Poland for Russia, caused further alarm. Talleyrand urged Castlereagh and Metternich to take action, and France, Austria, and Britain signed a treaty pledging to use force if necessary to prevent Prussia or Russia from gaining more power. As a result, both Russia and Prussia abandoned many of their demands.

Final Settlement at Vienna

The congress was nearing a final peace settlement in March 1815 when news reached Vienna that Napoleon had left the island of Elba and was on his way to Paris. The leaders of the Grand Alliance decided to unite their armies and finally rid Europe of Napoleon. In June, the allied forces, commanded by the Duke of Wellington, defeated Napoleon's army at Waterloo (in present-day Belgium). In the same month, the delegates of the congress put the finishing touches on the peace settlement.

Although the Congress of Vienna had settled the matters of encirclement, legitimacy, compensation, and balance of power, its delegates made few concessions to the causes of nationalism and liberalism. They redrew the map of Europe with little regard for the interests of various national groups. Though the major powers consented to cooperate to prevent a major war, France had established an explosive precedent in Europe. Soon the forces of nationalism and democratic liberalism stirred widespread revolt in Europe.

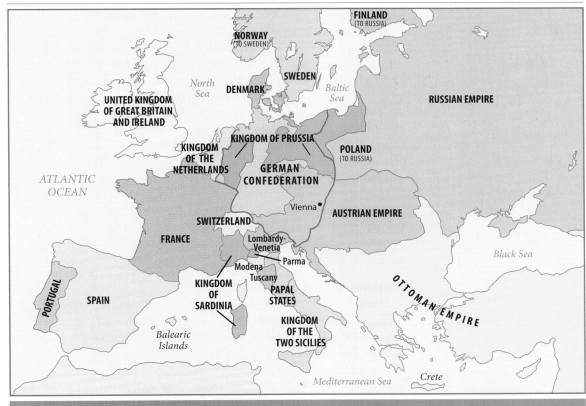

Europe After the Congress of Vienna (1815)

Concert of Europe: Protection of the Old Order
Establishing the Alliance System

In their concern to preserve peace in Europe, the delegates at the Vienna Congress established the **Quadruple Alliance**. In November 1815, the four nations of the Grand Alliance—Austria, Prussia, Russia, and Great Britain—signed an agreement designed to maintain the Vienna settlements. They agreed to convene new congresses when necessary to resolve problems affecting the peace and stability of Europe. In 1818, France was admitted to the Quadruple Alliance, making it the Quintuple Alliance. Through this "congress system" the major powers hoped to work together to avoid major wars and to suppress nationalism and liberalism. This international cooperation became known as the Concert of Europe.

Testing the Alliance System

During the Napoleonic Era, the spirit of "Liberty, Equality, Fraternity" had swept Europe. Governments adopted written constitutions, abolished feudal privileges, and granted freedom of speech. Small national groups hoped to gain independence. But the Congress of Vienna refused to acknowledge their demands when it redrew the map of Europe. It also attempted to return Europe to conditions that existed before the French Revolution. Yet even though conservatives were back in power, the spirit of revolution and democratic reform was still very much alive.

Suppressed Revolts in Spain and Italy

Following the defeat of Napoleon, the European leaders reinstated Ferdinand VII as king of Spain. Ignoring the liberal constitution adopted during the revolutionary period—limiting the power of the monarchy and guaranteeing basic freedoms for the people—Ferdinand reintroduced repressive measures to the country. He revived the Inquisition and punished those who spoke out for reform. In 1820 the Spanish people demanded that the king restore the constitution. Ferdinand, having lost the support of the Spanish army, gave in to their demands. The success of the Spanish revolt encouraged a similar uprising in Italy, where the people in the Kingdom of the Two Sicilies forced the king to grant a constitution.

Word of the revolts spread alarm among the rulers of Europe. Metternich feared that one revolution would lead to another and that soon all of Europe would be caught up in the revolutionary fervor. He called for a meeting of the Concert of Europe. At a congress in 1820, the Quintuple Alliance decided to send Austrian troops into Italy to suppress the revolution and restore the king's authority. Two years later, it sent French troops into Spain to crush the revolt. In both instances, the forces of the Quintuple Alliance briefly succeeded at suppressing the will of the people.

Weakness of the Congress System

When the alliance representatives met to settle the uprising in Spain, they also discussed the problem of the Spanish colonies in the New World. Several of the colonies in Latin America had revolted during the Napoleonic Era (see page 370). By the early 1820s, they had won their independence. Such success, in the eyes of Europe's leaders, set a bad example for Europe. One ardent supporter of monarchical government wrote, "If the New World ever becomes entirely Republican, the monarchies of the Old World will perish!"

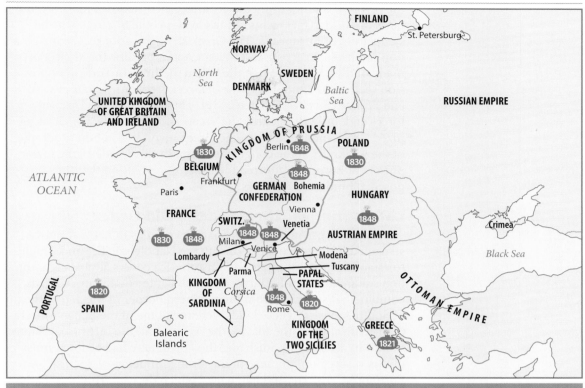

European Revolutions (1820–48)

The congress decided to send troops to help restore the colonies to the Spanish monarchy.

Not every member of the Quintuple Alliance, however, agreed with the plans for intervention in Latin America. Since the Congress of Vienna, Britain had become disenchanted with the congress system and more sympathetic to liberal reforms. It had not cooperated with the congress in suppressing the Spanish revolt. Now Britain strenuously objected to plans to restore the colonies to the Spanish monarchy. The colonies' independence had broken the Spanish trade monopoly in Latin America. As a result, Britain enjoyed a flourishing trade with that region. Britain threatened to use its navy to stop any European intervention in the New World.

In addition to British objections, U.S. president James Monroe, in a speech to the U.S. Congress, warned the European nations that any attempt to establish or reestablish colonies in the Western Hemisphere would be considered an act of aggression. Although the United States did not have the power to enforce the **Monroe Doctrine** (1823), the British navy was able to block any attempt on the part of the European alliance.

Weaknesses now appeared in the congress system. The Concert of Europe was successful only when it did not infringe on the special interests of one of the major powers. Then, as today, national interests superseded international cooperation. The defection of Britain signaled the decline of the congress system. Although Austria, Prussia, Russia, and France continued to suppress uprisings in Europe, their efforts became considerably less effective.

Success of the Greek Revolt

In 1821, the Greeks rebelled against the Ottoman Empire. During the early years of the struggle, European rulers basically ignored the revolt. It did not immediately affect their national interests. But news of Turkish massacres of the Greek people began to stir the sympathies of Europeans. The Greek struggle captured the imagination of European artists and writers, and it became the subject of many of their works. When the brutal methods of Turkish oppression seemed to doom the cause of Greek freedom, Britain, Russia, and France came to the Greeks' aid. They defeated the Turkish forces and, in 1829, secured the Treaty of Adrianople, which recognized Greek independence. The Greek revolt was another example of the weakness of the congress system. In this incident, the major powers of Europe supported the cause of revolution that they opposed at home.

Latin America: Threat to the Old Order

As previously mentioned, Spanish colonies in Latin America struggled for independence during the Napoleonic Era and sought to establish sovereign states. Latin America covers almost eight million square miles and is larger than the United States and Canada combined. It stretches from the northern border of Mexico to the tip of South America. These lands were the home of the major Amerindian civilizations—the Mayas, the Aztecs, and the Incas (see chapter 8). But by 1500 the Spanish and the Portuguese had claimed most of this vast region. Because of the strong influence of Spanish and Portuguese customs and languages, which derived from the "Latin" culture of ancient Rome, this region is known as Latin America.

Struggle for Independence

Unlike the English colonies in North America, which experienced a large measure of self-government, the Latin American colonies were tightly controlled by Spain and Portugal. Officials appointed by the crown directed colonial affairs. In the Spanish possessions, most of these civil officials were *peninsulares*, Spaniards born and reared in Spain. They controlled the government and economic wealth of the colonies. Often, they used their positions selfishly to amass personal fortunes with which they returned to Spain to live lives of ease. Their arrogant attitude angered the criollos (Spaniards born in the New World). There was also dissatisfaction among the rest of the people—Indians, me*stizos* (those of mixed Spanish and Indian blood), and black Hispanics—who were held in low esteem and used by the other two groups to achieve their own ends. Over the years, growing discontent with the economic restrictions and political corruption of Spanish rule gave rise to independence movements.

The Napoleonic Wars in Europe stirred these revolts. Napoleon removed the Spanish king and placed his brother Joseph Bonaparte on the Spanish throne. But the colonists, though dissatisfied with Spanish rule, would not tolerate French rule. Two men, **Simón Bolívar** (boh LEE vahr; 1783–1830) and **José de San Martín** (sahn mahr-TEEN; 1778–1850), dreamed of a Spanish South America free from outside control. They raised troops to fight "wars of liberation." Bolívar, called "the Liberator," led the struggle for freedom in the north. His troops crushed the Spanish forces and secured

Simón Bolívar

the independence of Gran Colombia (comprising what are now the countries of Colombia, Venezuela, Panama, and Ecuador). To the south, San Martín, backed by Argentina (which had already gained its independence), led an army over the Andes Mountains and freed Chile and then Peru from Spanish domination.

The Portuguese colony of Brazil experienced a more peaceful transition to independence. In 1807, French troops invaded Portugal, forcing the royal family to flee to Brazil. From his new capital in Rio de Janeiro, the king ruled the Portuguese empire. Brazil prospered during that period as trade and industry flourished. In 1821, the king returned to Portugal, leaving behind his son **Dom Pedro** as his regent. But when the Portuguese legislature attempted to reduce Brazil to its former colonial status, Dom Pedro declared Brazil independent and became the emperor of Brazil. Under his rule and that of his son Dom Pedro II, Brazil became a thriving nation. But eventually, growing sectional differences in the large country and discontent among Brazil's military leaders forced Dom Pedro II to abdicate. In 1889, Brazil was proclaimed a republic. In the years that followed, however, the military dominated the government.

The birth of liberty in Latin American nations that gained independence from Spain tended to follow a pattern. After gaining independence, the nation's new leaders fought among themselves until military leaders (*caudillos*) stepped in with armed gangs, seized power, and established dictatorships.

Mexico is an example of this pattern. Self-government in Mexico came slowly, although it had been promised in the election of Porfirio Diaz in 1876. He had campaigned as a champion of a free, constitutional democracy. Once elected, he restored order, increased investments by foreign businesses, and led Mexico to become the most prosperous Latin American nation.

Although elected under a constitution, Diaz eventually consolidated his power and became a dictator, ruling for more than thirty years. Gradually, the peasants came to view Diaz and his appointees as self-serving autocrats and puppets of foreign businesses. During Diaz's rule, Indians were reduced to virtual slavery, the Roman Catholic Church amassed great wealth, and foreign investors exploited Mexico. This foreign exploitation often led to a hatred of foreigners.

Resistance to the Diaz regime began as localized rebellions against the regional administrators. The critics of Diaz consolidated under the leadership of Francisco Madero, who denounced violent revolution and ran against Diaz in the presidential election. Diaz had Madero and ten thousand of his supporters jailed, ensuring his own victory in the election. Madero challenged the results in court, but the judges, all Diaz appointees, ruled against him.

In response to Diaz's schemes, the people revolted in 1910. The uprising succeeded, and Madero was elected president. As often happens in revolutions, however, Madero's own supporters disputed among themselves, split into several armed factions, and revolted against him. Madero was assassinated. Order was not fully restored until after World War I.

José de San Martín

Latin America After Independence

Problems of Self-government in Latin America

From the time of independence through the rest of the nineteenth century, the new Latin American nations often suffered from common problems. However, the following generalizations did not equally apply to every Latin American country.

Political Instability

After gaining their independence, most Latin American countries followed the example of the United States and established republics. Unlike the United States, however, they had little previous experience in self-rule. As previously mentioned, ambitious military leaders often seized power. They ruled as dictators, satisfying their own desires at the expense of their countries. As a result, Latin American countries experienced frequent changes in government as one military dictator was overthrown and another took his place. Several factors contributed to the political instability.

Monopoly of Land and Wealth By a Few—From early colonial days, Latin America was dominated by a wealthy, powerful upper class. Though a small minority, this social class owned most of the land, controlled the wealth, and manipulated the government in many Latin American countries. The vast majority of the people remained poor and had little voice in the everyday workings of the government. Without a large middle class to provide stability, Latin American countries suffered from the effects of political favoritism and class conflict.

Powerful Influence of the Roman Catholic Church—As the Spanish and Portuguese came to the New World, they firmly established Roman Catholicism in Latin America. This religious system became a dominant influence on Latin American culture. Church leaders gained control of large amounts of land in addition to controlling the educational system. As a result, church leaders often influenced the political process to benefit the Roman Catholic Church.

Ethnic Disunity—In addition to black Hispanics, Indians, and inhabitants of European descent, a large number of Latin Americans were of mixed ancestry. Hatred, jealousy, and conflicts of interest often existed among the ethnic groups.

Conflict Among Latin American Countries—Unlike the United States, the Latin American colonies did not form one nation after gaining their independence. Soon after the wars of liberation, the Latin American people divided into a number of small countries rather than several larger ones. This fragmentation led to several border wars among the nations.

Economic Weakness

During the nineteenth century, Latin America had virtually no industry. (Foreign investment from the United States and Europe accounted for the little industry that existed.) In most Latin American countries, the economy was built around only a few products, such as bananas, coffee, rubber, or wood. A poor growing season or a struggling world market could bring economic disaster to these countries.

European and U.S. Involvement

Political and economic problems within the Latin American countries prompted European nations to interfere in their domestic affairs. The Europeans wanted to protect their foreign investments and to ensure that loans made to these countries would be repaid. Such European involvement in Latin America worried the United States. As a result, the United States assumed a greater responsibility for policing Latin American affairs. But with the increased dominance of the United States in the Western Hemisphere came a growing resentment of the United States on the part of the Latin American countries.

Section Review

1–4. List the four major powers of the Grand Alliance that defeated Napoleon.

5–7. List three goals of the Congress of Vienna.

8–9. Did colonial revolts in Latin America strengthen or threaten the European alliance system? Briefly explain your answer.

☆ Evaluate the European challenge to the uprisings in the 1820s.

☆ How did the colonial revolts influence Latin America?

II. Rise of Nationalism

Conflicting motivations among the citizens of many European countries led either to a defense of existing conditions or the determination to fundamentally alter them. These conflicts often led to violence that seldom resulted in a satisfactory outcome.

Liberalism, Nationalism, and Conservatism

Two leading forces stirring discontent with the old order during the first half of the nineteenth century were liberalism and nationalism. **Liberalism** stressed individual rights such as life, liberty, and property, and personal freedoms such as religion, speech, and the press. Liberals advocated democratic reforms such as written constitutions that guaranteed rights and freedoms and limited the power of autocratic rulers. They promoted parliamentary government, economic freedom, and an increased public participation in government.

The middle class were the primary supporters of these liberal goals. They wanted a voice in government equal to their economic influence in society. Joining with the middle class to advance the liberal cause were the masses of urban factory workers and peasants. They, however, often differed with the upper middle class concerning the goals and extent of reform. Instead of the gradual, moderate changes advocated by the middle class, the lower classes often desired more immediate, sweeping changes. They hoped to gain a voice in government to improve their social and economic standing in society.

Closely associated with the cause of personal liberty was the cause of national liberty. A strong spirit of **nationalism** motivated small and large groups alike to seek their independence or to defend their ethnic interests. The cause of nationalism also promoted a strong drive for unification in both the Italian and German states.

Conservative leaders supported absolute monarchies, the aristocracy, and Roman Catholicism. Despite their resistance to political change in Europe, discontent with the old order continued to grow, leading to new revolts. In the early 1830s and again in 1848, a series

Guiding Questions

1. How did early nineteenth-century political labels differ from modern political labels?
2. What caused the revolts of the 1830s and 1848?
3. Why did some revolts succeed while others failed?

of revolutions erupted on the Continent. In both instances, the revolutionary fires sparked first in France and soon spread throughout Europe. Although the congress system was no longer effective in dealing with these outbreaks, individual rulers following Metternich's example actively sought to suppress liberalism and nationalism within their borders.

Revolts

1830s

When **Louis XVIII** (r. 1814–24) ascended the throne of France following the defeat of Napoleon, he accepted many of the reforms that had resulted from the French Revolution. He granted a constitution that guaranteed freedom of the press and religion, ensured equality before the law for all Frenchmen, and established a legislature similar to the British Parliament. But toward the end of his reign, Louis XVIII began to suppress these liberal trends. He muzzled the press, introduced a secret police, and raised property qualifications that determined voter eligibility. By the time of his death in 1824, France once again was beginning to simmer with discontent.

But it was the reactionary policies of the new king, **Charles X** (r. 1824–30), that brought things to a boiling point. Charles, brother of Louis XVI and Louis XVIII, believed in the divine right of kings and sought to restore not only absolute rule but also the privileges of the Roman Church and the nobility. In July 1830, the people of Paris rose in rebellion in what is called the **July Revolution**. They raised barricades in the streets and resisted attempts by government soldiers to end the revolt. After three days of fighting, Charles fled to England. The French produced a more liberal constitution and chose the Duke of Orléans, **Louis Philippe** (r. 1830–48), to serve as their king. Initially popular with the French people, Louis was hailed as the "citizen king." Many of the participants in the revolution, however, soon became disillusioned because Louis Philippe catered to the interests of the upper middle class.

News of the July Revolution soon ignited a series of revolts throughout Europe. One of the nations whose smoldering discontent burst into the flame of revolution was Belgium. That tiny state had been given to the Dutch Netherlands by the Congress of Vienna. But the Belgians were dissatisfied; many cultural differences separated them from the Dutch people. Whereas the Belgians were Roman Catholics, the Dutch were predominantly Protestants. The Belgians were farmers and textile workers; the Dutch were bankers and traders. The Belgians spoke Flemish; Dutch was the official language of the schools, the government, and the courts.

When news of the July Revolution reached the city of Brussels, rioting erupted. Belgian nationalists declared their independence and wrote a liberal constitution. The leading European nations, facing unrest at home, were not able to come to the aid of the Dutch government. Leaders of these countries, however, met at a congress in London and signed the **Treaty of London**, which recognized the independence of Belgium. It also declared Belgium to be a perpetually neutral state. Thus, the balance of power would be maintained, and Belgium would be protected from foreign aggression.

Stirrings of nationalism and liberalism caused revolts to erupt in many central European states, but the rulers of Austria, Prussia, and Russia zealously suppressed any disruption of the *status quo*. Aus-

Louis Philippe

trian and Prussian troops quelled small uprisings in the Italian and German states. In Poland, when nationalist leaders tried to break free from Russian control, Czar Nicholas I sent the Russian army to brutally crush the rebellion.

1848

Most of the revolts of the 1830s were suppressed, but resentment remained within the lower classes. They were bitter against the upper class, who often excluded them from the moderate gains the middle class had received during earlier revolts. Poor harvests and rising unemployment also increased the discontent among the peasants and city workers. In 1848, barricades went up across Europe as revolution once more rocked the continent.

As before, the revolutionary fires began in Paris. In February 1848, unemployed workers and disgruntled students gathered in the French capital. They protested Louis Philippe's policies, which favored the interests of wealthy businessmen. When Louis refused to listen to their demands for reform, rioting erupted. Barricades blocked the streets of Paris as mobs prepared to meet government troops. But when the National Guard joined the side of the workers, Louis Philippe fled to England.

The revolutionary leaders proclaimed the establishment of the Second French Republic and established a temporary government to restore order in Paris and compose a new constitution for France. At the urging of radical leaders, the government established "national workshops," a social program meant to provide food, shelter, medical care, and jobs for the growing number of unemployed workers. But instead of providing useful jobs, the workshops became a public-relief program, one of the earliest modern examples of socialistic (government-financed) programs.

The new French constitution established universal manhood suffrage (all men could vote). When elections were held for a new legislature, the voters sent a fairly conservative assembly to Paris. The message was clear—the rural portions of France did not agree with the more radical ideas of the city workers and students. They objected to being taxed to support the unemployed in Paris when they were themselves facing famine. Thus, the newly elected conservative majority abolished the workshops. In reaction, unemployed workers sought to overthrow the government. For three days in June, Paris was the site of a bloody battle. During those "June Days," thousands of Frenchmen lost their lives as the army restored order to the city.

In December, elections were held for the presidency of the Second Republic. Perhaps because of recent violent uprisings, the French people voted for a man whose name symbolized authority. **Louis Napoleon**, the nephew of Napoleon Bonaparte, won by an overwhelming majority. Seeming to champion the rights of the common people, he increased his power over the government. In 1852, he staged a *coup d'état*, proclaiming himself Emperor Napoleon III of the Second French Empire. (Napoleon Bonaparte's son, who died in 1832, was considered Napoleon II.) Once again, French attempts to achieve democratic reforms through revolution led to widespread violence and to the establishment of a dictatorship.

Despite Metternich's precautions, revolts spread throughout the Austrian Empire in 1848. For example, strong nationalistic uprisings

Louis Napoleon

occurred in Hungary and Bohemia. Venice and Milan also declared their independence from Habsburg control. Demonstrations by university students and workers in Vienna finally forced Metternich to resign.

Austrian emperor Ferdinand I readily submitted to the revolutionary demands. He granted a liberal constitution, abolished serfdom, and promised self-rule for the Hungarians. But as the summer wore on, differences among the revolutionaries gave reactionary forces an opportunity to suppress the revolution. Reactionary leaders forced Ferdinand to abdicate in favor of his nephew, **Franz Josef I** (1848–1916). The young emperor renounced the concessions of his predecessor and, with the backing of the army, crushed the nationalist revolts throughout the Austrian Empire.

Although the Napoleonic Wars had exposed the Russian people to the revolutionary battle cry of "Liberty, Equality, Fraternity," peasants in Russia still suffered under the burden of serfdom that bound them to the land. Likewise, the many national groups within Russia's borders still yearned for independence. However, democratic and nationalistic reforms made little progress in Russia.

Czar **Nicholas I** sought to prevent uprisings by instituting a policy of "Autocracy, Orthodoxy, and Nationalism." This domestic program called for increasing the czar's control over the state, recognizing only the Russian Orthodox Church, and uniting the diverse national groups within Nicholas's territory around the culture and traditions of Russia—a policy called **Russification**. Nicholas, as well as later Russian czars, suppressed domestic problems instead of trying to find workable and equitable solutions. Although Russia did not experience revolution in the 1830s and 1848, it suffered from devastating social upheaval in the early twentieth century.

The Napoleonic Era also had awakened liberalism and nationalism among the Italian and German states. They sought freedom from repressive rulers, worked for democratic constitutions, and longed for national unification. However, in these states, as in most of Europe, the bright prospects of concessions were soon dimmed. Conservative monarchs temporarily regained the support of the army and crushed the uprisings. Nevertheless, the force of nationalism would triumph later in the century.

Failure of the Revolts

The period following the Napoleonic Wars remained turbulent, with discontent, uprisings, and bloodshed becoming commonplace. Most who took part in the revolts of the 1830s and 1848 shared the common desire of advancing the causes of liberalism and nationalism. However, the revolts that swept across Europe shared something else—most ended in failure.

Discontent led to violent protests and uprisings, often winning concessions from weakened and frightened rulers. Nevertheless, these gains soon were threatened as the revolutionaries quarreled among themselves. Conflicting goals and backgrounds divided the forces that had previously joined in opposition to the government. Taking advantage of the disagreement and disunity among revolutionary factions, government forces were often able to rally and suppress the revolts.

Underlying this period of turmoil was the failure of governments and their citizens to fulfill their God-ordained civic responsibilities. Government should promote righteousness in a land, which includes right moral conduct and justice. However, many European rulers chose to oppress their subjects rather than show mercy. Citizens needed to submit to authorities that God placed over them while continuing to work for reform. During this period many citizens desired greater freedom. Several of these freedoms could be supported by Christians, but some people sought to eliminate all restraint. In contrast to this, a Christian view of liberty involves obedience to legitimate authority and self-control.

Section Review

1–4. From what country were the revolutionary fires of the 1830s and 1848 first ignited? List three additional European countries that revolted during this period.

5–7. What motivated European revolts during this period, and how did these motivations relate to justice, power, and nationalism?

8–9. Why did some revolts succeed and others fail?

✴ Briefly assess the reign of Nicholas I in light of Proverbs 28:16.

✴ Contrast nineteenth-century political labels (*conservatism* and *liberalism*) with contemporary labels. Evaluate these terms.

III. Triumph of Nationalism

By 1850, the spirit of conservatism and international cooperation established by the Congress of Vienna had waned, and the spirit of liberalism and nationalism had intensified. During the second half of the century, the mood of European politics gradually changed. The years of revolution had dispelled the zeal of romantic idealism; in its place arose a hardened realism. Like Machiavelli's *Prince*, European politicians and diplomats adopted a politics of necessity known as ***realpolitik*** ("the politics of reality"), in which they used whatever means necessary—including force—to advance their national goals. Although most of Europe escaped widespread war during the nineteenth century, the spirit of nationalism resulted in several smaller wars among the major powers.

Nationalism in Italy and Germany

National interests divided the congress members and often led to war instead of peace. Nationalism decreased international cooperation and increased the drive for unification in both Italy and Germany.

Italian Unification

By the mid-nineteenth century, Italy was still what Metternich contemptuously called a "geographic expression." The Italian peninsula remained politically divided; small kingdoms competed with one another, and foreign powers controlled large sections of the country. Nevertheless, the spirit of nationalism was on the rise, fueled by a movement called ***Risorgimento*** ("resurgence"). In 1832, **Giuseppe Mazzini** (maht TSEE nee; 1805–72) started a patriotic society called Young Italy, determining to fight, if necessary, for Italian unification.

The man primarily responsible for unifying Italy was Count **Camillo di Cavour** (1810–61), the prime minister of the Kingdom of Sardinia. Cavour was a wily diplomat who used whatever means

Guiding Questions

1. What circumstances resulted in the unification of Italy and Germany?
2. What reforms were achieved in Austria and Russia?

Camillo di Cavour

necessary to promote Italian unification. When the Crimean War began in 1854, Cavour joined Britain and France in sending troops to fight Russia. He had no quarrel with the Russians but hoped that the peace negotiations following the war would give him the opportunity to enlist support for his cause of unification. Cavour knew he would need an ally to wrest the provinces of Lombardy and Venetia from Austrian control. He found his ally in Napoleon III of France, who was seeking to win both territory and military glory.

Napoleon III secretly agreed to help Sardinia gain the Austrian-controlled provinces of Lombardy and Venetia. In return, Cavour promised to cede him the provinces of Nice and Savoy. In 1859, Cavour provoked the Austrians into declaring war on Sardinia. As the Franco-Sardinian armies successfully drove the Austrian troops out of Lombardy, revolts broke out across northern Italy. Rulers of small Italian states were overthrown as Italians joined Cavour's efforts for unification. Fearful of a strong, unified Italy, Napoleon III made a separate peace with Austria. Despite this infuriating setback, Cavour had made considerable progress in uniting most of northern Italy with the Kingdom of Sardinia.

Meanwhile in southern Italy, a follower of Mazzini, **Giuseppe Garibaldi** (gar uh BAWL dee; 1807–82), rose to prominence. Strongly patriotic and determined to unify Italy, Garibaldi gathered a band of loyal followers called "Red Shirts" and invaded the island of Sicily in 1860. Having conquered it, Garibaldi's forces landed on the Italian mainland and took Naples. Garibaldi next planned to march on Rome and take possession of the Papal States.

At that point, Cavour quickly intervened, fearing that an attack on Rome would draw the French into the conflict on the pope's side. (Since the days of Charlemagne, French troops had guarded the papal city.) Rushing southward with Sardinian troops, Cavour persuaded Garibaldi to hand over his conquests to **Victor Emmanuel II**, the king of Sardinia. On March 17, 1861, just a few months

Giuseppe Garibaldi

Victor Emmanuel II

	Sardinia prior to 1859		To Italy 1866
	To Sardinia		To Italy 1870
	Added to Sardinia 1860 (Sardinia becomes Italy)		

Unification of Italy (1859–70)

Pioneers of Military Medicine

Florence Nightingale (1820–1910) established the modern nursing profession through her efforts to help sick and wounded British soldiers during the Crimean War (see chapter 19). Newspaper reports detailing the appalling conditions in the Crimea shocked the British public; many people demanded that something be done to alleviate the suffering. The British government responded by recruiting thirty-eight nurses, many of whom had little or no training, to accompany the well-trained Florence Nightingale to the Crimea.

When this small band of nurses arrived, they found that the "hospital" was a filthy and damp former army barracks. Wounded soldiers—wrapped in bloody, vermin-covered blankets—died by the hundreds from their wounds and disease. Florence began her work. At first, she had few supplies, but through donations from Britain she was able to purchase many necessities. Florence believed in efficient organization and hard work, and before long her efforts saved lives.

Strain and overwork, however, ruined her health, and after returning from the Crimea a national heroine, she rarely ventured out into public again. During the American Civil War, however, Florence advised the United States on how to establish

Florence Nightingale

Mary Seacole

military hospitals. Having received many honors in her lifetime, Florence Nightingale in 1907 became the first woman to receive the British Order of Merit.

Mary Seacole (1805–81) became another pioneer of military medicine. When the Crimean War began, Seacole sought to serve as a nurse but was rejected because of her gender and ethnicity (Jamaican). Even Florence Nightingale refused to accept her offer to serve. Still determined to go to the Crimea, she used her own money to get there and set up the British Hotel. From there, Seacole helped many soldiers from Britain, France, Italy, and even Russia. Overcoming Nightingale's continued refusal to support her work, Seacole saved many lives and won the appreciation of the soldiers. She was the first woman allowed in Sevastopol after its surrender. For her efforts, Seacole was awarded the British Crimean Medal, the French Legion of Honor, and the Turkish Order of the Medjidie. After the war, she returned to Britain financially devastated and in poor health. British newspapers published her story, inspiring the British public to repay her wartime expenses and relieve her financial plight.

before Cavour's death, an Italian parliament officially proclaimed the establishment of the Kingdom of Italy with Victor Emmanuel II as the first king. With the exception of Venetia and the Papal States, Italian unification had been accomplished. By 1870, these last two territories were added to the Italian kingdom while the French were engaged in the Franco-Prussian War. In 1871 the city of Rome became the capital of the nation of Italy.

German Unification

Despite the failure of the revolts of 1848, the cause of German unification continued to advance. But it was in the economic, not the political, realm that great strides were made initially. Under the leadership of Prussia, the German states established a trade union called the **Zollverein**. The favorable results of this economic cooperation lent support to the movement for political unification.

Otto von Bismarck

The architect of political unification in Germany was Count **Otto von Bismarck** (1815–98), a loyal Prussian who was both crafty and opportunistic. Bismarck was not a romantic idealist but was devoted to the practice of *realpolitik*. He believed that the most practical way to achieve his goals was through the hard-nosed policy of "blood and iron," not through idealistic speeches. In 1862, King Wilhelm I made Bismarck the chancellor of Prussia. Bismarck immediately began seeking opportunities to promote German unification under Prussian domination.

War with Denmark and Austria

Bismarck's first opportunity came in 1864, when he deliberately involved Prussia in a dispute with the king of Denmark over the small territories of Schleswig and Holstein. The king of Denmark wanted to incorporate these territories into his kingdom, but Bismarck protested, claiming them as German territories. Posing as the protector of the German people, he persuaded Austria to join Prussia in a war against Denmark. The brief war ended in a Danish defeat. Following the Danish surrender, Austria and Prussia divided the spoils: Austria took control of Holstein, while Prussia administered Schleswig.

Next, Bismarck sought for a way to discredit Austria and to strengthen Prussia's influence in German affairs. He sought to isolate Austria from other European nations and then use the superior might of the Prussian army to assert Prussian domination. Through skillful diplomacy, Bismarck persuaded both Russia and France to remain neutral in the event of war between Prussia and Austria. He then enlisted the aid of the Italians in a war against Austria, promising Venetia in return for their support. Though Bismarck was now prepared for war, he did not want to be seen as the aggressor. So he stirred up trouble in Holstein, angering the Austrians to such a degree that they declared war first.

The **Austro-Prussian War**, also known as the Seven Weeks' War, erupted in 1866. The Prussians quickly gained the victory and forced the Austrians to agree to the Prussian peace proposal. Prussia acquired both Holstein and additional German territory. Furthermore, Austria agreed to end the German Confederation established by the Congress of Vienna. In its place, a Prussia-dominated North German Confederation was established.

The Franco-Prussian War

With Austria now out of the way, Bismarck began working to bring the southern German states under Prussian control. To accomplish this goal, he sought an opportunity to provoke a war with France. Such a war, he believed, would stir up such nationalistic feeling among the German states that it would be relatively easy to persuade them to join with Prussia. In France, an increasingly ill Napoleon III allowed himself to be pushed into war by a prowar party. They wanted to diminish Prussian power before it became too strong for France to handle.

The immediate cause for the **Franco-Prussian War** (1870–71) was the throne of Spain. A liberal revolution had overthrown the corrupt Spanish monarchy in 1868, and the new provisional government invited Leopold, a Hohenzollern prince, to become king. The French opposed such a plan because the Hohenzollern family also ruled Prussia. If Leopold became king of Spain, France would be encircled by the Hohenzollerns. Amid the furor and cries of the French for war, Leopold withdrew his candidacy.

Yet the French were not satisfied. The French ambassador met with the Prussian king, Wilhelm I, who was vacationing at Ems in the Rhineland. He demanded that Wilhelm promise in writing that no Hohenzollern would ever sit on the Spanish throne. Wilhelm refused and sent Bismarck a dispatch (report) of his discussions, granting him permission to publish it in the newspapers. Bismarck did publish the dispatch, but not before he changed the wording slightly to make

Unification of Germany (1866–71)

it seem as if Wilhelm and the ambassador had insulted each other. This "Ems dispatch" so angered the French that they declared war on the equally infuriated Prussians.

As Bismarck had hoped, the southern German states joined with Prussia in the war effort. The Germans invaded Alsace and Lorraine (French provinces) and in less than two months had trapped Napoleon III at the fortress of Sedan. There, Napoleon III and his army of 83,000 men were forced to surrender. On hearing of the surrender, mobs in Paris declared an end to the Second French Empire and established a republic, vowing to continue the war. But the Germans advanced to the outskirts of Paris, and the French cause became hopeless. On January 28, 1871, Paris surrendered after a 132-day siege. Ten days earlier, in the Versailles Palace outside Paris, Kaiser Wilhelm I had been proclaimed emperor of the German Reich (empire), fulfilling Bismarck's plans for unification.

Reforms in Austria and Russia

The Dual Monarchy

The Austrian Habsburgs ruled over a varied and increasingly restless group of nationalities. Of these nationalities, the Hungarians created the most problems for the Austrian government. In 1848, under the leadership of Louis Kossuth (KAH sooth), they had staged an unsuccessful revolt. Later, after the Prussian victory over Austria in the Austro-Prussian War (1866), the Hungarians again demanded self-government. But this time the Austrians were in no position to reject their demands. They made the Hungarians equal partners within the empire. Both countries remained under the Habsburg monarchy and cooperated in matters of finance, foreign affairs, and defense. However, each had its own constitution, official language, flag, and parliament. The Austrian Empire now became the Austro-Hungarian Empire, or **Dual Monarchy**, ruled by Franz Josef I.

Alexander II

Russia Under Alexander II

When Nicholas I died in 1855, his son **Alexander II** (r. 1855–81) became the Russian czar. He recognized that his father's policy of "Autocracy, Orthodoxy, and Nationalism" had caused widespread discontent. It had also weakened Russia's position as a major European power, resulting in Russia's defeat during the Crimean War. Consequently, Alexander implemented several social reforms.

The most important one came in 1861, when he abolished serfdom, giving the serfs personal freedom and the right to buy land. Radicals pressed for more extensive reforms, but Alexander rejected many of their demands. In 1881, revolutionaries used explosives to assassinate Alexander. When his son Alexander III (r. 1881–94) became czar, he returned to the harsh policies of Nicholas I.

Section Review

1. Who was the prime minister of Sardinia primarily responsible for the unification of Italy?

2–5. Who was the Prussian politician primarily responsible for the unification of Germany? Against what three European nations did he take Prussia to war to achieve his goal?

6. As a result of Austria's military defeat, what nationality within the Austrian Empire was able to achieve self-government?

☆ What events led to the unification of Italy?

☆ What did revolutionaries accomplish by assassinating Alexander II?

Guiding Questions

1. What were the prominent themes in romanticism?
2. How did romanticism influence nineteenth century Europe and the present?

Romanticism in Literature

Theme	Writer
Longing for distant lands	Sir Walter Scott Victor Hugo Samuel Taylor Coleridge
Fascination with the supernatural and mysterious	Jakob and Wilhelm Grimm Johann Wolfgang von Goethe Edgar Allan Poe
Glorification of the noble savage	James Fenimore Cooper
Emphasis on nature	William Wordsworth
Love of freedom	George Gordon, Lord Byron Percy Bysshe Shelley
Pride of nationalism	Aleksandr Pushkin

IV. Protest of Romanticism

The powerful feelings unleashed by the political revolutions of the late eighteenth and early nineteenth centuries resulted in **romanticism**. This cultural movement gave literary and artistic expression to the concepts of "Liberty, Equality, Fraternity."

Romanticism in Literature

The works of romantic writers exhibited a variety of themes. Most of these themes were not new; writers had expressed them in previous centuries but without protests against the status quo. During what we call the romantic age, however, scores of well-known writers from many countries contributed to this movement of protest. The table in the margin provides a representative sample of romantic themes and writers.

Romanticism in Music

Some composers of this period drew heavily on the conventions that had developed to that point, whereas others were eager to push the accepted rules of regularity, balance, and restraint that had defined previous music. As works by such innovators became popular, certain traits came to distinguish the music of this era from that which had come before. For instance, as in romantic literature and art, romantic music sought to stir the emotions of its audience.

During the romantic age, popular interest in music increased as new musical instruments such as the accordion, harmonium (reed organ), and piano improved in construction and became more accessible to the general public. Music lovers attended solo recitals by such popular performers as pianist Liszt and singer Jenny Lind, as well as the performances of national and city orchestras. The London Philharmonic Orchestra was formed in 1813 and the New York Philharmonic in 1842.

Nationalism exerted a major influence on romantic music. Many European countries could boast of a national composer: Poland had Chopin, Hungary had Liszt, Bohemia had Smetana, Russia had Tchaikovsky, and Italy had Verdi. These composers often used national folk songs and popular dance tunes in their compositions. Many romantic composers are still well known, and their music is still greatly enjoyed.

The man who bridged the gap between classical and romantic music was **Ludwig van Beethoven** (1770–1827). Although

Ludwig van Beethoven

born in Bonn, Germany, Beethoven spent most of his life in Vienna. His early music reflected the classical influence of his teacher, Franz Josef Haydn. Later, however, his music became more dramatic and explosive, blending classical and romantic elements. Beethoven increased the size of the orchestra and added two new instruments: the trombone and the piccolo. He also helped establish the piano as a popular instrument. In his late twenties, he began to lose his hearing; by his fiftieth birthday, he was completely deaf. In spite of this handicap, he continued to compose for the rest of his life.

The table in the margin provides a representative sample of romantic musical forms and composers.

Romanticism in Art

Like their literary counterparts, romantic artists appealed to the senses and feelings of the beholder. Their use of bright colors was intended to elicit an emotional response. Their paintings depicted local landscapes as well as faraway places. They chose themes from national legends and folklore and the medieval past. Their works demonstrate an appreciation for nature and a deep sensitivity to the feelings of the common man.

Most French painters of this period continued in the neoclassical style. The most famous neoclassical painter was **Jacques**

> ### Balancing Head and Heart
> In reacting against rationalism and restraint, romantics tended to go to extremes in the opposite direction, becoming rebels against all forms of rules. Many romantics made their feelings the standard—if it felt good, it must be good. In addition, many romantics exchanged the mind-centered humanism of the Enlightenment for a heart-centered humanism. The Bible, however, does not permit a reduction of either mind or heart. Christians are not simply to know or do the right things. The Great Commandments require loving God and others (Matt. 22:36–40). Nor does the Bible permit us to simply follow our hearts. Jeremiah 17:9 warns about the deceitfulness of our hearts. Both the mind and the emotions are part of the human person that God made, and both play a role in either sinful or righteous living.

Romanticism in Music	
Form	Composer
Piano music	Frédéric Chopin Franz Liszt
Orchestral music	Peter Ilich Tchaikovsky Johannes Brahms
Opera	Giuseppe Verdi Richard Wagner

Wivenhoe Park, Essex by John Constable

The "Fighting Temeraire" being tugged to her last Berth by Joseph M. W. Turner

Shipwreck on the Coast by Eugène Delacroix

Romanticism in Art	
Characteristic	**Artist**
Love for nature	John Constable (1776–1837)
Landscapes and seascapes	J. M. W. Turner (1775–1851)
Emphasis on color and movement	Eugéne Delacroix (duh lah KRWAH; 1798–1863)

Louis David (dah VEED; 1748–1825), whose works demonstrate the neoclassical interest in themes from classical Greece and Rome.

Romanticism's Influence on the 19th Century and Beyond

Advocates of romanticism led a reaction against (1) the restraint of the Age of Reason, (2) the violence of the French Revolution, (3) the repression following the Napoleonic Wars, and (4) the often harsh working conditions caused by the rapid growth of the Industrial Revolution (discussed in chapter 18).

In contrast to the Age of Reason, the romantic age turned from rationalism to idealism, from the intellectual to the emotional. Romantics emphasized originality above imitation, nationalism above internationalism, and self-fulfillment above the common good. Their attitude shifted from optimism to uncertainty, from contentment to desire. Many political changes can be traced to this philosophy.

The romantic concept of the noble savage also began during this period. Many of the *philosophes*, especially Jean Jacques Rousseau, assumed that civilization had corrupted man. Rousseau believed that man is at his best when living in a primitive environment apart from civilization.

Another characteristic of the romantics was their rebellion against the constraints of society. Many of them sought to live a life free from all restraint. The influence of romanticism has continued to the present.

Section Review

1. What cultural movement gave literary and artistic expression to the concepts of "Liberty, Equality, Fraternity"?

2–5. List four of the prominent themes prevalent in the works of romantic writers.

6–7. Nature was the primary subject matter of which two romantic artists?

✻ How did romanticism influence nineteenth-century Europe?

✻ How does romanticism influence the present?

Making Connections

1–2. Give two reasons the Vienna peace settlement failed to accomplish its goals.

3–6. List three goals of liberalism and explain why the middle class supported these goals.

7. Why did Giuseppe Mazzini start a patriotic society called Young Italy?

8. Explain how Beethoven bridged the gap between classical and romantic music.

Developing History Skills

1. What were the long-term results of the revolts of Latin American colonies from Spain?

2. What significant events in this chapter led to the unification of Germany?

Thinking Critically

1. Should national interests come before international cooperation? Explain your answer.

2. Evaluate the romantic attitude toward freedom in light of God's instruction to Adam in Genesis 2:16–17.

Living in God's World

1. During the late nineteenth century, an anti-revolutionary party was started by Christians in the Netherlands as an alternative to both the Conservative and Liberal Parties. Imagine that you are a newspaper editor for the *De Standaard*, the party newspaper. Write a brief article explaining why the Anti-Revolutionary Party would disagree with both liberals and conservatives. Explain why the name Anti-Revolutionary was chosen for the party.

2. Outline some of the key unbiblical tenets of romanticism and formulate biblical alternatives.

People, Places, and Things to Know

Congress of Vienna
Lord Castlereagh
Alexander I
Prince Klemens von Metternich
Charles Maurice de Talleyrand
Quadruple Alliance
Monroe Doctrine
peninsulares
criollos
mestizos
Simón Bolívar
José de San Martín
Dom Pedro
caudillos
liberalism
nationalism
Louis XVIII
Charles X
July Revolution
Louis Philippe
Treaty of London
Louis Napoleon
Franz Josef I
Nicholas I
Russification
realpolitik
Risorgimento
Giuseppe Mazzini
Camillo di Cavour
Giuseppi Garibaldi
Victor Emmanuel II
Zollverein
Otto von Bismarck
Austro-Prussian War
Franco-Prussian War
Dual Monarchy
Alexander II
romanticism
Ludwig van Beethoven
Jacques Louis David

CHAPTER

Industrial Revolution and European Society

18

I. The Industrial Revolution

II. Responses to the Industrial Revolution

III. Changing Outlooks in European Society

Houses of Parliament, London

Big Ideas

1. How did the Industrial Revolution develop?

2. How did Christians respond to the Industrial Revolution?

3. What challenges to Christianity occurred during this period?

"It was the best of times, it was the worst of times, it was the age of wisdom, it was the age of foolishness, it was the epoch of belief, it was the epoch of incredulity. . . ."

These opening lines of Charles Dickens's *A Tale of Two Cities* aptly describe European society in the second half of the nineteenth century. In the eyes of many Europeans, this period was the "best of times." Nationalism and democratic liberalism brought about great changes. In addition, the Industrial Revolution dramatically transformed European society. The advances in industrial development gave rise to a belief in progress that affected both intellectual and religious attitudes. Many people believed that both man and society were getting better and better. Yet, for many Europeans, this period was the "worst of times." Crowded slums and miserable working conditions caused many urban workers to despair. To them, it was apparent that the evils of society had not been remedied.

The situation became worse as many intellectual and religious leaders began to question the authority of God's Word. This gradual shift away from God and Scripture produced a secular humanism that replaced belief in God with faith in human potential. However, many skeptics ultimately turned to Christianity when they found secular humanism to be an empty promise. Some even became Christianity's strongest defenders.

This chapter traces the development of the Industrial Revolution, which began in Great Britain, and examines its impact on European society. We will also assess both the response of European society to the dramatic changes caused by industrial development and the changing outlooks and values that transformed European society.

I. The Industrial Revolution

Shortly before the French Revolution, Great Britain began to experience some sweeping changes of its own. Unlike the French Revolution, which was sudden and violent, the **Industrial Revolution** occurred gradually over several decades. Powered machines began to replace hand tools, and the modern factory system came into existence. These technological developments were revolutionary, not because of the speed with which they occurred but because of their tremendous impact on society.

Beginnings of Industrialism

During the eighteenth century, conditions in British society were favorable for industrial development. Three important factors combined to make the Industrial Age possible.

1. *An adequate food supply*—The Industrial Revolution was preceded by a revolution in agriculture. New machines and better farming methods led to an increased food supply that was sufficient to meet the demands of the growing urban population.

2. *A large and mobile labor force*—As a result of the increased efficiency and productivity in agriculture, fewer people were needed to produce the food. The unemployed farm workers moved to the centers of industrial development and formed the labor force of industry.

3. *Expansion of trade*—Throughout the eighteenth century, foreign trade became an increasingly vital part of the British economy. This trade expanded as the number of British

Guiding Questions

1. What three factors made the Industrial Revolution possible?
2. How did the Industrial Revolution develop?

colonial possessions increased. The newly acquired colonies not only supplied raw materials for British industry but also provided a growing market for British products.

In addition to these factors, Britain's social and political climate provided a favorable setting for industrial development. Because of Britain's geographic isolation from the Continent, it escaped the destruction of the Napoleonic Wars. While other nations experienced revolution in the nineteenth century, British society remained relatively stable and peaceful. Reforms came gradually through parliamentary measures rather than by violent uprisings. Furthermore, the British government encouraged industrial development by issuing patents for new inventions and removing many regulations that had previously hindered economic growth. Likewise, taxes were not excessive, and interest rates were low. These conditions encouraged businessmen to invest in new business ventures.

Agricultural Revolution

Jethro Tull and **Charles Townshend** are important figures in the history of agriculture. In the eighteenth century, Tull invented a seed "drill," or planter, that enabled farmers to plant more efficiently, increase crop yields, and end the wasteful scattering of seed. Later, Townshend developed a new system of crop rotation. Instead of leaving a field fallow for a year, he planted clover and turnips in the field. These crops returned needed minerals that other crops removed from the soil. In addition, the yield of turnips and clover could be used to feed farm animals. Townshend also used fertilizer in connection with his system and found that an increased crop yield resulted.

Robert Bakewell used selective breeding to produce larger and healthier farm animals. Since more feed was available (thanks to Townshend's system of growing turnips and clover), farmers no longer had to slaughter most of their animals in the winter. They now had the means to feed them until spring. Because of the work of Bakewell and others, today we have such well-known breeds as Hereford cattle and Berkshire hogs.

Another factor that influenced agricultural production was the enclosure movement. In the past, small farmers had benefited from using certain open fields as common pasture. In the eighteenth century, however, Parliament made it much easier for wealthy landowners to incorporate these common grazing lands into their own estates and form large farms. The small farmer, unable to survive on what little land he owned, often had to sell his land. In order to live, these farmers and their families had no choice but to move to the cities to find work. In spite of all the hardships and upheaval, the enclosure movement made British agriculture more efficient and profitable. Also, this painful transition ultimately provided workers to fill positions in Britain's growing industries.

The Textile Industry

The Industrial Revolution made its real breakthrough in the cotton textile industry. In the eighteenth century, cotton manufacturing was new to Britain and faced a strong challenge from the established wool industry. The manufacturers of woolen goods enjoyed government support and even persuaded Parliament to pass laws that were designed to hinder domestic cotton production. But with the inven-

Charles Townshend

tion of new machines, cotton production soon exceeded that of the wool industry.

Improvements in the textile industry began in 1733, when John **Kay** invented a "flying shuttle," which made it possible for a weaver to work faster and to weave cloth of greater width. One weaver, however, now needed four spinners to keep him supplied with thread. In 1769, James Hargreaves solved this problem with the invention of the spinning jenny. (The word *jenny* may be derived from *gin*, a regional term for *engine*.) That machine could spin up to eight threads at a time. But the thread it spun was coarser and weaker than the thread the old spinning wheel spun. It did not take long, however, for someone to find a solution to that problem too. That same year, **Richard Arkwright** invented a spinning frame that not only produced thread superior to the spinning jenny but also was powered by water. Because his spinning frames were too large for home use, he built special factories for them. For this contribution to the textile industry, Arkwright is sometimes called the Father of the Industrial Revolution.

Other improvements quickly emerged in the cotton industry. For example, in 1779 **Samuel Crompton** invented an even larger spinning machine called the spinning mule. His machine, operated by one person, could spin a thousand threads at a time. Six years later, both spinning and weaving machines were converted to steam power. The only remaining bottleneck in the production process was the harvesting of cotton, which involved a slow process by which cotton seeds had to be separated by hand from the cotton fiber. Before long, the demand for cotton exceeded the supply. But in 1793 the American inventor **Eli Whitney** devised a simple cotton gin with which one man could do the work of fifty people separating the fiber from the seed manually. Now spinning, weaving, and preparing raw cotton could keep pace with one another. As a result, the manufacture of cotton goods proceeded at a frantic pace.

(top) *Flying shuttle;*
(bottom) *Early spinning frame*

Spinning mule

The Factory System

In the earliest stages of the Industrial Revolution, there were no factories in the modern sense of the word. Workers lived in rural areas. They labored at home, using their own hand tools. For the most part, they were able to set their own work schedules and determine how much they wanted to produce. But the size and expense

Why the Demand for Cotton?

You might wonder why so much effort went into turning cotton into thread and why the demand for cotton quickly exceeded the supply prior to Eli Whitney's invention. Two important reasons are cost and versatility. Cloth woven from cotton thread was less expensive than cloth made from wool. Manufacturers then turned the less expensive cotton cloth into affordable clothing. In a society where wages were low but where everyone needed goods produced from cotton, this was revolutionary. With the introduction of cotton, even the working poor could save and buy a new shirt, a pair of socks, or some slacks, rather than continue to mend the more expensive woolen material. In addition, cotton was versatile. Manufacturers turned cotton thread into denim, underwear, bed sheets, and even fire hoses. While fire hoses are no longer made from cotton, cotton remains the most widely used natural fiber for cloth today.

of the new industrial machinery made it impossible for this domestic system to continue.

The factory system brought the workers, raw materials, and machinery under one roof. Factories were usually located near transportation routes, sources of water power, or natural resources. As the factory system replaced the domestic system, four significant changes took place for the worker. (1) The worker often moved to an urban environment to be near the factory. (2) He no longer owned his own tools but used those provided by the factory owner. (3) He no longer controlled the number of hours he worked per day or the pace at which he worked. (4) He now more often performed his work away from his family. Although these changes were a necessary part of industrialism, they created problems for both workers and society.

Development of Industrialism

During the last half of the nineteenth century, industrialism spread throughout much of western Europe. Britain remained the leader, but Germany became a fierce competitor. Although several European countries built factories and railroads, Russia, eastern Europe, and southern Europe remained economically backward and poverty stricken. The pace of industrial growth in the United States, Japan, and some regions of Canada also increased. In South America, Africa, and most of Asia, however, modernization and industrialization significantly lagged. In the latter areas, traditional economic patterns continued relatively unchanged by the new economic developments in Europe.

Iron and Steel Production

One of Britain's most abundant natural resources was iron ore. During the early stages of the Industrial Revolution, however, the production of cast-iron objects remained very costly. Before the Industrial Revolution, charcoal (a wood byproduct) had been used in the smelting of the ore. Charcoal was becoming increasingly scarce, so ironmakers began to use coke (a coal byproduct) in the smelting process. Britain had large coal deposits, and coke became a cheap fuel. In 1784, **Henry Cort** invented a process by which iron ore was "puddled" (stirred) in the furnace to rid it of impurities. He also developed a method of rolling and hammering the iron to produce a versatile product called wrought iron.

Not until 1856 was an inexpensive and efficient steel-making process devised. The man responsible for developing it was Sir **Henry Bessemer**, who found that shooting a jet of air into molten iron would help rid it of more impurities. Then, by adding carbon

Bessemer process

1. *Bessemer furnace in upright position*
2. *molten iron being poured into furnace*
3. *furnace returned to upright position, after which air is pumped in from the bottom to stir the molten iron and remove impurities*
4. *purified iron being poured from the furnace to the next step in preparing molten iron*

and other metals, he developed steel. With this process, steel production increased dramatically. For example, Britain, Germany, France, and Belgium produced 125,000 tons of steel in 1860; in 1913 they produced more than 32 million tons. For this reason, the first stage of the Industrial Revolution has been called the "age of iron," the later stage the "age of steel."

New Sources of Power

Many of the early factories were near rivers, streams, or lakes so that they could use water power to run their machinery. Discoveries of new sources of power made the modern factory system possible. In 1769, a Scotsman named **James Watt** designed the first practical and efficient steam engine by improving the design of an earlier model to provide enough power to run heavy machinery. Steam power made it possible for factories to be strategically located near markets or sources of raw materials instead of near a source of water power.

By the late nineteenth century, new energy sources began to replace the steam engine. Through the invention of the electric dynamo (a machine that turned mechanical energy into electrical energy), many factories converted to electrical power. By 1914, half of all the power used in British and German industries was supplied by electricity. Oil provided another energy source. The beginning of oil production followed the drilling of the world's first commercial oil well near Titusville, Pennsylvania, in 1859. Although the oil initially was used primarily to produce kerosene for lamps, the development of the internal combustion engine in 1885 provided new uses for petroleum products.

Transportation

Improvements in transportation aided the progress of the Industrial Revolution. Between 1754 and 1788, British roads were greatly improved under a system of turnpike trusts. In a turnpike trust, a group of men financed the building of a road and then charged a toll to those traveling on it. By 1788, Britain had eighteen thousand miles of roads, many of which were built using a method devised by **John McAdam**. Constructed with tightly packed crushed rocks, macadamized roads provided a smoother and more durable surface. Travel by stagecoach became faster than ever.

The construction of canals made it easier to transport heavy or bulky industrial goods. Canals also shortened the routes and lowered the cost of transportation. England had dug its first canal by 1757, and by 1850 five thousand miles of canals crisscrossed the nation, joining major rivers.

In addition to building roads and canals, Britain led in constructing railroads. The early rail lines were rather short, usually running from coal mines or stone quarries to a nearby port. The first "trains" moved to their destination with the help of gravity and horse power. In 1804 Richard Trevithick built a steam-powered locomotive, and ten years later the locomotive of George Stephenson pulled a train of cars for the first time.

As industry grew in the nineteenth century, the need for transportation increased as well. To meet this need, railroad building intensified. For example, in 1860 only about 30,000 miles of railroad existed in the entire world, but by 1890 the United States, Britain, and Germany had a combined total of 213,000 miles of railroad.

Blücher locomotive

Industrial Revolution in Great Britain

(above) *Robert Fulton;*
(inset) Clermont *steamboat*

(top) *Orville and Wilbur Wright;* (bottom) *Wright brothers' airplane*

About the same time that Trevithick put a steam engine on wheels, American **Robert Fulton** put a steam engine in a ship. Although not the first person to do this, he was the first to operate a steamboat as a commercial success. By the middle of the century, iron steamships were crossing the Atlantic Ocean in less than ten days, although at first those ships still carried sails because few people trusted the new steam engines.

The steamships and railroads met transportation needs in the nineteenth century; however, two developments at the beginning of the next century pointed the way to the future. In 1903, two brothers, **Orville** and **Wilbur Wright**, made the first successful airplane

Henry Ford

Model T

flight at Kitty Hawk, North Carolina. In 1908, **Henry Ford** began production of his famous Model T automobile.

Mass Production

In addition to the scores of inventions that improved industrial output, new production techniques helped manufacturers produce more goods at a cheaper price. Between 1870 and 1914, industrial production in Europe and North America more than tripled. Several new manufacturing methods made this tremendous growth possible.

1. *Automation*—In the early stages of industrialism, new machines helped workers perform their functions more quickly and efficiently. As the years progressed, other machines were invented to run the first machines. One result of this increased automation was that workers in many factories spent their time ensuring that machines functioned properly rather than directly making the products themselves.

2. *Interchangeable parts*—The expanding role of machines in industrial production gave rise to interchangeable parts. Whereas handcrafted items varied, machine-produced items were all the same. Previously, if some part of a product was damaged, the whole product had to be replaced or a new part custom-made. But with interchangeable parts, a product could be repaired easily and cheaply by replacing the broken piece with an identical piece.

3. *Division of labor*—In the past, skilled craftsmen worked on their products from start to finish. During the last part of the nineteenth century, this procedure changed. A number of workers divided the manufacturing process into several simple procedures, each worker performing a separate function.

4. *Assembly line*—Another method devised to accelerate production was the assembly line. Workers stationed along a conveyor belt each assembled a different specific part of a product. The item then moved down the line, where other workers

assembled different parts. Henry Ford's automobile plant became one of the first industries to use this new procedure. By 1913, Ford workers were able to assemble a complete car in only ninety-three minutes.

Science and Industry

As scientists made new discoveries, factory owners eagerly sought to apply the new knowledge to their particular areas of manufacturing. In the field of chemistry, for example, scientists discovered how to make synthetic products such as dyes and fertilizers. Inventors designed new products that aided not only industry but society as a whole. One of the most famous of the nineteenth-century inventors was Thomas Alva Edison, an American genius whose 1,093 patented inventions included the light bulb, the phonograph, and the motion picture projector.

Business Finance

When historians speak of industrial expansion before 1860, they refer to the increase in the number of small business partnerships. After 1860, large corporations began to replace the small businesses that found it difficult to meet the high cost of machinery, factories, and workers' wages. As corporations became more common, banks and other financial institutions became more important. These institutions not only helped to organize and finance new corporations but also controlled many of them.

Thomas Alva Edison

Consequences of Industrialism

British society changed dramatically during the age of industrialism. Some of the changes were good and others bad. This age saw sharp contrasts of prosperity and poverty, opportunity and oppression, morality and immorality, and hope and despair.

Living and Working Conditions

In the early stages of the Industrial Revolution, living and working conditions were wretched. The cities were ill equipped to meet the needs of the great number of rural unemployed who flocked to the industrial centers. Housing sprang up quickly to meet the heavy demand—so quickly that little thought was given to the comfort and health of the occupants. As a result, many families shared one-room dwellings. Crowded slums soon appeared in almost every factory town, and people were forced to live in the midst of disease and filth.

The working day in most factories was exhausting, and working conditions were often dangerous. It was not uncommon for men, women, and even children to work fourteen to sixteen hours a day. Mill owners, in order to maximize their profits, often took advantage of their workers. One owner who employed children told parliamentary investigators that during busy times of the year, he expected the children to work from 3:00 a.m. to 10:00 p.m. (They regularly worked from 6:00 a.m. to 8:30 p.m.) Conditions in the mines and factories were appalling. Coal mines, for example, were poorly ventilated, and factory machinery had few, if any, safety

(left) *A little spinner in a Georgia cotton mill;*
(right) *Breaker boys who worked in coal mines*

features. If a worker suffered serious injury on the job, the employer could simply hire another worker to fill his place.

Increased Population and Productivity

Many positive contributions also came from the Industrial Age. People were better nourished, enjoyed a higher standard of living, and had a longer lifespan than people of the previous century. It is estimated that the population of Europe increased from 190 million in 1800 to 460 million in 1900. The growth in population was especially noticeable in the cities. Before 1840, England had only two cities with more than 100,000 people. But by 1910, forty-eight English cities had more than 100,000 residents.

An increase in the food supply and industrial production accompanied the increase in population. Greater efficiency and productivity reduced the prices of many goods. As a result, people in the nineteenth century had a greater abundance of material possessions than did those of any previous century.

Evaluation of the Industrial Age

Some people today emphasize only the negative aspects of the Industrial Revolution. They condemn capitalism, which made the industrial growth possible, for producing the terrible living and working conditions. They blame the free enterprise system for allowing a few people to get rich while many others remained poor. But this view overlooks the fact that conditions in the rural areas were often no better than those in the crowded cities. Farm workers, including children, had to work long hours and under many adverse conditions, as did the factory workers. Also, one must remember that industrialism provided jobs for the increasing number of unemployed farm workers. To say that no one was concerned about the conditions in which the workers lived and worked is a distortion. The moral and social conscience of the Victorian Age initiated many reforms.

On the other hand, some people tend to minimize the problems that developed during the growth of industrialism. Although the Industrial Revolution created new opportunities and provided a greater abundance for more people, it also provided opportunity for many to demonstrate the extent of their fallen nature. Some who were blessed with wealth used it to help the less fortunate, but others used their wealth to satisfy selfish desires, even if it meant taking advantage of workers. A growing emphasis on material goods and a decline in spiritual concern became another consequence of the Industrial Revolution. People tend to forget God when they enjoy prosperity and seek material gain.

We must remember that problems—both individual and collective—are the result of sin. In the Industrial Age, as in any other time, greed and cruelty as well as discontentment and immorality resulted in human suffering.

Section Review

1–2. In what country did the Industrial Revolution begin? In what industry did the Industrial Age make its real breakthrough?

3–6. List two inventions that aided the development of the textile industry. Identify the inventor of each.

7. What is the name of the system in which workers labored at home, using their own tools and determining how much they wanted to work and produce?

8–9. Name two new methods of transportation that aided the progress of the Industrial Revolution.

10–11. List two new production methods that helped manufacturers produce more at cheaper prices.

* Why did the issuing of patents by the British government encourage the development of the Industrial Revolution?

* Analyze the Industrial Revolution's influence on justice or power (see p. 13). Was the impact good or bad?

Guiding Questions

1. What were political responses to the Industrial Revolution?
2. What forms of socialism emerged during this period?
3. How did the Industrial Revolution influence society?

II. Responses to the Industrial Revolution

Response of Government

Great Britain was the leader not only in industrial production but also in attempts to remedy the social and political problems resulting from the rapid industrial expansion. During the 1830s and 1840s, the British Parliament passed the first significant social reforms. The members of Parliament who sponsored this legislation attempted to correct the abuses of industry and the accompanying problems in society. However, they failed to realize that, over time, increased government involvement in many areas could eventually lead to government control of industry.

Except for a few isolated incidents, Great Britain avoided the violent uprisings that shook the European continent during the first half of the nineteenth century. The British prevented revolution by bringing about change through parliamentary reform. During this century, Parliament passed many political reform bills that broadened the electorate and enabled a greater percentage of people to have a voice in government.

Social Reform

Among the earliest pieces of social legislation passed by Parliament were acts intended to curb abuses in the factories. Parliament enacted several bills to restrict the long hours and harsh conditions under which many women and children worked. In 1833, it passed the first effective Factory Act to limit child labor. According to this law, no child under nine years of age was to work in a textile mill.

Children from nine to thirteen years old could work but no more than eight hours a day. In addition, they were to receive at least three hours of schooling daily. Those between the ages of thirteen and eighteen could work no more than twelve hours a day. To enforce the law, Parliament appointed inspectors to ensure that the mill owners obeyed it.

Other reforms soon followed the Factory Act of 1833. The Poor Law of 1834 placed the national government in charge of relief measures for those who were too old or too sick to work. The Mines Act (1842) barred from the coal mines all females as well as all males under ten years old. In a further effort to regulate working hours, Parliament passed the Ten Hour Bill in 1847, which limited women and children in any industry to a ten-hour day.

Some social reforms grew out of the humanitarian efforts of individuals. One prominent example was the antislavery movement led by **William Wilberforce**. Motivated by his Christian faith and a sincere compassion for his fellow man, Wilberforce campaigned

William Wilberforce: "No Common Christian"

In 1785, five years after he entered Parliament, William Wilberforce (1759–1833) underwent a conversion, what he later called "the great change." In his efforts to turn from his previously worldly lifestyle, he considered abandoning politics altogether. However, he heeded the advice of Anglican pastor John Newton to stay in Parliament. Newton said, "It is hoped and believed that the Lord has raised you up for the good of His church and for the good of the nation."

Wilberforce became a serious and fervent Christian. His pastor wrote, "He is no common Christian; his knowledge of divine things and his experience of the power of the Gospel are very extraordinary." Nor was he the kind of politician who makes a religious profession to sway voters but makes worldly wisdom his political philosophy. Wilberforce said, "A man who acts from the principles I profess reflects that he is to give an account of his political conduct at the Judgment Seat of Christ."

Although he supported many worthy causes, Wilberforce pressed none so hard or so consistently as the abolishing of the British slave trade. He declared on one occasion, "If it please God to honor me so far, may I be the instrument of stopping such a course of wickedness and cruelty as never before disgraced a Christian country." He faced tremendous opposition to his efforts. The slave trade was profitable, and the planters in Britain's Caribbean possessions predicted economic disaster if it were abolished. The economic arguments swayed many politicians who were concerned about financial prosperity—and their own reelection. Several times Wilberforce presented to the House of Commons a motion to abolish the slave trade. Sometimes he lost by wide margins, at other times by narrow ones. However, even when he managed to get his bill through the House of Commons, the House of Lords rejected it.

During these discouraging times, other Christians sought to encourage him. For example, John Wesley, shortly before his death, wrote to Wilberforce, "Unless God has raised you up for this very thing, you will be worn out by the opposition of men and devils. But if God be for you, who can be against you?"

Finally, in 1807, Wilberforce succeeded in guiding an abolition bill through both houses of Parliament. The slave trade was abolished. But Wilberforce was not finished. Although the trade was illegal, slavery continued to exist in British territory. The fight to abolish slavery, however, took more years than Wilberforce had left. Ill health forced him to retire from Parliament in 1825 and leave the battle to others. A few weeks after Wilberforce's death in 1833, the House of Commons voted to abolish slavery.

While others praised him for his humanitarian activities, Wilberforce remained painfully aware of his human failings and frailties, saying, "The genuine Christian . . . humbles himself in the dust and acknowledges that he is not worthy of the least of all God's mercies."

against the slave trade. His efforts were rewarded when in 1807 Parliament passed a law abolishing the slave trade in British territories. Another act in 1833 began the process of freeing all slaves in the British Empire.

Economic Reform

In 1846, Parliament repealed laws that had placed a high tariff on imported grain. Such tariffs limited foreign competition and allowed British landowners to sell their grain at higher prices. The repeal of these laws not only lowered the price of grain (thereby relieving a great financial burden on workers) but also signaled a shift toward free trade in British economic policy.

Political Reform
Reform Bills

At the outset of the nineteenth century, aristocrats and wealthy landowners controlled Parliament. Property qualifications prevented most of the British people from voting in parliamentary elections. In addition, voting districts (called boroughs) had not changed for almost 150 years. Thus, the landholding class retained control of Parliament, denying equal representation to residents of the growing industrial centers. Members of the middle class, therefore, demanded change. By 1830, they persuaded the House of Commons to pass a reform bill, but the House of Lords vetoed it. When the king threatened to create new lords to ensure that there would be a majority to pass the bill, the House of Lords backed down, and the **Reform Bill of 1832** became law.

The Reform Bill lowered property qualifications for voting, increasing the electorate by an estimated 50 percent. It also reorganized the voting districts, giving representation to middle-class citizens in the new industrial cities. Merchants, bankers, and factory owners now had a voice in government. But the Reform Bill had not extended the voting privilege to the average man. As a result, dissatisfied workers supported a new movement called **Chartism**. The Chartists advocated universal manhood suffrage, the secret ballot, equal electoral districts, pay for members of Parliament, no property qualifications for members of Parliament, and annual elections to Parliament. The Chartists presented several petitions, but each time Parliament refused to act. Although the Chartist movement failed, all of its demands—except annual elections to Parliament—eventually became law in Britain.

In 1867, Parliament passed a second major reform bill, which again reduced property qualifications for voting. This bill nearly doubled the electorate and shifted additional political power to Britain's industrial centers.

Disraeli and Gladstone

Reforms continued throughout the rest of the century as two dominant political figures, **Benjamin Disraeli** (diz RAY lee; 1804–81) and **William Gladstone** (1809–98), often alternated as prime minister of the British Parliament. Benjamin Disraeli began his political career as a liberal but later became the leader of the Tory, or Conservative, Party. Through his efforts, Parliament passed the Reform Bill of 1867. While he was prime minister, Parliament passed several bills related to public health and housing. But Disraeli was primarily involved in foreign affairs. Perhaps his greatest suc-

---

Wealth of Nations

One of the most influential books on political economics, *Wealth of Nations*, was written by **Adam Smith**. Published in 1776, it attacked mercantilism, the prevailing economic system of most European nations during the eighteenth century. Smith defined national wealth not by how much gold or silver a nation possessed, but by how many goods it could produce and sell. In other words, wealth depended on productivity.

Smith proposed a policy of free trade among nations. A nation, he said, should manufacture what it can best and most efficiently produce. What other goods it needs it should purchase from other countries. If each nation were driven by self-interest, all countries would do their best to produce superior products that other nations would want to buy. With increased demand, production would improve, and everyone would benefit.

Smith attacked the economic policies of the British government in his day as restrictive of free trade. He advocated a hands-off policy known as *laissez faire*, in which government does not interfere in business and trade but provides a favorable climate for business activity. Smith believed that the proper role of government, apart from maintaining law and order, is limited to providing an adequate education system, road system, and defense.

cess occurred when he, on behalf of the British government, bought 44 percent of the shares in the Suez Canal from the ruler of Egypt, thereby enhancing British dominance in the Mediterranean region and greatly aiding British trade.

Disraeli's political opponent was William Gladstone, the leader of the new Liberal Party. Gladstone, the son of a wealthy Scottish businessman, was a man of strong character. As a states-man, he placed his moral con-victions above political expedi-ency and earned the respect of both friends and enemies. As a man of strong religious faith, he diligently studied the Scrip-tures and regularly gathered his family for prayer. He also wrote several works on theol-ogy. Undoubtedly, his religious beliefs shaped his political outlook and made him a man of compassion toward those less fortunate than himself.

During his four terms as prime minister (1868–74, 1880–85, 1886, and 1892–94), Gladstone emphasized domes-tic reforms that established a single national court system, instituted voting by secret ballot, and in 1884 extended suffrage to rural communities. Gladstone also supported several education bills, believing that better education would promote wiser voting.

One particularly pressing problem during Gladstone's ministry was the matter of British rule of Ireland. Under James I (1603–25), Protestants had begun settling in Northern Ireland. The rest of the

Benjamin Disraeli

William Gladstone

Women's Rights Movement

The women's rights movement spanned more than one hundred years as women struggled to gain the right to own property and vote. Although the movement for "univer-sal suffrage" (right to vote) began with the Chartist movement in the late 1700s, women were excluded from that movement. However, women continued to push for suf-frage, and the issue received posi-tive attention in some 1865 election speeches in Britain. In 1867 the first petition for women's suffrage was introduced to Parliament. Support-ers introduced similar petitions every year thereafter with increasing support, but they failed to pass, due in part to the opposition of political leaders, including William Gladstone.

In 1881, leaders on the Isle of Man (located in the Irish Sea between Ireland and Great Britain) gave women property owners the right to vote. Later, women who lived on the island but did not own land also gained this right. Encouraged by this progress, women increased their efforts. Some groups applied pres-sure directly on elected officials and campaigned against the opponents of women's suffrage. Other women took more radical steps by violating laws and getting sentenced to jail. A few women prisoners even went on hunger strikes, drawing further attention to women's suffrage.

During World War I, activity for suffrage nearly ceased, but women resumed their efforts after the war. Their persistence resulted in women winning the right to vote in the United States in 1920 and in Great Britain in 1928.

The Grandmother of Europe

Queen Victoria (1837–1901) has become the symbol of nineteenth-century Britain. She reigned for sixty-three and a half years. Her moral standards and political ideas exemplified the attitudes of many Britons.

In 1840, Victoria married Albert, a German prince of strong character. During their twenty-one years of marriage, Victoria and Albert did much to restore respect for the British monarchy. They not only reduced court expenditures but also set an example of moral uprightness. The relationship between the queen and the prince was happy. When Albert died of typhoid fever in 1861, Victoria was heartbroken. For the next thirty-nine years, she lived in relative seclusion, doing everything in her power to perpetuate the memory of her beloved Albert.

Because many of her nine children and thirty-four grandchildren married into other royal families, Victoria has been called the grandmother of Europe. One of her grandsons was Kaiser Wilhelm II of Germany, and one of her granddaughters was the wife of Nicholas II, the last Russian czar. Other children and grandchildren married into the royal lines of Sweden, Norway, Spain, and Romania. Three monarchs during World War I —Kaiser Wilhelm II, Alexandra (the wife of Nicholas II), and King George V of Britain—were cousins.

island was primarily Roman Catholic. Catholic southern Ireland became increasingly restless under British rule and began demanding home rule. "My mission is to pacify Ireland," Gladstone had said as he took office for the first time. But despite diligent effort, he never achieved his goal. The "Irish Question" would not be easily settled.

The Parliament Bill of 1911

The capstone of Britain's political development came in 1911 with the passage of a bill that increased the power of the House of Commons so that it became the supreme governing body in Britain. As a result of this bill, the House of Lords could only temporarily delay legislation passed by the House of Commons, not veto it as before. Also, in 1911 the House of Commons approved a salary for its members, making it financially possible for poorer citizens to become members of Parliament.

As Britain's government became more representative of the people, the attitude toward the role of government began to change. Many people began to expect the government to be directly involved in establishing and funding various social programs. Britain began to develop into a welfare state (a state in which the government assumes the responsibility for the material and social well-being of every individual). Within a few years, Parliament passed bills providing for unemployment insurance, health protection, workman's compensation, and old-age pensions. In addition, it placed secondary education under state control. The result was greater government control and reduced individual freedom.

Ideas of the Socialists

Many people during the nineteenth century believed that humans are basically good. As a result, those people neglected the reality of sin, the root of all social evils, in their attempts to change society. This false teaching regarding human goodness found clear expression in socialism.

Most people today assume that **socialism** is only an economic term. It is defined as government ownership of the means of production and the distribution of goods for the presumed welfare of society. This definition is correct to a point, but socialism, like any other philosophy, is a worldview and therefore affects *every* area of life. For example, since socialism emphasizes the group rather than the individual, many socialists advocate an international government to replace independent national states. In addition, socialism rejects individual responsibility, limits individual choice, and replaces individual initiative with collectivism (rule by the group).

Four major types of socialism developed in the nineteenth century. Although each form sought to achieve the perfect society through different means, all were built on the same set of false ideas: (1) man is by nature good—it is society that has corrupted him; and (2) if society can be improved, then man will be improved, and all injustice will cease.

Utopian Socialism

Utopian socialism was a direct result of the French Enlightenment. Like many of the eighteenth-century *philosophes*, the utopian socialists believed that if the inequities in society could be abolished, man's natural goodness could be perfected. These socialists believed that the profit motive of capitalism was the basic source of evil and that it stimulated greed and hatred.

Because they assumed that one's environment produced social evil, the utopians believed that proper surroundings and a good education would solve all problems. To test these ideas, several men in Europe and America formed socialist communities that they hoped would set the example for sweeping changes in society. **Robert Owen** (1771–1858), a textile manufacturer, established one such community for his workers at his textile mill in Scotland. He later established an agricultural community at New Harmony, Indiana. But New Harmony failed after only a short time—people were not as unselfish and reasonable as he and others had assumed.

Marxism

Another form of socialism was advanced by **Karl Marx** (1818–83), the son of a prominent German lawyer. Marx abandoned the study of law to study philosophy and history. At the age of twenty-three, he received a doctor of philosophy degree, but no German university would hire him because of his radical political views. The Prussian government forced him to flee to Paris, where he became friends with **Friedrich Engels** (1820–95) and other socialists during the early Communist movement in France. During that time, Paris was the center of revolutionary gatherings and Communist leadership. In 1846, the Communists met in Brussels and asked Marx and Engels to compose a manifesto expressing the views and aims of communism. The two men became lifelong friends, and they produced the *Communist Manifesto*, which appeared during the revolutionary year 1848. The premise of their book is that the "history of all hitherto existing societies [was] the history of class struggles." The goal of history, according to Marx and Engels, is for the workers to unite in opposition to capitalism, smash the superstructure of society, and establish themselves as rulers, creating the "dictatorship of the proletariat."

From Paris, Marx went to England, where he spent the last thirty-three years of his life and wrote his most famous work, *Das Kapital*. In it, he explains in detail his socialist ideas. Marx thought the utopian socialists (a term that he and Engels coined) were im-

Karl Marx

Friedrich Engels

practical; he considered them idle dreamers. He believed that his ideas, which he called "scientific socialism," were based on provable economic principles. Yet his views were actually anything but scientific.

Marx believed that economic forces determined the course of history. To him, every social, political, or religious movement sprang from a desire by one group of people to take economic advantage of another group. According to that view of history, even the Protestant Reformation was not primarily a religious movement; religion was simply a veil that obscured the real economic issues. Marx also believed that history would naturally progress toward perfection. During this process, conflicts between various social, political, or religious movements would be inevitable. Each conflict, however, would somehow be resolved successfully, enabling man to "progress" to a higher stage of development. These conflicts are an essential feature of history, Marx said, and they will continue until man finally reaches the perfect society—a society in which everyone is equal and gladly shares the fruit of his labor with others. That perfect condition is what Marx called *communism*.

According to Marx, all of history had been dominated by class struggle and, from earliest times, the oppressed had fought their oppressors. For example, during the Roman Republic, the plebeians struggled against the patricians; during the Middle Ages, the serfs struggled against their lords; and during Marx's time, the **proletariat** (workers) struggled against the **bourgeoisie** (middle-class property owners, capitalists, and industrialists or factory owners). Marx believed that under communism such struggles would cease since all class distinctions would be eliminated.

Marx taught that one of the ways industrialists exploited (took advantage of) the workers was by paying them less than they deserved. According to Marx, the workers created wealth, and the value of a product was the amount of labor it took to produce it. Yet the wages that the workers received were always less than the value of the products they produced. Therefore, according to Marx, the capitalists were robbing the workers and living unjustly off the labor of others. However, Marx ignored the fact that the capitalists invested great funds in building the factories and buying machines and raw materials, without which industrial goods could not be produced.

How would communism end such so-called injustices and achieve the perfect society? Marx said that the answer lay in revolution. He believed that Communist revolutions were a necessary and inevitable part of Communist development and that they would begin in industrialized nations, which had a large, class-conscious proletariat. The proletariat would overthrow the capitalist bourgeoisie and establish their own rule, called the "dictatorship of the proletariat."

Once in power, the proletariat would begin to systematically eliminate anything that opposed the ideals of communism, such as private ownership of property and private business. In addition, they would destroy Christianity since, according to Marx, religion was "the opiate of the people," a "drug" that the ruling class used to keep the workers in subjection. Once the last remnant of capitalism had been erased, the dictatorship of the proletariat would disappear because it would then be unnecessary. Thus, Marx believed, man would become a perfect being in a perfect society and would no longer need a state to govern him. (Marxism is the form of socialism that most Communist countries pursued—including China, Cuba, North Korea, Vietnam, Laos, the Soviet Union, and other eastern European nations.)

Fabian Socialism

British socialists who sought to achieve a socialist society without revolution took their name from Quintus Fabius Maximus, a cautious Roman general who tried to wear down his opponent Hannibal gradually instead of engaging him in open battle. The Fabian socialists believed that the best way to destroy capitalism was to gradually undermine it rather than to seek its sudden overthrow. The Fabians and similar groups throughout Europe and America worked to bring about gradual change by urging the passage of welfare legislation.

Christian Socialism

Most of the so-called Christian socialists were theological liberals who believed that Christianity and capitalism were incompatible. They believed that unregenerate society could and should live according to the Sermon on the Mount (Matt. 5–7). They sought to establish an earthly millennium in which peace and justice would reign. Because many people opposed socialism in any form, the Christian socialists tried to portray it positively. They said that socialism is nothing more than "the embodiment of Christianity in our industrial system." In fact, according to an early Christian socialist paper, "Christianity and Socialism are almost interchangeable terms." Such men, although claiming to be Christian, failed to see that the very basis of socialism, the perfectibility of man by man, is contrary to the teaching of Scripture.

Concern of Christians

Following the admonition of the apostle Paul, who said, "As we have therefore opportunity, let us do good unto all men, especially unto them who are of the household of faith" (Gal. 6:10), Christians were among the first to respond to the needs and problems of an industrialized society. However, they were not simply social reformers hoping to improve living conditions, help the poor, and reduce crime; they realized that sin lies at the root of all social ills. As William Booth, the founder of the Salvation Army, said, "My only hope for the permanent deliverance of mankind from misery, either in this world or the next, is the regeneration or remaking of the individual by the power of the Holy Ghost through Jesus Christ."

One of the earliest movements to minister to the laboring classes in British cities was the Sunday school, founded during the late eighteenth century. Founder **Robert Raikes** sought to reach the poor, illiterate, working-class children, and he used the classes to teach the children about Jesus in addition to reading and writing. Over time, many churches made Sunday school a part of their regular ministry, not only to reach underprivileged children for Christ but also to provide further instruction in God's Word for the members of the church. Since most of the teachers were laymen, Bible institutes were founded to train laymen to be more effective Christian workers. Concerned Christians also established homes for juvenile delinquents and orphans. Perhaps the best-known orphanages were founded by **George Mueller** in Bristol, England.

George Mueller

Spiritual Impact on the Industrial Age

During the Industrial Age, England benefited from the ministry of one of the greatest preachers since Wesley—Charles Haddon Spurgeon (1834–92). Born in the home of a minister, Spurgeon had a godly upbringing and was converted at the age of fifteen. In 1854, he became pastor of the New Park Street Chapel, a Baptist church in London. His congregation grew so large that the church had to construct a new building. During the interim, Spurgeon used various buildings to house his congregation. In 1857, he even preached in the Crystal Palace to a crowd of more than twenty-three thousand. Completed in 1861, the London Metropolitan Tabernacle seated five thousand people and soon had to offer additional services to make it possible for everyone to hear Spurgeon preach. His earnest delivery, wonderful oratory, and searching style earned him the title "the Prince of Preachers."

In addition to preaching, Spurgeon oversaw numerous other ministries. He operated a college for preachers, an orphanage, and a tract society for the sale and free distribution of books and pamphlets. Spurgeon also published a magazine, *The Sword and the Trowel*, and wrote several works, the most famous of which is *The Treasury of David*, his commentary on the book of Psalms.

Near the end of his life, Spurgeon became concerned about the growth of theological liberalism within the Baptist denomination. Using *The Sword and the Trowel*, he began publishing articles attacking the "downgrading" of Scripture by those who denied its inerrancy and authority. Called the "Downgrade Controversy," this conflict led Spurgeon to withdraw from the Baptist Union (an organization of English Baptist churches). Many members of the Union refused to withdraw and instead attacked and rebuked Spurgeon for his stand, voting overwhelmingly to condemn him.

Spurgeon's importance today lies not in the size of his ministry, the number of converts he won to Christ, or even his unmatched eloquence. Spurgeon is remembered, in large part, because of his refusal to sacrifice principle for popularity. Many other popular ministers of the era (who are now little remembered) preached on sentimental or moralistic topics. Spurgeon, however, nourished his congregation with sound teaching regardless of the controversy it might arouse. To the end of his life, Spurgeon refused to yield to opposition—remaining obedient to the Word of God.

William Booth

In 1844, twenty-two-year-old George Williams established the Young Men's Christian Association (YMCA) in London. The purpose of the organization was to minister to young men who worked in the city and win them to Christ. Although the primary purpose of the YMCA was spiritual, Williams also emphasized educational, social, and athletic development. The YMCA soon became a worldwide organization. Before long, other people established a women's organization, the YWCA. Sadly, these organizations no longer have the spiritual concern of their founders.

As previously mentioned, **William Booth** (1829–1912) founded the Salvation Army, another ministry with worldwide impact. Booth began working in the London slums in 1865, preaching the gospel and seeking to meet the physical needs of those around him. Throughout his ministry, Booth tried to counteract the apathy of some Christians toward the plight of the poor. He wrote, "Why all this apparatus of temples and meeting-houses to save men from perdition in a world which is to come, while never a helping hand is stretched out to save them from the inferno of their present life?" Booth believed that an unconverted individual needed to see that Christians had a genuine concern for him, just as Christ showed compassion for people during His earthly ministry by healing them and feeding them.

The outpouring of Christian charity during the nineteenth century was due in large part to great revivals that swept across Great Britain and the United States. In the eighteenth century, the Wesleyan revivals prompted the first surge of Christian activity; in the nineteenth century, the revivals of **Dwight L. Moody** (1837–99) and other evangelists brought about a second surge. Moody and his partner, Ira Sankey (1840–1908), believed that conditions in society would improve only when those who lived in that society experienced true conversion. Beginning in 1873, Moody and Sankey held evangelistic campaigns in the large industrial cities of Britain and America, bringing thousands of people to Christ. Many of their converts went on to win others to the Savior, and some devoted themselves to various Christian ministries designed to bring those in the inner cities to Christ.

How many thousands or even millions of souls received the gospel through the efforts of Raikes, Mueller, Williams, Booth, Moody, and others will never be known in this life. Although their methods were inventive and unique, their message was the same: "Believe on the Lord Jesus Christ, and thou shalt be saved" (Acts 16:31).

Dwight L. Moody

Section Review

1–2. List two of the six goals of the Chartist movement.

3–6. Name the two dominant prime ministers of Britain during the latter part of the nineteenth century. Give the political party of each.

7–8. What force did Karl Marx believe determined the course of history? In what work did he explain his socialist ideas?

★ Analyze Disraeli's and Gladstone's influence on justice and citizenship in Great Britain.

★ Evaluate the various forms of socialism mentioned in this chapter.

III. Changing Outlooks in European Society

Faith in Scientific Progress

During the second half of the nineteenth century, Europe experienced a rapid expansion in scientific knowledge and technology. Practical inventions provided material comforts that previous generations had not known. The telegraph and telephone, for example, made rapid communication possible. Improved methods of transportation made travel easier. Better nutrition and methods of diagnosing and treating disease increased the average lifespan. Greater industrial output raised the material standard of living for most western Europeans. To many people, science became the source of hope for the future. They believed that mankind could achieve anything if given the opportunity. The impact of science on this age greatly influenced man's perception of himself and the world.

Evolutionary Outlook

Most scientists during the Age of Reason viewed the world of nature much like a machine that operates according to fixed, unchanging laws. To them, the order reflected by nature demonstrated the existence of God and His creative power. But in the second half

Guiding Questions
1. How did science influence society during this period?
2. What scientific and philosophical challenges to Christianity occurred during this period?
3. How did art and literature reflect the changes in Western society during this period?

Charles Darwin

Marie Curie

of the nineteenth century, scientists began to view man and nature as the products of an evolutionary process. The man who laid the basis for the modern theories of biological evolution was **Charles Darwin** (1809–82).

In his famous work *On the Origin of Species* (1859), Darwin tried to prove that organisms developed from simple to complex structures through natural causes. According to Darwin, no species is fixed and changeless; rather, it is shaped gradually by its environment over countless ages. Those creatures best able to adapt to their environment survive; those with inferior characteristics perish. This theory is called the "survival of the fittest." However, Scripture says that God made each different animal group to reproduce "after his kind" (Gen. 1:24). Hence, the Bible does not allow for one kind of organism to evolve into another.

In 1871, Darwin published a book titled *The Descent of Man*, which was even more shocking than his previous work. In this book, Darwin applied his evolutionary theory to humans. Darwin observed that man resembles other creatures. Instead of recognizing the hand of a common Creator, he taught that man developed from animals. His theory opposed the biblical doctrine of the special, direct creation of man by God. Scripture declares that God directly created man (Gen. 1:26–27; 2:7).

Revolution in the Physical Sciences

During the 1800s and early 1900s, significant developments in the physical sciences greatly expanded man's understanding of matter and energy, the components of the physical universe. Scientists of this period discovered that matter was made up of distinct units called chemical elements. An English Quaker named **John Dalton** (1766–1844) proposed that each chemical element was composed of particles called atoms, and these were distinct from the atoms of any other element. His ideas helped to explain the distinct characteristics of various substances. Today he is recognized as the formulator of the atomic theory.

Later scientists sought to identify and classify the chemical elements. Knowing that certain elements shared similar characteristics, the Russian chemist **Dmitri Mendeleev** (men duh LAY uf; 1834–1907) organized the chemical elements in a chart according to their atomic masses. His system of classification, with columns of elements having shared characteristics, was the basis for the modern periodic table.

As scientists continued to investigate, they found more characteristics that distinguished the chemical elements as unique particles. Aiding them in their discoveries was the x-ray tube. German physicist **Wilhelm Roentgen** (RENT gun; 1845–1923) accidentally discovered x-rays while working with vacuum tubes. He called them *x-rays* because he did not fully understand the energies he had discovered. Using x-rays, a young British scientist named Henry Moseley (1887–1915) was able to determine the number of protons in the atoms of an element. On the basis of this information, Moseley and others reordered the periodic table by atomic number (number of protons) rather than atomic mass (Mendeleev's arrangement).

The discovery of radioactive matter added new elements to the chart. The husband-and-wife team of **Pierre** (1859–1906) and **Marie** (1867–1934) **Curie** found two new elements in a type of uranium ore called pitchblende. Those radioactive elements naturally broke down into simpler elements, indicating that all atoms, and thus all matter, are composed of even smaller particles. Such an idea was advanced by British physicist Ernest Rutherford (1871–1937). He stated that the atom is composed of at least two distinct parts— a positively charged nucleus surrounded by negatively charged electrons. Danish physicist Niels Bohr (1885–1962) built on Rutherford's theory. Bohr's model of the atom shows a nucleus surrounded by electrons that move in orbits much like planets revolving around the sun. Bohr discovered that electrons were assigned to distinct energy levels, but they could move from one level to another by gaining or releasing energy.

The work of perhaps the greatest scientific thinker of the twentieth century, **Albert Einstein** (INE stine; 1879–1955), showed the relationship between matter and energy, which he demonstrated through the equation $E = mc^2$ (energy equals mass times the speed of light squared). Another of his contributions to science was his theory of relativity. Scientists in the past believed that measurements of time, mass, and length did not vary. According to Einstein's theory, however, moving objects increase in mass as they decrease in length. The amount of increase or decrease depends on the speed of the object.

Albert Einstein

Impact of Science on Society

The advances in science caused many people to look on science as the means of progress. People began to apply scientific theories of the physical world to the study of man and society. "Scientific" became a new standard by which society's institutions and values were measured. To many people, science became a religion. They rejected the authority of God's Word for the authority of scientific theory. Often, something done in the name of science was judged true and worthy regardless of whether evidence existed to support it. For example, many people praised Darwin's theory of evolution as scientific while dismissing the biblical account of Creation as mythical. In rejecting the Genesis record, they also rejected their responsibility to God as their Creator. Others incorrectly applied scientific theory to society. Philosophers, for example, embraced Einstein's theory of relativity as the guide for the study of ethics (questions of right and wrong). They claimed that since all things in the universe are relative, moral principles are relative too; moral principles simply evolved as man evolved. Through such belief and teaching, sinful people demonstrated their rebellion against God and His Word.

Challenges to Christianity

Although the nineteenth century was a time of great revivals and missionary activity, the Christian church, as we have seen, was besieged by many foes. Even many religious leaders embraced the false religion of science. They rejected the authority of Scripture as the inspired and inerrant (free from error) Word of God. Instead, they tried to "scientifically" discern what portions of God's Word are true and what portions are false. Basing their theories on the evolutionary ideas of Darwin, these men claimed that Judaism and Christianity slowly developed out of ancient Near Eastern civilizations. They rejected the fact that God revealed His truth directly to "holy men of God" (2 Pet. 1:21). Many liberal theologians claimed that Moses did not write the first five books of the Bible. They also rejected the miracles mentioned in the Bible, inventing their own natural explanations for those supernatural events. Likewise, because theological liberals rejected the possibility of prophecy, they claimed the Old Testament writers actually wrote down their "prophecies" after the events had happened.

The purpose and mission of the church also came under attack. Those who promoted the social gospel believed that the major purpose of Christianity was to change society and that by changing society individuals would be made better. They rejected the New Testament teaching that the only gospel is the story of the death, burial, and resurrection of Jesus Christ (1 Cor. 15:1–4). Instead, they preached a gospel of social improvement. The apostle Paul warned against such teaching in Galatians 1:7–8.

The work of Christ was also challenged by growing materialism and secularization of society. Many people began to concentrate on the things of this world and neglect spiritual things. The number of church members, especially in Europe, remained high, but the number of people who actually attended church declined significantly. In addition, a small but increasing number of people began to leave the church. Weakened by the worldly members who remained, the Christian church as an institution lost much of its influence on the lives of Europeans.

Common to all of the foes of Christianity was a spirit of humanism, the exaltation of man above God. Modern humanists accepted the evolutionary theories and the social gospel, which taught that man was neither created by nor responsible to God. Instead, man was responsible to himself and to society. They did not believe in heaven and hell but rather believed that whatever fulfillment man was going to receive would come through his efforts in this life.

In the late nineteenth century, humanists were a small minority, consisting primarily of unbelieving religious leaders, liberal theologians, and godless intellectuals. But the secularization of society and the spread of this humanistic spirit increased rapidly—permeating all areas of society during the twentieth century.

However, many people during the Victorian era did not undergo a crisis of faith. Faithful believers continued to believe the Bible and demonstrate Christ's redeeming power in their daily lives. Others, including secularists, eventually found their lives to be without meaning and experienced a crisis of doubt. Many former skeptics found Christ and became faithful believers in later years.

New Trends in the Arts
Realism

By the 1850s, a new form of artistic expression known as **realism** had become widespread in Europe. Realists had a growing awareness of the world around them. They rejected both the idealist emotion of romanticism and its fascination with exotic themes and faraway places. Realists believed that life should be portrayed as it really was. Although they did not abandon emotion, they sought to express feelings that touched their everyday lives. They were conscious of the social problems around them and sought to represent reality with scientific objectivity. They tended, however, to highlight the darker side of European society: poverty, injustice, and immorality.

One of the earliest realist writers was English novelist **Charles Dickens** (1812–70). Dickens was a social critic who attacked injustice in society through his vivid portrayals of such places as indus-

Charles Dickens

trial slums and debtors' prisons. In his famous novel *Hard Times*, he depicted the living conditions in industrial cities with the following description of the imaginary city of Coketown:

> It was a town of red brick, or brick that would have been red if the smoke and ashes had allowed it; but as matters stood it was a town of unnatural red and black like the painted face of a savage. It was a town of machinery and tall chimneys, out of which interminable serpents of smoke trailed themselves for ever and ever, and never got uncoiled. It had a black canal in it, and a river that ran purple with ill-smelling dye, and vast piles of buildings full of windows where there was a rattling and a trembling all day long.

Other writers wrote about man's struggles in this life. British novelist and poet **Thomas Hardy** (1840–1928) portrayed man as engaged in a hopeless struggle against impersonal forces beyond his control. American **Samuel Clemens**, better known by his pen name Mark Twain (1835–1910), viewed life as Hardy did; unlike Hardy, however, he used humor to convey his ideas. The famous Russian novelist **Leo Tolstoy** (1828–1910) realistically described life in Russia during the Napoleonic Wars.

In reaction to the romantic artists, who tended to paint faraway places, realist painters concentrated on observable, commonplace subjects. They tried to portray life as they saw it, not as they imagined it to be. According to Gustave Courbet (koor BEH; 1819–77), a famous realist painter, "an abstract object, invisible or nonexistent, does not belong to the domain of painting." "Show me an angel," he said, "and I'll paint one." Instead of painting angels, he and his fellow realists painted such works as *The Stone Breakers* and *The Third Class Carriage*.

The Grain Sifters *by Gustave Courbet*

Impressionism

Near the end of the nineteenth century, French artists created a new style of painting known as **impressionism**. The impressionists

Luncheon of the Boating Party *by Auguste Renoir*

Water Lilies *by Claude Monet*

turned away from photographic realism in their painting and instead made light and color their chief concerns. The impressionists did not outline their figures clearly but used short, choppy brush strokes to capture the vibrating nature of light. To the impressionists, light was all important; what the light revealed did not matter. The most famous of the French impressionists were **Auguste Renoir** (ren WAHR; 1841–1919) and **Claude Monet** (moh NAY; 1840–1926).

Another Frenchman, Auguste Rodin (roh DAN; 1840–1917), was one of the foremost sculptors of the nineteenth century. It is difficult, however, to place him within a particular style. His subject matter was romantic, but his technique was often impressionistic. Like the impressionistic painters, Rodin did not make his art photographically exact. As a result, many of his works are not finely polished and have an "unfinished" look. Perhaps his best known sculpture is *The Thinker*.

Postimpressionism

Not all artists agreed that color and light should be the ultimate objects of painting. **Paul Cézanne** (say ZAN; 1839–1906), a Frenchman, and **Vincent van Gogh** (van GOH; 1853–90), a Dutchman, believed that impressionism rejected too many traditional artistic concepts, so they advocated a style that became known as postimpressionism. Among other things, Cézanne and van Gogh tried to emphasize universal themes and to outline the figures more clearly in their paintings.

For example, Cézanne believed that the artist could reduce everything in nature to basic geometric shapes. He urged his fellow artists to "treat nature in terms of the cylinder, and the sphere and the cone" to make the outlines of various objects clearer. This geometric emphasis in his art made Cézanne a forerunner of cubism (see ch. 21). Van Gogh, on the other hand, often distorted the figures in his paintings in an effort to portray the intense emotions he felt toward his subjects. For this reason, he was a forerunner of expressionism (see ch. 21).

Section Review

1–2. What man laid the foundation for the modern theories of biological evolution? In what book did he set forth his theory of survival of the fittest?

3–7. Identify the contribution to science of each of the following men: Dalton, Mendeleev, Roentgen, Bohr, and Einstein.

8. What did advocates of the social gospel movement believe was the major purpose of Christianity?

9. What new form of artistic expression in the latter half of the nineteenth century sought to portray life as it really was?

★ Contrast the artistic works in this chapter with those in chapter 15.

★ Contrast impressionistic and post-impressionistic art.

Making Connections

1–2. In what two ways did mass production benefit society?

3–4. In what two ways did science contribute to the development of the Industrial Revolution?

5. How did Parliament respond to demands for increased representation?

6–9. Explain the four types of socialism discussed in the text.

10–11. What two related causes did William Wilberforce fight for in Parliament?

Developing History Skills

1. Survey the development of the Industrial Revolution.

2. Why did the Industrial Revolution begin in Britain rather than in a country in continental Europe?

Thinking Critically

1. Are the forms of socialism mentioned in this chapter harmful to society? Why or why not?

2. What impact did Christianity have on Britain during the nineteenth century? Support your answer.

Living in God's World

1. Evaluate the following possible responses to evolutionary science. Defend the one you believe to be best. (1) Accept evolutionary science as factual and reject the Bible's reliability. (2) Accept evolutionary science as factual and reinterpret the Bible's teaching on creation to accommodate evolutionary science. (3) Accept the Bible as factual and withdraw from scientific endeavor. (4) Accept the Bible as factual and allow it to shape Christian engagement with scientific study.

2. Write a brief paragraph describing how Christians could have responded to the impact of the Industrial Revolution on society.

People, Places, and Things to Know

Industrial Revolution
Jethro Tull
Charles Townshend
John Kay
James Hargreaves
Richard Arkwright
Samuel Crompton
Eli Whitney
Henry Cort
Henry Bessemer
James Watt
John McAdam
Robert Fulton
Orville and Wilbur Wright
Henry Ford
William Wilberforce
Reform Bill of 1832
Chartism
Benjamin Disraeli
William Gladstone
Adam Smith
laissez faire
socialism
Robert Owen
Karl Marx
Friedrich Engels
proletariat
bourgeoisie
Robert Raikes
George Mueller
William Booth
Dwight L. Moody
Charles Darwin
John Dalton
Dmitri Mendeleev
Wilhelm Roentgen
Pierre and Marie Curie
Albert Einstein
realism
Charles Dickens
Thomas Hardy
Samuel Clemens
Leo Tolstoy
impressionism
Auguste Renoir
Claude Monet
Paul Cézanne
Vincent van Gogh

19

Big Ideas

1. Why did some British territories gain independence?

2. How did imperialism affect Asia, Africa, and the Near East?

3. What were positive and negative results of imperialism?

American cartoon in 1882 depicting England as the octopus of imperialism

The early explorers who traveled around the world opened the door to a flood of European migration. During the seventeenth and eighteenth centuries, thousands of Europeans crossed the oceans in search of fortune, adventure, or religious freedom in these new lands of opportunity. Though they left their homelands, they did not leave behind their European heritage or culture. They established new settlements that were like "little Europes" overseas. Despite strong cultural and economic ties to Europe, many of these settlements gained political independence in the late eighteenth and early nineteenth centuries and began developing as new nations.

The period of European expansion was renewed during the nineteenth century. Industrialized nations sought new overseas territories as sources of raw materials for their factories and as markets for their industrial goods. Later in the century, nationalistic pride prompted other countries to seek to build overseas empires to symbolize their power and glory. As a result, European nations competed for control of much of the world—especially Africa and Asia. This new scramble for territory came to be known as imperialism.

Although imperialism was an economic and political movement, Christians used it as an opportunity for missionary outreach. The nineteenth century was the greatest period of missionary activity since the first three centuries of the Christian era. Godly men and women dedicated their lives to carrying out the Great Commission: "Go ye into all the world, and preach the gospel to every creature" (Mark 16:15). Although some secular historians claim that the missions movement was merely a form of colonialism, missionaries often served as a check on the abuses of colonial powers.

I. Independence for Some British Territories

After the Age of Exploration, European civilization was carried to all parts of the globe as Europeans settled in newly discovered regions. Most early settlers went to isolated lands—the Americas, Australia, New Zealand, and South Africa. Overcoming the dangers and obstacles of frontier life, transplanted Europeans built thriving colonies. As these colonies grew and prospered, they attracted more European immigrants. At the same time, they became more and more independent of their homelands.

In chapter 16, we traced the American struggle for independence. Since the United States was considered a model for developing colonies, let us begin by examining the growth of this young nation. The sections that follow will survey the settlement, development, and independence of the British colonies in Ireland, Canada, Australia, New Zealand, and South Africa.

Growth of the United States Following Independence

Geographic and Political Expansion

In the years following independence, the American nation rapidly expanded westward. Pioneers pushed westward across the Allegheny and Appalachian Mountains, laying claim to vast tracts of land. In 1803 President Thomas Jefferson purchased more than 800,000 square miles of French territory west of the Mississippi River from Napoleon for $15 million. Known as the **Louisiana**

Guiding Questions

1. How did the United States experience domestic and foreign expansion during the nineteenth century?
2. What led to the independence and nationhood of British colonies?

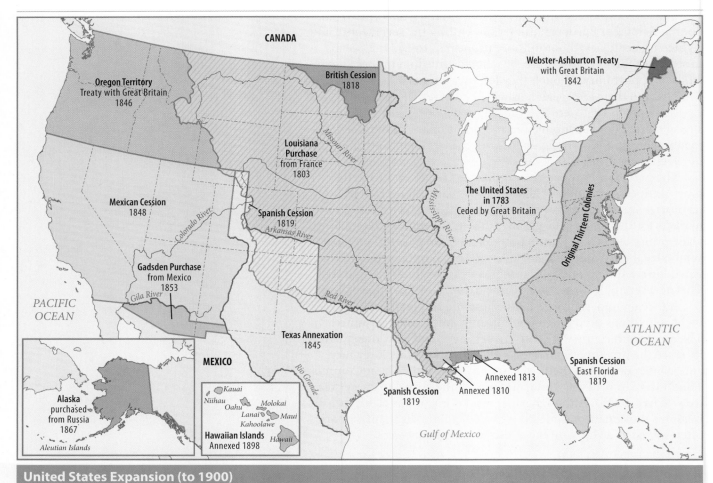

United States Expansion (to 1900)

Purchase, this land almost doubled the size of the United States. Much of the territory that comprises the southwestern portion of the United States today was acquired after a war with Mexico (1846–48). In 1848 the discovery of gold in California prompted a great rush to the far West. Thus—through settlement, purchase, and war—the United States expanded its borders from the Atlantic to the Pacific. This growth raised tensions as slave states and free states battled over the the status of slavery in newly acquired territory. In the end, the issue of slavery was settled by the Civil War. Additional territory was added in 1867 when the United States purchased Alaska from Russia. By the end of the century, the U.S. government also controlled Hawaii, Cuba, Puerto Rico, and the Philippines.

Growth in Industry and Population

Following the Civil War, the nation entered a period of rapid industrial expansion. A number of factors made this growth possible: the hardworking American spirit, an abundance of raw materials, new inventions, and the expansion of the railroads. God's blessing and provision also played a major role, as demonstrated by several spiritual revivals in America during the nineteenth century.

A growing population provided industry with a large labor force. The population of the United States rose from four million in 1790 to ninety-two million in 1910. More than one-third of that increase came from immigrants who each year entered this land of opportunity by the thousands. From 1821 to 1910, about thirty-four million immigrants from all over Europe came to the United States. Many of them remained in the cities, providing the backbone of America's rapidly developing industries.

Isolation in Foreign Affairs

The United States was not always as involved in world affairs as it is today. Since the presidency of George Washington, the government had largely followed a policy of neutrality and isolation from European politics. Americans were more interested in national security and trade than in "entangling alliances." In a message to Congress in 1823, President James Monroe enunciated what has come to be called the **Monroe Doctrine**. He told Europe that North and South America, "by the free and independent condition which they have assumed and maintain, are henceforth not to be considered as subjects for future colonization by any European powers." Monroe went on to say that the United States would regard "any attempt" by Europe to extend its control "to any portion of this hemisphere as dangerous to our peace and safety." In return, Monroe promised that the United States would not interfere in European affairs.

Although the United States avoided making foreign alliances, it could not remain isolated from world affairs. The first challenge to its isolation came as American merchants and businessmen expanded their foreign trade and investments. To protect and help Americans in their overseas business ventures, the U.S. government signed trade agreements with several European nations. Later in the century, the United States competed with European nations for trade opportunities in new markets such as China and Japan.

British Colonies Granted Independence

At the outset of the nineteenth century, while Spain was losing most of its colonial possessions, Great Britain was acquiring new territory. By the end of the nineteenth century, the British could boast that the sun never set on their empire. British emigrants had transplanted their culture into many lands, including Ireland, Canada, Australia, New Zealand, and South Africa. The British carried with them their tradition of self-government. As the colonies developed, Britain allowed them greater self-government—it had learned from its experience with the American colonies. As a result, most British colonies eventually gained independence without experiencing widespread revolts.

Ireland

The English seized control of land in Ireland beginning in the 1100s. Despite strong Irish resentment, the British maintained control and annexed Ireland in 1801. During the late 1800s the Irish intensified their efforts to gain a greater voice in government. British prime minister Gladstone unsuccessfully tried to "pacify Ireland" (see pp. 399–400). While some Irish people sought independence, others desired to achieve local control of internal issues while remaining under British protection for international affairs. At the beginning of World War I, this matter was still unresolved. However, Britain granted Irish independence shortly after the war.

Canada

Unlike other British possessions, Canada was originally a French colony. From the beginning of European settlement in North

America, relations between the French Canadians and the British colonists were unfriendly. The national rivalry between Great Britain and France in Europe often spilled over into the colonies, bringing war and unrest. When the Seven Years' War (known in North America as the French and Indian War) ended in 1763 (see chapter 14), Britain emerged victorious. As part of the peace settlement, France ceded Canada to Great Britain.

To ensure French Canadian loyalty to British rule, the British Parliament passed the **Quebec Act** in 1774. This legislation permitted the French Canadians to retain their language, law, and customs and to freely practice their Roman Catholic religion. Although the act alarmed the predominantly Protestant American colonies, its concessions temporarily pacified the French Canadians.

During the American War for Independence, thousands of British Loyalists fled to Canada. The French Canadians felt threatened by the growing British population. At the same time, the British colonists did not want to live under the long-established French customs and law. Attempting to end the friction, the British Parliament divided Canada into two provinces: Upper Canada (now Ontario), where most of the Loyalists lived, and Lower Canada (now Quebec), where most of the French lived. Each province was granted its own governor, legislative council, and elected assembly. Nevertheless, discontent continued.

The British government sent a new governor general, Lord Durham, to Canada to study problems in the colonies. He recommended that Britain grant Canada self-government in domestic matters while retaining control over foreign affairs. At the same time, he called for a united Canada. Parliament adopted the latter recommendation and combined Lower and Upper Canada by an Act of Union in 1840. In 1867, the government was reorganized again by the **British North America Act**, which created the Dominion of Canada, a federation of four provinces—Quebec, Ontario,

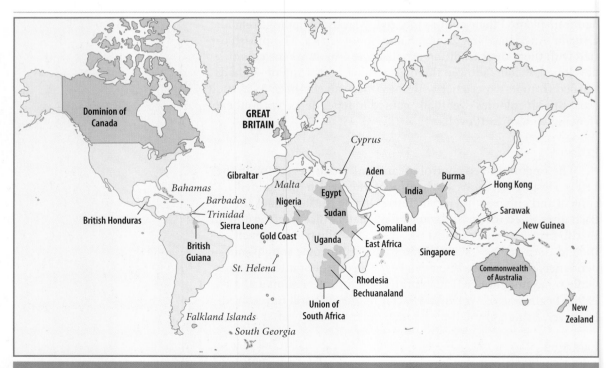

British Empire (1914)

Nova Scotia, and New Brunswick. (It also provided for new territories to be added to the union.) Canada remained a part of the British Empire, but it had a much greater degree of self-government than before.

Australia and New Zealand

Australia is an island continent located in the South Pacific. It is nearly as large as the continental United States. Despite its size, it remained virtually unknown before the seventeenth century. Dutch explorers discovered it in the early 1600s, but they did not establish a colony there. More than a century later in 1770, an Englishman, Captain **James Cook**, explored the eastern coast of Australia. His exploration became the basis for British claims to the area.

With the outbreak of the American Revolutionary War in 1775, Britain no longer had a place to send criminals from its overcrowded prisons. (Before the war, Britain had transported convicts to penal settlements in Georgia.) The British resolved this problem by establishing a British settlement at Port Jackson (now Sydney), Australia, in 1788. The first "settlers" were mostly convicts from British jails and soldiers sent to supervise them. Most of the convicts were not dangerous criminals but had been imprisoned for either minor crimes or debt.

During the nineteenth century, the Australian settlements grew economically and politically. Free settlers were attracted to Australia by the abundance of cheap land and the discovery of gold. By the end of the century, Australia had become a world producer of wool and meat. In 1901, the independent Australian colonies, with the approval of the British Parliament, united into a federal union, forming the Commonwealth of Australia.

The islands of New Zealand, located about one thousand miles southeast of Australia, were first sighted by the Dutch. Captain Cook later made five visits to the islands, exploring them extensively and mapping their coastlines. Among the first European settlers in New Zealand were escaped convicts from the penal colonies in Australia and seamen who had deserted their ships. In addition, the islands were inhabited by native New Zealanders, the **Maoris**.

In 1841, New Zealand became a British colony. In 1907, New Zealand became a dominion in the British Empire. The status of dominion allowed New Zealand to be virtually independent while still recognizing the British monarch as head of state. Dominion status preserved British control over defense, constitutional amendments, and foreign affairs in New Zealand. By 1947 New Zealand had declared itself a sovereign state, and the Constitution Act (1986) "unilaterally revoked all residual United Kingdom legislative powers." This settled New Zealand's status as an independent nation.

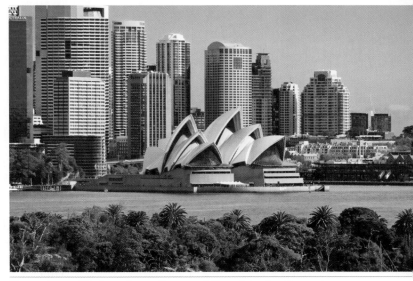

Three views of Sydney, Australia: two of the original settlement and one of the modern city

South Africa

The Dutch were the first Europeans to settle South Africa. In 1652, they established the Cape Colony on the southern tip of Africa. During the Napoleonic Wars, Britain seized the colony and encouraged British people to settle at the Cape. The Dutch colonists, called **Boers** (Dutch for "farmers"), resented British rule. Beginning in 1836, hundreds of them began a migration, called the **Great Trek**, east and north into the interior, where they founded the republics of the Transvaal and the Orange Free State. In the 1850s, Britain granted these republics their independence.

For several decades, the Boers lived in relative isolation from the British settlers along the coast. But in 1867 diamonds were discovered in the Orange Free State, and in 1886 gold was discovered in the Transvaal. Soon, thousands of miners—mostly British—poured into the region. Growing tension between the Boers and the British led to the **Boer War** (1899–1902). The British won the war and extended their control over those two republics. They were lenient with the Boers, however, providing them with financial help to recover from the war and allowing them to use their own language in schools and courts. In 1910, the British colonies at the Cape and the old Boer republics combined to form the Union of South Africa. South Africa joined the British Empire as a dominion in 1931. In 1961, a new constitution renamed South Africa the Republic of South Africa.

Section Review

1–4. List four possessions outside North America that the United States controlled by the end of the nineteenth century.

5–6. What man's exploration was the basis for the English claim on Australia? What was unusual about the first English "settlers" there?

7–8. What were Dutch colonists in South Africa called? What people did they fight for control of the mineral resources found in Transvaal and the Orange Free State?

★ Trace the steps toward the development of the Commonwealth of Australia.

★ Trace the steps toward the development of the Republic of South Africa.

Guiding Questions

1. How did the British gain control of India?
2. What caused the Opium Wars and the Boxer Rebellion?
3. Why was Japan isolated from the West, and what ended that isolation?

II. Imperialism in the East

Asia

When Europeans sailed to the New World, they found sparsely populated lands. Thus, they were initially able to transplant European culture into these lands with little opposition. But the situation in Asia was different. That densely populated continent was the home of strong and ancient cultures. Although the industrial and military might of Western nations successfully forced open many Asian lands to Western trade, attempts to establish Western culture met with determined resistance.

India

After Vasco da Gama discovered an all-water route to India, European nations set up trading posts along the Indian coast. By the

Imperialism in Asia and Africa

The quest for colonies in the sixteenth and seventeenth centuries was motivated primarily by the economic policy of mercantilism. (See chapter 13.) European countries looked upon their colonial possessions as a source of wealth. But by the late eighteenth century, they found it financially draining to maintain and protect their colonies, many of which were now seeking independence. Likewise, a free-trade policy was slowly replacing the one-sided trade of mercantilism. Revolts in Europe during the early nineteenth century further diminished the interest in overseas colonies.

However, between 1870 and 1914, the race for overseas possessions revived. Many European nations competed in a new form of empire-building known as **imperialism**, the dominance and power asserted by one nation over less-powerful nations. During the late nineteenth century, European nations eagerly sought to impose their spheres of influence over most of the world. Empire-building became increasingly important to the foreign policy of many European nations, resulting in fierce rivalries that would eventually contribute to World War I.

Reasons for Imperialism

The motives behind imperialism were diverse. In fact, the interests of any particular nation may have differed from one overseas possession to another or from one time to another.

1. The expansion of industrialism in the late nineteenth century increased the demand for raw materials and new markets. Industrialized nations did not want to depend on other nations for their supplies. They sought to control areas of the world that would meet their industrial needs and provide an outlet for manufactured goods. Unfortunately, the European powers often acted without regard for the rights and desires of the native populations.

2. Imperialism was also motivated by the intense nationalism that characterized Europe from 1870 to 1914. An overseas empire brought national honor and prestige. In addition to the ongoing rivalry between Britain and France, imperialism provided the newly formed nations of Germany and Italy the opportunity to display their growing national strength. European countries were quick to seize control of strategic locations to establish military bases and protect their worldwide interests.

3. "Humanitarianism" became an often-used excuse for imperialism. The British poet Rudyard Kipling expressed this popular nineteenth-century sentiment as he urged his contemporaries to "take up the white man's burden." It is difficult to overstate the racist attitude of Europeans who viewed their society as superior to the civilizations of Asia and Africa. Those who embraced this view assumed it was their responsibility to share the benefits of Western culture—education, medical care, industry, and technology. In truth, some Europeans did launch sincere efforts to improve education, abolish slavery, and stamp out disease and famine in colonial territories. Also, many people did profit from Western aid. However, the native populations found the superior attitude of many Europeans to be offensive. Furthermore, too often humanitarian concerns by the Europeans became nothing more than an excuse to exploit the wealth of these dominated countries.

4. While not a dominant motivation behind Europe's worldwide expansion, the dramatic spread of Christian missions accompanied this expansion. Despite opposition from some imperialist powers, the nineteenth century became the "great century" of missionary activity. As European countries built overseas empires, Christians became acquainted with the spiritual needs of people in distant lands. Even though in many countries Western political and economic control opened the doors for missionary activity, Christian missionaries were not motivated by a desire to exploit or subject foreign peoples. They desired to tell the good news of the Savior who died for the sins of the world. In some parts of Africa, the arrival of missionaries *preceded* the coming of traders and government officials. David Livingstone opened the interior of Africa as he preached Christ in thousands of villages. Livingstone and others also reported the terrible abuses of African slavery and pressed for its abolition. As a result of what the missionaries witnessed, and in their desire to help those who were oppressed, the missionaries often found themselves at odds with imperialists.

eighteenth century, French and British trade companies had established thriving bases in India. But early in the 1700s, the security of those bases was threatened by the collapse of the Mughal Empire (see ch. 12), which left India once again divided into small rival states. The British and French used this political unrest for their economic advantage. They extended their control in India by making alliances with local rulers or by outright conquest of territory.

Robert Clive and his Indian allies after the Battle of Plassey

The strong British-French rivalry that dominated European affairs during the eighteenth century extended to India. During the Seven Years' War (1756–63), an Indian ruler who sided with the French attacked the British settlement at Calcutta. In the **Battle of Plassey** (1757), British forces led by **Robert Clive** defeated the Indian ruler. Three years later, Clive defeated the French as well. The victories made the British East India Company the dominant authority in India; no individual Indian state was strong enough to challenge its power.

For the next hundred years, the British East India Company governed much of India. The British government supervised the company's affairs but did not exercise any direct rule over the country. Because the East India Company was primarily a commercial organization, financial considerations played an important role in determining its political policies. For example, the company tried to keep William Carey and other missionaries from preaching

William Carey in India

Young **William Carey** (1761–1834), from England, gave little indication of the great things God was going to accomplish through his life. As a student, he liked history, science, and mathematics, but he had little interest in the Bible. As a boy, he mastered Latin, then Greek, and later Hebrew. As a young man, he taught himself French and Dutch. It might have seemed odd that Carey, a cobbler's apprentice, had such a talent for learning languages. Time would show that God was preparing him for his future work in India. Around the age of eighteen, Carey trusted Christ and began to identify with Nonconformists. Later he was immersed and became an active member of a Baptist congregation.

Since his youth, Carey had been interested in foreign lands. Next to his workbench he had a crude, hand-drawn map of the world on which he wrote geographic and religious facts about each country. When he tried to get others interested in sending missionaries to those countries, however, they told him that the injunction "Go ye into all the world, and preach the gospel" was given only to the apostles. Later, at a meeting of Baptist ministers, Carey made his plea for missions:

"Expect great things from God; attempt great things for God." As a result of Carey's sermon, others joined him in establishing the Baptist Missionary Society. Carey, the first appointed missionary, took his family to India in 1794.

When the Careys landed in India they faced many hardships. But William Carey was well established in his faith, competent in linguistics, and firmly resolved to do God's will. He quickly went about establishing the work under two principles: (1) the missionary must be a companion to and an equal with the nationals, and (2) the missionary must, as soon as possible, become self-supporting. While on the mission field, Carey worked as both an indigo planter and a horticulturist. He established his first church by preaching to plantation workers. He also worked on translating the Bible into the native Bengali languages.

To master the various Indian dialects, Carey set about learning Sanskrit. He translated the Bible into Bengali in 1798. He went on to translate the Bible into twenty Indian dialects and supervised its translation into twenty more. In 1798, a printer joined Carey in his work. Together, they set up a printing press and produced the first Bible and tracts in the Indian dialects.

Carey never returned to England. Once he settled in India, he devoted his life to bringing the gospel to the Indian people. Because of his pioneering accomplishments in mission work, he became known as the Father of Modern Missions. Yet once when someone was talking about his remarkable accomplishments, Carey replied, "Do not talk about Dr. Carey's this or Dr. Carey's that. Talk about Dr. Carey's Savior." He lived by the verse "He must increase, but I must decrease" (John 3:30).

the gospel in India. They believed that such preaching might cause unrest among the Hindu and Muslim populations and thus hurt their business interests. Yet the expansion of the company's authority and the growing efforts by the British to impose Western ways on Indian society led to the very unrest the British had feared.

In 1857, *sepoys*, the native Indian troops employed by the East India Company, revolted. The immediate cause of the **Sepoy Mutiny** was the introduction of new rifle cartridges. The cartridges—the ends of which had to be bitten off—were greased to keep the powder dry. Rumors spread that the grease used was cow and pig fat. (Hindus consider the cow sacred, and Muslims consider the pig unclean.) The revolt symbolized the nation's dissatisfaction with Western rule. British troops were dispatched, and after several months of bloody fighting, the mutiny was brutally suppressed.

As a result of the mutiny, the British government assumed control of Indian political affairs. It appointed a viceroy to govern India, and in 1877 Prime Minister Disraeli conferred the title Empress of India on Queen Victoria. The British government also assumed the responsibility of providing for the welfare of the Indian people. They improved sanitation and medical care, built roads and railroads, and constructed factories (in areas most beneficial to the British). They also established new schools that imposed Western thought and culture. But as many young Indians studied the political ideas of the eighteenth century, their desire for self-government became even stronger. A movement for self-rule had begun to grow by the end of the nineteenth century.

China

Despite China's vast territory and its large population, the Chinese were not able to withstand European imperialism during the nineteenth century. Under the **Manchu dynasty**, which had ruled China since 1644, all Chinese ports except Canton were closed to foreign merchants. However, by the nineteenth century, internal problems had crippled Manchu leadership. Western nations took advantage of China's growing weakness and demanded greater trade privileges.

Chinese attempts to restrict foreign trade led to war between China and Great Britain. Initially, the Chinese demanded hard currency (gold, silver) from the British in exchange for tea and silk. This led to a negative trade balance between Britain and China. British merchants shifted the balance by delivering chests of opium (a dangerous and highly addictive drug) to sell in China. The horrible addiction that resulted enabled British merchants to demand Chinese goods for a continuous supply of opium. The results for China were devastating, but the British authorities largely ignored the problem because of the financial benefit for Britain. For a time, Chinese rulers did little to stop British traders from smuggling opium into China. When Chinese officials finally sought to stop this drug trade, British merchants objected. Tension over the opium trade and all foreign trade sparked the **Opium Wars**, in which British forces were used to preserve the profitable but destructive opium trade. In 1842, the British forced China to sign the Treaty of Nanking, which opened four more trade ports and gave Britain the island of Hong Kong. A second war (1856–60) further weakened China, as French and British forces joined to win additional trade concessions.

Sepoy Mutiny

J. Hudson Taylor in China

J. Hudson Taylor (1832–1905) was a man who set himself to do God's will and would not allow anything to stop him. At the age of five, after hearing his father talk about the need of taking the gospel to China, he declared that "one day he would go to that country." In 1849, at the age of seventeen, he dedicated himself to the Lord's service. That was when he knew that God was calling him to China. After earning a medical degree, he set sail for China in 1853.

In those days, missionaries were allowed to labor only in the coastal regions of China, near the treaty ports. Soon after he landed, however, Taylor became deeply burdened for the people living inland. During the next seven years, he made many trips inland. With each visit, his burden increased for the millions who had not heard the gospel. In 1860, poor health forced him to return to England. Yet his concern for the Chinese did not diminish. While in England, he revised the Chinese New Testament.

Five years went by, but his health did not improve. It seemed that he would never be able to return to China. But one weekend in the summer of 1865, while resting in Dover, he prayed that God would send twenty-four skilled and willing workers to the inland areas of China. After he prayed, he experienced a calmness of heart and body. When he returned to London, his wife remarked that Dover seemed to have been good for him. He told her of his request and about the renewed strength that the Lord had given him. Two days later, with less than £10, he opened a bank account in the name of the China Inland Mission, an organization dedicated to enlisting people and funds for missionary work in China. On May 26, 1866, Taylor, his family, and twenty-four others set sail for China.

Missionary work in inland China was difficult. The Chinese were reluctant to welcome the missionaries even though Taylor and the others adopted Chinese dress. But Taylor's faith was unwavering. He knew that he was doing God's work and that God would protect and prosper the work. God did exactly that. New areas in China opened, and more missionaries joined in the task of reaching the Chinese for Christ. Taylor, who had once asked the Lord for twenty-four colaborers, now prayed for one thousand; God answered his request.

In this 1898 French cartoon, the rulers from the United Kingdom, Germany, Russia, and Japan divide up China while France looks on and China protests without avail.

Although China never officially lost its independence, other nations heavily influenced its policies and forced it to bend to their will. By the end of the century, many Western countries had secured treaties forcing China to open its ports to their trade. Two demands found in many of those treaties especially angered the Chinese: the right of Western nations to station their warships in China's waters and the right of Westerners to **extraterritoriality**. This principle stated that Westerners who broke Chinese law had the right to be tried in their own national courts rather than in Chinese courts.

Particularly embarrassing to China was its loss to Japan in the **Sino-Japanese War** (1894–95). China had always considered Japan an inferior nation. After this humiliating defeat, Western nations increased their demands for more trade concessions, and China had little choice but to grant them.

Angered by Western actions, some Chinese organized secret societies, pledging to rid China of Western influences. In 1899, following orders from the Chinese empress, members of these societies began to terrorize both Westerners and Chinese Christians. Throughout the country, rebels destroyed railroads and bridges and murdered Western diplomats, missionaries, and merchants. This uprising, known as the **Boxer Rebellion** (named after a leading society called the "Righteous and Harmonious Fists"), became so serious that European, Japanese, and American troops finally intervened. The rebellion failed, but it contributed to the collapse of the Manchu dynasty.

Japan

Japan entered the nineteenth century with a feudal society dominated by the warrior class. Shoguns of the **Tokugawa** family ruled Japan as they had done since the beginning of the seventeenth century. Like China's rulers, Japan's rulers intended to exclude all Western influence and to maintain the country's traditions. But in July 1853 **Matthew Perry**, a U.S. naval commander, sailed into Edo Bay (later called Tokyo Bay) with a small fleet of ships. His mission was to persuade the Japanese to allow trade between the United States and Japan. After presenting the American request, Perry sailed away, telling the Japanese that he would return later for their answer. In February 1854 Perry returned with even more warships. The shogun realized Japan's weak position and reluctantly agreed to open trade. Both nations signed the **Treaty of Kanagawa**, the first treaty Japan ever signed with a Western nation.

The period of Japan's isolation had ended. But how were the Japanese going to respond to Western influences? Would they resist like the Chinese, or would they adopt some Western ways? A civil war settled the issue. The struggle overthrew the shogun and restored the Japanese emperor to his position of authority. The emperor, who adopted the name Meiji (MAY jee; "enlightened rule") for his reign, declared, "The uncivilized customs of former years shall be abandoned."

During the **Meiji Period** (1868–1912), Japan's leaders transformed the nation from a feudal society to a major industrial power. Japanese commissions were sent to Western nations to study their governments, industries, schools, and militaries. The Japanese copied what they considered to be the best methods and institutions. Within a relatively short time, Japan became the first industrial nation of Asia, and the Japanese government adopted a Western constitution. It also established new educational and judicial systems and reorganized the military forces according to Western models.

By adopting some Western ways, Japan was able to resist Western imperialism. Its new industrial and military might enabled Japan to compete with Western nations for territory and influence in Asia. As noted earlier, Japanese expansionism eventually led to the Sino-Japanese War (1894–95), a conflict that exposed the weakness of the Chinese state. Later, in the **Russo-Japanese War** (1904–5), Japan stunned the Western powers by defeating the supposedly mightier Russians on both sea and land (see ch. 21). The small island nation, by routing its much larger opponents, demonstrated that it was becoming a world power. During the first half of the twentieth century, Japan continued its expansionist policies. Its aggression would contribute to the outbreak of World War II.

(top) *Matthew Perry;* (bottom) *Artist's conception of Perry's second fleet*

Southeast Asia

Southeast Asia includes the territory east of India and south of China, as well as many of the islands in the Pacific and Indian Oceans. Before the nineteenth century, several parts of Southeast

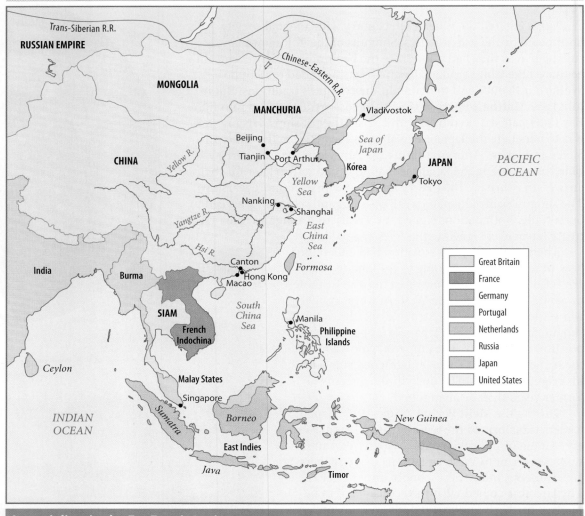

Imperialism in the Far East (1914)

Asia had come under European control. But during the nineteenth century, the Europeans seized virtually the entire area. The only major territory that remained independent was Siam (today called Thailand). The rulers of Siam successfully played the British and French against one another. Thus Siam became a buffer state between British and French possessions. (See map above.)

One of the most valuable British possessions was Ceylon (modern Sri Lanka), an island taken from the Dutch in the eighteenth century. Rubber trees and tea grew well there, and the island was also a source of lead and sapphires. Other important British possessions in Southeast Asia included Malaya, Burma (modern Myanmar), and Singapore. The French had one large colony in Southeast Asia, an area called Indochina that bordered the South China Sea and included the modern nations of Vietnam, Cambodia, and Laos.

The major Dutch possession in Southeast Asia was a group of islands known as the Dutch East Indies—modern Indonesia. The East Indies includes more than three thousand islands spread over several thousand miles. When the Dutch seized the islands, they established what they called a **culture system**. They forced the nationals to use one-fifth of their land and one-fifth of their time to grow crops for the Dutch.

Section Review

1–2. During what time period was the race among European nations for overseas possessions revived? What name was given to empire-building in which one country sought to dominate and assert its power over less powerful countries?

3–4. In what region of the world was it difficult for Western nations to impose Western culture? What form of control were they able to establish over that region?

5. What was the immediate cause of the Sepoy Mutiny?

6–7. Explain the cause of the Opium Wars. What long-term advantage did France and Great Britain extract from China following these wars?

✯ Outline the transformation of Japan from an isolated, feudalistic society to a major industrial power.

✯ Using activity 1 from chapter 19 of *Student Activities*, map the territorial claims of European powers in Southeast Asia.

III. African Slave Trade and Imperialism

As we learned in chapters 2, 5, and 12, Africa was the home of several thriving civilizations before 1500. African kingdoms traded profitably among themselves and with the Arabs, Asians, and Europeans. European expansion, however, reduced the African people from trading partners to subjects. Imperialism in Africa became an uneven mixture of exploitation, racism, and humanitarian impulses. The result was a transformed Africa.

African Slave Trade

European exploration of the African coast and the discovery of the New World indirectly prompted the rise of the West African slave trade. In 1441, Portugal became the first European nation to engage in this trade by bringing a small group of Africans to Europe. Yet until the opening of the New World in the sixteenth century, few Europeans owned slaves. They were first used on a large scale after the Spanish arrived in Latin America. The Spaniards enslaved the native Indians, forcing them to work in the mines or on large plantations. The Indians, however, were vulnerable to the new diseases that the Europeans brought. As a result, many of them died. To replenish the labor supply, the Spaniards began importing slaves from Africa. By the eighteenth century, black slavery was common in the New World, and traders from many European nations participated in it.

The slave trade proved to be very profitable and therefore expanded rapidly. The heaviest European trading occurred from 1700 to 1850, during which time approximately 80 percent of all slaves brought to the New World arrived. From the early sixteenth century to about 1870, when the Western slave trade ended, traders transported up to 9.5 million African slaves (some say as high as 15 million), most of whom came from western Africa, to the Americas and Europe.

The European slave traders did not usually capture the slaves themselves. Instead, they bought them from Muslim slave traders and African tribes on the coast. Often, victorious African chiefs sold

1. What role did Livingstone play in the opening of Africa?
2. What led to the Scramble for Africa?
3. How did Europe divide up Africa?

Muslim Slave Trade

Centuries before Europeans became involved in the dreadful practice of the slave trade, Muslim slave traders seized and transported vast numbers of Africans from North and East Africa to the Arabian Peninsula and the Middle East. Most of those taken were women and children; African males were routinely slaughtered. Slave traders sold the African women and children to men throughout the Muslim world. Muslim slave trading continued long after Western nations discontinued the practice and survives in some African nations to this day.

the prisoners they captured during tribal warfare. As the demand for slaves increased, some groups even launched raids on unsuspecting villages, capturing the inhabitants and selling them into bondage.

Before purchasing a boatload of slaves, the European slave trader had his surgeon examine the captives to determine their physical condition. He then selected only the slaves who seemed to be in good physical condition; weak or sickly slaves would reduce his profits. He wanted slaves who could withstand the inhumane conditions during the voyage across the Atlantic and still bring a good price. After paying for the slaves with guns, gunpowder, rum, tobacco, trinkets, cloth, iron, or copper, the trader had the slaves branded with a red-hot iron. The brand ensured that the slaves he purchased would not be confused with those purchased by others.

Not all of the slaves lived to see the New World. About one-fourth of those who left Africa died during the long voyage across the Atlantic. Crowded conditions allowed disease to spread rapidly. Lack of exercise and contaminated food and water supplies also contributed to illness and death. Some Africans chose to jump into the sea when allowed on deck rather than submit to a life of slavery.

Opening the Interior

Before the nineteenth century, few Europeans had ever traveled to the interior of Africa. It was an unknown land, often called the "Dark Continent." Among the first European explorers to travel inland was David Livingstone (1813–73). He had planned to be a medical missionary to China but was prevented by the outbreak of the Opium War. Livingstone went to Africa instead, motivated by reports from people who had seen the "smoke of a thousand villages" in the interior, where the gospel had never been heard.

Enduring great physical hardship, Livingstone journeyed into the African interior. He was devoted to opening Africa to the gospel and in the process ending the slave trade. While on one of his lengthy expeditions, he remained away from civilization for so long that people wondered if he was still alive. As part of a publicity campaign, a New York newspaper hired British explorer Henry Stanley to find Livingstone. In 1871, Stanley found him at Lake Tanganyika and casually greeted him: "Dr. Livingstone, I presume." Livingstone continued to travel and preach in his beloved Africa until he died there two years later.

Word of Livingstone's endeavors created great enthusiasm among prospective missionaries in Britain and the United States. Unfortunately, his journeys and those of other explorers who mapped rivers and recorded information about African resources also opened the door for European trade and imperialism in the areas they had explored.

Imperialism in Africa

Before 1880, Europe controlled only about 10 percent of the African continent. From 1880 to 1914, however, the race for territory in Africa became so intense that by World War I only Ethiopia and Liberia remained independent.

Britain was interested in the entire continent of Africa. In the 1880s the British secured a controlling interest in the newly built Suez Canal, which had been completed in 1869. To protect this lifeline of British trade with India and the Far East, the British government assumed control of the Egyptian economy and government.

Scramble for Africa

The transition from trading with Africa to seizing control of African states became a scramble, or race, between European nations to seize strategic regions in Africa. The **Scramble for Africa** often occurred in three phases. Phase one involved a European nation convincing one or more African states to sign a treaty that granted trade rights for the European nation and promised protection for the African state, a promise that proved to be empty. Phase two consisted of European nations meeting in secret and making agreements to avoid war as they carved up Africa. During phase three, European ships and troops arrived in Africa to subjugate various regions. As mentioned on page 419, motives varied from determination to protect raw materials and markets to intense nationalism.

David Livingstone and Mary Slessor in Africa

On his fifty-ninth birthday, **David Livingstone** wrote in his journal, "My Jesus, my King, my Life, my All; I again dedicate my whole self to Thee. Accept me, and grant me, O gracious Father, that ere this year is gone I may finish my task." He penned those words several months before his death. He had dedicated his life to reaching Africa for Christ. In his last days, he was often too sick to walk; yet, borne on the shoulders of faithful Africans, he continued to go to villages where the gospel had never been preached.

Finally, on May 1, 1873, his task on earth was ended. While on his knees in prayer, he went to be with his Lord.

Livingstone's body was transported to the coast and sent back to England. His heart, however, was left behind in Africa, buried by nationals at the foot of a mvula tree. Today, his earthly remains lie near the central nave in Westminster Abbey in London. The black slab that marks his resting place reads in part,

Brought by faithful hands
Over land and sea,
Here rests
DAVID LIVINGSTONE
Missionary, Traveler, Philanthropist

Born March 18, 1813
At Blantyre, Lanarkshire
Died May 1, 1873,
At Chitambo's Village, Llala

The slab also bears his favorite missionary text: "Other sheep I have, which are not of this fold: them also I must bring, and they shall hear my voice" (John 10:16).

Livingstone's life affected many; his death affected one woman in particular. **Mary Slessor** (1848–1915) was a petite Scottish girl with brilliant blue eyes and curly red hair. She was born into a poor family; her father was a drunkard, but she had a godly mother. At the age of eleven, Mary went to work at a spinning mill. She worked twelve hours a day, six days a week to help with the family's finances. In her heart, however, she dreamed of going to Africa as a missionary. When she heard the news of David Livingstone's death, she asked her mother if she could offer herself for missionary service. Her mother gave her permission. Learning of the heathen customs and poor living conditions in Calabar, West Africa, Mary believed that was the place God would have her labor.

In September 1876, she sailed for Calabar. She began her work with youthful impatience, wanting to see immediate results. But she was reminded to wait patiently on God. Among the many heathen practices that she found among the people, perhaps the most appalling was the custom of killing newborn twins. The nationals believed that twins were

the children of demons. Mary was able to rescue some of these children, whom she raised as her own. As the years went by, the children became teachers and missionaries to their own people.

After spending a few years at the mission station on the coast, Mary felt the call of God to go upriver to witness to several cannibal tribes. At first, the mission was opposed to the idea, but finally they allowed her to go. Taking her children with her, she settled in one of the cannibal villages. She clearly showed her love for the people; she tended their sick and cared for their unwanted. They returned her love by giving her the honored title of Ma ("mother"). Later, they came to consider her as their queen. When Calabar was taken over by the British government in 1889, she was made vice-consul for the interior of the Niger Coast Protectorate. She was responsible for establishing law and order among the nationals. Nonetheless, she remained true to her primary task of winning people to the Lord. She faithfully gave out God's Word, trusting that it would enlighten their hearts. When she moved to another area some fifteen years later, she left behind a thriving Christian community.

After thirty-nine years of self-sacrificing service, her frail body could take no more; she went to be with her Lord on January 13, 1915. What was the secret to her successful labor for the Lord? In her own words, "I have no idea how and why God has carried me over so many hard places, and made these hordes submit to me . . . except in answer to prayer at home for me. It is all beyond my comprehension. The only way I can explain it is on the ground that I have been prayed for more than most. Pray on—power lies that way."

An 1892 British cartoon depicting Cecil Rhodes stretching from Cape to Cairo; (inset) Cecil Rhodes

In southern Africa, British imperialism was eventually directed by **Cecil Rhodes** (1853–1902), called "the empire-builder." As a young man, Rhodes went to southern Africa and made a fortune in diamonds. He became a firm supporter of British imperialism, working tirelessly to advance British (and his own) interests in Africa. He dreamed of an uninterrupted line of British territory stretching from Egypt in northern Africa to the Cape Colony in southern Africa. Although his goal of British control "from Cape to Cairo" was only partially realized, he helped Britain acquire additional territory in Africa, including Rhodesia (modern Zambia and Zimbabwe), which was named in his honor. His name lives on in Britain's Rhodes scholarships, which provide funds for students, primarily from the British Commonwealth and the United States, to study at Oxford University.

While Britain seized African territory in the southern and northeastern parts of the continent, France subjugated most of the northern part and much of western Africa. In 1830, France began to build its African empire by invading Algeria. The following year, King Louis Philippe established an elite army group that would figure prominently in the history of French imperialism—the famous **Foreign Legion**. By the end of the century, France had extended its holdings to include most of West Africa, building the largest land empire in Africa (though it was mostly desert).

Belgium's African possessions consisted of one large mass of land in central Africa called the Congo. Between 1878 and 1884, King **Leopold II** of Belgium hired explorers to acquire as much of the region as possible. As a result, Leopold soon personally controlled the nine-hundred-thousand-square-mile Congo Free State, a land area more than seventy-five times larger than Belgium. Sadly, Leopold's agents severely mistreated the nationals. When the news of their atrocities reached Europe, such an outcry arose that the Belgian parliament forced Leopold II to turn over administration of the Congo to the Belgian government, which renamed it the Belgian Congo (modern-day Democratic Republic of the Congo).

Germany was late entering the race for colonies. The effort toward German unification kept German attention focused on domestic matters rather than imperial concerns. In addition, Bismarck was never very enthusiastic about acquiring overseas territories because he believed that they would dilute Germany's strength. After German unification had been achieved, however, Germany wished to prove its strength as a new nation. In the 1880s, it seized its first African colony—German Southwest Africa (modern-day Namibia). Of all of Germany's African possessions, the most valuable one geographically was German East Africa (modern-day Tanzania). The German explorer Dr. Karl Peters secured this area, preventing the British from acquiring an unbroken stretch of territory from the Cape to Cairo.

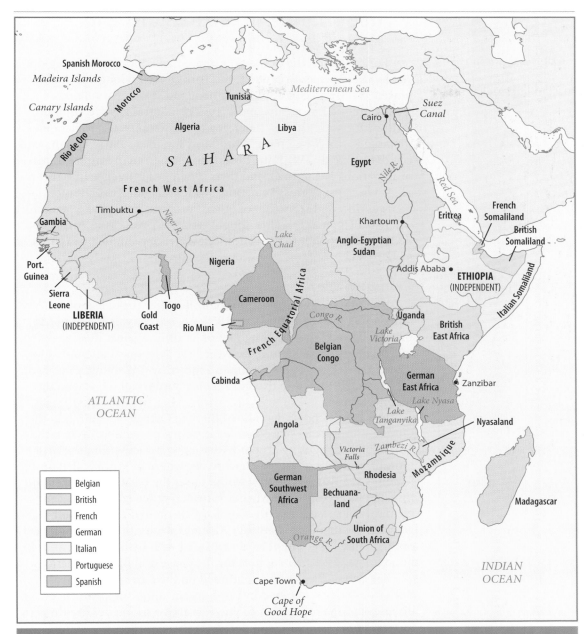

Imperialism in Africa (1914)

Section Review

1. What famous explorer opened the interior of Africa to the gospel message?

2. What role did Cecil Rhodes play in British imperialism?

3–4. What European king personally controlled an area in Africa seventy-five times the size of his own country? What was that area called?

5. How did Germany obstruct Cecil Rhodes's dream for British imperialism in Africa?

★ Evaluate the Scramble for Africa in light of the concepts of justice, power, and citizenship.

★ Using activity 3 from chapter 19 of *Student Activities*, map the territorial claims of European powers in Africa.

Guiding Questions

1. What led to the decline of the Ottoman Empire?
2. What characterized Russian imperialism?

IV. Imperialism in the Balkans and Near East

For centuries, the Ottoman Empire had controlled this region. But by the nineteenth century, the Turks were no longer a mighty power. Weak and corrupt government and strong nationalistic feeling among Europeans under Turkish control signaled doom for the Ottoman Empire. Referring to that empire, Czar Nicholas I remarked, "We have on our hands a sick man, a very sick man, who can die suddenly." With the decline of the Ottoman Empire, European nations began to extend their spheres of influence into this region. The most aggressive nation was Russia, but Russian imperialism was different from that of other European nations. For example, whereas Britain and France sought territory overseas in Africa and Asia, Russia sought to gain additional territory simply by expanding its borders.

Crimean War

The first major international conflict after the defeat of Napoleon was the **Crimean War** (1854–56; see chapter 17). It pitted Britain, France, and the Kingdom of Sardinia against Russia, which was pursuing expansion in the Near East. Nicholas I attempted to hasten the decline of the Ottoman Empire by provoking a war with the Turks. He hoped to expand Russia's borders all the way to the Mediterranean.

In 1853, Nicholas demanded that the Orthodox Church in the Ottoman Empire be placed under Russian "protection." When the Turks refused, fighting erupted. Russian victories within the first months of fighting created concern elsewhere in Europe. Britain feared that a Russian victory would upset the balance of power and threaten its access to the Mediterranean. France entered the war primarily because Emperor Napoleon III wanted to do something glorious to enhance his prestige. Count Cavour, the prime minister of the Italian kingdom of Sardinia, sided with Britain and France in hopes of gaining their support for the cause of Italian unification.

For two years, the war continued on the Crimean Peninsula. Both sides were hampered by poor organization, supply difficulties, disease, and inept leadership. The war ended soon after the Russian fortress of Sevastopol surrendered. At Paris in 1856, the nations that took part in the war met to discuss the peace settlement. Besides losing territory, Russia agreed to abandon its claim as protector of the Orthodox Church within the Ottoman Empire. It also agreed not to build any forts along the Black Sea or to station any warships in those waters. The major nations also promised to keep the Ottoman Empire from being destroyed, thereby preserving the balance of power.

Continued Russian Expansion

In 1877 Russia renewed its efforts to extend its influence into this region by initiating another war with the Turks. After suffering disastrous defeats, the Turks surrendered and signed the Treaty of San Stefano. The war strengthened Russia's position in the Balkans while virtually pushing the Ottomans out of Europe. But, once again, the European nations stepped in. At the Congress of Berlin (1878), they forced Russia to return some of the territories it had won from the Turks.

Crimean War

Russia continued its expansionistic designs, however. It made a concerted effort to push southward through Afghanistan and Persia toward the Persian Gulf. The British feared that such expansion would imperil both their prized possessions of India and the Suez Canal, which was their lifeline to India and the East. The rivalry between the two nations was temporarily settled in 1907 by the **Anglo-Russian Entente**. This agreement divided Persia (Iran) into three zones: the British dominated the southern zone, the Russians dominated the northern zone, and the middle zone remained neutral. In Afghanistan, the Russians recognized British influence and agreed not to interfere in Afghanistan's internal affairs.

Finally, Russia tried to expand eastward into Manchuria in hopes of establishing a warm-water seaport. Russia seized Port Arthur in 1897 and began work on the Chinese Eastern Railroad in Manchuria in 1898. Russian troops seized all of Manchuria in 1900 during the Boxer Rebellion but later lost this region in the Russo-Japanese War in 1904–5.

Section Review

1. What characterized Russia's imperialism in contrast with other European powers?

2–5. What motivated Russia, Britain, France, and Sardinia to participate in the Crimean War?

6. Why did a congress of European nations in 1856 force Russia to give up the territorial gains it made during the Crimean War?

✯ Why did Russia not seek territory overseas as many other European countries did?

✯ Given Russia's environment, explain the goal of Russia's eastward expansion.

V. Results of Imperialism

Negative Results

The military and industrial might of European nations enabled them to exploit the people and resources in their overseas empires. Too often, territorial officials and foreign merchants amassed personal fortunes at the expense of the native populations. Some Europeans even abused the native peoples. When dividing African territory, for example, imperial powers often ignored ancient tribal boundaries. This led to strife as tribes were arbitrarily grouped together or divided and ruled by different European countries.

While the Europeans improved the infrastructure of the conquered nations, the improvements were designed for the benefit of the Europeans rather than the native populations. As a result, rural areas and other regions considered less important were neglected. This created a large gulf between urban and rural areas that would linger long after the Europeans left. Later, many of these countries would have to bear the cost of providing a more effective infrastructure, even as they suffered from a large drain of capital because the Europeans took much of the country's wealth back to Europe.

It also became common for the Europeans to train and arm a professional army in some of these countries to protect against attacks by other European powers. While this seemed to be a practical

The Great Game

The *Great Game* was a political and diplomatic conflict between Great Britain and Russia for control of regions in Afghanistan and adjoining regions in Asia. Russia feared British expansion into Central Asia, and Britain feared Russian expansion into India. This sixty-five-year conflict ended in 1907 when both nations agreed to a defined border between Afghanistan and Russia.

Guiding Questions

1. What were the negative results of imperialism?
2. What were some positive results of imperialism?

matter at the time, it became a source of instability later when these colonies gained their independence. Dictators could easily step in and use the army to subjugate the people.

Even with the best of intentions, European imperialism delayed the natural development of these subjected countries. For example, several African countries were developing into modern states when European forces invaded and subjugated them. European interference set African development back several generations.

Positive Results

Although many aspects of imperialism were negative, some good things occurred as well. For example, some of the imperial nations instituted democratic governments and bureaucracies to administer them. The Europeans also established modern judicial systems that have proven to be successful.

From a Christian perspective, the most significant benefit to the nationals, however, was the missionary outreach. God used imperialism, a selfish and materialistic movement, to open foreign lands to the gospel. Christians in Great Britain, in particular, responded to the unique opportunities that imperialism afforded to send forth missionaries. By 1900, almost six thousand missionaries were from Great Britain, one-third of the total number of missionaries then ministering around the world.

Along with spreading the news of salvation, the missionaries modernized societies with schools and colleges, taught the people trades, opened orphanages, began hospitals and medical clinics, and helped eliminate life-threatening customs. Some missionaries developed written languages for the people and translated the Bible into the native tongues, enabling the people to read God's Word and other important documents.

Many missionaries also became advocates for the nationals. As they lived among the people and understood the harmful effects of European oppression, they spoke out against the poor treatment that the people were experiencing.

Making Connections

1. Summarize one motive that prompted European nations to establish overseas empires.
2. Explain the rise of British rule in India.
3–5. Outline the three phases of the Scramble for Africa.
6. Explain one cause of the Boxer Rebellion.
7. Summarize the decline of the Ottoman Empire.

Developing History Skills

1. Contrast the independence movements among early British colonies and the subjection of later British colonies in Africa.
2. Summarize the long-term consequences of Perry's visits to Japan.

Thinking Critically

1. Outline the domestic expansion and the foreign policy of the United States during the nineteenth century.
2. Cite some useful outcomes of imperialism or condemn the practice of imperialism. Support your answer.

Living in God's World

1. Imagine that you are a missionary working among a people in Central Africa. Write a letter to the British governor defending the people to whom you minister against imperialist confiscation of their land and forced relocation.
2. Imagine that you are a British leader during the early nineteenth century. Craft a policy for how the British government should relate to foreign peoples that it conducts trade with.

People, Places, and Things to Know

Louisiana Purchase
Monroe Doctrine
Quebec Act
British North America Act
James Cook
Maoris
Boers
Great Trek
Boer War
imperialism
Battle of Plassey
Robert Clive
William Carey
Sepoy Mutiny
Manchu dynasty
Opium Wars
J. Hudson Taylor
extraterritoriality
Sino-Japanese War
Boxer Rebellion
Tokugawa
Matthew Perry
Treaty of Kanagawa
Meiji Period
Russo-Japanese War
culture system
Scramble for Africa
David Livingstone
Mary Slessor
Cecil Rhodes
Foreign Legion
Leopold II
Crimean War
Anglo-Russian Entente

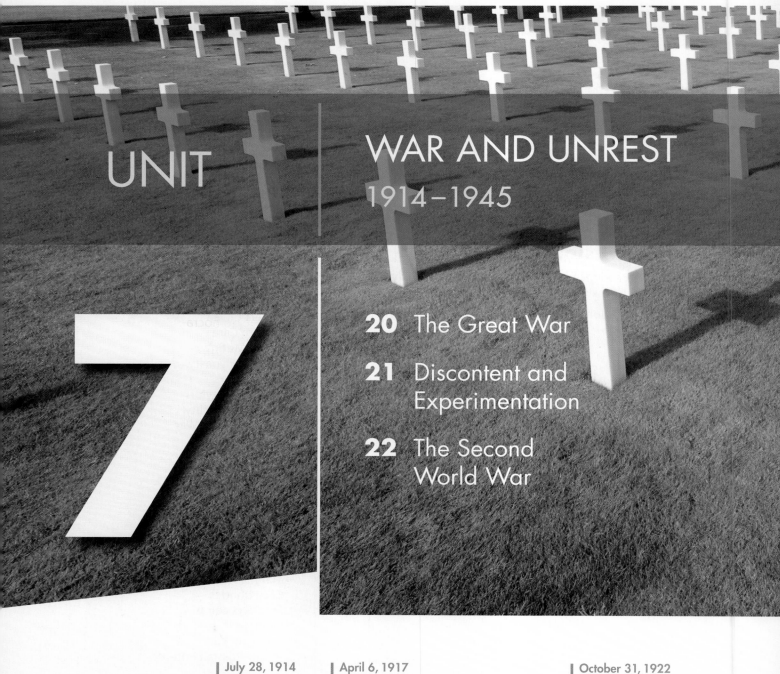

UNIT

WAR AND UNREST
1914–1945

7

July 28, 1914
WWI begins

April 6, 1917
U.S. enters WWI

October 31, 1922
Mussolini appointed prime minister of Italy

November 11, 1918
WWI ends

January 21, 1924
Lenin dies

1914–18
World War I

June 28, 1919
Treaty of Versailles

1927
Stalin becomes dictator of USSR

1910

1920

1917
Russian Revolution

1925
Mussolini/Fascist dictatorship established

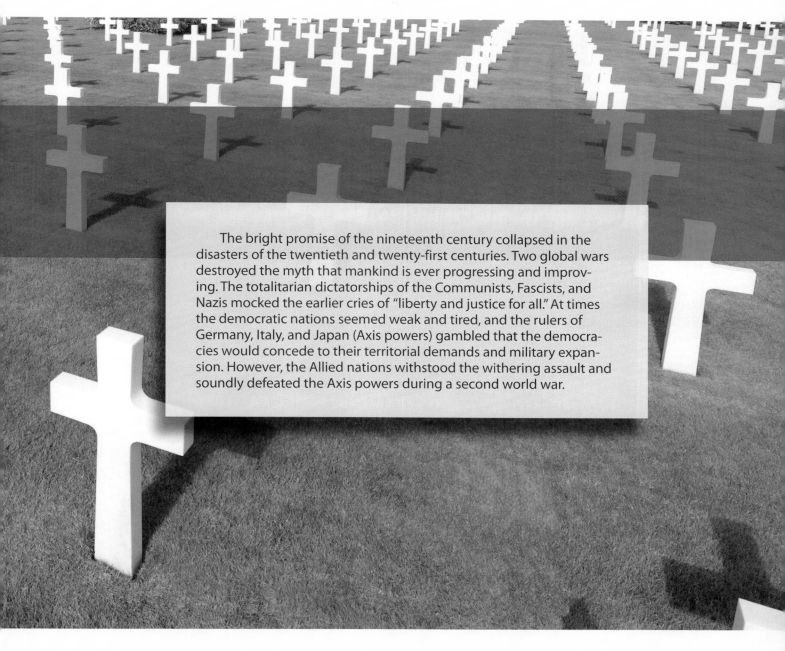

The bright promise of the nineteenth century collapsed in the disasters of the twentieth and twenty-first centuries. Two global wars destroyed the myth that mankind is ever progressing and improving. The totalitarian dictatorships of the Communists, Fascists, and Nazis mocked the earlier cries of "liberty and justice for all." At times the democratic nations seemed weak and tired, and the rulers of Germany, Italy, and Japan (Axis powers) gambled that the democracies would concede to their territorial demands and military expansion. However, the Allied nations withstood the withering assault and soundly defeated the Axis powers during a second world war.

October 29, 1929
U.S. stock market crash

September 18, 1931
Japan invades Manchuria

1933
Hitler/Nazi dictatorship begins in Germany

October 3, 1938
Czechoslovakia brought under German control

March 12, 1938
Austria brought under German control (*Anschluss*)

September 1, 1939
Germany invades Poland

1939–45
World War II

September 2, 1945
WWII ends

June 4, 1944
D-day invasion of Europe

1930

1940

November 8, 1932
FDR elected US president

October 3, 1935
Italy invades Ethiopia

1936–39
The Spanish Civil War

December 7, 1941
Attack on Pearl Harbor

August 23, 1942–February 2, 1943
Battle of Stalingrad

June 4–7, 1942
Battle of Midway

The Great War

French troops enter the Rhineland with a Renault FT-17 light tank in 1919 following the end of WWI.

Big Ideas

1. What events led to World War I?
2. How did World War I impact the participants?
3. What was significant about the post-war treaties?

A psychologist in the early twentieth century taught his patients to say, "Every day in every way, I'm getting better and better." Many people in the late nineteenth and early twentieth centuries thought the same of the world. The future seemed bright and full of promise. Some people even thought that man was on the verge of bringing in the millennial reign of Christ. Much of the earth appeared to be experiencing peace and prosperity, and many influential people thought that it was the result of mankind's power, intelligence, and innate goodness. But alongside man's pride in his own accomplishments lay the reality of his sinfulness. In 1914 a terrible war shattered the dreams of the optimists. Tension and discord confronted hope and enthusiasm. Peril replaced promise as nations rushed headlong into the catastrophe called "The Great War," now known as World War I.

I. Promise and Peril

Reasons for Hope

Winston Churchill, a leading statesman of the twentieth century, described the nineteenth century as a time when the "accumulation of health and wealth had been practically unchecked." The rise of industrialism made possible a higher standard of living for more people than ever before. Science seemed to be eradicating disease; efforts at peace and international cooperation increased as the century continued. Because of this apparent progress, most people were optimistic about the future.

International Cooperation

The late nineteenth century saw the rise of organizations to promote international cooperation. In 1864 Jean Henri Dunant, a Frenchman who believed that "all men are brothers," founded the Red Cross. This international organization seeks to help those who suffer from natural disaster or war. International cooperation also improved as communications improved. In 1868 the International Telegraph Union was founded, followed by the Universal Postal Union in 1875. In addition, many countries standardized their systems of weights and measures. In 1889 the Pan-American Union was established to promote trade and peace among the countries in the Western Hemisphere. In 1896, in a symbolic gesture of cooperation, a number of countries revived the Greek Olympic games.

International Efforts at Peace

Following the failure of the Concert of Europe (see p. 368), various individuals and organizations tried to maintain world peace. One individual who became famous for his promotion of international peace was the wealthy Swedish chemist **Alfred Nobel** (1833–96). In his will he established the Nobel Peace Prize to recognize men and women whose accomplishments furthered the cause of peace. Nobel had gained his fortune by inventing dynamite. Misgivings about his invention's great destructive potential prompted him to set aside funds for the cause of peace.

Nobel was not alone in his efforts; another philanthropist was **Andrew Carnegie** (1835–1919), an American steel manufacturer. Carnegie donated funds to build the Peace Palace at The Hague (the seat of government in the Netherlands). He intended that The Hague be a place where international disputes could be settled

(see p. 368)

Guiding Questions

1. Why were many people optimistic about continued peace and progress prior to World War I?
2. What were the underlying causes of World War I?
3. What events led to World War I?

Andrew Carnegie

Peace Palace at The Hague

Poetry Glorifying Militarism

"To set the cause above renown,
To love the game beyond the prize,
To honour, while you strike him down,
The foe that comes with fearless eyes;
To count the life of battle good,
And dear the land that gave you birth,
And dearer yet the brotherhood
That binds the brave of all the earth."

Excerpt from "Clifton Chapel" by Henry Newbolt

through peaceful means. Ironically, the Palace was completed just as World War I began. By 1910 about 160 peace organizations were in existence; between 1800 and 1914, 250 international disputes had been arbitrated (settled by a third party).

Reasons for Fear

Neither scientific progress nor attempts at international co-operation could prevent dark clouds of suspicion and hatred from forming on the European horizon. As the nineteenth century drew to a close, several developments made war an increasing possibility, despite continued talk of cooperation and peace. From the earliest chapters in this book, we have seen that despite man's efforts to maintain peace, "wars and rumours of wars" (Matt. 24:6) persist. In his epistle, James asks, "From whence come wars and fightings among you?" They come, he says, from "your lusts that war in your members" (James 4:1). This principle helps us understand the real source of tension that produces war. The issues described below are the outward, historical expressions of the pride, fear, and greed of men and nations that led to the Great War.

Extreme Nationalism

Although love for one's country is not wrong, many Europeans during the late 1800s developed an excessive patriotism. They began to consider other cultures inferior. Unbridled nationalism caused many people to desire war so that they could prove their superiority over other nations. As one German put it, war "is not only a necessary element in the life of a people, but also an indispensable factor in culture, indeed the highest expression of the strength and life of a truly cultured people."

Militarism

Many European nations during this time increased their military might far beyond what was necessary for a strong national defense. National glory became the primary purpose for such military buildup; a large standing army symbolized power. In several countries—Germany, for example—the military dominated the civil government. When disputes broke out among nations, it became very easy for a government to immediately resort to the use of force. Compounding the problem was the fact that many citizens glorified war, believing that war was the noblest task in which any nation could engage. Such militaristic attitudes in Europe helped foster the full-scale war that lay ahead.

Imperialism

Another cause of antagonism among countries was competition for colonies. Many European nations, jealous of Britain's colonial empire and industrial strength, desired colonies of their own. Germany and Italy, recently unified nations, were especially eager to prove their new national strength by acquiring territory in Africa and Asia. Since colonies provided economic benefits for the mother country's growing industries, European nations sought territories that were rich in natural resources. Conflicting claims nearly led to war on several occasions. Usually the nations involved worked out peaceful solutions, but they were not always satisfied with the results. As competition increased, so did jealousy, hatred, and suspicion.

Rival Alliances

Deep-seated fear and distrust among European nations led to the formation of protective alliances. Two (sometimes several) nations made agreements (often in secret) promising to come to one another's aid in the event of a foreign attack. By the late nineteenth and early twentieth centuries, Europe was divided into rival alliances. This alliance system helped to drag most of Europe into war.

Steps Toward War

The Building of Bismarck's System

Germany became a unified nation after its victory over France in the Franco-Prussian War (1870). Bismarck, who continued as chancellor of the new German state, feared that France would seek revenge for its humiliating loss. Therefore, he set out to create a system of alliances among the major nations of Europe to prevent France from finding a strong ally. By keeping France isolated diplomatically, Bismarck believed that Germany would be safe from French attack and that the political balance of power could be maintained. The system of alliances that Bismarck created is often called **Bismarck's System**.

The first alliance that Bismarck established was the Three Emperors' League (1873), by which Germany, Austria-Hungary, and Russia made vague promises of mutual aid in the event that war broke out with France or the Ottoman Empire. But despite its promising beginning, the league fell apart. Conflict arose between Russia and Austria-Hungary over the Balkans. Since Austria-Hungary and Russia would not cooperate, Bismarck realized that he would have to cultivate closer ties with one or the other. Fearing the growing power of Russia, he chose Austria-Hungary. In 1879, Germany and Austria-Hungary pledged mutual aid if Russia attacked one of them. This alliance, sometimes called the **Dual Alliance**, soon became the foundation of German foreign policy.

Bismarck continued his efforts to prevent France from finding a strong ally. In 1882, the **Triple Alliance** brought Germany, Austria-Hungary, and Italy together in an anti-French coalition. But Bismarck still was not satisfied; he wanted to bring Russia back into the circle of German allies. Through skillful diplomacy, he negotiated a secret alliance with Russia known as the **Reinsurance Treaty** (1887). In addition, he worked to bring Great Britain into the Triple Alliance. But Britain continued its long-standing policy of isolation, not wishing to get involved in European rivalries. Bismarck did not despair over the failure to create an Anglo-German alliance. As a determined foe of France and Russia, Britain was unlikely to unite with either nation. In effect, France was now isolated diplomatically.

The Breakdown of Bismarck's System

In July 1888, a young, impulsive **Wilhelm II** (r. 1888–1918) became kaiser (emperor) of Germany. Not yet thirty years old, he was a proud, arrogant man who resented the domination of Bismarck in German affairs. He determined that as kaiser he would be

Rival Alliances (1914)

Wilhelm II

DROPPING THE PILOT.

1890 cartoon about Bismarck resigning as chancellor of Germany following his disagreement with Kaiser Wilhelm II

the real leader of Germany and that no one would overshadow him. Therefore, in 1890, he forced Bismarck to resign as chancellor. Wilhelm assumed control of Germany's foreign policies, but he was not Bismarck's equal. His words and ill-advised actions only heightened European tensions.

One of Wilhelm's first mistakes was to allow the Reinsurance Treaty with Russia to expire. France quickly capitalized on this error and approached Russia with offers of an alliance. Fearing a possible alliance between Germany and Britain (which never took place), Russia joined France in a defensive alliance in 1894. According to this treaty,

> if France is attacked by Germany, or by Italy supported by Germany, Russia shall employ all its available forces to attack Germany. If Russia is attacked by Germany or by Austria supported by Germany, France shall employ all its available forces to fight Germany. . . . These forces will engage with all their might, so that Germany has to fight both on the East and West.

A second major mistake that Wilhelm made was to antagonize Britain. Germany began a massive shipbuilding program that threatened British naval domination and alarmed the British people. Britain traditionally had to rely on its fleet to maintain its empire and to protect its homeland. In addition, Germany began to interfere with British affairs in Africa. Germany was late entering the race for colonies, but Wilhelm was determined to build an overseas empire in one generation, although it had taken other nations many generations. As a result of these developments, Britain's fear of Germany soon became stronger than its fear of France. In 1904, contrary to every German hope or expectation, Britain and France put aside their differences and came to a "friendly understanding" in what is called the ***Entente Cordiale***.

That same fear of Germany impelled Britain to patch up its differences with Russia. For some time, Russia had been trying to expand into eastern Europe to acquire an outlet to the Mediterranean Sea. It had also attempted to expand into the Persian Gulf region. The British feared that such expansion would imperil both their prize possession of India and the commercial trade going through the Suez Canal. In spite of their deep-seated rivalry, Britain and Russia signed the Anglo-Russian Entente in 1907. This agreement, like the Entente Cordiale, tended only to lessen tension and promote cooperation between the two nations. Since Britain had previously formed a friendly understanding with France, its agreement with Russia paved the way for the **Triple Entente** between Britain, France, and Russia.

The Testing of the Alliance System

By 1907, secret agreements, friendly understandings, and formal alliances had divided Europe into two rival sides. Yet many questions remained unanswered: How strong were these alliances? How long would they last? Would a nation who promised to come to another's aid in the event of war actually fulfill its promise? During the early years of the twentieth century, Europe went through a series of crises that answered many of these questions and solidified the new alliances but at the same time increased international tension and fear.

Twice, in 1905 and 1911, Germany interfered with French plans to control Morocco (a country in northwest Africa). Germany hoped not only to block France's attempt to take Morocco as a colony but also to break up the entente between Britain and France. But Germany's actions had just the opposite effect; Britain gave France its firm support, and France succeeded in gaining Morocco. As a result, bad feelings between Germany and France mounted; they were becoming too intense to be settled peacefully.

Another series of crises occurred in the Balkans, where small national groups were struggling for independence from Turkish control. By 1900 several Balkan nations had won their indepen-

Settling "The Armenian Question"

The Armenians, who came under Ottoman control in the 1400s, were a minority in both ethnicity and religion. Most Armenians were at least nominal Christians, whereas the Turks were Muslims. As a result, the Turks viewed the Armenians as infidels with no rights. In addition, some Armenians became more wealthy than the Turks living around them, so the Turks tended to be jealous of their Armenian neighbors. Over time, Turkish leaders began to formulate an answer to the question "What will we do with the Armenians?"

In the two decades leading up to World War I, the Ottomans became more and more concerned that the Armenians posed a threat to Turkish rule. Their fears seemed to be confirmed when Armenians formed po-

litical organizations and voiced their desire for independence. The Turks responded with terrible and indiscriminate brutality.

The first wave of massacres occurred between 1894 and 1896, resulting in the deaths of over one hundred thousand Armenians. Renewed assaults on Armenian communities in 1909 led to the murder of another thirty thousand men, women, and children.

When World War I erupted, the Armenians may have been reluctant to support the oppressive Turkish government but answered the call when drafted. However, instead of equipping the Armenians for battle, the Ottomans marched them off to build roads and facilities to aid in the war effort. When the Armenian work crews had finished their tasks, the Turks summarily

executed them or marched them to distant prison camps with immense loss of life along the way.

To prevent any threat by the surviving Armenians, Taalat Pasha, the Turkish interior minister, ordered "the elimination of the Armenian element." He ordered local leaders to "destroy completely all Armenians living in Turkey." By the end of World War I, the Turkish government had murdered an estimated 1.5 to 2 million Armenians.

Sadly, most people have long forgotten the Armenians. When Hitler ordered the elimination of the Jews, he knew that his policy would cause revulsion and anger, but he believed that, as people had forgotten the Armenians, so they would forget the Jews. "Who does now remember the Armenians?" he asked.

Armenian refugees

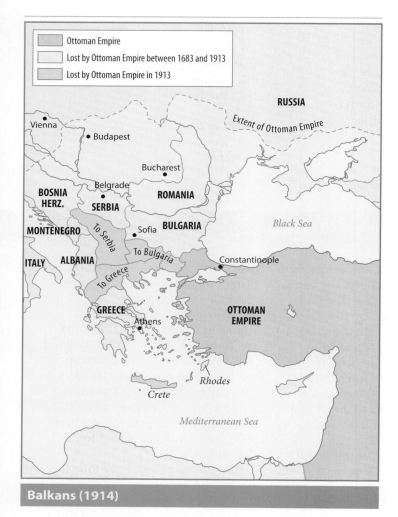

Ottoman Empire
Lost by Ottoman Empire between 1683 and 1913
Lost by Ottoman Empire in 1913

Balkans (1914)

dence from the Ottoman Empire. In 1912 they joined to drive the Turks out of the Balkans. In short order, the Balkan nations smashed Turkish resistance and gained the victory. But less than a month later, a new war broke out as the Balkan nations fought among themselves to decide who would control the remaining Balkan territory.

The weakness of the Ottoman Empire and the instability of the Balkans spurred the intervention of major European nations, especially Austria-Hungary and Russia. Austria-Hungary disliked having such unrest on its southeastern border; it also hoped to extend its borders farther into the Balkans. The Russians were of the same ethnic background (Slavic) as most of the peoples of the Balkans. By posing as the defender of its "brother Slavs," Russia too hoped to extend its influence in this region. While the major powers sought to keep the crisis in the Balkans a local war, their selfish interests and deep-seated hatred for one another only hastened the coming of widespread war. The Balkans were rightly called the "powder keg of Europe."

The spark that set off World War I ignited in the Balkans. On June 28, 1914, Archduke **Francis Ferdinand**, the heir to the throne of Austria-Hungary, was assassinated while visiting Sarajevo, the capital of Bosnia. (Austria had annexed that Balkan province in 1908 over the opposition of the Slavic nations.) A Bosnian revolutionary, acting on behalf of the Black Hand (an anti-Austrian terrorist organization based in Serbia), shot and killed the archduke and his wife. Austria accused the Serbian government of knowing about the plot and failing to inform Austria. Meanwhile, Kaiser Wilhelm of Germany promised Austria full support in any action it might take. Austria decided to crush Serbia once and for all and on July 23 sent a list of demands to the Serbian government. The ultimatum demanded not only an explanation and an apology for the assassination but also that Serbia undertake a thorough investigation of the crime. Austria further demanded that Serbia suppress all anti-Austrian publications and organizations.

Section Review

1. Who established the Nobel Peace Prize to recognize those who furthered the cause of world peace?

2. Why did Carnegie donate funds to build the Peace Palace at The Hague?

3–4. What two countries were eager to prove their new national strength by acquiring territory in Africa and Asia?

5. What country claimed to be the defender of "brother Slavs"?

6. Why were the Balkans called the "powder keg of Europe"?

7. Who was assassinated on June 28, 1914?

✭ Why did European states form alliances?

✭ Trace the events that led to World War I.

Francis Ferdinand

II. The Pressing Conflict

The Commencement of the War

Austria did not want, or expect, Serbia to meet its demands. Serbia, however, rejected outright only one of the demands; nonetheless, Austria used the assassination as an excuse to attack and, on July 28, 1914, declared war on Serbia. Two days later, Russia began to mobilize (make ready) its troops to come to Serbia's defense. Germany, realizing that full-scale war was imminent, warned Russia to cease mobilization within twelve hours. When Russia did not heed its warning, Germany declared war on Russia on August 1. Likewise, when France refused to give the Germans solid assurances of French neutrality, Germany declared war on France as well. Thus, the alliance system had effectively drawn the great powers into open conflict with one another. On one side were the **Central Powers** (Germany and Austria-Hungary), and on the other side were the Allies (Russia, Serbia, and France).

Much of Europe greeted the declaration of war joyfully. As the troops marched to the front, people cheered and threw flowers. In subsequent weeks, thousands of young men rushed to enlist in the army, eager to win glory on the field of battle. Since both sides expected that a few short campaigns would end the war (as had been the case in the wars of the 1860s and 1870s), neither side prepared for or expected the four terrible years of war that were to come.

Not everyone, however, cheered the outbreak of war. Sir Edward Grey, the British foreign secretary, uttered prophetic words: "The lamps are going out all over Europe; we shall not see them lit again in our lifetime." For him and many others, the apparent progress of the nineteenth century, with all of its aspirations and dreams, was soon to end on the fields of France and the plains of western Russia.

War in the West

With the outbreak of war, Germany found itself in a precarious position. It had an enemy on two fronts: Russia on its eastern front (or border) and France on its western front. But the Germans had prepared for such a situation. Several years before the war, a German general named Schlieffen devised a plan to be used in such an emergency. Acting upon this **Schlieffen Plan**, the German generals decided to put most of their forces in the west and attack France first. It would take Russia longer, they believed, to organize for war because its territory was more extensive than France's. The Germans planned to surprise the French by marching through the flat plains of neutral Belgium and attacking France from the north. The German generals believed that they could encircle Paris and defeat France within six weeks. The victorious German armies could then be quickly sent to meet the advancing Russians on the eastern front.

The Germans demanded that the Belgians allow the German army to pass through their country on the way to France, but the Belgians refused. On August 4, the German army crossed into Belgium, breaking a seventy-five-year-old treaty that guaranteed Belgian neutrality. "Necessity knows no law," the German chancellor said; "we shall try to make good the wrong we have thus committed as soon as we have reached our military goal." The British, angered over Germany's disregard of the neutrality treaty, joined the Allies and declared war on Germany. The Germans soon pushed on into France and within a month were outside of Paris. But at the Marne

Guiding Questions

1. What were key events in World War I?
2. How did new weapons and strategies affect the war?
3. What was the cost of the war on individuals and nations?
4. What were the religious dimensions of the war?

World War I

River, the French (with reinforcements brought to the front in Paris taxicabs) stopped the German advance. By the end of the year, both sides had solidified their positions by constructing a long series of trenches that stretched from Switzerland to the English Channel.

War in the East

In the east, the Russians mobilized their forces more quickly than the Germans expected. As a result, the Russian armies achieved several initial victories against the Austrians and the Germans. In the battles of Tannenberg and the Masurian Lakes, however, the German armies, under the leadership of General **Paul von Hindenburg** (1847–1934), defeated the Russians. They captured more than 200,000 prisoners and began to push the demoralized Russian troops back toward Russia. Although they continued to fight for several more years, the Russians did not threaten German borders again during the war.

The inadequacy of Russian factories to produce the needed supplies fatally weakened the Russian war effort. Few supplies were available from even its allies, because German warships had closed the Baltic Sea. In addition, Russia's northern ports were frozen for many months of the year. To remedy this desperate situation, the British decided to force open a sea route to Russia via the Black Sea by taking control of the Dardanelles.

The Ottoman Empire, which had entered the war in 1914 on the side of the Central Powers, controlled the straits between the Black Sea and the Aegean Sea. In 1915 Britain attempted to gain control of the strategic waterway by launching a naval attack and then landing Allied troops on the Gallipoli Peninsula. Poor planning coupled with strong Turkish resistance, however, doomed the invasion. After months of inconclusive fighting and more than 100,000 casualties, public opinion at home forced the British to withdraw their troops and abandon the project. Meanwhile, the Bulgarians had joined the Central Powers and helped conquer Serbia by the end of 1915.

The Course of the War

During most of the war, the situation on the western front was a stalemate (a situation in which both sides are at a standstill).

While in the east armies shifted back and forth across miles of open territory, in the west neither side could break through the intricate system of trenches that had been dug. During each year of the war, both sides conducted major offensives that cost thousands of lives but produced few gains. In 1916, for example, the British conducted an offensive along the Somme River in France. After four months of fighting, the Allies gained only 125 miles of mud while losing six hundred thousand men. On one day of that campaign, the British alone lost sixty thousand men. Earlier in 1916 the Germans had tried to break through the French lines at the fortress of Verdun. After six months of heavy bombardment and fierce fighting, the French held firm. The conflict in France became a deadly war of attrition in which both sides tried to wear each other down gradually.

Italy Joins the Allies

Although Italy was a member of the Triple Alliance, it remained neutral at the beginning of the war. Italy claimed that Austria and Germany were conducting an offensive, not a defensive, war; therefore, it did not feel obligated to come to their aid. Instead, Italy entered into secret negotiations with France, Britain, and Russia. The Allies promised Italy a loan and additional territory adjoining its borders if it would join them. In 1915 Italy ended its neutrality and declared war on the Central Powers. Fighting along the Italian border proved to be inconclusive, but it became yet another line for the hard-pressed Germans and Austrians to defend.

New Weapons of War

As the war continued to rage on many fronts, casualties multiplied, partly because of the introduction of new weapons. Entire industries developed to produce these weapons; nations launched major research and development programs to create more devastating weapons—and, in turn, inventions to protect soldiers against them. Infantrymen used machine guns, which dramatically increased both their firepower and the number of casualties inflicted on the enemy. For example, one Lewis machine gun could fire 450 rounds per

War on the Home Front

. . . [In Calais, France] refugees gathered in crowds hoping to get away by steamer. Like lost souls, [these refugees were] carrying all the possessions they could on their backs. . . . There was numbness in their movements and their faces were blank—the paralysis of brain from sudden disaster. The children did not cry, but munched the dry bread which their parents gave them mechanically.

The newspaper men said that "refugee stuff" was already stale; eviction and misery were stale. . . . What was going to happen? What might not happen? It was human helplessness to the last degree for all behind the [soldiers]. Fate was in the battleline. There could be no resisting that fate.

My Year of the Great War, Frederick Palmer, 74

British infantry assembled in trenches; (facing page) German infantry assembled in trenches

The Red Baron

World War I was the first war in which airplanes were used as weapons. They were used not only for reconnaissance (inspection to gain military information) and bombing but also for fighting the enemy's planes in "dogfights" (air battles). Pilots who shot down at least five enemy airplanes were called aces.

The most successful ace was a German nobleman, Baron Manfred von Richthofen (1892-1918), better known as the "Red Baron" (because of the scarlet-red Fokker Dr. 1 triplane he flew). Early in the war, Richthofen transferred from the cavalry to the air service. His first efforts proved less than impressive. He crash-landed on his first solo flight and failed his first pilot's exam. Once he had learned his skill, however, Richthofen proved a deadly foe to Allied fliers. He shot down eighty Allied planes during the war, more than any other pilot on either side.

Richthofen became a national hero in wartime Germany. He formed a special fighter squadron of aces, nicknamed the "Flying Circus" because all of the pilots flew colorfully painted planes and used tents as hangars (so they could move their base of operations quickly).

On April 21, 1918, the Flying Circus encountered a squadron of Allied fighters. A Canadian pilot, Captain A. Roy Brown, fired at a German plane that was chasing a friend of his. Although Brown did not know it at the time, he may have shot down the Red Baron. (Some researchers, however, suggest that the fatal shot may have been fired by a soldier on the ground.) Wounded, Richthofen managed to land his plane behind enemy lines but died in the cockpit. Although Richthofen was an enemy pilot, the British buried him with full military honors in recognition of his bravery and gallantry.

Richthofen (facing camera); (inset) Fokker triplane

German soldiers in a machine-gun nest

minute. Flame throwers and poisonous gas-filled artillery shells also increased the horrors of war. Gas masks and gas-detection devices were developed to protect against the poison attacks.

Near the end of the war, the Germans began using huge guns with a range of seventy-five to eighty miles. These "Big Bertha" guns launched shells 420 mm in diameter. In 1916 the British introduced the tank to pierce the entrenched lines of the Central Powers. Although the early tanks were slow and hard to maneuver, they had such power potential that all sides eventually used them. By the end of the war, the combatants had produced more than eight thousand tanks.

In the air, both sides used airplanes to observe the enemy's position and troop movements and, in some cases, to drop bombs. Adding a machine gun to a plane made it even more formidable. As more planes on both sides incorporated machine guns, aerial "dogfights" between opposing air forces resulted. Germany also used **zeppelins** (long, slender airships similar to modern blimps) to bomb eastern England and London. The submarine, discussed below, was another important weapon.

As each new weapon was introduced or further developed, the opposing side scrambled to develop ways to defend against it and new weapons to overcome it. The new weapons forced commanders to devise new tactics and strategies for conducting war. The innovative weapons and the resulting new tactics made World War I the deadliest war in history to that point.

The War at Sea

Both sides realized the importance of winning the war at sea. When the fighting began, British warships implemented a blockade of Germany to keep war goods from reaching that country. Germany,

German zeppelin

German U-Boats

In 1870 Jules Verne's novel *Twenty Thousand Leagues Under the Sea* was published. In it Verne described the fictitious adventures of the mad Captain Nemo, who sailed beneath the ocean surface in his submarine, the *Nautilus*. When the novel was published, it was considered a fantasy and was received with great skepticism (even though a few primitive submarines had been invented before Verne's time). Just forty-four years later, however, the *Nautilus* became a devastating reality in the form of the German U-boat.

The Germans launched an all-out attack on British shipping to stop the flow of war supplies into Britain. The Germans found that their surface ships were no match for the large British fleet. So they relied on their U-boats to enforce the blockade around the British Isles.

The U-boat crews realized that their task was of the utmost importance to the German war effort and were willing to endure appalling conditions onboard the submarines. One historian wrote, "On long patrols . . . crews lived in an atmosphere of increasing squalor. The heat was oppressive, the air stale and foul and reeking of bilge water [water that collects in a ship's hull], wet oilskins, rubber boots, sweat, and diesel fumes so thick that a man's hair became pitchy mire."

In the early years of the war, the German U-boats badly mauled British shipping. The British were hardpressed to stop this deadly menace. They used merchant ships equipped with guns to combat them. These ships, called Q-ships, could quickly alter their appearance from a British freighter to one of another country.

(Early in the war, German U-boats sank only British ships.) By posing as a merchant ship of a neutral nation, the Q-ships hoped to lure unsuspecting U-boats in close and then open fire. Sometimes, however, the British ships were unable to fool the captains of the U-boats and were sunk. As one courageous Q-ship captain said, "It was no use pretending to be something you were not unless you attended to every detail."

Later in the war, the Allies enjoyed much better success in defending against U-boat attacks. Allied ships traveled in large convoys and used blimps to spot U-boats. With the invention of depth charges, Allied surface ships had an effective means of destroying U-boats lurking below the ocean surface. Even so, German U-boats sank more than six thousand Allied ships during the war.

Lusitania

on the other hand, counted on its submarines (called **U-boats**, from *Unterseeboot*) to destroy ships of both Allied and neutral nations. Soon each side was attempting to stop all imports, including food, in an effort to starve its opponent into submission.

In 1915 Germany declared a submarine blockade against Britain, threatening to sink any enemy ship that entered the "war zone" around the British Isles. On May 1 the German Embassy issued a warning to passengers planning to leave New York for Liverpool, England, aboard the British liner *Lusitania*.

On May 7 a German submarine sank the *Lusitania* off the coast of Ireland, killing 1,198 people, including 128 Americans. The incident, as well as the sinking of various merchant ships, touched off a storm of protest in America and forced the Germans to temporarily curtail the sinking of merchant and passenger ships.

By 1916 the British had not only chased down and destroyed isolated German warships at sea but also effectively maintained their blockade of the German coastline. Facing shortages of supplies at home, the Germans decided to send their navy out to break the blockade. The fleets met in the Battle of Jutland, off the coast of Denmark. Although the British suffered more damage than the Germans, the blockade remained intact, and the German fleet returned to port, where it stayed for the rest of the war.

The German generals persuaded Kaiser Wilhelm that an all-out submarine campaign would win the war quickly for Germany. When Wilhelm and others voiced fear that such a campaign might bring the Americans into the war, the chief of German naval operations told the kaiser, "I give Your Majesty my word as an officer that

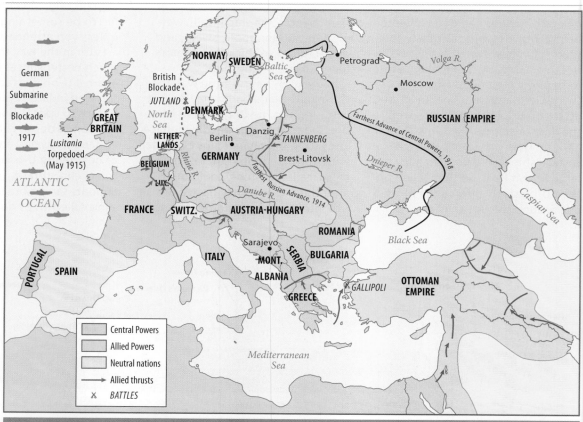

Sides in World War I

not one American will land on the continent." In February 1917 the Germans resumed unrestricted submarine warfare—the sinking of all ships, even if they were unarmed, that carried supplies to the Allies. By the end of the year, the Germans had sunk nearly three thousand ships. But the Allies overcame these losses by improving their methods of antisubmarine warfare.

Collapse of Russia

Russia was unprepared to fight a lengthy war. Its economy and government were inefficient and corrupt, and as casualties and shortages increased, the people's anger and frustration led to strikes and violence. An unplanned popular uprising that began in the Russian capital of St. Petersburg soon spread to other cities. Czar **Nicholas II** abdicated on March 15, 1917. For several months, a provisional government under Aleksandr Kerensky attempted to restore order and continue the war against Germany. But in November 1917 a second revolution occurred, bringing the Communists to power. In 1918 Vladimir Lenin, the new Russian leader, signed a peace treaty with the Germans. The **Treaty of Brest-Litovsk** effectively took Russia out of the war and gave Lenin time to consolidate his power. Russia gave up 1.3 million square miles of land that was inhabited by more than sixty million people (approximately one-third of its population). In addition, it lost nearly 90 percent of its coal mines and more than 50 percent of its industry. As a result, Germany gained access to badly needed raw materials; more importantly, Germany could now concentrate its troops in the west against France and Britain and possibly win the war.

The United States Enters the War

When war broke out in 1914, the United States remained neutral. At that time, most American citizens probably agreed with President Woodrow Wilson: "The United States must be neutral in fact as well as in name. . . . We must be impartial in thought as well as in action, [we] must put a curb upon our sentiments." Yet, only a few years later, President Wilson addressed Congress and called for a declaration of war against Germany. In his speech, he stated that Americans would "fight for the ultimate peace of the world, and for the liberation of its people. . . . The world must be made safe for democracy."

What caused this shift in American sentiment? Why did Wilson, who in 1916 won reelection to the presidency with the slogan "He kept us out of war," ask for a declaration of war five months later? The following reasons help to answer these questions.

1. *German Submarine Campaign*—Many Americans were angered by the loss of life and property resulting from Germany's unrestricted submarine attacks, which reached their height in 1917. They regarded the sinking of unarmed merchant ships without warning as immoral conduct and a violation of international law.

2. *Ties with Britain and France*—The United States enjoyed bonds of language and cultural heritage with England. It also believed it had a debt to repay to the French, who had helped the American colonies in their War for Independence. Furthermore, the United States had been on friendly terms with France and Britain throughout much of the preceding century.

Religious Dimensions of the War

During World War I, religious motivations were often given for young men to fight. When soldiers died, their sacrifice for the nation was often equated with sacrifice for God. Because the major participants in this conflict were viewed as Christian, many government officials and pastors declared that the war would further God's will on the earth. Influential liberal German theologians viewed the Germans as a chosen people who could use their military to advance God's kingdom. Some American leaders argued that the kingdom of God could be advanced by fighting Germany, home to much unorthodox theology and philosophy. By transforming national enemies into the foes of God, these opponents were dehumanized. Thus the massive death toll could be justified.

However, the destruction of the war led to deep pessimism and disillusionment. The teachings of the German theologians and the hopes of the social gospel now seemed foolish and naïve. Europeans soon realized that mankind was getting more brutal and destructive, not better.

Christianity was also discredited in the eyes of many people. Europe was thought by many to be a Christian continent. But the great nations of Europe had led their young men to terrible slaughter. After the war, many rejected not only civil religion (religion used by the state to advance its own purposes) but also true Christianity. Many people stopped attending church and rejected Christian morality.

3. *German Plot*—Great Britain uncovered a plot to bring Mexico into the war against the United States. The Germans planned to offer the Mexicans financial aid and the promise of territory in southwestern New Mexico and Arizona (territories that the United States had gained from Mexico in 1848) if Mexico would declare war on the United States.

4. *Allied Propaganda*—The turning of American opinion against the Germans was due, in part, to Allied reports of German atrocities. American newspapers received nearly all of their war news from the British, and the British often exaggerated stories and incidents to stir up anti-German sentiments.

5. *Monetary Ties*—The United States had close financial ties with the Allies. American businessmen and farmers profited from British and French purchases of American goods. In addition, American bankers had lent large sums of money to the French and British governments. These Americans did not want to lose either their markets or their investments.

6. *Balance of Power*—The United States also wanted to maintain the balance of power in Europe. Many Americans feared what would happen if a victorious Germany, with its strong militaristic ways, were to dominate Europe.

For these reasons, and at the request of the president, the U.S. Congress declared war on Germany on April 6, 1917. Initially, American soldiers provided little help to the struggling Allies, because the United States did not already have a large, well-trained army. In the last months of the war, however, more than 250,000 American troops landed in France every month. Under the leadership of General **John J. "Black Jack" Pershing**, the American Expeditionary Force (AEF) provided the necessary edge to defeat the Germans at last.

Gen. John J. "Black Jack" Pershing, commander, American Expeditionary Force

Conclusion of the War

Germany made a last attempt to win the war before American forces could turn the tide against them. With Russia out of the war, Germany was able to send its veterans from the eastern front into France for a final series of offensives that began in March 1918. At first, the German attacks were successful; the weary French and British soldiers were on the verge of collapse. However, under General **Ferdinand Foch** (FAWSH) who had just been named commander in chief of the Allied armies in France, the Allies stopped the German advance. Then, with reinforcements from the United States, they mounted a counterattack.

While the Allies were pushing the Germans slowly out of France, Germany's allies collapsed. Revolts of subject nationalities under Turkish and Austrian control had weakened an already faltering war effort and hastened the Central Powers' defeat. In September, Bulgaria surrendered, and by the beginning of November, the Ottoman Empire and Austria-Hungary had surrendered. Germany saw the end coming and appealed to President Wilson for an armistice (a temporary cessation of fighting) based on his proposals. Wilson, however, refused to negotiate with a government that he believed did not truly represent the German people. Meanwhile, mutinies and revolts erupted across Germany. The kaiser fled to Holland, and a German republic replaced the Second German Reich. Leaders of the new government agreed to an armistice. On

Profiles in Courage

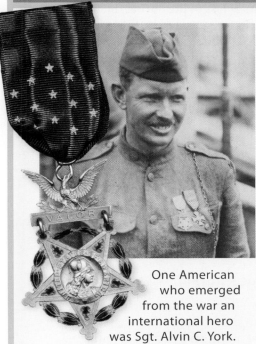

One American who emerged from the war an international hero was Sgt. Alvin C. York. A quiet, unpretentious Christian, York initially was a conscientious objector (one who believes it is wrong to fight in war). After intense soul-searching, however, York went to war with his unit, determined to do his duty. During the war York displayed such courage that the U.S. military awarded him the Congressional Medal of Honor. He also received numerous foreign decorations for heroism.

Another American soldier also demonstrated unparalleled courage but did not return home to parades. Furthermore, the awarding of his Medal of Honor was delayed for nearly eighty years. Born in Sandy Springs, South Carolina, Freddie Stowers was the grandson of a slave. Like York, he was a poor southern farmer who was drafted into the army in 1917. Because of the American military's low opinion of black soldiers, Stowers and other African American soldiers were prevented from fighting with American units. Instead, they were assigned to French units who badly needed reinforcements. On the morning of September 28, 1918, Corporal Stowers and his company took part in the assault on a tall, well-defended hill known as *Côte* 188. Facing heavy German machine gun and rifle fire, Stowers's company made a steady advance against the Germans. A few minutes into the battle the Germans signaled their desire to surrender. However, when the Allied forces advanced to within one hundred meters of the Germans, the Germans suddenly dropped into their trenches and renewed their attack, killing about half of the Allied force, including the officers. Stowers then took charge and led his men, crawling toward the closest German machine gun nest. Even though Stowers was wounded during this assault, he led his men to advance toward the second line of German trenches. Stowers continued to lead his men until he was wounded a second time and then encouraged his men to continue on to victory. Stowers died during the battle and was later buried at the Meuse-Argonne American Cemetery and Memorial.

Although Stowers's name was submitted for the Medal of Honor shortly after his death, no action was taken until 1990 when the Department of the Army discovered the unprocessed request. Seventy-three years after his death, his surviving sisters, Georgina and Mary, received Stowers's Medal of Honor at the White House from President George H.W. Bush.

November 11, 1918, at 11:00 a.m., German and Allied officials met in a railroad car in the Compiègne Forest in France and signed the armistice ending World War I.

Although the armistice brought an end to the fighting, it could not repair the damage that the war had done. The cost of the war in terms of human lives was staggering. Ten million of the approximately sixty-four million men who were mobilized died; approximately twenty million were wounded, and about six million were

The War and the Colonies

Although most attention in discussions of World War I focuses on the major European combatants, the colonies of those nations also played critical roles in the conduct of the war. For example, France mobilized 46,000 troops from its colonies. Great Britain mobilized troops from its colonies in Australia, New Zealand, Canada, South Africa, and India. The British enlisted the services of 100,000 soldiers in the Royal Gurkha Rifles alone. Most of the British troops at the Battle of Gallipoli were Australians and New Zealanders. Belgium used its colonial troops in the Congo to attack the German colony of East Africa. The colonies of Portugal and Italy were also involved. The Allies seized most of Germany's colonies early in the war.

But the colonies were also affected economically. The same war economies that were imposed on the people in the mother countries also were imposed on their colonies. Consequently, the colonists experienced some of the same conditions and restrictions that those in the mother country felt, including higher prices and scarcity of goods. They also faced increased taxes to pay for the war.

missing or unaccounted for. Civilian deaths through starvation, disease, massacres, submarine attacks, and so on probably equaled battlefield deaths. The average daily loss of life during the war was approximately fifteen thousand. In financial terms, the total direct cost of the war neared $200 billion; indirect costs totaled more than $151 billion. Combined, the war cost approximately $9 million an hour.

While these figures give a somewhat cold and approximate account of the cost of the war in lives and dollars, one cannot measure the total effect that the war had on the world, especially Europe. How does one measure personal suffering or the loss of a generation of young men? How does one measure the devastation to industry, countryside, and economy?

The only difference between this war and previous wars was that new technology increased man's destructive power. In fact, some people foolishly believed that the war had been so destructive that men would never again resort to warfare to settle their disputes. Their error would soon be exposed by yet another world war.

Section Review

1–2. What country's neutrality did the Germans violate as they invaded France? What European country declared war on Germany as a result of that attack on a neutral country?

3. What was the German policy that called for the sinking of all ships, armed or not, that carried supplies to the Allies?

4. What country left the struggle against Germany in 1918?

5. What country joined the struggle against Germany in 1917?

✶ Assess the religious dimensions of the war.

✶ Analyze the effect of new weapons and trench warfare on the course of the war.

Guiding Questions

1. What characterized the postwar treaties?
2. What were the effects of the postwar settlement?

III. The Pursuit of Peace

The Paris Peace Conference

In January 1919 the **Paris Peace Conference** opened. Seventy delegates representing thirty-two nations met to negotiate the peace settlement for World War I. Unlike the victorious nations at the Congress of Vienna, which had allowed France (the defeated nation) to participate in the negotiations (see p. 365), the Allies excluded the defeated Central Powers from the conference. Nor was Russia invited because it had withdrawn from the war in 1918 after the Communist revolution.

The dominant leaders at the conference were U.S. president **Woodrow Wilson**, French premier **Georges Clemenceau**, British prime minister **David Lloyd George**, and Italian prime minister **Vittorio Orlando**. These men largely determined the character and content of the peace treaties.

When the Germans signed the armistice ending World War I, they did so with the understanding that Wilson's peace program would be the basis of the peace treaty. Wilson had advocated a moderate settlement, known as the **Fourteen Points**, which would not seek revenge upon the defeated powers. When Wilson arrived in Europe, enthusiastic crowds welcomed him wherever he went. He did not receive such a hearty welcome by the diplomats at the (left) *The "Big Four" at the League of Nations (from left) Vittorio Emanuelle Orlando, Italy; David Lloyd George, Great Britain; Georges Clemenceau, France; and Woodrow Wilson, US;* (right) *The signing of the peace treaty at the Palace of Versailles*

conference, however; many of them considered him an idealist and found him stubborn and preachy.

Clemenceau, the leader of the French delegation, was known as the "Old Tiger." He was a cynical and crafty politician who had no use for Wilson's idealism. He once commented that "even God was satisfied with Ten Commandments, but Wilson insists on fourteen." Clemenceau's main concern was the security of France. He desired to keep Germany militarily weak and to make it pay for the war damages inflicted on France.

Lloyd George of Great Britain also wanted to see Germany punished, but his treaty proposals were not as severe as Clemenceau's. He hoped that German industry could soon be revived, since the staggering British economy desperately needed as many markets as possible. At the same time, he wanted to protect British colonial and naval interests.

The Treaty of Versailles

The Allies drew up five major treaties ending the war, the most important of which was the **Treaty of Versailles**—the treaty between the Allies and Germany. The Germans had expected the treaty to be in accord with Wilson's moderate proposals; instead, its provisions were very harsh.

Territorial Provisions

According to the Treaty of Versailles, Germany had to return Alsace and Lorraine to France and grant smaller amounts of land to Belgium and Denmark. Clemenceau had originally demanded that all German territory west of the Rhine River come under French control, but the United States and Britain would not agree to such a demand. So the Allies worked out a compromise whereby they would jointly occupy the Rhineland for fifteen years. During that time the French would be allowed to control the rich Saar coal field located in the Rhineland.

In the east, the treaty reestablished an independent Polish nation. East Prussia was detached from the rest of Germany to give Poland an outlet to the Baltic Sea. This territory became known as the Polish Corridor (because it ran between the two parts of

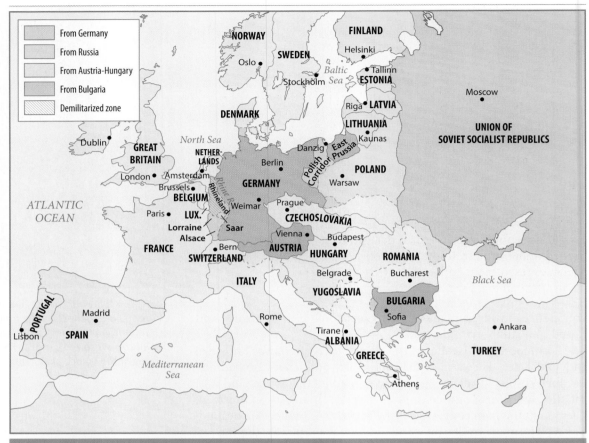

Territorial Changes in Europe After World War I

Germany) and included the port city of Danzig (Gdańsk), which came under the control of the League of Nations. A portion of the coal-rich province of Silesia went to Poland, and Lithuania received the German port of Memel. In addition, Germany lost its Asian and African colonies. Altogether, the Germans lost twenty-five thousand square miles of territory inhabited by six million people.

Economic Provisions

The Treaty of Versailles also specified that large amounts of coal from German mines had to be sent to several of the Allied nations for ten years. It required the Germans to turn over many of their merchant ships and fishing vessels to the Allies, in addition to building new ships for them. But the most damaging economic provision of the treaty was the Allied demand that Germany pay reparations (payment for war damages). In spite of the Allies' inability to agree on the amount of the war damages, the treaty demanded an immediate payment of $5 billion. The delegates established a special commission to decide on the final amount later.

Military Provisions

The German army was limited to one hundred thousand men. A thirty-mile-wide zone east of the Rhine River was to remain demilitarized (no armies could be in that area at any time). The army could have no tanks or large guns; the navy could have no submarines and only six warships. All military aircraft had to be destroyed; no new ones could be built.

The "War Guilt" Clause

The basis for all of these repressive provisions was Article 231 of the treaty, which stated, "The Allied and Associated Governments affirm and Germany accepts the responsibility of Germany and its allies for causing all the loss and damage to which the Allied and Associated Governments and their nationals have been subjected as a consequence of the war imposed upon them by the aggression of Germany and its allies." This so-called **war guilt clause** placed the entire blame for the war on Germany and its allies.

Germany at first refused to sign the treaty. Although it was willing to accept some blame for the war, it believed it unjust to shoulder all the blame. But when the Allies threatened to continue the war if the Germans would not cooperate, a German delegation at Versailles signed under protest. In the years following Versailles, German resentment and anger at this unjust provision soon changed to hatred, and thoughts of revenge began to mount. Before long, many Germans began to listen seriously to Adolf Hitler as he fiercely condemned the treaty and advocated the building of a new Germany that would right the wrongs of Versailles. (See chapters 21 and 22.)

Other Peace Treaties

The Paris Peace Conference drew up treaties with the other defeated Central Powers as well. Austria signed the **Treaty of St. Germain**, in which it turned over territory to Italy and recognized the independence of Czechoslovakia, Hungary, Poland, and Yugoslavia. It also had to pay reparations, limit the size of its army, and agree not to seek *Anschluss* (political unification) with Germany. Both Hungary and Bulgaria signed similar treaties.

The Treaty of Sèvres dismantled the Ottoman Empire. The Turks retained Asia Minor (modern Turkey), where the majority of the population was concentrated. Their Arabian territories, however, such as Syria, Palestine, and Iraq, came under British and French control. These territories, as well as the former German colonies, were called *mandates*, territories technically under the control of the League of Nations but administered by various Allied countries. Turkey retained control of the straits between the Black Sea and the Aegean Sea, but surrounding territory had to be demilitarized and the straits opened to ships of all nations.

Attempts to Maintain the Peace

The League of Nations

Woodrow Wilson was the one person most responsible for the creation of the **League of Nations**. He was convinced that future war could be avoided through the creation of an international organization in which nations could discuss their differences instead of fighting about them. Therefore, he was willing to compromise many of his other proposals at the Paris Conference to enlist support for the League.

Mandates in Africa, the Middle East, and the Pacific

Purpose

Leaders of several nations formed the League of Nations "to guarantee international cooperation and to achieve international peace and security." After its establishment in 1920, the League sought to maintain peace by seeking arms reductions and settling disputes through arbitration. Various commissions tried to ensure that Germany and its former allies carried out the provisions of the peace treaties. In addition, the League sought to promote the rights of colonial peoples and to improve economic and social conditions around the world through groups such as the International Labor Organization.

> The members of the League undertake to respect and preserve . . . against external aggression the territorial integrity and existing political independence of all Members of the League. . . . In case of any such aggression or in case of any threat or danger of such aggression the Council shall advise upon the means by which this obligation shall be fulfilled.
>
> —League Covenant, Article X

Ultimate Failure

Despite the League's success in settling minor disputes among weaker nations, it lacked the authority to settle major crises among powerful nations. Strong nations simply ignored or defied the League, and later some of them even withdrew their membership in the organization.

Compounding the problem was the organization's ineffectiveness. The League had the power only to recommend action on the part of its members; it could not require them to take action. In addition, important decisions required unanimous approval among the member nations. In the unlikely event that the League could get every member to approve an action, it had no armed forces of its own to police troubled areas. Even when member nations had the military capacity to enforce a decision, they were hesitant about using force, fearing it might lead to another war.

The League suffered a serious blow when the United States refused to join. Even though President Wilson was the chief proponent of the League, the U.S. Senate would not ratify the treaty. The

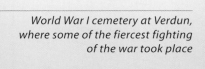

World War I cemetery at Verdun, where some of the fiercest fighting of the war took place

mood in the United States after the war was one of isolation from foreign involvement. Thus, the nation that emerged from the war as the strongest power did not become a member of the League.

Reparation Revisions

The Paris Peace Conference set up a special commission to determine how much Germany owed in reparations. In addition to the $5 billion that the Allies originally demanded, the reparations commission finally settled on an additional sum of $32 billion. Germany made several payments but soon stopped because its economy was not strong enough to bear the burden. When payments did not resume, France retaliated by invading the Ruhr Valley (an industrial district in Germany). British and American opposition forced France to withdraw.

Realizing Germany's financial problems, American banker Charles Dawes formed a committee in 1924 to find a solution. Taking as its slogan "Business, not politics," the committee decided to lend Germany money and allow it to spread the reparation payments out over a longer period. In 1929, Owen Young, an American lawyer, devised another plan that reduced the amount of reparations and gave Germany until 1988 to complete its payments. When economic problems continued, President Herbert Hoover in 1931 advocated a one-year moratorium (suspension) on all reparations payments. After this moratorium, however, Germany never resumed payments.

Closely associated with the German failure to pay reparations was the failure of Britain and France to pay their own war debts to the United States. During the war, Britain, France, and other countries had borrowed huge amounts of money from the United States. The Allies had planned to use some of the money Germany paid them in reparations to repay their war debt. But when Germany could not meet its reparation payments, the Allies in turn could not repay their creditors. Intending to reduce the problem, American and British bankers made loans to Germany, hoping that it would invest that money in its economy. As its economy became stronger, it would better be able to meet the reparation payments. But instead of investing the money, Germany immediately used most of it for reparation payments to Britain and France. Britain and France, in turn, used the money to pay off their war debts to the United States, and again Germany needed another loan. The Allies found this reparations/war-debt cycle impossible to break, and before long all war-debt and reparation payments ceased. This cycle contributed to the worldwide depression of the 1930s.

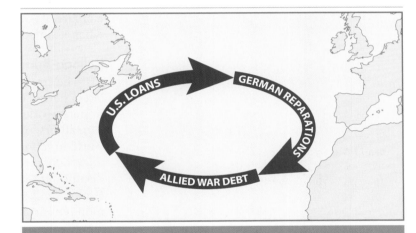

Postwar Debt Cycle

Disarmament and Nonaggression Pacts
The Locarno Pact

To a Europe apprehensive about the possibility of another war, the Locarno Conference seemed to offer hope. In the fall of 1925, several European nations met in Locarno, Switzerland. At this conference, Germany signed a treaty with France and Belgium in which it agreed to recognize its present borders with those two nations as permanent. In addition, all three nations promised not to go to war with one another except in self-defense. Although Germany did not recognize its eastern border as permanent, it did agree not to seek any change in that border through war. This **Locarno Pact**, which involved other agreements as well, seemed to hold the promise of peace in Europe. Nations that hated each other now seemed, at least on the surface, to be friends. European tensions relaxed somewhat, and for several years this "spirit of Locarno" gave Europeans a false sense of security.

Washington Naval Conference

Those who refuse to believe that wars result from the natural sinfulness of man will sometimes conclude that wars are caused by weapons. They believe that if they eliminate weapons, they can eliminate war. This elimination of weapons or arms is called **disarmament**. The best example of an attempt at disarmament in the 1920s was the **Washington Naval Conference** (1921–22). The great naval powers—Britain, the United States, Japan, and others—agreed to limit the number of warships each could build. They also established a ratio by which to limit the buildup of large warships. They decided, for example, that for every five tons of American shipping, Britain could have five tons, and Japan three tons. The conference failed, however, to reach any agreement on limiting the number of smaller warships and submarines. Ultimately, the conference was a failure; its participants—notably Japan—kept the agreement only when it suited their purposes.

Kellogg-Briand Pact

The crowning effort to preserve the peace in the post–World War I period came in 1928. Frank Kellogg, the American secretary of state, working with Aristide Briand, the French minister of foreign affairs, proposed an agreement calling upon the nations of the world to renounce the use of offensive war. Nations that signed the document pledged to use arbitration rather than force to settle their disputes. In short, this document, known as the **Kellogg-Briand Pact**, sought to unite "the civilized nations of the world in a common renunciation of war as an instrument of their national policy." Sixty-two nations eventually signed this idealistic agreement, which simply made war illegal. Three years later, one signatory—Japan—invaded Manchuria. Yet many people living at that time looked to this agreement as the start of a new era of international cooperation.

Section Review

1–5. What were the main provisions of the Treaty of Versailles? Which provision blamed the war on Germany and its allies?

6–7. With what country did the Treaty of St. Germain settle the terms of peace? What did that treaty forbid?

8. What major Allied nation did not join the League of Nations?

9. What agreement called on the nations of the world to renounce the use of offensive war and seek arbitration to settle international disputes?

★ Why were the Allied nations unable to repay their debts to the United States?

★ Evaluate the postwar settlement in terms of justice, power, and citizenship.

Making Connections

1–3. Identify three underlying causes of World War I.

4–6. Discuss three events that led the United States to enter the war on the side of the Allies.

7–8. Summarize two reasons why the League of Nations failed.

9. Explain why World War I utterly shattered European optimism about the goodness of humanity and the progress of civilization.

Developing History Skills

1. Defend or refute the following statement, "The peace settlements of World War I increased the likelihood of another major war."

2. How was World War I different from previous wars?

Thinking Critically

1. Assess the cost of the Great War on individuals and nations.

2. Based on the information in this chapter, evaluate the disarmament and nonaggression pacts and their ability to prevent war.

Living in God's World

1. Given James 4:1–3 and Matthew 5:9, write a brief Christian perspective on war and peace.

2. Given Matthew 5:7, write a proposal for how nations ought to treat each other after war.

People, Places, and Things to Know

Alfred Nobel
Andrew Carnegie
Bismarck's System
Dual Alliance
Triple Alliance
Reinsurance Treaty
Wilhelm II
Entente Cordiale
Triple Entente
Francis Ferdinand
Central Powers
Schlieffen Plan
Paul von Hindenburg
zeppelins
U-boats
Lusitania
Nicholas II
Treaty of Brest-Litovsk
John J. "Black Jack" Pershing
Ferdinand Foch
Paris Peace Conference
Woodrow Wilson
Georges Clemenceau
David Lloyd George
Vittorio Orlando
Fourteen Points
Treaty of Versailles
war guilt clause
Treaty of St. Germain
Anschluss
League of Nations
Locarno Pact
disarmament
Washington Naval Conference
Kellogg-Briand Pact

Discontent & Experimentation

Adolf Hitler, the Nazi party, and the swastika came to symbolize the rise of totalitarian regimes in Europe after World War I.

Big Ideas

1. What characterized the Era of Disillusionment following World War I?

2. What were the political and economic conditions of the major democracies following World War I?

3. What totalitarian dictatorships arose following World War I?

Shifting from war to peace proved to be extremely difficult for a world that was tired and disillusioned from four years of bloodshed. Economic weakness, political instability, and changing moral values multiplied in the years following World War I. During the 1920s, world leaders attempted to solve these problems through peace treaties and economic agreements. By the 1930s, however, it was clear that those efforts had failed. The Great Depression brought worldwide economic chaos. The rise of new dictators shattered President Wilson's idealistic promise of a world "safe for democracy." Standards of morality declined, and moral decay increased as a growing number of people abandoned belief in the authority of God's Word.

Edmund Burke, an eighteenth-century British statesman, said, "All that is necessary for the triumph of evil is that good men do nothing." The two decades following World War I were marked by widespread apathy, especially among the victorious Allied nations. Individual citizens and national governments allowed evil to multiply. Communist ideas crept into the economies of many nations. Self-serving dictators captured control of the governments of both small and large countries. Religious liberals infiltrated the churches, turning many away from the truth of God's Word. The attitude of indifference that allowed these forces of evil to triumph contributed to the outbreak of World War II.

I. Era of Disillusionment

During the latter half of the nineteenth century, many artists and writers reacted against the impact of industrialism on society. They rejected conventional art forms and embraced new, experimental techniques. This reaction continued in the early twentieth century as the arts reflected the death and destruction of the war period. The devastation of war, economic depression, and moral decay led to feelings of despair. As this mood affected modern art and literature, artists and writers portrayed a pessimistic and disjointed view of man, his world, and the future.

Science

In chapter 18 you read about scientific advances that included work by Pierre and Marie Curie in the area of radioactive matter and Albert Einstein's theories explaining the relationship between matter and energy. Charles Darwin proposed a scientific theory about the origin of life. During the same period, men developed a social science in the form of psychology. Ivan Pavlov (famous for his experiments with dogs) and **Sigmund Freud** developed theories to explain human behavior.

Freud

Freud divided the human mind into three levels: the conscious mind, the preconscious mind, and the unconscious mind. He theorized that the conscious mind contained thoughts that are the focus of human attention and the preconscious mind contained thoughts that could be retrieved from one's memory. Freud concluded that repressed thoughts caused by pain or trauma lay deeply buried in an individual's unconscious mind. He used psychoanalysis with his patients to retrieve these repressed thoughts. By encouraging the patient to relax and talk freely about his symptoms, Freud believed

Guiding Questions

1. How did World War I lead to disillusionment in philosophy and the arts?
2. What were the main ideas of Freudian psychology and eugenics?
3. What characterized the development of the arts and sciences during this period?

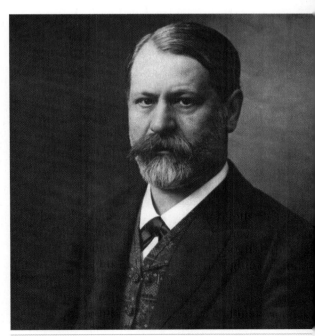

Sigmund Freud

that he could cure them. He was convinced that the unconscious mind controls how a person thinks and acts. Thus Freud found human nature to be often irrational. This concept contradicted the Victorian ideals of the day and challenged the optimistic view of human reason. Though Freud became very influential, his theories became less popular after World War II.

Eugenics

Eugenics focused on determining who was fit to reproduce and ways of preventing reproduction by those deemed unfit. This so-called science was popular among public health agencies during this period. However, the concept of selective breeding was not new. Similar ideas can be traced to Greek philosophers, including Plato. Some progressives, reformers, and elites embraced eugenics and used their influence to target those they believed to be racially inferior or of an inferior class. In a horribly misguided attempt to improve society, criminals and ethnic groups were sterilized or otherwise prevented from having children.

> The human race could be immensely improved in quality, and its capacity for happy living immensely increased, if those of poor physical and mental endowment were prevented from multiplying. . . . Certain types of criminals and paupers breed only their kind, and society has a right and a duty to protect its members from the repeated burden of maintaining and guarding such parasites.
>
> *Frank William Taussig,* Principles of Economics, vol. 2, 250-51

Using this reasoning, thousands of men and women were subjected to medical procedures against their will. This occurred even in free countries like the United States. Eugenics did not become unpopular until the late 1960s, following decades of opposition by human rights advocates and some scientists.

Philosophy

Existentialism as a philosophy is difficult to define, and there is no consensus regarding its definition. It is more accurately a label that was assigned to a widely divergent group of philosophers who lived in the late nineteenth and early twentieth centuries. However, there are some ideas that existentialists held in common. These include the lack of absolute or universal truths and the absence of true purpose for life. A common attribute of this philosophy is subjectivity and the belief that individuals must search for their own purpose. Friedrich Nietzsche and Jean-Paul Sartre are two examples of existential philosophers, and their writings were foundational in the development of this philosophy. Nietzsche declared that there is no purpose to life. Sartre asserted that people can find their purpose if they create their own meaning for life. While these writers attempted to answer the questions raised by the unthinkable violence and destruction brought about by World War I, their works contributed to the sense of hopelessness that typified this period.

Painting

Expressionism

In art, two of the best-known twentieth-century movements (or schools) were expressionism and cubism. In **expressionism**, the artist tried to paint how he felt about his subject rather than trying to realistically reproduce what he saw. Henri Matisse (1869–1954) was the best representative of this school. Figures in expressionistic paintings were of secondary importance. Color was the real subject; through this medium the artist could most graphically express his emotions. Bright colors, simplified designs, and clearly outlined figures characterized Matisse's work.

Cubism

The second major artistic movement of the twentieth century was **cubism**. Its best representative was the Spanish-born **Pablo Picasso** (1881–1973). To a much greater degree than Matisse, Picasso abandoned the Renaissance ideal that a painter should portray on canvas what he saw in nature. Picasso believed that what we see might not be final reality; therefore, he contended that art that simply copied the visible world was useless. Instead, he often reduced his figures to various geometric shapes (hence, the name cubism), which he portrayed from several different perspectives at once. His technique distorted the figures in his paintings. Picasso, as well as many other twentieth-century artists, tried deliberately to shock viewers and challenge their perception of the world.

Houses on a Hill *by Pablo Picasso*

Music

Music in the twentieth century was extremely varied, encompassing everything from jazz (which reached its peak of popularity in the 1920s) to electronic music. As in other art forms, radical experimentation increased after World War I as many composers abandoned traditional musical concepts. Russian composer **Igor Stravinsky** (struh VIN skee; 1882–1971) and Austrian Arnold Schönberg (SHURN behrg; 1874–1951) influenced modern musical trends. Stravinsky's compositions were particularly innovative. He developed a new musical theory known as polytonality, which involves the use of several keys simultaneously. In the past, composers had used only one musical key at a time. Stravinsky used polytonality in his famous orchestral work *The Rite of Spring*. Arnold Schönberg, on the other hand, abandoned all fixed tone patterns or keys and created what is called atonal music. Instead of using one of the common eight-tone scales, Schönberg based his compositions on a twelve-tone scale, giving no special emphasis to any one tone.

In spite of several technical differences among modern composers, their music exhibited certain common characteristics—and contrasted markedly with the music of earlier eras. Modern rhythms were often jarring and violent. In contrast to the harmony of earlier periods, modern music made greater use of dissonance (clashing tones).

Igor Stravinsky

Literature

Like music, the literature of the 1920s and 1930s reflected the attitudes prevalent between the wars. For example, poet **T. S. Eliot** (1888–1965), in his complex major work *The Waste Land*, tried to portray the desolation and meaninglessness of modern life. In his poem "The Hollow Men," Eliot replaced the cataclysmic view of the end of the world taught in Scripture (2 Peter 3:10, 12–13) with a bleak, feeble one: *"This is the way the world ends / Not with a bang but a whimper."* Another author, German novelist Thomas Mann (1875–1955), presented his central characters as passive figures, victimized by the uncontrollable forces that surround them.

T. S. Eliot

Much of the literature of the first half of the twentieth century was filled with hopelessness, pessimism, and pacifism. Many writers rejected the concept that literature should teach moral lessons. The techniques they used also demonstrated a break with the past. Modern poetry, for example, often lacked a rhyme scheme and a regular rhythm pattern. In addition, some prose writers and poets tended to be deliberately obscure. Despite their diverse forms and styles, painters, composers, and writers united in portraying a world that was hopeless, barren, and dehumanizing.

Section Review

1. What was the major goal of eugenics?
2. Why did existentialism emerge and have influence following World War I?
3. How was T. S. Eliot's work influenced by World War I?
* How did the music of this period reflect the attitude of many people after World War I?
* Summarize the main ideas of Freudian psychology.

Guiding Questions

1. What economic conditions did the democracies face after World War I?
2. What caused political instability in the democracies of this period?

II. Weakness Within the Democracies

One of the most serious problems facing Europe and America after World War I was the change from wartime to peacetime economies. Once the fighting stopped, governments relaxed their economic controls. But as inflation and then depression struck, many governments reestablished those controls.

Great Britain

As veterans returned home from the war, British prime minister Lloyd George promised that Britain would be a land "fit for heroes." The two decades between the world wars, however, did not match his optimistic promise. Britons witnessed the steady decline of their empire. In addition, the British economy suffered greatly; the war had seriously hurt the nation's trade, and debt was ten times greater than it had been in 1914. Hardest hit was the coal-mining industry. Strong foreign competition and increased use of other energy sources resulted in diminished demands for coal. Layoffs and miners' strikes resulted. Unemployment in all industries increased so dramatically that by 1932 almost one Briton in four was out of work. Many were on the dole (government relief for the unemployed). In the same year, Britain abandoned its policy of free trade and initiated protective tariffs (taxes on imported goods).

As economic problems deepened, Britain gradually developed into a welfare state. Parliamentary appropriations for social welfare programs dramatically increased during the 1920s and 1930s. Another indication of the trend toward socialism was the rise of the Labour Party led by Ramsay MacDonald (1866–1937). In 1924, MacDonald became the first Labour Party prime minister of Britain. Although he held the office for less than a year, the Labour Party established itself as a major force in British politics.

The war had not only increased Britain's economic woes but also stimulated demands for home rule, or complete independence, by several British possessions. After several years of fierce fighting, Britain finally agreed to Irish demands for independence and created the Irish Free State in 1921. (Northern Ireland—called Ulster—

remained part of the United Kingdom.) In Egypt, strong nationalism forced the British to recognize that country's independence, although Britain still maintained a naval base there to protect the Suez Canal. Nationalists in India continued clamoring for independence. In 1935, the British Parliament passed the Government of India Act, which granted the Indians greater self-government. In the **Statute of Westminster** (1931), Britain approved a 1926 report that had declared Canada, Australia, New Zealand, and South Africa to be "autonomous communities within the British Empire, equal in status, in no way subordinate one to another in any aspect of their domestic or external affairs, though united by common allegiance to the crown and freely associated as members of the British Commonwealth of Nations."

France

During World War I, France suffered heavier losses in life and property than Great Britain, yet France achieved greater economic recovery. New factories replaced those destroyed during the war. The recently returned territories of Alsace and Lorraine provided rich mineral deposits and important industrial plants. Even in the face of worldwide economic problems, unemployment never became as severe in France as it was in Britain. Many of the French people were small businessmen or farmers, and although violent strikes did occur, France weathered the economic storms better than much of Europe.

Nevertheless, France remained politically unstable. The Third French Republic (established after the French defeat in the Franco-Prussian War) was plagued by so many political parties that none was able to gain a majority. As a result, the government was established on shaky coalitions of several political parties. Between 1920 and 1940, France changed prime ministers some forty times. As successive governments failed to solve France's domestic problems, discontented radical groups, which threatened the republic, became increasingly popular. During this period various Socialist and Communist political parties became stronger. These parties, calling themselves the Popular Front, managed to gain control of the government in 1936, naming Léon Blum (1872–1950) as prime minister. This coalition soon fell apart, however, and France returned to more conservative control.

In foreign affairs, the French remained wary of Germany. They were determined to protect their border with Germany and questioned the League of Nations' ability to provide protection in case of another war. Furthermore, Britain and the United States refused to guarantee aid to France in the event of renewed German aggression, so France formed defensive alliances with some of the smaller European nations. Between 1924 and 1927, for example, France signed agreements with Czechoslovakia, Romania, and Yugoslavia.

In 1929, under the leadership of André Maginot, the French began building a line of fortifications stretching hundreds of miles, from Switzerland to the Belgian border, along its border with Germany. Below the fortifications was a network of underground chambers containing power stations, ammunition supplies, hospitals, recreation halls, theaters, and living quarters. Each fortification was to be joined to the others by an underground subway, which would make possible quick and safe transportation of troops along the line. Those fortifications became France's main line of defense

Ruins of La Ferté fortress on the Maginot Line

The Maginot Line was a line of fortifications that included an elaborate system of underground chambers containing whatever the soldiers might need or want.

on the east. Many Frenchmen confidently believed that the **Maginot Line**, as it was called, would stop any German attack. During World War II, however, the Germans simply bypassed those fortifications, rendering them useless.

The United States

World War I had thrust the United States into a strong leadership role in world affairs. After the war, however, many Americans wanted to return to a policy of isolationism. Although Wilson advocated U.S. participation in world affairs through the League of Nations, the Senate twice refused to ratify the Versailles Treaty, which contained the League provisions. In 1920 Americans turned away from the idealism and internationalism of Wilson. They elected as president Warren G. Harding, who promised a "return to normalcy." Harding's successor, Calvin Coolidge, continued to emphasize domestic well-being over foreign involvement. (That is what Harding meant by "normalcy.") Coolidge declared, "The chief business of the American people is business." By the end of the 1920s, conditions seemed so favorable that President Herbert Hoover stated in his 1929 inaugural address, "I have no fears for the future of our country. It is bright with hope."

Warren G. Harding *Calvin Coolidge*

The Great Depression

On the surface, all seemed well in the United States. New technology enabled factories to mass-produce a variety of consumer goods. People were enjoying more leisure time. But under the surface of this period known as the "Roaring Twenties" was great decay in the moral life of the nation. This decay became evident by the end of the decade. One of the characters in John Steinbeck's novel *The Grapes of Wrath* summarized the popular moral attitude of the day:

> There ain't no sin and there ain't no virtue, there's just stuff people do. . . . Some of the things folks do is nice and some ain't nice, but that's as far as any man got a right to say.

Heavy advertising and credit purchases helped to weaken old ideas about thrift. America was fast becoming a nation in which the rush for wealth and pleasure was the most important pursuit in life. But in 1929 the seeming prosperity of the 1920s came to a sudden end. The collapse of the stock market in October triggered a drop in prices, a decline in foreign trade, the closing of factories, the failure of banks, and a dramatic rise in unemployment. Unemployed workers receiving food in bread lines and soup lines became a common sight in many American cities. By the winter of 1932–33, an estimated thirteen to seventeen million people (approximately one-third of the work force) were unemployed. Though the crash occurred only a few months into his presidency, Herbert Hoover received most of the blame for America's economic woes. Looking for a solution to their problems, the American people elected **Franklin Roosevelt** (1882–1945) to the presidency in 1932.

The New Deal

After his inauguration, Roosevelt immediately began to promote his program of relief, recovery, and reform as a "**New Deal**." Job programs such as those connected with the Works Progress

Administration sought to provide immediate relief for the millions of unemployed. Other organizations, such as the Agricultural Adjustment Administration, were designed to meet long-term goals. Roosevelt promoted many economic changes that he hoped would end the threat of another depression and at the same time provide financial security for Americans. The Securities and Exchange Commission was established to regulate stock exchanges, and Congress passed the Social Security Act (1935).

Historians, economists, and politicians have debated the value of the New Deal. No one doubts that Roosevelt's policies dramatically affected the United States. The key question is whether that effect has been positive or negative. In retrospect, many people have concluded that the New Deal did more harm than good. It provided temporary relief for many Americans but failed to end the Depression or provide any real economic recovery. In addition, Roosevelt's policies were often experimental and increased government spending and the power of federal bureaucrats (the nonelected officials who handle government affairs). This led to increased government involvement in economic and social matters without resolving the core economic problems.

Hoover and FDR on Inauguration Day, 1933

Section Review

1–3. Name three possessions of Great Britain that were given self-rule, or complete independence, after World War I.

4. What factor contributed to political instability within the Third French Republic following World War I?

5. What was the purpose of the Maginot Line?

6–7. Which U.S. president sought to promote relief, recovery, and reform to get the country out of the Great Depression? What name was given to his programs?

* Identify the economic conditions that the democracies faced after World War I.

* Explain the causes of political instability in the democracies of this period.

III. Rise of Totalitarian Dictatorships

People often rely on strong leaders without being appropriately discerning of their integrity. As Europe struggled to overcome postwar problems, dictatorial governments became more common. Many Europeans supported ambitious, power-seeking men in hopes that they would bring economic and political stability to their countries. Despite the early successes of such rulers, their nations were brought to bitter mourning.

Once in power, these dictators established totalitarian states. Although no two such states were exactly alike, they did share the following characteristics:

1. The use of propaganda (materials and methods of indoctrination) to promote the ideas and programs of the state.

2. The use of an efficient secret police to arrest or assassinate those who opposed the state and its policies.

3. Emphasis on the goals of the state rather than on individual rights or concerns.

Guiding Questions

1. What were key elements of totalitarian regimes?
2. How did communism come to dominate Russia?
3. What political and economic conditions made the rise of dictatorships possible in Italy and Germany?

4. State control of every aspect of life—political, economic, cultural, educational, and religious.

5. A government maintained by force and not accountable to the people for its actions.

6. A one-party political system led by a powerful dictator.

All across Europe, in both established countries and newly created countries, dictators came to power. For example, Antonio de Oliveira Salazar became dictator in Portugal. In Spain, following a bloody civil war, Francisco Franco gained control of the government. In Turkey, Mustafa Kemal (keh MAHL), a champion of Turkish nationalism, established himself as dictator. But it was under dictators in Russia, Italy, and Germany that totalitarianism assumed its most terrible forms between the world wars.

Communism in Russia
Collapse of Czarist Russia

The reforms of Czar Alexander II came to an end with his assassination in 1881 (see p. 382). His successor, **Alexander III** (r. 1881–94), attempted to suppress revolutionary ideas and activities. He ordered the state police and courts to intensify their efforts and demanded a strict censorship of the press. Alexander also persecuted various minority national groups, such as the Poles and the Finns. He wanted to force them to become "Russian" in language, religion, and attitude. Alexander also supported organized government massacres called **pogroms**, which killed thousands of Jews living in Russia, in an effort to redirect Russian anger away from his abusive rule.

The harsh policies of Alexander III were continued under his son **Nicholas II** (r. 1894–1917). During his reign, popular discontent burst into revolutionary activity. Radicals and liberals of all kinds organized themselves into political parties, one of the most radical of which was the Social Democratic Party (1898). To escape arrest and imprisonment, some of its members fled to Switzerland, where they carried on their work and awaited an opportunity to return to Russia. But philosophical differences within the party caused a small group called the **Bolsheviks** to break away from the larger, more moderate group known as the **Mensheviks**. The Bolsheviks advocated change through violence; the Mensheviks desired change through more peaceful measures.

Czar Nicholas II

Prelude to Revolution

For a while, Nicholas II was able to maintain the authority and stability of the government. But disasters in the **Russo-Japanese War** (1904–5) brought popular discontent to the surface. Russian expansion in the Far East during the late nineteenth century had clashed with Japanese expansionist interest, leading to open hostility. Fighting erupted, but the war was brief; poor organization, incompetence, and low morale among the Russian troops helped Japan gain several important victories. At the urging of U.S. president Theodore Roosevelt, a humiliated and shaken Russian government met with Japanese leaders and signed the Treaty of Portsmouth. Russia surrendered both territory and economic advantages in the Far East to Japan.

The most dramatic illustration of popular discontent during the war was a workers' march to the czar's winter palace in St. Petersburg.

On January 22, 1905, a procession of two hundred thousand men, women, and children moved toward the palace. They carried a petition calling on Nicholas II to improve the lot of the workers, convene a national assembly, and order elections in which all the people could vote. But government soldiers met the marchers and opened fire, killing scores of people and wounding many more. The violent events of that day, known as **Bloody Sunday**, turned the loyalty of many Russians from the czar. They began to look elsewhere for an answer to their suffering.

Bloody Sunday

In the following months, unrest and disorder increased as peasant uprisings, strikes in the factories, and mutinies within the armed forces spread throughout the country. In October a strike among railway workers triggered strikes in all areas of the economy. To direct and maintain the general strike more efficiently, the workers in St. Petersburg organized themselves into a soviet (council). Groups of workers in other cities soon followed their example. After a few days, the czar's government yielded to the strikers. Nicholas issued the October Manifesto, promising a constitutional government with free speech and a national assembly (Duma) to be elected by the people.

Outbreak of Revolution

Over the next several years, however, the czar worked against the Duma while promoting his own social reforms. Economic expansion and industrialism resumed, but local strikes and other symptoms of unrest continued. Dissatisfaction with the czar's government remained strong, and the hardships and sufferings of World War I stirred that discontent into revolutionary action.

The Russian people at first seemed to support the war. But early disastrous defeats (see p. 444) caused serious morale problems. Poor planning created food shortages in the cities, and heavy casualties among the soldiers weakened Russia's ability to continue fighting. To try to save the military situation, Nicholas II personally took command of the troops, leaving the empress at home under the evil influence of the monk Rasputin. Though he was a religious fraud, Rasputin assisted the empress's son who suffered from hemophilia, a blood disorder, thereby winning the favor of the empress. He became an advisor to the royal family, but his greedy desires and corrupt influence only further weakened the czar's government. With Nicholas gone from the capital, the political situation rapidly deteriorated. Several Russian nobles murdered Rasputin, hoping that their action would restore public confidence in the government, but even this did not accomplish their purpose.

Rasputin

Aleksandr Kerensky

Vladimir Lenin

On March 8, 1917, the people's anger and frustration erupted. Strikes and riots broke out in the capital of St. Petersburg. As chaos gripped the city, the troops which had been ordered to quell the disturbances joined with the strikers. News of the uprisings spread quickly throughout the country, and in city after city, workers overthrew local authorities and organized revolutionary soviets. In St. Petersburg, Nicholas disbanded the Duma, but its members ignored his order and established a provisional government. Four days later, on March 15, Nicholas II abdicated, bringing to an end over three hundred years of Romanov rule. The royal family was imprisoned and then executed the following year.

In the months following the fall of the czar, a provisional government headed by **Aleksandr Kerensky** tried its best to restore order. But the radical Bolsheviks organized workers in opposition to his government. They sought an immediate end to the war and the implementation of radical social reforms. Worker opposition at home and the war abroad made the situation very difficult.

To make matters worse, the Germans, eager to remove the Russians from the war, helped exiled Bolshevik leaders return to their homeland. The Germans hoped that these extremist leaders would further complicate Russia's internal affairs and thereby disrupt Russia's war effort. Their plan succeeded.

Founding of the USSR
Bolsheviks Seize the Revolution

The leader of the Bolsheviks was **Vladimir Lenin** (1870–1924), a brilliant young man who became involved in revolutionary activities while attending a Russian university. Through his study of Karl Marx, he became a dedicated member of the Social Democratic Party and later assumed the leadership of the Bolshevik wing of that organization. Returning to Russia from exile in Switzerland with the help of the Germans in April 1917, Lenin rallied his followers in opposition to the provisional government.

On the morning of November 7, 1917, Lenin's followers seized the government offices in St. Petersburg and arrested many of the leaders of the provisional government. With very little bloodshed, the Bolsheviks came to power, with Lenin as a virtual dictator.

Lenin was successful for several reasons. The Russian people had not wholeheartedly supported the provisional government, which wanted to continue the war against Germany. Most of the Russian people, including the soldiers, desired an immediate end to the fighting. Discipline was so low among the armed forces that officers who might have opposed the Bolshevik takeover did not have the support of their troops. Besides wanting to end the war, the peasants and industrial workers expected the provisional government to solve Russia's economic problems. When the government failed to do so, many Russians turned to Lenin and the Bolsheviks.

Civil War Erupts

Once the Bolsheviks seized power, they faced serious problems of their own, the most serious of which was the war with Germany. Lenin realized that the Communists (the name that the Bolsheviks had adopted in 1918) could not consolidate their power and fight a war at the same time. Therefore, in 1918 they signed the Treaty of Brest-Litovsk, exchanging large amounts of Russian territory for peace. The Allies were angered that Russia had deserted the war

Union of Soviet Socialist Republics

effort and were disheartened by the radical change that had swept over Russia.

For the next four years, Russia suffered through a bloody civil war which raged throughout the country. Initially, the Communists seemed to be at a disadvantage; they lacked a strong, well-trained army. But through the efforts of **Leon Trotsky**, the Communists organized the so-called Red Army. Their opponents, known as the Whites, had the support of the Allies, including the United States. The Allies sent troops to several Russian ports in an effort to aid anti-Bolshevik groups in Russia. Although the Whites won some notable victories, they were never able to coordinate their efforts. Also, many Russians feared that the Whites wished to restore the old order of the czar. In the end, the Communists retained their power.

Russia Becomes a Communist State

Within the first years of its existence, the new Communist state underwent several official changes. For example, in 1918 Lenin moved the Russian capital from St. Petersburg (or Petrograd) to Moscow because of the threat of advancing German armies. After the war, Moscow remained the new capital and became the center of what was called the Russian Soviet Federated Socialist Republic (RSFSR). After the death of Lenin in 1924, the official name of the country became the Union of Soviet Socialist Republics (**USSR**). This new country was composed of fifteen regions called *republics*. But, unlike true republics, they were dominated by a central government that controlled virtually every aspect of the country and left the people with no real voice in their government.

During the violent civil war, Lenin instituted a tightly regulated system of economic controls that he called "war communism." In

Lenin's words, it was "a frontal attack" on "the citadel of capitalism" designed to implement pure Marxist economic principles. Among other things, the government nationalized (placed under state ownership) Russian industry and demanded that the peasants give their surplus crops to the state for a set price. Forced labor and lack of incentives brought an already ailing economy to the point of collapse. For example, by 1920 the production of iron ore had dropped 98.4 percent from its 1913 level; the manufacture of cotton goods had fallen 95 percent. Overall, industrial production was only 13 percent of what it had been in 1913. As signs of deep resentment against the Communist system began mounting, the government abandoned its policy of war communism and in 1921 instituted the **New Economic Policy** (NEP).

The NEP, which lasted from 1921 to 1928, was nothing new at all; it was simply a temporary retreat from communism to rescue the Russian economy and to quiet growing anti-Communist sentiment within the country. Various aspects of capitalism, such as some limited private trade and profit-making, became legal once again. By the time the program ended, the Russian economy had significantly improved. Ironically, Lenin used the capitalistic principles that he had vowed to destroy to save the Communist government and economy.

Strengthening of the USSR

When Lenin died in 1924, a power struggle developed between Leon Trotsky and **Joseph Stalin** (1879–1953). Trotsky was a brilliant and egotistical man known for his fiery speeches. Stalin, on the other hand, was a quiet, dependable, yet ruthless party man, little known outside the Soviet Union. By 1927 Stalin had established himself as the new dictator of the USSR. In the years before Lenin's death, Stalin had appointed many of his supporters to high government positions. After Lenin's death, he used his influence to force Trotsky and his supporters from the government.

Five-Year Plans

In 1928 Stalin ended the NEP and embarked on a series of programs called the **Five-Year Plans**. These programs turned the country back toward socialism by attempting to increase industrial production and collectivize (bring under central government control) agriculture. The government established production goals for each industry. Although some of the heavy industries met the government's demands, many other industries did not. Manufactured products were always in short supply. Inefficient bureaucratic mismanagement further illustrated the serious weaknesses in Communist economic theory.

Stalin's program to collectivize agriculture met with hostile resistance on the part of many peasants. The secret police and the army used whatever means they deemed necessary—execution, deportation, or the burning of peasants' homes—to force compliance with government demands. In desperation, many peasants fought back, burning their crops and killing their livestock. Yet, in the end, their resistance was crushed. The struggle had been so severe that between 1928 and 1933 more than half of the homes in the Soviet Union were destroyed. In addition, a severe famine struck the country during 1932 and 1933. This, along with the struggle over collectivization, led to the deaths of more than five million people.

Lenin and Stalin

Lenin and Stalin

The Soviet Union's first two Communist dictators—Vladimir Lenin and Joseph Stalin—were not actually named Lenin and Stalin. In 1901, Vladimir Ilyich Ulyanov assumed the alias Lenin in an effort to confuse the Russian police. Joseph Stalin was really named Iosif Vissarionovich Dzhugashvili. In his early writings, he used several pseudonymns, but his favorite was Stalin ("man of steel").

Peter Vins: "Choosing Rather to Suffer Affliction"

The suffering of Soviet Christians at the hands of their Communist government is well illustrated by the life of Russian Baptist pastor Peter Vins. He was born in 1898 into the family of Jacob Vins (or Wiens), a pastor among the Mennonites and Baptists in Russia. Persecuted by the czarist government, Jacob went into voluntary exile in North America in 1911, and his family joined him the following year. In 1919, after the Bolshevik Revolution, Jacob Vins returned to his homeland. Peter remained in the United States to attend seminary and prepare for the ministry. In 1926 he joined his father as an "American missionary" holding American citizenship.

In the years immediately following the Bolshevik Revolution, a surprising degree of religious freedom existed in the Soviet Union. The Communists allowed some liberty to win supporters to their side during the civil war. Jacob Vins began his ministry in 1919, for example, in a section of eastern Russia that was temporarily occupied by the Japanese.

Lenin had written, "We require that religion should be a private matter as far as the state is concerned. The state must have nothing to do with religion. . . . Religious and church societies must be completely free unions of like-minded citizens independent of the authorities."

Although the atheistic Lenin found it convenient to accommodate religion for a while, his successor Joseph Stalin moved ruthlessly to transform the Soviet Union into a religion-free state. When persecution began, Christians with foreign citizenship had the choice of leaving or becoming Soviet citizens. Peter, now with a wife and son, chose to give up his American citizenship and remain.

Peter Vins was able to minister to the Russian people for only two years before he was arrested and sentenced to three years in a labor camp. After his release, he moved to the city of Omsk. With meetings for worship forbidden, he sought to encourage believers privately in their homes, but he knew that it was only a matter of time before he was arrested again. He and his wife sewed parts of the Bible into his clothing so that he would have the Scriptures with him when he returned to prison.

In 1936 Peter Vins was arrested, served ten months, was released, and then was arrested again in 1937. This time he received a ten-year sentence for "anti-Soviet" views. He was denied visitors. Instead, his wife and young son would come to the street outside the prison, where they could look at him through the barred windows. The prison authorities, disliking even this distant contact between prisoners and their families,

began building boxes around the windows. These boxes allowed light in from the top but did not permit anyone to see in or out. Each time Peter's family visited, they saw the boxes getting closer to his window. Finally, his window was covered. Only many years later did his son learn that shortly after this, Soviet authorities had shot Peter Vins.

Appropriately, Peter Vins's favorite Scripture passage was Hebrews 11:24–26: "By faith Moses, when he was come to years, refused to be called the son of Pharaoh's daughter; choosing rather to suffer affliction with the people of God, than to enjoy the pleasures of sin for a season; esteeming the reproach of Christ greater riches than the treasures in Egypt."

Reign of Terror

As we have seen, Stalin often resorted to violence and terror to force his will on the Russian people. During 1936–38, he turned on some within his own Communist Party, determined to eradicate anyone who might prove disloyal to his regime. To accomplish his goal, Stalin instituted a system of **purges** in which at least eight hundred thousand Communist Party members were murdered, including many of the ruling elite. Even the military suffered, as Stalin ordered the execution of most of the army's top leaders and many of the lesser officers. These events created such fear in the Soviet Union that Stalin's power became more secure than ever.

Because communism seeks to control every aspect of life, the Soviet state under both Lenin and Stalin made a strong effort to destroy any form of Christianity within its territory. Within twenty years, the government had forced the closure of thousands of churches and schools and had killed many pastors and priests. The Soviet government's cruelty stemmed from the realization that Christian virtues (including love for one's neighbor and individual responsibility) posed a threat to Communist ideas and goals. The Communists' hatred for Christianity is well illustrated by Lenin, who described the idea of God as "unutterable vileness."

Foreign Policy

After the Bolshevik Revolution, Lenin believed that Communist revolutions would soon sweep across Europe. To further his goal, he established the "Communist International," commonly called the **Comintern**, to found Communist parties in other countries and to take an active role in stirring up discontent in hopes of producing revolution.

Section Review

1–2. Who was the last czar of Russia? In what year was his government overthrown?

3. What Communist leader instituted "war communism"?

4–5. When "war communism" failed and the Russian economy faced collapse, what did Lenin institute? What economic system was he restoring on a limited basis?

6. What Communist leader instituted a system of purges, eliminating all whom he considered a threat to his regime?

⋆ Explain the key elements of any totalitarian regime.

⋆ Trace the rise of Communist Russia.

Fascism in Italy and Germany

After the rise of communism in Russia, a new type of totalitarian government called **fascism** (FASH iz um) came to power in Italy and Germany. (German fascism is usually called **Nazism**.) Many of the citizens in those countries had grown discouraged with representative government, yet they feared communism. Fascism seemed to provide an attractive alternative because it promised stability and security. In theory, communism and fascism differ in the following ways.

1. Under fascism, businesses are privately owned but rigorously controlled by the government. (A fascist economy is often referred to as a corporate economy.) Under communism, however, the government both owns and controls business.

2. Fascism is highly nationalistic; communism ideally seeks a classless, international society.

3. A military dictatorship usually openly governs a fascist state; communism deceptively emphasizes the "dictatorship of the proletariat."

4. Fascism glorifies the state; communism teaches that the state will gradually wither away.

Despite the theoretical differences between communism and fascism, there is little difference in the everyday life of people living under these forms of governments. Both firmly control the people and severely restrict their liberties.

Mussolini in Italy

Italy entered the postwar era a disappointed and dispirited nation. Despite significant sacrifices in the Great War—including the loss of five hundred thousand men—the country gained very little in return, except additional problems. While Britain and France received former German and Turkish territory as mandates (regions to be governed), Italy received none. Furthermore, Italy's borders were not expanded as many Italians believed they should be (because of Italy's support for the Allies). Strikes, inflation, and debt plagued the Italian economy. Politically, small factions created disunity and hindered government action.

In the midst of the turmoil and confusion, the Italian people became increasingly disenchanted with the country's direction. Wealthy landowners and industrialists, fearful of a Communist revolution, wanted protection for their businesses and property. Returning war veterans found that jobs were in short supply and that few Italians appreciated their wartime services. Strong nationalists wanted Italy to become a great military power, to expand its borders, and to acquire additional colonies. The man who seemed to draw these groups together was **Benito Mussolini** (1883–1945).

Benito Mussolini

Mussolini and the Fascist Party

Mussolini, the son of a blacksmith, became a well-known Socialist while still in his twenties. He wrote for several Socialist newspapers. But his violent articles incurred the wrath of the authorities, and they imprisoned him on several occasions. He soon fell out of favor with the Socialists because he supported Italy's entrance into World War I. His political career, however, did not end. In 1921 Mussolini helped to organize the Fascist Party, which took as its emblem the symbol of authority in ancient Rome, the *fasces* (see p. 73); hence, the name *Fascists*.

Most Italians were not Fascists, but they were tired of the unrest and trouble caused by labor unions and Socialist political groups. Mussolini seemed to offer some promise of stability and order. He decided that the time was ripe to seize power. In October 1922 thousands of his followers marched on Rome and demanded that King Victor Emmanuel III appoint Mussolini premier of Italy. The king, believing he had no other choice, agreed to the Fascists' demands, and Mussolini became the new leader of Italy.

Mussolini and the Fascist State

Once in power, Mussolini slowly turned Italy into a totalitarian state. He established his authority by appointing Fascists to numerous government posts. By the end of 1925, he had manipulated the political process so completely that he had a firm grasp on the affairs of the state. Mussolini was now a dictator, but he maintained the appearance of a representative government.

In Fascist Italy, as in Communist Russia, the party was the real source of political power. Fascist political organizations began on the local level and provided the basis for a highly structured hierarchy that culminated in the Fascist Grand Council. In theory, that group of approximately twenty individuals ran the Italian government. The final authority, however, lay in the hands of *Il Duce* ("leader" or "commander"), a title that Mussolini used for himself.

One of Mussolini's major goals was to make Italy economically self-sufficient. He wanted Italy to be able to produce everything it needed, including manufactured goods and food. To achieve this goal he organized Italy's entire workforce into thirteen groups, or syndicates, each representing a different division of the workforce. Under the watchful eye of the government, the syndicates established wages, prices, business policies, and working conditions.

Unlike Stalin or Hitler, however, Mussolini had no clearly defined political program. Like most dictators, he suppressed freedom of speech, freedom of the press, and opposing political parties. But Mussolini's own political philosophy was rather vague and, according to one of his government officials, was based on "mystic sentiment" rather than "distinct ideas."

As dictator, Mussolini enacted a series of popular agreements known as the **Lateran Treaties** with the Roman Catholic Church. Since 1870, relations between the Roman Catholic Church and the Italian state had been strained. The state had taken territory that for centuries had been controlled by the papacy. With the unification of Italy, that territory became part of the Italian state. In retaliation, the Roman Catholic Church refused to recognize or cooperate with the new state. For nearly sixty years, successive popes remained isolated in the Vatican. In 1929, after lengthy negotiations, Mussolini and the Roman Catholic Church finally reached an agreement. The pope agreed to recognize the Italian government and to renounce all territorial claims. In return, the government granted the pope a large sum of money and established a small independent state known as the Vatican City and placed it under the pope's control. The Lateran Treaties remain in effect today.

Hitler in Germany

As World War I was coming to an end, German Kaiser Wilhelm II abdicated. Spontaneous revolutions had erupted throughout the country, forcing him to flee to Holland. The German people organized a republic to replace the monarchy. In 1919 delegates from around Germany assembled in the town of Weimar and wrote a constitution for the young republic. Among other things, the new constitution granted the German people the right to freely elect representatives to the Reichstag and to elect a president to a seven-year term. The president appointed a chancellor from the strongest political party in the Reichstag. In turn, the chancellor selected people to fill the various cabinet posts of the government. In addition, the constitution guaranteed the German people a number of basic freedoms, including the freedoms of speech, press, and religion.

Despite its promising start, the **Weimar Republic** had serious weaknesses. Many Germans did not support the republic; they were generally apathetic toward government. The German people also had no experience running a republic, nor did they have a strong traditional attachment to its ideals. Furthermore, having numerous political parties made it difficult for the government to function effectively because no party ever won a majority in the national elections. These weaknesses helped prepare the way for one of the worst dictators of modern history, **Adolf Hitler** (1889–1945).

Hitler and the Nazi Party

As a young man, Adolf Hitler had shown little promise. When his hopes of becoming an artist or architect ended in failure, he

Adolf Hitler in 1923

The Collapse of the German Mark

After World War I, Germany had severe economic problems that fueled discontent and created support for Nazism. Not only were government expenditures high, but Germany had a huge debt resulting from the war. One indication of the country's plight was the high rate of inflation. During World War I, prices had risen about 100 percent, but in the early 1920s, inflation increased at an even more alarming rate.

When French troops invaded the Ruhr Valley in 1923, many Germans in that region went on strike. To support the strikers while they were unemployed, the government began printing large amounts of paper money. Consequently, prices skyrocketed, bringing about the collapse of the German mark (the German monetary unit, similar to the American dollar).

As inflation climbed in 1923, more than three hundred paper mills and two thousand printing establishments worked twenty-four hours a day to supply the necessary paper

Date	Number of marks equal to a dollar (monthly average)
JULY 1914	4.2
JAN. 1919	8.9
JAN. 1921	64.9
JAN. 1922	191.8
JULY 1922	493.2
JAN. 1923	17,972
JULY 1923	353,412
AUG. 1923	4,620,455
SEPT. 1923	98,860,000
OCT. 1923	25,260,208,000
NOV. 15, 1923	4,200,000,000,000

money. By August 1923, the government was printing 46 billion marks per day. In light of the worsening conditions, employers began paying their employees twice a day and allowing them time off from work to rush to the stores and buy what they needed before prices rose again. Restaurants did not even price items on their menus. They figured a customer's bill only when he was ready

to leave because the value of the mark might have declined from the time he sat down at a table.

The following example may help illustrate the devastating nature of German inflation. In 1914, if someone possessed 100,000 marks, he could have exchanged them for nearly 24,000 American dollars. In November 1923, that same 100,000 marks would have been worth only a minute fraction of a cent— $0.00000024.

Finally, the German government abolished the old currency and instituted a new mark—the Rentenmark. People with the old currency could trade in one trillion of their old marks for the new Rentenmark. As a result of such terrible inflation, many Germans lost both their savings and their confidence in the Weimar Republic. As they searched for answers to their country's problems, many people began to listen to a man named Adolf Hitler, who promised a new and better Germany.

wandered about the city of Vienna, barely making a living. At the outbreak of World War I, he tried to enlist in the Austrian forces but failed to pass the physical exam required for entrance. He then volunteered for service in the Bavarian Reserve Infantry and was assigned to the messenger service. During the war, he was wounded in the leg, promoted to lance corporal, and awarded two Iron Crosses.

Hitler reacted bitterly to news of the armistice. After the war, he came in contact with a small political organization that soon became known as the National Socialist German Workers' Party, or Nazi Party. Finding many of its ideas to his liking, he promptly joined the group in 1920; a year later, he became its leader.

The name National Socialist German Workers' Party (*National-sozialistische deutsche Arbeiter Partei*) was chosen to appeal to a wide range of Germans. In 1920 the Nazis formed the *Sturmab-teilungen* (SA), also known as stormtroopers and Brownshirts, to help preserve order at party rallies. They were essentially street thugs.

As the Nazis increased in power, Hitler found it expedient to reduce the SA's power and purged it, killing many of its leaders. He later created an elite guard called the *Schutzstaffel* (SS). They were identified by their black shirts and special daggers. Their initial purpose was to protect Hitler. Later, under the leadership of Heinrich Himmler, the SS also operated both a secret police organization

Hitler was a powerful orator. To increase his effectiveness, he studied films of himself experimenting with various gestures and facial expressions. He selected the most dramatic gestures and expressions for use in his speeches.

known as the **Gestapo** and a system of concentration camps. The SS military units were among the most fanatical and formidable fighters during World War II and were responsible for horrendous war crimes in the concentration camps.

In 1923 Hitler led an uprising (called the "beer hall putsch" because of where it was staged) in the city of Munich, attempting to overthrow the government. Popular support was not behind the idea, however, and the revolt was short-lived. The government arrested the leaders of the revolt, and the courts sentenced Hitler and several other Nazis to prison. Hitler, who served less than a year of his five-year sentence, did not remain idle while in prison; he dictated a book to his cellmate titled ***Mein Kampf*** (*My Struggle*), in which he attacked the Weimar Republic, blamed the Jews for Germany's problems, and demanded the renunciation of the Versailles Treaty. He also proclaimed that the Germanic peoples were a "master race" called the Aryans. Upon release from prison, Hitler continued to spread these ideas in public speeches, and before long, large numbers of Germans began to believe him. He began reorganizing the party and planning a propaganda campaign designed to gain power without reliance on force alone. The Nazi movement was filled with symbolism, with no symbol more infamous than the **swastika**.

Hitler's Rise to Power

The reasons for Hitler's amazing rise to power are varied. (1) As we have seen, the Weimar Republic was weak and inefficient. The Nazis realized this fact and took advantage of those political weaknesses. (2) The Nazis exploited the anger of many Germans against the "war guilt" clause of the Versailles Treaty, using every opportunity to condemn it. (3) Economic problems, especially inflation and unemployment, caused many people to listen to the Nazi promises of economic recovery. (4) Hitler and the Nazis were violently anti-Communist, a position that reassured Germans who worried about their wealth. (5) Hitler's charisma, personal leadership, and brilliant use of propaganda techniques drew to the Nazi Party people who otherwise would have had little use for the organization.

As economic problems became more severe after 1930 because of worldwide depression, the Nazis steadily increased in strength and numbers. After each election, the number of Nazis in the Reichstag (the lower house of the German Parliament) grew, until by July 1932 they were the largest party in the German republic, although still not a majority. Because the Nazis had won such a large number of seats, however, the president of the republic, **Paul von Hindenburg**, asked Hitler to join a coalition government as vice-chancellor, but Hitler refused. Because no party held a majority of seats, his refusal made it difficult to form a government. New elections had to be held in November. When the results were in, the Nazis had received two million fewer votes than they had received in the July elections. In addition, they had lost thirty-four seats in the Reichstag. Despite the decline in Nazi strength, Hitler demanded the position of chancellor. Hindenburg, who saw no other way out of the political impasse, appointed Hitler chancellor of Germany on January 30, 1933.

Paul von Hindenburg

Hitler then realized that the power he craved was within reach. New elections would be held in March. In an effort to win a majority of the votes, the Nazis used propaganda, violence, and threats. The culmination of the election campaign occurred six days before the voting took place. A fire broke out in the Reichstag building, partially destroying it. The Nazis blamed the Communists and tried to whip up mass hysteria. (There was strong suspicion that the Nazis may have set the fire themselves.) When the election results were tallied, the Nazis found that they had won only 44 percent of the vote. Although they still lacked a majority, the Nazis persuaded enough Reichstag members to pass the Enabling Act, which suspended the republic and made Hitler dictator of Germany. He established the so-called Third Reich, an empire that he said would last for a thousand years.

Germany Under Nazi Rule

Once in power, Hitler clearly manifested the racist beliefs of Nazi ideology. Hitler blamed the Jews for causing Germany's defeat in the First World War. He accused them of corrupting the pure Aryan race and plotting to rule the world. "The wretched Jew," said Hitler, is the "enemy of the human race" and the "cause of all our miseries." Within months after coming to power, the Nazis turned this hatred of Jews into action. Initially, they deprived Jews of citizenship and forbade their marriage to other Germans. Then, on the night of November 9–10, 1938, which was later called *Kristallnacht* (night of shattered glass), the Nazis severely damaged or destroyed 7,500 Jewish businesses, 155 synagogues, and numerous homes and killed 35 Jews. Afterward, they rounded up thirty thousand Jews (for their "protection") and put them into concentration camps. Before long, many more Jews were sent to concentration camps and ruthlessly exterminated.

Christians also faced Nazi persecution. Hitler attempted to close all church-run schools. The Gestapo arrested pastors who opposed the state. To the Nazis, Christian virtues such as humility and gentleness encouraged a slave mentality and had to be eliminated.

To their shame, some German Protestants supported Hitler, and, under Nazi sponsorship, organized what they called the German Christians. Their motto was "The Swastika on our breasts, the Cross in our hearts." These religious leaders discarded most of the Bible because it was written by Jews. They allowed only Aryans to be members of their churches. These pastors claimed that Christ was not really a Jew and that through His death He had preserved the world from Jewish domination. To them, Hitler was a second messiah destined to perfect the work that Jesus had begun. One German pastor said, "Christ has come to us through Adolf Hitler. . . . We know today the Savior has come. . . . We have only one task: be German, not be Christian." As if the blasphemy of these so-called German Christians was not enough, some Nazis

German chancellor Hitler speaking at the Reichstag in March 1936

Kristallnacht

Nazi propaganda: (top) "The German student fights for Führer and people;" (bottom) "The League of German girls in the Hitler youth"

Hitler reviews Hitler Youth formation at a Nuremberg rally ca. 1935.

Hitler inaugurates the Autobahn, accompanied by cheering crowds and Nazi formations.

even abandoned all pretense of Christianity and openly promoted a return to the pagan idols of the ancient Germanic tribes.

On the economic front, Hitler advanced a series of Four-Year Plans. The first, begun in 1933, sought to end unemployment through a massive rearmament program and the building of public works such as the famous *Autobahnen* (superhighways). The *Autobahnen* provided a military highway system throughout Germany in anticipation of another two-front war. The second Four-Year Plan attempted to make Germany economically self-sufficient so that, in the event of war, Germany could not be hurt by a blockade. To accomplish these goals, the government outlawed strikes. In addition, all workers and employers came under the direction of the German Labor Front, which had the power to determine wages and settle labor disputes. To gain the cooperation of labor, the Nazis established the "Strength Through Joy" movement, which provided vacations and entertainment at low cost. The Nazis also intensely labored to indoctrinate young people with Nazi propaganda, organizing them into Hitler Youth clubs. Thus, Hitler successfully brought Germany under Nazi control, establishing a strong totalitarian state. Soon he would attempt to expand the territory of his Third Reich (see chapter 22).

Section Review

1–2. Who was the leader of the Fascist Party in Italy? In what year did he come to power?

3. What did the Lateran Treaties secure for Mussolini?

4–5. What was the name of the fascist movement in Germany? Who became its leader?

6–7. Whom did Hitler call the "master race"? What people did Hitler blame for Germany's problems?

★ Why did the German people allow Hitler to control their lives?

★ Analyze the political and economic conditions that made the rise of a dictatorship possible in Italy.

Making Connections

1–3. Survey examples of disillusionment in painting, music, and literature.

4. Describe the response in the democracies to postwar inflation and depression.

5. Explain a foundational similarity between fascism and communism.

6–8. Summarize three reasons why Hitler rapidly rose to power in Germany.

Developing History Skills

1. Evaluate the effects of Lenin's policy of war communism on the Russian economy.

2. Consider the following statement: "During difficult times, people often seek immediate solutions to their problems. Some 'solutions,' however, often bring harm rather than good." Support or refute this statement by providing examples from the leading democratic nations following the First World War.

Thinking Critically

1. Compare the themes of art produced during the Era of Disillusionment with the art produced during the Romantic Era (chapter 17).

2. Evaluate justice and power in the USSR and Germany.

Living in God's World

1. Both Communists and Fascists realized that Christian virtues stood in contrast to their forms of government. Make a list of key Christian virtues that relate to government, especially those that would have ensured a just use of power and protected citizens.

2. Choose one piece of art mentioned in this chapter and research it. Describe how it reflects the worldview of the creator. Be prepared to give a brief presentation to the class.

People, Places, and Things to Know

Sigmund Freud
existentialism
expressionism
cubism
Pablo Picasso
Igor Stravinsky
T. S. Eliot
Statute of Westminster
Maginot Line
Franklin Roosevelt
New Deal
Alexander III
pogroms
Nicholas II
Bolsheviks
Mensheviks
Russo-Japanese War
Bloody Sunday
Rasputin
Aleksandr Kerensky
Vladimir Lenin
Leon Trotsky
USSR
New Economic Policy
Joseph Stalin
Five-Year Plans
purges
Comintern
fascism
Nazism
Benito Mussolini
Lateran Treaties
Weimar Republic
Adolf Hitler
Gestapo
Mein Kampf
swastika
Paul von Hindenburg

22

U.S. Navy Douglas SBD-5 Dauntless flying over the battleship USS. Washington

Big Ideas

1. What events led to World War II?
2. What was the Holocaust?
3. What led to an Allied victory in World War II?
4. How did this war affect the international community?

Despite World War I being called "the war to end all wars," it was not long before the nations of the world faced an even more devastating conflict—World War II. For two decades, people had relied on vague promises of peace made by world leaders. They had trusted in well-meaning but ineffective treaties and organizations. But, as in the days of the prophet Jeremiah, people were crying, "Peace, peace; when there [was] no peace" (Jer. 6:14). Had they been alert, the leaders could have seen the signs of approaching war. Power-thirsty dictators were on the march, building large armies and stockpiling weapons. By the time the rest of the world realized the danger, it was too late to avert the outbreak of a war that was truly a "world war."

I. Global Tension

Dictators Defy the League of Nations

After World War I, world leaders met to organize the League of Nations. They hoped this organization would thwart any new military aggression and thus maintain world peace and security. But during the 1930s, the militaristic governments of Italy, Germany, and Japan began to threaten world peace. For Mussolini in Italy, Hitler in Germany, and the leaders in Japan, war became an accepted and legitimate means of achieving their personal and national goals. Although the League of Nations made several feeble attempts to stop such aggression, its system of collective security failed.

Japanese Expansion in Asia

Japan entered the twentieth century as a greatly transformed country. During the Meiji Period (see p. 423), Japan had thrown off centuries-old feudalistic customs and had adopted many modern ways. Its new industrial and military might enabled Japan to win decisive victories over the much larger countries of China and Russia. In the years before World War I, Japan continued to develop its industry and modernize its military forces. When World War I erupted, Japan joined the side of the Allies. In spite of its limited role, Japan emerged from the war a major power.

After World War I, the office of emperor became largely ceremonial, and civilian officials led the Japanese government. They followed a more restrained and conciliatory policy than that to which Japan was accustomed. In 1922, Japanese leaders signed the Nine Power Treaty, agreeing with other major powers to respect the sovereignty and territory of China. Japan also joined and participated in the activities of the League of Nations. But by the end of the decade, the young emperor allied with the military with the goal of gaining control of the country. Emperor **Hirohito** and the military leaders believed that Japan should take advantage of its position of strength and extend Japanese influence in the Pacific. They sought to use Japan's military might to create a new order in Asia. Several historians believe that when Japan's civilian government collapsed in the 1930s, Hirohito used the military to seize control of the government. Under his leadership, Japan actively embarked on a program of territorial expansion.

Chinese Weakness

Japan conducted its expansionist policy at the expense of China. China lacked a strong central government and was seething with

<table><tr><td>

Guiding Questions

1. What aggressive actions did Japan take against neighboring states?
2. How were Italy's invasion of Ethiopia and the Spanish Civil War used as preparation for World War II?
3. What aggressive actions did Germany take against neighboring states?

</td></tr></table>

Emperor Hirohito, 1945

Chiang Kai-shek

Mao Zedong

internal political turmoil. In 1911, there had been a revolt against the ruling Manchu dynasty. Within four months, the Manchu had fallen from power and a Chinese republic was proclaimed. Sun Yat-sen, the organizer of the Kuomintang (KWO min TAHNG), or Nationalist Party, led the revolt. To give direction to this new party, Sun enunciated what he called the Three Principles of the People: nationalism, democracy, and social progress. But Sun never gained the support he needed to establish a stable government. Years of anarchy ensued as local leaders known as warlords fought one another for political power.

After the death of Sun Yat-sen, **Chiang Kai-shek** (CHANG KYE-SHEK; 1887–1975) took control of the Kuomintang. He began a military campaign to reunite China under a national government. But in 1927 rival factions within the Kuomintang split the party. Civil war began between Chiang's conservative forces and the Communist forces led by **Mao Zedong** (MOU DZUH-DONG; 1893–1976). By stirring up peasant uprisings, Mao hoped to bring about a Communist revolution. Chiang countered by launching an all-out effort to drive the Communists from their strongholds in southern China. But the Communist forces slipped past Chiang's lines and in their famous Long March traveled some six thousand miles to northwestern China. Further attempts by Chiang to force the Communists out of the country failed because he had to focus his military forces on defending China from Japanese aggression during the 1930s.

Japanese Invasion

Japan's decisive defeat of China in the Sino-Japanese War (1894–95) had revealed the weakness and vulnerability of China. Working through the military, the Japanese emperor launched a daring program of territorial expansion. In 1931, Japanese troops seized the entire province of Manchuria. The Chinese government protested the Japanese action to the League of Nations. Though slow to act, the League eventually demanded that Japan return the area to China. In the end, Japan refused to withdraw from Manchuria and withdrew from the League of Nations instead.

Realizing that Japan was a continuing threat to China, the Communists under Mao and the Nationalists under Chiang called a truce in their civil war and united to defeat the Japanese. But even a united Chinese front could not withstand Japan's full-scale invasion of China, which began in 1937. The Japanese captured several major Chinese cities and most of China's valuable economic resources. Although the League of Nations condemned the invasion, no country was willing to go to war to halt Japanese aggression.

Italian Revenge in Africa

Italy was the second major nation to successfully defy the League of Nations. Mussolini sought to recreate the grandeur of the Roman Empire by building a new Italian empire. In doing so, he hoped also to illustrate the vitality of fascism. His first target was Ethiopia—an independent African nation that had defeated an invading Italian army in the late nineteenth century. In 1935, a large, well-equipped Italian army invaded Ethiopia. The Ethiopians, who fought with primitive weapons such as bows and arrows, were no match for the Italians. Using a combination of air power, tanks, and poison gas, the Italians easily conquered the country.

The League of Nations was unwilling to use military force against Mussolini because its most important members, Britain and France, wanted to stay on good terms with Italy to isolate Hitler's Germany. Instead, the League decided to impose economic sanctions—forbidding the sale of certain materials to Italy. These sanctions, however, did little to hinder Italy's war effort because they did not include oil, which fueled Mussolini's tanks, planes, and other motorized vehicles. Mussolini defied every effort of the League to halt his invasion and made Ethiopia a part of his growing empire. In addition, he seized the small Balkan nation of Albania in April 1939.

German Rearmament in Europe

Like Mussolini, Hitler also sought to build a new empire. Once he had firmly established himself in power, he began laying the foundation for a new German empire—the **Third Reich**. Hitler wished to provide the German people with additional *lebensraum* ("living space"). To accomplish this goal, he knew that he had to rearm Germany. In 1933, Hitler ended German participation in the Geneva Disarmament Conference (1932–33). He also withdrew Germany from the League of Nations. Two years later, in violation of the Versailles Treaty, he reestablished the German General Staff and reintroduced a military draft.

Only one task then remained before Hitler could begin actively building his empire—he had to fortify the Rhineland. According to the Treaty of Versailles and the Locarno Pact, German territory west of the Rhine River had to be demilitarized (kept free of troops and military equipment). But Hitler had no intention of abiding by these treaty provisions. On March 7, 1936, he ordered German troops to march into the Rhineland. France reacted angrily to Hitler's conduct but took no action against Germany. Furthermore, the League once again proved itself unable to prevent or solve an international crisis. No significant check was placed on Hitler's action.

Hitler Challenges European Security
Germany Forms Alliances

Until 1935, Germany remained diplomatically isolated in Europe; even Italy sided with Britain and France in verbal opposition to Hitler. European displeasure with Italy's conquest of Ethiopia, however, drove Mussolini closer to Hitler. In 1936, Germany and Italy formed an alliance known as the **Rome-Berlin Axis**, taking its name from a speech by Mussolini. Mussolini had described a "line" running between Berlin and Rome, a line that was "not a partition but rather an axis round which all European states animated by the will to collaboration and peace can also collaborate." That same year, Germany and Japan signed the **Anti-Comintern Pact**, which on the surface was an agreement generally directed against communism but in reality was aimed specifically at the Soviet Union. The following year, Italy and Japan signed a similar agreement, bringing together the three major nations that would constitute the Axis powers in World War II. The opponents of this Rome-Berlin-Tokyo Axis would come to be known as the Allies.

The Spanish Civil War

The outbreak of civil war in Spain in 1936 provided the opportunity to bring Germany and Italy together. The Fascist followers

Adolf Hitler

The Third Reich

German history has included three *reichs* (empires or kingdoms). Otto the Great established the first one in 962, when he became the first Holy Roman emperor. This reich lasted until 1806, when Napoleon abolished it. Later, Otto von Bismarck helped unify Germany, creating a second German empire that lasted from 1871 to 1918. Adolf Hitler created what he called the Third Reich. Although he declared that it would last for a thousand years, it lasted for only twelve (1933–45).

Mussolini and Hitler

of General **Francisco Franco** (1892–1975) revolted against Spain's republican government. Recognizing that Franco had a political philosophy similar to theirs, Mussolini and Hitler supported his war effort. The Germans provided primarily planes and tanks; Italy supplied fifty to seventy thousand troops and one thousand planes. The Soviet Union offered some material assistance to the Loyalists (supporters of the Spanish government), but France and Britain followed a policy of nonintervention in Spain's affairs. France and Britain opposed a Fascist victory because it would push Spain into alliance with Germany and Italy. But they were concerned about a Loyalist victory because of Russian support. Despite a lack of supplies and foreign support, the Loyalists resisted stubbornly; but when Madrid fell to the rebel forces in early 1939, the war ended. The victorious Franco became dictator of Spain.

In addition to the tremendous significance that this civil war had for the history of Spain, it also proved to be a "dress rehearsal" for World War II. By assisting Franco, Germany and Italy were able to test new weapons under actual battle conditions and to learn how to use them effectively. One such weapon was the dreaded *Stuka* dive-bomber, which Germany would soon use to terrorize its enemies. Consequently, when World War II began in Europe, these nations—Germany in particular—had an initial advantage over their opponents.

Hitler Takes Austria

According to a post–World War I treaty, Austria was forbidden to join Germany in a political union. Yet Austria was the first area of Europe that Hitler sought to add to his Reich. During the interwar years, economic and political weakness hindered the growth of a stable economy and threatened to undermine the new Austrian republic.

In 1934, Nazis had attempted to seize Austria, but their effort had failed, partly because of Mussolini's opposition. To soothe Austria's fear, Hitler promised to respect Austrian independence. This promise, however, was only one of many that he did not intend to keep. In 1938, Hitler was ready to try again. Taking advantage of the political turmoil in Austria, Hitler demanded that a Nazi be installed as chancellor of the country. Mussolini, by then on friendlier terms with Hitler, was heavily involved in the Spanish Civil War and did not give the Austrian government his support as he had in 1934. Austria was too weak to resist Hitler's demands. When the new Nazi chancellor of Austria was installed, he "requested" that Hitler send troops into Austria and reestablish order. As Europe stood by, Hitler seized the entire country, effecting the *Anschluss* (union).

Sudetenland Sacrificed at Munich

Encouraged by his success in Austria, Hitler next turned his attention to Czechoslovakia, where 3.5 million of the inhabitants were German. Most of them lived near the border of Germany and Austria in an area known as the Sudetenland. Unlike Austria, Czechoslovakia had a strong economy and a stable, republican government. Nevertheless, Hitler's agents stirred discontent among the German inhabitants of the country. Hitler brazenly demanded that the Sudetenland become a part of the German Reich.

As tension between Czechoslovakia and Germany increased, **Neville Chamberlain** (1869–1940), prime minister of Great Britain,

---

Fascist Worldview

Japan, Germany, and Italy exalted their nations as superior to other states or ethnic groups. In Germany especially, fascism identified the Jewish people as the ultimate evil. Thus something God created (the concept of nation) was idolized, and God's chosen people were demonized. In Italy, Fascists portrayed the middle class and Communists as despicable. These authoritarian states also intruded on every aspect of life and demanded unquestioning obedience.

met with Hitler three times to seek a solution to the Czech crisis. Convinced that Hitler was willing to go to war over the Sudetenland, Chamberlain—with the support of the French government—pressured Czechoslovakia to capitulate to Hitler's demands. In his efforts to avoid war, Chamberlain foolishly believed Hitler's promise that "after the Sudeten German question is regulated, we have no further territorial claims to make in Europe."

Although bordered by German territory on three sides, Czechoslovakia refused to surrender to Hitler's wishes. War seemed imminent. At the last minute, Hitler, at Mussolini's urging, invited Chamberlain and Édouard Daladier (the prime minister of France) to meet in Munich and settle the crisis. On September 29, 1938, after hours of negotiations, the other leaders gave Hitler the Sudetenland. Incredibly, representatives from Czechoslovakia had not even been allowed to participate in the **Munich Conference**.

When Chamberlain returned to Britain, he told an enthusiastic crowd, "I return from Germany bringing peace with honor." However, Chamberlain sought to halt Hitler's expansionistic plans through a policy of **appeasement** (concessions to an aggressor to avoid conflict). Chamberlain believed that he had helped to establish "peace for our time"; but within a year, Europe would plunge into World War II.

Neville Chamberlain returning to Britain following the Munich Conference with assurance that Germany would not seek more territory

Czechoslovakia Falls to the Germans

On October 3, 1938, Chamberlain stood in the House of Commons and spoke in defense of his appeasement policy. He claimed that the "great and imminent menace" of war had been removed and that "the new Czechoslovakia [would] find a greater security than she [had] ever enjoyed in the past."

Although the road to peace might be difficult, he said, "I believe that there is sincerity and good will on both sides." Two days later, **Winston Churchill** (1874–1965), a member of the House of Commons, stood in the same place and denounced appeasement. "We have sustained a total and unmitigated defeat," he declared. He predicted that all of eastern Europe would be subjected to Nazi tyranny. Furthermore, he concluded with a somber warning and challenge:

> And do not suppose that this is the end. This is only the beginning of the reckoning. This is only the first sip, the first foretaste of a bitter cup which will be proffered to us year by year unless by a supreme recovery of moral health and martial vigor, we arise again and take our stand for freedom as in the olden time.

Time was to prove Churchill right. On March 15, 1939, German troops marched into Prague (the capital of Czechoslovakia) and brought most of the country under Nazi rule. Poland and Hungary occupied the rest of Czechoslovakia.

In the past, Hitler had claimed that all he wanted to do was to bring all Germans in Europe under one rule. Several European nations, particularly Britain, thought that Germany had been treated unfairly in the Versailles Treaty. Many leaders regarded Hitler's seizure of "German" territory as a means of correcting that injustice. In addition, the people of Europe remembered the last great war. They wanted to avoid renewed bloodshed at all costs.

As it turned out, however, the policy of appeasement only made war certain. Following Hitler's seizure of Czechoslovakia, even the

Winston Churchill

most naive of political leaders (including Chamberlain) finally realized that appeasement had failed. Hitler did not intend to confine his territorial demands; instead he sought to incorporate as much territory into his empire as possible with little regard for boundaries. Afraid for their own safety, Britain and France now determined to use force if necessary to oppose any further Nazi aggression.

Stage Set for War

Hitler's next target was Poland. Within a week after taking Czechoslovakia, he demanded that Poland cede to Germany a strip of territory known as the "Polish Corridor," which would connect East Prussia with the rest of Germany. This time, however, France and Britain decided to resist German demands regardless of the cost. Chamberlain, in a complete reversal of his earlier appeasement policy, stated that in the event "of any action which clearly threatened Polish independence, and which the Polish government accordingly considered it vital to resist with their national forces, His Majesty's Government would feel themselves bound at once to lend the Polish government all the support in their power."

To increase their effectiveness against Hitler, Britain and France tried to reach a military agreement with the Soviet Union. They ran into difficulty, however. Not only had they ignored the Soviets in the crisis over Czechoslovakia, but Stalin also thought that the Soviets had been snubbed by Chamberlain all along. He was not about to meekly cooperate with Britain now.

Meanwhile, Hitler was not idle. In May, he and Mussolini finalized a military alliance known as the **Pact of Steel**. Then, on August 23, Hitler shocked the world by announcing that Germany and the Soviet Union had signed a nonaggression pact. Both sides agreed that for ten years they would "refrain from any violence, from any aggressive action, and any attack against each other, individually or jointly with other powers." Two nations that had been sworn enemies now seemed to be on friendly terms. As William Shakespeare once wrote, "'Tis time to fear when tyrants seem to kiss."

With this agreement, Hitler confidently believed that Britain and France would not try to stop him if he invaded Poland. He had seen them weakly give in to his demands in

Hitler addresses the Reichstag on April 28, 1939, and renounces the German-Polish Nonaggression Pact.

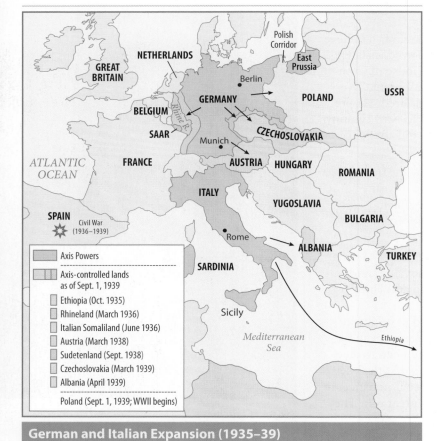

Axis Powers

Axis-controlled lands as of Sept. 1, 1939

Ethiopia (Oct. 1935)
Rhineland (March 1936)
Italian Somaliland (June 1936)
Austria (March 1938)
Sudetenland (Sept. 1938)
Czechoslovakia (March 1939)
Albania (April 1939)
Poland (Sept. 1, 1939; WWII begins)

German and Italian Expansion (1935–39)

the past. He had no doubt that in spite of their promise to defend Poland they would back down once again. Hitler miscalculated, however, and Europe was plunged into another war.

Section Review

1–2. What areas did Japan invade in 1931 and 1937?

3–4. What country did the Italians invade in 1935? How did the League of Nations respond?

5. What country experienced a civil war in which other nations—especially Germany and Italy—helped shape the outcome?

6–7. Where did European leaders meet in 1938 to settle the question of the Sudetenland? To what country did the Sudetenland belong?

✶ What role did the Spanish Civil War play in preparing for World War II?

✶ Evaluate the worldviews of the fascist nations.

II. Axis Successes

Sweep into Poland

On September 1, 1939, German forces numbering 1.7 million suddenly attacked Poland and rapidly advanced across the country. Britain and France immediately demanded that Germany cease hostilities. When the German government did not respond, Britain and France declared war on Germany. It was now too late for Hitler to turn back—World War II had officially begun. In less than four weeks, Germany, using its powerful armored divisions and superior air force—the **Luftwaffe**—defeated Poland. This fast-moving attack became known as **blitzkrieg** (lightning war).

As the Germans were invading Poland from the west, the Soviets were invading Poland from the east. According to the secret provisions of the August Nazi-Soviet Pact, the two countries divided Polish territory between themselves. In addition, Hitler agreed to recognize the Soviet claim to the small Baltic nations of Estonia, Latvia, and Lithuania. The Soviets forced those nations to allow the establishment of Soviet military bases within their countries. The Soviets then demanded that Finland grant them the same military concessions. When Finland refused, fighting broke out in late 1939. Although outnumbered five to one, the Finns held off the Russians for four months and won several victories. In the end, the Soviets broke the Finnish resistance and forced the Finns to cede territory, displacing about 400,000 citizens. The conflict, however, cast grave doubts on Russia's ability to wage war.

Invasion of Scandinavia

Meanwhile, little was happening in western Europe. The Allies, unprepared for a full-scale war, decided that a blockade of Germany would be the most effective strategy while they waited for the next German move. On the German side, Hitler wanted to attack in the west, but severe winter weather hampered his plans. For seven months a "phony war," or **sitzkrieg** (literally, "sitting war"), continued without either side launching a major offensive.

Guiding Questions

1. How did Germany advance from the invasion of Poland to the invasion of Russia?
2. What was the German strategy for conquering Europe?

German JU87 dive-bombers

In April 1940, Germany ended the military inactivity on the western front by attacking Denmark and Norway. Hitler feared the Allies would establish military bases in Norway, so he attacked and seized the country for the Axis powers. Both Norway and Denmark were caught by surprise and were easily conquered. Denmark, in fact, surrendered after only a few hours of fighting.

One factor that particularly aided the German conquest of Norway was the presence of traitors known as fifth columnists (a term coined during the Spanish Civil War to refer to individuals who secretly aid the enemy by spying, spreading enemy propaganda, and committing sabotage). In Norway, **Vidkun Quisling** became the most notorious of the fifth columnists. His subversive activities helped the Germans conquer his country. Today his name is a synonym for *traitor*.

The Fall of France

After the conquest of Norway and Denmark, Hitler began his long-awaited offensive in the west. Although the Low Countries (Belgium, the Netherlands, and Luxembourg) could provide little resistance, most observers thought that France would prove much more formidable than Germany's other foes. The French and the British had thousands of troops on the French-Belgian border to protect against a German attack across the flatlands of central Belgium. Also, along the French-German border, the French had established the **Maginot Line** (see pp. 465–66). No one expected a stunning blitzkrieg like the one in Poland.

On May 10, 1940, German forces attacked, easily crushing the Low Countries; Holland and Luxembourg fell in less than a week, and the Belgians held out for only two weeks. Meanwhile, the Allies swept into Belgium to meet the Germans. Britain and France had made a serious error, however. While they strongly defended most of the French border, the Allies stationed very few troops in the Ardennes region by southern Belgium. The Allies thought that the heavy forests there would be enough to stop any German attack through the Ardennes. Hitler thought otherwise and sent a large armored force through the forests, bypassing both the heavy fortifications of the Maginot Line along the French-German border and the massive buildup of Allied troops along the French-Belgian border. The heavy tanks pushed through the Ardennes with only minor difficulty and attacked a small and very surprised Allied force near the city of Sedan.

The German forces broke through the Allied lines and soon had a large Allied army encircled in northwestern France. The Allies had their backs to the English Channel and seemed doomed as the Germans pushed them relentlessly toward the coast. Soon, the French and the British were on the beaches at the port city of Dunkirk. Surprisingly, the Germans halted their advance, thereby giving the British time to send out a call for help. From all along the British coast, sailors and civilians came in barges, tugboats, and private yachts—more than eight hundred boats of all types and sizes—and ferried the Allied soldiers across the channel to Britain. Thus, an army of almost 350,000 men was saved from almost certain destruction. Churchill, however, told the House of Commons, "We must be very careful not to assign to this deliverance the attributes of a victory. Wars are not won by evacuation."

The German Offensive (May 1940)

Deliverance at Dunkirk

In May of 1940, news reached Britain that Hitler's panzer divisions had pushed through the Ardennes Forest into France. The surprised British Expeditionary Force and thousands of other Allied troops were forced to retreat to the port city of Dunkirk, and Christians throughout the British Empire began praying for God to deliver them. A close examination of the events of the rescue at Dunkirk shows how God granted deliverance in the midst of seemingly hopeless circumstances.

When the commander of the British forces realized that his army could not withstand the waves of German troops and tanks, he ordered the retreat to Dunkirk. Although this action was contrary to orders from Britain, he reasoned that at Dunkirk there would be a chance of escaping by sea. Had he remained in his present position, he would have been surrounded, with no means of escape.

To the surprise of the Allies, the advancing German panzer divisions stopped twelve miles short of Dunkirk. Hitler, thinking that the Allies had little hope of escaping, ordered the halt. He agreed with many of his top aides that the annihilation of the trapped Allied army should be left to the Luftwaffe, which could annihilate the British army in only three days.

But the Luftwaffe was thwarted by bad weather. Pouring rain, thick fog, and low cloud cover hindered their efforts. The British seized the opportunity to send for help. A flotilla of more than eight hundred ships, manned by British soldiers and private citizens, crossed the channel to ferry the men back to England.

The notoriously treacherous channel weather was unusually cooperative. Prevailing winds were light and westerly—had they been strong and

northerly, which is often the case, the rescue would have been much more difficult. In addition, wave heights were lower than normal. Above the rescue operation, haze and dense fog obscured the beaches from the Luftwaffe pilots. Luftwaffe records state that wave after wave of bombers reported "lack of good bombing conditions" and returned to base with their bombs.

For nine days—from May 26 to June 4, 1940—the rescue operation went on. In the end, almost 350,000 soldiers, two-thirds of whom were British, were rescued. This amazing evacuation was known as the "miracle at Dunkirk." God used both human instruments and the forces of nature to answer the prayers of concerned, but trusting, British Christians. Truly, "the effectual fervent prayer of a righteous man availeth much" (James 5:16).

British destroyers filled with evacuated British troops berthing at Dover, May 31, 1940

Meanwhile, another German force pushed southward into France. As a French defeat became more certain, Italy, hoping to gain more territory, declared war on France and Great Britain. "I need a few thousand dead," said Mussolini, "so that I can attend the peace conference as a belligerent [a nation that is an active participant in a war]." The French government, which had already fled Paris, rejected Britain's plea that the French army withdraw to North Africa and continue fighting. Instead, the political parties appointed Marshal Henri Pétain (1856–1951), a hero of World War I, to head a new French government. Pétain immediately asked the Germans for an armistice. On June 22, 1940, the French signed the surrender documents in the same railroad car in which the Germans had surrendered to the Allies in World War I. France had fallen in just forty-two days.

According to the agreement with France, the Germans would occupy more than half of France, including Paris, the entire Atlantic coastline, and the northern section of the country. The

Hitler and some of his senior officers standing in front of the railroad car where France signed the terms of surrender

Charles de Gaulle

General Erwin Rommel

rest of France would remain unoccupied, and a government under Marshal Pétain would rule for the Germans. Since the city of Vichy became the new seat of government, the entire region under Pétain's rule became known as **Vichy France**. Many of the Frenchmen who had escaped to Britain refused to recognize the leadership of the Vichy government. Instead, they joined the Free French movement led by **Charles de Gaulle** (1890–1970). These Frenchmen continued to wage war against the Axis powers.

Invasion of North Africa

Inspired by Hitler's impressive victories in Europe, Mussolini attempted to duplicate them in North Africa. He knew that Britain was facing terrific pressure from Hitler in Europe and therefore would not be able to send many additional troops to Africa. Consequently, Mussolini launched an invasion of Egypt. Such an invasion, he hoped, would not only seriously weaken Britain's position in the Mediterranean but also provide access to the oil fields of the Middle East. But Mussolini had underestimated the British, and his invasion proved a disaster. The British pushed the Italian invaders out of Egypt and back into Libya and captured more than 100,000 prisoners and much valuable war materiel.

To prevent a total Italian collapse, Hitler intervened. In the spring of 1941, a brilliant German commander, General **Erwin Rommel**, arrived in North Africa with specially trained German forces. Rommel, known as the "Desert Fox," often displayed tactical ability but was unable to win a crushing victory; he lacked sufficient supplies and reinforcements. Nonetheless, by 1942, his forces had advanced into Egypt, coming within seventy miles of the British naval base at Alexandria. Both sides were exhausted, however, and for four months there was a lull in the fighting.

Axis Blunders

At the beginning of Hitler's rule, many of his generals did not trust his military judgment or strategy. After the fall of France, however, his military prestige increased to the point that his ideas were rarely challenged. But Hitler's military success did not continue. We can now look back and see that many of his decisions proved to be military blunders.

The Battle of Britain

Although France was defeated, Hitler could not immediately direct his attention toward Britain. German troops had to first consolidate their position in the newly conquered territories. The British knew that the lull in the fighting was only temporary and that soon they too would experience the fierceness of Hitler's attack. Like France, they were in a precarious position, having already suffered several military setbacks and having little with which to defend themselves.

Although the future seemed dark, the British found hope in the courageous and energetic leadership of Winston Churchill, who had replaced Neville Chamberlain as prime minister. Churchill encouraged the British people with these words:

> We shall not flag or fail. We shall go on to the end. We shall fight in France, we shall fight on the seas and oceans, we shall fight with growing confidence and growing strength in the air. We shall defend our island, whatever the cost

may be. We shall fight on the beaches, we shall fight in the fields and in the streets, we shall fight in the hills. We shall never surrender.

The will of the British people to withstand the Nazis was soon tested. Hitler ordered not only a complete air and submarine blockade around Great Britain but also a Luftwaffe bombing campaign in preparation for an invasion. While the Luftwaffe bombed British airfields and radar installations, Hitler's generals began gathering a fleet of barges and training their troops for an amphibious assault (invasion by sea). He believed that once the Nazis had control of the skies over Britain, Operation Sea Lion (the code name for the invasion) could proceed.

Even though the German attacks against British airfields seemed to be succeeding, the Luftwaffe changed targets in early September. German bombers began dropping their loads on British cities. At the height of the bombing, three hundred to six hundred Londoners were killed daily. Hitler hoped that bombing civilian targets would destroy the British people's morale and thus break their will. But British morale did not weaken.

Hitler had underestimated the spirit of the British people. Their determined effort to resist the Nazis was demonstrated by the heroism of the British Royal Air Force (**RAF**). The Luftwaffe outnumbered the British fighters, but the British had better planes and the advantage of the newly invented radar. Before the war, Britain had begun to build an air defense system that allowed the RAF to track enemy planes and then direct the British planes to meet the attackers. Also, whenever a British plane was shot down, the pilot could often parachute to safety and fly again another day. Downed German pilots, however, were usually captured and lost to the Nazi cause. Time after time, the RAF met the oncoming waves of bombers and inflicted heavy losses. Between August 8 and October 31, 1940, official government estimates placed the number of German planes shot down at nearly 1,400 in contrast to 800 British planes. The German air force never recovered from these terrific losses. With each passing week, Hitler's invasion plans became less and

Britain Prepares for Invasion

Soon after the fall of France, the British were keenly aware of the threat of a German invasion and began making careful preparations. In a radio address, Anthony Eden, the secretary of war, said, "Those of you who are not in the Forces: Stay where you are! Refugees on roads and railways hamstring those upon whom your defense depends. . . . The mass of refugees helped to lose the battle of France; they will not lose the battle of Britain."

All across Britain, obstacles were placed on roads and in fields to prevent the enemy from landing planes. People were instructed to immobilize their cars and trucks by removing and hiding vital engine parts, thus denying the invading enemy an additional means of transportation. Public information leaflets further instructed the British people: "Do not give any German anything. Do not tell him anything. Hide your food and your bicycles. Hide your maps. . . . Think always of your country before you think of yourself." School children were taught that if German soldiers asked them for directions they should answer only "I can't say."

To confuse the Germans further in the event of an invasion, the government ordered that "no person should display or cause or permit to be displayed any sign which furnishes any indication of the name of, or the situation or the direction of, or the distance to any place." Consequently, all signposts were removed from the roads; wherever the name of a town was written, it was painted over. However, the invasion did not come, and the British people did not have to test their precautionary measures.

The Atlantic Charter

The President of the United States of America and the Prime Minister, Mr. Churchill, representing His Majesty's Government in the United Kingdom, being met together, deem it right to make known certain common principles in the national policies of their respective countries on which they base their hopes for a better future for the world.

First, their countries seek no aggrandizement, territorial or other;

Second, they desire to see no territorial changes that do not accord with the freely expressed wishes of the peoples concerned;

Third, they respect the right of all peoples to choose the form of government under which they will live; and they wish to see sovereign rights and self government restored to those who have been forcibly deprived of them;

Fourth, they will endeavor, with due respect for their existing obligations, to further the enjoyment by all States, great or small, victor or vanquished, of access, on equal terms, to the trade and to the raw materials of the world which are needed for their economic prosperity;

Fifth, they desire to bring about the fullest collaboration between all nations in the economic field with the object of securing, for all, improved labor standards, economic advancement and social security;

Sixth, after the final destruction of the Nazi tyranny, they hope to see established a peace which will afford to all nations the means of dwelling in safety within their own boundaries, and which will afford assurance that all the men in all lands may live out their lives in freedom from fear and want;

Seventh, such a peace should enable all men to traverse the high seas and oceans without hindrance;

Eighth, they believe that all of the nations of the world, for realistic as well as spiritual reasons must come to the abandonment of the use of force. Since no future peace can be maintained if land, sea or air armaments continue to be employed by nations which threaten, or may threaten, aggression outside of their frontiers, they believe, pending the establishment of a wider and permanent system of general security, that the disarmament of such nations is essential. They will likewise aid and encourage all other practicable measures which will lighten for peace-loving peoples the crushing burden of armaments.

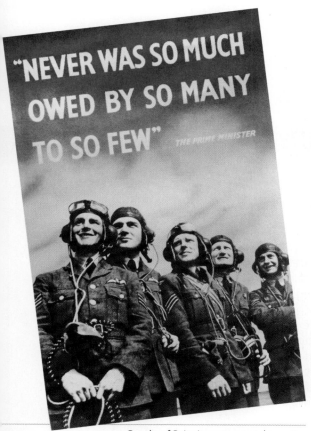

Battle of Britain propaganda poster

less likely to succeed. Summarizing the work of the British pilots, Winston Churchill said, "Never in the field of human conflict was so much owed by so many to so few."

Although the United States was not yet at war with the Axis powers, America clearly indicated its support for the Allied cause. First, the United States gave Britain fifty World War I destroyers in return for a ninety-nine-year lease on eight British military bases in the Western Hemisphere. Second, the U.S. Congress passed the so-called **Lend-Lease Act** in 1941, authorizing the president to "sell, transfer title to, exchange, lease, lend, or otherwise dispose of" military supplies to any country whose security was important to the United States. Third, Winston Churchill and Franklin Roosevelt signed the **Atlantic Charter**, an eight-point document that set forth the "common principles" on which both countries "base[d] their hopes for a better future for the world." The charter provided that after the "final destruction of the Nazi tyranny," the signatories would seek such things as the disarmament of aggressor nations, freedom of the seas, and equal economic opportunities.

The Invasion of Russia

Late in 1940, Hitler issued an order directing his generals to begin "preparation to crush Soviet Russia in a lightning campaign even before the termination of hostilities with Great Britain." Under the code name Operation Barbarossa, plans went forward in the spring of 1941 for an invasion of Russia. Although Stalin and Hitler had signed a nonaggression pact in 1939, Hitler decided to attack Russia to secure both *lebensraum* and needed natural resources such as oil. (The British naval blockade was preventing the German importation of needed raw materials.) In addition, Hitler hoped that a Russian surrender would put increased pressure on Britain by removing its last hope of finding a European ally.

But the attack on Russia proved to be another serious blunder. The Nazis underestimated not only the Soviet industrial capacity but also the length of time necessary to win a victory. Although some Russians initially welcomed the Germans as liberators from the cruel Stalin regime, the harshness of the German conquerors soon united the Russian people to fight for "Mother Russia." Like Napoleon in 1812, the Nazis made no provision for the severe Russian winters, and, like Napoleon, they found that in the end the weather helped defeat them.

The invasion was delayed one month while the Germans established Nazi control over Greece and Yugoslavia, but Hitler finally launched his attack on June 22, 1941. With thousands of planes and tanks and more than 600,000 other motor vehicles, three million Nazi soldiers advanced into Russia along an eighteen-hundred-mile front. For the first several months, the Nazi forces advanced rapidly, capturing thousands of prisoners and more than 500,000 square miles of territory. As the Russians retreated, however, they carried out a scorched-earth policy, just as they had done when Napoleon invaded in 1812. They destroyed or removed anything that the invading Germans might have used as supplies.

German tank unit in a Soviet village

By December 1, the Russian armed forces had suffered four to five million casualties, including more than one million prisoners of war. German forces had besieged Leningrad and had nearly reached Moscow, but the coming of winter ended their advance. Temperatures in early December fell to −40°F, bringing the earliest and coldest winter of the century. Machinery would not function, and soldiers suffered from lack of winter clothing. Hitler's campaign failed to knock Russia out of the war quickly. Now he had to wait until spring to try again.

In the spring, Nazi troops pushed farther into southern Russia, toward the oil fields. At the same time, they attacked Stalingrad, which not only was a strategic transportation center but also carried Stalin's name. Therefore, Hitler was determined to capture the city at all costs. For months, German troops shelled Stalingrad, but the Soviets refused to surrender. As the Nazis advanced slowly into the city, they found that the Russians were using the rubble of the destroyed buildings as fortresses. For several more months, desperate hand-to-hand fighting raged in the city. Neither side was able to defeat the other. Finally, the Russians managed to surround the Germans, and what was left of the German army surrendered in February 1943. Several days earlier, the Russians had also broken the German siege of Leningrad.

To this point, Russia had received only a limited amount of aid from the West. In a speech broadcast at the start of the German invasion of Russia, Churchill had promised that

> any man or state who fights against Nazism will have our aid. . . . We shall give whatever help we can to Russia and to the Russian people. . . . We have offered to the government of Soviet Russia any technical or economic assistance which is in our power.

Yet supply routes were few. British and American supply ships sailed regularly around Norway to the northern Russian ports of

Anti-Jewish posters:
(left) *"And at the back there is a Jew"*
(right) *"The Jew: warmonger, war elongater"*

The Holocaust

forced to live in deplorable conditions and given rationed food allotments. They were also forced to work in nearly unbearable conditions. The Nazis called the ghettos "death boxes."

When the German invasion of Russia began, Hitler instructed the SS to eliminate all Soviet Jews. In town after town and village after village, the Nazis systematically rounded up the Jews and shot them. In Kiev, for example, they herded the Jews to the cemetery, forced them to dig a large communal grave, undress, and then in groups climb into the grave. Each group was machine-gunned and covered with a layer of dirt.

In January 1942, Hitler called for a meeting of his top advisers to devise a way to annihilate the entire European Jewish community as quickly as possible. They rejected starvation and shooting; the first method was too slow and the second too costly.

In both *Mein Kampf* and his many speeches, Hitler said that the Jews were "culture destroyers" and had to be annihilated to save the "master race" (the Germans) from contamination. However, although the Jews were horribly mistreated and frequently placed in concentration camps, few people outside Germany (and only a few in Germany) believed that Hitler really meant what he said.

Early in the war, Hitler ordered that all Jews be rounded up and forced to live in restricted areas called *ghettos*. These areas were sealed off from the rest of the city, and the Jews were

Gas chamber at Auschwitz

Jews arriving by train at Auschwitz concentration camp

The Nazis decided that the most economical and efficient method was to build large gas chambers at the existing concentration camps. In those chambers, hundreds of Jews could be gassed at once. The disposal of the bodies, however, was a problem. In one camp, they were just stacked and allowed to decay, and in another they were placed in huge graves. But in most of the other camps, the Nazis built large crematoriums (furnaces for cremating bodies).

The Germans built the largest "disposal" center in the Polish village of Oswiecim (in German, *Auschwitz*). Three camps were built there to receive thousands of Jews from all over eastern Europe. They were brought to the camps in closed railroad cars made to accommodate forty people, but as many as one hundred fifty people were crammed into each car. With little food or water and no toilet facilities, the Jews traveled for days before reaching the camp. Usually by the time the train reached its destination, scores of people in each car were dead. Upon arrival at the camp, the Nazis divided the victims into two groups: those who were fit to work and those who were not (the old, sick, or very young). The Nazis took the second group to the "showers," as the gas chambers were called, and disposed of them. They put the rest to work until they were no longer useful, and then they sent them to the "showers" as well.

Toward the end of the war, as the Germans grew desperate, most incoming victims were sent directly to the gas chambers. The slaughter was so immense that the crematoriums could not keep up with the demand.

Millions of Europeans (including communists, Gypsies, the mentally and physically handicapped, Jehovah's Witnesses, and members of many other groups) died in the Nazi concentration camps from the awful brutality of the SS. But the Jewish people remained Hitler's primary target. An estimated six million Jews (about one million at Auschwitz alone) were methodically murdered, supposedly to save the "master race" from destruction.

This horrible event has become known as the Holocaust by many. However, many Jews prefer the term *shoah*, which means "calamity." They reject the term *holocaust* because it refers to a burnt sacrifice, and some Jews find this image objectionable.

(left) *Crematorium at a concentration camp at Weimar, Germany*

(top right) *Surviving prisoners at a concentration camp at Langenstein*

(bottom right) *German civilians were forced to view rows of corpses at a concentration camp.*

Murmansk and Archangel, but the ships were in danger from Nazi submarine and air attacks. Consequently, the Allies opened up an alternative supply route into southern Russia through Iran. By 1943, supplies began to pour into Russia. By the end of the war, the United States alone had supplied the Soviets with $11 billion in Lend-Lease aid.

Attack on Pearl Harbor

Japan was already at war in Asia before World War II officially began. In September 1939, when war erupted in Europe, Japan took advantage of the situation and moved into Southeast Asia. The free nations of Europe were struggling against Hitler for their very survival and could do little to halt Japanese aggression. Japan needed only to neutralize the military power of the USSR and the United States to proceed with its plans of conquest in the Pacific. In April 1941, Japan and Russia signed a nonaggression pact. Only the United States remained an obstacle.

Although U.S.-Japan relations had become increasingly strained because of Japanese aggression, the United States remained officially neutral. However, in the fall of 1941, Japanese emperor Hirohito appointed **Hideki Tojo** (1885–1948) to serve as the virtual dictator of Japan. With the emperor's approval, he and his fellow generals decided that if the American fleet stationed at Pearl Harbor, Hawaii, were destroyed, there would be no power strong enough to stop Japanese expansion into Southeast Asia. Such expansion was necessary, they believed, if Japan was to become economically self-sufficient.

Just before 8:00 a.m. on Sunday morning, December 7, 1941, nearly four hundred Japanese planes descended on Pearl Harbor. In a well-coordinated surprise attack, the Japanese knocked out American airfields and seriously crippled the U.S. Pacific Fleet, which was anchored in the harbor. Through a combination of carelessness and miscalculation, the Americans at Pearl Harbor were caught by surprise. The Japanese attack killed more than two thousand Americans, destroyed two-thirds of the American aircraft, and sank or seriously damaged five battleships and three cruisers.

In a day when a nation's naval strength rested on its battleships, the American losses seemed insurmountable. But the American aircraft carriers were not at Pearl Harbor and thereby escaped the devastation of the Japanese attack. These carriers would play a critical role in defeating the Japanese in the Pacific.

Although the Japanese considered their attack on Pearl Harbor a resounding success, it stirred the American people to action. On December 8, President Roosevelt declared the unprovoked attack a "date which will live in infamy" and asked Congress to declare war on Japan, which it did. Three days later, Germany and Italy declared war on the United States. The entrance of the United States into the war brought renewed vigor to the Allies in Europe. Soon, the U.S. Navy—led by its aircraft carriers—began to turn back Japanese expansion in the Pacific. The fears of the Japanese admiral Yamamoto had come true: the attack on Pearl Harbor had awakened a "sleeping giant."

Japanese bombers preparing to attack Pearl Harbor

Planes and fuel burning on Hickam Field

Ship sinking during the attack

Section Review

1–2. The German invasion of what country triggered the beginning of World War II? When did that invasion—and thus the war—begin?

3. What is the significance of Dunkirk?

4. Explain the beliefs that motivated the Holocaust.

5. What people, whose systematic extermination he ordered, did Hitler label as "culture destroyers"?

6. When (month, day, and year) did the Japanese attack Pearl Harbor?

☆ Explain the German strategy for conquering Europe.

☆ Analyze the effects of the Battle of Britain, the invasion of the USSR, and the attack on Pearl Harbor on the war's outcome.

III. Allied Advances
From North Africa to Italy

The year 1942 witnessed the halt of the Axis advance and proved to be the turning point for the Allies. In spite of Rommel's brilliant leadership in North Africa, the Germans were defeated by the British general **Bernard L. Montgomery** at the battle of El Alamein. At the same time, an American invasion force under General **Dwight D. Eisenhower** landed on the Algerian coast. By May 1943, the outnumbered Axis troops in Africa had surrendered.

British 5th Royal Tank Regiment in North Africa, February 1942

Two months later, a force of 160,000 men under Eisenhower landed in Sicily, bringing the war directly to the Italian people. This invasion not only cost Mussolini what little popular support he still had but also turned some of the top-ranking members of his own Fascist Party against him. Having no alternative, Mussolini was removed from his position and was quickly imprisoned. A new Italian government headed by one of his former associates immediately began secret negotiations with the Allies about terms of surrender. As Allied troops landed on the Italian peninsula itself, Italy surrendered unconditionally in September 1943. Nevertheless, hundreds of thousands of German troops continued fighting in Italy until the surrender of Germany.

Guiding Questions

1. How did the Allies advance from the invasion of North Africa through to final victory?
2. How did the war lay the groundwork for the postwar settlement in Europe?
3. How did the use of the atomic bomb end World War II?

The United States Strikes Back

Unprepared for war and reeling from the attack on Pearl Harbor, the United States was fighting a purely defensive war against both Germany and Japan. The first two U.S. offensive actions occurred in the Pacific. In China, the American Volunteer Group, a small band of fighter pilots led by Col. Claire Chennault, helped China oppose the Japanese invasion there. Flying P-40 Warhawks, the noses of which they painted with a distinctive shark's mouth, the American pilots became known as the Flying Tigers. In China they developed the techniques that American pilots would use throughout the war.

But America needed the boost in morale that could come only from striking the enemy on his own soil. That opportunity came with a top-secret bombing raid led by Gen. Jimmy Doolittle, who trained army pilots to fly B-25 bombers from the deck of an aircraft carrier. Doolittle and his "raiders" steamed secretly across the Pacific and bombed Tokyo on April 18, 1942. Although the raid did little actual damage, it shook the confidence of Japan's military leaders and forced them to keep at home some of the military resources they might otherwise have used elsewhere in the Pacific.

Mussolini himself met a violent end. German troops rescued him from prison and established him as a puppet ruler in the German-controlled areas of Italy. In April 1945, as the Axis collapsed, Mussolini, his mistress, and some friends attempted to escape to Switzerland. But Italian partisans (fighters who harass an enemy occupying their territory) captured them. They shot both Mussolini and his mistress, took their bodies to Milan, and hung them upside down in front of a gas station.

From Britain to Normandy
Allied Summit Conferences

In 1943, the Allies held two conferences that greatly influenced the outcome of the war. In January, Churchill and Roosevelt met for ten days at Casablanca, Morocco, where they declared that nothing less than the "unconditional surrender" of the Axis would be acceptable to them. The reason for such a declaration was that after World War I many Germans began to believe the myth that they had not really been defeated; Churchill and Roosevelt wanted to ensure that this time Germany would know without question that it had been beaten. But by establishing the principle of unconditional surrender, the Allies unintentionally lengthened the war, uniting the Germans more firmly behind their government.

In late 1943, Churchill, Roosevelt, and Stalin held a major summit (a conference of high-level officials) at Tehran, Iran, to discuss military strategy. Churchill wanted the Western Allies to concentrate their military efforts in the Mediterranean to check Soviet expansion there and in Eastern Europe. Stalin, on the other hand, wanted to control Eastern Europe, so he opposed any plans that would call for American and British troops in Eastern Europe. Roosevelt sided with Stalin, so Churchill had to abandon his ideas and agree to an invasion of France instead.

The Normandy Invasion

After the Tehran Conference, the United States and Britain began planning an invasion of France under the code name **Operation Overlord**. It would be impossible to conceal from the Germans the tons of supplies and thousands of aircraft and motor vehicles being stockpiled in Britain, so the Allies attempted to mislead the Germans as to the time and place of the invasion. To accomplish that deception, work crews built fake military installations in southeastern England across from Calais in France. They constructed rows of dummy tanks that looked real to German airmen flying over the island. The military then created a nonexistent invasion force complete with its own commander, sent false messages, which they allowed the Germans to intercept, and even conducted naval movements off that section of the French coast. All this activity was designed to make the Germans believe that an attack was coming near the French-Belgian border. The plan succeeded. When the real Allied attack came, the Germans had amassed their best troops in the area of France where they expected the invasion to come.

The Allies actually planned to invade Europe by way of Normandy. Dwight Eisenhower, the supreme Allied commander, decided to plan **D-day** (the day when an attack is to be launched) for June. Everything had to be just right for the attack, including the weather, the tides, and the amount of moonlight. Finally, on June 6, 1944, despite threatening weather, Eisenhower ordered the attack to

American propaganda poster

proceed on five different Normandy beaches. The assault, the greatest amphibious operation in history, had been thoroughly rehearsed to ensure its success. More than ten thousand planes bombed coastal targets and provided aerial cover for the invasion forces. Battleships shelled the enemy's beach defenses. Paratroopers landed behind the German lines before the amphibious assault and secured important objectives. Five thousand large ships and four thousand smaller landing craft followed minesweepers across the English Channel to the designated landing spots.

In the end, D-day succeeded in spite of underwater barriers, explosive mines, and stiff German resistance at several of the beaches. Within three weeks after the invasion, the Allies had landed nearly one million men, 500,000 tons of supplies, and 177,000 vehicles in France. Germany's defeat was assured; it was only a matter of time before the Germans surrendered.

If defeat seemed so certain, why did the Germans continue fighting for another year? First, Hitler and his staff believed that new "miracle weapons" would turn the tide and save Germany from defeat. For example, in 1944, the Nazis began launching rocket bombs (the British called them "buzz bombs") against the Allies. But the V-1 rockets (short for *Vergeltungswaffe*, "retaliatory weapon"), the more sophisticated V-2 rockets, and the newly developed jet aircraft all came too late to save the Nazis from defeat. Had German scientists succeeded in their efforts to develop the atomic bomb before the end of the war, the outcome might have been different.

A second reason that the Nazis prolonged the war is that Hitler expected the United States and Britain to fall into serious disagreement with Russia and split their alliance. He and his staff did not believe that the Western democracies would allow the Soviet Union to conquer Germany.

Third, the Nazis stirred up a fear of Russian communism among the German people. Nazi propaganda began to emphasize the importance of Fortress Europe (*Festung Europa*) rather than the concept of *lebensraum*, which had been so prominent in their ideology a few years earlier. With the cry of "Victory or Bolshevism" ringing in their ears, many Germans tried wearily to do their part in salvaging the collapsing Third Reich.

From Island to Island
The Fall of the Philippines

After the attack on Pearl Harbor, the Japanese military command ordered attacks throughout the Pacific. One of those attacks struck the Philippines. American defenders on the islands had too few aircraft and too few men to defend the entire territory, so they decided to concentrate on defending the largest and most important of the islands, Luzon. American and Filipino forces on the Bataan peninsula held out for several months, making their final stand on the fortress island of Corregidor. With surrender in May 1942, however, all organized resistance in the Philippines ceased. The American commander, General **Douglas MacArthur**, escaped but vowed, "I shall return." The Japanese forced the prisoners they captured on Bataan and Corregidor to march nearly seventy miles through the jungle and under the most inhumane conditions to a prison camp. Brutality on the "Bataan Death March" was commonplace, and thousands died. A few managed to escape and became guerrilla fighters.

The U.S. Coast Guard manned USS LST-21 *unloads British Army tanks onto a "Rhino" barge during the early hours of D-day.*

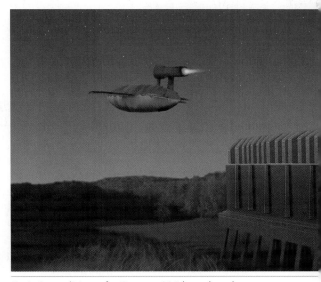

Artist's rendition of a German V-1 buzz bomb being launched toward Allied forces

Elsewhere in the Pacific, Japanese troops overran the British colonies of Hong Kong, Malaya, Singapore, and Burma, as well as the Dutch East Indies (Indonesia). Other nations were also unprepared for war, and Japan won a series of relatively easy victories.

But Japan had overextended itself. Its resources were no match for America's industrial potential. Soon, American war production surpassed that of the Japanese. By the end of 1942, only one year after Pearl Harbor, most of the ships that had been damaged in the attack had been repaired or replaced. The Allies had suffered serious reverses, but under the leadership of General MacArthur, who became the supreme Allied commander in the Pacific, the tide slowly turned against Japan.

Island-Hopping Campaign

In 1942, the United States defeated Japan in two major naval battles, halting Japanese expansion. In the Battle of the Coral Sea, American planes launched from aircraft carriers sank 100,000 tons of Japanese shipping. These losses prevented the Japanese from launching a full-scale invasion of Australia. A month later, a Japanese force of eighty ships converged on Midway Island, an American naval base 1,300 miles northwest of Honolulu, Hawaii. Although seriously outnumbered, the Americans struck first, sinking several Japanese aircraft carriers and turning back the Japanese attack. After that defeat, Japan was on the defensive for the rest of the war.

American forces soon began an island-hopping campaign, recapturing strategic Japanese-held islands in the Pacific. Instead of conquering every island in their path, the Americans seized only those that offered good sites for air bases. They simply bypassed Japanese troops on other islands. Fighting was intense, with great loss of life on both sides. Few Japanese troops surrendered, and most chose to die in battle or to commit suicide rather than face the dishonor of surrender.

Artist's rendition of the aircraft carrier USS Yorktown *under attack by Japanese planes during the Battle of Midway*

Breaking the Japanese Codes

Because radio transmissions can be intercepted easily by an enemy, both the Allies and the Axis forces took pains to maintain the secrecy of their communications. Most often they used ciphers and codes in transmitting their radio messages. (In a cipher, the letters and numbers in a message are exchanged for different letters and numbers. In a code, a word, phrase, or sentence is replaced by one letter or several letters or numbers.) Most messages are sent in both cipher and code.

By World War II, Americans had broken many of the Japanese military ciphers and codes. This knowledge became a vital help to the Allied war effort, especially after the devastating American losses at Pearl Harbor. The significance of such code breaking is illustrated by the Battle of Midway.

Having cracked a new Japanese code, the Americans learned of a planned Japanese attack on an undisclosed target coded "AF." Though Navy intelligence had a hunch that "AF" referred to Midway Island, they were not certain. They had to be sure if they were to stop the Japanese invasion. To confirm their suspicions, Navy intelligence had personnel at Midway send an uncoded message to headquarters at Pearl Harbor stating that the freshwater distilling plant on Midway was broken. Pearl Harbor radioed back that they would send a barge with fresh water. Knowing that the Japanese monitored such messages and reported such routine matters to Tokyo, the Americans waited for the Japanese transmission. Soon, the Americans intercepted a Japanese message that said that "AF" was short of fresh water. Now the Americans knew for sure that the target was Midway.

Because of this advance warning, the American fleet—led by three aircraft carriers—was able to surprise the Japanese invasion fleet and severely cripple it. Midway was saved, and the tide of Japanese expansion was stopped.

As American forces moved ever closer to the home islands of Japan, some Japanese soldiers engaged in suicide attacks against U.S. forces. For example, American forces sometimes faced banzai charges (so named because of the war cry shouted by the Japanese troops). Waves of Japanese soldiers, some with improvised weapons, charged American infantry positions only to be slaughtered. In the air, Japanese suicide pilots, known as **kamikaze** pilots, crashed their bomb-laden planes into American ships in desperate attempts to sink them. Although such attacks caused great damage, they failed to halt America's advance toward Japan. They did, however, illustrate just how determined the Japanese forces were.

In the fall of 1944, General MacArthur returned to the Philippines as promised, bringing a large American force. As his troops advanced on the ground, American naval forces engaged the Japanese off the coast in the Battle of Leyte Gulf. In three days of fighting, the Japanese navy lost forty ships and any opportunity to launch another naval attack. On the ground, American forces had some success, but Japanese resistance continued in the Philippines until the end of the war.

In 1945, U.S. troops targeted two strategic islands—Iwo Jima and Okinawa—that would provide good air bases on which pilots

General Douglas MacArthur wades ashore at Lingayen Gulf in the Philippines, fulfilling his vow to return to the islands.

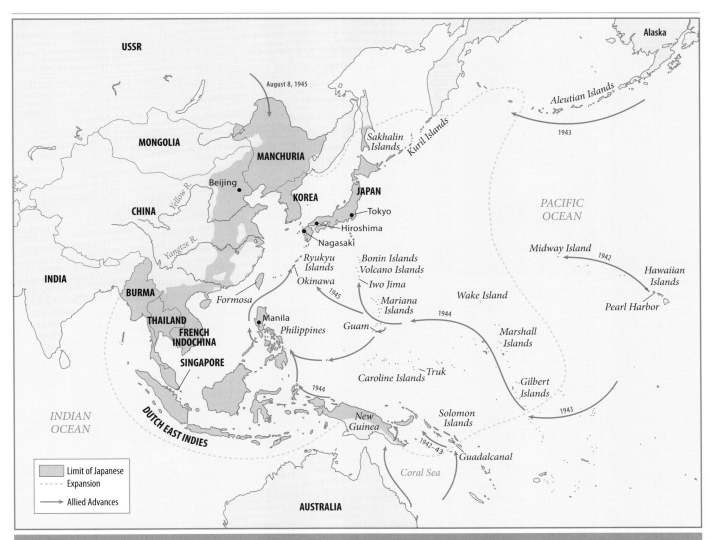

WWII Pacific Theater of Operations

The Navajo "Code Talkers"

Just as American code experts worked to break Japan's codes, the Japanese tried to break U.S. military codes—and Americans tried to prevent it. Philip Johnson, the son of a missionary to the Navajo Indians in the American Southwest, suggested a method by which the American code was never broken: using Navajos speaking their own language.

Navajo has no alphabet or symbols, so it is not written. It is also very complicated, and few people knew it. In early tests of the method, Navajos could decode a three-line message in only twenty seconds, whereas a decoding machine re-quired thirty minutes to decode the same message.

The U.S. Marine Corps recruited and trained more than 375 Navajos

as "code talkers," and they served in every major engagement in the Pacific. For example, during the first two days of the battle for Iwo Jima, six code talkers worked around the clock, sending and decoding more than eight hundred messages without making any mistakes.

The Navajo code talkers were critical to the Allied victory over Japan. For years, few people knew about their invaluable contribution because the program was so secret. They were finally honored for their service in 1992.

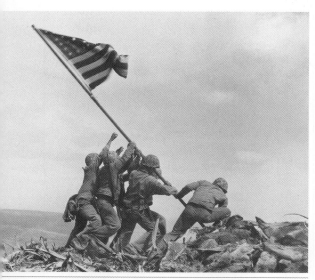

Marines raising the flag atop Mount Suribachi on Iwo Jima

could land safely and from which they could launch bombing raids and even an invasion of the main islands of Japan. Iwo Jima was less than seven hundred miles from Tokyo. For seventy-two days American planes bombed Iwo Jima, hoping to "soften up" the defenses before ground troops landed on the beaches. Nevertheless, American casualties during the invasion were high. After five weeks of intense fighting, Iwo Jima was in American hands. Of the estimated 21,000 to 23,000 Japanese troops on the island, only 216 surrendered. In June 1945, American forces also captured Okinawa, a large island only 350 miles south of Japan.

Allied Victory in Europe
Germany's Last Stand

Throughout 1943 and 1944, Soviet troops, well-supplied by the West, relentlessly pushed the German troops back toward Germany. They drove the Nazis out of eastern Europe and established their own form of totalitarianism over that region. In western Europe, Allied troops liberated Paris. They intensified their bombing of German cities and by December 1944 had reached the border of Germany. Hitler decided to order one final effort to shatter the Allied advance. In December, German armored troops suddenly attacked a weakly held section of the Allied line and pushed back the American forces there. Despite some initial success, the German drive halted as the Allies forced the Germans back to their original position. The **Battle of the Bulge** (as it came to be known) wasted much of Germany's remaining strength and probably hastened the end of the war in Europe.

In February 1945, as Allied victory seemed certain, Churchill, Roosevelt, and Stalin met at the **Yalta Conference** in the Crimea to determine the policies they would follow in the months ahead. "We have considered and determined the military plans for the final defeat of the common enemy," they proclaimed. Although they had agreed on surrender terms, they said, "these terms [would] not be made known until the defeat of Germany has been accomplished."

Yalta Conference

Churchill, Roosevelt, and Stalin

The Yalta Conference recognized Soviet control of eastern Europe. In fact, at the time of the conference, Russian troops already controlled large portions of that region. Unless the United States and Great Britain wanted war with Russia, Stalin intended to maintain Russian control over the area. Roosevelt and Churchill were eager to gain Soviet aid in the war against Japan; therefore, they consciously tried not to antagonize Stalin. Stalin promised Churchill and Roosevelt that he would allow free elections in eastern Europe following the war, but within a few years even the most naive Western observers realized that Stalin did not intend to keep his word.

Although they avoided specific public statements, the Allies did make certain general principles clear to the public: Germany would have to pay reparations, German war criminals would be brought to trial, all German forces would be disarmed and disbanded, and Germany would be divided into zones of occupation. Stalin also promised America and Britain that he would go to war against Japan within three months after the war ended in Europe.

Advance to Berlin

Although American forces could have taken Berlin, Eisenhower ordered American troops to halt on the Elbe River, in fulfillment of a promise made at Yalta, to allow the Russians to close in on the city. On April 30, 1945, before Russian troops arrived, Adolf Hitler committed suicide in his underground bunker in Berlin. His aides then burned his body with gasoline. The next day, however, German radio announced that Hitler had died at the head of his troops, fighting to his last breath against bolshevism. On May 7, the Germans surrendered unconditionally, and the Allies declared May 8, 1945, **V-E Day** ("Victory in Europe"). The war in Europe was over.

Amid the jubilation, however, was the discovery of unbelievable horrors and atrocities committed by the Third Reich in the numerous concentration camps the Nazis had run. These and other atrocities became known as the **Holocaust**. The Allies forced captured German guards from the camps and civilians who had lived near the camps to look on their ghastly work and then bury the dead. Jews and Gentiles the world over vowed, "Never again."

Two months later, the leaders of the three victorious powers met at Potsdam, Germany, where they drew up a declaration charting the future course of Germany according to the decisions reached at Yalta. Roosevelt had died in April 1945, so President **Harry Truman** represented the United States. Near the end of the conference,

WWII European Theater of Operations

Clement Attlee, who had been elected the new British prime minister, replaced Churchill at Potsdam. During this time, plans for the demilitarization of Germany and its division into four zones was decided. In addition to discussing Germany, the United States and Britain issued an ultimatum to Japan, warning that unless the country surrendered, it would face "prompt and utter destruction."

Allied Victory in the Pacific

After the surrender of Germany, war continued in the Pacific. American bombers leveled whole sections of Japanese cities using incendiary bombs (bombs designed to start fires). In a one-night raid against Tokyo, for example, fire destroyed nearly sixteen square miles of the city, and more than eighty thousand people died. Although many Japanese people wanted to see the war end, Japan's emperor and military leaders refused to surrender. Instead, they gathered as much war materiel as they could, including eight thousand planes, which they intended to use against the Americans should they attempt to invade Japan.

American and British troops advanced steadily toward Japan. Allied leaders, however, dreaded the long and bloody struggle that lay ahead of them. President Truman and his military staff believed that Japanese and American casualties would reach into the hundreds of thousands if American troops actually invaded the home islands of Japan. In an effort to shorten the war and save lives, Truman ordered that an atomic bomb be dropped on the Japanese city of **Hiroshima**. On August 6, 1945, the bomb was dropped. Its blast wiped out 4.7 square miles of the city and killed an estimated eighty thousand people immediately, while another thirty-five thousand were injured, and another sixty thousand died within several months. When Truman announced the dropping of the bomb to the American people, he issued another stern warning to Japan: "We are now prepared to obliterate more rapidly and completely every productive enterprise the Japanese have above ground in any city." If the Japanese leaders did not accept Allied terms of surrender, they could "expect a rain of ruin from the air, the like of which has never been seen on this earth."

Realizing that the war against Japan would end quickly and wanting to gain territory in the peace negotiations, the Soviets finally declared war on Japan on August 8. Since the Japanese leaders still refused to surrender, the United States dropped a second atomic bomb on the city of **Nagasaki** on August 9. Five days later on August 14, the Japanese government surrendered with the sole condition that their emperor be allowed to retain his throne. On September 2, 1945 (**V-J Day**), hostilities formally ended as Japanese and Allied representatives signed the surrender document aboard the USS *Missouri* in Tokyo Bay. World War II was finally over.

Section Review

1–3. Which "Big Three" Allied leaders met at Tehran in 1943?

4. Where did the Big Three decide to invade Europe to get a foothold on the continent?

5. Who was the Allied leader of the Normandy invasion?

6. How did Yalta and Potsdam prepare for postwar settlement of Europe?

7. What new weapon did the United States use against two Japanese cities in August 1945?

★ Why do you think the Japanese emperor and military leaders refused to surrender until the United States dropped two atomic bombs?

★ Evaluate the use of the atomic bomb to end World War II.

IV. Efforts for Global Peace

Even before the end of World War II, the Allies had called for the formation of an international peace-keeping organization. The "Big Three" Allied powers discussed that hope in conferences in Tehran (1943), Dumbarton Oaks (1944), Yalta (1945), and San Francisco (1945).

At the San Francisco conference, representatives of fifty governments formally organized the **United Nations** (UN). The UN Charter defined its purpose as the maintenance of international peace and security. In addition, the UN sought to foster cooperation

Guiding Questions

1. Why was the United Nations formed?
2. What were the major bodies of the United Nations?

among nations in solving worldwide social, economic, and humanitarian problems. These goals expressed the same kind of optimism that had characterized the ill-fated League of Nations after World War I—the desire for lasting world peace and cooperation among all nations. The verse inscribed on the UN headquarters building in New York City summarizes the organization's dream:

> They shall beat their swords into plowshares, and their spears into pruninghooks: nation shall not lift up sword against nation, neither shall they learn war any more. (Isa. 2:4)

To accomplish their goals, member nations created three major bodies within the UN: the **Secretariat**, the **General Assembly**, and the **Security Council**. The Secretariat, headed by the Secretary-General, is the administrative arm of the UN. All member nations are represented in the General Assembly, where they debate world issues in annual sessions. The Security Council embodies the executive, or enforcement, power of the UN. Five permanent members—the United States, Russia (formerly the Soviet Union), China, Great Britain, and France—and ten nonpermanent members, elected by the General Assembly to two-year rotating terms, make up the Security Council.

In addition to these bodies, the UN bureaucracy includes various special agencies. For example, the Economic and Social Council promotes better living standards and human rights throughout the world, the Trusteeship Council assists colonial peoples, and the International Court of Justice resolves disputes among nations as the judicial arm of the UN. Other specialized agencies include the International Labor Organization; the World Health Organization; and the UN Educational, Scientific, and Cultural Organization (UNESCO). The United States, which earlier had shunned the League of Nations, not only joined the UN but became its host as well.

The UN displays the shortcomings that often characterize international organizations. As with the League of Nations, the primary weakness of the UN has been its lack of authority. As a voluntary international organization, it has lacked the power to enforce its actions, even upon member nations. Furthermore, each of the five permanent members of the Security Council has veto power over any council decision. In the first ten years of the UN, the council experienced seventy-eight vetoes, seventy-five of them by the Soviet Union. During the Cold War era that followed World War II, the superpowers clearly dominated the world organization, but their competing differences rendered the Security Council ineffective. The threat of nuclear war, not the UN, has prevented the outbreak of another world war.

Section Review

1. How many nations were represented in the formal organization of the United Nations?

2. What is the goal of the Security Council?

3. What is a primary weakness of the United Nations?

4. What country exercised the veto more than any other nation during the first ten years of the UN?

5. What has prevented the outbreak of another world war?

☆ Why do nations not turn their weapons into farm implements?

Making Connections

1–3. Describe three of Japan's advances to control the Pacific region.

4–5. Give two examples of new techniques that Nazi Germany used to advance through Europe.

6–9. Summarize a significant agreement reached at each of the four conferences.

Developing History Skills

1. Why did the Allied declaration of war in September 1939 surprise Hitler?

2. Evaluate the overall effectiveness of the United Nations in keeping peace in the world. Defend your answer.

Thinking Critically

1. Defend or refute the following statement: "The dropping of the atomic bombs saved many lives and was justified."

2. Why did the Axis powers have an advantage at the beginning of the war? Why do you think they were unable to maintain that advantage?

Living in God's World

1. Imagine you are a Christian living in Germany during World War II. What would your responsibility toward the government be?

2. Critique the beliefs and actions that led to the Holocaust.

People, Places, and Things to Know

Hirohito
Chiang Kai-shek
Mao Zedong
Third Reich
Rome-Berlin Axis
Anti-Comintern Pact
Francisco Franco
Neville Chamberlain
Munich Conference
appeasement
Winston Churchill
Pact of Steel
Luftwaffe
blitzkrieg
sitzkrieg
Vidkun Quisling
Maginot Line
Vichy France
Charles de Gaulle
Erwin Rommel
RAF
Lend-Lease Act
Atlantic Charter
Hideki Tojo
Bernard L. Montgomery
Dwight D. Eisenhower
Operation Overlord
D-day
Douglas MacArthur
kamikaze
Battle of the Bulge
Yalta Conference
V-E Day
Holocaust
Harry Truman
Hiroshima
Nagasaki
V-J Day
United Nations
Secretariat
General Assembly
Security Council

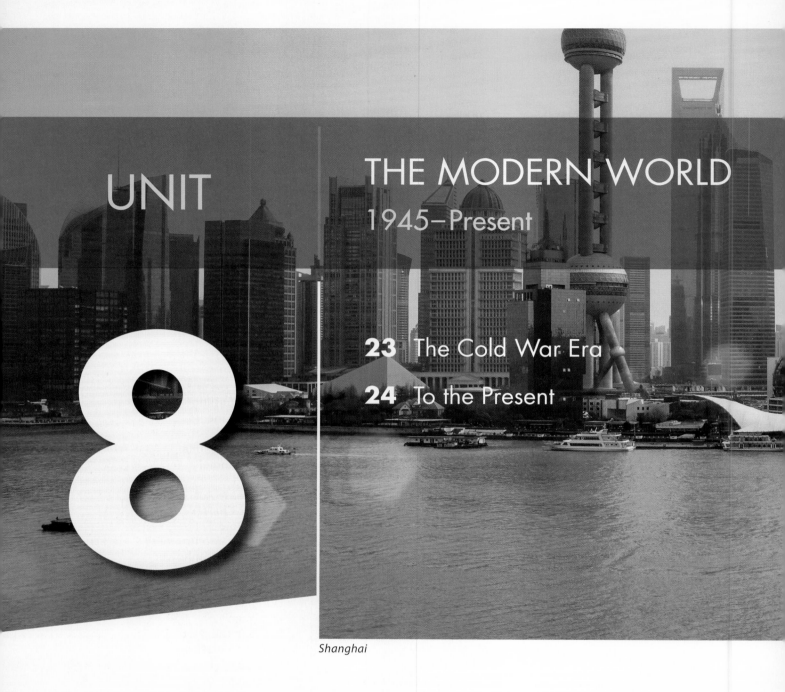

UNIT

8

THE MODERN WORLD
1945–Present

23 The Cold War Era

24 To the Present

Shanghai

1948
Nation of Israel born

1949
Fall of China to Communists

1950–53
Korean War

1959
Castro seizes power in Cuba

1961
Construction of Berlin Wall begins

1963–75
Vietnam War

1973
Yom Kippur War

1979
Egypt–Israel
Peace Treaty

1950 **1960** **1970** **1980**

1967
Six-Day War

1979
Islamic revolution
in Iran

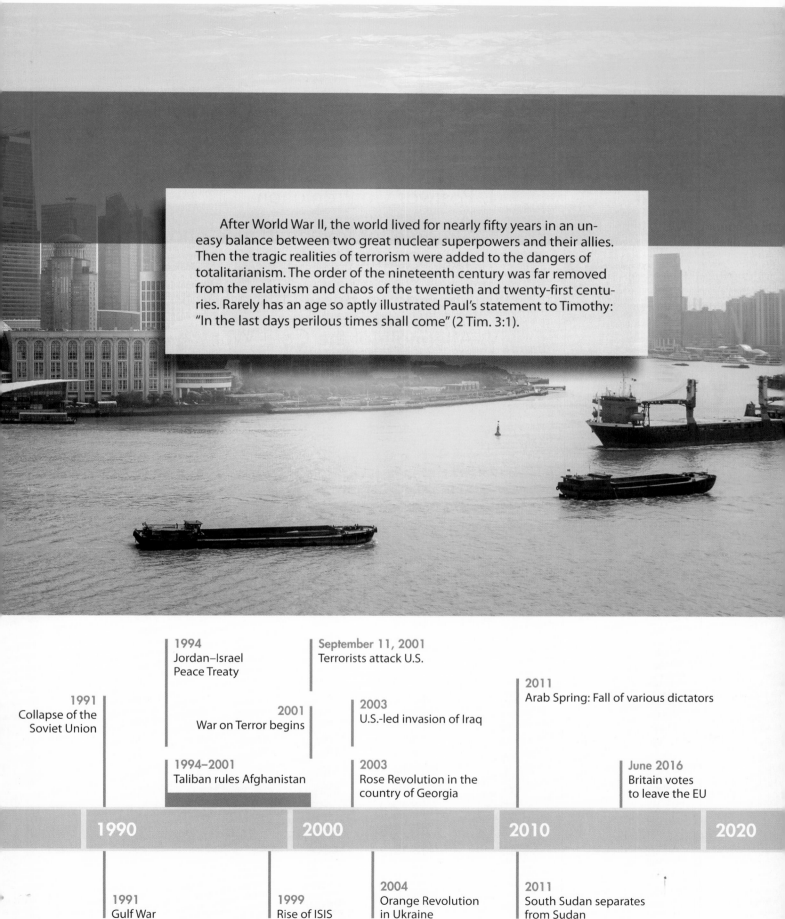

After World War II, the world lived for nearly fifty years in an uneasy balance between two great nuclear superpowers and their allies. Then the tragic realities of terrorism were added to the dangers of totalitarianism. The order of the nineteenth century was far removed from the relativism and chaos of the twentieth and twenty-first centuries. Rarely has an age so aptly illustrated Paul's statement to Timothy: "In the last days perilous times shall come" (2 Tim. 3:1).

1994
Jordan–Israel
Peace Treaty

September 11, 2001
Terrorists attack U.S.

1991
Collapse of the
Soviet Union

2001
War on Terror begins

2003
U.S.-led invasion of Iraq

2011
Arab Spring: Fall of various dictators

1994–2001
Taliban rules Afghanistan

2003
Rose Revolution in the
country of Georgia

June 2016
Britain votes
to leave the EU

1990

2000

2010

2020

1991
Gulf War

1999
Rise of ISIS

2004
Orange Revolution
in Ukraine

2011
South Sudan separates
from Sudan

23

Opening of the Berlin Wall

Big Ideas

1. What characterized the interaction of the West and the Soviet Union during the Cold War?

2. How did independence movements develop during the Cold War?

3. What led to the collapse of the Soviet Union?

4. How did the collapse of communism affect Eastern Europe?

During the months following World War II, Soviet expansion threatened to enslave the Europe that the Allies had so recently freed from the grips of Hitler and Mussolini. "Nobody knows what Soviet Russia and its Communist international organization intends to do in the immediate future, or what are the limits, if any, to their expansive and proselytizing tendencies," Churchill warned. But what was already apparent to Churchill was that much of Europe had fallen under Soviet domination. "From Stettin in the Baltic to Trieste in the Adriatic," Churchill observed, "an iron curtain has descended across the Continent."

Before long, that so-called **iron curtain** came to symbolize an even greater division. The world that emerged from World War II split into two competing camps—the Communist world, dominated by the Soviet Union, and the free world, led by the United States. Decades of apprehension, hostility, and competition between the Soviet Union and the United States followed. Because those super-powers never actually fought each other in open combat, people referred to the decades following World War II as the **Cold War**. After forty-five years of costly struggle, communism proved to be a failure, and the Soviet Union dissolved.

I. Postwar Confrontation

Background of the Cold War

The end of World War II brought a new set of challenges. The United States and the Soviet Union emerged as the world's greatest military powers, or superpowers. The world was divided politically and economically into three groups: the "industrialized nations," comprising North America, Western Europe, and Japan, which combined democratic government with capitalistic economies; the Communist world of the Soviet Union, Eastern Europe, and China, all of which were controlled economies; and the developing countries in Africa, Asia, and the Middle East, which were known collectively as the third world and were a mixture of military dictatorships and fledgling democracies.

A Heritage of Mistrust

Since the Bolshevik Revolution of 1917, relations between the Soviet Union and the West had been characterized by suspicion and mistrust. Lenin created ill will among the Allies when he pulled Russia from World War I and made a separate peace with Germany.

Relations between the Soviets and the West worsened when the Soviets signed a nonaggression pact with Nazi Germany in 1939. In June 1941, when Hitler violated that pact and invaded the Soviet Union, the Communists joined Britain to fight the common threat of Nazism and remained allies throughout the war. The United States later entered the war.

Communist Motives

Three motivations fueled Soviet expansion. First, the Soviet Union remained suspicious of the West, in part because of centuries of Russian isolation but even more because of the nature of the totalitarian Communist system. Since their own rule was built on fear and repression, the Soviets assumed the worst motives in their opponents.

Guiding Questions

1. Why did confrontation develop between the West and the Soviet Union?
2. What did America do to contain communism during this period?
3. What confrontations occurred between the West and the Soviet Union?

A second factor was Communist ideology. Communist philosophy required its expansion around the world. In fact, one of Lenin's enduring contributions to Communist thought was his conviction that violence was the primary means of spreading the Communist revolution. If the workers of the free world would not overthrow their governments, then the Communist powers would do so by force.

Finally, a simple desire for power motivated the Communists. Like the Nazis, they wanted to increase their empire's wealth, power, and prestige by adding territories. Although they constantly criticized Western imperialism, the Communists built an empire that dwarfed the ancient empires of Persia and Rome.

Soviet Expansionist Policies

The Soviet Union was especially interested in Eastern Europe. Twice in the twentieth century, Germany had invaded Russia; Soviet leaders wanted to ensure that it never happened again. The Soviet Union sought to extend its sphere of influence over the bordering territories in Eastern Europe, creating a buffer zone between the Soviet Union and the West. Soviet control over this territory also would supply raw materials for rebuilding the Soviet economy, which had been devastated by the war.

In the wartime conferences at Tehran, Yalta, and Potsdam, the Allied leaders had wrestled with the question of what to do with Germany and Eastern Europe. They agreed that Germany should be divided and occupied by Western and Soviet forces. They could not agree, however, on the issue of Eastern Europe. Great Britain and the United States wanted to set up democratic republics, but the

The Iron Curtain

Beware, I say, time may be short. . . . A shadow has fallen upon the scenes so lately lighted by the Allied victory. Nobody knows what Soviet Russia and its Communist international organization intends to do in the immediate future, or what are the limits, if any, to their expansive and proselytizing tendencies. . . . From Stettin in the Baltic to Trieste in the Adriatic, an iron curtain has descended across the Continent. Behind that line lie all the capitals of the ancient states of central and eastern Europe. Warsaw, Berlin, Prague, Vienna, Budapest, Belgrade, Bucharest, and Sofia, all these famous cities and the populations around them lie in what I must call the Soviet sphere, and all are subject, in one form or another, not only to Soviet influence but to a very high and, in many cases, increasing measure of control from Moscow. . . . In a great number of countries, far from the Russian frontiers and throughout the world, Communist fifth columns are established and work in complete unity and absolute obedience to the directions they receive from the Communist center. Except in the British Commonwealth and in the United States, where communism is in its infancy, the Communist parties, or fifth columns, constitute a growing challenge and peril to Christian civilization. These are sober facts. . . . But we should be most unwise not to face them squarely while time remains. . . . What the Russians desire is . . . the indefinite expansion of their power and doctrines.

Winston Churchill, March 5, 1946

Cold War (1982)

Soviet Union, with its Red Army already in that region, insisted on regimes friendly to Soviet interests.

The Soviets managed to place Communists in power in several countries in Eastern Europe. In 1945 both Poland and Romania fell under Communist control. Soviet puppet governments were established the following year in Bulgaria and Albania. In 1947 Hungary succumbed to Soviet domination, as did Czechoslovakia in 1948. In Yugoslavia, Josip Broz (1892–1980), better known as Marshal Tito, came to power. Tito established a Communist government but dismayed Stalin by insisting on a greater degree of independence from Moscow than did other Eastern European countries. Since Stalin had no common border with Yugoslavia, he could not use his army to enforce his will. The Soviet dictator could only fume and denounce Tito.

Elsewhere in Eastern Europe, though, the Soviet Union exercised virtual colonial control over the Communist-bloc countries for nearly fifty years. Soviet leaders dictated the political, economic, and social affairs of their satellite states. When any Soviet-dominated country in Eastern Europe attempted to overthrow the imperialistic yoke, Soviet tanks and troops crushed the revolt swiftly and brutally. Such was the case in both Hungary in 1956 and Czechoslovakia in 1968. And the free countries of the world did nothing militarily to help those people gain their freedom. Although leaders in the United States hinted that they would support the Hungarians, they did not deliver on those perceived promises.

American Containment Policies

American Ideals

When World War II ended, the United States was undoubtedly the most powerful nation in the world; its economic and military might were without equal. The only nation with the atomic bomb, the United States could not retreat to its traditional prewar isolationism. In another break with tradition, America began a peacetime defense buildup.

The United States enjoyed an enormous amount of prestige and goodwill among the nations that benefited from its assistance during the war. America entered the postwar period with a clear sense of superiority and mission. Its goal was to spread democracy and promote free trade throughout the world. In actions unprecedented in history, the United States began to rebuild its defeated foes, helping them recover from the ravages of war and get back on their feet economically and politically.

Containment

Americans became alarmed, however, at the spread of communism. They denounced Soviet aggression. When President Harry S. Truman (1884–1972) sternly lectured the Soviet foreign minister about the issue, the Soviet official indignantly replied that he had never been talked to like that in his life. Truman shot back, "Carry out your agreements and you won't get talked to like that." But little changed. With a dwindling Allied presence in Eastern Europe and the continued influence of the Soviet Union, one country after another fell to communism. In response, Truman implemented a foreign policy designed to contain the spread of communism.

The **Truman Doctrine** underscored the major objective of American foreign policy during the Cold War—**containment**. This policy, developed by George Kennan, stated that the best strategy against Soviet power would be "long-term, patient but firm . . . containment of Russian expansive tendencies." Kennan also noted prophetically that Soviet power bore within itself the seeds of its own destruction.

Hungarian uprising, 1956

The Marshall Plan

The United States also worried about Western Europe, where the economic chaos following the war encouraged the growth of Communist parties in Italy and France. In June 1947, one month after Truman signed the bill of aid to Greece and Turkey, U.S. secretary of state George Marshall announced plans to provide massive economic assistance to war-ravaged Europe. In April 1948 Truman signed the European Recovery Act, or **Marshall Plan**, as it was popularly called, which provided $13 billion for the program. Western European countries eagerly accepted the funds. Over the next four years, their economies dramatically improved.

The long-term purpose of the Marshall Plan was to thwart any advance of communism in Western Europe by rebuilding those countries economically. This plan not only reduced the appeal of communism in Western Europe but also helped create strong trade partners. Not surprisingly, the act further intensified the Cold War.

The Soviet Union and the puppet governments of its satellites rejected the American offer of economic assistance, fearing a scheme that meant greater American influence. Acceptance or rejection of the aid divided Europe into pro-American and pro-Soviet sides.

Western/Soviet Confrontation

Germany

After World War II, the Allies divided Germany into zones, each occupied by France, Great Britain, the United States, or the Soviet Union. Berlin, the German capital, was also divided: the Western Allies occupied West Berlin, and the Soviets occupied East Berlin. In 1949 the Western Allies organized the Federal Republic of Germany, which included West Germany and West Berlin, with Bonn as its capital. The Soviet Union responded by establishing the German Democratic Republic, composed of East Germany and East Berlin. Unfortunately, West Berlin lay deep inside hostile East Germany.

Occupation of Germany After World War II

In 1948 Berlin became a test for the policy of containment. The Soviets, upset with the Marshall Plan and the unification of West Germany, cut all highway and rail access between West Berlin and Western Europe, bringing the Communist-bloc nations and the free world to the brink of war. With Truman's leadership, American and British authorities ordered an airlift to provide the people of West Berlin with vital supplies. For nearly a year, the West flew fuel and food to the besieged city. At the height of the airlift, planes were landing every ninety seconds, twenty-four hours a day. So successful was the airlift that the Soviet Union lifted the blockade. The West had scored a major victory in the Cold War without resorting to armed conflict.

NATO

Containment took a more militaristic turn, however, in 1949. Tensions were high over the Berlin crisis and the inability of the United Nations to provide peace and security. The West sought a more effective means of ensuring its defense against Soviet expansion. The solution was a regional military alliance called the North Atlantic Treaty Organization, or **NATO**. Organized in 1949, NATO originally included the United States, Canada, Great Britain, France, and Italy, along with less powerful nations in the North Atlantic region. In 1952, during the Korean War, NATO added Greece and Turkey. In 1955 West Germany joined the alliance. The Soviet Union reacted by creating its own regional military alliance, the **Warsaw Pact**, which included its Eastern European satellite states.

Arms Race

Also in 1949, the Soviet Union exploded its first atomic bomb, bringing more uncertainty to the Cold War. The West wondered how this achievement would affect Soviet behavior. Since 1945 the United States had exercised restraint with its exclusive control of atomic weapons. Americans feared that the Communists would use their nuclear capability to blackmail and intimidate their foes. The

Soviet production of the atomic bomb also marked the beginning of the **arms race**. In January 1950 President Truman ordered the production of the hydrogen bomb, or H-bomb, which was hundreds of times more powerful than the atomic weapons dropped on Japan. Over the next three decades, both the Soviets and the Americans increased their peacetime production of nuclear and conventional weapons. Both sides wanted to maintain a position of strength and prevent the other side from gaining a military edge.

U.S. Domestic Conditions

Some experts predicted economic decline in the United States after World War II. Instead, what followed was an economic boom. Consumers demanded items that they could not purchase during the war. They had sacrificed consumer goods for the greater good of the war effort; now they wanted to make up for it. One writer nicknamed American culture "the affluent society" because of its enormous wealth and productivity. The United States was the undisputed leader among nations during the first twenty years following the war.

Nonetheless, internal difficulties troubled the nation. Many black Americans still did not receive equal treatment. Launching what became known as the **civil rights movement**, African Americans began to make significant gains in politics and society. The U.S. Supreme Court declared segregation of public schools by race to be unconstitutional. **Martin Luther King Jr.**, the movement's most visible spokesman, emerged in the 1950s and 1960s to lead a crusade for voting rights and equal access to public facilities for black Americans. Congress passed the 1964 Civil Rights Act and the 1965 Voting Rights Act. But violence also erupted as different ethnic groups clashed during civil rights protests. Riots devastated poor sections of large American cities.

Added to the ethnic conflict was a generational conflict. In the 1960s many young people revolted against authority—parental, educational, and governmental. Long hair, rock music, drugs, and sexual immorality symbolized their revolt. The Vietnam War (see p. 526) particularly divided the older and younger generations. Demonstrations against the war sometimes ended in bloodshed, and many young men refused to serve in the armed forces, dodging the draft by fleeing to Canada.

Vietnam did more than divide Americans; it diminished their prosperity. President Johnson attempted to pay for the war without cutting the massive spending needed to support his social programs. Soon, economic stagnation set in, and the United States suffered high unemployment and high inflation in the 1970s.

A national drift occurred in leadership as well. Johnson's successor, Richard Nixon, was forced to resign in 1974 amid charges of political corruption. Many viewed his successors, Gerald Ford and Jimmy Carter, as uninspiring, and voters rejected them. The apparently growing military strength of the Soviet Union seemed only to heighten the perception that the United States was on the decline.

A change occurred, however, with the election of **Ronald Reagan** in 1980. He was the first president since the 1930s to question the premise of the welfare state. He sought to reduce government regulation and lower taxes, and Congress obliged with huge tax cuts. Reagan enjoyed the support of religious and social conservatives, who were offended by the radicalism of the 1960s. He supported

Martin Luther King Jr.

Ronald Reagan

issues important to such conservatives, notably an end to legalized abortion.

Reagan's successor, George H. W. Bush, continued Reagan's policies. During his term, the Soviet Union collapsed, and he led a successful war against Iraqi dictator Saddam Hussein. Yet in 1992 a sluggish economy and an uninspiring campaign resulted in the rejection of Bush in favor of the Democrat Bill Clinton.

Postwar Conditions in Western Europe and Japan

Western Europe

The postwar era saw the decline of the remaining dictatorships in Western Europe. When Spanish dictator Francisco Franco, who had seized power in the Spanish Civil War in the 1930s (see chapter 22), died in 1975, Spain restored the monarchy under King Juan Carlos. The new king restored democratic government to the nation, paving the way for Spain to join the European Community in 1985.

The end of the dictators did not mean the end of strong rulers in Europe. Within the democracies, leaders with strong views and even stronger character dominated the politics of their countries as well as the Continent.

Germany

Germany traveled a remarkable road after the war—from a ruined shell of a nation to a world economic giant. The Cold War, however, divided Germany. West Germany had the fastest-growing economy in Europe by the 1950s, in large part because of the policies of Chancellor Konrad Adenauer. Adenauer became mayor of Cologne in 1917 but was dismissed from his office by the Nazis in 1933. In 1944 the Gestapo put him in prison, where the warden told him, "Now, please do not commit suicide. You would cause me no end of trouble. You're sixty-eight years old, and your life is over anyway."

Adenauer's life was far from over, however. In 1949 he became the first chancellor of West Germany, an office he held for fourteen years. The chancellor fashioned what was called the *Wirtschaftswunder* ("economic miracle"). Rejecting socialism and following free-market principles, he rebuilt Germany. Income tripled while he was chancellor, and by 1955 the nation was producing more goods than it had before the war, despite West Germany's being only about half the size of prewar Germany. Although not a military power, West Germany became an economic superpower.

France

France experienced two new governments in the decades after World War II. After the liberation of the French from the Nazis in 1944, **Charles de Gaulle**, leader of the Free French during the war, led a provisional government until 1946. He angrily rejected the new constitution for the Fourth Republic, however, because it did not give sufficient power to the president. De Gaulle retired, and his predictions about the weaknesses of the Fourth Republic proved true. Multiple parties dominated the legislative branch, and a succession of cabinets made it difficult to solve major problems. The French army, humiliated by the Germans in 1940, sought to restore its honor by holding on to the French empire. Instead, the army endured bitter defeat at the hands of Vietnamese Communists and withdrew from Indochina in 1954. In 1956 the French joined

Konrad Adenauer

Charles de Gaulle

Margaret Thatcher

the British and the Israelis in an attempt to recapture the Suez Canal from Egypt, but international opposition forced France and Britain to relinquish their gains, further humiliating the French.

Following a crisis in Algeria in 1958, the French army forced the government to recall de Gaulle. He led the French to replace the Fourth Republic with the Fifth Republic, a government with a constitution that provided for a strong president. De Gaulle and the new government brought stability and order to France. It became the leading military power of the Continent and was surpassed by only West Germany in economic might. After de Gaulle's retirement in 1969, his system endured. Even the 1981 election of François Mitterand, the first socialist president of the Fifth Republic, did not shake the nation. Since the French Revolution in 1789, the Third Republic (1870–1940) is the only French government to have lasted longer than the Fifth Republic.

Great Britain

The postwar era was a period of transition and decline for Great Britain. The sun finally set on the British Empire as her once-glorious holdings began to slip away. India, Pakistan, and Burma gained independence in the late 1940s, and by the 1960s few territories remained under British rule.

The weak British economy was not helped when the Labour Party took power after World War II and began to pursue socialist policies to build a welfare state. While the British people welcomed greater personal security through reforms such as a national health insurance plan, they learned too late that the cost included higher taxes and stifling government regulation. The Labour Party nationalized (placed under government control) many major industries, such as coal and the railways. Government control resulted in inefficient industries, which reduced Britain's competitiveness.

In 1975 Margaret Thatcher became leader of the Conservative Party and campaigned against Great Britain's "slither and slide toward socialism." Voters swept her and her party into power in 1979, marking a sense of renewal in the nation. Thatcher sold many of the nationalized industries to private investors and slashed the nation's tax rates, spurring economic growth. She confronted the powerful labor unions, which were stifling economic growth, and broke their power. Thatcher appropriately became known as the "Iron Lady."

In foreign affairs Thatcher supported the anti-Communist policies of the Reagan administration. She also led Britain to victory in a war against Argentina over the Falkland Islands in 1982. To her opponents and those who warned of possible defeat in the war, Thatcher responded, "Defeat—I do not recognize the meaning of the word." Likewise, when Iraq invaded Kuwait in 1990, she provided invaluable support to the international coalition created by President George H. W. Bush.

Winning three elections and holding office from 1979 to 1990, Thatcher served longer than any other British prime minister since the late nineteenth century. Next to Winston Churchill, she is considered by many people to have been the most important British political leader in the twentieth century.

Japan

Like West Germany, Japan made great strides politically and economically after World War II. General MacArthur headed the occupation government that oversaw the rebuilding of the devastated nation. When Emperor Hirohito publicly repudiated claims to deity, MacArthur became the real leader of the Japanese nation. Launching a massive reform movement, he called for women's suffrage, promoted the formation of labor unions, requested Christian missionaries to come to Japan, and, ultimately, imposed a new constitution on Japan. The result was a stable democracy, a remarkable contrast to Japan's recent militaristic tradition.

With the removal of the occupation government, Japan proved competent to rule itself. The Liberal-Democratic Party took control in 1955 and held power continuously until 1993. Political stability contributed to striking economic growth. In addition to providing billions of dollars in financial aid to Japan, America supplied technology, markets, and raw materials for a strong industrial base. Military protection by the West allowed Japan to pour its wealth into industrial development. (The new constitution strictly forbade Japan to have an army.)

The bullet train speeds by rice harvesters near Mount Fuji, Japan

In addition, Japan's own hard work and a superior educational system pushed the Japanese to the economic forefront. The Japanese excelled in heavy industry. In automobile manufacturing, their well-built, fuel-efficient cars allowed the nation to displace the United States as the leader in auto production. The Japanese pioneered the development of electronics by stressing the use of transistors and other technological innovations. In the 1950s critics joked that "Made in Japan" was a synonym for cheap, shoddy products; by the 1980s Japan was cornering the world market in high-quality televisions, stereos, radios, and other electronic equipment. Japanese companies such as Mitsubishi, Toyota, Sony, and Nintendo became household words around the world. The Japanese also developed a passenger rail system that became the envy of the industrialized world.

Japan still faced problems, however. Foreign nations resented the Japanese government's high tariffs and trade restrictions that protected Japanese industries from competition. Although such actions did protect Japan, they prompted Japanese trading partners to retaliate with their own trade barriers. Still, the rise of a prosperous, democratic Japan from the rubble of totalitarianism and military defeat was one of the great success stories of the postwar era.

Section Review

1. What was the purpose of the Truman Doctrine?

2. What role did the city of Berlin play in the postwar confrontation between the West and the Soviet Union?

3–4. What Western regional military alliance was organized in 1949? What was its Soviet counterpart?

5–6. Summarize two reasons for Germany's remarkable recovery following World War II.

7–8. Outline two reasons for Japan's monumental recovery following World War II.

★ Analyze reasons for confrontation between the West and the Soviet Union during the Cold War.

★ Explain the West's containment policies after World War II.

Guiding Questions

1. What was the significance of China's fall to communism?
2. What were the key events of the Korean War?
3. What were the important events of the Vietnam War?
4. How did communism and the West engage in proxy conflicts in the third world?

II. Struggle for Independence and Cold War Conflict

Eastern Europe was not the only critical region in the Cold War era. Bolstered by the Soviet Union, the unrelenting march of communism continued around the world. In Asia, the Middle East, Africa, and Latin America, country after country fell under the yoke of communism. The Soviet empire alone encompassed one-fourth of the world's land area. During the postwar period, tension between the free world and the Communist bloc flared several times into wars limited to specific geographic areas, often called contained or **limited wars**. Instead of confronting each other directly in these military actions, the United States and the Soviet Union supported other nations to protect and maintain their respective spheres of influence around the world. For example, the Soviets supported North Vietnam against the United States in the 1960s and early 1970s, and the United States aided Afghan forces against the Soviets in the 1980s.

China
The Fall

One of the first areas outside Europe to face the threat of communism was China. After the defeat of Japan in 1945, civil war between the Nationalist forces of Chiang Kai-shek and the Communist forces of Mao Zedong resumed in China. The conflict continued until 1949. Despite receiving more than $2 billion in American aid, the Nationalist forces could not defeat the Communists. As that aid was reduced, the leaders of China, who had relied on American help to defeat the Communists, found themselves militarily and economically vulnerable. By 1949 Mao's forces had captured the major cities of China, sealing the fate of Chiang. The Communist forces drove the Nationalist armies off the mainland and to the nearby island of Formosa (Taiwan).

Chiang's collapse was a major blow to American interests in Asia. America had fought World War II, in part, to secure the freedom of China from Japanese militarism, but the country fell to the Communists. For the next thirty years, the United States recognized Taiwan as the real China and refused diplomatic ties with the Communist government in Beijing. A huge landmass encompassing the Soviet Union and China was under Communist rule, posing a serious problem for the West during the Cold War era.

Communist Rule

After taking the mainland from the Nationalist government in 1949, Mao Zedong and his Communist forces established a cruel dictatorship in China. Thousands of people who were considered enemies of the Communist state—former Nationalists, intellectuals, businessmen, Christians—were sent to prison camps or executed. Like the Soviet Communists in the 1920s, the Chinese sought to establish an atheistic state through force and repression.

Seeing the need to compete with the free world and the Soviet Union, Mao initiated programs to modernize China. With the "Great Leap Forward" in the late 1950s, Mao sought to improve Chinese agriculture and bring the steel industry up to Western standards. Instead, his ill-planned reforms wrecked the Chinese steel

Mao Zedong

industry and caused a famine that resulted in the deaths of twenty to thirty million Chinese. In the late 1960s, Mao launched the **Cultural Revolution**, an attempt to stir up zeal for radical communism. Young Communists, called the Red Guard, held rallies and indulged in acts of violence designed to promote revolutionary fervor. They disrupted the Chinese educational system until it could be "purified" in an acceptably radical manner. The result of the Cultural Revolution was civil chaos and economic decline. Mao abandoned it after only a few years, and Chinese authorities suppressed Mao's radical supporters.

Western leaders were somewhat relieved when Mao died in 1976. The Communist leaders who succeeded him—Deng Xiaoping, Hu Yaobang, and Zhao Ziyang—seemed to be more moderate in their rule. China's Communist overlords allowed limited free-market reforms and scaled back some of Mao's more repressive measures.

Chinese Cultural Revolution propaganda poster

The true nature of the Communist state had not changed, however, as was shown tragically in 1989. In a year when communism seemed to be collapsing around the world, a reform movement sprang up among Chinese students. They called for the reform of the Chinese state, particularly the granting of greater political freedom. In April 1989 a group of students began a demonstration in **Tiananmen Square** in the Chinese capital of Beijing. More and more people joined the demonstration, and people around the world watched on television as the students protested repressive rule. News of the event quickly spread, making it difficult for the Communists to misinform the world or spin the events in their favor. Then the Communist authorities cracked down. In early June tanks rolled into Tiananmen Square. Hundreds, perhaps thousands were killed as the government quashed the student movement. There was no rebirth of freedom in China as there had been elsewhere in the former Communist bloc. The students, though, had demonstrated that strong dissent still existed within Communist China despite forty years of oppression.

Often overlooked in many histories of China is the violent persecution that Chinese Christians have endured under communism. Many stories have emerged of arrests, imprisonment, and brutal treatment of Christians by the Communist Chinese. However, many of those Christians have stood firm and spread the gospel even under the most trying circumstances. Despite harsh treatment by authorities, the church in China is thriving. Chinese Christians are now estimated to number over one hundred million and continue to multiply even as the Communist authorities frequently harass and imprison the leaders of the church.

Korea

Communist Invasion and Western Reaction

Asia remained a hot spot in the East-West confrontation when Communist North Korea invaded South Korea and sparked the **Korean War** (1950–53). At the close of World War II, Korea had been divided, like Germany, into Communist and non-Communist occupation zones. North Korean forces, trained and financed by the Soviet Union, now sought to unite all of Korea under Communist rule. In June 1950 North Korean forces invaded South Korea, confirming the worst fears of the West—that Communists intended to continue expanding their influence.

President Truman viewed this invasion as another example of Soviet expansion; such aggression, he believed, had to be stopped. Therefore, he called on the free world, led by the United States, to halt the Communist conquest of South Korea. Rather than appealing to Congress for a declaration of war, however, President Truman appealed to the United Nations. Although other nations joined the fight against the North Koreans, the war was primarily an American effort.

Success and Stalemate

The initial North Korean advance had overrun most of the Korean peninsula. However, under the command of General **Douglas MacArthur**, UN forces composed primarily of American and South Korean troops mounted a daring counteroffensive. Following an amphibious assault at Inchon, UN forces secured South Korea, driving the enemy across the **38th parallel** (the border between North and South Korea). They pursued the enemy deep into North Korea, pushing all the way to the Yalu River (the border between North Korea and Communist China). Just as the UN forces seemed on the verge of victory, waves of Communist Chinese troops swept across the Chinese border, overwhelming MacArthur's army and forcing a retreat to the 38th parallel.

General MacArthur, wanting to gain a military victory, proposed a major assault on North Korea that would have included bombing Chinese bases in Manchuria. Such action would escalate the conflict but would be necessary for ultimate victory. However, the risk of widening the war in Asia and possibly involving both China and the Soviet Union led Truman to fight a limited war with a negotiated settlement. Truman's chairman of the Joint Chiefs of Staff, General Omar Bradley, expressed the administration's sentiment that MacArthur's plan would provoke "the wrong war, at the

Korean War

U.S. forces in the Korean War: (left) *Machine gun crew near the Chongchon River;* (right) *Loading a 105 mm howitzer*

wrong place, at the wrong time, and with the wrong enemy." Frustrated, MacArthur bypassed regular channels for expressing his views to the government and made his views public. On April 11, 1951, an angry Truman responded by relieving MacArthur of his command. That same year, negotiations to end the war began.

For two years, both hostilities and peace negotiations continued. Finally, in July 1953, an armistice was signed, ending the fighting. It provided for a demilitarized zone between North and South Korea and called for a conference to settle questions about Korea's future, but the conference was never held. The years of bloodshed ended in a stalemate with the Korean peninsula returning to its prewar divided state. Communism had been contained—not defeated—but at a great price. More than a million Koreans and Chinese lay dead from the conflict; about 54,000 Americans would not return home.

Vietnam

The French Phase

Another significant challenge to the containment of communism during the Cold War came in the Southeast Asian country of Vietnam. The Japanese had captured French Indochina, which included Vietnam, during World War II. After the war, the French wanted to recover their colony, but Vietnamese Communist **Ho Chi Minh** declared his country's independence, and a struggle with the French ensued. The Indochinese war increased in significance with China's fall to communism in 1949 and the beginning of the Korean War the next year.

The year after the Korean armistice, the Vietnamese Communists scored a major victory over the French in the Battle of Dien Bien Phu, annihilating a major French army. The French, no longer able or willing to reclaim their former colony, sought a negotiated settlement. At the Geneva Conference of 1954, the Communists won a diplomatic victory: Vietnam was divided into two parts at the 17th parallel—the Communist north and the non-Communist south. Almost immediately, Communist guerrillas, known as the **Viet Cong**, began subversive activity in the south. Their goal was to weaken the South Vietnamese government so that they could unite Vietnam under a Communist government led by Ho Chi Minh.

To keep South Vietnam and other Asian nations free from communism, the United States, Great Britain, France, and several non-Communist Asian nations formed the Southeast Asia Treaty Organization (**SEATO**) in 1954. In theory, the member nations agreed to consult with each other concerning any Communist aggression in that part of the world. In practice, they were pledging military assistance against the Communist menace.

As the chief member of SEATO, the United States began supporting the non-Communist government in South Vietnam economically and militarily. Behind America's foreign policy lay what U.S. president Dwight Eisenhower called the **domino theory**: if South Vietnam fell to communism, then other countries of Asia would fall like a row of dominos. The United States was determined that South Vietnam would not be that first domino. Although presidents Eisenhower and Kennedy sent only a limited number of American military advisers to help South Vietnam, their aid marked the beginning of a major military commitment. American leaders had decided to settle the conflict through direct military involvement.

Ho Chi Minh

The American Phase

In 1964 North Vietnamese torpedo boats allegedly attacked American destroyers that were in international waters in the Gulf of Tonkin. Through the **Gulf of Tonkin Resolution**, the American Congress authorized President Lyndon Johnson to "take all necessary measures to repel any armed attack against forces of the United States and to prevent further aggression." Congress also authorized the president to take "all necessary steps, including the use of armed force, to assist any member . . . of the Southeast Asia Collective Defense Treaty requesting assistance in defense of its freedom." The number of American military personnel in Vietnam jumped from 23,000 in 1964 to a high of 542,000 in 1969. In 1965 the United States also began bombing Communist supply routes and bases in North Vietnam.

U.S. soldiers deploying from a helicopter

A pivotal year in American involvement in the Vietnam War was 1968. Military officials believed that they were making progress against the Communist enemy. But the Viet Cong demonstrated surprising strength in their **Tet** (New Year) **offensive** on South Vietnamese cities. In that coordinated attack, the Communists temporarily occupied many major cities of South Vietnam and even briefly captured part of the American embassy compound. In purely military terms, the offensive was a failure; American and South Vietnamese forces drove the Communists back and inflicted heavy casualties. Its propaganda value, however, was enormous. Tet showed that the war was not almost won, as the American government was claiming. For many Americans, frustration increased, and victory seemed even further away.

President Johnson, faced with growing public dissatisfaction with American involvement in the war, saw no likely prospect of military success through limited war. He decided not to seek reelection, halted the bombing of North Vietnam, and initiated peace talks with the Communists.

Richard Nixon, who won the 1968 presidential election, began a gradual American withdrawal from Vietnam and turned the burden of the fighting over to the South Vietnamese in a program that he called **Vietnamization**. However, to keep pressure on the North, he continued heavy bombing in that region and in the spring of 1970 ordered an invasion of Cambodia to cut Communist supply routes. Nixon finally achieved what he called "peace with honor" by negotiating a peace settlement with the North Vietnamese in January 1973. According to that agreement, U.S. troops evacuated South Vietnam. However, without American troops, the South Vietnamese could neither defeat the Communists nor hold on to their own country. In 1975 the war ended with the achievement of Ho Chi Minh's goal: a unified Vietnam under Communist control. The Communists also took over the neighboring countries of Laos and Cambodia. The domino theory had proved partially true.

The Middle East

The Middle East is also part of the developing world. The region is important as a strategic source of wealth and a troubled center

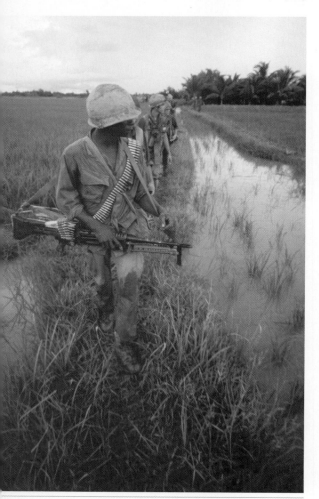

U.S. soldiers crossing a flooded rice paddy

of conflict, and it has great significance for the Western industrial nations because it holds some of the world's largest oil reserves. In addition, several countries in the Middle East are or have been controlled until recently by brutal dictators or radical groups.

Two of the most disruptive elements in the Middle East are ethnic and religious factors. Except for Iran and Turkey, most countries in the area are Arab. Israel, though controlled by Jews, also has a large Arab population. Islam is the dominant religion in the region, although pockets of Jews and Christians also exist there.

All of these features combine to make the Middle East a volatile region. This should come as no surprise for the Christian, since history after the Flood began in the Middle East and will end in the Middle East with the return of Christ (Rev. 19).

Energy Resource

While man has discovered many energy sources, oil remains one of the main sources of energy for transportation, heat, and production of electricity. Even though oil is available in many regions of the world, most nations import much of their oil from the volatile Middle East. These imports grant significant importance to an area dominated by Islam. Since oil continues to produce most of the energy consumed in many countries, those who provide this resource will continue to exercise a great influence over the nations that import it.

Arab-Israeli Conflicts

Much of the postwar tension in the Middle East has resulted from the return of the Jews to Palestine and the creation of the national state of Israel. The history of Israel and its neighbors has been one of armed truces punctuated by open warfare. In each conflict Israel has shown amazing strength and military cunning to overcome its more numerous foes, but military victory has not brought peace.

The modern state of Israel was literally born of war in 1948. The United Nations attempted to divide Palestine peacefully between the Jews and the Arabs. Instead, war followed as Arab forces from Egypt, Jordan, Syria, Lebanon, and Iraq tried to drive the Jews from Palestine. Against great odds, the Israelis defeated their opponents and won their war for independence. However, the uneasy peace provided no final settlement. The Arab states refused to recognize the existence of Israel and dedicated themselves to Israel's destruction.

The Suez Crisis

The tension between Israel and the Arab community led to war again in 1956, when Egypt unilaterally took control of the Suez Canal. Fearing Egyptian moves against their nation, the Israelis agreed to aid Britain and France by moving into the Sinai Peninsula, thereby giving those nations an excuse to take control of the Suez Canal. The Israeli army conquered Sinai with surprising ease, but it had to withdraw when international pressure forced Britain and France to back down.

The Six-Day War

A UN peacekeeping force remained in Sinai until 1967, when the Egyptian government asked them to leave before it launched a new attack on Israel. Realizing that Egypt, Syria, and Jordan were preparing to attack, Israel launched a preemptive strike. The Israeli air force caught the Egyptian planes on the ground, destroyed them, and then turned on Syria and Jordan. The Israelis again routed a larger foe. They captured the Sinai Peninsula, the West Bank (territory on the west bank of the Jordan River, including Jerusalem), the Gaza Strip (along the Mediterranean coast), and the Golan Heights (along the Israeli-Syrian border).

The Yom Kippur War

Victory still did not bring peace. In 1973 Egypt and Syria attacked without warning on October 6, Yom Kippur, the Jewish Day of Atonement. In that war the Arab allies enjoyed initial success, but the Israelis, led by defense minister Moshe Dayan and resupplied by the United States, ultimately repulsed the Arab forces.

The Palestinian Question

While there are various opinions about what *Palestinian* means, the term usually refers to a group of Arab-speaking people who trace their lineage to people who, over the past several centuries, lived in Palestine. Because they have lived in the land for so long, Palestinians consider land currently occupied by the modern state of Israel to be their own and insist on its return. Organized as the Palestine Liberation Organization (**PLO**) in 1964 under the leadership of Yasser Arafat, the Palestinians have continued to demand that Israel give them land in order to form a separate Palestinian state. During two periods, 1987–93 and 2000–2005, the war of words escalated to a violent outburst known as *intifada* ("uprising"), resulting in several thousand deaths. *Hamas*, a radical Islamic group recognized as a terrorist organization by the UN, developed during the first *intifada* as a more radical Islamic counterpart to the PLO. *Hamas* gained popularity through social and religious leadership, physical aid to Palestinians, and terrorist activities against Israel. *Hamas* won an election and gained control of the Palestinian government in 2007. Despite seemingly endless peace negotiations and U.S. diplomatic involvement at the highest levels, peace has eluded this region.

Africa and Latin America
Africa

As in Asia, Moscow had an opportunity to extend its influence in Africa in the wake of the disintegration of European colonial empires. Following World War II, one African country after another gained its independence from European colonial rule. Many of these countries turned to the Soviets for assistance in their struggle against the imperialistic forces of the West. In other countries, Communist forces used the turmoil and discontent to encourage revolution. Communist regimes enjoyed some success in Ethiopia, Mozambique, and Angola. Newly independent countries also sought financial and military assistance from the Soviet Union and its Communist allies. However, many African countries soon began to realize that their pro-Soviet alliances came with strings attached. These countries fell prey to a new form of colonial control, that of Soviet, Cuban, and Chinese Communists. Sadly, the West responded to Communist expansion in Africa with little more than words.

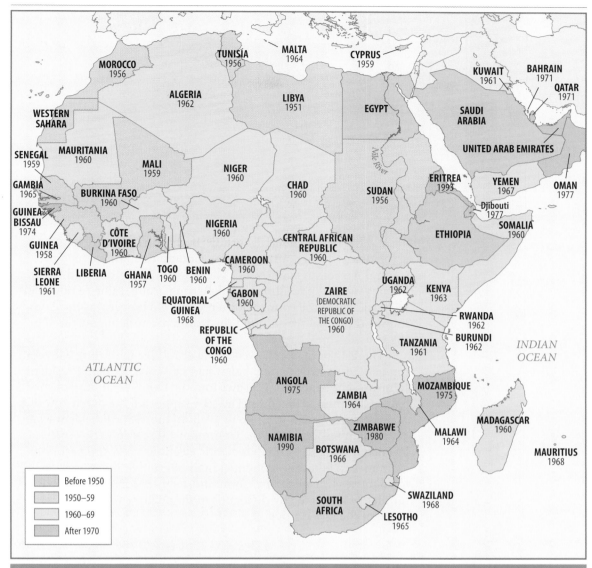

Map legend:
- Before 1950
- 1950–59
- 1960–69
- After 1970

Decolonization of Africa Since WWII

Latin America

The cause of containing communism moved closer to home for the United States as communism gained a foothold in Latin America. In the decades following World War II, Latin American countries were still suffering from social and political inequality, poverty, poor education, and dictatorial governments. As the Communists began to exploit the unsettled conditions in the region, Americans became more alarmed. Some Latin American countries looked to the Soviets instead of the United States for economic assistance in reaction to what they called "Yankee imperialism."

In 1959 Communist dictator **Fidel Castro** seized power in Cuba and allied his country with the Soviet Union. Cuban exiles, supported by the U.S. Central Intelligence Agency (CIA), attempted an invasion to oust Castro in 1961. However, Castro learned of the planned invasion, and President Kennedy aborted the American support of the mission. This resulted in a fiasco known as the **Bay of Pigs**.

Fidel Castro

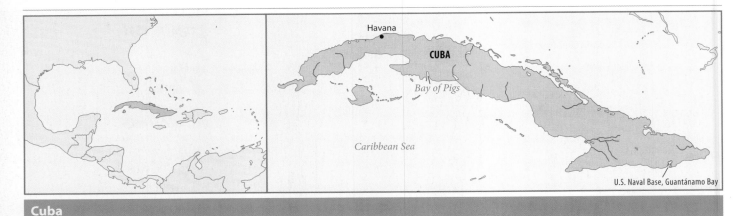

Cuba

Castro-backed guerrilla groups began stirring up revolutionary activity throughout the region. Communism threatened the Central American countries of Nicaragua, El Salvador, and Panama. In Nicaragua, the Sandinistas, a left-wing group, came to power in 1979 and ruled the country for ten years. No longer was the Communist threat halfway around the world; it was being nurtured in the United States' backyard.

The United States showed stronger resolve in dealing with communism in Latin America than it had in Africa. In 1965 President Johnson sent American Marines into the Dominican Republic to halt a Communist takeover. The CIA supported the overthrow of a Marxist government in Chile in 1973. In the 1980s President Ronald Reagan responded to the Communist threat in Latin America by encouraging free and democratic elections, providing economic assistance to faltering economies, and offering military assistance to countries threatened by Communist aggression. His firm stand ultimately began to pay dividends in the collapse of Marxist regimes south of the U.S. border.

Section Review

1. What was the significance of the island of Formosa?
2. How did Communist China influence the outcome of the Korean War?
3. Explain the domino theory.
4. What was the purpose of the Gulf of Tonkin Resolution?
★ Trace the course of the Korean War.
★ Why did the United States respond more aggressively to the Communist threat in Latin America than it had in Africa?

Guiding Questions

1. What strategies emerged during the Cold War?
2. What led to the collapse of the Soviet Union?

III. Showdown Between the Superpowers
Coexistence and Tension

Despite the ongoing struggle between the free and Communist worlds regarding the spread of communism, relations between the United States and the Soviet Union improved during the 1950s. In 1953 Stalin died and **Nikita Khrushchev** (KROOSH chef) emerged as the new leader of the Soviet Union. He and the new American president, Dwight Eisenhower, pursued a course of **peaceful coexistence**. According to Khrushchev, "The main thing is to keep to the

Nikita Khrushchev

Sputnik

positions of ideological struggle without resorting to arms to prove that one is right."

The prospect of peaceful coexistence was short-lived, however. By the late 1950s, East-West relations were once again stormy. In 1957 the Russians launched *Sputnik*, the first man-made earth satellite, causing great alarm for the people of the United States. Americans looked upon their country as the world leader in science and technology; they now found themselves in second place in what would become the race for space. They particularly feared that the Soviets would use this new capability for a possible nuclear missile strike.

America responded with a renewed resolve to strengthen education (especially in science) and an intense acceleration of its own space program. President Kennedy pledged to put a man on the moon by the end of the 1960s—a promise that the government fulfilled during the Nixon presidency.

While attempting to keep track of Soviet activities, the United States suffered an embarrassing setback in May 1960. Two weeks before a major summit conference between the Western allies and the Soviet Union, an American U-2 reconnaissance (spy) plane piloted by Gary Powers was shot down while flying over Russian territory. Khrushchev used the **U-2 incident** as an excuse for breaking off talks at the Paris summit conference. The Soviet defense minister announced that if further flights over the USSR occurred, the Soviets would fire rockets on the base from which the plane took off. Powers was tried by the Russians and found guilty of espionage and imprisoned. He was released in 1962 in a prisoner exchange.

Spy plane

The U-2 incident was only a mild prelude to clashes between the free world and Soviet totalitarianism in the early 1960s. The first center of tension was Berlin. The constant flow of refugees from Communist East Germany into Western Europe was a living testimony to the failures of communism. Embarrassed by the mass exodus, the Soviets in August 1961 built a concrete-and-barbed-wire wall separating East and West Berlin. The **Berlin Wall** became the most recognizable symbol of the Cold War struggle between the free world and communism. In a sense, it was an admission of failure by the Communists, but it kept their most productive citizens within the Communist bloc.

In addition to the wall itself, would-be escapees had to contend with more barbed wire, attack dogs, land mines, and armed guards with shoot-to-kill orders. But that did not keep people from trying to escape. Some people tried to climb over, jump over from nearby multistoried buildings, tunnel under, or even sail over in a home-made hot-air balloon. Many died in their attempts.

The Cold War heated up briefly in 1962 when the United States discovered that the Soviets were installing nuclear missiles in Castro's Cuba. In what has been called the **Cuban missile crisis**, President Kennedy insisted that the Soviets remove the missiles. To enforce his demand, he ordered a blockade of the island. Khrushchev backed down and had the missiles removed. The United States and the Soviet Union narrowly avoided a full-scale war.

Thaws in the Cold War

In the early 1970s, President Nixon took dramatic steps to end the Cold War. In 1972 he became the first American president to visit mainland China, even though the United States at that time did not recognize the Communist Chinese government. His secretary of state, Henry Kissinger, worked toward a policy of **détente** (relaxation of tensions) with the Soviet Union. Cooperation and summit meetings replaced the harsh language and hostile positions of the superpowers. In 1972 Nixon visited the Soviet Union and signed the Strategic Arms Limitations Talks (SALT) treaty with the Soviets, which limited the number of nuclear weapons that each superpower could possess.

The United States entered the 1980s in a weakened position. Economically, recession gripped the country. Militarily, years of disarmament talks and broken Soviet promises left the United States in a precarious position of having to catch up with the military production of its Soviet counterpart. But the American resolve to stand against the threat of communism found a champion in President Reagan, elected in 1980. He was determined to restore America's prestige in the world; at the same time, he denounced the evils of communism. Wanting to deal with the Soviets from a position of strength, Reagan gained support for a buildup of America's military. He proposed a new weapons system, the Strategic Defense Initiative (**SDI**), called "Star Wars" by its detractors, which was designed to use American space, laser, and satellite technology to provide a shield against incoming Soviet missiles.

Although some people in the United States were skeptical of SDI, the Soviets were alarmed. The arms race, which had been balanced in their favor, was now tipping toward the United States. They withdrew from arms-control negotiations, insisting that they would not return until the United States was willing to stop work on SDI.

Collapse of the Soviet Empire
Reasons for Decline

In spite of this renewed confrontation between the superpowers, the relationship between the Soviet Union and the free world began to change. Several factors made this dramatic development possible. One was the growing unrest of Eastern Europeans who suffered under the yoke of Soviet rule. They expressed their opposition to Soviet control through demonstrations and uprisings.

True Soviet Intentions

By the end of the 1970s, it was apparent that the Soviets were still intent on military aggression. This was clearly demonstrated in December 1979 when Soviet troops invaded neighboring Afghanistan. The free world was alarmed over not only the Soviet invasion of Afghanistan but also the possible Soviet threat to the world's oil supplies in the Persian Gulf region.

Another factor contributing to change was unsettled leadership in the Soviet Union. In the first five decades following the creation of Communist Russia, the leadership of the Soviet government had been vested mainly in the hands of three brutal and deceptive men: Lenin, Stalin, and Khrushchev. When Khrushchev left office in 1964, a brief power struggle occurred between Aleksei Kosygin and Leonid Brezhnev (1906–82). Kosygin thought that the Soviet Union should relax tensions with the West while strengthening the Soviet economy. Brezhnev, however, favored a hard line toward the West, an extensive development of the Soviet military, and continued export of communism to other countries. Brezhnev's views won, Kosygin passed into oblivion, and Brezhnev ruled with an iron hand for almost twenty years. But the continuity and longevity of leadership was broken in 1982 with the death of Brezhnev. Over the next three years, two men headed the Soviet state: Yuri Andropov and Konstantin Chernenko, neither of whom was in office for much more than a year. When Ronald Reagan was criticized for his lack of success in negotiating with the Soviets, he replied with exasperation, "Well, they keep dying on me!" This rapid change in Soviet leadership was partially the result of the advancing age of the elite within the Communist Party. A battle began to emerge between the younger, more pragmatic leaders and the aging hard-liners.

The economic woes so prevalent under the Communist system caused many younger Soviets to recognize the need for reform. Communism had built basic industries in Russia early in the century but could not match the material abundance of the West's consumer society. Soviet farms consistently performed poorly. Central planning rather than market forces guided the economy, and the lack of incentives for Soviet workers resulted in low productivity. In the high-technology, scientific world of the 1980s, the Soviets were lagging far behind the West.

Contributing to the Soviet economic decline was the enormous drain of national wealth spent on defense. The arms race during the Cold War ultimately bankrupted the Soviet Union, especially in the 1980s after Reagan increased the pressure with America's defensive buildup.

Perestroika and Glasnost

By the mid-1980s, the defects in the Soviet political and economic system could no longer be hidden. The new Soviet premier, **Mikhail Gorbachev**, called for a wide range of social, political, and economic reforms called *perestroika*, or "restructuring." Through *perestroika*, he sought to increase industrial productivity; stimulate technological development; restructure the stagnant, inefficient bureaucracy; decentralize management of the economy; and experiment with a free-market system.

Gorbachev knew that his quest for reform would be in vain unless he could gain public support to put pressure on the "Old Guard" in the Communist Party. In addition, he desperately needed financial assistance from the West to implement his programs.

Ronald Reagan and Mikhail Gorbachev

Therefore, he linked to *perestroika* the concept of **glasnost**, or "openness." Gorbachev hoped to create a more democratic atmosphere in which the Soviet government would be more forthright and accountable to the people. He encouraged open discussions of the problems facing the country and a self-examination of the Soviet state. Under *glasnost*, the Soviet people were encouraged to evaluate and even criticize their leaders to promote better government. But given an opportunity they had not experienced for nearly seventy years, the Soviet people voiced opposition to the very foundation of the Soviet state—communism. They did not want to reform that corrupt system; they wanted to abolish it.

Gorbachev, whether purposely or inadvertently, set in motion forces that led to the undoing of the Soviet state and the rejection of communism. As a former White House official said, "Gorbachev has let the genie out of the bottle, and his successors will not be able to stuff it back in."

Unrest in Eastern Europe

As the 1980s drew to a close, the Soviet empire began unraveling with amazing speed. Gorbachev's internal reforms encouraged new waves of protest against the Soviet Union in Soviet-dominated Eastern Europe. In Poland, resistance to the Communist government had been maintained by Solidarity, a powerful labor union. In 1989 Solidarity-led forces secured the election of the first non-Communist prime minister in Poland since World War II. In 1990 **Lech Walesa**, the head of Solidarity and leader of the movement for reform and resistance, was elected president. Hungary and Czechoslovakia, nations in which the Soviets had crushed democratic movements in 1956 and 1968 respectively, began distancing themselves from the Soviets and ultimately repudiated communism.

Lech Walesa

The Fall of the Berlin Wall

On June 12, 1987, President Reagan stood on the West German side of the Berlin Wall and challenged the Soviet leader: "General Secretary Gorbachev, if you seek peace, if you seek prosperity for the Soviet Union and Eastern Europe, if you seek liberalization: Come here to this gate! Mr. Gorbachev, open this gate! Mr. Gorbachev, tear down this wall!" In November 1989 East German protesters attacked that symbol of Communist isolationism and totalitarianism. They began hammering away at the concrete structure. Soon even the guards, who had once shot people for getting too close to the wall, joined the protesters in tearing it down. Through its breaches, East Germans poured into West Berlin, reuniting with family members and experiencing freedom for the first time. Soon the government of East Germany collapsed, and in 1990 the two Germanys became one nation.

Berlin Wall memorial with photos of those who were killed while trying to go over the wall

Hungary and Czechoslovakia opened their borders to the West. This action had an unexpected effect on East Germany, supposedly one of the most prosperous Soviet-bloc countries. The East Germans expressed discontent with the Communist regime by a mass exodus. By hundreds and then thousands, they went around the Berlin Wall and guarded borders, escaping to the West through Hungary and Czechoslovakia. By the time the Communist government tried to act, it was too late. The momentum of protest was out of hand and would not be satisfied until communism and Soviet control were overthrown. The Berlin Wall fell in 1989, and freedom became contagious.

Unrest in the USSR

While Soviet leaders witnessed the disintegration of their domination over Eastern Europe, they struggled to maintain control at home. Many internal challenges threatened to tear the country apart. Ethnic unrest in the Soviet republics of Armenia and Azerbaijan led to widespread violence. The Baltic republics of Latvia, Lithuania, and Estonia moved toward separation from the Soviet Union. Reformers, upset at the slow pace of Gorbachev's reforms, called for his resignation. They supported the decentralization of government, the independence movements of the republics, a speedier transition toward a free-market economy, and more freedom of expression. Leading the opposition to Gorbachev was Boris Yeltsin, an ex-Communist whose support of reform helped him to be elected president of Russia, the largest of the Soviet republics.

In August 1991 the hard-line Communists made a last stand. Soviet Communist leaders detained Gorbachev and announced that he was ill. Furthermore, the Communist Party ordered a six-month "state of emergency." Soviet citizens, led by Yeltsin, resisted, launching a general strike as Yeltsin denounced the action of the hard-liners. The army refused to obey orders to fire on the crowds, and the Communist coup collapsed.

In December 1991 eleven of the Soviet republics declared their independence from the Soviet Union. Following the leadership of Russia, they formed the Commonwealth of Independent States (CIS). Gorbachev was a ruler without a country. On December 25, with little fanfare, he resigned. The Soviet Union dissolved into independent republics, and, with its demise, communism was repudiated.

Section Review

1. What term did Khrushchev use to indicate that the United States and the Soviet Union could agree to disagree without resorting to arms?
2. What crisis close to the U.S. border almost led to war between the United States and the Soviet Union in 1962?
3. What does the word *perestroika* mean?
4. Explain the significance of *glasnost*.
5. Who was the last leader of the Soviet Union?
* Why did the Soviet invasion of Afghanistan alarm the free world?
* Compare or contrast the strategies used to address Cold War conflicts.

Guiding Questions

1. Why was transitioning from communism difficult for Eastern European countries following the collapse of the USSR?
2. Why did Eastern Europe fragment after the end of Soviet control?

IV. Aftermath of the Cold War

The collapse of the Soviet Union signaled "a new birth of freedom" for many oppressed peoples. With that freedom, however, came many problems. The people in some countries noticed little difference in their lives; the change in governments was more like the changing of jailers in a prison than the opening of the prison doors. In some cases, not even the jailers changed.

The Former Soviet Union

The events within the former Soviet Union illustrated the blessings and difficulties of the collapse of communism. Some former republics of the USSR—notably the Baltic states of Estonia, Latvia, and Lithuania—wanted little to do with their former overlords. Some of the newly independent republics merely maintained repressive rule under another name. Three republics in particular dominated the new Commonwealth of Independent States. Ukraine and Belarus, located the farthest west, were among the most populous, most prosperous, and most industrialized of the new republics. Their transition to independence, therefore, was a little easier. The most important of the new republics, however, was Russia. With more than half of the population and more than three-fourths of the landmass of the former Soviet Union, Russia is a notable world power on its own. The United Nations recognized this fact by granting Russia the Soviet Union's seat on the UN Security Council.

The Russians now enjoyed greater freedom than they had at any other time in their history, but the drastic change from communism to a free-market economy created inflation and unemployment. The troubles of the Soviet economy, which had sparked the drastic political changes, did not disappear with the overthrow of communism. With its antiquated technology, inefficient management policies, poor system of transportation, and nearly worthless currency, Russia had to begin almost from scratch to rebuild its economy.

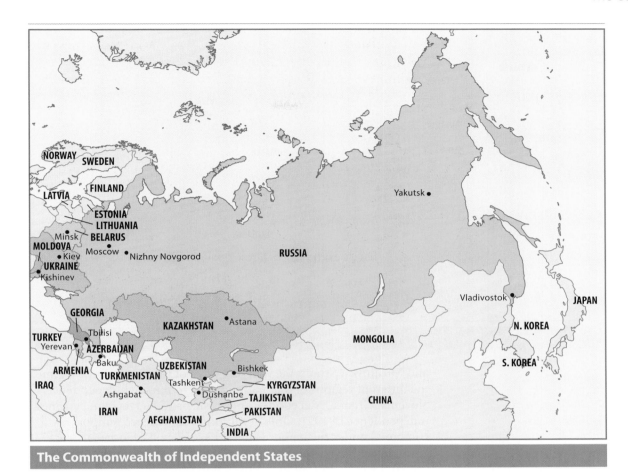

The Commonwealth of Independent States

President Boris Yeltsin, who had been praised for standing up to the Communist coup in August 1991, found himself roundly criticized for problems that he could do little to solve. Shortages and unrest marked the difficult transition from tyranny to freedom.

Eastern Europe

The former Soviet empire in Eastern Europe likewise endured a difficult transition. Some nations, such as Poland and Hungary, made the transition to democratic government and a free economy without violence, though not always without pain. In other nations, physical suffering overshadowed the economic suffering. Romania overthrew its Communist leader in violent revolution, executing dictator Nicolae Ceausescu and his wife on Christmas Day 1989. The violence did not stop with that act, however. Riots continued to rend the nation after the Communist overthrow, and Romania found itself exchanging one form of dictatorship for another.

Czechoslovakia was an unusual case. The western half of the nation, dominated by the Czechs, was eager to embrace a Western-style economy. The less prosperous eastern half, dominated by the Slovaks, preferred a slow transition from a controlled economy. Faced with an irreconcilable conflict, the two halves decided peacefully to pursue separate paths. In 1993 Czechoslovakia became two nations: the Czech Republic and Slovakia.

The division of Yugoslavia, however, was not peaceful. Ever since its creation after World War I, Yugoslavia had been an uneasy mixture of different ethnic groups (including Serbs, Croats, and Slovenes) and religious groups (Eastern Orthodox, Roman Catholic,

Immediate Post-Communist Eastern Europe

and Muslim). Without the unifying force of the Communist regime, the different regions of that nation began to pursue independence. Slovenia, Croatia, Macedonia, and Bosnia and Herzegovina claimed independence in 1991. Only Serbia and Montenegro temporarily combined under the name "Federal Republic of Yugoslavia." Violence marred the breakup of Yugoslavia. The Serbs particularly resented the reduction of their power and feared for the fate of Serbs, who were now minorities in the other former Yugoslav republics.

The result was bloody civil war. Thousands of civilians died, particularly in Bosnia, where the Serbs sent arms and troops to "protect" Serb minorities—and carve out more territory for the Serb-dominated government of Yugoslavia. To help knit the acquired regions to Yugoslavia, the Serbs began the forced removal or even killing of non-Serbs in the conquered regions. Anarchy reigned even as the UN sought a peaceful solution. Described as the powder keg of Europe before World War I, the Balkans had again become a center of terror and violence by the end of the twentieth century. Years of Communist rule had done little to bring a sense of unity to that troubled region.

Section Review

1–2. Which of the former Soviet republics became the most important player in world politics? Who was its first president?

3–4. Over what European country did dictator Nicolae Ceausescu rule? How did his rule end?

5. After the collapse of communism in Eastern Europe, what former Communist nation broke into several smaller republics and engaged in ethnic civil war?

✶ Analyze the difficulties of transitioning away from communism after the collapse of the USSR.

✶ Why have the Balkans been described as the powder keg of Europe, what forces have restrained this region in the past, and how did the collapse of the USSR lead to renewed hostilities?

Making Connections

1. Why was this period in history called the Cold War?

2–6. Summarize five events that could have led to another major war.

7–8. Contrast the leaders who struggled to rule China during this period.

9–10. Summarize two conditions that contributed to the fall of the Soviet Union.

Developing History Skills

1. Compare/contrast the U.S. military action in Vietnam with the Soviet invasion of Afghanistan.

2. Briefly summarize the consequences of Mao Zedong's victory over Chiang Kai-shek in China. (You may want to refer to chapter 22 to help answer this question.)

Thinking Critically

1. Assess the decision of President Truman to relieve General MacArthur of his command during the Korean War.

2. Why was the United States in a weak military position when Ronald Reagan became president?

Living in God's World

1. The Soviet Union was a military threat to the United States during much of the last half of the twentieth century, yet it fell swiftly. What are some biblical reasons the Soviet Union may have fallen so quickly?

2. During the Cold War, Americans championed the ideals of liberty rather than oppressive communism. What are some of the dangers that America faces in its emphasis on freedom?

People, Places, and Things to Know

iron curtain
Cold War
Truman Doctrine
containment
Marshall Plan
NATO
Warsaw Pact
arms race
civil rights movement
Martin Luther King Jr.
Ronald Reagan
Charles de Gaulle
limited wars
Cultural Revolution
Tiananmen Square
Korean War
Douglas MacArthur
38th parallel
Ho Chi Minh
Viet Cong
SEATO
domino theory
Gulf of Tonkin Resolution
Tet offensive
Vietnamization
PLO
intifada
Hamas
Fidel Castro
Bay of Pigs
Nikita Khrushchev
peaceful coexistence
Sputnik
U-2 incident
Berlin Wall
Cuban missile crisis
détente
SDI
Mikhail Gorbachev
perestroika
glasnost
Lech Walesa

CHAPTER | To the Present

24

Skyscrapers in Hong Kong

Big Ideas

1. What are some of the economic challenges and opportunities in the global economy?

2. What is the impact of military conflict around the world?

3. What are some political challenges in the modern world?

4. How has religion influenced the modern world?

Since the end of the Cold War, several trends have emerged. One is **globalization**: nations now tend to have an international focus rather than a purely national focus. The United States remains a leader in the West, while European states have struggled to play a significant role. In the East, China and India have become leading economic and political powers.

A second trend is the spread of democracy. Having survived in many of the former Communist countries, democracy has now spread to countries in Africa and Asia. Exceptions to this trend include North Korea and Communist China, which have staunchly resisted movement toward democracy. Nevertheless, Communist China has emerged from self-imposed isolation to develop extensive trade ties with the West.

The advance of Christianity around the world is a third trend. The most significant growth has occurred in global-south countries, though persecution often accompanies this growth.

Finally, even though the Cold War ended nearly thirty years ago, conflict remains. Wars in this new era have tended to be regional, as evidenced by flare-ups in parts of Africa, Eastern Europe, and the Middle East. In addition, acts of terrorism—the use of indiscriminate violence, or the threat of its use, for political ends—have been on the rise. Terrorism, often motivated by militant Islam, has replaced communism as the primary international threat.

I. The Americas
North America

The North American continent is the home of three nations: Canada, the United States, and Mexico. North America extends over 8.4 million square miles and has a great variety of geographic features. Over 476 million people occupy this vast region, with population densities per square mile varying from one to over 1,200 people, depending on the province.

Trade/Economy

The combined Gross Domestic Product (**GDP**—the monetary value of all goods and services produced within a geographic border) was $21.15 trillion in 2017. North America's **per capita GDP** (goods produced per person) varied from $42,158 in Canada and $57,800 in the United States to $9,005 in Mexico.

Canadian trade reached $1 trillion in 2016. Canada's primary trade partner is the U.S. at 75 percent. Its next trade partner is the EU at 8 percent, followed by 4 percent with China and 3 percent with the United Kingdom. Other nations account for 1 percent or less of Canada's trade.

In 2017 U.S. trade totaled $4.6 trillion. However, the United States continues to suffer a trade deficit, with $1.3 trillion in exports and $3.3 trillion in imports. The largest trade deficit is with China. China imports $100 billion worth of U.S. goods while exporting over $400 billion of Chinese goods to the United States.

Mexico's trade reached $412 billion in 2017. Its primary trade partner is the U.S. at 81 percent. Mexican trade with Canada is just under 3 percent, followed by China at about 1.5 percent.

Canada, the United States, and Mexico developed a trade agreement that was signed by President George H.W. Bush and went into effect under President Bill Clinton in 1994. The North American

Guiding Questions

1. What are some challenges related to trade in North America and Latin America?

2. How has terrorism influenced North America?

3. How has immigration affected North America and Latin America?

4. How have Latin American nations exercised stewardship of the environment?

Free Trade Agreement (**NAFTA**) was intended to lower trade barriers and enhance trade between these countries. While this trade agreement may have had good intentions, it resulted in a trade deficit/imbalance for the United States. In 2017 the U.S. had a trade deficit with Canada of $29 billion and a $59 billion trade deficit with Mexico. President Trump initially threatened to pull out of NAFTA. However, Canada and Mexico asked to renegotiate the trade agreement rather than end it.

9-11 and the War on Terror

Nine months after George W. Bush became president of the United States (2001), nineteen Islamic terrorists staged a large-scale attack on the United States. This attack used two commercial airplanes to destroy the World Trade Center towers in New York, and a third plane was used to severely damage the Pentagon in Washington, D.C. A fourth plane crashed in Pennsylvania after passengers attempted to wrest control from the hijackers. Authorities quickly determined that a Saudi citizen, **Osama bin Laden**, had masterminded the attack from Afghanistan and that members of the **al-Qaeda** Islamic terrorist network had staged it. A strong military response by several nations, led by the United States, invaded Afghanistan and drove the Taliban out of power.

Attacks on nations sponsoring or supporting terrorism continued, with military operations in Iraq and other states. Allied states used diplomatic pressures in an attempt to end support for Islamic terror by Pakistan and other countries with large Muslim populations. The United States and its allies have also sent troops to regions of North Africa to train national troops and equip them for the ongoing struggle against militant Islam and the violence this ideology brings to African nations.

Immigration

While the most-cited statistic refers to eleven million illegal immigrants having entered the United States since the year 2000, the number could be much higher. Illegal immigration occurs in many ways, including foreign visitors coming to the United States on a temporary visa and then staying after their visa has expired. The largest number of illegal immigrants have entered the country via the southern border with Mexico. Extending nearly two thousand miles, the border between the United States and Mexico is one of the most frequently crossed borders in the world, despite miles of barriers, including sections of walls, to control illegal crossings. The United States Border Patrol has over 21,000 agents patrolling the border in an effort to inhibit unauthorized entrance or capture those who have entered illegally.

One reason for the large influx of immigrants since the 1980s is the process of **chain migration**. Under this process, aliens who were granted amnesty by Congress in 1986 were able to apply for immediate family members to come to the United States. Thus a chain of migration occurred, and the number of immigrants granted access to the United States multiplied exponentially.

Some see the large number of migrations as a benefit for the United States because many migrants are hard-working individuals who simply desire a better life. Others fear that unrestricted migration allows criminals and terrorists easy access to the country and threatens the safety of American citizens.

Osama bin Laden

Border patrol taking illegal immigrants from Central America into custody

Drugs

Drug cartels from many parts of the world have amassed billions of dollars of revenue by transporting huge quantities of illegal drugs into North America to satisfy the growing demand for these destructive substances. Drug traffickers use every conceivable form of transportation to bring illegal drugs into North America.

In addition to the rapid growth of illegal drug use, the misuse of opioids, or painkillers, has become epidemic in many parts of the United States. These powerful prescription medicines are designed to bring relief to those who have debilitating pain following surgery or some type of injury. Abundant prescriptions by physicians of newer drugs, such as OxyContin, have led to addiction and death. In 2016, over 64,000 Americans died from opioid overdoses; this was a 21% increase from the previous year. Officials estimate that this crisis cost the United States over $504 billion in 2015, and the cost is rapidly rising. Healthcare officials and law enforcement personnel are working to address this epidemic. Several state attorneys general have also filed lawsuits against manufacturers of these addictive medicines, claiming that the producers promoted their prolific use and did not properly warn physicians of the great danger of addiction.

OxyContin pills

Latin America

Many countries in this region have struggled with political revolutions, economic crises, and social upheaval. Latin America has one of the world's fastest-growing populations and is experiencing the growing pains of a developing region. It is rich in human and natural resources and has great potential for growth in a variety of sectors. Latin America covers 7,412,000 square miles, and is composed of nineteen or twenty countries (depending on whether Mexico is included in this region). The combined GDP of this region was $7.3 billion (2017), and the population was around 600 million people. The per capita GDP was $13,730.52 (2017). Natural resources include precious metals, sugar, rubber, grains, coffee, copper, and oil.

Economy/Trade

Several Latin American economies are utilizing technology and developing this region's many resources. Brazil, for example, has enjoyed one of the highest economic growth rates in the developing world through the development of technologies including aviation and energy. The production of oil has also led a growing number of Latin American countries to enjoy sustained wealth and prosperity. Effective methods of extracting and processing crude oil and related resources give this region tremendous promise for sustained growth and development.

The Amazon Rain Forests

The Amazon rain forests contain enormous resources for countries like Argentina and Brazil. However, the deforestation of this region has also endangered many of these resources. The Amazon forest generates nearly half the rainfall in the area. Cutting down too many trees can reduce the rainfall and make the forest unsustainable. While there is a growing demand for more land to grow crops and raise livestock, wise stewardship is needed to ensure the survival and health of regions like the Amazon rain forests.

Argentina's president Mauricio Macri shakes hands with Chinese president Xi Jinping at the G20 Summit in Hangzhou, China (2016).

Growing Influence of China

While the United States has historically exercised a strong influence in Latin America, China has recently extended its influence in that region. China has invested billions of dollars in Latin American industries. It has gained significant economic penetration, even as U.S. companies have divested themselves of economic activity in the less stable regions of Latin America. As a result, China has become the top trade partner with Latin American countries such as Brazil, Chile, Peru, and Venezuela. One industry of particular interest is telecommunications. Heavy investment in this industry has enabled China to use this technology to monitor many foreign communications, which represents a huge asset for Chinese intelligence.

Chinese investments come with many risks for Latin America. Chinese exports to Latin America have created a trade imbalance that has drained the wealth of this region. Chinese imports of Latin American raw materials, such as oil, have also made this region subject to the fluctuation of commodity prices when demand for their raw materials experiences periodic decline.

China has also destabilized regions of Latin America by giving financial support to leftist regimes and dictators. In exchange for favorable access to raw materials, China has propped up governments that are repressive and disregard the welfare of their people. This influence has also promoted a strong bias against the United States and the values that Americans have sought to promote in Latin America, including democracy and political transparency.

Global South

The world's largest population growth is occurring in Latin America, India, China, and Africa. At the same time, Christianity is growing at an accelerated rate in these regions, which are known as the global south. Accurate numbers are difficult to obtain, and the numbers available often combine Roman Catholics, and Mormons along with mainline Protestants and Evangelicals. However, the continued growth of biblical Christianity is exciting. In one significant development, missionaries are now coming from the global south to evangelize the traditionally Christian-influenced nations of the West.

Christianity is spreading throughout Latin America. Distinct from Roman Catholic and traditional Protestant churches, Evangelical and Charismatic congregations are growing and multiplying in many Latin American countries.

Section Review

1. What was the goal of NAFTA?

2. What is the significance of al-Qaeda?

3. Using the example of the Amazon rain forests, summarize the problem of managing the environment while promoting economic expansion in Latin America.

4. What nation is beginning to have great influence in Latin America?

★ Discuss the impact of terrorism on North America.

★ Propose some ideas to address the opioid crisis.

II. Europe

European Union

In an effort to multiply their effectiveness in the world economy, various countries united by treaty to form economic unions. The most significant economic union in Europe to date is the European Union (**EU**). Composed of twenty-eight states, this organization manages agriculture, fisheries, and regional development in its member states. The EU presides over 1.7 million square miles and a population of 512 million people. It was formally established with the Maastricht Treaty and became effective in 1993. Brussels serves as the capital of the EU, and this organization represents twenty-four language groups. In 2012 the EU received the Nobel Peace Prize "for over six decades contributed to the advancement of peace and reconciliation, democracy and human rights in Europe." In 2013 Croatia became the twenty-eighth and latest (to date) member of the EU.

Some problems encountered by the EU include a debt crisis experienced by several member states, most notably Greece. Migration from the Middle East, due in part to a civil war in Syria, has also placed economic and social stress on EU members. However, the greatest difficulty for the EU occurred in the United Kingdom (UK).

Growing frustrations with the EU's interference in and domination of the UK's economy and use of resources, including fishing rights, developed into a referendum to exit the EU. This movement became popularly known as **Brexit** (British exit). In June 2016, the proposed Brexit passed by a 51.9% vote, and the departure is scheduled to be completed on March 29, 2019. The long-term consequences of the UK's exit have yet to be determined.

Immigration

While people from non-European countries have been migrating to Western Europe for many years, the large displacement of people from the Middle East due to a Syrian civil war, seizing of regions in Iraq by militant Islamists, and continued instability in Afghanistan resulted in a refugee crisis of a proportion not seen since World War II. In 2015 about 1.2 million people fled the Middle East and migrated to Western Europe. This group was composed of asylum seekers, economic migrants, and Islamic militants

Middle Eastern immigrants passing through Slovenia en route to western Europe (2015)

Guiding Questions

1. What are the key events in the development of the European Union?
2. How has immigration affected Europe?
3. How has terrorism affected Europe?
4. What are significant challenges in Eastern Europe?

EU building in Brussels

Nigel Farage helped lead the British movement to exit the EU.

pretending to be victims of the violence. Most of these people came from Muslim-dominated countries, with the top three home countries being Syria (46.7%), Afghanistan (21%), and Iraq (9.4%). Over one million people became first-time asylum applicants in Western Europe, and chaos often ensued. Germany, Hungary, Sweden, and Austria received about two-thirds of these immigrants and attempted to provide them a safe haven.

Islamic Terrorism

Most states in Europe have become secular, and the role of religion has continued to diminish over the last fifty years. One consequence of a secular society is the diminished role of the family and the tendency to have smaller families. This has resulted in a vacuum that Muslim immigrants have tended to fill. Bringing their religious values with them and often having large families, Muslims have assumed a greater significance in European society. The failure of many Muslim immigrants to adapt to Western society and the difficulty many young Muslim males have in finding employment have created a significant opportunity for Muslim terror recruitment. It seems clear in restrospect that some of those fleeing the Middle East in 2015 were actually Islamic militants who took advantage of European generosity and set up operations in European cities. There has been a significant increase of Islamic terror attacks in several European cities as a result. Attacks range from detonating explosive devices to using an automobile to run down people on city streets, where many victims can be killed with no warning.

Eastern Europe

At the beginning of the twenty-first century, Eastern Europe continued to be a source of both hope and despair. Freedom from communism meant a better life for some people but strife and trouble for others.

Bosnia

Bosnia-Herzegovina formed from the breaking up of Yugoslavia in the early 1990s. This region was inhabited by three ethnic groups: Bosniaks, Slavic Serbs, and Croats. The Serbs favored remaining a part of Yugoslavia, while the Bosniaks and Croats preferred to become independent. The disagreements between these groups led to growing violence and ethnic cleansing.

Serbia, populated by Orthodox Christians, had dominated the area for centuries and tried to maintain its dominance over Muslims and Catholics there, even if it meant wholesale slaughter. One simmering battleground was Bosnia, where Serbs fought Muslims. NATO intervened in the former Yugoslavia to stop ethnic and religious war between the dominant Serbs and two other groups. In 1995 a peace agreement was signed in Dayton, Ohio. Peacekeepers remained in Bosnia to control the violence. This region has made significant progress toward long-term stability and has a growing economy based largely on tourism.

Russia

As we saw in chapter 23, Russia emerged as the dominant power in Eastern Europe following the fall of the Soviet Union. At 6.6 million square miles, Russia is the largest country in the world measured by surface area and has one of the lowest population densities per square mile at 8.8. The population of Russia is 144 million people. Russia has one of the largest mineral and energy reserves in the world. The development of its vast oil and gas reserves contributed to the recovery and growth of Russia's economy, but periodic slumps in oil prices have had a disruptive effect on its economy. Russia's GDP reached $1.47 trillion in 2017, and its per capita GDP in 2015 was $9,092.58.

Russia also has a large military force and the third-largest military budget in the world, behind the U.S. and China. As Russia has recovered from the collapse of the Soviet Union, it has used its military and economic influence to restrict or halt some of the independent activities of nations previously under Soviet control. Russian leaders have been quick to use the state's military might to force its will on neighboring regions, including Georgia, Crimea, and Ukraine.

Georgia

In 2003 the country of Georgia overthrew the pro-Russian government in the peaceful **Rose Revolution**. However, Russia resisted Georgian independence by supporting two secessionist regions in Georgia. In 2008 South Ossetians (separatists) set off an explosion and killed Georgian troops. Shots were fired between Georgian and separatist forces, and Georgian troops moved toward a separatist city to force it into submission. This provided Russia with the excuse it wanted to wage war against Georgia. A ceasefire was later brokered, and Russia declared two separatist regions of Georgia to be independent republics, despite strong objections by the country of Georgia. Russia used this event to demonstrate its power in Eastern Europe and to put the West on notice that it remained a force to be reckoned with.

Ukraine and Crimea

In 2004 the country of Ukraine gained its independence from Russian dominance during the **Orange Revolution**. Moscow's response was to secretly send Russian forces across the border to occupy territory in Ukraine. More serious was Moscow's outright

Vladimir Putin

Clashes in Ukraine resulted in the ouster of President Yanukovych (2014).

Rose Revolution

Russian soldiers nicknamed "Little Green Men" seized control of Crimean sites.

seizure of Crimea, a region that had been part of Ukraine since the 1950s. Elite Russian troops moved quickly to secure key Crimean sites. Some Crimeans referred to the masked Russian troops as "Little Green Men" because they were dressed in green uniforms but had no military insignia.

Section Review

1. What is the most significant economic union in Europe to date?
2. What is the significance of Brexit?
3. What country is the dominant power in Eastern Europe?
4. What country overthrew the pro-Russian government in the Rose Revolution?
★ What effect has recent immigration had on Europe?
★ What plan of action would you implement to reduce terrorism in Europe?

Guiding Questions

1. What are some opportunities and challenges regarding economies and trade for Africa?
2. What are key political challenges for the nations of Africa?
3. How severe is the problem of human trafficking in Africa?
4. How have Christianity and Islam expanded in modern Africa?

III. Africa

Africa also witnessed a rapid series of independence movements in the postwar period. In 1950 only four states on the continent were independent; by 1977 fifty-seven had gained their freedom from colonial control. In 1960 alone eighteen former colonies gained independence. In their rush for independence, the African states encountered many problems. However, since 2000 many African nations have enjoyed increasing stability and prosperity.

Economy and Trade

The continent of Africa encompasses 11.73 million miles and has a population of 1.22 billion people. The population density varies, but the average is 39.1 people per square mile. Africa's GDP varies by nation from $1.6 billion to $3.5 trillion. As a result, the per capita GDP ranged from $300 to $20,581 in 2010.

Although African states are gradually turning their enormous natural resources into sustained growth, many of them are still among the poorest in the world. Problems that have limited economic growth and increased trade include poor infrastructure and colonialism. Ongoing hindrances include language diversity and, in some cases, poor governance. Bribery, cronyism (awarding positions to friends and colleagues), and kleptocracy (using political office to gain wealth and power) remain serious problems that must be solved. One observer noted that "Africa will be the future growth engine of the world."

Ethnic Conflict and Political Struggle

When European colonial powers divided Africa in the late nineteenth century and created colonies, the boundaries were often arbitrary and artificial. Western interests were deemed more important than African interests, and many ethnic groups were split or moved from their homelands. European rule held the diverse populations together, but as African countries began to gain their independence, ethnic loyalties superseded national unity. Rivalries often led to bloody civil wars. Civil conflict plagued young nations such as Kenya and the Congo (today known as the Democratic Republic of the Congo).

Human Trafficking

Kidnapping people to sell to others is an age-old problem that continues to thrive in many nations, including many in Africa. Women and children are most often the victims of this crime. While reliable statistics are difficult to verify, this terrible abuse generated an estimated $150 billion in 2014. It is considered to be one of the fastest growing transnational crimes in the world.

Expansion of Christianity and Islam

As previously mentioned, some of the world's largest population growth is occurring in Africa. At the same time, Christianity is growing at an accelerated rate in the global south. Significantly, much of the recent growth has resulted from African outreach rather than foreign missionary activity. Another important development is that missionaries are now coming from the global south to evangelize the traditionally Christian-influenced nations of the West.

Islam has also expanded throughout Africa. While Islam spread quickly across North Africa within this religion's first century, it has experienced a renewal with the literal interpretation of the Qur'an and the popularity of sharia law (legal system based on Islamic writings). Groups such as Boko Haram in Nigeria have used extremely violent means to impose a strict and brutal interpretation of Islam on many in Africa.

South Sudan

This African state formed in 2011 when it formally separated from Sudan. The population is 12.23 million, and the GDP is $3.62 billion. The area is 248,777 square miles. South Sudan contains the third-largest oil reserves in Sub-Saharan Africa, and revenue from that oil accounts for over 90 percent of the nation's GDP. Disagreements with Sudan regarding the percentage of profits from the oil have led to political and social strife. A civil war that erupted shortly after South Sudan became independent has threatened the survival of this state. This country has a very high infant mortality rate and the world's highest maternal mortality rate (mothers dying during or shortly after giving birth). In many parts of South Sudan there is only one doctor for every half million people. Half of the country's people have no access to clean water. In 2017 South Sudan suffered from a severe famine, and medical authorities warn that one million children in South Sudan are malnourished.

Section Review

1–2. Summarize two challenges Africa has faced relating to the economy and trade.

3. How were boundaries set in Africa in the late nineteenth century?

4. What religions are growing in Africa?

✶ What are possible solutions to the problem of human trafficking?

✶ What factors contribute to the political challenges for the nations of Africa?

✶ Briefly trace the expansion of Christianity in modern Africa.

Guiding Questions

1. Why is the Middle East important to the nations of the world?

2. What conflicts have occurred in the Middle East since the first Gulf War?

3. What roles do Iran and Saudi Arabia play in the Middle East?

4. How has the Israeli-Arab conflict developed since the 1970s?

IV. The Middle East

Persian Gulf

The Persian Gulf is a body of water in western Asia that extends from the Indian Ocean. It is nearly surrounded by eight states, including Iran and Saudi Arabia. This region has become the focal point of many in the world primarily due to its vast supply of oil and natural gas. States bordering this region have gained significant importance because of the abundant supply of resources and because of the potential threat to the unrestricted access to these resources. In addition, the countries that border the Persian Gulf are almost exclusively Muslim, and the vast wealth from this region has frequently been used to support the spread of militant Islam.

The Middle East and Environs

The Gulf Wars

Seeking power and fame, dictator Saddam Hussein of Iraq invaded Kuwait in August 1990, seizing Kuwait's huge oil reserves and threatening the security of Saudi Arabia. Led by the United States, under President George H.W. Bush, and Great Britain, a coalition launched massive air strikes against Iraqi forces in Kuwait in January 1991. For five weeks coalition forces pounded Iraqi forces in Kuwait and even struck targets in Iraq with bombs and missiles. In February coalition ground forces attacked, driving Iraqi forces from Kuwait and quickly defeating Hussein's army.

As previously mentioned, following the terrorist attack on September 11, 2001, President George W. Bush launched the United States and much of the world into a second war in the Persian Gulf region. A U.S.-led multinational coalition invaded Afghanistan, destroyed terrorist training camps, and toppled the Taliban government, which had hosted bin Laden and al-Qaeda. Coalition forces secured areas of the country and began the process of establishing a representative government. Afghanistan had its first free presidential election in 2004.

In 2003 American military forces led a coalition against Iraq to remove Hussein from power. The coalition quickly crushed Iraqi military opposition, removed Hussein's Ba'athist party from power, and captured Hussein. A newly established Iraqi government held war crimes trials in 2005, after which several leaders, including Hussein, were executed by the Iraqi government.

Following the initial invasion of Iraq, U.S. forces quickly found themselves having to deal with violent clashes between Shia and Sunni Muslims, who have been at war for centuries. President Bush responded by sending in additional troops to stabilize the country. Following his election in 2008, President Obama initially called for the withdrawal of U.S. forces. Then he briefly supported the build-up of forces before abruptly calling for the pullout of American troops. The last U.S. forces left Iraq in December 2011. Violence between Shia and Sunni Muslims resumed shortly after the departure of U.S. forces.

Arab Spring and Syria

Long pent-up frustration from dictatorships, corruption, and human-rights abuses erupted in a violent event often referred to as the Arab Spring. The first uprising occurred in Tunisia in December 2010. Similar revolts spread to a number of Arab states, including Algeria, Egypt, Libya, Yemen, and Syria. Most revolts were suppressed, and little positive change occurred. The uprising in Syria developed into a civil war with the ruling Assad family and has taken on international relevance due to the participation of Iran, Russia, the United States, and other nations.

ISIS

With the abrupt departure of U.S. forces from Iraq, a power vacuum resulted. Added to this was the sustained resistance of Syrians against the Assad family. In this unstable region, a group of militant Islamists formed an organization that became known as The Islamic State in Iraq and Syria (ISIS). Headed by a religious leader (Abu Bakr al-Baghdadi), who took the title of caliph (chief Muslim civil and religious leader), ISIS forces seized territory in Syria and northern Iraq. Iraqi forces supported by U.S. and other nations pushed ISIS out of Iraq in 2017.

Destroyed Iraqi tank in the Gulf War with oil well fires in the background

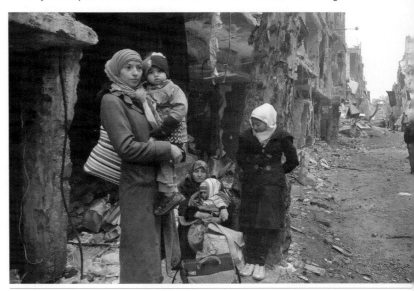
Syrian refugees in Yarmouk, Syria

Abu Bakr al-Baghdadi

Iran

Iran extends over 636,372 square miles and has a population of 80.28 million people. It has a GDP of $438 billion and a per capita GDP of $5,383. It is an Islamic republic, and all decisions are made by the current religious leader (ayatollah). This Muslim state is unusual because a majority of the population is Shiite (90–95%), with Sunnis being in the minority (5–10%). Iran has a standing army of around 523,000 that is considered one of the most powerful in the region, second only to Israel's. Iran also maintains a strategic alliance with other powerful nations, most notably China.

Beginning in the 1970s, Islamic elements stirred hostilities in the Middle East. Iran, for example, had been a longtime ally of the United States. However, in 1979 Islamic forces overthrew the shah and installed the **Ayatollah Khomeini** as ruler. (*Ayatollah*, Persian for "reflection, or sign, of Allah," is the highest title of honor that a Shiite Muslim can hold.) Iranian radicals instituted an Islamic republic in which Muslim religious law guides the state. The Iranians viewed their revolution as a first step toward worldwide change.

Iran returned to the spotlight in 2005 with the election of Mahmoud Ahmadinejad (ah mah DIH nee zhahd) as president. He frequently attacked the West in defiant speeches. Ahmadinejad also led his country to develop nuclear technology, with the suspected goals being to strengthen Iran's military capabilities and to support terrorist groups abroad. He won reelection in 2009, despite large protests in Iran. Many protesters were detained or murdered by Iranian security forces.

In addition to having Iraq on its western border, Iran has Afghanistan and Pakistan on its eastern border. Across its long borders, Iran has extended its influence into these other troubled countries. Leaders in Iran have worked tirelessly to destabilize this region and have opposed Western attempts to develop democracies.

Continued development of nuclear technology for possible military use led the United States and other nations to apply sanctions to limit trade and resources for Iran. The effort to convince Iran's leaders, including the current president, Hassan Rouhani, to abandon pursuit of nuclear weapons has done little or nothing to deter their actions. In addition, Iran's support of Islamic groups across the Middle East has reduced any hope for stability and heightened the possibility of war.

Chinese President Xi Jinping meets with Iranian President Hassan Rouhani and Supreme Leader Sayyed Ali Khamenei

Hassan Rouhani

Israel

The state of Israel is a tiny, narrow strip of land along the eastern shore of the Mediterranean Sea. Despite its small size, with an area around 8,500 square miles, Israel boasts a GDP of $348.6 billion and a per capita GDP of $39,974. Israel's population is 8,785,020 and is made up of Arabs, Jews, and other nationalities. There is an average of 1,023 people per square mile. One reason for such a dense population is immigration. Large migrations of Jews occurred between 1980 and the 1990s and included immigrants from Ethiopia and the former Soviet Union.

Following the Camp David Accords (see chapter 23), Israel continued to struggle for survival against Muslim groups, such as the Palestinian Liberation Organization (PLO), and neighboring states, including Iraq and Syria. With the effective collapse of government in Lebanon, the PLO launched repeated attacks against northern Israel from Lebanese territory. Israel responded by invading Lebanon in 1982 and destroying many PLO bases. In 1986, Israel bowed to international pressure and withdrew from most of Lebanon, with the exception of a buffer zone along the border of Lebanon and Israel. Palestinian uprisings known as The First (1987–1993) and Second Intifada (2000–2005) resulted in thousands of deaths as Israeli and Palestinian forces attacked one another. Elected to the office of prime minister in 2001, Ariel Sharon withdrew Israeli forces from the Gaza Strip and erected the Israeli West Bank barrier (concrete wall) that effectively ended the Second Intifada. Continued conflicts included the Second Lebanon War in 2006 and the brief Gaza War that lasted three weeks (2008–9). Increasing rocket attacks from the Gaza Strip led, in 2012 and 2014, to Israeli military operations within Gaza to seize weapons and reduce Palestinian military capabilities.

Israel-Jordan Peace Treaty

One positive development occurred in 1994 when Israel and Jordan signed a peace treaty. Jordan became the second Arab state after Egypt to recognize Israel as a nation.

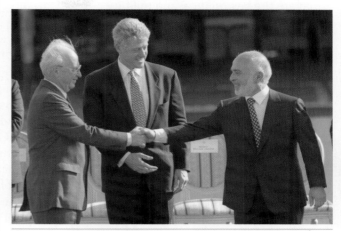

U.S. president Bill Clinton with Israeli Prime Minister Yitzhak Rabin and Jordan's King Hussein

Section Review

1–2. Identify two major conflicts following the Gulf War.

3. What dictator of Iraq was executed following the war crimes trials in 2005?

4. What was the significance of ISIS?

5. What is the status of Israel with many of its Arab neighbors?

✶ Discuss the roles of Iran and Saudi Arabia in the Middle East.

✶ What can the West do to curb the potential nuclear power of Iran?

West Bank barrier

Guiding Questions

1. What role does Asia play in the global economy?

2. What are the key political and military challenges in the nations of Asia?

3. What is the state of Christianity in Asia?

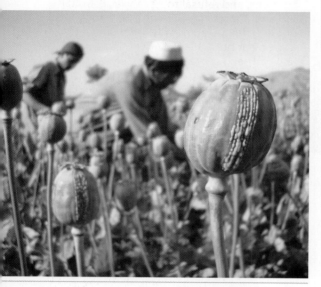

Harvesting opium in Afghanistan

Taliban

Beginning in the late 1990s, the **Taliban** (literally "students"; trained in not only radical Islamic doctrine but also terrorist tactics) gained control in Afghanistan, enforcing radical Muslim rule and providing safe haven and training camps for Muslim terrorists. These and other groups committed acts of terrorism to undermine secular Muslim regimes. Saudi Arabia has a large number of such radicals. With the decline of communism, many people view Islamic expansion as the new ideological threat to international peace and stability.

V. Asia

Afghanistan and Pakistan

Afghanistan is located in Central Asia and is bordered by Iran and several countries whose names end in "istan," such as Turkmenistan and Pakistan. Pakistan is located in South Asia and is bordered by India and China, in addition to Afghanistan.

Afghanistan

Afghanistan stretches over 252,000 square miles and has a population of thirty-five million people. Given its vast size, the population density is a mere 49.82 people per square mile. Despite years of war and instability, Afghanistan has a GDP of $64 billion and a per capita GDP of $2,000. This nation is rich in resources such as crude oil, natural gas, natural-gas liquids, lithium, copper, gold, iron, and rare earth elements. Its agricultural output is impressive, with large crops of pomegranates, grapes, apricots, and melons. However, it is also the world's largest producer of opium, which accounts for 11 percent of the country's economy.

Afghanistan is an Islamic republic, and the majority of its population is Muslim. Despite all of its human and natural resources, Afghanistan is considered one of the most corrupt countries in the world. Corruption is woven into the fabric of Afghan society, and removing it would be a major challenge. Even so, Afghanistan is beginning to experience an economic recovery, in part due to the return of five million expatriates (Afghans who fled and have since returned). A leading industry in Afghanistan is construction, as the country seeks to rebuild following decades of conflict.

Construction site in Kabul, Afghanistan

Pakistan

Pakistan is a large country that extends over nearly 882,000 square miles. It has a population of 208 million people. The population density averages 245 people per square mile. Pakistan has the sixth largest standing army in the world and is one of the handful of nations that are nuclear powers. Like Afghanistan and Iran, Pakistan is an Islamic republic, and 96 percent of the population is Muslim. Its GDP was $304 billion in 2017, and its per capita GDP was $1,468. Pakistan is the fifth-largest producer of cotton and the fourth-largest producer of milk.

India

As one of the largest countries in the world, India spans 1.27 million square miles. With a population of 1.34 billion people, India competes with China for the title of most populous country in the world. Not surprisingly, India's population density is 962 people per square mile. Given the potential for threats from neighboring nations, India has developed the third-largest standing army in the world.

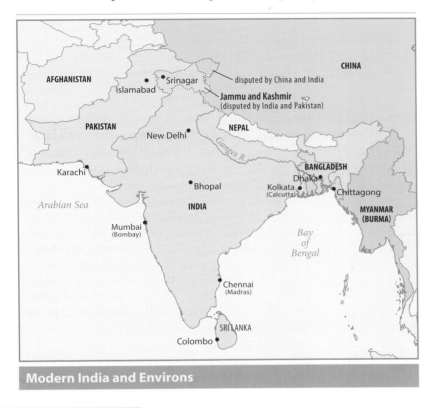

Modern India and Environs

Street scene in Old Delhi

India Gains Independence

The first major developing nation to gain independence was India, the "Jewel in the Crown" of the British Empire. **Mahatma Gandhi**, the leader of the Indian nationalists, mounted a campaign of **passive resistance**, a nonviolent program designed to defy British rule through strikes (including hunger strikes and sit-down strikes), mass demonstrations, and refusal to pay taxes. Between the world wars, the British government granted the Indian people more political power, but not until 1947 did India achieve full independence.

Economic Growth and Democracy

In 1991 market reforms transformed India's economy into one of the world's fastest-growing major economies. In 2017 India had the sixth-largest economy in the world by GDP ($1.47 trillion); it had the third-largest economy by purchasing power. Ongoing challenges include poverty, corruption, malnutrition, and inadequate public healthcare. India, the "world's largest democracy," has struggled to remain a representative government, but leaders in India have increasingly embraced capitalism over socialism. One result is the emergence of areas with strong economic growth, including Mumbai, Gujarat, Haryana, and Delhi. Leadership has shifted from the Nehru family to Hindu nationalists, who have won elections since 1998.

Growth of Christianity

Although India is primarily a nation of Hindus (74%), there is also a large Muslim minority (14.2%). While Christians remain a tiny minority (5.8%), there is a definite growth in the number of Indians who are turning from other religions to embrace the truths of Christianity. While India has tried to remain a secular state, religion continues to play a dominant role in every aspect of Indian society. Tension between the sizable Muslim minority, the Hindu majority, and a growing Christian population is ongoing, and violence against Christians and other religious groups has continued to escalate.

China

China remains the most influential Communist nation, with North Korea, Vietnam, and Cuba continuing their totalitarian ways in its shadow. Since the 1990s, China has developed one of the largest and fastest-growing economies in the world. China covers 3.7 million miles and has a population of 1.37 billion people. Its population density is 146 people per square mile. It had an $11 trillion GDP in 2015 and a per capita GDP of $8,123. This growth is due primarily to increased world trade and foreign investment. Five of the world's fastest-growing cities are located in China.

Beijing

Economic Growth

Beginning in the 1990s, China's leaders embraced modernization and some capitalism so their nation could improve its standard of living. In 1997 Great Britain's control of Hong Kong ended, and it passed into China's hands. The Chinese shrewdly let Hong Kong keep its capitalist economy, one of the best in Asia, while exercising firm political control. In 2001 China joined the World Trade Organization, another measure of its economic progress. Walmart opened its first store in China in 1996, and the company became a major employer through its 424 retail units by the end of 2016. Other so-called big-box stores, including Home Depot and Best Buy, opened several stores in China but were unable to successfully compete there.

Military Expansion

The Chinese military benefited from the growing wealth of the nation. The military made significant advances in missile technology, purchased and refitted Soviet aircraft carriers, and built stealth fighters and bombers. While much of this technology was appropriated from the West, the Chinese have aggressively used this technology to increase their political and military clout in Asia.

The Chinese have recently built several bases in the South China Sea with the potential of threatening sea trade in this busy region. Vietnam and other nations have vigorously protested Chinese construction and expansion in these disputed waters. Several nations have overlapping claims to these areas in the South China Sea.

Population Crisis

An ongoing tragedy is China's attempt to stabilize its population growth. In the 1970s the Communist government instituted a policy that limited Chinese families to one child. This policy resulted in the murder through abortion of up to thirteen million Chinese babies each year for the last forty years. One unintended consequence of this slaughter has been the imbalance of male and female babies born. Since many Chinese families prefer a male child so that the parents will be provided for in their final years, gender-selective abortion resulted in the murder of many Chinese baby girls. There are now millions more Chinese men looking for wives than there are Chinese women to meet this need. It is projected that by 2025 China will have 96.5 million men in their twenties but only 80.3 million young women. Another long-term consequence of this imbalance is that by 2050 there will not be enough workers to support an aging Chinese society. Despite recent changes that allow families to have two children, forced abortions continue in many regions of China.

Chinese WZ-10 attack helicopter

Chinese DF-26 hypersonic long-range antiship missiles

Growth of Christianity

Communist China continues to persecute religious groups, from Christians and Tibetan Buddhists to sects such as the Falun Gong. However, despite this persecution and the brutal prison conditions imposed upon believers, Christianity is growing. The number of Christians in China has exceeded one hundred million and shows no sign of decline. One reason for official concern about the growing church is the fact that there are now more Christians than Communists (estimated to be around eighty million) in Communist China.

Korean Peninsula
North Korea

North Korea stretches 46,540 square miles along the northern half of the Korean peninsula. It has a population of twenty-four

Kim Jong Un

The Korean peninsula at night (note the absence of lights in North Korea)

million people and a population density of 544 people per square mile. North Korea has a GDP of $28 billion (2013) and a per capita GDP of $1,800. Despite North Korea's modest population, it has a standing army of 950,000 and 5.5 million in reserve.

As noted in chapter 23, North Korea came under Communist control during the early days of the Cold War. Kim Il Sung (r. 1948–1994) became the first Communist dictator and ruled until his death. His son, Kim Jong Il (r. 1994–2011), continued the ruthless dictatorship until his death. One of his sons, **Kim Jong Un** became the third-generation dictator of North Korea in 2011. He has displayed an even more belligerent attitude against the United States than his predecessors, has demonstrated an unusual brutality in disposing of perceived rivals, and has rapidly accelerated the development of missile technology with the goal of being able to strike the United States with a nuclear-tipped warhead.

South Korea

South Korea has thrived following the armistice with North Korea during the Cold War. It spans 38,502 square miles and has a population of forty-nine million people, with a population density of 519.26 people per square mile. South Korea's rejection of communism and embracing of a free market has enabled this state to achieve a GDP of $1.38 trillion (2015). In sharp contrast to the meager per capita GDP of its northern counterpart, South Korea enjoys a per capita GDP of $32,400.

Having developed beyond military dictatorships, South Korea has a stable democracy and many of the benefits that accompany a free society. The nation even survived a scandal at the highest level of government in 2017 and peacefully resolved the issue with a newly elected leader. Despite the constant threat of aggression and even war with North Korea, South Korea continues to thrive and prosper.

South Korea embraces religious freedom, and around 31 percent of the population affiliates with some form of Christianity. Buddhism also has many adherents and represents about 24 percent of South Korea's population.

Japan

The islands of Japan total an area of 145,925 square miles, with a population of 126.4 million people. Its population density is 348.25 people per square mile. Japan enjoys a GDP of $4.38 trillion, and its per capita GDP was $34,523.70 in 2015.

After World War II, Japan experienced a remarkable economic recovery and became one of the leading economies in the world. Nevertheless, it has had significant problems in recent years. From 1990 to the early twenty-first century, Japan suffered its longest economic downturn since 1945. Critics blamed bureaucratic regulation and recommended greater economic freedom. Bad loans during the good economic times of the 1970s and 1980s weakened banking in Japan. Competition from South Korea, Taiwan, Hong Kong, and Singapore also hurt Japan's economy. Ironically, the success of those Asian neighbors came from their imitation of Japanese industry.

In addition, Japan faced traditional challenges. Its people live on a relatively small area of land, and its natural resources are limited. The Japanese must import most of their food as well as raw materials for their factories. Trade with the world remains vital for both importing and exporting. If the Asian, European, or American economies suffer, so does the Japanese economy.

However, Japan stands apart from most of Asia, not only because it is a democracy and a major economic power but also because its culture and society have certain special characteristics. Most Asian countries are very traditional, but urbanization is changing Japan rapidly. Young people, moving to the cities for work, often leave their rural customs behind. When they marry, they establish their own homes rather than living with their extended families, and Western influences, especially American popular culture, are strong.

Religion in Japan is a collection of religious beliefs (including elements of Buddhism and Confucianism) under Japan's native religion of Shintoism. Christians are a tiny minority of 2 or 3 percent in Japan. While some Japanese do turn to Christ, conversions are rare because of the emphasis on family traditions and Japanese culture. Recently, some Korean missionaries have moved to Japan and are serving as a witness to the Japanese people.

Southeast Asia

Composed of eleven countries, Southeast Asia has a combined area of 1.7 million square miles. Its combined population is around 642 million people with a population density of 377.64. Southeast Asia has a GDP of $7.6 trillion, with a per capita GDP of $4,018.

Southeast Asia was under Japanese domination during World War II, but nationalist movements began to take hold after the war's end. Some nations in Southeast Asia continue to face serious ethnic and religious tensions. Terrorism and separatist movements also threaten the stability of some governments. While the economies of some of those nations improved dramatically in the late twentieth century, by the late 1990s severe economic decline gripped the area, worsening social and political conditions. Many nations in this region continue to be heavily dependent on agriculture, but several states have made steady progress in developing industrial sectors such as textiles, microprocessors, and heavy industrial products. This region also has great potential in its abundant oil reserves that have yet to be fully developed.

Various religions are found in Southeast Asia, including Islam, Buddhism, Hinduism, and Christianity. With approximately 240 million Muslims, Islam is clearly the predominant religious force in the region. Christianity, in various forms, varies from less than 1 percent of a given population to nearly 8 percent. While relatively small as a percentage, Christians continue to witness of Christ and see people added to the local churches, wherever they may meet.

* * *

At the beginning of our journey through world history we studied God's creative work. Soon we found humanity turning in disobedience as we considered the Fall. Much of this book has

			Fast Facts		
Country/ Region	Area (sq. mi.)	Pop.	Pop. Density (per sq. mi.)	GDP (US$)	Per Capita GDP (US$)
North America	8.4 (M)	476 (M)	Canada (3.9) U.S. (Varies from 1 to 1,218) Mexico (65)	$21.15 (T)	Canada ($42,158) U.S. ($57,800) Mexico ($9,005)
Latin America	7.4 (M)	600 (M)	81	$7.6 (B)	$13,230
Europe	1.7 (M)	512 (M)	Varies from 5 to 173	Varies from $1.6 (B) to $3.5 (T)	$36,448 (2014)
Russia	6.6 (M)	144 (M)	9	$1.47 (T)	$9,093 (2015)
Africa	11.73 (M)	1.22 (B)	39	Varies from $35 (B) to $406 (B)	Varies from $300 to $20,581 (2010)
Iran	636,372	80.28 (M)	131	$438 (B)	$5,383
Israel	8,500	8.79 (M)	1,023	$348.6 (B)	$39,974
Afghanistan	252,000	35 (M)	50	$64 (B)	$2,000
Pakistan	882,000	208 (M)	245	$304 (B)	$1,468
India	1.27 (M)	1.34 (B)	962	$1.47 (T)	$1,709
China	3.7 (M)	1.37 (B)	146	$11.01 (T)	$8,123
North Korea	46,540	24 (M)	544	$28 (B) (2013)	$1,800
South Korea	38,502	49 (M)	519	$1.38 (T)	$32,400
Japan	145,925	126.4 (M)	348	$4.38 (T)	$34,524
Southeast Asia	1.7 (M)	642 (M)	378	$7.6 (T)	$4,018

recorded the consequences of the Fall and God's work to redeem humans from their fallen condition by sending His Son "in the fullness of time" to live a perfect life, die a perfect death, and purchase redemption for those who trust in Him. We find the conclusion to history described in various Scripture passages, including portions of the books of Daniel, Ezekiel, and the Revelation.

For the secularist, history must be very frustrating and ultimately without meaning. However, for the Christian, history has a wonderful beginning followed by a period of tragedy and suffering, but it concludes with a glorious victory for God and those who have become His children through faith in His Son. To the Christian, history has purpose and a magnificent conclusion that no human author could adequately describe.

Section Review

1. What is the primary religion of India?
2. What is the economic system of Hong Kong?
3. What Chinese policy has had a significant impact on the population?
4. Who is the dictator of North Korea?
5. What culture are many young Japanese beginning to adopt?
* Discuss the challenges that face Christianity in Asia.
* How does Asia influence the global economy and vice versa?

Making Connections

1. Define *globalization*.

2. What religion is growing in the global south?

3. Why have many African countries endured ethnic conflict since World War II?

4. What was the significance of Osama bin Laden?

5. What is the significance of the term *ayatollah*?

Developing History Skills

1. Outline the Israeli-Arab conflict since the Camp David Accords.

2. What are two major positions regarding how to address illegal immigration in the United States? Identify the arguments each side makes in support of its position.

Thinking Critically

1. Evaluate the U.S. response to terrorism beginning with President George W. Bush following the attacks on September 11, 2001.

2. Discuss key politcal and military challenges in Asia.

Living in God's World

1. Globalization has affected not only trade but also religion. You are more likely to work or associate with people from other religions than previous generations of Americans were. Research a religion such as Islam or Buddhism, and write a gospel tract that addresses the gospel specifically to adherents of that religion.

2. Most people recognize the horrors that totalitarian governments have brought about in the last one hundred years. Is democracy the solution to these horrors? Why or why not?

People, Places, and Things to Know

globalization
GDP
per capita GDP
NAFTA
Osama bin Laden
al-Qaeda
chain migration
EU
Brexit
Rose Revolution
Orange Revolution
Ayatollah Khomeini
Taliban
Mahatma Gandhi
passive resistance
Kim Jong Un

GLOSSARY

A

Abbasid caliphate that marked the peak of the Muslim empire

Abrahamic Covenant God's covenant with Abraham in which He promised Abraham descendants, a land for his descendants, and a Messiah that would come through his seed

absolute power unlimited and unrestrained power

Act of Settlement Act of Parliament that established its right to grant the throne to whomever it wished

Adena group of Indians who were mound builders and lived in large dome-shaped structures

Age of Reason a term for the seventeenth and eighteenth centuries

Aksum kingdom that defeated the Kushites around AD 330; embraced a form of Christianity

Allah the god of Islam

al-Qaeda terrorist network headed by Osama bin Laden; attacked the United States on September 11, 2001

amphibious related to an invasion by sea

Anabaptists group that rejected infant baptism and rebaptized each other

anarchy the breakdown of government and order

ancestor worship worship of a family's ancestors

Anglican Church Church of England; the established state church of England, which has as its creed the Thirty-Nine Articles

Anglo-Russian Entente 1907 agreement between England and Russia; divided Persia into three zones of control

Anglo-Saxon Chronicle document that traces the history of England from Roman times to Alfred the Great's day

Anglo-Saxons Germanic tribes from northern Europe who invaded Britain after the Romans left

Anschluss political unification between Austria and Germany; forbidden by the Treaty of Versailles but later accomplished by Hitler

anthropomorphic having human form or attributes

Anti-Comintern Pact 1936 treaty between Germany and Japan directed against communism, specifically the Soviet Union

appeasement concessions to an aggressor to avoid conflict

apprentice first class of a craft guild; lived in the home of a master for two to seven years and learned trade skills and proper conduct

aqueducts designed to supply water to cities

archon chief magistrate of the Athenian council of nobles

armistice a temporary cessation of fighting

arms race a build-up of weapons between two or more nations in order to maintain a position of strength and to prevent the other side from gaining a military edge

artifacts objects made by people

Aryans a warlike people who came from central Asia sometime after 1500 BC and subdued the non-Aryan people of northwest India; established Sanskrit

assembly line workers stationed along a conveyer belt assembling specific parts of a product as the item moves down the line

Assembly of Centuries the chief assembly of the early Roman Republic

assignats French Revolutionary paper money backed by Roman Catholic land that was confiscated

astrology the practice of trying to interpret human events and destiny by the position of the planets and stars

astronomy the study of celestial bodies

Athena according to Greek mythology, patron of the city of Athens; goddess of wisdom

Atlantic Charter eight-point document between Winston Churchill and Franklin Roosevelt that set forth the "common principles" on which both countries "based their hopes for a better future for the world"

atonal music music style that abandoned fixed tone patterns or keys; no special emphasis on any one note

attrition situation in which opposing sides try to gradually wear each other down

Augsburg Confession a confession written by Philipp Melanchthon that set forth the chief doctrines held by Luther and his followers

Austro-Prussian War also called Seven Weeks' War; 1866 war in which Prussia defeated Austria

Autobahnen superhighways in Germany

autocratic ruling with unlimited authority

automation machines running the machines that make the products

Avesta the sacred writings of Zoroastrianism

Aztec Central American civilization that flourished after the Mayan civilization; conquered by the Spanish

B

Baal one of the pagan gods of the Canaanites

Babel city in Shinar (probably located in southeastern Mesopotamia) that had a great tower; place where languages were born

Babylonian Captivity (1) seventy-year exile of Israelities in Babylon; (2) the period from 1309 to 1377 when the papal court dwelt in Avignon, France

baillis French royal officials whom the king appointed and paid

balance of power the goal of European nations to ensure that no nation would dominate Europe; involved the formation of alliances

Balfour Declaration British declaration to provide a home for the Jews in Palestine

banca "bench"; the table of the moneychangers

Bantu migration migration of a people group who used a family of languages that became known as the Bantu language

banzai war cry shouted by Japanese troops

barbarians a Roman term for all those outside the empire who did not share in the Greek or Roman cultures

baroque period in art history from 1600 to about 1750; having a grand, dynamic, heroic, active, swirling, sensual, and emotional style

barter exchanging goods for goods

Battle of Dien Bien Phu battle in which the Communist Vietnamese annihilated the French army

Battle of Hastings battle in England between the Normans and the Anglo-Saxons; won by William "the Conqueror," who established the Norman dynasty

Battle of Manzikert battle in Asia Minor between the Seljuk Turks and the Byzantines; established Turkish control of Asia Minor

Battle of Plassey battle in which the British defeated an Indian ruler during the Seven Years' War

Battle of the Bulge Germany's final attempt to push back the Allied advance into Germany after D-day

Battle of Tours defeat of the Muslims by the Franks; stopped the Muslim advance into Europe

Bay of Pigs failed American attempt to invade Cuba and overthrow Castro

Bedouins Arab nomads who traveled through the harsh desert wilderness in independent bands, searching for pastureland and water for their livestock

Benedictine Rule a standard of discipline and order that strictly regulated the life of monks; the most popular system of rules in medieval Europe; designed by Benedict of Nursia

Benin perhaps the most important kingdom in western Africa from 1440 to 1897

Beringia a possible ice or land bridge that may have facilitated crossing from Asia via the Bering Strait

Berlin Wall a concrete-and-barbed-wire wall physically separating East and West Berlin; most recognizable symbol of the Cold War

"Big Three" Winston Churchill, Franklin D. Roosevelt, and Joseph Stalin

Bill of Rights (1) 1689 English document that limited royal power, established certain civil liberties, and forbade future kings or queens from being Roman Catholics; (2) the first ten amendments of the United States Constitution, which defined liberties and placed restraints on governmental interference

Bismarck's System German system of alliances created by Bismarck to prevent French attack and to maintain the balance of power

blitzkrieg "lightning war"; fast-moving attack that sought to penetrate enemy lines

Bloody Sunday January 22, 1905; when the troops of the Russian czar massacred peaceful protesters

Boers Dutch colonists in South Africa

Boer War conflict between the Boers and the British; won by the British, who gained control over the Orange Free State and the Transvaal

Bolsheviks wing of the Social Democratic Party in Russia that advocated change through violence

Bourbon French royal family; descended from Louis IX

bourgeoisie middle-class property owners, capitalists, and industrialists or factory owners

Boxer Rebellion Chinese uprising against Western influences; put down by European and American troops

Brahman the great Hindu god who is believed to permeate everything in the universe

Brexit British exit from the European Union

British North America Act Act of Parliament creating the Dominion of Canada, a federation of four provinces—Quebec, Ontario, Nova Scotia, and New Brunswick

Brunswick Manifesto declaration of the Duke of Brunswick calling upon the French people to rally behind their king and to protect him from the leaders of the Revolution

Buddhism religion founded by Siddhartha Gautama (Buddha); a religion built on the Four Noble Truths

bull an official papal document

bureaucracy the nonelected officials who handle government affairs

Bushido an unwritten military code that governed the conduct of the Japanese samurai

Byzantine Empire the Eastern Roman Empire after the Western Roman Empire fell

C

cabinet government a group of advisors to the English king who met to discuss matters of state

caesar the assistant of an augustus

cahiers lists of grievances from the Estates in France

caliphs successors of Muhammad who directed the affairs of Islam and exercised spiritual, political, and military authority

calligraphy the art of beautiful writing

capital supply of money

capitalism economic system designed to advance wealth

caravel a ship with large square sails to provide power and smaller triangular sails to provide maneuverability

Carolingian House the Frankish royal house named after Charlemagne

caste system a system of rigid social groups in India

castle the center of life for the nobility; the lord's home, the local jail, the treasury, the armory, the court, and the seat of government

catholic "universal"; "encompassing all"; the term of early Christians for the church

caudillos ambitious military leaders who ruled as dictators

Cavaliers supporters of the king in the English Civil War

ceiba tree the sacred tree of the Mayas

Central Powers Germany, Austria-Hungary, and the Ottoman Empire during World War I

chain migration result of allowing aliens who were granted amnesty by Congress in 1986 to apply for immediate family members to come to the United States

Champa a kingdom that thrived in central and southern Vietnam until the Dai Viet gained control of the territory

charter a legal document that outlined the privileges granted to a town by a feudal lord

Chartism nineteenth-century British reform movement that advocated universal manhood suffrage, the secret ballot, equal electoral districts, pay for members of Parliament, no property qualifications for members of Parliament, and annual elections to Parliament

Chichén Itzá Mayan city that was a center of power and influence

chivalry a knight's strict code of behavior

Christian socialism philosophy held by theological liberals who viewed socialism as "the embodiment of Christianity in our culture"

Christian worldview composed of three central truths: (1) God made the world and everything in it; (2) this world has fallen into a sad and broken condition because of human sin; and (3) God is working to redeem this world to Himself; see **worldview**

circumnavigation sailing around the world

Cistercians monastic order that adopted lives of seclusion and strict discipline; made popular by Bernard of Clairvaux

cities central locations for a particular group of people where government, religion, and culture are found

citizenship the status a person has within a community that gives this person certain rights, priviliges, and duties

Civil Constitution of the Clergy placed the French church under state control, provided for the election of all the clergy by the people, and required the clergy to take an oath of loyalty to the state

civilization human culture lived in cities or under their influence

civil rights movement African American movement to gain fair and equal treatment in matters such as voting and access to public facilities

clan (1) a number of families from a common ancestor; (2) a group of families claiming descent from a common ancestor; the basic social, political, and religious unit in Japan

clergy those who took "Holy Orders" in special service to the church

coalition a temporary alliance of nations

Code Napoleon Napoleon's codification of French laws

Cold War post–World War II state of apprehension, hostility, and competition between the Soviet Union and the United States

collectivize bring under central government control

College of Cardinals a Roman Catholic assembly of cardinals that chooses a new pope; created to ensure that churchmen rather than Roman nobles or German kings would choose the popes

Comintern "Communist International"; a group established to found Communist parties in other countries and to take an active role in stirring up discontent in hopes of producing revolution

Commercial Revolution the economic changes in European business practice and thinking during the fifteenth and sixteenth centuries

Committee of Public Safety twelve-man committee headed by Robespierre that managed the everyday affairs of the French Revolutionary government; see **Reign of Terror**

common law uniform laws in England determined by justices

Commonwealth of Independent States CIS; organization of former countries of the USSR

company an organization of men who pool their resources, sharing gains as well as losses

compass a magnetized navigation device that greatly aided sailors during the age of exploration

Concert of Europe international cooperation set up through the congress system to avoid major wars and to suppress nationalism and liberalism

Concordat of Worms recognized the right of the church to elect its own bishops and abbots and to invest them with spiritual authority; required that elections be held in the presence of the emperor or his representatives

Confucianism religion founded by Confucius that is based on relationships

Congress of Vienna a meeting of European statesmen at the end of the Napoleonic Wars

conquistadors "conquerors" sent from Spain to the New World to search for riches, convert the Indians to Catholicism, and establish Spanish authority

consul annually elected leaders of the Roman Republic who held the imperium

containment the use of a variety of means to curtail the further advance of communism

Continental System attempt by Napoleon to blockade British trade by closing Europe's ports to British ships

Cortés Spanish council composed of nobles, clergy, and representatives of the cities

corvée French system of forced labor

Council of Constance fifteenth-century Roman Catholic Church council that ended the Great Schism

Council of Nicaea church council in 325 that affirmed the doctrines of Christ's deity and the Trinity

Council of Trent the Counter Reformation council that condemned justification by faith alone and the sole authority of Scripture, set forth a complete doctrinal position of the Roman Church, and sealed the break between Protestant and Roman Catholic churches

Counter Reformation another term for the Catholic Reformation, which opposed the Protestant Reformation

coup d'état a sudden and illegal seizure of power

Creation Mandate first command from God revealing that man's reason for being is to subdue the earth and exercise dominion over it; found in Genesis 1:28

Crimean War war in which Britain, France, and the Kingdom of Sardinia defeated Russia

criollos Spaniards born in the New World

Crusades military expeditions from the West to free the East from the Muslims

Cuban Missile Crisis confrontation between the United States and the USSR after the USSR placed offensive missiles on Cuba

cubism second major artistic movement of the twentieth century; often portrayed reality by geometric shapes seen from various perspectives at once

Cultural Revolution Communist China's attempt to stir up zeal for radical communism; resulted in civil chaos and economic decline

culture the physical and mental environment developed through human thought and labor

culture areas areas in which several tribes lived near each other and shared similar customs, means of livelihood, and level of civilization

culture system Dutch colonial system that required natives to use one-fifth of their land and one-fifth of their time in growing crops for the Dutch

cuneiform the earliest known form of writing

curia regis the Great Council; an English feudal body composed of chief vassals; "king's council"

D

D-day the day when an attack is to be launched; June 6, 1944, the day that the Allied forces invaded France

Declaration of Independence document whereby the American colonies declared their independence from Britain

Declaration of the Rights of Man French Revolutionary document that outlined what the National Assembly considered to be the natural rights of all people and the rights that they possessed as citizens

deductive method reasoning from the general to the specific

deism belief in God as the First Cause; denies supernatural prophecy and miracles; teaches that man is born good; regards reason as the standard for truth

deists those who regard reason as the standard of truth and the guide to understanding the universe and the proper way to worship God

Delhi Sultanate one of the few kingdoms in Asia to successfully repel a full-scale Mongol invasion for nearly three hundred years

Delian League defensive alliance of Greek city-states led by Athens against the Persians

democracy rule by the people

détente relaxation of tensions

Diaspora the scattering of the Jewish people

Dai Viet a kingdom formed by Vietnamese that broke from Chinese domination

Diet the German equivalent of the English Parliament and the French Estates-General

Diet of Worms the Diet in 1521 at which Martin Luther held to the contents of the books that he had written

Diplomatic Revolution radical changes in traditional European alliances prior to the Seven Years' War

Directory French Revolutionary government after the National Convention; two chamber legislature; five Directors; overthrown by Napoleon

disarmament elimination of weapons or arms

dividends profit given to the stockholders of a joint-stock company

divine providence biblical teaching that there is no event that is out of God's control or that does not help to accomplish His purpose for this world

divine right belief that the king was established by God and therefore had absolute power and was not bound by human law

division of labor dividing the manufacturing process into several simple procedures among a number of workers

Djenné-Djeno perhaps the oldest city in West Africa

"do-nothing kings" seventh-century Merovingian kings who reigned but did not rule, the real power being held by the mayor of the palace

Domesday Book a survey of property taken in England when William "the Conqueror" conquered England

domestic system workers living at home and working there with their own hand tools

domino theory the Cold War theory that once Vietnam fell to communism, then other countries of Asia would fall like dominos toppling against one another

Dorians invaders that conquered the Mycenaean civilization around 1200 BC

Dual Alliance the alliance between Germany and Austria-Hungary; the foundation of pre–World War I German foreign policy

Dual Monarchy the Austro-Hungarian Empire under one crown

dualism philosophical system in which there are two types of reality (e.g., spiritual and physical)

Duma Russian national assembly

dynastic rule the rule of one family

E

Eastern Orthodox Church made up of various national churches that refused to recognize the Church of Rome's claim of control

Eastern Woodlands Indians American Indian civilization that developed in the Southeast and along the Atlantic coast into the Northeast

Edict of Milan edict of Constantine in 313 that made Christianity legal

Edict of Nantes edict of Henry IV that gave the Huguenots a certain amount of religious toleration

empire the rule of one people over another

empiricism the idea that all knowledge comes through experience

Ems dispatch report of a meeting between William I of Prussia and a French ambassador that was altered and published by Bismarck; immediate cause of the Franco-Prussian War

enclosure movement the incorporation of common grazing lands into the estates of wealthy landowners to form large farms

Enlightenment the eighteenth-century intellectual movement that looked to reason as the solution for all of life's problems

Entente Cordiale agreement between Britain and France

environment the physical geography in which civilizations are located

Epic of Gilgamesh Sumerian literature that describes the adventures of Gilgamesh and includes an account of a universal flood

Epicureanism philosophy that teaches that true happiness comes only as man frees his mind from fear and his body from pain

Estates-General French representative body composed of clergy, nobility, and townspeople

Etruscans one of Italy's earliest civilizations, which lived along Italy's western coast, just north of the Tiber River, and possibly contributed to the development of Roman culture

EU European Union; union of European countries

euro single currency of the member nations of the European Union

evaluation of historical sources examination of a given record for its internal consistency and believability

excommunicate to punish an individual by depriving him of the sacraments and excluding him from the fellowship of the church

existentialism philosophy that rejected absolute truth and the idea of purpose in life; taught that individuals must search for their own meaning

expressionism artistic movement in which the artist tries to paint how he feels about his subject rather than trying to reproduce realistically what he sees

extraterritoriality an individual's right to be tried in his own national court for breaking the law of another country

F

Fabian socialism British socialists who sought to achieve a socialist society without revolution

factory system production system that brought the workers, raw materials, and machinery under one roof

fasces a small bundle of rods that enclosed an axe; symbol of the king's power

fascism totalitarian government characterized by corporate economy, strong nationalism, military dictatorship, and a glorification of the state

federalism delegating specified powers to the national government and reserving all other powers for the state governments or the people

Fertile Crescent crescent-shaped fertile region encompassing Mesopotamia and the land of Canaan

feudalism a political system in which local rulers offered the people protection in return for their services

fiefs land grants given in return for services

fifth columnists individuals within a country who secretly aid the enemy by spying, spreading enemy propaganda, carrying out acts of sabotage, or other similar activities

Fifth Republic French government established by Charles de Gaulle that provided for a strong president

First Estate composed of upper clergy of the Roman Catholic Church

Five Pillars of Islam certain religious duties that Islam requires every Muslim to perform in order to reach paradise; (1) reciting the simple confession "There is no God but Allah, and Muhammad is his prophet"; (2) reciting prayers five times daily while facing toward Mecca; (3) giving alms (money) to the poor; (4) fasting from sunrise to sunset during the sacred month of Ramadan; (5) making a pilgrimage to Mecca, if physically and financially able

Five-Year Plans economic program of Joseph Stalin that increased the socialization of the Russian economy

footbinding a Chinese custom that involved breaking toes in order to bind a girl's foot to keep them dainty

Foreign Legion elite French army that was used throughout France's colonial empire

Four Noble Truths the center of Buddha's teachings; (1) Suffering is part of all existence; (2) Suffering has a cause—selfish desires; (3) Suffering can be overcome by destroying selfish desires; (4) If man follows the Eightfold Path, he will destroy selfish desires and end all suffering.

1492 the year that Ferdinand and Isabella completed the reconquest by driving the Moors out of Granada; the year that Christopher Columbus, under Spanish sponsorship, landed in the New World

Fourteen Points Woodrow Wilson's proposed peace plan after World War I

Franco-Prussian War war between France and Prussia immediately caused by the Ems dispatch; won by Prussia, ending the Second French Empire

Franks the most powerful Germanic people in the early Middle Ages; kingdom ruled by the Merovingian House and the Carolingian House

freemen more privileged peasants who served as manorial officials or provided skilled labor, such as blacksmiths, millers, and carpenters

frescoes paintings on wet plaster

Fujiwara a clan that took over Japan by marrying their daughters to the sons of the imperial family and forcing the ruling emperor to abdicate when a son was born

G

GDP Gross Domestic Product; the monetary value of all goods and services produced within a geographic border

General Assembly body of the United Nations where all member nations have representation

geocentric theory earth-centered theory of the universe

Gestapo Nazi secret police

Ghana prominent African kingdom from 700 to 1200; became a major destination for commercial caravans crossing Africa

ghettos Jewish areas of a city sealed off from the rest of the city

glasnost "openness"; Soviet policy of encouraging open discussions of the problems facing the USSR

globalization characterized by an international rather than a purely national focus

Glorious Revolution peaceful revolution in which Parliament dethroned James II and installed William and Mary as joint rulers

Golden Bull established the Diet of the Holy Roman Empire

Golden Horde Mongol state based in Russia; founded by Batu Khan; the strongest Mongol state in western Asia

gospel the teaching that Jesus Christ died in the place of sinful humans so that they might be forgiven of their sins and be able to claim as their own the righteousness of Jesus Christ

Gothic light and delicate architecture beginning in the thirteenth century with flying buttresses, higher ceilings, thinner walls, larger windows and doors, and stained glass windows

Grand Alliance an alliance of European nations—especially England and the Netherlands—against Louis XIV of France

Grand Canal built by conscripted workers; connected the Yellow and Yangtze Rivers in China

Great Awakening eighteenth-century revival in Britain's American colonies

Great Leap Forward Mao's attempt to modernize China's agrarian economy; wrecked the Chinese steel industry and caused a famine

Great Northern War war in which the Russians, led by Peter the Great, defeated Sweden and won additional territory along the Baltic Sea

Great Schism the period from the late fourteenth to early fifteenth century during which the Roman Catholic Church had two to three men claiming to be the pope

Great Serpent Mound famous effigy mound

Great Trek migration of the Boers northward from Cape Colony in South Africa

"Greek fire" an explosive mixture of chemicals possibly including quicklime, sulfur, naphtha, and potassium nitrate

guerrillas "little wars"; small bands of troops that attack a superior force

guilds organizations whose primary function was to regulate the business activity of a given town

Gulf of Tonkin Resolution congressional authorization for American President Lyndon Johnson to "take all necessary measures to repel any armed attack against forces of the United States and to prevent further aggression"

Gupta Empire fourth-century Indian empire under which India had perhaps its greatest era of prosperity and achievement

H

Habeas Corpus Act made it illegal for the British government to arbitrarily hold someone in jail

Hagia Sophia finest example of Byzantine architecture; built by Justinian

Hamas a radical Islamic group recognized as a terrorist organization by the UN; developed during the first *intifada* as a more radical Islamic counterpart to the PLO

Hanseatic League an association composed of more than seventy German cities in northwestern Europe; sought to organize and control trade in Sweden, Russia, Flanders, and England

Habsburgs German noble family who built a strong base of power (Austria) among the southern German states

Hegira the flight of Muhammad from Mecca to Medina; year 1 of the Muslim calendar

heliocentric theory theory that the sun is the center of the universe and that the earth and other planets orbit around it; promoted by Copernicus

Hellenic Greek culture

Hellenistic similar to Greek culture

Helots original Spartans who were enslaved by the Dorians

hierarchical describes a structure with levels of authority

hieroglyphics a form of picture writing

Hinduism Indian religion that has no formal statement of doctrine but is based on the *Vedas* and *Upanishads*; serves as a unifying influence in India's diverse society

Hiroshima the Japanese city where the first atomic bomb was dropped

historical interpretation interpreting events by integrating the perceived meaning and significance of the events

historical synthesis gathering the useful information and weaving the information together into a narrative of the past

history the study of the record of the past acts of God and man on earth from its creation to the present, based on the best surviving evidence

Hohenstaufens German royal family that rose to prominence in the twelfth century

Hohenzollern rulers of Prussia; rivals of the Habsburgs; united the German states into one country in the nineteenth century

Holocaust Nazi Germany's attempt to exterminate the Jews

Holy Roman Empire the name of the German empire because of its alliance with the Roman Catholic Church and its symbolic association with the empire of ancient Rome

homage the ceremony by which a man became a vassal and thus eligible for a fief

Hopi Indian tribe in the Southwest known for its peaceful culture

Hopewell a dispersed group of related Indian populations that were probably united by a network of trade routes

Huguenots French Protestants

humanism a renewed focus on man's capacities

humanists those who studied the liberal arts

humanities (1) formal study of human thought and culture; (2) the liberal arts; the study of history, science, and grammar, as well as classical literature and philosophy

Hundred Years' War war between England and France during the fourteenth and fifteenth centuries; won by the French

Huns nomadic tribe led by Attila whose advance forced Germanic tribes to seek refuge in Roman territory

I

icon a painted image of Christ or a saint

Il Duce title of Mussolini; the head of the Italian Fascist government

Île-de-France the small area around Paris owned by the Capetians

Iliad an epic poem of the Greek Dark Ages written by Homer

image of God a quality possessed by all humans that reflects part of God's own personality

imperator an ancient title given to the commander of a victorious army; head of the Roman Empire

imperialism the extension of power by one people or country over another country

imperium the king's authority in Rome

impressionism nineteenth-century French art style; focused on light and color and used short, choppy brush strokes

Inca South American kingdom from the thirteenth to sixteenth centuries

indemnities compensation to other nations for war damages

Index of Prohibited Books a list of books that the Roman Catholic Church has condemned

indictment accusation

inductive method reasoning from specific cases to a general conclusion

indulgences certificates which, according to Catholicism, granted pardon from the punishment of sins

Industrial Revolution a period in the eighteenth and nineteenth centuries when technological developments radically changed industry

Inquisition a special church court commissioned by the pope to stamp out heresy

The Institutes of the Christian Religion theological book written by John Calvin; one of the most significant and influential books on theology ever written

interchangeable parts identical parts that could be used to replace broken parts in manufactured goods

interdict the suspension of public church services and of the administration of all sacraments (except baptism and extreme unction) in a given location

intifada the "uprising" of the Palestinians against the Israelis

investiture symbolic act by which the lord gave to the vassal the right to use a fief

iron curtain the dividing line between Western Europe and Communist Eastern Europe

ISIS Islamic State in Iraq and Syria; led by Abu Bakr al-Baghdadi

Islam a religion based on the teachings of Muhammad

J

Jacobins French revolutionaries who advocated the most radical changes; appealed to Paris workers known as the *sans-culottes*

Jamestown first English permanent settlement in the New World; located in Virginia

Jesuits Roman Catholic religious order founded by Ignatius Loyola that suppressed heresy and promoted Roman Catholic education

jihad Islamic "holy war"

joint family extended family that includes the children, grandchildren, wives, and close blood relatives of a common ancestor

joint-stock company a company in which people invested money and in return were issued stock certificates showing the amount of money they invested; the company used this capital to finance a business venture; if the company made a profit, the stockholders received payment in the form of dividends

journeyman second class of a craft guild; "day laborer"; could seek employment and earn wages as a skilled worker

July Revolution revolution in France in 1830 that brought down Charles X and established Louis Philippe as king; sparked other revolutions throughout Europe

June Days attempted overthrow of the French government in June 1848

justice a social condition in which people do right and respect the rights of others

"just price" a price that included the cost of materials, a fair return for the labor expended, and a reasonable profit

Justinian Code a systematic arrangement of laws that clarified Roman legal principles

K

Ka'bah a sacred shrine at Mecca that housed hundreds of pagan idols; was turned into the center of Islamic worship by Muhammad, who destroyed the idols of the Ka'bah—except the Black Stone

kamikaze Japanese suicide pilots

karma a person's deeds in life that Hindus believe determine his status in the next

Kellogg-Briand Pact document that outlawed war, but failed to stop it; crowning effort to preserve peace in the post–World War I period

Khmer an empire that developed sometime between the ninth and thirteenth centuries in Cambodia

Kilwa a prosperous city-state in East Africa

knight medieval warriors who protected life and property and lived by the code of chivalry

Korean War war between Communist North Korea and non-Communist South Korea from 1950 to 1953

Kush province of Egypt that eventually won independence from Egypt

L

laissez faire hands-off policy in which the government does not interfere in business and trade but provides a favorable climate for business activity

laity common church parishioners who did not take Holy Orders

language families groups of Indian languages that are believed to have had a single ancestral language

Lateran Treaties treaties between Benito Mussolini and the Roman Catholic Church that established Vatican City and gave Italy's government recognition by the Roman Catholic Church

latitude distance from the equator

Law of the Twelve Tables foundation of Roman civil law

lay investiture claim of kings and nobles not only to appoint church officials but also to invest them with their religious authority

League of Nations post–World War I international organization that sought to guarantee international cooperation and to achieve international peace and security

League of the Seven Hills league of seven villages on the banks of the Tiber River; the beginning of the city of Rome

lebensraum "living space"; Hitler's early reason for expanding German territory

Lend-Lease Act Act of Congress authorizing the president to "sell, transfer title to, exchange, lease, lend, or otherwise dispose of" military supplies to any country whose security was important to the United States

levée en masse a nation calling upon all its citizens to take an active part in the war effort; employed during the French Revolution

liberalism political theory supporting an increase in civil and political freedoms and less government interference with the individual (early nineteenth century)

limited wars wars limited to specific geographic areas

Line of Demarcation line of separation in the Atlantic Ocean that decided the areas that could be colonized by Spain and Portugal

Locarno Pact 1925 treaty in which Germany agreed to recognize its post–World War I boundaries with France and Belgium as permanent and to not seek to change its eastern border through war

Lollards followers of John Wycliffe

Lombards Germanic tribe that conquered most of Italy

longbow English bow that could shoot arrows able to penetrate certain types of armor

Long Count calendar name for the precise calendar developed by the Mayas

lord landholding noble in feudalism

Louisiana Purchase 1803 land purchase by the United States that almost doubled the size of that nation

Luftwaffe Nazi Germany's air force

Lusitania British ocean liner that was sunk by a German submarine in 1915

M

Maastricht Treaty treaty between many European countries to form the European Union

Maginot Line a series of French fortifications along France's border with Germany

Magna Carta a guarantee of feudal rights; one of the most important documents in English history because it showed that the king was under the law

Magyars Asiatic nomads who terrorized southeastern Europe in medieval times

Mali western African kingdom noted for its agricultural productivity as well as its transdesert trade in gold, salt, and copper

Manchu dynasty ruling dynasty in China that began in 1644 and underwent wars and uprisings related to foreigners

mandates territories technically under the control of the League of Nations but administered by various Allied countries

mannerism artistic style that was prevalent throughout much of the sixteenth century; characterized by distortions and exaggerations

manor the center of medieval society; a self-contained farming community controlled by a lord and farmed by peasants

Maoris New Zealand natives

Mare Nostrum the Roman term for the Mediterranean Sea; "our sea"

Marshall Plan European Recovery Act; provided massive economic assistance for post–World War II Europe

Marxism theory that every social, political, or religious movement springs from a desire by one group of people to take economic advantage of another group; taught that history would naturally progress toward perfection (communism)

mass the Roman Catholic service in which the Holy Eucharist is offered

master third class of a craft guild; could open his own shop and take on apprentices and journeymen

Maya Central American civilization (ca. 2000 BC–AD 1539) whose culture was centered on their religious beliefs

Mayflower Compact a temporary agreement establishing civil authority for the Plymouth Colony

mayor of the palace the real power behind the throne under the Merovingian House

Medici family prominent Italians who had become extremely wealthy through commerce and banking; used their riches and prominence to gain political control of the city of Florence

Meiji Period period during which Japan was transformed from a feudal society to a major industrial power

Mein Kampf "My Struggle"; book by Adolf Hitler

Mensheviks wing of the Social Democratic Party in Russia that advocated change through peaceful measures

mercantilism economic system that held that the wealth of colonies should benefit the mother country

Merovingian House first royal line of the Franks

Mesopotamia the fertile region between the Tigris and Euphrates Rivers

mestizos those of mixed Spanish and Indian blood

middle class social class primarily composed of merchants, bankers, craftsmen, and skilled laborers

Middle Kingdom Chinese term reflecting their belief that China was the center of the earth

minaret a tower that is a part of or adjacent to a mosque

Ming dynasty restored Chinese rule and reestablished Chinese ways

Minoan civilization an early civilization in the Aegean region based on the island of Crete; established trade with the Fertile Crescent and Egypt

Mississippian Indian culture that broadly covered the central Mississippi River Valley and extended to the Ohio River Valley and south to parts of Kentucky, Tennessee, Alabama, and Mississippi

monarchy rule by one

moneychangers men experienced in judging the approximate value of coins, discovering counterfeit currency, and determining one currency's value in relation to another

monotheism belief in only one God

Monroe Doctrine warning by James Monroe that the United States would resist any efforts to colonize the Americas; included a promise that the United States would not interfere in European affairs

Moors Spanish Muslims

moratorium suspension

mosaic inlaid pieces of glass or stone in wet cement or plaster

mosque place of Muslim worship

Mound Builders North American Indians known for their large burial mounds and effigy mounds

movable type separate printing blocks for each character

muezzin one who calls faithful Muslims to prayer five times a day from a minaret

Mughal Turkish-Mongol dynasty in India; founded by Babur

Munich Conference 1938 conference in which Britain and France gave the Sudetenland to Hitler

Muslim follower of Islam; "submitter to Allah"

Mycenaean civilization early Greek civilization on the mainland of Greece; borrowed heavily from the Minoan civilization

N

NAFTA North American Free Trade Agreement; intended to lower trade barriers and enhance trade between these countries; resulted in a trade deficit/imbalance for the United States

Nagasaki the Japanese city where the second atomic bomb was dropped

nation very large group of people (usually including many cities) who have in common the same land area and the same language

nationalism a longing for independence and local autonomy

nation-state an independent group of people having common traditions and ruled by a king

NATO North Atlantic Treaty Organization; a regional military alliance to defend against Soviet expansion

Nazism German fascism

neoclassical artistic style that used themes of ancient Greece and Rome

Neolithic Age the period from 10,000 BC to about 4,000 BC called the New Stone Age; framework of the evolutionary worldview

New Deal Franklin Roosevelt's program of relief, recovery, and reform in response to the Great Depression

New Economic Policy capitalistic program to revitalize the economy of the USSR after the Russian Revolution

"New Rome" Constantine's name for Constantinople

Nika Revolt a popular uprising crushed by Justinian early in his reign; the turning point of Justinian's reign

Ninety-five Theses a list of statements concerning the sale of indulgences that Martin Luther proposed as topics for a scholarly debate

Nok culture the earliest evidence for civilization in West Africa

O

Odyssey an epic poem of the Greek Dark Ages written by Homer

Old Regime political and social order in France before the French Revolution

oligarchy rule of a few

Olympiad four-year period between Olympic games; became a Greek means of dating historical events

Operation Overlord code name for the Allied invasion of France during World War II

Opium Wars wars between China and European powers led by Great Britain; fought over the issue of importing opium into China

Orange Revolution uprising by which Ukraine gained independence from Russian dominance in 2004

organization a system of rules, regulations, and accountability that governs all who take part in the functions of a city

Ottoman Turks the Muslim invaders who conquered Constantinople

P

pacifism refusal to take up arms against anyone, even in time of war

Pact of Steel German-Italian military alliance prior to World War II

page a boy placed under the care of a knight for the purpose of becoming a knight

Paleolithic Age time period in history when man used very simple stone tools; framework of the evolutionary worldview

pantheism the belief that everything in the universe, whether it be spiritual or physical, is all part of one great substance called "god"

Paris Peace Conference conference that negotiated the peace settlement for World War I

Parliament the English representative body consisting of two houses, the House of Commons and the House of Lords; had the "power of the purse"

Parliament Bill of 1911 capstone of Britain's political development; made the House of Commons dominant; limited the House of Lords

partisans fighters who harass an enemy occupying their territory

passive resistance a nonviolent program defying the current rule through strikes (including hunger strikes and sit-down strikes), mass demonstrations, and refusal to pay taxes

Parthenon most spectacular temple in ancient Athens; dedicated to the city's patron goddess Athena

patriarch bishop of one of the most important cities of the empire; appointed in Jerusalem, Antioch, Alexandria, Rome, and Constantinople

patrician the aristocratic class in ancient Rome made up of wealthy landowners and noble families

patrons sponsors of artists

Pax Romana "Roman Peace"; 31 BC to AD 180

Pax Sinica "Chinese Peace" established by the Han Dynasty

"peaceful coexistence" the Cold War policy that sought "to keep to the positions of ideological struggle without resorting to arms to prove that one is right"

Peace of Augsburg allowed each German prince the right to choose whether his territory would be Lutheran or Roman Catholic

Peace of God medieval decree by which the church forbade the pillage of its property and extended protection to all noncombatants in society

Peace of Westphalia name for the peace treaties that ended the Thirty Years' War

Peloponnesian League a league of Greek city-states led by Sparta with the intention of protecting against foreign invasion and to prevent tyranny and democracy

Peloponnesian War Greek civil war between Athens and her allies and Sparta and her allies

peninsulares Spaniards born and raised in Spain

per capita GDP goods produced per person

perestroika Soviet policy during the 1980s of a wide range of social, political, and economic reforms; "restructuring"

Petition of Right document sent by Parliament to Charles I which stated that the king did not have the right to make people pay taxes without parliamentary consent and that Parliament would not tolerate arbitrary imprisonment of any subjects

Petrine theory the Roman Catholic theory that Christ made Peter the first pope and gave him supreme authority over the church on earth; also states that Peter subsequently transferred this office and its authority to those who succeeded him as bishop of Rome

pharaoh ruler of ancient Egypt

philosophers men who sought the answers to the basic questions of life through human reasoning

philosophes mistakenly believed that the right philosophy could solve society's problems and that perfectibilty was attainable for both society and man

Pietism movement that began in the seventeenth century; dedicated to spiritual renewal

Pilgrims group of English Separatists that left for the New World in 1620

plebeian the "common" class in ancient Rome made up of farmers, traders, and craftsmen

plebiscite a resolution of the Council of Plebeians

PLO Palestinian Liberation Organization; demanded a separate Palestinian state and initiated intifada

pogroms organized government massacres in Russia

polis "city-state"; basic political unit of Greece

polygamy marriage of a husband to more than one wife

polytheism belief in many gods

polytonality the use of several musical keys simultaneously

pontifex maximus "greatest priest"; title of the Roman emperors

pope the bishop of Rome; first used of the bishop of Rome in 452 and generally accepted as his title by the end of the sixth century

popular sovereignty government based upon the consent of the governed

power the ability to bring things under one's control

"power of the purse" a representative body's power to approve all new taxes; a means of forcing the king to hear grievances

Pragmatic Sanction agreement among European rulers to respect the territorial boundaries of Austria when Maria Theresa came to the throne

primary sources records produced during the time period being studied, usually by those involved in the events being studied

princeps "first citizen"; a title taken by Octavian

proletariat the workers in a Marxist society

propaganda materials and methods of indoctrination

prospectus details of a proposed business venture

Protectorate English government established by Oliver Cromwell

publican tax collector for the Roman Republic in provinces

Pueblo Indians group of Southwest tribes who lived in small villages or caves and ledges of canyons

Punic Wars three wars between Carthage and Rome

purgatory a place of temporary punishment where souls bound for heaven must go after death to atone for their "minor" unconfessed sins

purges Stalin's practice of murdering those who might threaten his power

Puritans those who wanted to purify the Anglican Church of those practices that reminded them of Roman Catholicism; Anglicans who sought to purify the Church of England

Q

quadrivium liberal-arts curriculum consisting of arithmetic, geometry, astronomy, and music

Quadruple Alliance alliance between Austria, Prussia, Russia, and Great Britain to maintain the Congress of Vienna's settlements

Quebec Act act permitting French Canadians to retain their language, law, and customs and to freely practice their Roman Catholic religion

quipu also known as khipu; collections of knotted strings used for accounting and recording data

Qur'an the sacred book of the Muslims

R

RAF British Royal Air Force

rationalism the belief that reason is the only sure source of knowledge and truth

realism an artistic style that sought to portray life as it really was

realpolitik "politics of reality"; using whatever political means necessary—including force—to advance national goals

recant renounce one's beliefs

Reconquista the reconquest of the Iberian Peninsula, which was held by the Muslims

Reformation a protest against the corruption in the Roman Catholic Church during the sixteenth century

Reform Bill of 1832 1832 bill that reorganized the electoral system for the House of Commons

regular clergy clergy who lived in monastic communities under strict regulations

Reichstag the lower house of the German Parliament

Reign of Terror most destructive and violent phase of the French Revolution

Reinsurance Treaty Bismarck's alliance with Russia

religion a system of basic values, beliefs, and behaviors that are directed in worship toward God and lived out in community with others

Renaissance the revival of learning in Europe from the fourteenth century through the sixteenth century

reparations payments for war damages

republic form of government in which voting citizens exercise power through elected officials under law

Restoration reestablishment of the Stuart monarchy in 1660

Risorgimento Italian nationalist movement

Roman Forum the section of ancient Rome that was the center of government

Romanov Russian royal dynasty; overthrown by the Revolution of 1917

Roman sacramental system a system of religious acts which Roman Catholics believe grants grace (spiritual benefit) based on the recipient's right intentions

Romanesque the prevalent architectural style in Europe from 1050 to 1150; means "Roman-like"

romanticism late eighteenth-century European literary and artistic movement characterized by a reaction against rationalism and an embrace of idealism and emotions

Rome-Berlin Axis alliance between Nazi Germany and fascist Italy

Rose Revolution the country of Georgia's peaceful overthrow of the pro-Russian government in 2003

Roundheads supporters of Parliament in the English Civil War

Rus the Slavic designation of the Norsemen; "rowers" or "seafarers"

Russification Nicholas I's policy of uniting the diverse national groups within Nicholas's territory around the culture and traditions of Russia

Russo-Japanese War war between Japan and Russia; won by Japan in 1905

S

St. Bartholomew's Day Massacre massacre of Huguenots throughout France on August 27, 1572

Salian House German royal house that tried, unsuccessfully, to bring the German nobles under royal control

SALT Strategic Arms Limitation Talks; limited the number of nuclear weapons that the United States and the USSR could possess

samurai Japanese warrior

sanctions forbidding the sale of certain materials to a country

Sanskrit early Indian language established by the Aryans

satrapies provinces in the Persian Empire

Schlieffen Plan Germany's plan for a two-front war

Scholasticism a twelfth-century intellectual movement that was characterized by a renewed interest in theology and philosophy

scientific revolution a period from the Renaissance to the eighteenth century when scientific inquiry and achievement advanced rapidly

scorched-earth policy burning everything that might be of value to the enemy

Scramble for Africa a race between European nations to seize strategic regions in Africa

SDI Strategic Defense Initiative; American defense program designed to use American space, laser, and satellite technology to provide a shield in space against incoming Soviet missiles

SEATO Southeast Asia Treaty Organization; formed to keep Asian nations free from communism

secondary sources records that explain or interpret primary sources

Second Estate nobility; segment of French society

Secretariat administrative arm of the United Nations; headed by the Secretary General

secular clergy conducted religious services, administered the sacraments to the laity, and supervised the business and property of the church

Security Council the executive, or enforcement, power of the United Nations; consists of five permanent members and ten non-permanent members, elected by the General Assembly to two-year rotating terms

seed of the serpent humans yet to be born who would prove to have the same deceptive, God-defying nature that Satan evidenced in the Garden of Eden

seed of the woman refers primarily to Christ but also includes future humans who are united to Him in faith

Seljuk Turks nomadic tribes from central Asia that adopted Arab culture and the Islamic religion

Senate the most important and most powerful body of the Roman Republic

Separatists those who removed themselves from the Anglican Church

Sepoy Mutiny 1857 revolt by the sepoys, native Indian troops employed by the East India Company, due to the introduction of rifle cartridges rumored to be greased with cow and pig fat (offensive to Hindus and Muslims)

serfs majority of those living on a manor; their status was midway between the ancient slave and the medieval freeman

seven sacraments baptism, confirmation, penance, the Holy Eucharist, matrimony, Holy Orders, and Extreme Unction

Seven Years' War war with Britain and Prussia on one side and France, Russia, and Austria on the other; won by Britain and Prussia in 1763

17th parallel the 1954 border between North Vietnam and South Vietnam

shamanism based on the belief that a gifted person can interact with spirits

Shintoism originally a form of nature worship that attributed deity to anything in nature that was awe-inspiring or extraordinary; stressed the supremacy of the sun goddess and the divine descent of the emperor; a religion of feeling

shogun "great general"; military ruler of Japan; held the real power over the Japanese government from 1192 to 1868

Sikhism from the Punjabi term meaning "disciple" or "learner;" founded around 1500 by a Hindu man named Nanak; promotes meditation to sense god's presence and maintain control over the "Five Thieves"—lust, rage, greed, attachment, and conceit

simony the buying and selling of religious articles as well as church offices

Sino-Japanese War war between China and Japan (1894–95); won by Japan

Sistine Chapel a chapel in the Vatican; ceiling painted by Michelangelo

sitzkrieg "sitting war"; the beginning of World War II in the West when there were no major offensives

Six-Day War war in which Israel launched a preemptive strike against Egypt, Syria, and Jordan; won by Israel

Slavs a group that settled in Eastern Europe after the Germanic tribes migrated west; the largest people group in Russia

social classes composed of people with specific functions

socialism government ownership of the means of production and the distribution of goods for the presumed welfare of society

sola fide justification by faith alone; Reformation doctrine that a man is not justified before God by his works or by faith and works but by faith alone

Solidarity a powerful labor union in Poland that opposed the Polish Communist government

Song dynasty restored order under Emperor Taizu; politically weak compared to China's previous dynasties

Songhai Empire overthrew the Mali Empire but was ended by invading Moroccan forces

Spanish Armada a fleet of 130 ships that was to sail to the Netherlands, pick up a large Spanish army, and transport the invasion force to England; defeated by the English and storms in 1588

specialization an individual's focus on a specific job or skill

Sputnik the Russian satellite that was the first manmade satellite launched into space

squire the personal servant of a knight

Statute of Westminster act of Parliament declaring Canada, Australia, New Zealand, and South Africa to be "autonomous communities within the British Empire" and "members of the British Commonwealth of Nations"

steppes vast grassy plains from western China to eastern Europe

Stoicism philosophy that taught that the highest good is the pursuit of courage, dignity, duty, simplicity of life, and service to fellow men

sub-Saharan Africa the part of Africa south of the Sahara

Suez Crisis 1956 event in which Egypt took control of the Suez Canal and Israel took control of the Sinai Peninsula

Sui dynasty Chinese dynasty that briefly united China through marriage alliances and military expansion; emerged under the leadership of Yang Jian and his son, Yangdi

summit conference of high-level officials

Swahili the native African language of the east African city-states; contains elements of the Arabic, Persian, and Indian languages

swastika Nazi symbol

syllogism a three-step logical process of thinking

synagogues Jewish centers of worship

T

Table of Nations Genesis 10; lists the descendants of Shem, Ham, and Japheth according to the nations that arose from their families

Taika Reform mid-seventh-century restructuring of Japanese government to weaken the strength of the local clan chieftains; known as the "Great Change"

taille French tax on real and personal property

Taj Mahal a stunning example of Mughal architecture

Taliban radical Muslims that gained control in Afghanistan

Tang dynasty became the second golden age in Chinese history (the Han dynasty being the first golden age)

Taoism founded by Laozi (also Lao-tzu); encouraged men to live in harmony with nature ; became the basis of mystical, magical, and superstitious elements in Chinese society

Tartars European name for fierce Mongolian warriors from central Asia that attacked Russia in the thirteenth century

Tennis Court Oath oath of the French Third Estate declaring that they would not disband until a written constitution was established

Tenochtitlán famous city of the Aztecs known as "the Venice of the New World"; present-day Mexico City

terrorism the use of indiscriminate violence, or the threat of its use, for political ends; often motivated by militant Islam

Tet Offensive failed surprise attack of the North Vietnamese on South Vietnam; adversely affected the American attitude toward the Vietnam War

theocracy government directly by God

Third Estate largest estate in France comprising all who were not high clergy or nobility

Third Reich empire of Nazi Germany from 1933 to 1945

Thirty Years' War the last great religious war fought in Europe; won by the Protestants in 1648 with France's aid

38th parallel the border between North and South Korea

Three Emperors' League pre–World War I alliance between Germany, Russia, and Austria-Hungary

Tiananmen Square public square in Beijing, China; site of a deadly confrontation between the Chinese army and college-aged dissidents in 1989

Tikal Mayan city that was a center of power and influence

Timbuktu capital of ancient Mali; important trade center

Tokugawa family of shoguns that ruled Japan from the beginning of the seventeenth-century to the mid 1800s

topography the physical features of a land

totalitarian states one-party political system led by a powerful dictator who typically maintains control by force

tournament a mock war; included two types of contests, the joust and the melee

tradition the handing down of information by word of mouth from generation to generation

transubstantiation Roman Catholic belief that during the Holy Eucharist the priest transforms the bread and wine into the actual body and blood of Christ

treasury of saints Roman Catholic doctrine of the storehouse of the "excess works" of the saints and the works of Christ; used in the dispensing of indulgences

Treaty of Aix-la-Chapelle treaty ending the War of Austrian Succession; returned Europe to the status quo before the war, except for Silesia being given to Prussia

Treaty of Brest-Litovsk treaty between Russia and Germany after the Russian Revolution; pulled Russia out of World War I

Treaty of Kanagawa treaty between Japan and the United States in 1854; first treaty Japan ever signed with a Western nation

Treaty of London treaty that recognized the independence and perpetual neutrality of Belgium

Treaty of Paris (1) treaty ending the Seven Years' War; (2) treaty ending the War for Independence between the United States and Britain

Treaty of Sèvres treaty between the Ottoman Empire and the Allied Powers of World War I; dismantled the Ottoman Empire

Treaty of St. Germain treaty between Austria and the Allied Powers of World War I

Treaty of Utrecht ended the War of the Spanish Succession

Treaty of Verdun treaty between Charles the Bald, Louis the German, and Lothair to divide Louis the Pious's kingdom

Treaty of Versailles treaty between Germany and the Allied Powers of World War I; included the war guilt clause, which demanded that Germany pay reparations

Tribal Assembly another name for the plebeian assembly in Rome

tribe several families sharing common customs

tribunes ten men, elected by the Council of Plebeians in Rome, who protected the rights and interests of the common people

Triple Alliance (1) Indian alliance composed of the Aztecs and the city-states of Texcoco and Tlacopan; (2) anti-French coalition of Germany, Austria-Hungary, and Italy

Triple Entente pre–World War I agreement between Britain, France, and Russia

triumvirate rule of three men

trivium liberal-arts curriculum consisting of grammar, rhetoric, and logic

Truce of God medieval decree which limited fighting to specified weekdays by forbidding combat from Wednesday evening to Monday morning

Truman Doctrine the principle, enunciated by Harry S. Truman, of assisting countries in a struggle against communism in an effort to contain the spread of communism

Tudor family the ruling family of England during the sixteenth century

tyranny government headed by a tyrant who gained complete control of it, usually by force

U

U-2 incident the shooting down of an American U-2 reconnaissance (spy) plane over the Soviet Union in 1960

U-boat *unterseeboot*; German submarine

Umayyad Muslim caliphate that was a hereditary dynasty centered in Damascus

Unam Sanctam papal bull by Boniface VIII; stated that obedience to the pontiff was necessary for salvation

underwriter one who wrote his name below the prospectus, pledging to help share the cost of the enterprise

United Nations an international organization founded in 1945 that seeks to maintain international peace and security

universitas scholars who united for the common purpose of education

unrestricted submarine warfare German policy of sinking all enemy ships, whether armed or not

Upanishads philosophical essays elaborating on the teaching of the *Vedas*

USSR Union of Soviet Socialist Republics

usury the practice of charging interest for the use of lent money

utopian socialism belief that if the inequities in society could be abolished, man's natural goodness could be perfected

V

Vandals a Germanic tribe that established a kingdom in North Africa; plundered Rome after the Visigoths

Varangians Swedish Norsemen who plundered Slavic villages during the eighth and ninth centuries

vassal the recipient of a fief who owed allegiance to a king or lord

Vedas collection of religious literature that contains the early traditions and religious beliefs of ancient India

V-E Day Victory in Europe during World War II; May 8, 1945

vernacular common spoken language

Versailles palace of Louis XIV; built twelve miles southwest of Paris

veto a way for tribunes to stop the unjust acts of patrician officials

viceroy an "assistant king" that the Spanish king appointed to oversee affairs in the New World

Vijayanagara empire established in 1336 when Delhi Sultanate forces were pushed out of the Deccan Plateau

Vichy France area of France unoccupied by Nazi Germany, with Vichy as the seat of the new government

Viet Cong Communist guerillas who launched subversive activity in South Vietnam

Vietnam War war between Communist North Vietnam and non-Communist South Vietnam

Vietnamization the policy of gradually turning the burden of the fighting of the Vietnam War over to the South Vietnamese

Vikings Germanic tribes from Scandinavia that were feared invaders in medieval times

Visigoths a Germanic tribe that settled in the Eastern Roman Empire; defeated Rome at the battle of Adrianople and later plundered Rome

V-J Day Victory in Japan during World War II; Sept. 2, 1945

W

war communism tightly regulated system of economic controls imposed on Russia by Lenin

war debts debts incurred during the course of a war

war guilt clause clause in the Treaty of Versailles that placed the blame for World War I on Germany

War of the Austrian Succession war with Great Britain and Austria on the one side and Prussia, Spain, and France on the other; fought when Maria Theresa ascended the Austrian throne

War of the Spanish Succession war between the Grand Alliance and Louis XIV over the succession to the throne of Spain

Warsaw Pact Soviet regional military alliance that included Soviet satellite states in Eastern Europe; organized to counter NATO

Wars of the Roses series of conflicts between the houses of York and Lancaster over the English throne

Washington Naval Conference the 1920s conference that established ratios to limit the number of warships that each maritime nation could build

Weimar Republic German government after World War I

welfare state a state in which the government assumes the responsibility for the material and social well-being of every individual

wheel of life cycle of rebirths in reincarnation

witan Anglo-Saxon assembly of the great men of the kingdom

world soul another name for the Hindu concept of Brahman

worldview a perspective from which we may examine and interpret the universe and everything in it

written language a form of language in addition to spoken language

written records records of the past that are more accurate than oral traditions; include such things as private letters, inventory lists, inscriptions, diaries, and journals

Y

Yahweh the only true God

Yalta Conference meeting between Churchill, Roosevelt, and Stalin to determine the policies they would follow in seeking to end World War II

Yamato clan Japanese clan that forged a unified state; claimed divine lineage for the emperor

YMCA Young Men's Christian Association

Yom Kippur War 1973 war between Israel and the combined forces of Egypt and Syria that began on the Jewish Day of Atonement; won by Israel

Z

zeppelins long, slender airships similar to modern blimps

Zeus "king of gods and man" according to Greek mythology; ruler of Olympus

ziggurats pyramid-like structures that had terraces at different levels along their exterior

Zollverein nineteenth-century German trade union under the leadership of Prussia

INDEX

PHOTO CREDITS

326 Fine Art Images / Super-Stock; **328** Private Collection / Bridgeman Images; **329** "John Wesley by George Romney"/ Wikimedia Commons/ Public Domain; **330** Library of Congress; **331t** "George Whitefield" by John Russell/ Wikimedia Commons /Public Domain; **331b** "Jonathan Edwards engraving" by R Babson & J Andrews/Wikimedia Commons/Public Domain; **334bg** starryvoyage/Shutterstock.com; **334** "The Agony in the Garden of Gethsemane" by El Greco/Wikimedia Commons /Public Domain; **335tl** "The Hippopotamus and Crocodile Hunt" by Peter Paul Rubens /Wikimedia Commons/Public Domain; **335tr** "The Storm on the Sea of Galilee" by Rembrandt /Wikimedia Commons/Public Domain; **335bl** "Claudio Monteverdi" by Bernardo Strozzi/Wikimedia Commons /Public Domain; **335bc** Universal Images / SuperStock; **335br** API /Gamma-Rapho/Getty Images; **336l** © North Wind Picture Archives; **336r** akg-images / SuperStock

Chapter 16

338 Peter Barritt / SuperStock; **341** © iStock.com/jmoor17; **342t** "Washington Crossing the Delaware" by Emanuel Leutze /Wikimedia Commons/Public Domain; **342b** © Janice Barchat /Fotolia; **344** © trekandphoto /Fotolia; **346** "Antoine-François Callet (circle) King Louis XVI" /Wikimedia Commons/Public Domain; **348t** "Couder Stati generali" by Auguste Couder /Wikimedia Commons/Public Domain; **348b** akg-images / SuperStock; **349** Ian Woolcock / SuperStock; **351** "The Death of Marat" by Jacques-Louis David/Wikimedia Commons /Public Domain; **352** Artepics / age fotostock / SuperStock; **353** French School/Getty Images; **354** Library of Congress, LC-USZC4-2799; **355l** "Portrait of Nelson" by George Peter Alexander Healy/Wikimedia Commons/Public Domain; **355r** Everett - Art/Shutterstock.com; **356** Heritage Images/Hulton Archive/Getty Images; **357** "The Battle of Austerlitz, 2nd December 1805" by François Gérard/Wikimedia Commons/Public Domain; **359** A. Burkatovski / Fine Art Images / SuperStock; **360t** "Arthur Wellesley, 1st Duke of Wellington (1769–1852)" by Thomas Lawrence/Wikimedia

Commons/Public Domain; **360c** Denis Dighton/Getty Images; **360b** DEA/M. SEEMULLER/De Agostini/Getty Images

Chapter 17

364 © Simon Jakubowski | Dreamstime.com; **365** "Alexander I of Russia by Jean-Laurent Mosnier (1806, GIM)" /Wikimedia Commons/Public Domain; **366t** "Talleyrand 01" by Pierre-Paul Prud'hon /Wikimedia Commons/Public Domain; **366b** DeAgostini / SuperStock; **370** sourabhj /iStock/Thinkstock; **371** DEA /M. SEEMULLER/De Agostini /Getty Images; **374** Art Archive, The / SuperStock; **375** "Napoleon III" by Alexandre Cabanel /Wikimedia Commons/Public Domain; **377** Imagno/Hulton Fine Art Collection/Getty Images; **378t** "Gustave-Le-Gray Giuseppe-Garibaldi Palermo-1860 1-1000x1500"/Wikimedia Commons/Public Domain; **378b** De Agostini/A. Dagli Orti /De Agostini Picture Library/Getty Images; **379t** "Florence Nightingale three quarter length" /Wikimedia Commons/Public Domain; **379b** "Seacole photo" /Wikimedia Commons/Public Domain; **380** Hulton Archive /Getty Images; **382** "Alexander II of Russia (Nikolay Lavrov 01)" /Wikimedia Commons/Public Domain; **383t** "Ludwig van Beethoven when composing the Missa Solemnis" by Joseph Karl Stieler/Wikimedia Commons /Public Domain; **383b** "Wivenhoe Park, Essex" by John Constable /Wikimedia Commons/Public Domain; **384l** Bridgeman Art Library, London / SuperStock; **384r** "Shipwreck on the Coast" by Eugène Delacroix/Wikimedia Commons/Public Domain

Chapter 18

386 © Spiroview Inc. | Dreamstime.com; **388** "Portrait of Charles Townshend, 2nd Viscount Townshend (1674-1738)"/Wikimedia Commons/Public Domain; **389l** Wellcome Library, London /CC By 4.0; **389tr** Rob Byron /Shutterstock.com; **389cr** "Arkwright Water Frame (replica)" by Morio/Wikimedia Commons/GFDL/CC By-SA 3.0; **389br** zhuda/iStock/Thinkstock; **391, 392tr** Science Source; **392tl** Iberfoto / SuperStock; **392i** Library of Congress, LC-DIG-ggbain-00005; **392b** "Kitty hawk gross"/Library of Congress /Wikimedia Commons/Public Domain; **393l** "Henry Ford cph

.3b34530"/Library of Congress /Public Domain; **393r** © iStock .com/horse1asia; **394** "Thomas Alva Edison" by Abraham Archibald Anderson/Wikimedia Commons/Public Domain; **395l** "A little spinner in a Georgia Cotton Mill" by Lewis Hine /NARA/Wikimedia Commons /Public Domain; **395r** "Breaker boys. Smallest is Angelo Ross. Hughestown Borough Coal Co. Pittston, Pa." by Lewis Hine /NARA/Wikimedia Commons /Public Domain; **397, 407** Pantheon / SuperStock; **398** Stefano Bianchetti/Corbis Historical/Getty Images; **399l** "Benjamin Disraeli by H Lenthall"/Wikimedia Commons/Public Domain; **399r, 404t, 406b** Hulton Archive /Getty Images; **400** "Queen Victoria by Bassano" /Wikimedia Commons/Public Domain; **401t** "Karl Marx 001" by John Jabez Edwin Mayal /Wikimedia Commons/Public Domain; **401t** "Friedrich Engels portrait"/Wikimedia Commons /Public Domain; **403** "George Muller"/Wikipedia Commons /Public Domain; **404b** Time Life Pictures/The LIFE Picture Collection/Getty Images; **405** Library of Congress, LC-USZ61-264; **406t** "Charles Darwin by Julia Margaret Cameron 3" /Wikimedia Commons/Public Domain; **408** Rischgitz/Hulton Archive/Getty Images; **409** "The Grain Sifters" by Gustave Courbet/Wikimedia Commons /Public Domain; **410t** "Luncheon of the Boating Party" by Pierre-Auguste Renoir/Wikimedia Commons/Public Domain; **410b** "Water Lilies" by Claude Monet /Wikimedia Commons/Public Domain

Chapter 19

412 Sarin Images / Granger, NYC; **417t, c** John Bean; **417b** © Paul Liu/Fotolia; **420t** "Lord Clive meeting with Mir Jafar after the Battle of Plassey" by Francis Hayman/Wikimedia Commons/Public Domain; **420b** Private Collection / © Look and Learn / Elgar Collection / Bridgeman Images; **421** Private Collection / Bridgeman Images; **422t** Alpha Historica / Alamy Stock Photo; **422b** "China imperialism cartoon" by Henri Meyer /Wikimedia Commons/Public Domain; **423** "Commodore Matthew Calbraith Perry" by Mathew Brady/Wikimedia Commons/Public Domain; **427t** Rischgitz/Hulton Archive/Getty

Images; **427b** Dundee Central Library, Mary Slessor Collection; **428l** Photos.com/Thinkstock; **428r** "No-nb bldsa 1c031" by Alexander Bassano/Wikimedia Common/Public Domain

Chapter 20

436 Three Lions/Hulton Archive/Getty Images; **437** Library of Congress, LC-USZ62-88699; **438** Fedor Selivanov/Shutterstock.com; **439** Print Collector/Hulton Archive /Getty Images; **440** Sarin Images / Granger, NYC; **441** "Armenian woman kneeling beside dead child in field"/Wikipedia/Public Domain; **442** "Ferdinand Schmutzer - Franz Ferdinand von Österreich-Este, um 1914" /Wikimedia Commons /Public Domain; **444** FPG /Archive Photos/Getty Images; **445** "A raiding party from the 9th Battalion, Scottish Rifles (Cameronians), leaving a sap and making for the German lines, 11 April 1917. Q5101" by John Warwick Brooke /Wikimedia Commons/Public Domain; **446** © iStock.com /ChiccoDodiFC; **446c** ullstein bild/Getty Images; **446b** Hulton Deutsch/Corbis Historical/Getty Images; **447** Hulton Archive /Getty Images; **448** "Lusitania" by Norman Wilkinson/Wikimedia Commons/Public Domain; **450** 4X5 Collection / SuperStock; **451tl** Library of Congress; **451tr** Pictorial Parade/Archive Photos/Getty Images; **451b** "Stowers MOH ceremony - Palmer, Bowens and Bush" by Robert Ward, DOD PA /Wikimedia Commons/Public Domain; **453l** Bettmann /Getty Images; **453r** "Interior of Versailles"/Woodrow Wilson Presidential Library Archives /Flickr/Public Domain; **456** © iStock.com/stockcam

Chapter 21

460 Hugo Jaeger/The LIFE Picture Collection/Getty Images; **461, 467** Bettmann /Getty Images; **463t** ACME Imagery / SuperStock; **463c** ullstein bild Dtl./Getty Images; **463b** E. O. Hoppe/The LIFE Picture Collection/Getty Images; **465** Mondadori Portfolio /Mondadori Portfolio Premium /Getty Images; **466l** "Warren G Harding-Harris & Ewing" /Wikimedia Commons/Public Domain; **466r** Library of Congress; **468** Apic/Hulton Archive/Getty Images; **469t** Oronoz / Album / SuperStock;

469b "Rasputin pt"/Wikimedia Commons/Public Domain; **470**t "Alexander Kerensky LOC 24416"/Library of Congress /Wikimedia Commons/Public Domain; **470**b A. Burkatovski / Fine Art Images / SuperStock; **472** "19220900-lenin stalin gorky-02" by Maria Ilyinichna Ulyanova/Wikimedia Commons /Public Domain; **473** Russian Gospel Ministries; **475** ullstein bild Dtl./ullstein bild/Getty Images; **476** Roman Nerud /Shutterstock.com; **478**t March Of Time/The LIFE Picture Collection/Getty Images; **478**b Schultz Reinhard / Prisma / SuperStock; **479**t Keystone /Hulton Archive/Getty Images; **479**b, **480**tl, tc Everett Historical /Shutterstock.com; **480**tr © SZ Photo / Scherl / Bridgeman Images; **480**b FPG/Archive Photos/Getty Images

Chapter 22

482 "SBD VB-16 over USS Washington 1943"/U.S. Navy /Wikimedia Commons/Public Domain; **483** ullstein bild/Getty Images; **484**t Jack Birns/The LIFE Picture Collection/Getty Images; **484**b, **497**tr Bettmann /Getty Images; **485**t Everett Historical/Shutterstock.com; **485**b, **489** ullstein bild Dtl. /ullstein bild/Getty Images; **487**t Central Press/Hulton Archive /Getty Images; **487**b, **488** Keystone/Hulton Archive/Getty Images; **491**t, **499**, **505** IWM /Imperial War Museums/Getty Images; **491**b Keystone-France /Gamma-Keystone/Getty Images; **492**t Mirrorpix/Getty Images; **492**b Photo 12/Universal Images Group/Getty Images; **494** Universal History Archive /Universal Images Group/Getty Images; **495** INTERFOTO / Alamy Stock Photo; **496–7**bg, **496**bl Sueddeutsche Zeitung Photo / Alamy Stock Photo; **496**tl De Agostini Picture Library /De Agostini/Getty Images; **496**tr Courtesy of Calvin College; **496**br robertharding / Alamy Stock Photo; **497**l, **498**c National Archives; **497**br Hulton Deutsch/Corbis Historical /Getty Images; **498**t Historical /Corbis Historical/Getty Images; **498**b "Naval photograph documenting the Japanese attack on Pearl Harbor, Hawaii which initiated US participation in World... - NARA - 295980"/U.S. National Archives and Records Administration/Wikimedia Commons/Public Domain; **500** "THIS MAN MAY DIE IF

YOU TALK TOO MUCH"/U.S. National Archives and Records Administration/Wikimedia Commons/Public Domain; **501** "US Navy LST Landing Sherman" by John H. Kellers GM3/c USS LCT-539, U.S. Navy/ Wikimedia Commons/Public Domain; **503** "Gen. Douglas MacArthur wades ashore" by U.S. Army Signal Corps officer Gaetano Faillace/National Archives/Wikimedia Commons /Public Domain; **504**t National Archives and Records Administration; **504**b AP Photo/Joe Rosenthal, File

Chapter 23

512, **518**b National Archives; **514** Popperfoto/Getty Images; **516** Hulton Archive/Archive Photos /Getty Images; **518**t Flip Schulke Archives/Corbis Premium Historical/Getty Images; **519** ullstein bild Dtl./ullstein bild /Getty Images; **520**t AP Photo /files; **520**b David Cole / age fotostock / SuperStock; **521** Dean Conger/National Geographic/Getty Images; **522** World History Archive / Super-Stock; **523** David Pollack/Corbis Historical/Getty Images; **524**l "Warkorea American Soldiers" /U.S. National Archives and Records Administration /Wikimedia Commons/Public Domain; **524**r "A United States Army artillery crew fires a 105-millimeter howitzer against North Korean Communist positions during a battle in the Republic of Korea HD-SN-50-00931"/Wikimedia Commons /Public Domain; **525**, **526**t, **533** Bettmann/Getty Images; **526**b tim page/Corbis Historical /Getty Images; **529** ullstein bild /Getty Images; **531**tl Universal Images / SuperStock; **531**tr © Anton Barashenkov | Dreams-time.com; **531**b Lockheed; **534**t Forum / Bridgeman Images; **534**b AFP/Getty Images; **535** Novarc Images/Christian Reister/Media Bakery

Chapter 24

540 © iStock.com/DKart; **542**t, **545**l, **547**l AFP/Getty Images; **542**b © iStock.com/vichinter-lang; **543**t Lawrence K. Ho/Los Angeles Times/Getty Images; **543**b Westend61/Florian Kopp /Media Bakery; **544** Lintao Zhang/Getty Images News /Getty Images; **545**tr © iStock .com/Jorisvo; **545**br Jack Taylor /Getty Images News/Getty Images; **547**tr Mikhail Svetlov /Getty Images News/Getty Images;

547br © Taraspolatayko | Dreamstime.com; **548** FILIPPO MONTEFORTE/AFP/Getty Images; **551**t AP Photo/David Longstreath, File; **551**c AP Photo/SANA, File; **551**b World History Archive / SuperStock; **552**t Anadolu Agency/Getty Images; **552**b Majid Saeedi/Getty Images News/Getty Images; **553**t Universal History Archive /Universal Images Group/Getty Images; **553**b AHMAD GHARABLI/AFP/Getty Images; **554**l Adobe Stock/Venelin Petkov; **554**r Ton Koene / age fotostock / SuperStock; **555**t Everett Collection / SuperStock; **555**b © iStock.com/Asian-Dream; **556** © iStock.com/SeanPavonePhoto; **557**t, b Imaginechina via AP Images; **558**t AFP PHOTO/KCNA VIA KNS/Getty Images; **558**b "Korean peninsula at night (2012)" by NASA/Wikimedia Commons/Public Domain

All maps from Map Resources